CISSP
The Official (ISC)²®
CISSP® CBK® Reference

Fifth Edition

CISSP: Certified Information Systems Security Professional

The Official (ISC)²® CISSP® CBK® Reference

Fifth Edition

JOHN WARSINKSE

WITH: MARK GRAFF, KEVIN HENRY, CHRISTOPHER HOOVER, BEN MALISOW,
SEAN MURPHY, C. PAUL OAKES, GEORGE PAJARI, JEFF T. PARKER,
DAVID SEIDL, MIKE VASQUEZ

SYBEX®
A Wiley Brand

Development Editor: Kelly Talbot
Senior Production Editor: Christine O'Connor
Copy Editor: Kim Wimpsett
Editorial Manager: Pete Gaughan
Production Manager: Kathleen Wisor
Associate Publisher: Jim Minatel
Proofreader: Louise Watson, Word One New York

Indexer: Johnna VanHoose Dinse

Project Coordinator, Cover: Brent Savage

Cover Designer: Wiley
Copyright © 2019 by (ISC)²

Published simultaneously in Canada

ISBN: 978-1-119-42334-8
ISBN: 978-1-119-42332-4 (ebk.)
ISBN: 978-1-119-42331-7 (ebk.)

Manufactured in the United States of America

For general information on our other products and services or to obtain technical support, please contact our Customer Care Department within the U.S. at (877) 762-2974, outside the U.S. at (317) 572-3993 or fax (317) 572-4002.

Wiley publishes in a variety of print and electronic formats and by print-on-demand. Some material included with standard print versions of this book may not be included in e-books or in print-on-demand. If this book refers to media such as a CD or DVD that is not included in the version you purchased, you may download this material at `http://booksupport.wiley.com`. For more information about Wiley products, visit `www.wiley.com`.

Library of Congress Control Number: 2019936840

V10009071_032819

Lead Author and Lead Technical Reviewer

Over the course of his 30-plus years as an information technology professional, **John Warsinske** has been exposed to a breadth of technologies and governance structures. He has been, at various times, a network analyst, IT manager, project manager, security analyst, and chief information officer. He has worked in local, state, and federal government; has worked in public, private, and nonprofit organizations; and has been variously a contractor, direct employee, and volunteer. He has served in the U.S. military in assignments at the tactical, operational, and strategic levels across the entire spectrum from peace to war. In these diverse environments, he has experienced both the uniqueness and the similarities in the activities necessary to secure their respective information assets.

Mr. Warsinske has been an instructor for (ISC)² for more than five years; prior to that, he was an adjunct faculty instructor at the College of Southern Maryland. His (ISC)² certifications include the Certified Information Systems Security Professional (CISSP), Certified Cloud-Security Professional (CCSP), and HealthCare Information Security and Privacy Practitioner (HCISPP). He maintains several other industry credentials as well.

When he is not traveling, Mr. Warsinske currently resides in Ormond Beach, Florida, with his wife and two extremely spoiled Carolina dogs.

Contributing Authors

Mark Graff (CISSP), former chief information security officer for both NASDAQ and Lawrence Livermore National Laboratory, is a seasoned cybersecurity practitioner and thought leader. He has lectured on risk analysis, cybersecurity, and privacy issues before the American Academy for the Advancement of Science, the Federal Communications Commission, the Pentagon, the National Nuclear Security Administration, and other U.S. national security facilities. Graff has twice testified before Congress on cybersecurity, and in 2018–2019 served as an expert witness on software security to the Federal Trade Commission. His books—notably *Secure Coding: Principles and Practices*—have been used at dozens of universities worldwide in teaching how to design and build secure software-based systems. Today, as head of the consulting firm Tellagraff LLC (`www.markgraff.com`), Graff provides strategic advice to large companies, small businesses, and government agencies. Recent work has included assisting multiple state governments in the area of election security.

Kevin Henry (CAP, CCSP, CISSP, CISSP-ISSAP, CISSP-ISSEP, CISSP-ISSMP, CSSLP, and SSCP) is a passionate and effective educator and consultant in information security. Kevin has taught CISSP classes around the world and has contributed to the development of (ISC)^2 materials for nearly 20 years. He is a frequent speaker at security conferences and the author of several books on security management. Kevin's years of work in telecommunications, government, and private industry have led to his strength in being able to combine real-world experience with the concepts and application of information security topics in an understandable and effective manner.

Chris Hoover, CISSP, CISA, is a cybersecurity and risk management professional with 20 years in the field. He spent most of his career protecting the U.S. government's most sensitive data in the Pentagon, the Baghdad Embassy, NGA Headquarters, Los Alamos Labs, and many other locations. Mr. Hoover also developed security products for RSA that are deployed across the U.S. federal government, many state governments, and internationally. He is currently consulting for the DoD and runs a risk management start-up called Riskuary. He has a master's degree in information assurance.

Ben Malisow, CISSP, CISM, CCSP, Security+, SSCP, has been involved in INFOSEC and education for more than 20 years. At Carnegie Mellon University, he crafted and delivered the CISSP prep course for CMU's CERT/SEU. Malisow was the ISSM for the FBI's most highly classified counterterror intelligence-sharing network, served as an Air Force officer, and taught grades 6–12 at a reform school in the Las Vegas public school district (probably his most dangerous employment to date). His latest work has included *CCSP Practice Tests* and *CCSP (ISC)² Certified Cloud Security Professional Official Study Guide*, also from Sybex/Wiley, and *How to Pass Your INFOSEC Certification Test: A Guide to Passing the CISSP, CISA, CISM, Network+, Security+, and CCSP*, available from Amazon Direct. In addition to other consulting and teaching, Ben is a certified instructor for (ISC)², delivering CISSP, CCSP, and SSCP courses. You can reach him at www.benmalisow.com or his INFOSEC blog, securityzed.com. Ben would also like to extend his personal gratitude to Todd R. Slack, MS, JD, CIPP/US, CIPP/E, CIPM, FIP, CISSP, for his invaluable contributions to this book.

Sean Murphy, CISSP, HCISSP, is the vice president and chief information security officer for Premera Blue Cross (Seattle). He is responsible for providing and optimizing an enterprise-wide security program and architecture that minimizes risk, enables business imperatives, and further strengthens the health plan company's security posture. He's a healthcare information security expert with more than 20 years of experience in highly regulated, security-focused organizations. Sean retired from the U.S. Air Force (Medical Service Corps) after achieving the rank of lieutenant colonel. He has served as CIO and CISO in the military service and private sector at all levels of healthcare organizations. Sean has a master's degree in business administration (advanced IT concentration) from the University of South Florida, a master's degree in health services administration from Central Michigan University, and a bachelor's degree in human resource management from the University of Maryland. He is a board chair of the Association for Executives in Healthcare Information Security (AEHIS). Sean is a past chairman of the HIMSS Privacy and Security Committee. He served on the (ISC)² committee to develop the HCISPP credential. He is also a noted speaker at the national level and the author of numerous industry whitepapers, articles, and educational materials, including his book *Healthcare Information Security and Privacy*.

C. Paul Oakes, CISSP, CISSP-ISSAP, CCSP, CCSK, CSM, and CSPO, is an author, speaker, educator, technologist, and thought leader in cybersecurity, software development, and process improvement. Paul has worn many hats over his 20-plus years of experience. In his career he has been a security architect, consultant, software engineer, mentor, educator, and executive. Paul has worked with companies in various industries such as the financial industry, banking, publishing, utilities, government, e-commerce, education, training, research, and technology start-ups. His work has advanced the cause of software and information security on many fronts, ranging from writing security policy to implementing secure code and showing others how to do the same. Paul's passion is to help people develop the skills they need to most effectively defend the line in cyberspace and advance the standard of cybersecurity practice. To this end, Paul continuously collaborates with experts across many disciplines, ranging from cybersecurity to accelerated learning to mind-body medicine, to create and share the most effective strategies to rapidly learn cybersecurity and information technology subject matter. Most of all, Paul enjoys his life with his wife and young son, both of whom are the inspirations for his passion.

George E. Pajari, CISSP-ISSAP, CISM, CIPP/E, is a fractional CISO, providing cybersecurity leadership on a consulting basis to a number of cloud service providers. Previously he was the chief information security officer (CISO) at Hootsuite, the most widely used social media management platform, trusted by more than 16 million people and employees at 80 percent of the Fortune 1000. He has presented at conferences including CanSecWest, ISACA CACS, and BSides Vancouver. As a volunteer, he helps with the running of BSides Vancouver, the (ISC)² Vancouver chapter, and the University of British Columbia's Cybersecurity Summit. He is a recipient of the ISACA CISM Worldwide Excellence Award.

Jeff Parker, CISSP, CySA+, CASP, is a certified technical trainer and security consultant specializing in governance, risk management, and compliance (GRC). Jeff began his information security career as a software engineer with an HP consulting group out of Boston. Enterprise clients for which Jeff has consulted on site include hospitals, universities, the U.S. Senate, and a half-dozen UN agencies. Jeff assessed these clients' security posture and provided gap analysis and remediation. In 2006 Jeff relocated to Prague, Czech Republic, for a few years, where he designed a new risk management strategy for a multinational logistics firm. Presently, Jeff resides in Halifax, Canada, while consulting primarily for a GRC firm in Virginia.

David Seidl, CISSP, GPEN, GCIH, CySA+, Pentest+, is the vice president for information technology and CIO at Miami University of Ohio. During his IT career, he has served in a variety of technical and information security roles, including serving as the senior director for Campus Technology Services at the University of Notre Dame and leading Notre Dame's information security team as director of information security. David has taught college courses on information security and writes books on information security and cyberwarfare, including *CompTIA CySA+ Study Guide: Exam CS0-001, CompTIA PenTest+ Study Guide: Exam PT0-001, CISSP Official (ISC)² Practice Tests,* and *CompTIA CySA+ Practice Tests: Exam CS0-001,* all from Wiley, and *Cyberwarfare: Information Operations in a Connected World* from Jones and Bartlett. David holds a bachelor's degree in communication technology and a master's degree in information security from Eastern Michigan University.

Michael Neal Vasquez has more than 25 years of IT experience and has held several industry certifications, including CISSP, MCSE: Security, MCSE+I, MCDBA, and CCNA. Mike is a senior security engineer on the red team for a Fortune 500 financial services firm, where he spends his days (and nights) looking for security holes. After obtaining his BA from Princeton University, he forged a security-focused IT career, both working in the trenches and training other IT professionals. Mike is a highly sought-after instructor because his classes blend real-world experience and practical knowledge with the technical information necessary to comprehend difficult material, and his students praise his ability to make any course material entertaining and informative. Mike has taught CISSP, security, and Microsoft to thousands of students across the globe through local colleges and online live classes. He has performed penetration testing engagements for healthcare, financial services, retail, utilities, and government entities. He also runs his own consulting and training company and can be reached on LinkedIn at `https://www.linkedin.com/in/mnvasquez`.

Technical Reviewers

Bill Burke, CISSP, CCSP, CRISC, CISM, CEH, is a security professional with more than 35 years serving the information technology and services community. He specializes in security architecture, governance, and compliance, primarily in the cloud space. He previously served on the board of directors of the Silicon Valley (ISC)² chapter, in addition to the board of directors of the Cloud Services Alliance – Silicon Valley. Bill can be reached via email at billburke@cloudcybersec.com.

Charles Gaughf, CISSP, SSCP, CCSP, is both a member and an employee of (ISC)², the global nonprofit leader in educating and certifying information security professionals. For more than 15 years, he has worked in IT and security in different capacities for nonprofit, higher education, and telecommunications organizations to develop security education for the industry at large. In leading the security team for the last five years as the senior manager of security at (ISC)², he was responsible for the global security operations, security posture, and overall security health of (ISC)². Most recently he transitioned to the (ISC)² education team to develop immersive and enriching CPE opportunities and security training and education for the industry at large. He holds degrees in management of information systems and communications.

Dr. Meng-Chow Kang, CISSP, is a practicing information security professional with more than 30 years of field experience in various technical information security and risk management roles for organizations that include the Singapore government, major global financial institutions, and security and technology providers. His research and part of his experience in the field have been published in his book *Responsive Security: Be Ready to Be Secure* from CRC Press. Meng-Chow has been a CISSP since 1998 and was a member of the (ISC)² board of directors from 2015 through 2017. He is also a recipient of the (ISC)² James Wade Service Award.

Aaron Kraus, CISSP, CCSP, Security+, began his career as a security auditor for U.S. federal government clients working with the NIST RMF and Cybersecurity Framework, and then moved to the healthcare industry as an auditor working with the HIPAA and HITRUST frameworks. Next, he entered the financial services industry, where he designed a control and audit program for vendor risk management, incorporating financial compliance requirements and industry-standard frameworks including COBIT and ISO 27002. Since 2016 Aaron has been working with startups based in San Francisco, first on a GRC SaaS platform and more recently in cyber-risk insurance, where he focuses on assisting small- to medium-sized businesses to identify their risks, mitigate them appropriately, and transfer risk via insurance. In addition to his technical certifications, he is a Learning Tree certified instructor who teaches cybersecurity exam prep and risk management.

Professor Jill Slay, CISSP, CCFP, is the optus chair of cybersecurity at La Trobe University, leads the Optus La Trobe Cyber Security Research Hub, and is the director of cyber-resilience initiatives for the Australian Computer Society. Jill is a director of the Victorian Oceania Research Centre and previously served two terms as a director of the International Information Systems Security Certification Consortium. She has established an international research reputation in cybersecurity (particularly digital forensics) and has worked in collaboration with many industry partners. She was made a member of the Order of Australia (AM) for service to the information technology industry through contributions in the areas of forensic computer science, security, protection of infrastructure, and cyberterrorism. She is a fellow of the Australian Computer Society and a fellow of the International Information Systems Security Certification Consortium, both for her service to the information security industry. She also is a MACS CP.

Contents at a Glance

Contents

DOMAIN 4: COMMUNICATION AND NETWORK SECURITY

DOMAIN 7: SECURITY OPERATIONS

Foreword

BEING RECOGNIZED AS A CISSP is an important step in investing in your information security career. Whether you are picking up this book to supplement your preparation to sit for the exam or you are an existing CISSP using this as a desk reference, you've acknowledged that this certification makes you recognized as one of the most respected and sought-after cybersecurity leaders in the world. After all, that's what the CISSP symbolizes. You and your peers are among the ranks of the most knowledgeable practitioners in our community. The designation of CISSP instantly communicates to everyone within our industry that you are intellectually curious and traveling along a path of lifelong learning and improvement. Importantly, as a member of (ISC)² you have officially committed to ethical conduct commensurate to your position of trust as a cybersecurity professional.

The recognized leader in the field of information security education and certification, (ISC)² promotes the development of information security professionals throughout the world. As a CISSP with all the benefits of (ISC)² membership, you are part of a global network of more than 140,000 certified professionals who are working to inspire a safe and secure cyber world.

Being a CISSP, though, is more than a credential; it is what you demonstrate daily in your information security role. The value of your knowledge is the proven ability to effectively design, implement, and manage a best-in-class cybersecurity program within your organization. To that end, it is my great pleasure to present the *Official (ISC)² Guide to the CISSP (Certified Information Systems Security Professional) CBK*. Drawing from a comprehensive, up-to-date global body of knowledge, the *CISSP CBK* provides you with valuable insights on how to implement every aspect of cybersecurity in your organization.

If you are an experienced CISSP, you will find this edition of the *CISSP CBK* to be a timely book to frequently reference for reminders on best practices. If you are still gaining the experience and knowledge you need to join the ranks of CISSPs, the *CISSP CBK* is a deep dive that can be used to supplement your studies.

As the largest nonprofit membership body of certified information security professionals worldwide, (ISC)² recognizes the need to identify and validate not only information security competency but also the ability to connect knowledge of several domains when building high-functioning cybersecurity teams that demonstrate cyber resiliency. The CISSP credential represents advanced knowledge and competency in security design, implementation, architecture, operations, controls, and more.

If you are leading or ready to lead your security team, reviewing the *Official (ISC)²* *Guide to the CISSP CBK* will be a great way to refresh your knowledge of the many factors that go into securely implementing and managing cybersecurity systems that match your organization's IT strategy and governance requirements. The goal for CISSP credential holders is to achieve the highest standard for cybersecurity expertise—managing multiplatform IT infrastructures while keeping sensitive data secure. This becomes especially crucial in the era of digital transformation, where cybersecurity permeates virtually every value stream imaginable. Organizations that can demonstrate world-class cybersecurity capabilities and trusted transaction methods can enable customer loyalty and fuel success.

The opportunity has never been greater for dedicated men and women to carve out a meaningful career and make a difference in their organizations. The *CISSP CBK* will be your constant companion in protecting and securing the critical data assets of your organization that will serve you for years to come.

Regards,

David P. Shearer, CISSP
CEO, (ISC)²

Introduction

THE CERTIFIED INFORMATION SYSTEMS Security Professional (CISSP) signifies that an individual has a cross-disciplinary expertise across the broad spectrum of information security and that he or she understands the context of it within a business environment. There are two main requirements that must be met in order to achieve the status of CISSP. One must take and pass the certification exam, while also proving a minimum of five years of direct full-time security work experience in two or more of the domains of the (ISC)² CISSP CBK. The field of information security is wide, and there are many potential paths along one's journey through this constantly and rapidly changing profession.

A firm comprehension of the domains within the CISSP CBK and an understanding of how they connect back to the business and its people are important components in meeting the requirements of the CISSP credential. Every reader will connect these domains to their own background and perspective. These connections will vary based on industry, regulatory environment, geography, culture, and unique business operating environment. With that sentiment in mind, this book's purpose is not to address all of these issues or prescribe a set path in these areas. Instead, the aim is to provide an official guide to the CISSP CBK and allow you, as a security professional, to connect your own knowledge, experience, and understanding to the CISSP domains and translate the CBK into value for your organization and the users you protect.

SECURITY AND RISK MANAGEMENT

The Security and Risk Management domain entails many of the foundational security concepts and principles of information security. This domain covers a broad set of topics and demonstrates how to generally apply the concepts of confidentiality, integrity and availability across a security program. This domain also includes understanding compliance requirements, governance, building security policies and procedures, business continuity planning, risk management, security education, and training and awareness, and most importantly it lays out the ethical canons and professional conduct to be demonstrated by (ISC)² members.

The information security professional will be involved in all facets of security and risk management as part of the functions they perform across the enterprise. These functions may include developing and enforcing policy, championing governance and risk management, and ensuring the continuity of operations across an organization in the event of unforeseen circumstances. To that end, the information security professional must safeguard the organization's people and data.

ASSET SECURITY

The Asset Security domain covers the safeguarding of information and information assets across their lifecycle to include the proper collection, classification, handling, selection, and application of controls. Important concepts within this domain are data ownership, privacy, data security controls, and cryptography. Asset security is used to identify controls for information and the technology that supports the exchange of that information to include systems, media, transmission, and privilege.

The information security professional is expected to have a solid understanding of what must be protected, what access should be restricted, the control mechanisms available, how those mechanisms may be abused, and the appropriateness of those controls, and they should be able to apply the principles of confidentiality, integrity, availability, and privacy against those assets.

SECURITY ARCHITECTURE AND ENGINEERING

The Security Architecture and Engineering domain covers the process of designing and building secure and resilient information systems and associated architecture so that the information systems can perform their function while minimizing the threats that can be caused by malicious actors, human error, natural disasters, or system failures. Security must be considered in the design, in the implementation, and during the continuous delivery of an information system through its lifecycle. It is paramount to understand secure design principles and to be able to apply security models to a wide variety of distributed and disparate systems and to protect the facilities that house these systems.

An information security professional is expected to develop designs that demonstrate how controls are positioned and how they function within a system. The security controls must tie back to the overall system architecture and demonstrate how, through security engineering, those systems maintain the attributes of confidentiality, integrity, and availability.

COMMUNICATION AND NETWORK SECURITY

The Communication and Network Security domain covers secure design principles as they relate to network architectures. The domain provides a thorough understanding of components of a secure network, secure design, and models for secure network operation. The domain covers aspects of a layered defense, secure network technologies, and management techniques to prevent threats across a number of network types and converged networks.

It is necessary for an information security professional to have a thorough understanding of networks and the way in which organizations communicate. The connected world in which security professionals operate requires that organizations be able to access information and execute transactions in real time with an assurance of security. It is therefore important that an information security professional be able to identify threats and risks and then implement mitigation techniques and strategies to protect these communication channels.

IDENTITY AND ACCESS MANAGEMENT (IAM)

The Identity and Access Management (IAM) domain covers the mechanisms by which an information system permits or revokes the right to access information or perform an action against an information system. IAM is the mechanism by which organizations manage digital identities. IAM also includes the organizational policies and processes for managing digital identities as well as the underlying technologies and protocols needed to support identity management.

Information security professionals and users alike interact with components of IAM every day. This includes business services logon authentication, file and print systems, and nearly any information system that retrieves and manipulates data. This can mean users or a web service that exposes data for user consumption. IAM plays a critical and indispensable part in these transactions and in determining whether a user's request is validated or disqualified from access.

SECURITY ASSESSMENT AND TESTING

The Security Assessment and Testing domain covers the tenets of how to perform and manage the activities involved in security assessment and testing, which includes providing a check and balance to regularly verify that security controls are performing optimally and efficiently to protect information assets. The domain describes the array of tools and methodologies for performing various activities such as vulnerability assessments, penetration tests, and software tests.

The information security professional plays a critical role in ensuring that security controls remain effective over time. Changes to the business environment, technical environment, and new threats will alter the effectiveness of controls. It is important that the security professional be able to adapt controls in order to protect the confidentiality, integrity, and availability of information assets.

SECURITY OPERATIONS

The Security Operations domain includes a wide range of concepts, principles, best practices, and responsibilities that are core to effectively running security operations in any organization. This domain explains how to protect and control information processing assets in centralized and distributed environments and how to execute the daily tasks required to keep security services operating reliably and efficiently. These activities include performing and supporting investigations, monitoring security, performing incident response, implementing disaster recovery strategies, and managing physical security and personnel safety.

In the day-to-day operations of the organization, sustaining expected levels of confidentiality, availability, and integrity of information and business services is where the information security professional affects operational resiliency. The day-to-day securing, responding, monitoring, and maintenance of resources demonstrates how the information security professional is able to protect information assets and provide value to the organization.

SOFTWARE DEVELOPMENT SECURITY

The Software Development Security domain refers to the controls around software, its development lifecycle, and the vulnerabilities inherent in systems and applications. Applications and data are the foundation of an information system. An understanding of this process is essential to the development and maintenance required to ensure dependable and secure software. This domain also covers the development of secure coding guidelines and standards, as well as the impacts of acquired software.

Software underpins of every system that the information security professional and users in every business interact with on a daily basis. Being able to provide leadership and direction to the development process, audit mechanisms, database controls, and web application threats are all elements that the information security professional will put in place as part of the Software Development Security domain.

Security and Risk Management

IN THE POPULAR PRESS, we are bombarded with stories of technically savvy coders with nothing else to do except spend their days stealing information from computers connected to the Internet. Indeed, many security professionals have built their careers on the singular focus of defeating the wily hacker. As with all stereotypes, these exaggerations contain a grain of truth: there are capable hackers, and there are skilled defenders of systems. Yet these stereotypes obscure the greater challenge of ensuring information, in all its forms and throughout its lifecycle, is properly protected.

The Certified Information Systems Security Professional (CISSP) Common Body of Knowledge is designed to provide a broad foundational understanding of information security practice, applicable to a range of organizational structures and information systems. This foundational knowledge allows information security practitioners to communicate using a consistent language to solve technical, procedural, and policy challenges. Through this work, the security practice helps the business or organization achieve its mission efficiently and effectively.

The CBK addresses the role of information security as an essential component of an organization's risk management activities. Organizations, regardless of type, create structures to solve problems. These structures often leverage frameworks of knowledge or practice to provide some predictability in process. The CISSP CBK provides a set of tools that allows the information security professional to integrate security practice into those frameworks, protecting the organization's assets while respecting the unique trust that comes with the management of sensitive information.

This revision of the CISSP CBK acknowledges that the means by which we protect information and the range of information that demands protection are both rapidly evolving. One consequence of that evolution is a change in focus of the material. No longer is it enough to simply parrot a list of static facts or concepts—security professionals must demonstrate the relevance of those concepts to their particular business problems. Given the volume of information on which the CBK depends, the application of professional judgment in the study of the CBK is essential. Just as in the real world, answers may not be simple choices.

UNDERSTAND AND APPLY CONCEPTS OF CONFIDENTIALITY, INTEGRITY, AND AVAILABILITY

For thousands of years, people have sought assurance that information has been captured, stored, communicated, and used securely. Depending on the context, differing levels of emphasis have been placed on the availability, integrity, and confidentiality of information, but achieving these basic objectives has always been at the heart of security practice.

As we moved from the time of mud tablets and papyrus scrolls into the digital era, we watched the evolution of technology to support these three objectives. In today's world, where vast amounts of information are accessible at the click of a mouse, our security decision-making must still consider the people, processes, and systems that assure us that information is available when we need it, has not been altered, and is protected from disclosure to those not entitled to it.

This module will explore the implications of confidentiality, integrity, and availability (collectively, the CIA Triad) in current security practices. These interdependent concepts form a useful and important framework on which to base the study of information security practice.

Information Security

Information security processes, practices, and technologies can be evaluated based on how they impact the confidentiality, integrity, and availability of the information being communicated. The apparent simplicity of the CIA Triad drives a host of security principles, which translate into practices and are implemented with various technologies against a dizzying array of information sources (see Figure 1.1). Thus, a common understanding of the meaning of each of the elements in the triad allows security professionals to communicate effectively.

FIGURE 1.1 CIA Triad

Confidentiality

Ensuring that information is provided to only those people who are entitled to access that information has been one of the core challenges in effective communications. Confidentiality implies that access is limited. Controls need to be identified that separate those who need to know information from those who do not.

Once we have identified those with legitimate need, then we will apply controls to enforce their privilege to access the information. Applying the principle of least privilege ensures that individuals have only the minimum means to access the information to which they are entitled.

Information about individuals is often characterized as having higher sensitivity to disclosure. The inappropriate disclosure of other types of information may also have adverse impacts on an organization's operations. These impacts may include statutory or regulatory noncompliance, loss of unique intellectual property, financial penalties, or the loss of trust in the ability of the organization to act with due care for the information.

Integrity

To make good decisions requires acting on valid and accurate information. Change to information may occur inadvertently, or it may be the result of intentional acts. Ensuring the information has not been inappropriately changed requires the application of control over the creation, transmission, presentation, and storage of the information.

Detection of inappropriate change is one way to support higher levels of information integrity. Many mechanisms exist to detect change in information; cryptographic hashing, reference data, and logging are only some of the means by which detection of change can occur.

Other controls ensure the information has sufficient quality to be relied upon for decisions. Executing well-formed transactions against constrained data items ensures the system maintains integrity as information is captured. Controls that address separation of duties, application of least privilege, and audit against standards also support the validity aspect of data integrity.

Availability

Availability ensures that the information is accessible when it is needed. Many circumstances can disrupt information availability. Physical destruction of the information, disruption of the communications path, and inappropriate application of access controls are only a few of the ways availability can be compromised.

Availability controls must address people, processes, and systems. High availability systems such as provided by cloud computing or clustering are of little value if the people necessary to perform the tasks for the organization are unavailable. The challenge for the information security architect is to identify those single points of failure in a system and apply a sufficient amount of control to satisfy the organization's risk appetite.

Taken together, the CIA Triad provides a structure for characterizing the information security implications of a concept, technology, or process. It is infrequent, however, that such a characterization would have implications on only one side of the triad. For example, applying cryptographic protections over information may indeed ensure the confidentiality of information and, depending on the cryptographic approach, support higher levels of integrity, but the loss of the keys to those who are entitled to the information would certainly have an availability implication!

Limitations of the CIA Triad

The CIA Triad evolved out of theoretical work done in the mid-1960s. Precisely because of its simplicity, the rise of distributed systems and a vast number of new applications for new technology has caused researchers and security practitioners to extend the triad's coverage.

Guaranteeing the identities of parties involved in communications is essential to confidentiality. The CIA Triad does not directly address the issues of authenticity and nonrepudiation, but the point of nonrepudiation is that neither party can deny that they participated in the communication. This extension of the triad uniquely addresses aspects of confidentiality and integrity that were never considered in the early theoretical work.

The National Institute of Standards and Technology (NIST) Special Publication 800-33, "Underlying Technical Models for Information Technology Security," included the CIA Triad as three of its five security objectives, but added the concepts of accountability (that actions of an entity may be traced uniquely to that entity) and assurance (the basis for confidence that the security measures, both technical and operational, work as intended to protect the system and the information it processes). The NIST work remains influential as an effort to codify best-practice approaches to systems security.

Perhaps the most widely accepted extension to the CIA Triad was proposed by information security pioneer Donn B. Parker. In extending the triad, Parker incorporated three additional concepts into the model, arguing that these concepts were both atomic (could not be further broken down conceptually) and nonoverlapping. This framework has come to be known as the Parkerian Hexad (see Figure 1.2). The Parkerian Hexad contains the following concepts:

- **Confidentiality:** The limits on who has access to information
- **Integrity:** Whether the information is in its intended state
- **Availability:** Whether the information can be accessed in a timely manner
- **Authenticity:** The proper attribution of the person who created the information
- **Utility:** The usefulness of the information
- **Possession or control:** The physical state where the information is maintained

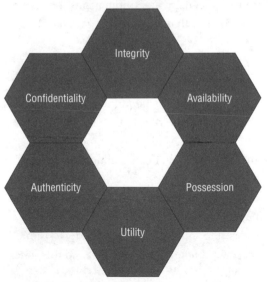

FIGURE 1.2 The Parkerian Hexad

Subsequent academic work produced dozens of other information security models, all aimed at the same fundamental issue—how to characterize information security risks. For the security professional, a solid understanding of the CIA Triad is essential when communicating about information security practice.

EVALUATE AND APPLY SECURITY GOVERNANCE PRINCIPLES

A security-aware culture requires all levels of the organization to see security as integral to its activities. The organization's governance structure, when setting the vision for the organization, should ensure that protecting the organization's assets and meeting the compliance requirements are integral to acting as good stewards of the organization. Once the organization's governance structure implements policies that reflect its level of acceptable risk, management can act with diligence to implement good security practices.

Alignment of Security Functions to Business Strategy, Goals, Mission, and Objectives

Information security practice exists to support the organization in the achievement of its goals. To achieve those goals, the information security practice must take into account the organizational leadership environment, corporate risk tolerance, compliance expectations, new and legacy technologies and practices, and a constantly evolving set of threats. To be effective, the information security practitioner must be able to communicate about risk and technology in a manner that will support good corporate decision-making.

Vision, Mission, and Strategy

Every organization has a purpose. Some organizations define that purpose clearly and elegantly, in a manner that communicates to all the stakeholders of the organization the niche that the organization uniquely fills. An organization's mission statement should drive the organization's activities to ensure the efficient and effective allocation of time, resources, and effort.

The organization's purpose may be defined by a governmental mandate or jurisdiction. For other organizations, the purpose may be to make products or deliver services for commercial gain. Still other organizations exist to support their stakeholders' vision of society. Regardless, the mission clearly states why an organization exists, and this statement of purpose should drive all corporate activities.

What organizations do now, however, is usually different from what they will do in the future. For an organization to evolve to its future state, a clear vision statement should inspire the members of the organization to work toward that end. Often, this will require the organization to change the allocation of time, resources, and efforts to that new and desired state.

How the organization will go about achieving its vision is the heart of the organization's strategy. At the most basic level, a corporate strategy is deciding where to spend time and resources to accomplish a task. Deciding what that task is, however, is often the hardest part of the process. Many organizations lack the focus on what it is they want to achieve, resulting in inefficient allocation of time and resources.

Protecting an organization's information assets is a critical part of the organization's strategy. Whether that information is written on paper, is managed by an electronic system, or exists in the minds of the organization's people, the basic challenge remains the same: ensuring the confidentiality, integrity, and availability of the information.

It is a long-held tenet that an organization's information security practice should support the organization's mission, vision, and strategy. Grounded in a solid base of information security theory, the application of the principles of information security should enable the organization to perform its mission efficiently and effectively with an acceptable level of risk.

Governance

The organization's mission and vision must be defined at the highest levels of the organization. In public-sector organizations, governance decisions are made through the legislative process. In corporate environments, the organization's board of directors serves a similar role, albeit constrained by the laws of the jurisdictions in which that entity conducts business.

Governance is primarily concerned with setting the conditions for the organization's management to act in the interests of the stakeholders. In setting those conditions, corporate governance organizations are held to a standard of care to ensure that the organization's management acts ethically, legally, and fairly in the pursuit of the organization's mission.

Acting on behalf of the organization requires that the governing body have tools to evaluate the risks and benefits of various actions. This can include risks to the financial health of the organization, failure to meet compliance requirements, or operational risks. Increasingly, governing bodies are explicitly addressing the risk of compromises to the information security environment.

In 2015, the Organization for Economic Cooperation and Development (OECD) revised its Principles of Corporate Governance. These principles were designed to help policymakers evaluate and improve the legal, regulatory, and institutional framework for corporate governance. These principles have been adopted or endorsed by multiple international organizations as best practice for corporate governance.

✔ The OECD Principles of Corporate Governance

The Principles of Corporate Governance provide a framework for effective corporate governance through six chapters.

- **Chapter 1:** This chapter focuses on how governance can be used to promote efficient allocation of resources, as well as fair and transparent markets.

- **Chapter 2:** Chapter 2 focuses on shareholder rights such as the right to participate in key decisions through shareholder meetings and the right to have information about the company. It emphasizes equitable treatment of shareholders, as well as the ownership functions that the OECD considers key functions.

- **Chapter 3:** The economic incentives provided at each level of the investment chain are covered in this chapter. Minimizing conflicts of interest and the role of institutional investors who act in a fiduciary capacity are covered, as well as the importance of fair and effective price discovery in stock markets.

- **Chapter 4:** This chapter focuses on the role of stakeholders in corporate governance, including how corporations and stockholders should cooperate and the necessity of establishing the rights of stockholders. It supports Chapter 2's coverage of stockholder rights, including the right to information and the right to seek redress for violations of those rights.

- **Chapter 5:** Disclosure of financial and operational information, such as operating results, company objectives, risk factors, share ownership, and other critical information, are discussed in this chapter.

- **Chapter 6:** The final chapter discusses the responsibilities of the board of directors, including selecting management, setting management compensation, reviewing corporate strategy, risk management, and other areas, such as the oversight of internal audit and tax planning.

Governance failures in the both the private and public sectors are well known. In particular, failures of organizational governance to address information security practices can have catastrophic consequences.

✔ Ashley Madison Breach

In July 2015, a major Canadian corporation's information systems were compromised, resulting in the breach of personally identifiable information for some 36 million user accounts in more than 40 countries. Its primary website, AshleyMadison.com, connected individuals who were seeking to have affairs.

Founded in 2002, the company experienced rapid growth and by the time of the breach was generating annual revenues in excess of $100 million. Partly due to the organization's rapid growth, the organization did not have a formal framework for managing risk or documented information security policies, the information security leadership did not report to the board (or board of directors) or the CEO, and only some of the organization's employees had participated in the information security awareness program for the organization.

The attackers subsequently published the information online, exposing the personal details of the company's customers. The breach was widely reported, and subsequent class-action lawsuits from affected customers claimed damages of more than $567 million. Public shaming of the customers caused a number of high-profile individuals to resign from their jobs, put uncounted marriages at risk, and, in several instances, was blamed for individuals' suicides.

A joint investigation of the incident performed by the Privacy Commissioner of Canada and the Australian Privacy Commissioner and Acting Australian Information Commissioner identified failures of governance as one of the major factors in the event. The report found, among a number of failings, that the company's board and executive leadership had not taken reasonable steps to implement controls for sensitive information that should have received protection under both Canadian and Australian law.

Almost without exception, the post-compromise reviews of major information security breaches have identified failed governance practices as one of the primary factors contributing to the compromise.

Information security governance in the public sector follows a similar model. The laws of the jurisdiction provide a decision-making framework, which is refined through the regulatory process. In the United States, this structure can be seen in the legislative adoption of the Federal Information Security Management Act of 2002, which directed the adoption of good information security practices across the federal enterprise. The several chief executives, interpreting the law, have given force to its implementation through a series of management directives, ultimately driving the development of a standard body of information security practice.

Other models for organizational governance exist. For example, the World Wide Web Consortium (W3C), founded by Tim Berners-Lee in 1994, provides a forum for developing protocols and guidelines to encourage long-term growth for the Web. The W3C, through a consensus-based decision process, attempts to address the growing technological challenge of diverse uses of the World Wide Web using open, nonproprietary standards. These include standards for the Extensible Markup Language (XML), Simple Object Access Protocol (SOAP), Hypertext Markup Language (HTML), and others. From a governance perspective, this model provides a mechanism for active engagement from a variety of stakeholders who support the general mission of the organization.

Due Care

Governance requires that the individuals setting the strategic direction and mission of the organization act on behalf of the stakeholders. The minimum standard for their governance action requires that they act with due care. This legal concept expects these individuals to address any risk as would a reasonable person given the same set of facts. This "reasonable person" test is generally held to include knowledge of the compliance environment, acting in good faith and within the powers of the office, and avoidance of conflicts of interest.

In this corporate model, this separation of duties between the organization's ownership interests and the day-to-day management is needed to ensure that the interests of the true owners of the organization are not compromised by self-interested decision-making by management.

The idea of duty of care extends to most legal systems. Article 1384 of the Napoleonic Code provides that "One shall be liable not only for the damages he causes by his own act, but also for that which is caused by the acts of persons for whom he is responsible, or by things which are in his custody."

For example, the California Civil Code requires that "[a] business that owns, licenses, or maintains personal information about a California resident shall implement and maintain reasonable security procedures and practices appropriate to the nature of the information, to protect the personal information from unauthorized access, destruction, use, modification, or disclosure." In defining *reasonable* in the *California Data Breach Report* in February 2016, the California attorney general invoked the Center for Internet Security (CIS) Critical Security Controls as "a minimum level of information security that all organizations should meet [and] the failure to implement all of the Controls that apply to an organization's environment constitutes a lack of reasonable security."

In India, the Ministry of Communication and Information Technology similarly used the ISO 27001 standard as one that meets the minimum expectations for protection of sensitive personal data or information arising out of the adoption of the Information Technology Act of 2000.

A wide variety of actions beyond adoption of a security framework can be taken by boards to meet their duty of care. These actions may include bringing individuals into the governing body with specific expertise in information security, updating of policies which express the board's expectations for managing information security, or engaging the services of outside experts to audit and evaluate the organization's security posture.

Widespread media reports of compromise and the imposition of ever-larger penalties for inappropriate disclosure of sensitive information would suggest that the governance bodies should increase their attention to information security activities. However, research into the behavior of publicly traded companies suggests that many boards have not significantly increased their oversight of information security practices.

A 2017 Stanford University study suggests that organizations still lack sufficient cybersecurity expertise and, as a consequence, have not taken actions to mitigate the risks from data theft, loss of intellectual property, or breach of personally identifiable information. When such failures become public, most announce steps to improve security, provide credit monitoring, or enter into financial settlements with injured parties.

Almost without exception, corporations that experienced breaches made no changes to their oversight of information security activities, nor did they add cybersecurity professionals to their boards. Boards held few executives directly accountable, either through termination or reductions in compensation. In other words, despite widespread recognition that there is increasing risk from cyber attacks, most governance organizations have not adopted new approaches to more effectively address weaknesses in cybersecurity governance.

Compliance means that all the rules and regulations pertinent to your organization have been met. Compliance is an expectation that is defined by an external entity that has some means to enforce its expectation. In any enterprise, one of the governing body's primary responsibilities is to identify the ways in which the organization must comply with an outside expectation. These compliance requirements may be expressed through legislation, regulation, or through a contract. Regardless, once the organization has identified the expectations for compliance, it is the responsibility of the management to implement processes to ensure those expectations for compliance are met.

DETERMINE COMPLIANCE REQUIREMENTS

Organizations always have expectations placed on them by outside entities or legal arrangements. The information security practitioner must be able to identify the source of the compliance expectation, the information to be protected, the level of protection, and the means by which proof can be supplied to demonstrate the effectiveness of the controls.

Legal Compliance

Many compliance expectations come from statutory or regulatory expectations and apply broadly to all industries. Others are specific to certain industries or for certain periods of time. This ever-changing set of expectations requires a continuous review of organizational practices to ensure that information is properly protected.

Jurisdiction

The first challenge in identifying compliance expectations requires knowing which jurisdiction has the legal authority to set rules. It is not enough to know the relevant geography or political boundaries. Jurisdiction may be established based on the activity of the organization and influenced by international treaties, agreements, or any number of other factors.

International dealings are complicated not only by the national laws but also by the existence of supranational organizations. Examples include the United Nations, the European Union (EU), the International Tribunal for Law of the Sea (ITLOS), the Organization of Petroleum Exporting Countries (OPEC), and the North American Free Trade Agreement (NAFTA). While the individual details and level of compliance varies, participating nations in these arrangements usually agree to implement the regulations within the supranational organization's jurisdiction or to abide by the decisions of the supranational entity.

With more than 190 individual nation-states in the world (the actual number depends on who is counting), the complexities of compliance increase. What is legal and required in one jurisdiction may, for the same information set, be illegal and unauthorized in another.

To further add to the complexity, sub jurisdictions may further add unique compliance expectations. Whether they are states, counties, parishes, cities, boroughs, provinces, territories, or prefectures, these entities have latitude to establish rules within the boundaries set by their parent jurisdictions.

Because of the complexities of the legal environment, it is impossible to address the unique aspects of each sovereign jurisdiction. While the CISSP CBK focuses on the laws and structures of the United States and the European Union, information security practitioners must be aware of the nuances of the jurisdictions in which they operate.

Legal Tradition

Much of the basis for the practice of information security has been created within the context of common law. This legal system relies heavily on precedent to determine the just course of action. More than a third of the world's population, including much of the British Commonwealth and the United States, relies on common law as a significant part of their legal tradition.

Civil law specifies conduct through a legal code, which the judge applies to the matter at hand. In this tradition, the sitting judge's interpretation of the code takes precedence over previous circumstances. The Napoleonic Code has been used to form the basis of law in various regions, including much of the European Union.

Other legal traditions place value on the religious teachings of their respective books of faith. In the Islamic tradition, the teaching of the Qur'an and the Hadith are used to set rules for the faithful, both in the expression of religious faith (Ibadah) and in the conduct of business (Muamalat). In the Hebraic tradition, Halakha defines the way an individual should behave.

Other nations' legal traditions reflect a mix of these traditions and local practice. For example, the legal tradition in China includes aspects of Confucian practice but is strongly influenced by Western civil law and the socialist law adopted following the establishment of the People's Republic of China in 1949.

Each of these traditions has had to address technological change and increased international contact in different ways. Privacy and intellectual property protections differ, as do limits on the use of technical protections like encryption. The CISSP CBK provides a broad overview of legal practice and information security law. The practitioner must take into account the complexities of the legal environment in which he or she operates and engage the assistance of trained legal professionals when appropriate.

Legal Compliance Expectations

In most jurisdictions, laws are established to define what is permissible and what is not. In U.S. law, the word *law* refers to any rule that, if broken, subjects a party to criminal punishment or civil liability. Laws may be generally broken into two parts: statutes and regulations. Statutes are written and adopted by the jurisdiction's governing body, while regulations are more detailed rules on how the execution of a statute will be performed. Both statutes and regulations are enforceable, but the regulations are subordinate to statutes.

UNDERSTAND LEGAL AND REGULATORY ISSUES THAT PERTAIN TO INFORMATION SECURITY IN A GLOBAL CONTEXT

Information security practice transcends borders. Threats can materialize in seconds from across the globe, actors are often difficult to identify, and they may attempt to compromise the confidentiality, integrity, and availability of information for a variety of purposes.

They range from otherwise-trusted individuals inside organizations to nation-state actors to individual criminals and organized criminal elements.

The weaknesses that the threat actors leverage are equally dynamic. Through the use of technical tools, social engineering, and other means, the systems that process and protect information assets are vulnerable because of their broad access, weak technical controls, and the complexity of managing the diverse array of interconnected systems.

In many cases, the unique information processed by the systems is of particular value to the attacker. Personally identifiable information can be used for fraud in a variety of forms. The intellectual property of an organization is also a target, where a compromise would allow attackers to gain competitive advantage in the marketplace. The information security professional must be aware of the international environment to develop appropriate strategies to protect the information under their control.

Cyber Crimes and Data Breaches

The explosive increase in the number of interconnected systems has created unprecedented opportunities to compromise records and processes using computer-related technology. These cyber crimes are growing not only in number but in severity, and the sheer volume of the information compromised is staggering. The information security practitioner must have a sound, yet current, appreciation for the range of potential criminal acts and actors.

The computer may be the target of the criminal act, or it may simply facilitate a traditional criminal act. Whether the attacks are for profit or notoriety, tools are readily available to enable malicious actors with minimal technical skills to effect great damage to the information environment. Given the constantly improving capabilities of nation-state actors to target information and infrastructure, today's information security professional is faced with an ever more difficult task of securing their environment from compromise.

Facilitating the Traditional Criminal Act

Criminal behavior is remarkably adaptable to new technologies. Fraud in various forms, extortion, and extortion are only some of the traditional criminal acts that are now leveraging computer technology.

Fraud

According to Black's Law Dictionary, *fraud* is defined as "All multifarious means which human ingenuity can devise, and which are resorted to by one individual to get an advantage over another by false suggestions or suppression of the truth. It includes all surprises, tricks, cunning or dissembling, and any unfair way which another is cheated." While the precise legal definition varies between jurisdictions, there is no doubt that the legal prohibition of fraud goes back to the earliest legal codes.

✔ Nigeria Money Scam

Virtually everyone who has ever had an email account has received a message similar to the following:

> Subject: CHARITY DISTRIBUTION
> From:
> Mr. Peter David Smith
> URGENT – HELP ME DISTRIBUTE MY $15 MILLION TO CHARITY
> IN SUMMARY:- I have 15,000,000.00 (15 million) U.S. Dollars and I want you to assist me in distributing the money to charity organizations. I agree to reward you with part of the money for your assistance, kindness and participation in this Godly project. This mail might come to you as a surprise and the temptation to ignore it as unserious could come into your mind but please consider it a divine wish and accept it with a deep sense of humility....

This "Nigerian money scam" or "419 scam" (for the part of the Nigerian criminal code that makes these scams illegal) asks the recipient to provide banking information in exchange for a percentage of the amount being transferred. This classic confidence scam has been going on since the 1920s, originally using postcards, but the ease with which email reaches millions of people has greatly reduced the overall cost to the criminal to deliver their initial message and to maintain contact with the victim, extracting ever increasing amounts of money.

The reason the scammers do this is simple: it works. Psychological experiments by Stanford University psychologists Jonathan Freeman and Scott Fraser suggest that a person who does a simple favor one time is more likely to help in the future. (See https://www.sciencefriday.com/articles/the-first-nigerian-prince-scam/ for more information on the experiments.) If the greed motivation is coupled with our desire to be helpful and sympathetic, the result is that some people will give large sums of money to the perpetrators.

People who fall for the scam come from all walks of life. Further, tracking down the criminals is difficult, requiring international cooperation. Occasionally, it results in high-profile arrests, but more often than not, the scammers make away with millions of dollars. With thousands of variants, the scam remains one of most profitable, low-risk opportunities for fraud available to technically unskilled thieves.

Individuals are often targeted to give to charities, often taking advantage of real disasters to solicit donations for relief. The scammers often tell their victims that the donation is tax-deductible under the U.S. tax code. The victims are then surprised when their deductions are disallowed and they are expected to pay federal and state tax on the money that they gave to the scammers!

Other forms of fraud include the use of online sales sites to entice a potential car buyer into fronting the money for the purchase of a vehicle, only to be told that the vehicle is "overseas" and must be transported to the United States, a story that gives the thieves the opportunity to disappear. Still others use a form of offering tickets to sold-out sporting events or concerts, with the scam being revealed only when the person tries to use the forged e-tickets at the event.

The technical sophistication of thieves is clearly increasing. According to FBI statistics from 2017, $969 million was "diverted or attempted to be diverted" from real estate transactions in the United States. Thieves either spoof or, in many cases, hack the email systems of legitimate title or escrow companies and provide instructions to potential homebuyers, who send payments to accounts controlled by thieves. This represents a marked increase in attacks from 2016, when only $19 million in such transactions were reported.

With so many different scams and potential victims, it is not surprising that criminals increasingly take advantage of the electronic movement of information to illegally profit.

Fencing Stolen Goods

Stolen goods are often resold online, where it is difficult to track the source of the goods. Most online retailers have strong policies against selling stolen goods, yet billions of dollars in losses were reported by businesses. In the 2017 Organized Retail Crime Report by the National Retail Federation, 57.6 percent of retailers in the United States have recovered property being sold through online auction sites, an increase of 18.8 percent from the previous year.

Turning the goods into cash quickly is of interest to most thieves, and thieves have taken advantage of new services to quickly turn their ill-gotten gains. With an auction site, the auction must close before the money is collected. Other social media sites operate as classified advertisements, allowing the transaction to close as quickly as a buyer is found. Even faster turnaround is possible through sites that are dedicated to selling used items, and tools allow prospective buyers to set triggers when items of interest become available.

In a somewhat ironic twist, online marketplaces are also used by police to sell unclaimed goods recovered from the thieves. Depending on the jurisdiction, many police agencies are allowed to keep all, or a portion, of the revenue to support policing activities. Traditionally done at police auctions, this new approach simplifies for the lawmen the same problem as it does for thieves—getting rid of the goods!

Cyber Extortion

Compelling someone to give money or goods or take actions by threatening harm to their person, reputation, or property is illegal in virtually all modern legal systems. Using computer technology has made it easier for criminals to extort from their victims. While extortion takes many forms, the rise in ransomware is a classic example of criminals leveraging technology for their nefarious ends.

Early malware attacked systems by hiding files or threatening to reformat hard drives. With sufficient technical knowledge, repairs could often be implemented without paying the ransom. Later compromises demanded that users send premium-rate SMS messages to receive a code that would stop their machines from displaying pornographic images.

Advances in technology, including the widespread availability of public key cryptography and relatively anonymous methods of receiving payment methods, allowed criminals to construct attacks that increased the effectiveness and profitability of malware. In late 2013, the malware Cryptolocker began spreading, encrypting drives, and demanding payment in Bitcoin.

The ease of delivery through email and SMS messaging, along with the relative anonymity afforded to the extortionists, created new opportunities for entire supply chains dedicated to the delivery of malware. Like any other business, specialists have begun to emerge, with some developing the malware, others managing the distribution, still others collecting the ransoms; some even have help desks to assist victims in purchasing bitcoins in hopes of being able to get back their data.

The technical capabilities of the extortionists increased when a number of exploits developed by the U.S. intelligence agencies were publicly released. These previously unknown compromises provided a vector that allowed the delivery of the malware to vast numbers of systems. The Petya and WannaCry exploits accelerated the impact of ransomware attacks, and one estimate suggests the collective financial impact to business is more than $11 billion, and the market is still growing.

Pornography

Erotic imagery has been around since the first cave-dwellers drew pictures with charcoal smudges. The early adopters of many technologies and industries, including books, photography, motion pictures, and video games, did so precisely to indulge their prurient interests. The widespread availability of pornography and the borderless nature of the Internet combine to make distribution of erotic content to a large audience a simple matter of bandwidth.

The type of content legally available is often regulated by the jurisdiction. More than half of the Interpol member states have laws specifically related to pornography depicting children, commonly referred to as child sexual abuse material (CSAM).

The adoption of legislation specifically prohibiting such depictions has been encouraged by a number of international organizations, including the United Nations and the European Commission.

The Internet has significantly changed how illegal pornography is reproduced and disseminated. The perpetrators actively swap images, often encrypted using steganographic or other cryptographic protections. The end result is that the use of non-electronic means to reproduce and transmit child pornography has been substantially eliminated.

Depending on the jurisdiction, owners of data services can be held accountable for the illegal use of their services. In the European Union, the ratification of Electronic Commerce Directive 2000/31/EC caused member states to implement legislation that requires service providers to "act expeditiously to remove or to disable access" when they are made aware of illegal content under their control. This was further strengthened by the Combating the Sexual Abuse and Sexual Exploitation of Children and Child Pornography Directive 2011/93/EU, which required member states to remove CSAM material on websites hosted in their countries.

Nevertheless, CSAM material continues to be available, particularly on the "dark web," where the lack of governmental enforcement has inspired others to take vigilante action. The hacker collective Anonymous has used several techniques to disrupt the flow of CSAM, including a well-publicized distributed denial of service (DDoS) attack against 40 child-porn websites in 2011. In 2016, a hacker claiming association with Anonymous took down some 10,000 sites they claimed were hosting such materials.

The Computer as the Target

The increasing reliance on electronic information systems to communicate provides the attacker with an opportunity to disrupt the flow of information by attacking the systems themselves. Unlike a physical attack where some piece of equipment is damaged, a logical attack often leaves the physical infrastructure intact but configured in a way that it cannot fulfill its function.

In other cases, the manipulation of the technology may cause physical damage. In extreme cases, these attacks can put lives in danger. Regardless, the information security professional must be able to identify threats to the systems themselves and devise appropriate controls to minimize the risk of such compromise.

Operational Disruption

The interconnected world has exposed a number of methods to disrupt the normal movement of information. As these activities directly affect the availability of services, security professionals should be able to identify how such disruptions would be addressed.

Distributed Denial of Service

Communications between electronic systems is conducted using a number of diverse services and technologies. Disrupting one of those technologies may deny access to legitimate users of the system. Various forms of denial of service (DoS) events can disrupt the access control processes, disrupt the directory processes, or even damage physical interconnections. However, the most common forms of denial of service involve leveraging weaknesses in the TCP/IP communications suite.

While the technical details of the various forms of DoS will be discussed in Chapter 3, suffice it to say that many different methods exist. However, in a pure DoS attack, the attacker uses only a single device to achieve service denial. A distributed denial of service attack uses multiple devices simultaneously to execute the attack, overwhelming the capabilities of the target by sheer volume of activity. Often, in a DDoS attack, the owner of the attacking system will not be aware that their device is being surreptitiously used for the nefarious purpose.

Domain Name System

The Domain Name System (DNS) processes that map IP addresses to names is essential to the operation of the Internet. However, security considerations were never prime considerations in the development of the protocol. Consequently, a number of attacks took advantage of the lack of authentication in zone file transfers to compromise the name resolution process.

The importance of the proper operation of the DNS environment was highlighted by an attack in October 2016. The commercial DNS provider Dyn.com, which provides services to hundreds of the Internet's most heavily trafficked sites, was subjected to multiple waves of a DDoS attack that originated from a wide array of Internet-connected devices. These devices had been compromised with the Mirai malware, which achieved persistence by leveraging default factory usernames and credentials for Linux-based baby monitors, home routers, and printers. While three individuals ultimately pleaded guilty in a U.S. court for their involvement in the botnet that was used in the compromise, the software that they developed has been used by others to execute similar attacks.

Hacktivism

Some attackers are interested in notoriety or making a political statement with their attacks. These ideologically motivated attackers seek to spread their political message by compromising their target's systems or by exposing sensitive information that will damage the reputation of the victim. These attacks have targeted private individuals, corporations, and nation-state actors.

Unlike in the physical world, when damaging information is published, holding the perpetrators to account in the virtual world is much more difficult. First, the perpetrators have to be identified, and often the attackers go to great lengths to anonymize their actions. Second, the question of which legal forum has jurisdiction is complicated, as many of the actors are not in the same jurisdiction as their victims.

Often, the perpetrators will argue that their actions are simply expressions of free speech. In some countries, the Internet is heavily censored by the government. By posting information that the government doesn't want made available, the perpetrators argue that they are achieving a greater social good.

Cult of the Dead Cow

One of the earliest groups associated with hacking was formed in 1984, before the broad adoption of Internet technology. Operating initially through dial-up bulletin boards, the Cult of the Dead Cow (cDc) shared with hackers various techniques to compromise systems, hosted early hacker conventions, distributed music, and occasionally made political news pronouncements. Their work provided a forum for like-minded individuals to communicate, share ideas, and collaborate on tools.

Some of the tools developed by cDc members include Back Orifice (demonstrating remote access to early Windows systems), Camera/Shy (a steganographic tool), and tools designed to compromise NetBIOS and SMB. These early tools demonstrated some of the most glaring weaknesses of the distributed computing environment.

However, their work has left a lasting impression on the language of security professionals. The cDc popularized communications methods such as ASCII art and the use of letter substitution with similar ASCII codes (i.e., $ for the letter S, as in "ki$$ my…"). The cDc is widely credited with originating the term 31337, an alternative spelling of the word *elite*, eventually leading to an entire "leetspeak" vernacular.

Anonymous

Under the moniker Anonymous, a rather amorphous collection of hackers and political activists have conducted a series of high-profile attacks against governments, religious groups, and corporations. The group has launched disruptive campaigns against groups as diverse as the Church of Scientology, the Recording Industry Association of America, PayPal.com, the New York Stock Exchange, and the Islamic State (ISIS).

"Anons" often appear in public or on video wearing Guy Fawkes masks. However, their Internet anonymity has been compromised on a number of occasions, as members of (or those claiming association with) Anonymous have been convicted of cyber attacks in the United States, the United Kingdom, Australia, Spain, Turkey, and others.

The arrests have slowed but not stopped Anonymous's efforts. While the group has spawned imitators as well as aligning with other hacktivist groups, they have also disclaimed hacking done by others. For example, claims that Anonymous was involved in the 2016 U.S. presidential election were denied on the group's Anonymous Official YouTube.com site. Regardless, the group, its imposters, and surrogates remain a real threat to organizations that spark their wrath.

Doxxing

One of Anonymous's preferred tactics is to release sensitive information about its targets. This attack, often referred to as *doxxing*, has been used against NASA, various pornographic websites, the Bay Area Rapid Transit system, and the information security firm HBGary Federal, which was engaged in researching the Anonymous group. Others, too, have used the attack to harass their targets, causing them to lose their jobs, friends, or families.

Depending on the source and content of the information, doxxing may or may not be illegal. If the information is legally obtained, the doxxer may claim that simply republishing the information isn't a crime. A wide variety of information sources, including public records, credit reports, and aggregated information from multiple legal sources, may result in legal disclosure of sensitive information. On the other hand, if the information is illegally obtained through hacking or some other means, then the victim may have legal recourse.

Doxxing can also take the form of cyberextortion, where the perpetrator will encrypt sensitive files or information about their victim and demand some sort of payment or action. Recent victims include Disney, Netflix, and HBO, all of which have seen content stolen by attackers.

WikiLeaks

The website WikiLeaks.com has taken doxxing to a new level. WikiLeaks is an international nonprofit organization that "specializes in the analysis and publication of large datasets of censored or otherwise restricted materials involving war, spying, and corruption." As of 2017, WikiLeaks claims to have published more than 10 million sensitive documents.

WikiLeaks claims no political ideology and indeed has released sensitive information from a wide variety of organizations. Among the high-profile document releases orchestrated by WikiLeaks are materials related to the war in Afghanistan, U.S. presidential elections, Russian monitoring of cell phone communications, Saudi Foreign Ministry cables, and other sensitive information. The sensitive nature of the materials released, however embarrassing to governments, has also included personally identifiable information on individuals.

WikiLeaks is often accused of acting on behalf of intelligence agencies as an outlet for disinformation. Not surprisingly, WikiLeaks has claimed it is the subject of nation-state actor attacks to silence its publications. Regardless, the site claims relationships with dozens of news organizations throughout the world.

Often, the information on these sites comes from insiders disillusioned with their organizations. Leaking information for traditional investigative journalism has a long tradition predating the Internet. Further, WikiLeaks is by no means the only site to provide an anonymous outlet for the disclosure of sensitive information. However, the ease with which inappropriate disclosure can now occur increases the need for information security professionals to understand and implement appropriate control over their organizations' sensitive information.

Growth of Criminal Activity Against Data

The value of data varies greatly, and criminal elements are acutely aware of which data will bring the best return with the least risk. Identity theft and credit card fraud, according to the FBI and other law enforcement organizations, are significantly underreported, and the cases are often complex, making prosecution difficult. Other forms of intellectual property, such as source code, digital media content, and research are also frequently the target of criminal actors.

Individual Actors

The widespread availability of personal data, coupled with lax controls, have made it relatively easy for individual criminals to target digital assets. Many significant and costly breaches have been accomplished by individuals with single computers and a dial-up Internet connection.

This is likely to continue as connectivity spreads to parts of the world where the return on hacking and identity theft relative to the risk of being caught is significantly in favor of the hacker. In many developing countries, the lack of cybersecurity expertise is even greater than in other parts of the world, precisely because talented and trained individuals seek more lucrative employment opportunities. Further compounding the problem is that information security practices in developing countries often lag behind the industry, and this allows attacks that would be unsuccessful elsewhere to be effectively used in these areas.

The development of simplified tools that make attacks available to less technical actors also create opportunities for individuals to profit from theft of media. Dozens of tools, like Metasploit, w3af, Core Impact, and others, can be misappropriated to compromise the systems they are designed to evaluate.

Individual actors are often motivated by the publicity or professional recognition of their skills. To take advantage of this, many organizations offer bug bounties to reward individuals who identify security flaws so they can be remediated.

Organized Crime

While attacks have traditionally been perpetrated by individuals, recent investigations suggest that continuing criminal enterprises (organized criminal gangs) are targeting sensitive information. In June 2017, a group of individuals in New York associated with the Bloods gang imprinted credit cards with stolen identity information and charged hundreds of thousands of dollars in shopping trips to local stores. The gang created the cards using blank Visa, MasterCard, and American Express cards, including some that used chip-and-pin technology.

Credit card information remains one of the most valuable commodities for thieves internationally. In May 2106, members of the Yakuza executed 14,000 withdrawal transactions against accounts held by the South Africa Standard Bank using ATMs at 7-Eleven convenience stores over a 3-hour period, withdrawing 1.4 billion yen ($13 million). The carefully selected targets, timing, and synchronization of the attack are typical of the actions of organized criminal elements.

Cyber Warfare—Nation-State Actors

Nation-state actors are acutely aware that more information is now made available electronically and greater reliance is placed on information systems to manage that information. The larger goals and constraints under which the cyberwarfare activities occur are unique to each country, but it is clear that some nation-state actors are using cyber means to sustain their economies, disrupt other nations' political processes, gain economic advantage, or provide a collateral capability to disrupt their enemies as part of a larger military effort.

To accomplish their respective goals, the various nation-state actors have developed sophisticated tools, identified weaknesses in their targets' infrastructures, and deployed sophisticated monitoring solutions directed at compromising the security of the information. Many of these nation-state actors make no distinction between private- and public-sector organizations and often find lucrative information in private corporations with relatively lax security controls. It is not unfair to say that any organization that has unique intellectual property either has been or will be the target of nation-state actors.

Nation-state actors are equally interested in developing appropriate defenses against cyber threats. The same skills that allow the development of technical capabilities to compromise systems are closely aligned with the skills necessary to secure the same systems. Consequently, most of the nation-state organizations dedicate part of their resources to defending against threats in cyberspace by identifying best practices, providing research, and, where appropriate, communicating vulnerability information to others to allow them to remediate weaknesses.

The nation-state actors have often been closely associated with industries inside their borders. It is not surprising that individuals who develop skills inside their governments' cyberwarfare operations would subsequently seek to profit from that knowledge by developing products in the private sector. Nevertheless, their previous association may create concerns for their customers, who want to ensure that their supply chain has not been compromised. Information security professionals should be aware of those potential associations so appropriate control can be applied.

Organizations that become targets of nation-state actors face a daunting challenge. Not only do the attackers have interests in a wide range of information, their sophisticated tools combined with the skill, numbers, and persistence of the attackers make defending against a nation-state actor a difficult proposition. Proper threat modeling and well-deployed defenses provide the best chance for organizations to defeat nation-state actor attacks.

United States

The United States government has a number of organizations that develop technical capabilities to compromise information systems. The largest of these organizations, the National Security Agency (NSA), has more than 30,000 employees.

Tasked with monitoring communications outside the United States, the NSA has developed sophisticated tools to exploit target infrastructures. Some sense of the scope of these capabilities were revealed when Edward Snowden, an NSA contractor, exfiltrated approximately 1 million documents from classified networks using his privileges as a systems administrator. These documents detailed a wide range of zero-day attacks and other methods that the U.S. government had developed to support intelligence collection activities. WikiLeaks subsequently published thousands of the documents.

The NSA has also developed capabilities to protect U.S. government networks from compromise. Through the work of the Information Assurance Directorate, the NSA publishes best practices for securing systems, networks, and devices.

The United States, like other countries, often shares intelligence information with its partners. In 2017, the director of the NSA testified before Congress that the United States had warned France, Germany, and the United Kingdom that the Russian government was actively working to influence elections in their respective countries. While this did not prevent the theft and republication of nine gigabytes of data from one of the candidates in the French elections, the forewarning allowed the French candidate time to inject false messages into the information set, degrading the overall impact of the disclosure.

Some of the other agencies with separate but sophisticated capabilities include the Department of Defense (DoD), the Central Intelligence Agency, and the Department of Justice. All of these agencies rely on specific legislative authority to conduct their monitoring and other activities.

United Kingdom

The National Cyber Security Centre (NCSC) provides similar capabilities for the United Kingdom much as the NSA does for the U.S. government. Pulling together a number of organizations that had separate functions under the Government Communications Headquarters (GCHQ), the NCSC provides technical capabilities to support governmental requirements and publishes best-practice security guidance that is widely applicable to both private- and public-sector organizations.

The GCHQ and its predecessor agencies have been at the forefront of cryptographic work for decades. The team of Allied cryptanalysts stationed at Bletchley Park during World War II succeeded in compromising many Axis ciphers, notably the Enigma system. Later, in the 1970s, the development of public key exchange mechanisms was first accomplished by UK cryptographers.

China

The People's Republic of China has a well-funded and highly capable technical capability to gather intelligence against both military and civilian targets. At the forefront of Chinese hacking efforts are members of Unit 61398, which has deployed advanced persistent threat agents against governments and companies in the United States, Canada, Australia, members of the European Union, and others to collect a wide variety of intellectual property, personally identifiable information, and information on critical infrastructures.

Internally, the Chinese government conducts extensive monitoring of the use of the Internet inside China, limiting access points and censoring materials believed to violate Chinese law. The Chinese government has acknowledged that it has more than 2 million people employed as content censors.

North Korea

North Korea presents a unique problem to information security professionals worldwide. Not only do they have a well-funded and technically capable cyberwarfare capability, but they have actively used that capability to steal information and money and compromise entities that they feel threaten their regime. While the Democratic People's Republic of Korea does not publicly admit that they are behind these attacks, private researchers and intelligence services worldwide have come to recognize the unique signatures of North Korean hacking operations.

International sanctions imposed on the regime have caused their cyberwarfare operators to focus on targets with a significant financial return. Some of the attackers' primary targets have been banks, with intrusions documented in more than 18 countries. Other targets include casinos and software developers in the financial services industry. According to the *New York Times*, the North Korean hacking efforts generate more than 1 billion dollars in revenue annually to the regime.

Probably the most recent area of focus by the attackers has been to use and compromise cryptocurrency. The WannaCry virus, although it leveraged an exploit allegedly developed by the NSA, was attributed to North Korean hackers. The virus infected more than 200,000 computers in more than 150 countries, but the effect was amplified in organizations that lacked effective patch management and used legacy operating systems. Analysis of the attack suggests that the financial return to the attackers was fairly limited, particularly when security researchers publicly announced that few who paid the ransom actually recovered their data.

Subsequent attacks on multiple bitcoin exchanges were probably more lucrative. South Korean officials have identified at least four separate attacks on bitcoin exchanges, each generating tens of millions of dollars and in one case causing the exchange to declare bankruptcy.

Others

The long-simmering animosity between India and Pakistan has been escalated to cyberspace on several occasions. While both countries have skilled cyberwarfare specialists, the respective national interests are often abetted by hackers outside the governments. Both countries had multiple websites compromised on their respective independence days in 2017, events not likely to be the work of intelligence operatives trying to maintain anonymity.

The Ukrainian government has attributed a series of cyber attacks on its infrastructure to the work of Russian intelligence services. Russian attackers have been credited with compromising the accounts in the Yahoo.com mail service and have been accused of using Kapersky antivirus/antimalware tools to extract information from machines where it was installed.

Most other nation-states have some level of technical capability, often purchased from companies like Lench IT Solutions' FinFisher, Trovicor, and Hacking Team, among others. Their tools are used by law enforcement and other governmental organizations in dozens of countries, within the legal framework of the nation-state.

Nation-state actors will continue to use technical tools to compromise systems when they believe it is in their national interest to do so. Whether to gain economic advantage, acquire information on military capabilities, or monitor internal political dissent, the tools to accomplish these ends exist. Security professionals must remain aware of the changing threat environment and their areas of vulnerability to protect their information assets from inappropriate disclosure.

Responding to Cyber Crime

While the technical defenses against cyber crime evolve in response to the threat, the governance and policy frameworks have been slower to adapt. Nevertheless, a variety of legal and organizational responses to minimize the impact of cyber crime and to hold perpetrators accountable have been initiated.

International Legal Frameworks

Recognizing the international nature of cyber crime, a number of existing international organizations have taken action to address such activities within the context of their current agreements and obligations. Other efforts have addressed cyber crime between individual states. Regardless of the forum, cyber crime has become a major issue in international engagement and diplomacy, which ultimately sets the terms for technical cooperation between nations.

NATO Article 5

Article 5 of the treaty that established the North Atlantic Treaty Organization (NATO) states in part, "The Parties agree that an armed attack against one or more of them in Europe or North America shall be considered an attack against them all and consequently they agree that, if such an armed attack occurs, each of them…will assist the Party or Parties so attacked by taking…such action as it deems necessary, including the use of armed force…." Although it has been invoked on only one occasion (following the 9/11 attacks), Article 5 binds members to actions in defense of the alliance if any of them are attacked.

In 2014, NATO members agreed on an updated defense policy that explicitly included cyber attack as an event under which a NATO country could invoke Article 5. NATO has been engaged in a broad range of training, coordination, and developing technical capabilities to defend NATO's operations in cyberspace.

Convention on Cybercrime

In 2001, the Council of Europe, together with representatives from the United States, Canada, Japan, and South Africa, met in Budapest to increase cooperation on cyber crime. The resulting Convention on Cybercrime, or the Budapest Convention, addressed such areas as copyright infringement, computer-related fraud and forgery, pornography, and violations of network security.

The convention created a set of common standards for the investigation of cyber crime, handling of evidence, and the commitment to provide mutual legal assistance in the prosecution of crimes. Ultimately, it is up to each individual nation to modify its laws to conform to the convention, and many of the signatories have stated reservations about various aspects of the convention that are in conflict with their respective laws. As of 2017, more than 56 nations are signatories to the convention.

Directive 2013/40/EU on Attacks Against Information Systems

On August 12, 2013, the European Union put standards in place for each member state to implement minimum sanctions for attacks against information systems and to increase the coordination between the member nations, law enforcement bodies, and cyber-response organizations. The directive specifically calls out identity theft, deployment of cybercrime tools such as botnets, illegal access, and illegal data interference as requiring additional criminal sanctions.

U.S.–China Agreement on Cyber Security

In 2015, following years of cyber attacks on U.S. firms attributed to Chinese actors, the leaders of both countries agreed not to attack companies based in the other's territory solely for economic advantage. That position was reaffirmed in 2017 by the new U.S. president and the president of China, and subsequent discussions agreed on these five key tenets:

>(1) that timely responses should be provided to requests for information and assistance concerning malicious cyber activities;

>(2) that neither country's government will conduct or knowingly support cyber-enabled theft of intellectual property, including trade secrets or other confidential business information, with the intent of providing competitive advantages to companies or commercial sectors;

>(3) to make common effort to further identify and promote appropriate norms of state behavior in cyberspace within the international community;

>(4) to maintain a high-level joint dialogue mechanism on fighting cyber-crime and related issues; and

>(5) to enhance law enforcement communication on cyber security incidents and to mutually provide timely responses.

Analysis by independent firms suggests that while the overall volume of attacks attributable to Chinese actors have decreased, there are still a significant number of attacks against U.S. corporations originating from China. This agreement was the first to recognize a distinction between economic and government/military espionage. For more information on the agreement, see https://www.justice.gov/opa/pr/first-us-china-law-enforcement-and-cybersecurity-dialogue.

Information Sharing

The sharing of cyberthreat information has evolved in complexity and grown in scale by orders of magnitude. Since traditional approaches to mandating information sharing are often limited to data breach events, a broad range of organizations supporting governments, the private sector, various industries, and other communities of interest have been formed to share cyberthreat information.

These organizations may be bilateral or multilateral, but in the absence of regulation mandating sharing, establishing trust between the partners is essential. Governance processes must exist to ensure that members sharing information are not harmed by their reporting.

Cyberthreat information is any information that can help an organization to identify, assess, monitor, and respond to cyber threats. Examples of cyberthreat information include indicators such as system artifacts or other "observables" associated with an attack, security alerts, threat intelligence reports, recommended security tool configurations, and other tactics, techniques, and procedures (TTPs).

Best Practices

International security frameworks have begun to coalesce around best practices for responding to cyber crime. These are only a few examples of best practice activities:

- **Traffic Light Protocol (TLP):** The Traffic Light Protocol was developed in the United Kingdom in the early 2000s to simplify the handling of information by the recipient. It has been incorporated into a number of other specifications. The use of the TLP is one means by which trust between organizations is supported.

  - **RED:** Not for disclosure, restricted to participants only

  - **AMBER:** Limited disclosure, restricted to participants' organizations

  - **GREEN:** Limited disclosure, restricted to the community

  - **WHITE:** Unlimited disclosure, subject to standard copyright rules

- **NIST 800-150:** NIST Special Publication 800-150, "Guide to Cyber Threat Information Sharing," is one of the most comprehensive sources describing how organizations can share cyberthreat information to improve their own and other organizations' security postures.

- **ISO/IEC 27010:2015:** ISO Publication 27010, "Information security management for inter-sector and inter-organizational communications," provides a structure for communicating information security information between industries in the same sectors, in different industry sectors, and with governments.

Mandatory Reporting and Disclosure

Many entities are required by law or compliance expectations to report cyber attacks. In the European Union, Directive 2016/1148, Concerning Measures for a High Common Level of Security of Network and Information Systems, across the European Union requires member states to set up or identify "competent authorities" who must be notified without undue delay when operators of essential services experience "incidents having a significant impact on the continuity of the essential services they provide." In India, government and "critical-sector organizations" are required to report cyber incidents to the Indian Computer Emergency Response Team (CERT-In) cyber incidents when they occur.

Certain industry sectors have specific compliance expectations for reporting incidents. The State of New York's "Cybersecurity Requirements for Financial Services Companies" requires regulated entities to report within 72 hours any cybersecurity events that have a "reasonable likelihood of materially harming any material part of the normal operations of the covered entity."

Separate from cyberincident reporting, most jurisdictions have mandatory reporting requirements for breaches of personally identifiable information. While this issue is discussed elsewhere in the chapter, the trend among regulators is to require more stringent reporting for both cyber incidents and data breaches.

Voluntary Information Sharing

Voluntary information sharing occurs through a diverse array of forums. The organizations listed here are only examples of the many organizations that support the sharing of cyberthreat information:

- **Asia-Pacific Computer Emergency Response Team (APCERT):** The APCERT is a coalition of Computer Emergency Response Teams (CERTs) and Computer Security Incident Response Teams (CSIRTs) within the Asia-Pacific region. Formed in 2003, the APCERT currently includes more than 30 members and partners with other organizations worldwide to share cyberthreat information.

- **European Cybercrime Centre (EC3):** As part of Interpol, the EC3 facilitates information sharing between policing organizations and provides technical expertise and cyber-related intelligence between member countries and non-EU law enforcement partners. The investigative arm, the Joint Cybercrime Action Task Force (J-CAT), works against cross-border cyber crimes, coordinating the efforts of the law enforcement community on high-priority cases.

- **U.S. Automated Information Sharing:** The U.S. Computer Emergency Readiness Team (US-CERT) has initiated a voluntary program that enables the exchange of cyberthreat indicators between the federal government and the private sector at machine speed. The Automated Indicator Sharing (AIS) capability relies on the Structured Threat Information Expression (STIX) and Trusted Automated Exchange of Indicator Information (TAXII) specifications for machine-to-machine communication.

Corporate Information Sharing

A number of private threat intelligence companies exist that market general or sector-specific threat intelligence. In many cases, these companies are founded by individuals who formerly served in similar roles in their countries' intelligence organizations.

The sector-specific Information Sharing and Analysis Centers (ISACs) provide another mechanism for private organizations to collaborate on cyber threats. In the United States, the National Council of ISACs recognizes more than 20 sector-specific ISACs, providing detailed threat information to their members. In the European Union, the ISAC model has taken advantage of the U.S. experience, while acknowledging that in the European Union, the state has a greater responsibility to protect private industry from attack.

General threat intelligence is also freely available from many companies as well. Google's VirusTotal evaluates URLs and files for malicious content, while Project Zero identifies previously unknown flaws in vendor products. In the spirit of "responsible disclosure," Google does not release the details of the flaws to the public until after the vendor issues a patch or 90 days have passed without vendor remediation.

Licensing and Intellectual Property

Intellectual property (IP) refers to creations of the mind. This includes physical creations or intellectual constructs, but both are worthy of protection to ensure that the creator receives proper recognition and can control the use of the idea. The World Intellectual Property Office divides intellectual property into two general categories: industrial property, including patents, trademarks, designs, and geographical indications of source, and copyright, which addresses the artistic expressions of ideas, including literary works, films, music, drawings, photographs, broadcasts, and a wide range of other creative work.

There are a number of reasons why legal protections exist for intellectual property. Inventions and new works benefit humanity. However, invention takes effort, and if anyone could copy the idea after it was created, there would be little incentive for innovation. Protecting IP encourages the commitment of resources to innovation and creation precisely because the creators will be able to benefit.

Innovation in one area begets further innovation. This creates an economic engine for growth, jobs, and improved quality of life. Consequently, a vibrant economy will provide some protection for an individual's work.

In practice, the protection of intellectual property is of paramount importance to the economic well-being of a nation. The growth of the U.S. economy can be directly traced to the intellectual property protections built into the U.S. Constitution that direct Congress to "promote the progress of science and useful arts, by securing for limited times to authors and inventors the exclusive right to their respective writings and discoveries." More than half of the economic growth in the United States in the last 60 years is attributable to technological innovation, while just the value of U.S. intellectual property is greater than the GDP of any other nation.

The four main forms of intellectual property are patents, trademarks, copyrights, and trade secrets. Each affords a different level of protection to the creator.

Patents

In simplest terms, a patent provides legal protection for rights over inventions. In many jurisdictions, the duration of protection extends for 20 years, at which time the knowledge of the invention becomes part of the public domain. In the United States, patents can be issued when someone creates a new and useful process, machine, manufacture, or composition of matter.

The invention must be novel or not have been described elsewhere. *Prior art* exists when someone else came up with the idea before the claimant. Many times, patent enforcement hinges on whether someone else came up with the idea first. Patent protection remains the "strongest form of intellectual property protection," but once the patent expires, others can leverage the patent without restriction.

Software has been eligible for patent for many years, but in Europe such patents are often more difficult to obtain than in the United States. However, recent case law in the United States suggests this will change. In *Alice Corp. v. CLS Bank*, the complainant argued that Alice Corporation's patent over software escrow practices was not unique and that escrow had existed for centuries before Alice Corporation created software to do the task. In a unanimous verdict finding for CLS Bank, Justice Clarence Thomas wrote, "[T]he mere recitation of a generic computer cannot transform a patent-ineligible abstract idea into a patent-eligible invention."

Trademark

A trademark identifies certain goods or services produced or provided by an individual or a company. A trademark could be a device, symbol, name, sound, product shape, logo, or some combination of those by which a product can be recognized. This allows vendors to build a brand association with the consumer, reflecting the quality, origin, or characteristics of a product.

The rapid growth of the Internet and, particularly, the Domain Name System created new challenges for trademarks. Often, organizations would want a particular domain name for which they already had a trademark, but that domain name was registered to another individual. *Cyber squatters* register Internet domain names that contain trademarks but have no intention of creating a legitimate website, instead hoping to sell the domain to the organization holding the trademark. In 1999, the United States enacted the Anti-Cybersquatting Consumer Protection Act (ACPA), which allows civil lawsuits against organizations for registering, trafficking in, or using a domain name confusingly similar to an existing trademark. Other countries have similar laws, and the Internet Corporation for Assigned Names and Numbers (ICANN) has developed a process to manage complaints regarding domain names.

Cyber squatting is often leveraged by malicious actors to facilitate the distribution of malware as well. *Typo squatting*, a form of cyber squatting, often fools unsuspecting users into visiting malicious sites by registering names like a well-known site, differing only in a single character. Depending on which fonts are displayed, it is often difficult to distinguish between an *I* and one that has been replaced by an *l*. The unsuspecting user ends up downloading malicious code due to the misdirection to a near copy of a legitimate site.

International harmonization of trademarks began in the late 1800s. Today, that work continues through the World Intellectual Property Organization (WIPO). Through WIPO, administration of trademarks is simplified for many countries, as approval of a single application is necessary for trademark protection in more than 90 countries.

Trademarks do not have an expiration date. As long as the organization continues to use the trademark, it can be renewed and enforced. However, if the organization does not renew the registration, it may fall into the public domain.

Copyright

A copyright protects the artistic expression of an idea. While individual jurisdictions vary, copyright protections are generally extended to printed works, audio recordings, photographs, motion pictures, and source code. The duration of the protection depends on the jurisdiction, but the Berne Convention requires all signatory nations to protect all works for at least 50 years after the author's death, with the exceptions of photographic (25 years) and cinematographic (50 years from first showing) work. Countries may have longer terms; in the United States, the minimum term is generally for the life of the author plus 70 years.

Trade Secrets

Proprietary information that is essential to the operation of a business can include recipes, processes, technical configurations, designs, or practices. If the organization takes active steps to maintain the confidentiality of the information, the information may be protected indefinitely. Unlike a patent, the contents of a trade secret do not have to be disclosed.

The active protections afforded to the product will vary depending on the organization. Nondisclosure agreements (NDAs), access rosters, and physical controls are often used. In the case of Coca-Cola, some of the measures taken to protect the secret formula include keeping the recipe in a company vault in Atlanta. The combination to the vault is known to only two employees, who are not allowed to fly on the same airplane and who are not permitted to open the vault without a resolution of the company's board.

Competing organizations may reverse engineer the secret, and doing so is generally legal. However, if the secret is inappropriately disclosed, the competing organization could be enjoined from using the information. As with other forms of intellectual property, the legal status of a trade secret depends on the jurisdiction. Trade secrets cannot be invoked to protect the company from disclosing wrongdoing. In other countries, source code and proprietary techniques may have to be disclosed to the government for evaluation to meet information security requirements, as is the case under China's Cybersecurity Law.

Licensing

Legal protections over intellectual property allow creators and inventors to profit from their work. Unfortunately, the ease with which information can be duplicated and transmitted has made it easier for people to copy information in violation of the legitimate owner's rights.

From an economic perspective, the effect is tremendous. By 2022, the global trade in counterfeited and pirated products, both physical and online, will grow to between 1.9 and 2.8 trillion dollars. Estimates by the Business Software Alliance (BSA) suggest that more than 40 percent of the software in use worldwide was not properly licensed.

Counterfeit goods also present significant economic as well as physical risks. A $460 billion a year industry, counterfeiting has been simplified by the e-commerce platforms and expedited international shipping, which has accompanied the lowering of trade barriers. The secondary impacts of illegal use of intellectual property are equally surprising. One estimate suggests that 23 percent of all bandwidth is consumed by activities that infringe on intellectual property.

While emerging technologies present opportunities for improving licensing methods, lack of enforcement remains one of the largest hurdles. With more applications transitioning to a cloud-enabled model, ensuring legal software licensing goes hand in hand with software as a service.

The use of unlicensed software increases the risk of software vulnerabilities, as the users are unable to get patches and updates. This leaves the users of bootleg software at risk when compromises are found in the software. While the vendors patch their legitimate versions, the unlicensed versions don't get the updates. It is somewhat ironic that by illegally using unlicensed software, individuals are more likely to be targeted by other illegal actors. The effect of this was seen most clearly in the rapid distribution of the WannaCry malware in China, where estimates suggest that 70 percent of computer users in China are running unlicensed software and state media acknowledged that more than 40,000 institutions were affected by the attack.

Corporate Espionage

Corporations constantly research the capabilities of their competitors to identify new opportunities, technologies, and markets. Unfortunately, some corporate actors extend their research beyond the usual venue of trade shows and reviewing press releases and seek to conduct surveillance and gather intelligence on their competitors in ways that move along the ethical continuum from appropriate to unethical and, in some cases, into illegal actions. Just as security professionals must consider the actions of nation-state actors or criminal elements, intellectual property must also be protected from legitimate competitors.

In 2011, an executive of the St. Louis Cardinals baseball team began illegally accessing information from his former employer—the Houston Astros—that was used to analyze player performance and personnel decisions. The hacking led to the criminal conviction of the employee, and the league imposed sanctions on the St. Louis organization, including fines and forfeited draft choices.

There is a close relationship between national security and economic activity. Often, nation-states assist local industries by sharing the results of their espionage on foreign competitors.

International Enforcement

While national laws are essential to the enforcement of some aspects of intellectual property protection, the growth of global markets and simplified means of information transmission requires international collaboration to protect the rights of creators and inventors. A number of international frameworks and organizations exist to address the transnational aspects of intellectual property.

World International Property Organization

One of 17 specialized agencies of the United Nations, WIPO has 191 member states and administers more than 20 international treaties. In addition, WIPO provides technical assistance to members in the areas of intellectual property and maintains various databases and registrations to simplify the administration of patents and trademarks internationally. WIPO has also worked with ICANN to build processes to resolve disputes related to domain names and with other multilateral organizations to support enforcement.

WIPO relies heavily on members' voluntary cooperation to enforce IP infringement complaints. Usually, this means taking legal action within the jurisdictions where the infringements have occurred. Often, this has resulted in less-than-aggressive actions to protect creative rights. WIPO does provide support for mediation and arbitration services as alternatives to litigation.

World Trade Organization

Originally created to govern trade between nations, the World Trade Organization (WTO) provides a somewhat stronger mechanism to protect intellectual property rights. The WTO has a structured process to hear complaints, present evidence, and handle appeals. As a result of complaints, compensation can be provided or, in extreme cases, an organization's participation in the WTO can be suspended.

There are a number of other organizations that could also be involved in enforcing intellectual property rights, including the World Health Organization, the EU, the World Customs Organization, and others.

Privacy

> *What I may see or hear in the course of the treatment or even outside of the treatment in regard to the life of men, which on no account one must spread abroad, I will keep to myself, holding such things shameful to be spoken about.*
>
> The Oath of Hippocrates

The concept of privacy in Western culture, that information about an individual should have protection against disclosure, dates back thousands of years. The concept of privacy has extended when considering the individual's expectation of privacy against intrusion by government.

New technology has challenged our traditional view of privacy. Our cellular phones track us everywhere on the planet, either through the cell network itself or through the use of global positioning systems. Our shopping is monitored in detail, from the time and place we make purchases to the order in which we pick out groceries. Each transaction is then aggregated with other data and analyzed to determine how better to meet the customer's needs.

Governments actively and passively track our activities. In many countries, the widespread use of facial recognition technology gives security forces the ability to know who is in the airport or driving on a highway. It can also give them the ability to monitor who a suspected drug dealer is meeting or who is being interviewed by a reporter.

The challenge for security professionals is to ensure that the organization's activities that affect privacy are compliant with the relevant laws of the jurisdiction and that the organization addresses the risks of managing personal information throughout the information lifecycle.

International Privacy Frameworks

A number of international frameworks exist that define privacy expectations. These vary in breadth and applicability, and most require some level of adoption by member states. In many cases, these frameworks have evolved to address the ability of new technologies to compromise traditional expectations of privacy.

Universal Declaration of Human Rights

Following World War II, there was great interest in ensuring that governments did not act in an arbitrary manner against citizens. The United Nations drafted the Universal Declaration of Human Rights that set forth these expectations for members. Article 12 states, "No one shall be subjected to arbitrary interference with his privacy, family, home or correspondence, nor to attacks upon his honour and reputation. Everyone has the right to the protection of the law against such interference or attacks."

The Organisation for Economic Cooperation and Development (OECD)

The Organisation for Economic Cooperation and Development (OECD) promotes policies designed to improve the economic and social well-being of people around the world. In 1980, the OECD published "Guidelines on the Protection of Privacy and Transborder Flows of Personal Data" to encourage the adoption of comprehensive privacy protection practices. In 2013, the OECD revised its Privacy Principles to address the wide range of challenges that came about with the explosive growth of information technology. Among other changes, the new guidelines placed greater emphasis on the role of the data controller to establish appropriate privacy practices for their organizations.

✔ OECD Privacy Principles: Basic Principles of National Application

The OECD Privacy Principles are used throughout many international privacy and data protection laws and are also used in many privacy programs and practices. The eight privacy principles are as follows:

1. **Collection Limitation Principle:** This principle states that data that is collected should be obtained by lawful and fair means, that the data subject should be aware of and consent to the collection of the data where appropriate, and that the quantity and type of data should be limited.

2. **Data Quality Principle:** This principle is aimed at the accuracy and completeness of data, whether it is appropriately maintained and updated, and whether the data retained is relevant to the purposes it is used for.

3. **Purpose Specification Principle:** Purpose specification means that the reasons that personal data is collected should be determined before it is collected, rather than after the fact, and that later data reuse is in line with the reason that the data was originally obtained.

4. **Use Limitation Principle:** This principle notes that release or disclosure of personal data should be limited to the purposes it was gathered for unless the data subject agrees to the release or it is required by law.

5. **Security Safeguards Principle:** Reasonable security safeguards aimed at preventing loss, disclosure, exposure, use, or destruction of the covered data are the focus of this principle.

6. **Openness Principle:** The principle of openness is intended to ensure that the practices and policies that cover personal data are accessible and that the existence of personal data, what data is collected and stored, and what it is used for should all be disclosed. Openness also requires that the data controller's identity and operating location or residence is openly disclosed.

7. **Individual Participation Principle:** This includes an individual's right to know if their data has been collected and stored and what that data is within a reasonable time and in a reasonable way. In addition, this principle allows the subject to request that the data be corrected, deleted, or otherwise modified as needed. An important element of this principle is the requirement that data controllers must also explain why any denials of these rights are made.

8. **Accountability Principle:** The final principle makes the data controller accountable for meeting these principles.

The OECD Privacy Guidelines can be found at `http://www.oecd.org/internet/ieconomy/privacy-guidelines.htm`.

In developing the guidelines, the OECD recognized the need to balance commerce and other legitimate activities with privacy safeguards. Further, the OECD recognizes the tremendous change in the privacy landscape with the adoption of data breach laws, increased corporate accountability, and the development of regional or multilateral privacy frameworks.

Asia-Pacific Economic Cooperation Privacy Framework

The Asia-Pacific Economic Cooperation (APEC) Privacy Framework establishes a set of common data privacy principles for the protection of personally identifiable information as it is transferred across borders. The framework leverages much from the OECD Privacy Guidelines but places greater emphasis on the role of electronic commerce and the importance of organizational accountability. In this framework, once an organization collects personal information, the organization remains accountable for the protection of that data regardless of the location of the data or whether the data was transferred to another party.

The APEC Framework also introduces the concept of proportionality to data breach—that the penalties for inappropriate disclosure should be consistent with the demonstrable harm caused by the disclosure. To facilitate enforcement, the APEC Cross-Border Privacy Enforcement Arrangement (CPEA) provides mechanisms for information sharing among APEC members and authorities outside APEC.

Privacy Law and Regulation

The levels and ways in which countries protect the individual's privacy vary tremendously. While this sampling of laws is by no means comprehensive, it reflects some of the different traditions and privacy practices in effect today.

U.S. Privacy Law

The concept of privacy is expressed in many ways. Certainly, an individual should have an expectation that they are not being observed without their knowledge. Privacy is integral when there is information uniquely identifying an individual; the individual should be able to control who has access to that information. In a more specific context, an individual's relationship with their government or other organizations also contains expectations and assumptions regarding those relationships.

In the drafting of the U.S. Constitution, the founders expressed great concern regarding the ability of the government to monitor and control the lawful activities of citizens. To further clarify the relationship between government and the people, a number of amendments were ratified designed to limit the government from controlling speech and association. Through the founder's experience with the English common law, they sought to ensure that the government could not unreasonably conduct searches and other activities that intruded on the private affairs of a person.

While the Constitution never uses the word *privacy*, the Constitution's explicit protections are only part of the broader rights to privacy guaranteed to citizens. Justice William O. Douglas wrote that the Constitution's explicit rights existed within the broader "penumbral rights of privacy and repose" that the founders intended to guarantee.

Consequently, a wide variety of legislation addresses privacy rights in the United States. At the federal level, privacy legislation often addresses a particular type of information or the practices of a specific industry. This approach is challenging because of the differing standards for protecting personal information. Among the many U.S. laws that relate to privacy are the following:

- **The Federal Trade Commission Act (FTC Act):** The FTC Act protects consumers from unfair or deceptive commercial practices. This act gives the FTC authority to ensure that companies implement appropriate privacy protections for personally identifiable information, complies with posted privacy policies, and holds companies accountable for unauthorized disclosures of personal data.

- **The Financial Services Modernization Act (also known as the Gramm–Leach–Bliley Act, or GLBA):** The GLBA regulates how financial services organizations use and protect financial information. Banks, securities firms, insurance companies, and other businesses that provide financial services and products must provide notice of their privacy practices and give data subjects the opportunity to opt out of having their information shared with third parties. The GLBA also addresses the disclosure of nonpublic personal information. In addition to the GLBA, financial services organizations are subject to certain FTC rules relating to the disposal and destruction of financial information.

- **The Fair Credit Reporting Act (FCRA):** The FCRA controls how consumer credit reporting agencies, those who use the agencies' reports (lenders), and those who provide consumer-reporting information (such as a credit card company) collect, use, and manage consumer financial information. The broad definition of consumer reports includes any communication issued by a consumer reporting agency that relates to a consumer's creditworthiness, credit history, credit capacity, character, and general reputation that is used to evaluate a consumer's eligibility for credit or insurance. Individuals can, under the act, receive information on their credit history and then challenge inaccurate information so credit decisions can be fairly made by lenders.

- **The Electronic Communications Privacy Act (ECPA):** A number of laws apply to the collection and use of electronic communications. The ECPA and the Stored Communications Act (SCA) address the circumstances and methods by which government may access electronic communications, including email and other communications means. Presidential Policy Directive 28 further sets privacy limits for U.S. intelligence agencies engaged in collecting signals intelligence.

- **The Health Insurance Portability and Accountability Act (HIPAA):** HIPAA regulates personal medical information. The law broadly applies to healthcare providers, data processors, pharmacies, and other entities that use or access individuals' medical information. HIPAA identifies standards for privacy when collecting and using individually identifiable health information in its Privacy Rule, while the Security Standards for the Protection of Electronic Protected Health Information sets standards for protecting this information.

  These HIPAA rules were revised in early 2013 under the HIPAA Omnibus Rule. The HIPAA Omnibus Rule revised the Security Breach Notification Rule requiring covered entities to give notice when there has been a breach of protected health information. The level of notification depends on the size of the breach, but the consequences for organizations that fail to take appropriate action can be severe and can include both civil and criminal penalties.

- **Genetic Information Non-Discrimination Act (GINA):** GINA provides protections from the inappropriate disclosure, use, or sale of an individual's genetic information. The law was enacted in 2008 in response to the increasing availability of medical tests that might suggest a person had an increased chance of medical conditions.

These laws are only a sampling of the privacy-related legislation at the federal level. Further complicating the privacy landscape is the regulation of personally identifiable information (PII) at the state and local levels. For example, while federal law addresses inappropriate disclosures of PII, as of 2017, 48 of the 50 states had enacted some level of additional breach legislation for their respective jurisdictions.

The European Union General Data Protection Regulation 2016/679

Since its inception, the European Union has supported strong protections for its citizens' personally identifiable information. These protections have evolved over time, taking into account the increasing technical capabilities to monitor and track the activities of individuals, both by governmental as well as commercial organizations. The latest iteration of the EU privacy effort is the General Data Protection Regulation (GDPR).

Prior to the formation of the European Union, many member states had well-established privacy expectations in law and custom that afforded individuals protections as to how their personally identifiable information would be collected, used, and shared. For many member states, these expectations mirrored the OECD's privacy principles.

The OECD principles were nonbinding. However, many future EU member states were also members of the Council of Europe, which negotiated a privacy framework in 1981, "Convention for the Protection of Individuals with Regard to Automatic Processing of Personal Data." This agreement restated the same general principles defined in the OECD work and required signatories to adopt local laws to enforce the privacy protections.

In 1995, the European Union adopted the Data Protection Directive 95/46/EU, which required member states to legally address privacy protections in a consistent manner. The Data Protection Directive continued to leverage the basic principles identified in the OECD work but extended the implications of the principles in three areas: transparency, legitimate purpose, and proportionality.

The directive created a consistent floor for privacy protections in the European Union, but nuances in the EU national laws made compliance difficult. In 2012, the European Union proposed the GDPR to harmonize the national laws and extend privacy protections over EU citizen information to any organization that processes data related to those citizens. As opposed to the Data Protection Directive, the GDPR has the force of law and does not require any additional enabling legislation from the member states in order to implement its provisions. The GDPR superseded the Data Protection Directive on May 25, 2018.

The GDPR significantly increases the expectations on data controllers and data processors to implement strong protections over personally identifiable information. By extending protections to "natural persons, whatever their nationality or place or residence," the GDPR asserts that the laws of the EU protect EU citizens *outside* the traditional geographical boundaries of the EU. This extraterritoriality aspect of the GDPR is particularly troubling to organizations that do not have a presence in the European Union but are potentially subject to sanctions by the European Union if EU privacy expectations are not met.

Article 17 of the GDPR expects data controllers to have in place processes to review requests from subjects for the removal of data. Subjects may request removal for a number of reasons: the data is no longer necessary for the purpose for which it was collected, the subject withdraws consent to use the data, the data has been unlawfully processed, or the controller needs to meet other legal obligations. The process set in place by the data controller must delete the personal data "without undue delay." These expectations extend the rights of individuals over their data, effectively creating a "right to be forgotten."

However, the "right to be forgotten" is not absolute. If the information subject to the request would affect the freedom of expression, is required to meet some legal obligation on the part of the controller, or has public interest, scientific, or historical research purposes, the request can be refused by the controller.

The GDPR also adds additional types of information to the categories that require special protection. Biometric and genetic data about an individual are now considered sensitive personal data and must be appropriately protected. The protections over this type of information may be increased by the individual EU nations.

The GDPR also requires controllers to integrate privacy expectations and controls into the development processes for applications and systems. This concept, *privacy by design*, is extended through the concept of *privacy by default*. When an individual is being given a choice about which information is to be gathered, the default choice should be the option that provides the highest level of privacy to the individual.

For organizations subject to the GDPR that experience data breaches, the consequences are much higher than in the past. First, all breaches that place sensitive information at risk, regardless of size, must be reported within 72 hours of becoming aware of the breach. While notifications to affected individuals may not be required depending on whether the controller has "implemented appropriate technical and organizational protection measures in respect of the personal data affected by the breach," the timeline alone remains a significant challenge for many organizations' incident response processes.

Organizations that fail to implement the protections of the GDPR are potentially subject to significant penalties. The state supervisory authorities will review the circumstances of the breach, taking into account a number of factors. The maximum fines depend on which aspects of the GDPR are violated.

✔ GDPR Fines

The GDPR imposes stiff fines on data controllers and processors for noncompliance.

Determination

Fines are administered by individual member state supervisory authorities (83.1). The following 10 criteria are to be used to determine the amount of the fine on a noncompliant firm:

- **Nature of infringement:** Number of people affected, damage they suffered, duration of infringement, and purpose of processing
- **Intention:** Whether the infringement is intentional or negligent
- **Mitigation:** Actions taken to mitigate damage to data subjects
- **Preventative measures:** How much technical and organizational preparation the firm had previously implemented to prevent noncompliance

CONTINUES

- **History:** Past relevant infringements, which may be interpreted to include infringements under the Data Protection Directive and not just the GDPR, and past administrative corrective actions under the GDPR, from warnings to bans on processing and fines

- **Cooperation:** How cooperative the firm has been with the supervisory authority to remedy the infringement

- **Data type:** What types of data the infringement impacts; see special categories of personal data

- **Notification:** Whether the infringement was proactively reported to the supervisory authority by the firm itself or a third party

- **Certification:** Whether the firm had qualified under-approved certifications or adhered to approved codes of conduct

- **Other:** Other aggravating or mitigating factors, including financial impact on the firm from the infringement

Lower Level

Up to €10 million, or 2 percent of the worldwide annual revenue of the prior financial year, whichever is higher, shall be issued for infringements of:

- Controllers and processors under Articles 8, 11, 25–39, 42, 43
- Certification body under Articles 42, 43
- Monitoring body under Article 41(4)

Upper Level

Up to €20 million, or 4 percent of the worldwide annual revenue of the prior financial year, whichever is higher, shall be issued for infringements of:

- The basic principles for processing, including conditions for consent, under Articles 5, 6, 7, and 9
- The data subjects' rights under Articles 12–22
- The transfer of personal data to a recipient in a third country or an international organization under Articles 44–49
- Any obligations pursuant to member state law adopted under Chapter IX
- Any noncompliance with an order by a supervisory authority

The GDPR addresses privacy from a much broader perspective than previous efforts by the European Union to guarantee the appropriate use of personally identifiable information. The security professional should have a working understanding of the GDPR and how it is implemented in their organization.

India

Although it is not explicitly stated, the Indian Constitution has been interpreted as protecting the individual's right to privacy as a fundamental and integral part of the rights guaranteed by Article 21. The Indian IT Act of 2008 also provides certain privacy protections in the workplace.

Saudi Arabia

Saudi Arabia's legal tradition comes from the implementation of Shari'ah. The importance of the religious tradition in the kingdom cannot be overstated. Article 7 of the Basic Law of Governance (promulgated by the Royal Decree No. A/90 dated 27/08/1412H [March 1, 1992]) states that the government of the kingdom is derived from the Holy Qur'an and the Sunnah of the Prophet, while Article 8 is based on the premise of justice, consultation, and equality in accordance with the Islamic Shari'ah.

There is no overarching privacy law in Saudi Arabia. Rather, there are a number of sector-specific laws that address aspects of privacy within the context of the industry and Shari'ah. The Anti-Cyber Crime Law of 2007 establishes heavy civil and criminal sanctions on the encroachment of personal data privacy. Similarly, the Telecommunications Act implements the provisions of the Basic Law of Governance Article 40, providing protection from monitoring of communications.

Import/Export Controls

Many countries closely regulate the movement of technology through their borders. This might be done to protect local industries from external competition, limit the exportation of sensitive technologies, or meet other policy goals of a particular nation.

United States

Industries in the United States continue to drive innovation at a rate far beyond most other economies. The development of new technologies, methods of communication, and military capabilities requires strong protection for intellectual property as well as provides a way to ensure such technologies are not used to endanger national security. In the United States, the Arms Export Control Act (AECA) of 1976 and the Export Administration Act provide the statutory basis for controlling the export of sensitive technologies.

The State Department uses its authority under the AECA to develop the International Traffic in Arms Regulation (ITAR). The primary focus of ITAR is to control sensitive military technologies. These are identified by the U.S. government through the United States Munitions List (USML). The USML is maintained by the U.S. Department of State, with extensive consultation with other agencies, and is routinely updated as technology changes.

The U.S. Department of Commerce's authority focuses on technologies that have both military and civilian purposes. These are commonly referred to as *dual use* technologies. Examples of dual-use technologies might include encryption systems, high-speed computers, and telecommunications systems. To identify these technologies, the Department of Commerce publishes the Commerce Control List, similar to the USML. If the technology being exported falls on either list, approval is required to sell the technology. In some cases, after the technology has been exported, the use of the technology by the purchasing country will be subject to ongoing monitoring under End Use Checks (EAR/CCL) or the Blue Lantern (ITAR/USML) program.

Both the EAR and the ITAR require U.S. residents to obtain permission before releasing controlled technology or technical data to foreign people in the United States. When information is released to a foreign person, the information is deemed to be an export to the person's country or countries of nationality. To avoid a "deemed export" situation, organizations that make information available to foreign nationals must seek and receive a license from the U.S. government before releasing controlled technology or technical data to its nonimmigrants. This may include individuals in the United States on a work visa, tourists, students, businesspeople, scholars, researchers, technical experts, sailors, airline personnel, salespeople, military personnel, and diplomats.

European Union

The European Union also places restrictions on dual-use technology. European Council Regulation (EC) No. 428/2009 of May 5, 2009, requires member states to participate in the control of exports, transfer, brokering, and transit of dual-use items. In 2017, these regulations were updated to reflect controls over cyber weapons.

International Import Restrictions

A number of countries have adopted laws or regulations that require security reviews to be conducted or, in some cases, denied companies the authority to import products to their countries altogether. In 2016, China passed a broad cybersecurity law that requires information technology vendors to submit their products to the Ministry of State Security for technical analysis. The law allows the Ministry to demand source code for inspection as part of the review process. Similar expectations have been placed on software products by Russia and other nations. In 2017, the U.S. government, citing security concerns, singled out Kaspersky Labs, legislating that the company's products would not be allowed on any U.S. government computer system.

Wassenaar Arrangement

International cooperation is vital to ensuring that import/export controls work as designed. The Wassenaar Arrangement sets a regulatory scheme that defines how weapons are exchanged between the 42 signatories to the agreement. The Wassenaar Arrangement promotes "international security and stability" by regulating exchanges of conventional weapons such as guns, bombs, torpedoes, grenades, and mines; dual-use goods; and technologies. The agreement's categories of coverage also include advanced telecommunications, information systems, and cryptographic products. In 2013, the agreement was revised to address cyber weapons, including malicious software, command-and-control software, and Internet surveillance software.

Applying traditional arms control mechanisms to cyber weapons has raised significant concerns about the effectiveness of the controls. Implementing the agreement itself requires action by each of individual signatories to implement the restrictions. Further, a great number of nonsignatory nations, including China and Israel, have cyber weapons that are not subject to regulation. The agreement has also been cited as an obstacle to the transfer of information related to researching and supporting cybersecurity-related systems.

Transborder Data Flows

For many years, jurisdictions have sought to regulate the movement of information gathered inside their borders to other countries. In some cases, regulation sought to protect the private information of individuals; in others, the interest of the state was to be able to access the information for legitimate governmental purposes. With the rise of cloud computing and the massive collection of information on individuals by both public and private organizations, even greater scrutiny is being placed on the movement of such data.

Data Economy

The world economy runs on data. As a matter of trade, data itself, even if devoid of privacy-related material, generates vast amounts of trade and revenue. Further, data that is legal in one jurisdiction might be illegal in another. As a result, the protection of the movement of data has become a significant policy concern.

Data Localization and Jurisdiction

Many jurisdictions require that certain types of data must be processed inside their borders. This trend has been increasing in recent years, on the assumption that the information, by default, will be more secure, will be available to governments on legal request, and will have the economic benefit of inducing operators of data processing centers to locate facilities within their countries. More than 34 countries have some sort of data localization requirement.

Data localization law took on greater importance following the Snowden disclosures of the range of collection activities performed by the National Security Agency. Data localization laws were seen as providing some protection against the intelligence activities of foreign powers.

The economic argument for data localization is not necessarily convincing. A substantial body of research suggests that the costs of barriers to data flows in terms of lost trade and investment opportunities, higher information technology (IT) costs, reduced competitiveness, and lower economic productivity and GDP growth are significant. The estimates suggest that localization reduces the GDP by 0.7 to 1.7 percent in Brazil, China, the European Union, India, Indonesia, Korea, and Vietnam.

Nevertheless, many countries have adopted such laws.

Russia

In 2015, Russia became one of the first regimes to require all data collected inside Russia on Russian citizens to be stored inside Russia. The regulations implementing the law may not require localization if the information service is not directed at Russia (i.e., use of Russian language, use of Russian top-level domains, etc.); this has still had significant impact on information providers. Some providers, including Google, Apple, and Twitter, have acquired computing capabilities in Russia to comply with the law. Others, most notably LinkedIn, have resisted the law, and their services have been blocked or curtailed inside Russia.

China

In China, the enforcement of the Cybersecurity Law will place new restrictions on the movement of information. China has asserted sovereignty over the Internet operating within its borders and has installed network protections, including limiting access points and strict firewall rules to censor data made available inside China. Article 37 of the Cybersecurity Law requires network operators in critical sectors to store all data that is gathered or produced by the network operator in the country on systems in the country. In particular, the law requires data on Chinese citizens gathered within China to be kept inside China and not transferred abroad without the permission of the Chinese government.

Unites States

The U.S. federal government requires certain types of data to be stored in the United States. For example, any information that would be subject to Export Administration Regulation cannot be transferred outside of the United States without a license. However, if the information is encrypted, the information can be stored in a cloud service.

LICRA v. Yahoo

The case of *Ligue contre le racisme et l'antisémitisme et Union des étudiants juifs de France c. Yahoo Inc. et Société Yahoo France* (in other words, *LICRA v. Yahoo*) was one of the first civil cases that addressed the presentation of information across jurisdictional boundaries. At issue was whether an organization could be prevented from providing information across the Internet that violated French law, despite the fact that the information was stored legally in the United States. In 2000, the French court found that Yahoo's advertisement of Nazi-era artifacts should be prohibited in France.

Yahoo subsequently filed suit in the United States, arguing that the judgment should be unenforceable under U.S. law, as doing so would violate Yahoo's right to free speech. The U.S. courts rejected Yahoo's claim on the basis that U.S. courts lacked jurisdiction over the matter. In 2006, the French courts issued a final ruling, and Yahoo responded by removing all advertisements for Nazi-era artifacts and memorabilia.

The precedent of *LICRA v. Yahoo* extended the jurisdictional boundaries over free speech beyond traditional geographic borders. As a result, content providers must be aware of the legal status of their content in each jurisdiction where it is provided.

UNDERSTAND, ADHERE TO, AND PROMOTE PROFESSIONAL ETHICS

Ethical decision-making is essential to professional information security practice. This section provides an overview of the concept of professional ethics, describes a number of international standards and ethical codes of practice, and explains the information security professional's responsibility to apply the (ISC)² Code of Ethics when faced with ethical choices.

Ethical Decision-Making

Whether consciously or not, every professional applies their ethical decision-making processes many times each day. Whether it is as simple as a "rolling stop" at a road intersection or as complex as the questions faced by someone confronted with potential illegal activity on the job, ethical decision-making requires a solid understanding of the moral, legal, and organizational expectations against which individuals apply their personal ethical standards.

The Context of Ethical Decision-Making

Ethical decision-making expectations have been placed on professionals for centuries. Ethical expectations for medical professionals were put forward in the Hippocratic Code's famous statement, "First, do no harm." However, determining harm in many contexts is difficult. Not only do we have to consider the direct results of our actions, but the unintended consequences may also give reason to reconsider our actions.

Ethical decision-making practices challenged early computing pioneers. Alan Turing's early writings on artificial intelligence suggest that building a machine whose responses are indistinguishable from the choices made by a human requires some level of ethical standard to be developed that would allow machines to make decisions consistent with the ethical standards held by their human evaluators. Absent such instructions, we would be faced with the certainty that, eventually, AI would advance to the point where the AI systems would find humans inefficient and therefore unnecessary.

The intersection of technology and ethical behavior presents other unique challenges. Today, our ability to monitor the activities of individuals through their computers, smartphones, cars, home automation, and the broad Internet of Things provides opportunities for business to target precise demographics. In doing that, does the business compromise the privacy expectations individuals have, and more important, what should the information security practitioner's role be in facilitating that monitoring?

In many professions, ethical standards bridge the gap between what is legally permissible and what the industry expects for best practice. As the legal environment evolves, a clear set of expectations for professional conduct becomes embodied in the legal code. This process has been occurring rapidly in the information security profession, as governments deal with significant financial, operational, and reputational harms that are caused by unethical behavior.

Failing to set and enforce acceptable standards of conduct creates risk for organizations that they might be held responsible for an employee's or member's actions. Due care requires that the organization ensure that the users of its resources know what is acceptable behavior and what is not. Due diligence extends the expectations of due care in developing the plans and programs to educate the users. Regardless, both the governance bodies and the management have responsibilities to ensure that ethical standards of conduct are set and enforced.

Ethical Decision-Making Challenges

Information security practitioners have to make decisions related to ethical conduct on a regular basis. When faced with similar circumstances, two professionals might make different choices. Often, these choice result from good initial intentions or from choosing between competing priorities. The following two examples highlight the challenge of good security decision-making.

Hacking in Flight

In 2015, a hacker claimed in an interview with the FBI that he had accessed the in-flight control systems by removing the cover to an access port under his seat and connecting a modified Ethernet cable to the interface. He then claimed that he had issued a CLB command (climb), which he believes resulted in a lateral or sideways movement of the plane. He stated in the interview that he had done this a number of times on different flights and on different aircraft. The hacker claimed his motivation for this was to force the aircraft manufacturers to "fix" the alleged weakness. In the aftermath of the incident, then-Yahoo chief information security officer Alex Stamos argued that "You cannot promote the (true) idea that security research benefits humanity while defending research that endangered hundreds of innocents."

Mass Surveillance

Mr. Stamos's ethical standard was again tested in 2015, when he resigned from his position at Yahoo. Subsequent news reports suggested that Mr. Stamos resigned when he became aware that the then-CEO of Yahoo, Marissa Mayer, authorized a program that enabled the U.S. government to monitor the incoming emails of Yahoo.com users. Mayer likely did so to comply with a secret subpoena issued by the Federal Intelligence Surveillance Court. It was widely reported that Stamos's decision to resign was driven by the breadth of the collection and the extent to which Yahoo went to enable the collection.

Established Standards of Ethical Conduct

Statements of ethical conduct have been developed by a wide number of international organizations, industries, and regulatory bodies. While these standards generally cover the appropriate collection and protection of sensitive information, they nevertheless represent unique industry viewpoints. The following is a sampling of some of these different standards.

International Standards

A number of organizations have struggled with establishing ethical standards, with varying degrees of success and influence. New technologies have required organizations to reevaluate the meaning of ethical conduct.

Internet Activities Board

The Internet Architecture Board is an Internet Engineering Task Force (IETF) committee charged with providing technical oversight to the RFC process and managing the protocol registries. In 1989, this organization, then known as the Internet Activities Board (IAB), published RFC 1087, "Ethics and the Internet" (`https://www.ietf.org/rfc/rfc1087.txt`). While the IAB's ethics statement reflects that the Internet was then substantially a research tool funded by the U.S. government, the ethical expectations have continued to shape the development of ethical computing practice. Among other things, the IAB's "Ethics and the Internet" states the following:

> The IAB strongly endorses the view of the Division Advisory Panel of the National Science Foundation Division of Network, Communications Research and Infrastructure which, in paraphrase, characterized as unethical and unacceptable any activity which purposely:
>
> (a) seeks to gain unauthorized access to the resources of the Internet,
> (b) disrupts the intended use of the Internet,
> (c) wastes resources (people, capacity, computer) through such actions,
> (d) destroys the integrity of computer-based information, and/or
> (e) compromises the privacy of users.

Subsequent RFCs addressed the ethical standards and security practices in detail. For example, RFC 1359, "Connecting to the Internet," was one of the first to reference the development of an acceptable use policy, leveraging previous work by the National Science Foundation.

Computer Ethics Institute

The Computer Ethics Institute discussion framework for ethical computing practice has been widely used in the development of acceptable use policies and in the education of users about the appropriate use of computing resources. The Computer Ethics Institute's "The Ten Commandments of Computer Ethics" states the following:

1. Thou shalt not use a computer to harm other people.
2. Thou shalt not interfere with other people's computer work.
3. Thou shalt not snoop around in other people's computer files.
4. Thou shalt not use a computer to steal.
5. Thou shalt not use a computer to bear false witness.
6. Thou shalt not copy or use proprietary software for which you have not paid.
7. Thou shalt not use other people's computer resources without authorization or proper compensation.

8. Thou shalt not appropriate other people's intellectual output.

9. Thou shalt think about the social consequences of the program you are writing or the system you are designing.

10. Thou shalt always use a computer in ways that ensure consideration and respect for your fellow humans.

National Laws and Ethical Behavior

Many countries place specific, legally enforceable expectations on certain industries to codify their ethical practices. In many cases, these industry expectations have significant implications for the information security professional to protect PII, protected health information (PHI), or financial information.

U.S Sarbanes-Oxley Act (SOX)

Following several high-profile corporate and accounting scandals, the Sarbanes–Oxley Act of 2002 (Public Law 107–204) required companies to implement a wide range of controls intended to minimize conflicts of interest, provide investors with appropriate risk information, place civil and criminal penalties on executives for providing false financial disclosures, and provide protections for whistleblowers who report inappropriate actions to regulators. The subsequent rules also require companies to disclose their internal Code of Ethics and put controls in place to ensure the organization acts according to those ethical principles.

U.S. Health Information Portability and Accountability Act

In developing HIPAA, regulators incorporated the longstanding ethical practice of doctor-patient confidentiality. The Privacy Rule provides specific guidance on the handling of sensitive patient information, breach and notification responsibilities, and the organization's responsibility to ensure the information is accurate. Further, in such areas as biomedical research, it provides specific expectations for patient notification, handling of information, and putting protocols in place to ensure the ethical conduct of the research.

China Cyber Security Law

In 2017, China enacted legislation that will compel companies doing business in China to maintain the information they have on individuals in such a way that it is both accessible on demand by the Chinese government and physically located in China. As a direct result of this law, Apple has begun to eliminate security capabilities from its products, like virtual private networks and other applications that allow individuals to communicate anonymously, while continuing to provide those same capabilities in other countries. In 2010, Google pulled out of China rather than accede to demands to censor content and capabilities, while Tim Cook, Apple's CEO, "believe[s] in engaging with governments even when we disagree."

Industry Efforts

Many industry organizations recognize the ethical challenges that face the information security industry. To address ethical decision-making by their members, the various organizations provide a set of ethical guidelines applicable to their particular industry organizations.

The IEEE Computer Society

The Institute of Electrical and Electronics Engineers Computer Society (IEEE-CS) is one of a number of professional societies that constitute the IEEE. Central to its mission is to support the education and professional development of its members. In conjunction with the Association for Computing Machinery (ACM), it has developed a detailed, comprehensive ethical standard for software engineering. Recognizing the professional's "commitment to the health, safety and welfare of the public," the IEEE-CS/ACM expects that "[s]oftware engineers shall commit themselves to making the analysis, specification, design, development, testing, and maintenance of software a beneficial and respected profession."

American Health Information Management Association (AHIMA)

Founded in 1928 to improve health record quality, AHIMA continues to play a leadership role in the effective management of health information to support the delivery of quality healthcare to the public. Active in advancing informatics, data analytics, and information governance for healthcare, the AHIMA Code of Ethics addresses in detail the privacy and security responsibilities that AHIMA's members must address in their professional roles. Their Code of Ethics consists of 11 principles, including support for privacy, confidentiality, a commitment to service before self-interest, efforts to protect health information, and ethical requirements. Like other codes, it also seeks to advance the profession and to ensure that practitioners represent the profession well throughout their work.

The full text of the AHIMA Code of Ethics can be found at `http://bok.ahima.org/doc?oid=105098`.

Cyber Security Credentials Collaborative

The mission of the Cyber Security Credentials Collaborative (C3) to provide awareness of, and advocacy for, vendor-neutral credentials in information security, privacy, and related IT disciplines. Members, including (ISC)², the Information Systems Audit and Control Association (ISACA) CompTIA, the EC-Council, and others, have put forth a set of security principles that encourage their members to monitor and enforce ethical practices. "A Unified Principles of Professional Ethics in Cyber Security" recognizes four high-level objectives in the ethics framework, but each participating organization in the C3 has integrated these principles into their unique ethical expectations for their members. The four principles are as follows:

- **Integrity**, including the duty to perform duties in line with existing law, ethical, and moral structures, in the interest of stakeholders. This also includes avoiding conflicts of interest and reporting any ethical violations or conflicts to an appropriate oversight body.

- **Objectivity**, which requires practitioners to remain unbiased and fair in the exercise of their profession. This includes noting opinions as opinions when they are provided, rather than allowing them to be seen as fact.

- **Confidentiality**, including due care and safeguarding of confidential and proprietary information that practitioners may encounter in the course of their work. The confidentiality principle specifically carves out an exclusion for disclosure of information-related criminal acts, setting the expectation that practitioners will disclose such information appropriately.

- **Professional competence**, which requires practitioners to do their jobs well, to perform only the tasks they are qualified and competent for, and to otherwise behave in a professional manner. This includes continued development, recognizing the work of others, and avoiding misconduct.

Cultural Differences in Ethical Practice

Individuals learn their personal ethical standards from their religion, their family, and their personal study. These are also powerful influences on how a person makes decisions. One of the reasons organizations conduct background investigations is to determine how individuals have made decisions in the past, because they are likely to react in predictable ways to similar challenges.

It is well documented that different societies set different ethical standards. For example, it is generally accepted that accessing computer systems without the owner's permission is unethical. However, when governmental organizations secretly access another nation's information assets in support of national security objectives, the same ethical standard may not apply.

Similarly, intellectual property is treated differently depending on cultural and social expectations and norms. In the People's Republic of China, *shanzhai*—the imitation and piracy of name brands—is a well-respected business model. Not only is it legally tolerated, it is often encouraged to support the development of local industry and technical capability. Consequently, the information security practitioner must be cognizant of the laws of the jurisdiction, the corporate or organizational ethics standards, and the cultural expectations for ethical behavior.

(ISC)² Ethical Practices

Members of (ISC)² are expected to behave in an ethical manner. This requires an understanding of both the Code of Ethics and the enforcement processes. Individuals are routinely held to account for their ethical choices through this process.

The (ISC)² Code of Ethics

(ISC)² has established a Code of Ethics for its members. Located at `https://www.isc2.org/ethics`, the code consists of a preamble that introduces four *canons*, or general principles, for information security:

Code of Ethics Preamble:

- The safety and welfare of society and the common good, duty to our principles, and to each other, requires that we adhere, and be seen to adhere, to the highest ethical standards of behavior.
- Therefore, strict adherence to this Code is a condition of certification.

Code of Ethics Canons:

- Protect society, the common good, necessary public trust and confidence, and the infrastructure.
- Act honorably, honestly, justly, responsibly, and legally.
- Provide diligent and competent service to principles.
- Advance and protect the profession.

In enforcing the code, (ISC)² recognizes that implementing the high-level expectations will require interpretation and professional judgment.

All information security professionals who are certified by (ISC)² recognize that such certification is a privilege that must be both earned and maintained. In support of this principle, all (ISC)² members are required to commit to fully support this Code of Ethics (the "Code").

Ethics Complaints

The full text of the current complaint procedure is maintained on the (ISC)² website (`https://www.isc2.org/ethics`). This summary is to provide members (and potential members) of (ISC)² with a working understanding of the complaint process, the expectations on the complainant, the protections for the members involved, and the potential outcomes from a complaint.

Complaint Process

(ISC)² members who intentionally or knowingly violate any provision of the code are subject to action by a peer review panel, which may result in the revocation of certification. (ISC)² members are obligated to follow the ethics complaint procedure upon observing any action by an (ISC)² member that breaches the code. Failure to do so may be considered a breach of the code pursuant to canon IV.

While the board recognizes its obligation to provide the certificate holder with guidance on making ethical decisions, it does not expect to supervise or judge professionals in making difficult decisions. The board does, however, recognize its responsibility to maintain the integrity of the certification. It accepts that, from time to time, the good of the profession may require it to disassociate the profession from egregious behavior on the part of a particular certificate holder. The use of the ethics complaint process is for the sole purpose of protecting the reputation of the profession. The ethics complaint process is not intended to be used to coerce or punish certificate holders.

The board will take actions to keep the identity of the complainant and respondent in any complaint confidential. While disclosure of the identity of the complainant will be avoided where possible, upon filing a complaint, the general rules of due process require that the board may disclose his or her identity to the respondent. Similarly, due process holds the board to address complaints in a timely manner.

We live in a world where we are faced with difficult choices every day. Doing "the right thing" is often the same as "doing the hard thing." (ISC)² expects professionals holding the CISSP to be able to identify when ethical decisions need to be made and to have a frame of reference that allows them to act consistently and with justification.

DEVELOP, DOCUMENT, AND IMPLEMENT SECURITY POLICY, STANDARDS, PROCEDURES, AND GUIDELINES

As an organization grows and matures, the need to effectively communicate expectations to the workforce becomes increasingly important. Organizations communicate through a series of documents, aimed at different audiences with different levels of detail.

A well-structured set of organizational policies, standards, procedures, and guidelines give consistent guidance to members of the organization, specifying responsibilities for individuals and making clear the consequences for noncompliance. Clear policies allow management to define the bounds of decision-making at different levels in the organization. This in turn creates a predictable, stable management environment where energies are spent solving new problems instead of constantly reinventing the wheel.

Many organizations use these terms in different and often interchangeable ways. As it relates to the CISSP CBK, understanding the hierarchical structure of the organizational documents is necessary, as the respective documents communicate to different levels of the organization.

Organizational Documents

For most organizations, the taxonomy of organizational documents sets high-level expectations at the policy level, while other documents provide the details on implementation. These documents establish expectations for behavior and performance in the organization, while providing appropriate levels of discretion to adjust to changing circumstances and events.

Policies

Policies are at the heart of what the organization is trying to accomplish. At a high level, policies provide critical instruction to management to implement measures to achieve external compliance expectations or support the larger strategic vision of the organization.

As governance documents, the responsibility for creating and maintaining policy rests with the board. As such, policies are one of the ways in which the board demonstrates due care.

Policies, relative to other organizational documents, are less likely to change. They provide consistency to the organization's management, allowing the leadership to shape standards and create procedures that achieve the policy end. They should provide management with sufficient flexibility to adapt to new circumstances or technologies without a policy revision.

Mature organizations routinely review their policies within their governance processes. Changing external compliance expectations or shifts in business strategy must be taken into account. The policy review process must address the changing needs of external stakeholders to support predictability in execution of the policies by management.

The use of the term *policy* when implementing security practice in an organization is often confusing. For example, a password policy may, or may not, be of interest to the governing organization—but it certainly would be of interest to the management team! The organization's governance structure would likely express interest in ensuring that access controls are present, meet the compliance expectations appropriate to the organization's needs at the policy level, and leave to management the decision of how many times a password should be rotated. That management chooses to refer to the outcome of their due diligence as a policy is an organizational decision.

Often referred to as *sub policies*, these amplifying instructions further set behavior expectations for the organization. Some of the areas that might be addressed include passwords, cryptography, identity management, access control, and a wide range of other topics. The critical distinction is whether the instruction comes from the governance body (making it a policy) or whether it is derived from a higher-level policy by the organization's management.

This broad use of the term *policy* reflects one of the major challenges in our industry. A lack of a common language for information security practice has been repeatedly identified as one of the factors inhibiting the development of a common body of practice in the information security community. It is further complicated in an international environment, where translations and cultural differences affect how people perceive information. However, the various standards bodies have published specific definitions for information security terms that may have nuanced differences between each other.

Standards

Once the organization has decided on what it wants to accomplish, management can execute against the policies. One tool to support efficient management of resources is the use of standards. Standards simplify management by providing consistency in control. They are promulgated by management to support the achievement of the organization's strategic goals and are tied directly to the organization's policies.

Organizations may be required to adopt certain standards to do business in a particular market. For example, if an organization wants a web presence, it has to take into account the standards of the World Wide Web Consortium (W3C) in developing applications.

While standards are a management tool, standards often evolve out of organizational practice. For example, selecting a particular vendor to provide a product may force a standard where none was originally contemplated. De facto standards often evolve inside organizations as different parts of the organization adopt a new technology, not as a conscious management decision.

Well-structured standards provide mechanisms for adaptation to meet local conditions. Through the use of baselines, an organization can shape a standard to better reflect different circumstances. Baselines enable the delegation of decision-making within strict parameters to lower levels of management.

Nevertheless, standards are directive in nature; compliance is not optional. Organizations that adopt standards must put in place performance measures to determine whether the standards have been implemented.

Procedures

Procedural documents provide highly detailed task-oriented instructions. Procedural documents are useful when a high degree of compliance is necessary and the precise steps to achieve the outcome are not readily apparent to individuals not familiar with the environment.

Management, as part of its diligence responsibilities, enforces organizational procedures through routine oversight and audit. Compliance is not optional, and well-structured organizations track compliance with procedural steps.

In certain environments, procedural compliance is achieved through the use of various separation-of-duties methods. For example, in cloud environments, an organization might require that every action applied to the cloud environment be performed through a script function—a Chef recipe or a Puppet task—and the author of a script cannot be the individual who approves the script.

Baselines

Once a standard has been established, a baseline is derived from the standard to meet a specific set of implementation requirements. Once a baseline has been established, any deviation from the baseline would be formally approved through the organization's change management practice. As with standards, baselines establish a compliance expectation.

As a subset of baselines, security baselines express the minimum set of security controls necessary to safeguard the CIA properties for a particular configuration. Scoping guidance is often published as part of a baseline, defining the range of deviation from the baseline that is acceptable for a particular baseline. Once scoping guidance has been established, then tailoring is performed to apply a particular set of controls to achieve the baseline within the scoping guidance.

Guidelines

Guidelines are necessary when an organization determines that some level of flexibility in implementation is necessary to achieve business objectives. Guidelines often rely upon best practices for a particular discipline or are the codification of an organization's experience in a particular area.

Guidelines may be useful when a range of options exist to achieve a particular control objective and it is acceptable to encourage creativity and to experiment to compare the effectiveness of different options. Guidelines may also be useful when the organization's staff has a broad base of experience and a shared vision for an outcome. In that case, the explicit directions of procedures, standards, and baselines may provide too much structure and impede the adoption of more efficient methods.

There are many sources of guidelines for information security practice. Certainly, the CISSP CBK is one, as it reflects a broad range of security practices but is not prescriptive inside an organization's information security environment. The ISO/NIST/ITIL frameworks are often leveraged as guidelines; however, they may become policies or standards if the organization has a compliance expectation. Other sources of guidelines include manufacturers' default configurations, industry-specific guidelines, or independent organizations such as the Open Web Application Security Project (OWASP) work in software development.

There is no single correct answer for the number and breadth of policies, standards, baselines, and guidelines an organization should have. Different regulatory environments, management expectations, and technology challenges will affect how the organization expresses and achieves its goals.

Policy Development

This hierarchy of instructions allows different levels of the organization to shape the security practice. In setting the rules for the expected behavior, the organization can require individuals to account for performance. A formal informational hierarchy communicates to a broad range of stakeholders the importance of information security practice to the organization.

Critical to the enforcement of organizational expectations are clarity and simplicity. If the policy or procedure is too detailed or complex, it is less likely to be followed. If it is too laden with jargon or inside terminology, it will be difficult for new people to understand and comply. Similarly, the instructional documents should be readily available and consistent in format and structure.

In enforcing the organization's expectations, consideration should be given to exceptional circumstances, particularly those where compliance in one area will result in non-compliance in another. Some method of resolving internal conflicts and approving variance to the organization's usual expectations must be addressed within the documentation.

Policy Review Process

Regular review of policies provides a way to ensure that the policy continues to meet the organizational objectives and compliance requirements. It is important to define your development and review process for your suite of policies. A well-structured policy review process should provide for the following:

- Develop methods to capture new policy requirements based on new technologies or new business models. The impact of new systems on an organization's policies should be reviewed as part of the systems development lifecycle.

- Set a regular schedule for the review of every policy. Even if the policy is not changed, the review itself demonstrates due care by the management. Reviews are often aligned with other organizational processes, such as annual audits.

- Set a protocol for gaining input from all stakeholders when reviewing policies. Structured input ensures that stakeholders' concerns are documented and addressed.

- Define your conditions for policy change and adhere to them. Policies should be more enduring than the management documents, which would be expected to change more frequently.

- Have a waiver or exception process. A formal process to request, evaluate, and, where appropriate, waive policies allows unique circumstances to be addressed by the organization. As the policies themselves are an expression of an organization's risk, a formal waiver ensures that the risk accepted by the waiver is within the organization's risk tolerance.

- Assign explicit ownership for the policy. This provides a measure of accountability to ensure the policy is properly managed and reviewed.

Information security policies are one of the strongest preventative tools against cyber-attacks. They define appropriate permissible behavior among all parties who access data in your enterprise. When properly crafted and maintained, well-structured policies and related documents set expectations for organizational behavior, direct work in a consistent manner, and are a critical area of control for the organization.

IDENTIFY, ANALYZE, AND PRIORITIZE BUSINESS CONTINUITY REQUIREMENTS

Business continuity (BC) and disaster recovery (DR) planning provide organizations with a structure to prepare for major disruptions. Under the more general heading of business continuity management (BCM), these separate, but related, activities ensure that the organization identifies its critical business functions, assesses the risk to those functions, and applies the appropriate level of control to the risks to ensure the efficient restoration of services.

While organizations operate under different compliance requirements, one thing is clear: the number and severity of disaster events are both increasing. The increasing risk can be attributed to many factors, including climate change, increasing urbanization, or the ability of threat actors to achieve broad effects with minimal resources. Regardless of the cause, a prudent organization would take steps in advance to minimize the likelihood and consequence of disaster and return the organization as quickly as possible to normal operations.

Develop and Document Scope and Plan

Recognizing the organization's obligations and risks is an essential part of governance. Whether this is accomplished through a formal governance, risk management, and compliance (GRC) process or through a more informal means, identification allows the management to take appropriate steps to respond to the risks. Ultimately, this will lead the governing body to establish policies and set an organizational expectation for resilience.

Compliance Requirements

There are many independently developed bodies of practice to assist organizations in developing BCM programs. Inevitably, one organization will define terms or use language in a manner that is not consistent with other organizations. The purpose of the CISSP CBK is to provide a base of good practice, recognizing that there is going to be some divergence in implementation based on the business models, compliance expectations, and the standards and practices of different organizations. To become overly wedded to one dogmatic interpretation of BCM practice is to exclude the potentially valuable perspectives of other organizations.

Business continuity is not simply a technology problem. Rather, BC involves the people, processes, and systems that are necessary to deliver the organization's services or meet compliance requirements. Business continuity is inherently proactive, as the research, analysis, and development of the organizational response are done before the disruption occurs.

The intent of BCM is to build organizational resilience. Resilience is the ability to quickly adapt and recover from any known or unknown changes to the environment through holistic implementation of risk management, contingency, and continuity planning. A resilient organization will be able to address a broad range of disruptions efficiently and minimize the likelihood and effects of a disaster.

Not every disruption in service is a disaster. For the purposes of the CISSP CBK, a disaster occurs when the organization is not able to restore normal services/functions before reaching the maximum tolerable downtime (MTD) set by the business. The MTD expresses in business language the total length of time a process can be unavailable without causing significant harm to the business. The MTDs are identified by the business owners through the business impact analysis process. Control is applied to ensure the people, processes, and systems are available and functioning to deliver the organization's services to its customers. If an event occurs but the organization is still able to deliver on its commitments, it is not a disaster.

NOTE Maximum tolerable downtime (MTD), maximum acceptable outage (MAO), maximum allowable disruption (MAD), minimum business continuity objective (MBCO), maximum acceptable outage time (MAOT), and other similar terms have created great confusion in the industry. Certain terms are preferred within certain frameworks. Semantic differences aside, the overarching concept is the important thing to remember: the business must decide how long it can be without the system/process/information and still meet its mission, contractual, and compliance expectations.

Compliance Frameworks

Most information security compliance frameworks, including the NIST Risk Management Framework and the ISO 27000 framework, expect the organization to perform some level of business continuity planning. In many regulated sectors, such as healthcare or financial services, specific levels of planning and verification are required by the regulatory organizations.

Further compliance expectations may come from contractual obligations that the organization assumes. Both the PCI-DSS framework and circumstances where the organization has negotiated service level agreements (SLAs) with its customers would fall under this category.

Healthcare

The HIPAA Security Rule requires all covered entities to have performed an appropriate level of contingency planning. The Contingency Plan standard includes five implementation specifications:

- Data Backup Plan (Required)
- Disaster Recovery Plan (Required)
- Emergency Mode Operation Plan (Required)
- Testing and Revision Procedures (Addressable)
- Applications and Data Criticality Analysis (Addressable)

In the United Kingdom, the Civil Contingencies Act of 2004 places contingency planning expectations on all Category 1 responders, which includes healthcare organizations and the National Health Service. The legislation expects that entities will follow good practice and relies heavily on the British Standard for Business Continuity Management, BS25999*.

NOTE British Standard for Business Continuity Management (BS25999) was withdrawn by the British Standards Institute (BSI) with the 2012 publication of ISO 22301, "Societal Security – Business continuity management systems – Requirements." The ISO standard heavily reflects the influence of the BSI work. As of 2018, Cabinet Office guidance continues to reference the BS25999 standard.

For information systems operated by the U.S. government, NIST Special Publication 800-34, "Contingency Planning Guide for Federal Information Systems," provides a base of practice for the development of resilience in information systems operations. NIST, through its collaborative process of standards development, took into account a broad range of industry and nongovernmental BCM practices. As a result of this process, the framework has been widely adopted by non-U.S. government organizations.

Financial Services

The Financial Industry Regulatory Authority (FINRA) Rule 4370 requires that all financial institutions operating in the United States must create and maintain a BC plan, reasonably designed to enable the member to meet its existing obligations to customers. Each plan must be tailored to meet the specific needs of the company but must include provisions for the following elements:

- Data backup and recovery (hard copy and electronic)
- All mission-critical systems
- Financial and operational assessments
- Alternate communications between customers and the firm and between the firm and employees
- Alternate physical location of employees
- Critical business constituent, bank, and counterparty impact
- Regulatory reporting
- Communications with regulators
- How the firm will assure customers' prompt access to their funds and securities in the event that the firm determines that it is unable to continue its business

The Basel II Accords were developed to provide an international framework for addressing financial and operational risk in the banking industry. The Basel Committee on Banking Supervision in 2003 published "Sound Practices for Management and Supervision," which requires that banks put in place disaster recovery and business continuity plans to ensure continuous operation and to limit losses. The Basel Accord views these activities as being among the tasks that management would perform to limit residual risk.

International Standards

A number of international standards exist to support business continuity practices. ISO 22301, "Societal Security — Business continuity management systems — Requirements," specifies requirements to "plan, establish, implement, operate, monitor, review, maintain and continually improve a documented management system to protect against, reduce the likelihood of occurrence, prepare for, respond to, and recover from disruptive incidents…." The ISO standard is a generic process intended to apply to any type of organization, but it has also been adopted as a standard by the EU standards body CEN, and as an EU standard it places an obligation on member states to implement at a national level.

ISO 22301 places an emphasis on early planning, leadership, and understanding the context in which the organization operates. The standard also recognizes that organizational competence hinges on people—trained, knowledgeable, and experienced—to both develop the BC processes and support the organization during incidents. As with all ISO standards, the business continuity management activities integrate a continuous process improvement model that ensures that the organization refines its BCM processes to meet changing conditions. While ISO 22301 identifies the high-level processes, ISO 22313:2012, "Societal Security — Business continuity management systems — Guidance," provides best-practice perspective for organizations implementing BCM processes.

ANSI/ASIS SPC.1-2009, "Organizational Resilience Maturity Model American National Standard," is the codification of one of several voluntary industry bodies that have developed independent standards for BCM practice. This particular ANSI/ASIS standard provides adoptees with generic auditable criteria on which to structure a BCM practice, addressing prevention, preparedness, mitigation, and response.

Other industry organizations that have well-structured business continuity practices include the Business Continuity Institute (BCI) and the Disaster Recovery Institute International (DRII). These organizations also provide training and certification to their members in BC/DR practice.

Business Continuity Policy

A reasonable person would recognize that bad things happen and that taking steps to minimize the likelihood and consequence of those bad circumstances is a prudent course of action. The responsibility for the development of the BCM policy rests with the board of directors or governing body. Failing to have a BCM policy may well violate the fiduciary standard of due care.

A business continuity policy sets the tone for the organization's management to place an appropriate emphasis on developing and maintaining a resilient organization. At a minimum, the policy will identify the organization's compliance obligations; assign responsibility for planning, executing, and evaluating the organization's state of readiness; and establish a routine review process to ensure that the policy remains relevant to the business context.

Planning Processes for Business Continuity

Planning for resilience must take into account the people, processes, and systems necessary for the organization to achieve its mission. It is not simply a technology exercise. The business leadership must be actively engaged to identify organizational priorities, properly resource the BCM work, and ensure the organization is prepared to address disruption. A holistic approach to addressing organizational resilience minimizes the risk that disruptions will occur and, in responding to disruption, ensures that the right people are doing the right things at the right time.

Initiate Planning

Most people come to work every day and do the work their boss wants them to do. If it's not important to the organizational leadership—whatever the task—no organizational resources will be applied to address the issue. The breadth of skills and range of processes that are necessary to recover even simple services or capabilities demands high-level management support to effectively plan for and implement BCM practices.

For some organizations, particularly private-sector organizations, the primary goals of the senior management is to grow the organization and to protect the brand. BCM is generally not seen as an activity that grows the organization. It is an expense the organization incurs as part of doing business.

Instead, BCM is focused on protecting the brand. Organizations that value their customers want those customers to know that the organization will reliably and predictably deliver their goods and services, while protecting information that has been entrusted to the care of the organization by the customers. Failing to do so will have devastating consequences to the organization's reputation and ability to convince potential customers that they should do business with the organization.

In the public sector, the motivation is somewhat different. Damage to the brand, while still an issue, is also of lesser importance, since public-sector organizations usually have a monopoly on the delivery of service within a jurisdiction. Similarly, the need to grow the business is much less important, as the boundaries of service are generally established through a political process. The primary driver for BCM services becomes ensuring the predictable delivery of services to the constituents.

Understanding the organizational motivations allows the BCM professionals to communicate the value of BCM to the business leadership in their terms. The organization generally recognizes that, as senior leadership often has so many issues pressing on their time, when they *do* spend time on an issue, that issue is of importance to the organization. A BCM strategy that does not address the interests of governance (compliance and strategy) and management (growing the business and protecting the brand) is unlikely to have the resources or organizational emphasis to succeed.

Scope, Objectives, Assumptions, and Constraints

Once the organization has committed to increasing its resilience, it is essential to determine the scope of the work. Limiting the scope in BCM planning is essential, as the number of potential disruptive events and circumstances is vast. Planning control for each potential event that could affect an organization is well beyond the capabilities of any organization. Reasonable limits on scope might include defining which disruptive events should be included in the analysis, the resources to be devoted to the planning effort, and the amount of time to be devoted to planning. The end result of this is to create a charter establishing the parameters for the planning activities.

Clear *objectives* will have to be defined for the planners. An objective is an end state to be achieved in the planning process without specifying the means by which it will be accomplished. For example, an objective might be "Reestablish minimum services to support communications for first responders within 1 hour of disruption" or "Develop annual training events in which the organization's response capability can be demonstrated." This type of statement gives the planners a degree of latitude in the planning process, while focusing the planning on larger compliance expectations or management goals.

Often, additional *constraints* will be placed on the planning activities. Resources (limited budget, key personnel), time, or areas that will require specific attention are often defined in the initiation process. These statements of fact are often more specific than the objectives and also represent an expression of acceptable risk by the management.

Assumptions made during the planning process will also have to be explicitly defined. An assumption is a statement believed to be true to allow planning to continue. "The plan assumes that the primary data center will not be usable" is an example of an assumption. The planning process reduces uncertainty by documenting the assumptions and then working to prove their validity.

The scope, objectives, constraints, and assumptions will be documented in the charter and formally acknowledged by the senior leadership. This process makes clear to the entire organization the importance of the BCM activities. Finally, the charter is the tool by which the end result of the planning will be measured.

Resources for Planning

Comprehensive BCM efforts span the entire organization. Getting the right people in the process, however, to provide sufficient information and effectively address organizational issues within the planning cycle is often a challenge. Since getting timely, appropriate input into the planning process is so important, often the planning team will include representatives from each of the affected areas of business.

Finding the right people is made more difficult because of the personal and group dynamics at work in the planning process. Having wildly different levels of supervisors and workers on the same planning team often inhibits free and open communication—the senior people don't participate because they are guarding turf or don't want make a foolish statement in front of their juniors, and the juniors are often reluctant to disagree with the statements made by the seniors for fear of offending them. Creating a team dynamic that encourages open collaboration and interpersonal trust is one of the most challenging aspects of the planning process.

✔ Case Study: Google Project Aristotle

For several years, Google studied the effectiveness of various teams. It was clear from the outset that certain teams of people did well on tasks, regardless of the task, while other teams consistently underperformed. The size of the team, the level of the participants, the psychological predispositions of the team members, and other factors did not correlate with results. Even putting the "best" people on a team did not guarantee success. Something else was at work.

In 2018, Google published the results of Project Aristotle. Two significant traits stood out. Higher-performing teams tended to communicate in ways that allowed each participant to equally share their ideas. While sometimes the communication would be verbal, other times it would be in writing, but regardless, everyone on the team equally expressed their thoughts and ideas.

Second, higher-performing teams tended to have a higher degree of "social sensitivity." The team members quickly picked up on the nonverbal communications clues—the facial expressions, tone of voice, and nervous movements that were displayed by the other team members. The team members generally were able to detect when someone was distressed or feeling left out.

High performance teams create a norm for their team in which it is safe to communicate to not worry that your ideas, contributions, or perspectives will be ridiculed or rejected. This idea, characterized as psychological safety, is not new, but Google's research, backed by data and empirical testing, suggests that the most effective teams develop a high degree of trust with the other team members.

There are areas of expertise that should be integrated into the planning process. Areas represented must include the lines of business, human resources, legal, compliance, information technologists, and, of course, information security professionals. Finding the right balance is always difficult, however. As teams get larger, the speed with which they generate results tends to increase.

Deliverables and Timeline

The outputs of the planning process should be defined in the charter. These outputs will include a risk assessment identifying the likelihood and consequence of threats; a business impact analysis (BIA), identifying the critical business functions, recovery priorities, and the recovery strategy; and the business continuity plan itself. These materials, along with additional materials that may be specified to meet specific compliance requirements, will allow the organization to approve the plan. Subsequent implementation of the plan, conducting training and awareness activities, incident response, plan activation, and recovery will be discussed in Chapter 7.

The charter should also be clear on when the results of the planning process are to be completed. The complex, interconnected nature of many systems can become an analytic nightmare, with endless dependencies to be considered. The planning team should know they must deliver their plan on a schedule so that the concrete actions to mitigate risk can be implemented.

This is often disconcerting for the perfectionists in the group—they want the final answer. However, resilience is not an end—it is a characteristic that an organization exhibits. The process of improving an organization's resilience is never-ending: systems change, people come and go, and compliance expectations change. Thus, no plan is ever complete, and no plan is perfect. It just has to be good enough.

Risk Assessment

Risk can present itself through a variety of events and actors. Traditional business continuity planning inherently relied on an attacker-centric threat model. What is the likelihood and consequence of an earthquake? A hack? An active shooter? A fire? A flood? Godzilla? Making planning and response more difficult, resources often flowed based on a particular risk—flood insurance, tornadoes, terrorist events.

While this approach allowed organizations to more specifically tailor their response to circumstances, the level of planning and coordination required to implement controls for each circumstance was very high. This made it difficult to effectively prioritize response and increased the complexity of incident identification and detection, corrective actions, and recovery.

Many standards, including ISO 22301, structure the BCM planning process around an all-hazards model. In this paradigm, there is a single base plan for all disasters. This base plan addresses issues such as communications, incident command, prioritization and escalation, disaster declaration, and other highly generic processes.

Once the base plan is established, the planners then identify a broad range of threats. This is further refined as the planners identify the *likelihood* and *consequence* of a particular circumstance, allowing them to prioritize the greatest threats. (Risk assessment methods are discussed later in this chapter.) Detailed analysis and planning are then continued against those threats that pose the greatest risk through a separate annex in the plan for each of those threats. Given the threats mentioned, fires, flood, and earthquakes might deserve additional emphasis; because of low likelihood, Godzilla probably won't make the list.

By building on the base plan, the organization simplifies the training and coordination activities that will be necessary to implement the plan. This risk-based planning approach has been widely adopted at all levels of government and in private industry as best practice.

Business Impact Analysis

The business impact analysis is at the center of the BCM activities. Once the scope of the plan has been set, the critical business functions will be identified and assessed in a consistent manner. This will allow the organization to prioritize the risks it faces and apply control appropriately. Figure 1.3 shows an overview of a partial BIA.

Business Impact Analysis									
Functional Area	Function	CBF?	Description	Risk Code	Impact Category	MTD	RTO	RPO	Recovery Priority
		Y/N		F=Financial C=Customer R=Regulatory	S=Severe M=Moderate L=Low				
Human Resources	Onboarding	N	Onboard new employees						
Human Resources	Identity	Y	Identity-badging, access, etc.	R	S	1 hour	45 min	Last transaction	1
Human Resources	Payroll	Y	Employee payroll processes	R	S	1 day	8 hours	Last transaction	2

FIGURE 1.3 **BIA**

The BIA is a formal, structured method of identifying and determining the impact to the organization due to disruption of critical business functions (CBFs) by identifying various measures of impact. Once the organization impacts have been measured, the BIA will be used to identify resource requirements to resume minimum operating capabilities necessary for that CBF to resume meeting the organization's requirement. Finally, the recovery priorities for that particular CBF will be identified.

Critical Business Functions

CBFs are those activities that a business must perform to meet obligations to customers or compliance expectations. Expressed in some fashion in all of the major frameworks, CBFs are always expressed as a *business* function, not a technology.

Identifying CBFs requires input from a broad range of stakeholders. The perspectives of the system owners, subject-matter experts, customers, and suppliers all help in identifying an organization's potential CBFs. In taking input into the BIA process, only those functions that are specifically excluded by the charter's scope should be discarded from analysis. This helps to ensure that the broadest range of stakeholder perspectives are captured and addressed at an appropriate level.

Many CBFs cut across organizational lines. For example, the ability to authenticate and authorize system users affects a variety of systems. Depending on the authentication and authorization scheme employed by the organization, this underlying functionality may well be a CBF.

The initial set of CBFs will usually be specified as part of the scope in the BCM charter. However, as the planning work proceeds, other CBFs may be uncovered. It is the responsibility of the planning team to bring these functions to senior management so that a formal determination can be made as to whether planning for the discovered CBF is within the scope of the planning work.

Measures of Impact

Determining the level of impact of a disruption is done in several ways. Collectively, these measures identify how much disruption the business is willing to accept and how much control they are willing to resource.

Maximum Tolerable Downtime

As mentioned, MTD expresses in business language the total length of time a process can be unavailable without causing significant harm to the business. This must be defined by the system owner, who is ultimately responsible to the organization for the proper operation of the process. Exceeding the MTD is an expression of *unacceptable risk* (or, properly, a disaster) by the business owner.

Recovery Point Objective

The Recovery Point Objective (RPO) represents the measurement of tolerable data loss. Many systems are designed to log every committed transaction, and thus the RPO can be set to the last successful commit. As with the MTD, this must be defined by the business, and the business is responsible for resourcing the controls to achieve the RPO.

Recovery Time Objective

The Recovery Time Objective (RTO) is the planned time and level of service necessary to restore a system to the point where it meets the minimum service expectations of the system owner. Since a disaster occurs when the MTD is exceeded, the RTO, by definition, must be less than or equal to the MTD. The RTO must be adjusted by the application of additional controls to bring it within the MTD. At the point where the business owner is no longer willing to apply control, they have accepted the risk of operation.

For many system owners, this last point is often a difficult point to accept. A system owner may want 99.999 percent availability (MTD) but will fund only 99.0 percent availability (RTO). In choosing to not apply additional control, the system owner is acknowledging that the cost of the control outweighs the benefit of achieving the additional .999 percent. When the organization is no longer willing to apply control, it is accepting the residual risk. In other words, knowing that recovering from a disruption will exceed the MTD is planning for a disaster.

In practice, however, when the BIA indicates that the RTO will exceed the MTD, the system owner will resource the additional control and accept the risk for a period of time while the control is being implemented. The period of time while the corrective action plan or plan of action and milestones (POAM) reflects the acceptance of risk by the business owner.

As the CBFs are being identified and evaluated, a comprehensive inventory must be made of the systems and their dependencies to enable planning for recovery. The inventory may be captured through the BIA process, or the organization may have an existing asset inventory database as part of its change management activities that can provide the information.

Finally, the risk assessment and the BIA will be used to identify recovery priorities. This prioritization is essential to ensure the efficient recovery of the business functions. In many cases, one CBF will rely on underlying systems for proper operation. If the critical business function is sharing files across a team, that simply cannot happen until the authentication and authorization system is in place. The resulting system recovery priorities will shape the development of the recovery plans.

In actual practice, the development of recovery priorities may change because of business cycles, recovery strategies, and political decisions. BCM planners must be clear with the senior management that deciding how a recovery will be implemented will result in prioritization, and it is often stressful for one system owner to be told that the recovery of their particular process is lower on the priority list than others. Open, clear communication between the team, stakeholders, and management is essential in the prioritization process.

Develop the Business Continuity Plan

The BCP itself is the organization's commitment to maintaining the operations of the business. This plan focuses on the people, processes, and infrastructure on which the business relies to deliver goods and services to its customers. Based on the information derived from the BIA work, the organization can now begin to evaluate appropriate controls to align the MTDs with the RPO/RTOs. The full range of control categories is available to the planners. Controls that affect the likelihood of the event are generally preferable to those that affect the consequence, but the decisions will have to be made at the organizational level.

A number of high-level strategies can be incorporated into the plan to address various aspects of the people-processes-infrastructure challenge. By addressing the preferred approaches to control, the BCP will shape the subsequent planning efforts.

Preventive Strategies

One of the best ways to ensure business continuity is to prevent events from happening in the first place. Some of the more common preventive approaches include the following:

- **Training:** Organizational resilience relies on a competent workforce with sufficient depth to ensure that critical business functions can be recovered. Many organizations often have people in roles where that individual is the only one who can perform the function. These single points of failure can be addressed in many ways, including training others to perform the task and identifying outside resources with the skills, knowledge, and ability to perform the work. Regardless, the BIA process should identify these critical roles, and the BCP should address the organization's preferred approach to addressing these risks.

- **Hardening the infrastructure:** Decreasing the likelihood that a compromise will occur may lead to developing a more disaster-resilient infrastructure. Implementing highly available environments such as system clusters, private clouds, mirrored systems working in conjunction with environmental redundancy such as backup power supplies, redundant electrical generation, and HVAC systems will decrease the likelihood of system failure. Beyond supporting the individual information systems, the environmental redundancies may also speed recovery of the business processes.

- **Advanced backup technologies:** For most enterprise organizations, the range of availability services in the current storage environments have broadly replaced legacy approaches to backing up large data stores. The ability to snapshot datasets, maintain multiple data mirrors, and use new approaches to engineering the storage environment for geographical distribution can enhance both the availability and the performance of the storage pools. Cloud-based storage can be provisioned relatively easily as objects and presented as block or volume storage, and in some cases, raw storage can be implemented as well. The cost of cloud-based storage can also be adjusted based on the performance tier needed by the organization. For some legacy environments, however, the legacy approach of full system backups supported by incremental and differential backups remains the practice of choice.

- **Load balancing:** Whether it is across systems in a single data center or whether the processing load is distributed to multiple data centers, load balancing increases system availability. Planning must take into account minimum expected loads, however, to ensure that the minimum service levels are available in the event of the partial failure of the environment.

- **Threat monitoring:** Threat monitoring provides the system operators with changes in the threat environment, potentially providing time to implement protections against the threat event. In many cases, this includes increased system logging and monitoring, but it may include reporting from outside threat monitoring services.

Strategies to Prepare for Handling Events

Once the event has occurred, a number of other strategies and controls may become relevant.

Recovery in place is often the only alternative for an organization that is tied to serving a geographical area. In a large-scale disaster, it may be difficult to get employees back to the site, to transport equipment and supplies, and to provide for the physical security of the environment. Many times, a recovery-in-place will leverage a mobile site, brought to the location of the original (but now compromised) location.

Alternate sites are often used by organizations to meet their RTOs. Alternate sites are characterized as mirror, hot, warm, or cold, depending on the level of readiness to handle the processing activities from the primary site. Regulatory constraints often dictate that organizations maintain an alternate processing site.

Mirror sites are completely duplicated environments, with either site being able to support the entire processing load at any point in time. Supported through load balancing or hot swapping, this is one of the most expensive approaches but has the highest levels of availability.

Hot sites have all of the same processing capabilities as the primary site and data captured up to the RPOs. When activated, the hot site would be operational within the organization's RTO. Hot sites can be internal (owned by the organization) or external (contracted through a vendor).

Cold sites are an empty shells that must be provisioned to meet the processing demand. Cold sites are often characterized as only having four walls, a roof, and a power plug. In the event of a disaster, the lead times for the build-out must be taken into account in the RTOs.

Warm sites have some level of infrastructure and/or data available to support the recovery. The presence of any recovery capability less than a hot site or more than a cold site is a warm site.

Another alternate site approach is through some mutual assistance agreement. When two organizations have similar infrastructures, it may be possible for one organization to provide support to the other in a disaster. While attractive from a financial perspective, this approach is often challenging to implement, as most organizations run with little spare capacity and hosting another organization may have significant operational impacts on the host as well. This approach is most often found in governmental entities, implemented through a memorandum of agreement or similar vehicle.

Cloud bursting/hopping is one of the newest approaches to disaster recovery. For organizations with private cloud environments, it may be possible using provisioning tools such as Puppet/Chef, or vendor proprietary tools, to transition from an internal infrastructure to an external cloud infrastructure. For non–cloud-ready applications, or where large volumes of data must be moved to the cloud, additional planning must be undertaken to ensure the viability of the approach.

Documenting the Plan

The BCP identified in the chartering process sets an organizational tone for resilience. Focused on shaping the subsequent planning activities, the BCP should minimally address the following issues:

- **Organizational resilience vision:** The overall tone for the organization's resilience activities should be characterized. It should reflect the compliance expectations, the commitments to customers, and a recognition of the general range of risk faced by the organization. If the organization is adopting an all-hazards approach to planning, this should be included in the vision to ensure that subsequent planning is properly aligned.

- **Organizational resilience priorities:** From the prioritization work performed in the BIA process, the organization should identify the critical business functions to focus the organization's resources properly. The inclusion of a CBF as a priority should be explained in terms meaningful to the organization. Senior management's identification of priorities should serve to minimize the 'turf battles" inside the organization.

- **Organizational risk framework:** The processes and preferred strategies for addressing resilience should be identified. This should include the expectations for training and plan exercises.

- **Roles and responsibilities:** The organization should reaffirm the ownership of the BC process and explicitly identify who is responsible for maintaining the BCP, how the plan will be reviewed and on what schedule, and how BC information will be reported through the organization.

Once adopted, the BCP will allow the next level of planning to begin. Organizational requirements may dictate a number of separate plans; however, they should be integrated into, or aligned with, the overall BCP. As an example, NIST 800-34 identifies plans in the areas shown in Table 1.1.

TABLE 1.1 Plans Identified by NIST 800-34

PLAN	PURPOSE	SCOPE	PLAN RELATIONSHIP
Business continuity plan (BCP)	Provides procedures for sustaining mission/ business operations while recovering from a significant disruption	Addresses mission/ business processes at a lower or expanded level from COOP Mission Essential Functions (MEFs)	Mission/business process-focused plan that may be activated in coordination with a COOP plan to sustain non-MEFs
Continuity of operations (COOP) plan	Provides procedures and guidance to sustain an organization's MEFs at an alternate site for up to 30 days; mandated by federal directives	Addresses MEFs at a facility; information systems are addressed based only on their support of the mission-essential functions	MEF-focused plan that may also activate several business unit-level BCPs, ISCPs, or DRPs, as appropriate
Crisis communications plan	Provides procedures for disseminating internal and external communications; means to provide critical status information and control rumors	Addresses communications with personnel and the public; not information system focused	Incident-based plan often activated with a COOP or BCP but may be used alone during a public exposure event
Critical infrastructure protection (CIP) plan	Provides policies and procedures for protection of national critical infrastructure components, as defined in the national infrastructure protection plan	Addresses critical infrastructure components that are supported or operated by an agency or organization	Risk management plan that supports COOP plans for organizations with critical infrastructure and key resource assets
Cyberincident response plan	Provides procedures for mitigating and correcting a cyberattack, such as a virus, worm, or Trojan horse	Addresses mitigation and isolation of affected systems, cleanup, and minimizing loss of information	Information system–focused plan that may activate an ISCP or DRP, depending on the extent of the attack

CONTINUES

PLAN	PURPOSE	SCOPE	PLAN RELATIONSHIP
Disaster recovery plan (DRP)	Provides procedures for relocating information systems operations to an alternate location	Activated after major system disruptions with long-term effects	Information system–focused plan that activates one or more ISCPs for recovery of individual systems
Information system contingency plan (ISCP)	Provides procedures and capabilities for recovering an information system	Addresses single information system recovery at the current or, if appropriate, alternate location	Information system–focused plan that may be activated independent from other plans or as part of a larger recovery effort coordinated with a DRP, COOP, and/or BCP
Occupant emergency plan (OEP)	Provides coordinated procedures for minimizing loss of life or injury and preventing property damage in response to a physical threat	Focuses on personnel and property particular to the specific facility; not mission/business process or information system–based	Incident-based plan that is initiated immediately after an event, preceding a COOP or DRP activation

While different organizations may have unique requirements for planning, the subsequent plans themselves should address a number of areas.

- **Invocation (or declaration):** Clear standards should exist as to what circumstances invoke a particular plan and who in the organization is authorized to invoke a particular plan. Invoking an organizational response may incur both financial and reputational consequences, so it is essential that the appropriate level of management decide that the plan should be implemented. This includes identifying compliance requirements that the plan addresses, the potential event anticipation milestones, and the triggers that would cause changes in the organizational response.

- **Recovery strategies:** The plan should clarify the organization's preferred recovery strategies for the incident. Unfortunately, not all incidents fall neatly into the plans that have been created. A well-designed plan will provide responders with some flexibility, including addressing workarounds and alternative recovery approaches. The recovery strategies should be refined to clarify the recovery priorities for the event.

- **Organization:** In an event, traditional lines of communication and authority may be disrupted or modified. These changes need to be specified in the individual plans. The organization should identify the crisis event leadership, span of control and span of authority for each leadership level, in-band and out-of-band communications flows for notification and reporting, and the roles of the individual recovery teams and individuals.

- **Communications:** The range of stakeholders affected when any response plan is invoked may vary greatly. Internal and external customers and suppliers, vendors, regulators, various levels of management, and the individuals involved in the execution of the recovery will require different levels of detail from the organization. In a broad disaster, media and the general public might also have to be notified. All stakeholders must receive appropriate, timely information on which to act or make decisions. Failing to provide timely communications may also have financial or reputational consequences to the organization, separate from the actual impact of the event.

- **Human resources:** In many organizations, invocation of a plan may affect the use of people in the response. The scope and nature of the disaster, the effect the event has on the ability of people to do their work, labor or union contracts, and various statutory or regulatory requirements may affect who can respond to the event.

- **Finance:** The event may require the expenditure of funds in a very short time frame. Organizations that have complex contracting processes may often find themselves unable to acquire the goods and services necessary to effect a timely response. Indeed, in certain disasters, traditional mechanisms for acquiring goods through credit cards or purchase orders may simply be unavailable. Capturing the costs of the recovery itself for subsequent insurance or other recovery claims must also be handled in such a way as to facilitate the documentation of claims.

- **End state:** The plan should be clear on what level of capability must be recovered for the organization to declare the end of the response, and the milestones that mark the transition to normal business operations.

- **Training and awareness:** The plan should clarify the level to which the organization can demonstrate its response capability. The techniques for training the employees' will vary depending on the level of capacity that the organization needs.

One of the challenges that planners face is to determine the level of detail the plan should contain. There is no easy answer, as this will be different for each organization. Best practice is that the plan should provide enough detail for an experienced individual, having never executed the plan, to meet the performance expectations for that role. This expectation takes into account the real possibility that the person who would be expected to fill the role or perform the task may be unavailable in the actual event.

Keep in mind that the broader topic of business continuity has many well-defined bodies of practice, often specific to a particular industry segment. The role of the CISSP is to advocate for good security practices in the business continuity process to guarantee the confidentiality, integrity, and availability of information throughout the BCM continuum.

CONTRIBUTE TO AND ENFORCE PERSONNEL SECURITY POLICIES AND PROCEDURES

The security of our information systems relies on people to make a myriad of decisions relative to the information. We rely on people inside our organizations to know which information is to be controlled, in what manner, throughout the information lifecycle. Multiple studies confirm that people remain the weak link in protecting our information assets. One study by IBM suggests that 95 percent of all security incidents involve human error.

Information security decisions start with identifying the right people for the organization—people with the proper knowledge, skills, and abilities (KSAs) to do the tasks we expect of them. Verifying their KSAs is only the start. At the time of hire, the organization must set good expectations for personal behavior.

Once inside the organization, the potential for an individual to cause harm increases exponentially. Their actions can be deliberate or accidental, but the misuse of their privileges and authority in the organization opens the possibility of harm. Control now has to focus on providing only the privileges they need to do their work and monitoring the work to ensure it is done properly.

When the individual leaves the organization, control over the sensitive information must still be exercised to reduce the likelihood and consequence of bad actions by the individual. The organization needs to ensure that their privileges to organizational information have been appropriately revoked. Further, the organization must take steps to ensure the individual does not misuse their knowledge of the organization's sensitive information.

Systems work only because people are doing the right thing. The information security practitioner must understand not only the technical means by which control is established but the administrative tools available to set expectations for behavior before, during, and after employment.

Key Control Principles

Several control principles must be taken into account when developing sound personnel security programs. These basic principles are applied in different ways and with different control mechanisms. However, a solid understanding of the principles is essential to evaluating a control's effectiveness and applicability to a particular circumstance.

Separation of Duties

When a single individual is responsible for a critical function from beginning to end, potential exists for the individual to act maliciously or to make mistakes that are not readily noticeable. Financial fraud is often perpetrated by individuals who are able to conceal their misdeeds because they are in control of the entire transaction path. Information security professionals must be able to identify the process flows to ensure appropriate controls are applied based on the risk of the process.

Separation (or segregation) of duties can be accomplished in a number of ways. The simplest is to break the process into a set of steps, where each step results in an output that must be used in the next step. Having different individuals perform the steps ensures that nonconforming inputs are identified.

If the task being performed requires multiple inputs, these factors, though not sequential, can be split among multiple actors with the inputs combined for the end result. Geographical or spatial separation may also be appropriate if some of the tasks are performed in one physical location and then moved to another location for completion.

Individual control may also be appropriate. Sometimes referred to as the *four eyes principle*, this form of control requires two individuals to separately validate the process. A form of this is when the CEO and CFO have to countersign checks for a purchase. In this case, the work does not have to be completed simultaneously.

The *two-person rule* can be implemented where simultaneous presence and action is required. Many countries require two people to be in the cockpit of commercial airliners at all times. Nuclear missile launch procedures require multiple individuals to authenticate the order to launch. In life-critical environments, the two-person rule provides a check and balance to ensure one person does not act alone.

Of course, all controls must be balanced against the risks presented against the cost of the control. Implementing separation of duties can be difficult in small organizations simply because there are not enough people to perform the separate functions! Nevertheless, separation of duties remains an effective internal control to minimize the likelihood of fraud or malfeasance.

Least Privilege

To perform a task or function, an individual should have only those privileges necessary to do the work but no more. While the concept of *least privilege* predates information technology systems, least privilege is widely used to enforce separation of duties. Least privilege is taken into account in personnel settings by clearly defining job roles and functions.

Need to Know

Related to least privilege, *need to know* deals with the information that is being accessed, not the process by which it is accessed. Since the same information can be accessed in many forms, it is important to understand which information an individual must have in order to perform their duties. Need to know is authorized by the information owner and provisioned by the information custodian.

Need to know and information classification are closely related. Information is defined by its sensitivity, and a person who is judged to need to know information will become cleared, or approved, to handle information at that level of sensitivity. The classification relates to the information, the clearance is associated with the person.

Candidate Screening and Hiring

Hiring the right employees is an act of due diligence. Failing to hire the right employees can result in significant legal risk to the organization. On the other hand, the employment process itself has specific legal expectations to ensure fair treatment of candidates. Information security professionals must understand the laws of their jurisdiction, the organization's security expectations, and the legal, appropriate way to ensure that the organization's interests are protected.

What Skills Are Needed

Many organizations do not have a comprehensive skill inventory relative to the skills required to perform their mission. Evaluating the current skills gap and projecting the required skills and competencies into the future are particularly difficult with information security talent because the industry is changing rapidly and the demand for talent exceeds the supply.

The 2017 Global Information Security Workforce Study conducted by the Center for Cyber Safety and Education reinforced the shortage of qualified talent available to meet information security requirements. Over the next five years the study estimates a worldwide shortfall of more than 1.8 million professionals. Further, nearly 90 percent of the global cybersecurity workforce is male, and as there are fewer young people coming into the workforce, the average age of the information security professional is rising. These factors suggest that new approaches to information security recruiting and skills expansion will be necessary to address the overall industry skills gap.

Further complicating the skills shortage is the increase in compliance demands on organizations for demonstrating that their workforce is trained. As of 2017, changes in the New York Financial Services Law require covered entities to "utilize qualified cybersecurity personnel" and provide them with "cybersecurity updates and training sufficient to address relevant cybersecurity risk." Other compliance frameworks place similar diligence expectations on organizations to ensure that the staff is both sufficient and competent.

Position Descriptions

Most organizations identify the competency and skills requirements in standard job or position descriptions. A well-written job description defines the job duties and responsibilities, identifies the qualifications necessary to perform the role, identifies the supervisory relationships, identifies the salary or rate of pay, and sets the baseline expectations for performance. If the role has special demands such as heavy lifting, travel, or other circumstances that would affect a person's ability to perform the essential tasks, these should also be captured.

The importance of the position description increases depending on the legal framework in which the organization operates. In some jurisdictions, accurate job descriptions are required for compliance with labor laws; in other circumstances, the job descriptions are required by, and negotiated through, a labor union agreement.

The position description also allows organizations to identify roles and responsibilities that require a higher level of trust. Ensuring the person filling the role has been fully vetted will provide some assurance that the person presents a minimal risk. Stating the assurance expectations in the position description makes any additional responsibilities clear to both the employee and the organization.

Information security requirements should be carefully stated in position descriptions to ensure that individuals know what is expected of them in their roles and that they could be held accountable for failing to meet those expectations. This might include maintaining professional certification, completing security awareness training, and referencing (or inclusion, where appropriate) NDAs and other supporting organizational security policies.

Screening and Interviewing

Once a job requirement has been identified and applications solicited, the organization has additional responsibilities to ensure that the recruitment action is, at a minimum, conducted legally. For example, in most jurisdictions, discrimination on the basis of gender, age, and race is illegal. Many labor agreements have seniority requirements defining how positions are to be filled. In some jurisdictions, nepotism (the hiring of friends and family) is restricted, while in other jurisdictions, it is acceptable or even encouraged. Similarly, some jurisdictions make it illegal to ask an applicant's prior salary. In short, the hiring practices your organization will follow depend on the applicable jurisdiction and legal framework.

Legal expectations for hiring extend to the interviewing of individuals. Questions must have a bona fide relationship to the position being filled. Improper questions may open the organization to legal challenge by the individual or, depending on the jurisdiction, criminal or regulatory action by the state.

In many cases, to evaluate the suitability of a candidate for a sensitive role, the organization may have to disclose proprietary or sensitive information. The use of NDAs in pre-employment situations has increased greatly in recent years. The organization must take care to ensure that the agreement is not overbroad, as it would be unenforceable in court, but sufficient to protect the organization's legitimate interests over its intellectual property.

✔ **Best Practices for Conducting Interviews**

The following are some best practices for conducting interviews:

1. Define the interview process in advance.
2. Define the evaluation criteria that will be used to assess all candidates.
3. Prepare all questions asked of candidates in advance and verify that the questions do not violate the employment laws of the jurisdiction.
4. Ask behavioral or situational questions relevant to the position, such as "Describe a circumstance where…" or "Given this scenario, what would you do?"
5. Ask objective knowledge questions such as "What is TCP Port 53 used for?"
6. Never interview a candidate alone.
7. Take formal notes and save them for reference.
8. Ask all candidates the same questions.

Selecting the right people for positions of responsibility inside organizations is difficult. Due diligence requires that we vet each individual's claims of experience, professional education, and certification. Failing to exercise due diligence in the hiring process can increase the organization's liability for negligent hiring if the individual subsequently misuses his access or authority.

As part of the hiring process, it is common to request that the applicant provide professional and personal references. These individuals should be able to speak to the applicant's job history, performance, technical skills, and work habits. As with any interview, a standard set of questions should be employed when speaking with a personal or professional reference.

Background Investigations

Background investigations are a more formal method of verifying an employee's claims. Many industry studies have shown that résumés frequently misrepresent the qualifications of the individual. However, the degree to which an applicant's background can be examined depends on the laws of the jurisdiction.

In the United States, background checks may not be used to discriminate based on race, color, national origin, sex, or religion; disability; genetic information (including family medical history); or age. Similarly, under federal law it is legal to ask about an employee's criminal history, but it may be illegal to use that information to discriminate in employment. Many states have a more stringent standard, prohibiting asking anything about an employee's criminal background in employment decisions.

The importance of knowing the local law cannot be overemphasized. In the United Kingdom, criminal background checks are only allowed to be performed for certain occupations and industry sectors. As in many other jurisdictions, India requires the individual provide "informed consent" prior to the collection of sensitive information. The information security professional is well advised to consult their legal counsel in regard to the local employment law prior to conducting any investigation into the background of a prospective employee.

Financial Information

In the United States, employers are limited in the amount of financial information they can use in making hiring decisions. The Fair Credit Reporting Act sets a national standard for employers to follow when conducting background checks. Further, the employer must follow specific procedures when conducting background checks using consumer reporting agencies for information. These include getting the person's written permission, telling how they want to use the information, not misusing the information, providing a copy of the credit report if they decide to not hire or to fire the person, and providing an opportunity to dispute the information contained within the credit report before making a final adverse decision.

Social Media

Most professional organizations that conduct background investigations will also review an applicant's social media accounts. While these public postings may give information that would help in a hiring decision, organizations have faced criticism by applicants who felt they were not considered because the employer knew their race, gender, nationality, sexual preference, or other protected category. One approach to help mitigate this risk is to ensure the searches are conducted by someone outside the hiring process, so any potentially protected content may be eliminated before it enters the hiring decision.

Organizations should have clear policies that define the appropriate uses of Internet and social media research, standardize which information is to be taken from the social media sites, verify the accuracy of the information, and disclose to applicants the potential use of Internet and social media in deciding which applicants to consider.

Criminal History

People with criminal histories are often barred from future employment in certain positions or sectors. However, individuals applying for jobs are much less likely to be considered for an interview if the application asks if they have a criminal record, and in some jurisdictions such discrimination may be illegal. Consequently, many jurisdictions limit when and under what circumstances a criminal record can be used in a hiring decision.

Driving Records

If an individual will be operating a motor vehicle as part of their job, it is generally acceptable to verify that they have a legal motor vehicle license. The driving record may show citations, accidents, license suspensions or revocations, or impaired operation of a motor vehicle. Hiring an individual with a known history of improper operation of a vehicle may expose the organization to risk if that individual subsequently commits a similar act during employment.

Medical Records

Medical records are generally considered to be among the most private of records. Most countries (and many subjurisdictions) specifically regulate pre-employment access to records and, almost without exception, require the applicant to explicitly grant permission for the employer to do so. For example, in the United States, prior to extending a job offer, an employer generally may not ask any disability-related questions and may not require medical examinations of applicants. After a conditional offer of employment is made, the employer may request information on disabilities or require examinations, but the Americans with Disabilities Act prohibits employers from revoking an offer based on the information.

Many countries also limit whether an employer is entitled to access genetic information on applicants or employees. In the United States, the Genetic Information Nondiscrimination Act of 2008 currently prohibits genetic information discrimination in employment. Similarly, in the European Union, Title 2, Article 21 of the Treaty of Lisbon prohibits discrimination based on genetic information. (For more information, see https://www.eeoc.gov/eeoc/foia/letters/2011/ada_gina_confidentrequre.html.)

Other countries have fewer restrictions. In Mexico, the Federal Labor Law does not limit the employer's ability to request medical information from a potential employee. However, limits on how that information can be used are subject to other antidiscrimination statutes.

Drug Testing

Many jurisdictions allow employers to require applicants to pass screening tests for illegal drugs. In the United States, there is no comprehensive federal law that regulates drug testing in the private sector; however, certain regulated industries, such as transportation or contractors for the Department of Defense, have mandatory drug testing requirements. Many states, however, have provisions imposing drug-testing restrictions of various forms, including no regulation, allowing all employers to test, and allowing testing only when "reasonable suspicion" or "probable cause" exists. Several states authorize random testing under certain circumstances, and others impose restrictions on public-sector employers but not on private companies.

In Canada, pre-employment medical testing is limited to determining whether an applicant can perform the essential tasks of the job. Consequently, drug testing is generally prohibited prior to employment. In Mexico, employers can require drug screening but must keep the results private.

Prior Employment

An employee's work history is one of the most valuable indicators of job success. Verifying dates of employment, job title, performance, and eligibility for rehire are generally acceptable practices prior to employment. Periods of unemployment should also be identified, and it is generally acceptable to have applicants explain why they were unemployed.

Attempting to avoid defamation lawsuits by former employees, many organizations have limited the information that can be passed to other employers. However, these restrictions are often much greater than the legal standard. In the United States, many states have "job reference shield" laws. For example, in Alaska, "If reference is presented in good faith, the employer is not liable for the disclosure regarding job references, provided they are not reckless, malicious, false or deliberately misleading." (Alaska Stat §09.65.160).

Other Tests

A wide variety of other tools are available to employers. These include tests for personality, integrity, cognitive, and emotional intelligence.

Handwriting analysis, or *graphology*, has gained in popularity in recent years. The science (or pseudoscience) behind this controversial method is subject to intense debate over whether it can indeed predict employee behavior. In France, surveys suggest that more than 80 percent of private companies use this tool; in the UK, 30 percent; while in the United States, between 3 and 5 percent of companies report that they use it to evaluate candidates. Interestingly, graphology has been used by agencies like the NSA and the FBI to evaluate applicants.

Regardless of the tool, however, it is essential to use only those tools that meet the legal tests in the applicable jurisdiction. Handwriting analysis has been shown to reliably predict the sex of the writer or could be affected by a person's medical conditions. Using the results of the handwriting analysis could create a conflict with U.S. antidiscrimination law where a subsequent hiring decision was based on the person's gender.

Polygraphs, commonly referred to as *lie detectors*, have also been generally banned in commercial pre-employment settings in the United States by the Employee Polygraph Protection Act of 1988. Similar, and even more stringent, laws are in place in Canada, Australia, and other countries. However, many other countries (e.g., Singapore, South Africa, etc.) allow for their use. While polygraph use in national security environments is widely accepted, there is significant scientific debate as to whether the testing accurately identifies individuals who are not trustworthy. The legal status of polygraph testing is another example where an understanding of the applicable law is important to the security practitioner.

Employment Agreements and Policies

Most organizations will put policies in place to set appropriate expectations for behavior in the workplace. In many cases, comprehensive policies are required by compliance frameworks, and compliance with the policies is evaluated as part of the audit framework.

Comprehensive policies also support a variety of other organizational goals. They give management a set of rules, procedures, and guidelines with which they can make consistent, appropriate decisions and support the delegation of routine decision-making to lower levels in the organization.

From the standpoint of the employee, policies demonstrate that the organization acts in good faith in treating employees equally, fairly, and within the legal constraints of the jurisdiction. They also provide a means to effectively communicate information to new employees. Mature organizations do not have to rely solely on "tribal knowledge" to fit new workers into the team.

There are a number of policies that are essential to setting good security expectations for employees.

Background Investigations

As discussed, background investigations are a vital tool in evaluating the skills, knowledge, and abilities of potential employees. A well-structured background investigation policy will ensure all applicants are treated equally and fairly. The policy should state the requirements for notification and obtaining the permissions from the people being investigated, identify who is responsible for performing the checks, the level of documentation of the results of the checks, and the processes for informing applicants of the results of the checks.

Many organizations will also do routine background checks on existing employees. People's life circumstances change, and routine background investigations after employment may identify individuals who, subsequent to their hire, would present an unacceptable risk to the organization. The policy should address the circumstances that trigger an investigation, the means by which they will be conducted, and the extent to which an individual's background will be verified. Aligning the pre- and post-employment background checks supports the organization's commitment to the fair and equitable treatment of all individuals in the organization.

Nondisclosure Agreement

Many organizations will use nondisclosure agreements to protect sensitive organization information from inappropriate disclosure. Often, NDAs are used to protect trade secrets, but they can protect physical assets, processes, customer relationships, or any nonpublic information. In some jurisdictions, deeds of confidentiality and fidelity serve the same purpose as an NDA.

NDAs can be unilateral (one party provides information, and the other party receives and protects the information), mutual (both parties provide and protect the other's information), or multilateral (multiple parties sharing and respectively protecting the others' information.) Depending on the nature of the information, the agreements can become complex and should be drafted with professional legal advice.

The terms and conditions of an NDA are generally enforced under civil law as a contractual relationship. Relying on the courts to enforce the terms of the agreement can be problematic, as courts have found NDAs unenforceable when they are overbroad or, depending on the jurisdiction, lack a time limit on how long the agreement is in force. Further, as contracts, the NDA must provide some "consideration" (exchange of value) between the parties. If signed at the time of employment, the value can be demonstrated by being hired. Further, NDAs cannot be enforced if they attempt to protect information about criminal activity or behavior.

Nevertheless, the use of NDAs is on the rise in many industries. While NDAs are used widely in the technology industry, companies as diverse as fast-food restaurants, summer camps, coffee shops, and hair salons have also required employees to sign NDAs as a condition of employment.

In many countries, trade secrets have specific legal protections regardless of whether an NDA is in place. The NDA's function is to protect the non–trade-secret information (for example, an organization's customer relationships). Regardless, it is incumbent on the organization with sensitive information to ensure the agreement is in place prior to sharing the information.

Nondisclosure agreements are often used in national security organizations to ensure that individuals with access to classified information understand their responsibilities. As opposed to the limitations on information protected by private-sector organizations, the NDAs related to national security information tend to be broad, unlimited by time and geography. As disclosure of sensitive national security information is a violation of criminal law in most jurisdictions, violations of these agreements are usually enforceable.

Acceptable Use

Organizations have a compelling interest in ensuring that their assets are used legally and in ways that support the organization's mission. Acceptable use policies set out the legitimate ways the information assets can be used and define consequences for inappropriate use. Acceptable use agreements should be presented to applicants prior to hire and then reinforced through the organization's information security awareness programs.

Conflict of Interest

A conflict of interest comes about when an individual has a duty of care to one organization and has other interests or obligations that conflict (or might conflict) with their obligation to the organization. In hiring situations, conflicts of interest often arise when an applicant has a second business relationship or has a relationship with someone in the organization. Conflict of interest can also occur because of financial obligations, access to confidential information, or any number of other factors.

Conflicts of interest may be actual or potential. Regardless, the organization should clearly state how it expects conflicts of interest to be addressed and resolved and the consequences for failing to do so.

Gift Handling

The giving and receiving of gifts plays an important role in establishing and maintaining relationships. In many cultures, it is an insult not to bring a gift when meeting or when recognizing life events. Similarly, to refuse a gift can also be considered an insult. Since gift giving has such cultural sensitivity, organizations are well advised to have rules in place to distinguish between acceptable and unacceptable gifting.

In many countries and business contexts, paying for your guest's meal at a restaurant is considered good business etiquette. In parts of eastern Europe, the Middle East, and other countries, small displays of gratitude for service are often expected even when dealing with government officials, physicians, and law enforcement. *Baksheesh*, broadly defined as tipping or giving alms, is a time-honored tradition in many countries where the practice is viewed as an augmentation to an official's low government salary. Often it is illegal but is nevertheless condoned — or even encouraged — to have requests for service addressed by government officials. In most Western countries, government officials accepting personal payments is illegal.

Many organizations will set different limits on how gifts are handled, depending on the culture and other factors. In the U.S. government, depending on departmental policy, individuals can accept gifts on behalf of the U.S. government but may, if they are willing to reimburse the U.S. Treasury the fair market value of the gift, take ownership of the item. A somewhat similar standard exists in the United Kingdom. According to the

UK's Ministerial Code, "Ministers should not accept any gift or hospitality which might, or might reasonably appear to, compromise their judgement or place them under an improper obligation…Gifts given to Ministers in their Ministerial capacity become the property of the Government and do not need to be declared in the Register of Members' or Peers' Interests. Gifts of small value, currently this is set at £140, may be retained by the recipient. Gifts of a higher value should be handed over to the department for disposal unless the recipient wishes to purchase the gift abated by £140."

Through a gift policy, most organizations set limits on gifting in the workplace, defining the value and circumstances under which gifting is acceptable. The policy should also identify which employees are covered by the gifting policy and when variance from the policy is permitted.

Mandatory Vacations

Many organizations define the amount of time away from a position, and often the period of time, in which employees must take vacations. The obvious health and quality of life benefits aside, mandatory vacations are one of the most effective tools for identifying fraud inside an organization.

The Federal Deposit Insurance Corporation (FDIC) considers this basic control effective in identifying fraud because "perpetration of an embezzlement of any substantial size usually requires the constant presence of the embezzler in order to manipulate records, respond to inquiries from customers or other employees, and otherwise prevent detection." The Basel Committee on Banking Supervision similarly expects this control to be implemented to reduce operational risk.

From a security perspective, best practice for individuals who are subject to mandatory vacation rules should have their access privileges suspended during the period of absence. This provides a check to minimize the likelihood that they are remotely performing the work (or maintaining a coverup).

Mandatory vacations are often part of a larger resilience strategy for organizations to ensure that critical functions can be performed in the absence of the principal individual assigned to the role. Individuals often become single points of failure in critical systems, precisely because they are competent and they then become the person who exclusively performs the critical function. Often, they fail to document the processes sufficiently for others to perform the task in their absence. These issues are generally brought to light when someone else performs the task in the absence of the principal.

Onboarding and Termination Processes

The processes that bring people into an organization set the tone for their work behavior. Similarly, the termination processes should clarify their obligation to respect the protection of the organization's intellectual property and security. The security practitioner should be actively engaged with the business to ensure that the proper tone is set for behavior in the workplace.

Onboarding

Setting good expectations for work behavior should start before the employee walks in the door.

Orientation

Part of the employee orientation program should address information security expectations and requirements. Employees should be reminded of their obligations to protect information and current threats to the organization's information assets, particularly if they are likely to be the targets of malicious actors. Further, orientation practices should inform new employees of the processes for reporting security incidents, their role in maintaining the security of their work area, and the classification and categorization processes so they can identify the level of control necessary for particular information.

Employees should also be made generally aware of the existence of controls that monitor their use of the organization's assets. Not only does this provide them with assurance that the organization does indeed take action to protect its information, but the information alone may act as a deterrent to inappropriate behavior. The intent is not to provide the employee with sufficient technical detail to defeat the controls, but to make sure they understand that their actions may be scrutinized.

The ability of the organization to monitor employees will depend on the legal jurisdiction, union agreements, and the risks faced by the employer. For example, a recent court case in the European Union found that a private employer may monitor employee activity, provided that the employees had been given sufficient notice.

By comparison, practices in Japan and India are generally consistent with this approach. In Japan, the Personal Information Protection Law regulates the collection, storage, and use of employee information, and guidelines published by the various ministries specifically call out the responsibility to notify the employees that they are being monitored. In India, privacy is not a constitutional right, but privacy practices have been legislated into the IT Act of 2000/2008. In short, if monitoring is performed and the capture of information could affect the privacy of the person being monitored, best practice is to ensure that the employee is made aware of and acknowledges in writing that they have been informed of the potential for monitoring.

Tribal Knowledge

Employee orientations set the initial expectations for employees, but the most influential information source for new employees is their supervisor and co-workers. Creating a security-aware culture is essential to ensure that new employees properly protect the organization's information.

A common example of this is in the healthcare industry, where patient confidentiality requires that only individuals involved in the circle of care should access a patient's records. In the past, paper records made it difficult to detect unauthorized access. However, with the broad adoption of electronic healthcare records (with attendant capabilities to monitor access), hundreds of employees at dozens of healthcare organizations have been reported as fired as a result of patient snooping. This suggests that the past practices that made it possible (while still against policy) to allow the workforce to snoop can now be enforced.

Organizations have been held in greater liability for having policies that they do not follow than if they had no policy at all. Consequently, it is up to management to perform their diligence ensuring the organizational policies are made available, implemented, and enforced.

Employment

Once an individual is accepted into the workforce, many organizations significantly reduce their evaluation of the employee's suitability for access to sensitive information. As discussed, life circumstances and organizational expectations change, and formerly acceptable backgrounds may no longer meet the security expectations of the organization.

Periodic Reinvestigation

Holders of U.S. government security clearances are routinely required to resubmit for periodic reevaluation of their suitability. While the length of time between reinvestigations varies depending on the level of the clearance, the process nevertheless provides an opportunity to reassess whether the individual is still worthy of access to sensitive information.

The problem with periodic reinvestigation is that it is periodic—and changes to one's life can happen within the period. Starting in 2015, the U.S. Department of Defense began moving many positions to a continuous evaluation model. In this approach, various social media forums and networks, as well as big data sources such as music-sharing and dating websites, are examined to determine whether individuals with clearances are potentially engaged in conduct that would affect their clearance. The DoD has already revoked dozens of clearances in advance of what would have been their scheduled periodic reinvestigation.

In the private sector, periodic reinvestigations are often conducted when individuals are involved in cash handling or sensitive transactions in the financial services industry.

However, periodic reinvestigation remains the exception rather than the rule for other positions.

Demotion or Reduction

Disgruntled employees often are motivated to take actions against their employers. The U.S. CERT's Insider Threat Center has identified a number of causes of disgruntlement that have led to malicious insider actions, including the following:

- Insufficient salary increase or bonus
- Limitations on use of company resources
- Diminished authority or responsibilities
- Perception of unfair work requirements
- Feeling of being treated poorly by co-workers

A well-structured insider threat program will have processes in place to coordinate management actions, identify circumstances and individuals who are likely to cause greater risk, and be able to take actions to minimize the risk without violating the individual's privacy rights.

Termination

Taking appropriate care when people depart organizations or roles is just as important as ensuring they are properly brought into the organization. These transitions can happen for a number of reasons, from changing business priorities, different skill requirements, new career opportunities, or transfers within the organization. These former insiders represent a risk to the organization, and appropriate actions must be taken to ensure they do not compromise the operations, intellectual property, or sensitive information with which they have been entrusted.

Voluntary

When an individual leaves an organization on good terms, it is relatively easy to go through the standard checklist: suspending electronic access; recovering their access badges, uniforms, and equipment; accounting for their keys; and changing the key codes on cipher locks that the departing employee used are among many other standard practices. Most organizations have well-structured off-boarding processes to ensure the removal of access when an individual is no longer entitled to organizational information or resources.

When individuals have elevated access, this often becomes more difficult, particularly in smaller organizations that lack effective controls. Access points such as shared passwords, encryption keys, various portals such as dial-in points, or even employee parking passes can be inappropriately used after access should have been terminated. Often, the organization will continue to rely on the departed individual as a consultant or volunteer, and this makes managing access even more difficult. Good organizational controls and processes to manage exceptions are essential in minimizing organizational risk.

The Insider Threat Center also identified a number of circumstances where individuals left to take a job with a competitor on apparently good terms but exfiltrated sensitive organizational information prior to their departure. This is far from unusual. A 2015 survey suggests that almost 87 percent of departing employees take information from their employers that they created during their employment.

The departure of key individuals due to voluntary reasons, death, illness, or other unforeseeable events place many organizations at risk. One estimate is that 55 percent of small businesses would not survive if a key person departed the organization. While key personnel insurance is available, a much smaller percentage (22 percent, in the United States) of organizations take advantage of it.

Involuntary

Involuntary termination of employment is an emotionally charged event for all involved. In virtually all cases, an involuntary termination forces the employer to assume the terminated individual is a threat to the organization, and appropriate action should be taken to protect organizational assets. Termination procedures at most organizations include specific processes to notify the information security organization to disable access to electronic and physical systems.

Where possible, recovery of property (uniforms, keys, equipment, etc.) that the employee used should be attempted. Where appropriate, the recovered material should be tracked as evidence and retained for subsequent forensic analysis. Finally, once the individual has left the organization, the staff should be informed that the terminated individual is no longer allowed access and that any attempts by that individual to access resources or property should be reported. Organizational policies will dictate how much information is to be conveyed, but generally minimizing the disclosure of the circumstances to those with a direct need to know is considered best practice.

It is not unusual for the terminated individuals to have taken steps to harm the organization in the event that they were terminated. The most obvious forms of this are the theft of data by the terminated individual, who hopes either to sell back the key to the organization, use the information to begin or join a competing organization, or disclose the information to discredit the organization.

Other malicious strategies include logic bombs placed inside programs and encryption of data, sometimes while retaining the key in hopes of extorting money or retaining some other access to organizational assets. Good data processing practices, including a well-developed insider threat program, availability controls, and managing elevated privilege, are essential in defeating malicious actions by terminated employees.

Vendor, Consultant, and Contractor Agreements and Controls

Many organizations require expertise or talent that does not exist inside their organizations. These relationships may exist for goods or services, but both types of acquisition open the organization to risk. Ensuring that these relationships do not expose the organization's sensitive information requires integrating the vendors, contractors, and consultants into the larger organizational security framework.

Industrial Espionage

Many organizations that rely on contractors have multiple contractors working side by side. While this can create a positive collaboration, care must be taken to ensure that the intellectual property of one vendor does not spill to another. Economic studies have shown it is far cheaper for organizations to steal technology from others than it is to independently develop the technology. In May 2014, the U.S. government indicted a number of Chinese military officers, alleging in part that to pursue business opportunities in China, Westinghouse Electric partnered with a Chinese state-owned nuclear power company (SOE-1). The Chinese partner "stole from Westinghouse's computers, among other things, proprietary and confidential technical and design specifications for pipes, pipe supports, and pipe routing within the nuclear power plants that Westinghouse was contracted to build, as well as internal Westinghouse communications concerning the company's strategy for doing business."

Protecting an organization's intellectual property from compromise in part requires a robust and comprehensive approach to personnel security.

Assessing Risk

At a minimum, the contracting organization should require its vendors to provide an equivalent, or greater, level of control than is maintained by the contracting organization in the absence of the vendor. This applies to the entire information lifecycle for the information being shared. Conducting risk assessments of vendor engagements, consistent with the organization's practice, should be performed as part of the contracting process, and the vendor's controls should be monitored during the period of performance.

The personnel assurance expectations should be identified as early as possible in the contracting process. This would typically occur as the statement of work or tender is being prepared, so vendor offerings can be evaluated within the context of the security expectations. From the standpoint of the vendor, knowing the expectations allows them to more accurately assess the cost of providing the services to the contracting organization.

There is a broad range of controls that may be appropriate for contractors or vendors. These include nondisclosure agreements, background investigations, training requirements, site escorts, badging, physical and logical access controls, monitoring of information systems use, and dozens of others. It is essential that the controls provide a defense in depth against information disclosure.

Background investigations leading to security clearances are not sufficient to prevent loss. Many of the significant information security breaches that have occurred in recent years were caused by cleared individuals. In the U.S. National Security Agency, contractor misbehavior by Edward Snowden, Hal Martin, Reality Winner, Nghia Hoang Pho, and others has inappropriately managed volumes of sensitive information. All of these individuals had security clearances and used their access to disclose sensitive information.

One of the challenges in placing specific expectations on vendors is the additional overhead in meeting the customer's requirements. It may well mean increasing the costs of using the vendor. Further, more onerous requirements may discourage competent firms from offering their services simply because of the burdens of compliance. This is particularly true if the method of control is specified, rather than identifying the effect of the control. Finding the right balance between the cost of the control and the level of risk must be determined for each unique circumstance.

Compliance Framework Requirements

Many of the risk management and compliance frameworks require organizations to address controls over third-party personnel. In the United States, NIST Special Publication 800-171, "Protecting Controlled Unclassified Information in Nonfederal Systems and Organizations," identifies personnel security controls that vendors must address when managing certain types of sensitive information under federal contracts. Third-party compliance with the Health Insurance Portability and Privacy Act also places expectations on contracting organizations to ensure that their partners use appropriate assurance practices with their personnel.

The ISO 27001 framework and, specifically, ISO 27005, "Information Security Risk Management," also addresses security risk management activities in outsourcing. Similarly, the Control Objectives for Information and Related Technologies (COBIT) framework identifies third-party management activities in the process area DS2, "Manage Third-party Services."

Privacy in the Workplace

The rapid pace of technological change has challenged our traditional notions of privacy. The widespread use of electronic technologies allows an unprecedented level of monitoring of the activities of employees through email, GPS, cell phones, video, and other means. While the general idea of privacy has been discussed previously, the application of the concept to the workplace presents unique challenges.

Reasonable Expectation of Privacy

The idea that some level of privacy exists in the workplace is based on the concept of the reasonable expectation of privacy. In deciding whether an employee has an expectation of privacy in the workplace, courts have to determine whether the employee had a reasonable expectation of privacy considering the operational realities of the workplace.

Employers have several legitimate reasons for wanting to control and monitor workplace communications. These include maintaining a professional work environment, meeting specific compliance expectations, enhancing employee productivity, and limiting the dissemination of trade secrets or other proprietary and confidential information to people who are entitled to the information.

Privacy expectations are higher if the employee has a dedicated space, such as a private office with a door and locked filing cabinets. On the other hand, privacy expectations are lessened in common areas, such as break rooms and open cubicles. Courts in the United States have also found that the privacy expectations for public employers and private employers are different, with private employers having greater latitude in monitoring employee conduct.

In Canada, courts have recognized that, in certain circumstances, employees do have an expectation of privacy when using the employer's computer systems. In the European Union, the High Court has found that while employers may monitor employee activities, they must ensure that safeguards are in place to ensure that the privacy rights of the employees are not violated.

Protection extends to the information that is in the care of the employer. In India, Section 43A of the Information Technology Act, 2000, requires that employers adopt reasonable security practices to protect sensitive personal data of employees that is in their possession. This includes information found in medical records or financial records. If an employee suffers a loss because of a lack of reasonable security practices, the employee is entitled to compensation.

Best Practice

In general, employers should notify employees that they are subject to monitoring, the types of monitoring employed, and the consequences for inappropriate use of the systems. Clear policies on workplace use should be included in awareness training, and users should formally recognize that they are subject to those expectations. Finally, consistent application of those policies should provide some assurance against selective enforcement.

UNDERSTAND AND APPLY RISK MANAGEMENT CONCEPTS

Information security activities are conducted within the context of risk. A common understanding of risk management principles, concepts, and approaches is essential when structuring an information security program.

Risk

The International Standards Organization Guide 73:2009, "Risk management – Vocabulary," was developed to standardize the language, terms, and high-level concepts related to risk management. *Risk*, in the context of the ISO standards, "is the effect of uncertainty on objectives." While the ISO definition is sufficiently broad to accept both negative and positive effects of uncertainty, other frameworks define the term differently.

Federal Information Processing Standard 200 defines *risk* as follows: "The level of impact on organizational operations (including mission, functions, image, or reputation), organizational assets, or individuals resulting from the operation of an information system given the potential impact of a threat and the likelihood of that threat occurring." While the FIPS addresses risk within the context of information systems in the U.S. federal government, this definition is widely used and applicable to other organizations as well.

For the security professional, such ambiguities in language can be frustrating, particularly when relating an organization's work practice to the CISSP CBK. The (ISC)[2] definition of *risk* is as follows: "The possibility of damage or harm and the likelihood that damage or harm will be realized."

Risk Management Frameworks

A number of frameworks have been developed to identify and evaluate risk. These frameworks have evolved to address the unique needs of different industries and processes. Individually, these frameworks address assessment, control, monitoring, and audit of information systems in different ways, but all strive to provide internal controls to bring risk to an acceptable level. While there are several internationally accepted risk frameworks, a number of industry-specific frameworks have also been developed to meet specific needs.

Regardless of the framework, to effectively address risk in an organization, standard processes to evaluate the risks of operation of information systems must take into account the changing threat environment, the potential and actual vulnerabilities of systems, the likelihood that the risk will occur, and the consequence to the organization, should that risk become manifest.

From a governance perspective, the selection of a framework should create a controls environment that is as follows:

- **Consistent:** A governance program must be consistent in how information security and privacy are approached and applied.

- **Measurable:** The governance program must provide a way to determine progress and set goals. Most control frameworks contain an assessment standard or procedure to determine compliance and, in some cases, risk as well.

- **Standardized:** As with measurable, a controls framework should rely on standardization so results from one organization or part of an organization can be compared in a meaningful way to results from another organization.

- **Comprehensive:** The selected framework should cover the minimum legal and regulatory requirements of an organization and be extensible to accommodate additional organization-specific requirements.

- **Modular:** A modular framework is more likely to withstand the changes of an organization, as only the controls or requirements needing modification are reviewed and updated.

There are dozens of different risk management frameworks. While many of the frameworks address specific industry or organizational requirements, the information security professional should be aware of the broad characteristics of the more common frameworks.

Comprehensive Frameworks

Many frameworks have been developed to address risk in different contexts. Many of these are general in nature, while others are limited to a single industry or business practice. Organizations use comprehensive frameworks to take advantage of the consistency and breadth offered by the framework. This simplifies a wide range of challenges, including a consistent evaluation of performance, the conduct of audits for compliance, and the standardization of training the workforce in the activities and processes of a particular methodology.

International Standards Organization

The International Standards Organization (ISO) has developed the ISO 31000 series of standards to identify principles for general risk management and to provide a set of guidelines for implementation. Developed using the consistent language contained in ISO/IEC Guide 73:2009, the ISO 31000:2018 is intended to be applicable to any organization, regardless of the governance structure or industry. The standard encourages the integration of risk management activities across organizational lines and levels to provide the organization with a consistent approach to management of operational and strategic risks.

The original ISO 31000 standard extends the work of Standards Australia in developing the risk management processes by addressing the design, implementation, and maintenance of risk, while leveraging a continuous process improvement model (see Figure 1.4). The standard was not intended to replace other industry-specific standards, but rather to harmonize practices between standards.

FIGURE 1.4 **ISO 31000**

ISO 31000:2018 is based on a set of eight principles that drive the development of a risk framework. That framework, in turn, structures the processes for implementing risk management. Continual process improvement is an essential component of the ISO 31000 process. The ISO 31000 principles characterize an effective risk management framework that creates and protects organizational value through structured processes.

- **Proportionate:** The framework should be customized and proportionate to the organization and the level of risk.
- **Aligned:** The appropriate and timely involvement of stakeholders is necessary.
- **Comprehensive:** A structured and comprehensive approach is required.
- **Embedded:** Risk management is an integral part of all organizational activities.
- **Dynamic:** Risk management anticipates, detects, acknowledges, and responds to changes.
- **Best available information:** Risk management explicitly considers any limitations of available information.

- **Inclusive:** Human and cultural factors influence all aspects of risk management.
- **Continual improvement:** Risk management is continually improved through learning and experience.

To assist organizations in implementing the ISO 31000 standard, ISO 31004, "Risk Management-Guidance for the Implementation of ISO 31000," was published to provide a structured approach to transition their existing risk management practices to be consistent with ISO 31000, consistent with the individual characteristics and demands of the implementing organization.

While the 31000 series addresses general risk, information security practices are addressed in the ISO 27000 series. The use of the ISO/IEC Guide 73 allows for a common language, but ISO/IEC 27005:2011, "Information technology – Security techniques – Information security risk management," gives detail and structure to the information security risks by defining the context for information security risk decision-making. This context includes definition of the organization's risk tolerance, compliance expectations, and the preferred approaches for assessment and treatment of risk.

ISO 27005 does not directly provide a risk assessment process. Rather, it provides inputs to, and gets outputs from, the risk assessment practice used by the organization. In this framework, the assessment process may be performed in a quantitative or qualitative manner but must be done consistently so that prioritization can be performed. ISO 27005 further emphasizes the need for communication with stakeholders and for processes that continuously monitor for changes in the risk environment.

The ISO standards have seen broad adoption, in part because of the broad international process in the development of the standards. Further, the standards themselves, while constantly under review, connect to other standards managed within the ISO. This enables organizations to adopt those standards that are appropriate for their businesses and provides a more holistic view of organizations' compliance activities.

U.S. National Institute of Standards

Through a hierarchy of publications, the National Institute of Standards and Technology (NIST) provides direction to U.S. government agencies in implementing information security practices. In the current incarnation, the Risk Management Framework (RMF) provides a structured analytical process to identify, control, evaluate, and improve the organization's information security controls. Documented in NIST Special Publication 800-37, "Guide for Applying the Risk Management Framework to Federal Information Systems," it prescribes a six-step process through which the federal government manages the risks of operating information systems.

The Federal Information Processing Standards (FIPS) are mandated for all federal computer systems, with the exception of certain national security systems that are governed by a different set of standards. Authorized under a series of related laws, the FIPS addresses a range of interoperability and security practices for which there are no acceptable industry standards or solutions.

Two standards are critical to the Risk Management Framework. FIPS 199, "Standards for Security Categorization of Federal Information and Information Systems," requires agencies to categorize all of their information systems based on the potential impact to the agency of the loss of confidentiality, integrity, or availability. Implied in this process is that the agencies must have a comprehensive inventory of systems to apply the categorization standard.

Once security categorization has been performed, a baseline set of controls must be selected in accordance with FIPS 200, "Minimum Security Requirements for Federal Information and Information Systems." Using a "high watermark" approach, the security controls are selected, consistent with the categorization of impact developed under FIPS 199. FIPS 200 identifies 17 security-related areas of control, but the details of which specific control is to be applied are found in NIST Special Publication 800-53, "Recommended Security Controls for Federal Information Systems."

Once the system has been categorized and baseline controls are selected, the controls must be implemented and monitored to ensure that they "are implemented correctly, operating as intended, and producing the desired outcome with respect to meeting the security requirements for the system." This will produce a set of documents certifying the technical application of the controls.

The organizational leadership then makes a formal decision whether to authorize the use of the system. This decision is based on the ability of the controls to operate the system within the organization's risk tolerance. Finally, the organization will monitor the effectiveness of the controls over time against the security environment to ensure that the continued operation of the system takes place within the organization's risk tolerance.

While focused on the computing activities of the U.S. government, the NIST standards and guidelines have had a pervasive effect on the security community because of their broad scope, their availability in the public domain, and the inclusion of industry, academic, and other standards organizations in the development of the standards. Further, the NIST standards often set the expectations for security practice that are placed on regulated industries. This is most clearly shown in the Health Information Privacy and Portability legislation, where healthcare organizations must demonstrate that their controls align with the NIST security practice.

Committee of Sponsoring Organizations

The Committee of Sponsoring Organizations (COSO) of the Treadway Commission provides a comprehensive, organizational-level view of risk management. Its framework, "Enterprise Risk Management—Integrating with Strategy and Performance," recognizes that the pursuit of any organizational objectives incurs some level of risk, and good governance must accompany risk decisions.

Based on five components, the framework captures the responsibilities of governance to provide risk oversight and set an appropriate tone for ethical, responsible conduct.

The complementary "Internal Control—Integrated Framework" extends the COSO practice to the organization's internal control environment. The three objectives (operations, reporting, and compliance) are evaluated against five components: control environment, risk assessment, control activities, information and communication, and monitoring activities. The objectives and the components are further evaluated within the context of the organizational structure. Ultimately, the system of internal control requires that each of these components be present and operating together to bring the risk of operations to an acceptable level.

In short, the framework provides a high-level set of tools to establish consistency in process in the identification and management of risks to acceptable levels.

The COSO organization originally came about to address weaknesses in the financial reporting environment that allowed fraud and other criminal activities to occur without detection, exposing financial organizations to considerable risk. While the framework evolved out of the need for better internal control in the financial services industry, the framework is now broadly applied to corporations operating in a wide variety of industries. As a result, it is not designed to address industry-specific issues. Further, the breadth of the framework requires management at all levels to apply considerable judgment in its implementation.

IT Infrastructure Library

The IT Infrastructure Library (ITIL) was developed over the course of 30 years to address the service delivery challenges with information technology. Emphasizing continuous process improvement, ITIL provides a service management framework, of which risk management is an integrated element.

The ITIL framework is organized into five volumes that define 26 processes.

- Volume 1 – Service Strategy seeks to understand organizational objectives and customer needs.

- Volume 2 – Service Design turns the service strategy into a plan for delivering the business objectives.

- Volume 3 – Service Transition develops and improves capabilities for introducing new services into supported environments.

- Volume 4 – Service Operation includes processes that manage services in supported environments.

- Volume 5 – Continual Service Improvement achieves incremental and large-scale improvements to services.

The ITIL Framework has been substantially incorporated into other standards, notably ISO 20000, "Information technology – Service management," and has strongly influenced the development of ISACA's COBIT framework and others.

ITIL does not directly address risk management as a separate process. However, the emphasis on continuous improvement, leveraging metrics to identify out-of-specification activities and processes to address information security management systems, availability, incident, and event management clearly incorporate the concepts of an enterprise risk management process. Indeed, if the goal of risk management is to reduce uncertainty, the ITIL framework emphasizes the importance of predictability in the processes.

COBIT and RiskIT

In the late 1990s the audit community in the United States and Canada recognized that there was a significant gap between information technology governance and the larger organizational management structures. Consequently, information technology activities were often misaligned with corporate goals, and risks were not comprehensively addressed by the control structure's risk or consistently reflected in financial reporting. To address this gap, ISACA developed a framework through which the information technology activities of an organization could be assessed.

The COBIT framework differentiates processes into either Governance of Enterprise IT (five processes) or Management of Enterprise IT (32 processes). Each process has a set of objectives, inputs, key activities, and outputs, and measures to evaluate performance against the objectives. As the framework is closely aligned with other management frameworks and tools (ISO20000, ISO27001, ITIL, Prince 2, SOX, TOGAF), it has gained wide acceptance as an encompassing framework for managing the delivery of information technology.

Based on the ISACA COBIT IT governance framework, the RiskIT framework provides a structure for the identification, evaluation, and monitoring of information technology risk. This simplifies the integration of IT risk into the larger organization enterprise risk management (ERM) activities.

Unlike the more generic risk management frameworks of COSO and ISO 31000 and the industry-specific risk structures of PCI-DSS or HITRUST, RiskIT fills the middle ground of generic IT risk. The framework consists of three domains—risk governance, risk evaluation, and risk response—each of which has three processes. The framework then details the key activities within each process and identifies organizational responsibilities, information flows between processes, and process performance management activities. Additional detail on how to implement the framework and link it to other organizational management practices is contained in the RiskIT Practitioner Guide.

Industry-Specific Risk Frameworks

Many industries have unique compliance expectations. This may be the result of requirements to meet the security expectations from multiple different regulatory entities or because of unique business processes. Some of these industry-specific frameworks are described next.

Health Information Trust Alliance Common Security Framework

The Health Information Trust Alliance Common Security Framework (HITRUST CSF) was developed to address the overlapping regulatory environment in which many healthcare providers operate. Taking into account both risk-based and compliance-based considerations, the HITRUST CSF normalizes the many requirements while providing an auditable framework for the evaluation of the security environment. In many ways, the HITRUST CSF is a "framework of frameworks."

North American Electric Reliability Corporation Critical Infrastructure Protection

The responsibility for protecting the electrical power grid in North America falls on the individual bulk electrical system (BES) operators. However, as the systems are interconnected, a failure of one operator to secure their environment may leave weaknesses that could affect the delivery of power throughout the continent. Over the past two decades, the North American Electric Reliability Corporation Critical Infrastructure Protection (NERC CIP) published a set of standards designed to enforce good cybersecurity practice and provide an auditable framework for compliance. This framework has been influenced by the NIST standard but is a standalone framework specific to the power industry.

✔ CIP Version 5 Standards

CIP 5 standards exist that cover a range of areas:

- **CIP-002:** Identifies and categorizes BES Cyber Assets and their BES Cyber Systems. This is where an impact rating is specified.

- **CIP-003:** Specifies consistent and sustainable security management controls that establish responsibility and accountability.

- **CIP-004:** Requires an appropriate level of personnel risk assessment, training, and security awareness.

- **CIP-005:** Specifies a controlled Electronic Security Perimeter with border protections.

- **CIP-006:** Specifies a physical security plan with a defined Physical Security Perimeter.

- **CIP-007:** Specifies select technical, operational, and procedural requirements for the BES Cyber Assets and BES Cyber Systems.

- **CIP-008:** Specifies incident response requirements.

- **CIP-009:** Specifies recovery plan requirements.

- **CIP-010:** Specifies configuration change management and vulnerability assessment requirements.

- **CIP-011:** Specifies information protection requirements.

ISA-99 and ISA/IEC 62443

The International Society of Automation has developed a series of standards to address the unique needs of the industrial controls environment. Organized into four groups, 13 different standards provide a policy, operational, and technical framework to increase the resilience of the industrial controls environment. See Figure 1.5.

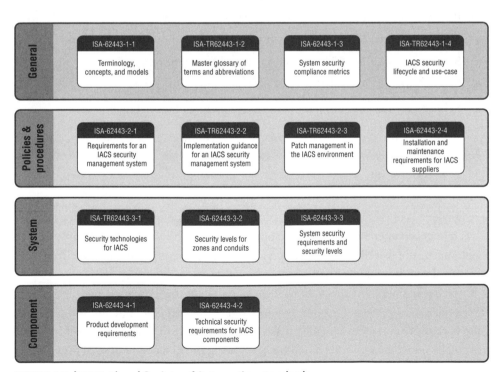

FIGURE 1.5 International Society of Automation standards

Industrial controls provide a clear example of the competing interests at work in the application of the CIA Triad to a technical environment. The failure of an industrial control might endanger thousands of lives and destroy assets worth millions of dollars. Consequently, the CIA focus of industrial control has always been on availability—creating resilience to ensure the control was always present. Adding functionality (with the attendant cost and complexity) to provide support for confidentiality controls had, in many implementations, not been a priority. One of the major motivations in the development of the ISA/IEC 62443 body of standards was to provide an appropriate emphasis on all aspects of the security challenge.

Payment Card Industry Data Security Standard

The PCI Security Standards Council (PCI SSC) developed the PCI-DSS standard to define a set of minimum controls to protect payment card transactions. Developed in response to increasing levels of credit card fraud, the PCI-DSS standard has undergone several modifications to increase the level of protection offered to customers. The current version of the standard, 3.2, identifies six goals with 12 high-level requirements that merchants are contractually obligated to meet. (See Figure 1.6.) The level of compliance is dependent on the volume of transactions processed by the merchant. Failing to meet the requirements can result in fines levied by the credit card processor. The number of annual transactions for each service provider level is as follows:

- **Service provider level 1:** More than 6 million annual transactions
- **Service provider level 2:** 1–6 million annual transactions
- **Service provider level 3:** 20,000–1 million annual transactions
- **Service provider level 4:** Fewer than 20,000 annual transactions

The PCI SSC also has published standards for PIN entry devices, point-to-point encryption (P2PE), token service providers, and software applications (PA-DSS).

Risk Assessment Methodologies

There are dozens of risk assessment methodologies. Many are specific to industry sectors, such as government or software development. Still others differentiate themselves through their emphasis on either a quantitative or qualitative method. For the CISSP, a foundational understanding of risk assessment methods is necessary.

At its core, risk assessment is a formal determination of the likelihood and impact of an event relative to an asset. Typically conducted as a method of identifying and prioritizing the controls necessary to bring the risk to an acceptable level, the assessment process varies greatly depending on the framework, asset being protected, and desired outputs of the risk assessment process.

PCI-DSS Goals and Requirements	
Goals	PCI DSS Requirements
Goal 1: Build and Maintain a Secure Network	1. Install and maintain a firewall configuration to protect cardholder data
	2. Do not use vendor-supplied defaults for system passwords and other security parameters
Goal 2: Protect Cardholder Data	3. Protect stored cardholder data
	4. Encrypt transmission of cardholder data across open, public networks
Goal 3: Maintain a Vulnerability Management Program	5. Use and regularly update anti-virus software or programs
	6. Develop and maintain secure systems and applications
Goal 4: Implement Strong Access Control Measures	7. Restrict access to cardholder data by business need-to-know
	8. Assign a unique ID to each person with computer access
	9. Restrict physical access to cardholder data
Goal 5: Regularly Monitor and Test Networks	10. Track and monitor all access to network resources and cardholder data
	11. Regularly test security systems and processes
Goal 6: Maintain an Information Security Policy	12. Maintain a policy that addresses information security for employees and contractors

FIGURE 1.6 **PCI-DSS**

One of the most widely used risk assessment methodologies is the process characterized in NIST 800-30, "Guide for Conducting Risk Assessments." (See Figure 1.7.)

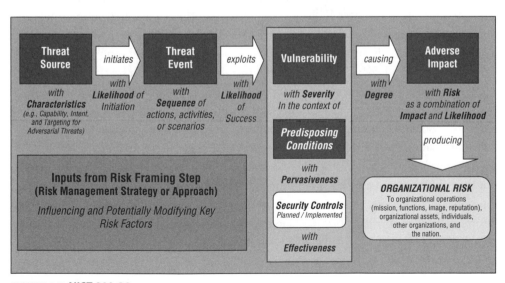

FIGURE 1.7 **NIST 800-30**

The first step in the four-step process is to properly frame the risk. To initiate the process, a number of inputs from the risk management strategy are necessary. This includes an understanding of the organization's risk tolerance, the scope of the assessment, any assumptions or constraints that would affect the assessment, the organization's preferred methods of risk response, the processes for managing communications with stakeholders, and other information to conduct the risk assessment process in the context of the organization's practices.

The second step in the process is to conduct the assessment. Four major activities will be performed to fully evaluate risk. Enumeration of the threats to the system must be undertaken, taking into account the threat's means and motivations. The threats could be actors or events, but their relevance to the system and the organization is an essential input to the subsequent prioritization of control activities.

Identification of vulnerabilities is also performed. Vulnerabilities are weaknesses that a threat could potentially exploit. Identification and enumeration of potential vulnerabilities allows the organization to assess their severity. This leads to the identification of necessary predisposing conditions, which may affect the actual presentation of the vulnerability to the threat actor.

The NIST process explicitly recognizes the relationship between the threats and the vulnerabilities. A single threat event might exploit multiple vulnerabilities. A single vulnerability might be exploited by multiple threats. Regardless, the size and complexity of the environment require that the risk assessment processes be conducted across multiple levels—tiers—to address uncertainty at the organizational, mission/business process, and information systems levels.

Once the threats and weaknesses are known, the likelihood and impact of the threat actually exploiting the vulnerability are evaluated. Existing and planned countermeasures may affect the likelihood or impact and thus affect the eventual determination of the level of risk. Ultimately, in this step, the level of risk is determined through the evaluation of the likelihood and consequence of a particular threat exploiting a specific vulnerability.

These activities, while they are often presented in a linear fashion to simplify explanation of the concepts, are often iterative and recursive. An identified vulnerability may reveal new potential threats. Part of the challenge in conducting assessments is placing constraints around the planning process to minimize "paralysis by analysis."

The third step in the process is to effectively communicate to stakeholders throughout the risk assessment process. Communication between organizational stakeholders must take into account the organization's communication and reporting requirements to ensure that decision-makers have sufficient information on which to act. Further communication to a variety of other stakeholders inside and outside the organization should also occur, consistent with organizational policies and guidance.

The fourth step in the process is to maintain the assessment. This includes monitoring the level of risk based on changes to the risk factors (threat sources and events, vulnerabilities and predisposing conditions, capabilities and intent of adversaries targeting the organizational operations, assets, or individuals) and communicating the changes in the risk appropriately in the organization. The activities in this step overlap processes identified in other parts of the NIST Risk Management Framework. This overlap is intended to explicitly recognize the integrated and holistic nature of the NIST 800 series processes.

Although there are many excellent risk management and risk assessment processes to choose from, it is more important to consistently apply risk practices across the organization. Consistent application and execution ensures that everyone knows what their role is relative to the risk activities and supports the evaluation and prioritization of risk. The security professional should be exposed to multiple methodologies to shape the risk management processes of their organization to meet the unique requirements of their business.

UNDERSTAND AND APPLY THREAT MODELING CONCEPTS AND METHODOLOGIES

Some of the key tasks that the CISSP must perform are to identify, categorize, and prioritize the threats faced by the organization. This skill must scale from a single application through enterprise-level attacks. The results of threat modeling will drive a wide range of security practices, including software development, communications, network design, monitoring, and incident response.

At a personal level, we do threat modeling every day, often unconsciously, as a way to prioritize and control risk. Even a simple decision such as crossing the street involves a threat model: I could get hit by a fire truck, bus, or bicycle, so I need to decide what level of control is appropriate given the risk to my health. (This is why systems like painted crosswalks and crossing signs are helpful!) Threat modeling applies consistency to uncovering the multiple threats that can affect the security of a system.

Threat Modeling Concepts

A *threat* is an actor who potentially can compromise the operation of a system. That actor might be a human actor, or it might be an event or circumstance. Similarly, the system in question may be a computer system, a physical environment, or a business process. *Threat modeling*, applied broadly to systems, takes into account a wide range of potential actors so that an appropriate response strategy can be developed.

The *attack surface* is the total range of potential areas where an attacker can potentially execute a compromise. With an information system, this might include the methods of communication, the access controls, or weaknesses in the underlying architectures. With a physical environment, the attack surface might include the construction techniques, the location, or the means of entrance and egress. Limiting the attack surface to the minimum number of areas of exposure reduces the opportunities for a threat to become an attack.

Related to the concept of attack surface, trust boundaries are created where a different type or level of threat exists between interacting parts of the system. As a result, the controls on one side of the boundary must be adjusted to ensure that the confidentiality, integrity, and availability aspects of the system are maintained.

The threat is going to act against a vulnerability, or weakness, in the system. Often, the vulnerability may only be exploitable in the event of certain precursing conditions. The combination of the attacker and the vulnerability can then be evaluated through the risk assessment process to prioritize response and apply control where appropriate.

One of the most important tools in threat modeling is the use of various diagramming techniques to identify where data is stored and manipulated, the relationship between processes, the location of security boundaries, and the movement of information. Data flow diagrams (DFDs) are often used for this purpose. In addition to their use as a threat modeling tool, DFDs are useful for other purposes, including the development of monitoring strategies, certifying systems, and as audit artifacts. Other diagramming techniques include swim lane diagrams, attack trees, state diagrams, or Unified Markup Language (UML) diagrams. Regardless of the tool that creates the DFD, diagramming is useful in virtually any form of threat modeling process by enforcing consistency of documentation and creating a common way of communicating threat modeling information across teams.

Threat Modeling Methodologies

There are three general approaches to threat modeling. Different risk methodologies, compliance frameworks, or systems prefer one or another, but the security professional should be able to apply all three approaches to a particular environment.

- **Attacker-centric:** This threat modeling approach starts by identifying the various actors who could potentially cause harm to a system. This approach can be helpful when narrowly approaching a problem by limiting the number of scenarios under analysis. Tactical military intelligence is typically driven by an attacker-centric threat model, as are many business continuity/disaster recovery planning processes. As a result, many people have had experience with this form of threat modeling elsewhere in their professional lives. This approach is often helpful when the analysis is being conducted by nontechnical professionals, as capturing the means, methods, and motivations of the attackers to build a profile (or persona) of an attacker encourages active engagement.

- **Asset-centric:** As opposed to an attacker-centric approach, an asset-centric threat model identifies the assets of value first. The value of the asset should be characterized by the value of the asset to the organization and the value of the asset to the attacker. The means by which the asset is managed, manipulated, used, and stored are then evaluated to identify how an attacker might compromise the asset. Many compliance regimes focus on protection of an asset (e.g., protected health information under HIPAA, personally identifiable information under the GDPR, or the Primary Account Number under PCI-DSS), so this approach is helpful when establishing or verifying compliance. Tools that supports asset-centric analysis include classification and categorization of information, identifying information that is sensitive to disclosure, and the importance of the information to the organization's business processes. As is done with the attacker-centric model, organizations typically maintain an inventory or library process to identify those assets of value.

- **System (Software)-centric:** For many information systems environments, the system- or software-centric model is most useful. In this approach, the system is represented as a set of interconnected processes, often using DFDs as mentioned. These diagrams are then evaluated by the analysts to determine whether control is necessary, exists, and achieves the control effect. Clarifying trust boundaries is essential to define, as the level and type of control changes as information transits the boundary.

There are many different threat modeling methodologies. Some of the most widely used are STRIDE, NIST 800-154, PASTA, and OCTAVE, each of which are explored next.

STRIDE

Microsoft developed the STRIDE methodology in the late 1990s as a way to standardize the identification of threats across their product line. Given the popularity of the Microsoft tools, the approach found wide acceptance within the development community. STRIDE is a classic software-centric threat model.

The acronym STRIDE is a mnemonic for spoofing, tampering, repudiation, information disclosure, denial of service, and elevation of privilege. When evaluating an interaction between processes, these six threats to a system's CIA state are reviewed. Finally, this model has been influential in the development of other models, notably the OWASP threat modeling process. This model is more fully discussed in Chapter 8.

NIST 800-154 Data-Centric Threat Modeling

In 2016, NIST placed for public comment a threat modeling approach centered on protecting high-value data. This approach is known as NIST 800-154, "Data-Centric Threat

Modeling." It explicitly rejects that best-practice approaches are sufficient to protect sensitive information, as best practice is too general and would overlook controls specifically tailored to meet the protection of the sensitive asset. In this model, the analysis of the risk proceeds through four major steps.

1. Identify and characterize the system and data of interest. The data and information should be defined narrowly to a particular logical set of data on a single host or small group of hosts. Then the information is characterized, taking into account the authorized locations for the data within the system, how the information moves within the system between authorized locations, the security objectives for the data using the CIA construct, recognizing that not all of the objectives are of equal importance for a particular data set, and then defining the people and processes that are authorized to access the data within the context of the security objectives.

2. Identify and select the attack vectors to be included in the model. Identify potential attack vectors and then prioritize those that meet the likelihood and consequence criteria established for the data or system.

3. Characterize the security controls for mitigating the attack vectors. Identify the security control alterations that would address the risk and are reasonably feasible to accomplish. Next, for each selected control alteration, estimate the effectiveness of the control on the attack vector. Finally, estimate the negative consequences of the control, taking into account issues such as cost, functionality, usability, and performance.

4. Analyze the threat model. Taking into account the characteristics documented in the previous steps, evaluate the controls to identify which controls give an acceptable level of risk reduction while minimizing the negative impacts of the control.

Most data-centric models emphasize one of the aspects of the CIA Triad over the others. In the case of national security information, confidentiality would receive more weight. In the case of information regarding hurricane forecasting, confidentiality might be low on the list of interests, but integrity and availability of the information might be of greater importance.

The Process for Attack Simulation and Threat Analysis

The Process for Attack Simulation and Threat Analysis (PASTA), as the full name implies, is an attacker-centric modeling approach, but the outputs of the model are focused on protecting the organization's assets. Its seven-step process aligns business objectives, technical requirements, and compliance expectations to identify threats and attack patterns. These are then prioritized through a scoring system. The results can then be analyzed to determine which security controls can be applied to reduce the risk to an acceptable level. Advocates for this approach argue that the integration of business concerns in the process takes the threat modeling activity from a technical exercise to a process more suited to assessing business risk.

Operationally Critical Threat, Asset, and Vulnerability Evaluation

Operationally Critical Threat, Asset, and Vulnerability Evaluation (OCTAVE) is an approach for managing information security risks developed at the Software Engineering Institute (SEI). While the overall OCTAVE approach encompasses more than threat modeling, asset-based threat modeling is at the core of the process. In its current form, OCTAVE Allegro breaks down into a set of four phases with eight steps. (See Figure 1.8.)

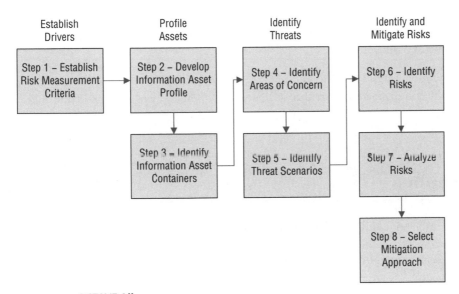

FIGURE 1.8 OCTAVE Allegro

These are the four phases of OCTAVE Allegro:

1. Establish drivers, where the organization develops risk measurement criteria that are consistent with organizational drivers.

2. Profile assets, where the assets that are the focus of the risk assessment are identified and profiled and the assets' containers are identified.

3. Identify threats, where threats to the assets—in the context of their containers—are identified and documented through a structured process.

4. Identify and mitigate risks, where risks are identified and analyzed based on threat information and mitigation strategies are developed to address those risks.

As compared with previous versions of OCTAVE, Allegro simplifies the collection of data, improves focus on risk mitigation strategies, and provides a simple quantitative model (as opposed to the qualitative approaches previously emphasized). Proponents argue that this makes the model easier to understand and use, simplifying training and increasing the likelihood that the approach will be consistently adopted as a risk method inside organizations.

Other Models

Other threat modeling methodologies include the following:

- TRIKE is an open source threat modeling approach and tool.
- Construct a platform for Risk Analysis of Security Critical Systems (CORAS), also open source, relies heavily on UML as the front end for visualizing the threats.
- Visual, Agile, and Simple Threat Modeling (VAST) is a proprietary approach that leverages Agile concepts.

Implementing a structured threat modeling program allows an organization to consistently identify and characterize the threats it faces and then apply appropriate control to the risks.

APPLY RISK-BASED MANAGEMENT CONCEPTS TO THE SUPPLY CHAIN

The interconnected nature of today's information systems places a high degree of reliance on the confidentiality, integrity, and availability of systems from multiple vendors spread across the globe. This ecosystem has been shown to be vulnerable to disruption from both accidental and intentional events. Securing the supply chain requires organizations to evaluate the risk of supply chain disruption to ensure the application and operation of appropriate controls.

Evaluating the supply chain for compromise integrates many of the information security disciplines and organizational practices. Integrating the organization's information security activities is a due diligence responsibility of the organization's management. In many cases, the adoption of a supply chain management framework provides an efficient mechanism to effect the integration activities.

Supply Chain Risks

Compromising an organization's supply chain has proven effective at disrupting the delivery of value to customers. To minimize supply chain risk, appropriate controls must be applied to verify the security practices of the involved parties. In most cases, controls have been identified that would address the risk; the security challenge is to ensure that the third parties actually do what they should to protect an organization's information.

Intellectual Property

Protecting an organization's intellectual property from loss or compromise when third parties have access to the information is a tremendous challenge. Best practice is to ensure that the control follows the intellectual property, regardless of its location. However, this is not easily accomplished.

Consider the following examples:

- In December 2016, an audio post-production company working for several major studios, including ABC, Fox, and Netflix, was compromised through an unpatched computer. The post-production company paid a bitcoin ransom, hoping to protect their clients' intellectual property. The attackers ultimately decided to approach Netflix directly for additional payments, where the additional extortion demand was refused. The attackers then released the stolen content.

- In December 2017, a subcontractor for the real estate data aggregator CoStar admitted in federal court that they had been stealing data on behalf of Xceligent, one of the data aggregator's competitors. In the filing, the subcontractor stated, "At Xceligent's direction, the REBO/MaxVal operations team used measures to circumvent CoStar's security measures and thereby hack into CoStar sites in order to populate the Xceligent databases with content copied from CoStar." This event took place as competing lawsuits between CoStar and Xceligent were being litigated between the two companies.

- In 2017, the Australian Cybersecurity Centre reported that a subcontractor working on a number of weapons systems projects, including the F-35 Joint Strike Fighter, antisubmarine aircraft, and precision munitions, was compromised by a nation-state actor. The ensuing investigation determined that while the 30 gigabytes of information was not classified, it was protected from disclosure under ITAR. In accomplishing the compromise, the attacker leveraged vulnerabilities for which patches had been available for more than a year.

Counterfeits

Losing intellectual property to a less scrupulous competitor creates an opportunity to create counterfeits of the original product, often with lower quality or imperfections. Marketing these duplicates as the genuine article, not only do the counterfeiters steal market share and revenue from the creator, the duplicates may fail prematurely or inject flaws into a process where the original article would not. Globally, losses due to counterfeiting are estimated at more than 1.8 trillion dollars annually.

Counterfeit technology has been detected in industries as diverse as weapons systems, medical devices, and auto parts.

To address this, a number of schemes have been proposed to identify and guarantee the provenance of a system from the point of origin to the point of use. Starting in May 2017, medical device manufacturers in the European Union will be required to apply a unique device identifier for each medical device. Similar regulatory requirements exist in the United States. Other technologies being developed include the use of blockchain to track systems from production through use, and DARPA has been developing chip-level microtag technology that will allow manufacturers to guarantee provenance.

Malicious Code

The widespread use of proprietary commercial off-the-shelf (COTS) software requires customers to trust the security practices of the vendors. However, many instances have been documented where that trust has been abused, and the COTS vendors become a vehicle to introduce vulnerabilities or compromise the CIA aspects of the customers' data.

This method has become increasingly popular for malware authors precisely because the updates are from a trusted source. In 2017, the developer of the antivirus product CCleaner distributed a routine update to its users that contained a remote access Trojan. As the malicious software had been inserted into the code before it was signed, the entire update package was seen by most users as a legitimate update. More than 2 billion downloads of the compromised software were reported.

Software of Unknown Pedigree

The use of standard code libraries, the proliferation of open source projects, and object-oriented programming have simplified the development process for many new systems. However, the quality of code written by third parties may vary widely. In life safety or medical systems, the use of Software of Unknown Pedigree (SOUP) is often explicitly regulated.

SOUP is not, necessarily, COTS or open source. SOUP typically has no vendor support, no record of development, and no formal testing or validation processes, where many of the COTS and open source projects provide higher levels of transparency and documentation. Regardless, development that incorporates SOUP may create risk for the organization.

In 2013, Toyota settled a lawsuit contending that the firmware in the Engine Control Module (ECM) contributed to a woman's death following the unintended acceleration of the car in which she was a passenger. Expert testimony presented in court stated that

Toyota's software development practices, including reliance on third-party code, resulted in poor-quality code and led to the accident.

Supply Chain Risk Management

Supply chain information security risk cuts across many organizational disciplines (see Figure 1.9). Existing governance, risk management, and compliance frameworks provide a starting point to evaluate, control, and monitor supply chain risk. Other areas where supply chain risk must be considered include acquisitions, software engineering, software assurance, and personnel security.

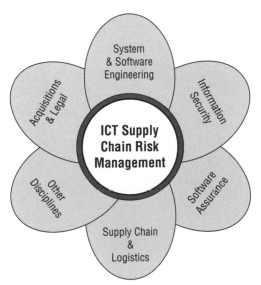

FIGURE 1.9 Supply chain information security risk management

A number of regulatory and statutory expectations explicitly require regulated organizations to address supply chain risk. The HIPAA legislation requires covered entities in the United States to evaluate the risk presented by business associates. The U.S. government (and organizations doing business with the U.S. government) have similar expectations in place.

The security of the supply chain is not solely addressed by ensuring the effectiveness of the security practices of the upstream (supplier) organizations. Customers of the organization may also create supply chain risk. Loss of control over intellectual property and misuse of privilege often occur because of ineffective control over the downstream (customer) practices.

Frameworks

Several of the frameworks explicitly address supply chain risks. This is an evolving area of risk management, but the complexities of managing the information systems supply chain have been evident for many years.

NIST

The U.S. government began directly addressing cyber supply chain risk as a separate issue with the publication of NIST IR 7622, "Notional Supply Chain Risk Management Practices for Federal Information Systems." This work recognizes that the actions required of the entities in the supply chain will change depending on their role, as will the level and type of control to be applied. The document identifies 10 practices that should be taken into account in addressing supply chain risk.

- Uniquely identify supply chain elements, processes, and actors
- Limit access and exposure within the supply chain
- Establish and maintain the provenance of elements, processes, tools, and data
- Share information within strict limits
- Perform supply chain risk management awareness and training
- Use defensive design for systems, elements, and processes
- Perform continuous integrator review
- Strengthen delivery mechanisms
- Assure sustainment activities and processes
- Manage disposal and final disposition activities throughout the system or element lifecycle

The U.S. government has a number of other supply chain risk management initiatives, including the Committee on National Security Systems Directive 505, "Supply Chain Risk Management," which specifically addresses security requirements for strategic national systems and the Comprehensive National Cybersecurity Initiative Number 11, which provides a set of tools to agencies to manage their cybersecurity supply chain through a risk-driven approach.

ISO

ISO 28000:2007, "Specification for security management systems for the supply chain," provides a broad framework for managing supply chain risk. While not specific to cybersecurity, ISO 28000 is useful for organizations that leverage other ISO specifications (ISO 9001, ISO 27001) to align supply chain risk with the organizations' audit processes or that seek to use a standardized, risk-based approach to evaluating supply chain risk.

ISO 28000:2007 relies heavily on the continuous process improvement model of plan, do, check, act (PDCA) to improve the security management system and to assure organizational conformance to the security practice. This approach facilitates the integration of supply chain risk with broader organizational risk management activities.

Supply Chain Operations Reference

Managing global supply chains involves a much broader risk set than cyber security. The American Production and Inventory Constrol Socient (APICS) developed the Supply Chain Operations Reference (SCOR) model to support diverse organizations in its supply chain management activities. The SCOR model integrates business process improvement, performance benchmarking, best practices, and organizational design into a single framework, which in turn drives a set of processes, performance metrics, best practices, and skills. The six primary management processes include the following:

- **Plan:** Processes that balance aggregate demand and supply to develop a course of action that best meets sourcing, production, and delivery requirements
- **Source:** Processes that procure goods and services to meet planned or actual demand
- **Make:** Processes that transform a product to a finished state to meet planned or actual demand
- **Deliver:** Processes that provide finished goods and services to meet planned or actual demand, typically including order management, transportation management, and distribution management
- **Return:** Processes associated with returning or receiving returned products for any reason. These processes extend into post-delivery customer support
- **Enable:** Processes that prepare, support, or handle information or relations on which depend the processes of planning and execution

Cybersecurity practices are one of the key enablers for the process areas.

ESTABLISH AND MAINTAIN A SECURITY AWARENESS, EDUCATION, AND TRAINING PROGRAM

It is a common characterization that people remain the weakest link in the security posture of organizations. Whether the victims of social engineering, complacency in security practice, serving in roles as single points of failure, or any of a myriad of other causes, the vulnerabilities associated with the people in a system provide a tremendous opportunity for bad actors.

Creating awareness within the organization requires providing information to a broad community of stakeholders. The most effective security awareness programs make security risks relevant and meaningful to those stakeholders. In this way, changing people's behavior and actions can be seen as making people the greatest asset to the security program.

Many security frameworks, including the NIST, ISO, PCI-DSS, and others, require organizations to implement security awareness programs. Simply having a program does not mean the program is effective. Truly reducing the risks associated with these programs requires creativity, effort, and genuine commitment by the management.

Security Awareness Overview

Developing an organizational capacity to effectively identify and respond to security risks requires a broad range of skills and knowledge. The level of security expertise will vary in focus and depth depending on the individual's role in the organization. Education, training, and awareness each address a different aspect of professional development.

Education is a formal process by which an individual develops conceptual understanding of a CBK. This understanding of the concepts, principles, and issues gives the ability for an educated person to proactively design programs to address a broad range of often ill-defined problems. A four-year university program is an example of education, as is developing an understanding of the CISSP CBK.

Where education is conceptual, training is more practical. Training teaches specific skills to address known circumstances. Training might include instruction on how to operate or configure a system to meet organizational requirements. If the desired outcome is known and the steps needed to achieve that outcome are well defined, learning that set of skills generally falls into the area of training. While training and education often overlap—and good education programs require more than a theoretical understanding of a technical issue—they each require different levels of knowledge.

Awareness is yet a third learning perspective. Awareness gives focus and attention to a particular issue so that the learner can identify out-of-normal circumstances and respond appropriately. Awareness might include user-focused lectures that provide information on how to recognize social engineering attempts, or it might include an email phishing campaign to identify individuals who do not follow good email practices.

Everyone cannot be an expert in everything. The challenge for the information security practitioner is to identify where education, training, and awareness fit into their overall security program and to ensure that those activities are properly resourced.

As the threats adapt to the weaknesses in our environment, organizations too must continuously monitor and adjust their security posture. Changes to the security awareness programs must reflect the adaptive nature of the malicious actors.

Over the course of the last five years, the rise of ransomware, the movement to the cloud, and the security issues with the Internet of Things are only a few of the changes to the security landscape. The pace of change requires all stakeholders to maintain currency in their areas and to keep the awareness activities relevant and timely.

A classic example of this is in the area of two-factor authentication. Many organizations rely on SMS messages for two-factor authentication. Over the past several years, we have seen bad actors compromise this method of identity verification by leveraging weaknesses in the transmission of the messages. Individuals have lost millions of dollars of cryptocurrency, have had social media accounts compromised, and have had their bank accounts drained. As a result, what had been believed to be a highly secure means of verifying identity now presents an unacceptable risk to most enterprise environments.

From an education perspective, the discovery of the weaknesses in SMS should have been predictable; the history of technology is that the longer a system is used, the more likely it is that bad actors will increase their ability to compromise the system, and new authentication mechanisms need to be developed and implemented. From a training perspective, technologists need to know how to implement the new systems and ensure their proper operation. From an awareness perspective, the larger user community must be advised of the security flaws so that they understand why the changes are necessary and how the new authentication processes will affect their activities, and can evaluate whether they want to rely on nonorganizational resources that leverage that technology.

Developing an Awareness Program

Developing an awareness program requires deliberate, sustained effort to ensure that the program is effective at improving the security posture of the organization. Driven by the level of risk, the program requires senior management support while respecting organizational culture, resources available, and the compliance expectations for the organization.

Perform Assessment

When developing an awareness program, assessing the organization's compliance obligations, risk environment, organizational capacity, and resources must be evaluated. Understanding the organizational culture is also important, as security behavior by individuals tends to follow the examples of their co-workers and the instructions of their supervisors. In this initial stage, establishing the level of organizational support and identifying senior management champions will set the tone for the entire awareness program.

The implementation of the information security awareness program will depend heavily on the organization's size, mission, and management structure. Smaller organizations tend to centralize the entire program into a single entity responsible for policy, content, and delivery, while other organizations will set policy and rely on decentralized delivery. Successfully implementing security awareness programs must take into account the organizational culture.

Compliance Requirements

Many frameworks have specific expectations for an organization's security awareness program. Compliance obligations, however, do not guarantee effectiveness; rather, they establish a minimum expectation that leads to an organization developing a program tailored to its unique requirements.

ISO

ISO 27001 sets a high-level expectation for information security awareness programs that address awareness for new and current employees and regular follow-up events. This is further described in ISO 27002-Information Security Code of Practice. In human resource control 7.2.2, "An Information Security Awareness Program should aim to make employees and, where relevant, contractors aware of their responsibilities for information security and the means by which those responsibilities are discharged."

SWIFT

The SWIFT network supports financial services institutions through secure financial messaging services. In 2017, SWIFT published its Customer Security Controls Framework. Control 7.2 states, "Ensure all staff are aware of and fulfil their security responsibilities by performing regular security training and awareness activities." SWIFT relies on self-attestation by member organizations, and facilitates the sharing of compliance status between member organizations.

The Federal Information Security Management Act

In the United States, the Federal Information Security Management Act (FISMA) requires that agencies establish information security awareness programs. This requirement has led to the development of a comprehensive body of practice inside the U.S. government for security awareness. NIST Special Publications 800-50 and 800-16 discuss the strategic/policy implications and the tactical implementation of awareness programs, respectively.

Others

Many other frameworks identify security awareness as a key information security control. These include the U.S. government's Risk Management Framework, the voluntary Cyber Security Framework, the PCI-DSS framework, and many others. Further, organization policies may dictate security awareness independent of an external framework.

Needs Assessment

Once the minimum expectations for compliance are identified, a needs assessment must be conducted. A needs assessment will identify gaps between the organization's requirements and the capabilities of its stakeholders. It will provide information on the organization's current level of awareness and the preferred methods of delivery and identify the different levels of awareness that stakeholders may have.

There are many tools that will support needs assessments. These include reviews of existing job responsibilities and roles, questionnaires evaluating current security practices and understanding, reviews of past information security events, evaluation of comparable programs in like organizations, and analysis of current threats and risks. Further, the needs assessment must take into account any organization-specific requirements that can affect the delivery of training and awareness content. These might include labor agreements, hours of operation, or delivery to populations that require adaptive technology.

The result of the needs assessment will be a report to management identifying the gaps between requirements and capabilities.

Security Awareness Strategy and Plans

The needs assessment report will be used by management to develop an awareness strategy and appropriate plans to resource the development and delivery of the awareness content. The strategy will also set the baseline for evaluating the effects of the awareness program. The plans themselves will reflect the organization's training and awareness priorities to ensure that the areas of highest risk are addressed.

As the assessment will identify different awareness levels and gaps in the organization, different delivery approaches and detail in the content will be necessary to achieve the desired awareness outcome. Whether if the organization develops a single master plan or multiple, synchronized separate plans, addressing the differences in approach and content is essential to a successful awareness program. If the target audience is too broad and the instructional content too generic, it will not have the relevance it needs to motivate changes in workplace behavior. If it is too specific, it becomes unwieldly to manage.

Striking the right balance is difficult, and awareness plans should be built around a continuous process improvement model. This allows for the refinement of the awareness plans and content over time.

Develop Content

With awareness programs, the intent is to shape and reinforce behaviors. Consequently, the level of detail in awareness programs is generally less than for training programs. Ensuring that the content is relevant and meaningful goes a long way toward achieving that end.

The identified gaps in awareness from the needs assessment will form the basis for the security awareness program. The content should be developed to answer these three questions:

- What change in behavior is needed?
- What information will motivate that change?
- How will the change in behavior be evaluated?

For example, the needs assessment may identify that individuals in the organization are susceptible to phishing attacks from outside the organization. The behavior change is to have users evaluate their emails to ensure their legitimacy. The information they need to do this is information on types of phishing threats, common techniques used by attackers, and the effects of phishing on the organization. The method of evaluation is to use an external phishing vendor to create a phishing campaign sending messages before (to establish a performance baseline) and after (to evaluate the change in behavior resulting from the awareness event.

The range of topics that could be addressed is broad. In developing content, the issues with the highest level of risk to the organization should be addressed. In most organizations, unique business requirements will drive awareness topics.

Deliver Content

Just as there is a wide range of content, the delivery of the content can occur in many different ways. Multiple methods of delivery further emphasize the importance of the issue to the organization, and often one method will not reach part of the target audience, while another method is successful.

Some of the more common techniques include the following:

- **Instructor-led events:** While the effectiveness varies depending on the delivery skills and knowledge of the instructor, this remains one of the most popular forms. Supporting materials (slides, handouts, etc.) should reinforce the message.

- **Computer-based training:** As an awareness delivery method, this approach ensures that everyone in the target audience receives the same message, and it is relatively simple to build an evaluation tool to determine whether the message was received. This method can also simplify the timing of the delivery, as the audience can view the message at their convenience. The effectiveness of computer-based delivery varies as well, as it is influenced by the sophistication of the message, relevance to the audience, and quality of the supporting technology and infrastructure.

- **Blended events:** In some cases, delivery of live instruction through computer broadcast can be an effective mix of methods. However, consideration should be given to ensuring that participant questions and feedback can be addressed.

The strategy should identify the broad timelines during which the awareness and training programs should demonstrate success, while the timing of the delivery should be refined in the implementation plan(s). Awareness programs built around a single event (annual awareness training) are generally less successful at changing behavior than campaigns that stress the importance of a security-aware culture.

Monitor Results

Once the program has begun, monitoring the delivery of the awareness content and measuring the level of change in behavior provides important information to refine the program. In a continuous process improvement model, the information generated becomes an important input in the next round of needs assessment.

It is relatively easy to tell whether people have been exposed to the awareness material. Sign-in rosters and automated course attendance tracking give information on which individuals have participated. Behavior change, which is the best measure of program success, is more difficult to measure.

Behavior change can be subtle, and it often takes time to change behavior, especially in large, diverse organizations. In the earlier phishing example, baselining the organizational behavior is an important step in the process, so that subsequent email campaigns can measure the delta of change.

Training

The complexity of the information security environment is such that a comprehensive discussion of training practices for all aspects of information security is beyond the scope of this volume. Generally speaking, the four-step process identified earlier would align well with the development of a training practice in an organization.

Training is also addressed within many of the compliance frameworks. Many times, people will have roles or responsibilities that they do not have the proper level of skills or knowledge to perform. The introduction of new technology also presents challenges for training, as installing, configuring, operating, and monitoring all require specific tasks to be performed.

Best practice is to ensure that cybersecurity personnel are qualified and receive ongoing training to remain current with the changing cybersecurity environment. For example, the COBIT Framework identifies in objective PO 7.4, "Personnel Training: Provide IT employees with appropriate orientation when hired and ongoing training to maintain their knowledge, skills, abilities, internal controls, and security awareness at the level required to achieve organizational goals." Other frameworks provide similar guidance.

This best-practice expectation is being incorporated into a number of regulatory regimes as well. Increased emphasis has been placed on control over regulated organizations' cybersecurity practices, including training and awareness. The resulting New York State Department of Financial Services regulation, "Cybersecurity Requirements for Financial Services Companies," provides an example of this growing trend:

"Section 500.10 Cybersecurity Personnel and Intelligence.

(a) Cybersecurity Personnel and Intelligence. In addition to the requirements set forth in section 500.04(a) of this Part, each Covered Entity shall:

(1) utilize qualified cybersecurity personnel of the Covered Entity, an Affiliate or a Third Party Service Provider sufficient to manage the Covered Entity's cybersecurity risks and to perform or oversee the performance of the core cybersecurity functions …

(2) provide cybersecurity personnel with cybersecurity updates and training sufficient to address relevant cybersecurity risks; and

(3) verify that key cybersecurity personnel take steps to maintain current knowledge of changing cybersecurity threats and countermeasures."

To meet these challenges, many organizations will place training expectations on their employees as a condition of hire or to remain in employ. A typical expectation would be for an individual to hold a certification like the CISSP at the time of hire and then maintain that certification over time. (ISC)² requires members, as part of remaining in good standing, to participate in continuing education activities that enable members to stay current with changes in the industry.

The dynamic nature of cyber security and the risks that organizations face can no longer be defended by the sharing of tribal knowledge and reliance on dated control processes. Information security practitioners must continue to learn and evolve their skills throughout their careers.

SUMMARY

The breadth of the security activities demands that the security practitioner possess a wide range of knowledge and skills. The ever-changing threat environment, imposition of new laws, and compliance expectations and changes in technology are only some of the areas that require constant attention.

Good security practice must be aligned with the organization's business objectives and practices. This is one of the greatest benefits of leveraging a security controls framework to integrate security best practice into the organizational risk management activities. This chapter highlights the importance of a controls framework in establishing an effective security environment.

Organizational resistance to change is often great. Strong senior management support is essential to the adoption of effective security practices. Communicating good security practices is an area where security practitioners continue to struggle. Through the use of good risk management processes, security practitioners have the greatest opportunity to transform their organizations to be proactive and security aware.

Asset Security

TO APPLY AND ENFORCE effective asset security, you must concentrate on inventorying all sources of value, called *assets*. Assets can be tangible or intangible, existing in the form of information stores, databases, hardware, software, or entire networks. In this domain, we cover significant elements of strategy to identify, categorize, secure, and monitor those assets. Although assets can also be buildings and real estate, those are not within the purview of this domain. Physical security is substantially addressed in Chapter 7. This chapter will focus on the best policies, practices, and methods to properly assure the confidentiality, integrity, and availability of an organization's assets.

ASSET SECURITY CONCEPTS

Asset security is a broad subject, and it deals with a vast array of knowledge and terminology, some more technical than others. The term *asset* describes computing devices, IT systems, software (both an installed instance and a physical instance), virtual computing platforms (common in cloud and virtualized computing), and related hardware (e.g., locks, cabinets, and keyboards). This matches definitions common to industry and regulatory entities, such as the National Institute of

Standards and Technology (NIST). Data is also an asset to an organization. The terms are not interchangeable, as data is a subset of valuable assets to an organization. It is important for the security professional to have a grounding in some key concepts that relate to securing assets. This chapter begins with asset security concepts as they relate to data protection, particularly those that relate to data policy, governance, quality, documentation, and organization.

Data Policy

Data management has to be guided by a set of principles and procedures that apply broadly to the organization. Each department in the organization may choose to customize the policy to fulfill unique requirements, but must remain in alignment with the authority of the top-level policy. A sound data policy should guide the organization to collect only the required information, keep it safe, and securely destroy any information once the asset is no longer needed.

A sound data policy helps an organization address important considerations that impact the practice of data protection. Because the nature of asset security is dynamic as threats change, the data policy will need to be flexible and able to accommodate change. However, the data policy must be aligned with prevailing law and regulatory requirements in all cases. For instance, privacy law may dictate the use of end user agreements or consent notices when collecting, sharing, storing, and disposing of information.

Establishing a data policy is important in an organization for more than just compliance or due diligence. Data policy also plays a significant role in data governance. A well-defined data policy provides direction for the management to set practices and standards related to quality, format, access, and retention of data.

Data Governance

In many large organizations, a data governance office oversees data policy and outlines roles and responsibilities for the cross-functional stakeholders. An organization should determine how it wants to manage the creation, transformation, and usage of data valued by the organization. This function describes data governance. The concept of data governance includes the people, processes, and IT organizations used to handle data properly and consistently, both internally and externally. There are several guiding principles that an organization should use to establish their data governance model:

- Establish responsibilities
- Plan to best support the organization
- Acquire validly

- Ensure performance when required
- Ensure conformance with rules
- Ensure respect for human factors

A data governance model establishes authority and management and decision-making parameters related to the data produced or managed by the enterprise. The function of data governance should be under the purview of an organizational data governance office or committee. The structure and formality of the data governance office or committee depends on the organization. A large, multinational organization that handles volumes of sensitive data likely wants to have a formal data governance organization made up of a centralized data governance office, with key stakeholders and members of executive leadership serving on a data governance committee, for example. Conversely, a small community bank has a need for a data governance committee, but that group may be less formal and led by an individual named to lead the group. In any case, as ISO/IEC 38500, *Governance of IT for the Organization*, states, data governance applies to organizations of all sizes, including public and private companies, government entities, and not-for-profit organizations.

A data governance committee is needed to oversee the development of common data definitions, standards, requirements, and processes. The committee should have the authority to enforce policies and procedures. The governing body manages implementation and integration of data governance principles into business processes.

Data governance in an organization has the goal of stopping data-related problems before they begin. The policies and procedures they establish reduce ambiguity, establish clear accountabilities, and disseminate data-related information to all stakeholders.

NOTE There are several components of data policy that are common across most organizations. Costs of providing access will drive policy decisions, for instance. The roles and responsibilities of data owners and custodians are also considerations. In some cases, responsibilities overlap because of shared accountability, for instance with in an asset who manages both financial and human resources data sets.

TIP There is a connection between the issues of concern in a data policy and an organization's risk tolerance. The organization's data policy should be part of the overall risk management program.

Data Quality

Data quality involves the integrity and reliability of data. To maintain its data quality, it is important to verify and validate data throughout useful life. In fact, the quality of the data is related to the fitness for use or potential use of the information. Factors such as accuracy, currency, and relevance top the list of items to check for when measuring data quality.

- **Quality assurance (QA):** Use of prescribed standards to assess and to discover inconsistencies and other anomalies in the data and apply data cleansing to deliver a final product. QA addresses the question, "Is the data fit for the purpose?"

- **Quality control (QC):** An assessment of data quality based on internal standards, processes, and procedures to control and monitor quality as informed by QA. QC addresses the question, "Is the data fit for use?"

The purpose of performing QA and QC in data quality procedures is to reduce errors in the data sets to acceptable levels. The cost of eliminating all errors may be prohibitive, but the organization should establish a threshold based on the frequency of incorrect data in a data field or record and the significance of the error.

NOTE   To view a good QA procedure guide, see the tools available at `https://www`
`.measureevaluation.org/resources/tools/health-information-systems/`
`data-quality-assurance-tools`.

The following are the general types of errors that good data quality practices aim to reduce:

- **Errors of commission:** Data entry mistakes or inaccurate transcription that should be reduced by having a sufficient QA process in data acquisition.

- **Errors of omission:** Harder to detect, these are missing data that can lead to inaccurate values or interpretation of data sets or calculations made on the data.

TIP   Data quality principles are relevant at all stages of data management: capture, digitization, storage, analysis, presentation, and use.

Data Documentation

The practice of documentation and organization of data assets is useful in organizations to manage the increasingly large sets of data critical to business processes. Proper data documentation helps to ensure that data users will understand and use data efficiently. It also helps organizations ensure that data will be usable far into the future. The general components of data documentation are how the data was created, what the context is for the data, the structure of the data and its contents, and any manipulations that have been done to the data. The objectives of data documentation are as follows:

- Longevity and reuse of data.
- Data users should understand content, context, and limits of data.

- Easier discovery of data within the organization.
- Data interoperability and exchange of data.

There are some general practices that can help accomplish data documentation objectives:

- **Metadata:** Metadata management is an inextricable part of records management, serving a variety of functions and purposes. It is descriptive information about the data set. It is data describing the context, content, and structure of records and their management through time. Some information to include in the metadata are name, title, subjects, keywords, description, date of creation, geolocation, and any other relevant information the organization desires by policy. The metadata requirements are established by the organization, but some types of metadata used are as follows:

  - Information describing the record

  - Business rules, policies, and mandates

  - Agents (or people) related to the record

  - Business activities and processes

  - Information about records management processes

  - Metadata about the metadata record

  In some cases, data quality control processes would prohibit data from being published if required fields are not completed. Metadata ensures authenticity, reliability, usability, and integrity over time and enables the management and understanding of information objects.

- **Readme file:** This is a type of data documentation used primarily for application or programming files. The use of a Readme file in .txt or .pdf format helps explain the data set beyond the metadata description. It can also describe multiple files in the directory if applicable. The Readme file helps explain the who, what, why, and any other contextual information the author might think is helpful to an external user of the data set. The Readme file may also contain directions for file handling, processing steps, field abbreviations, and data definitions.

- **File contents:** There is no mandatory formatting or requirements for file organization, but in general, files should be named something unique, consistent, informative, and easily sortable. Using project names or author names is encouraged while the use of special characters is not, except for dashes, underscores, and numbers. Users must understand the content of the file or data set. This would include knowing parameter names, units of measure, formats, and definitions of coded values. In files containing a large amount of data, it is acceptable to include all the descriptive information in a separate linked document.

NOTE   Different types of files have different methods to store the file content information. For instance, programming code may contain this information in the header area at the top of the file. In office automation files, this information is found in the properties area where author, filename, last accessed, and last printed fields are documented.

Data Organization

The process organizations use to arrange and control data is called *data organization*. This chapter covers specific components of data organization, like data classification, categorization, structure, and schema. The purpose of these components is to make data more useful. Data organization applies to both unstructured and structured data.

A data structure is important to enable access and modify data efficiently; it is used to organize and store data. A *data structure* is described as a collection of data values, the relationships among them, and the functions or operations that can be applied to the data. The aggregate data structure is referred to as a *record*. The record (or tuple) is a data set that can contain other values, typically in fixed number and sequence and typically indexed by name. The elements within a record are usually called *fields* or *members*.

For most organizations, the bulk of the information is stored as unstructured data. *Unstructured data* is data that lacks a formal data model. An example of this kind of data is a simple text document, where names, dates, and other pieces of information are scattered throughout random paragraphs.

Structured data is acquired, maintained, and analyzed within the context of a formal data model. For example, in a relational database, the data is stored in predefined tables that can be easily integrated into other applications and, from there, fed into analytics software or other particular applications. The existence of the data model provides context for the information, defines the format for the stored information, and simplifies data integration efforts.

Data Schema

A *data schema* is a concept that would be covered in great depth if this were a data science book. Limited to the topic of asset security, it is important to note that the data schema is an element of data organization. Decisions on security controls such as encryption, access and authorization levels, and disposition schedules will be informed by the data schema. A working definition of a data schema is that it is a blueprint of how a database is constructed. For example, in a relational database, the data schema is organized into tables. A data schema is established to document the elements that can enter the database or those of interest to the possible end users. A database generally stores its schema in a reference repository called a *data dictionary*.

Data Classification

Data collected, stored, and used in an organization needs to be classified or organized into tiers or classes based on the level of sensitivity the organization ascribes to the information. The classification helps to determine the security controls to be used to manage and safeguard the data against unauthorized access, improper retention, and unsafe destruction.

Although it is always a best practice to classify data, the concept is most formalized in military or government organizations or in heavily regulated organizations. The actual labels will differ in each organization.

✔ Examples of Classification Schemes

Commercial organizations might use this scheme:

- **Confidential:** Generally considered the highest level of classification outside of government or military organizations. The loss or theft of this data can cause serious risk to the organization. This category of data is usually subject to regulation, considered proprietary, or controlled by contractual agreement.

- **Sensitive:** A level of relative value less than confidential but still important to protect. Losing the data will raise the risk to the organization, even if it is just reputational damage. Strategy documents or interorganizational correspondence can be considered sensitive.

- **Private:** Usually compartmental data that might not do the company damage but must be kept private for other reasons. Employee retention statistics or salary ranges are often classified as private.

- **Proprietary:** Data that is disclosed outside the company on a limited basis or contains information that could reduce the company's competitive advantage, such as the technical specifications of a new product.

- **Public:** This data, if lost, would have little or no impact on risk levels. A briefing on proper antiphishing techniques that does not disclose specific results or personal information beyond the author's name or general best practices is suitable for sharing outside the organization.

NOTE   Other labels used to designate documents (but not considered classifications) include For Official Use Only (FOUO) and Limited Official Use. If you do not work in a military or government organization, you will want to collaborate with the organizational legal department to determine proper terminology to establish document designation. Some organizations have strict policies on allowable terminology.

Having a data classification policy and procedure in place allows the organization to begin designing security controls for the most efficient and effective segmentation and protection of the information. Sufficient policy and procedure around access and authorization for data at each classification assures the protection of privacy or welfare of an individual and the trade secrets of a business. In the case of military and government organizations, proper classification aids in the prevention of loss, misuse, modification, or unauthorized access that could lead to a security crisis or an international relations debacle.

Data Categorization

Once you know where information assets reside, you can assign categorization to them. Categorization has two principle functions. First, it assigns or reflects the value the organization attributes to the asset or information. Second, categorization embodies the risk tolerance established by management. How an organization, handles assets to assure confidentiality, integrity, and availability is determined by the classification process. The categories reflect the assessed potential impact to the organization, should certain events occur that jeopardize information confidentiality, integrity, and availability.

A simple method for categorization can start with a high, medium, and low set of categories. For U.S. government entities, the Federal Information Processing Standard (FIPS) Publication 199 outlines guidelines for applying the qualitative categories. Each of the levels has a precise definition against which the information is evaluated to determine the appropriate categorization level. In Table 2.1, categorization is summarized and depicted as security objective against potential impact.

TABLE 2.1 Potential Impact Definitions for Security Objectives

SECURITY OBJECTIVE	LOW	MODERATE	HIGH
Confidentiality Preserving authorized restrictions on information access and disclosure, including means for protecting personal privacy and proprietary information.	The unauthorized disclosure of information could be expected to have a **limited** adverse effect on organizational operations, organizational assets, or individuals.	The unauthorized disclosure of information could be expected to have a **serious** adverse effect on organizational operations, organizational assets, or individuals.	The unauthorized disclosure of information could be expected to have a **severe or catastrophic** adverse effect on organizational operations, organizational assets, or individuals.

SECURITY OBJECTIVE	LOW	MODERATE	HIGH
Integrity Guarding against improper information modification or destruction, and includes ensuring information non-repudiation and authenticity.	The unauthorized modification or destruction of information could be expected to have a **limited** adverse effect on organizational operations, organizational assets, or individuals.	The unauthorized modification or destruction of information could be expected to have a **serious** adverse effect on organizational operations, organizational assets, or individuals.	The unauthorized modification or destruction of information could be expected to have a **severe or catastrophic** adverse effect on organizational operations, organizational assets, or individuals.
Availability Ensuring timely and reliable access to and use of information.	The disruption of access to or use of information or an information system could be expected to have a **limited** adverse effect on organizational operations, organizational assets, or individuals.	The disruption of access to or use of information or an information system could be expected to have a **serious** adverse effect on organizational operations, organizational assets, or individuals.	The disruption of access to or use of information or an information system could be expected to have a **severe or catastrophic** adverse effect on organizational operations, organizational assets, or individuals.

Source: NIST Special Publication 199)sd1

The value in properly categorizing data is to permit appropriate security controls based on the level of risk. Oversecuring data is a waste of resources, while undersecuring data presents risk that may be unacceptable. At the enterprise level, the combination of mismanaging data categorization can be profound.

IDENTIFY AND CLASSIFY INFORMATION AND ASSETS

At a high level, the importance of identifying and classifying information assets as a first task in providing information security is significant. Without attending to these tasks, you will not be able to know where your assets are. You will not be able to know which assets are more valuable than others. The result will be an inefficient, costly information security plan attempting to secure all assets, with an assumption that the assets are located in all parts of the organization (local storage, shared storage, in the cloud, etc.). Worse, some assets requiring minimal protection, like public information, will be secured the same as confidential information. You will want to be able to locate, categorize, and differentiate the security approaches to your assets.

Creating the inventory of what assets an organization has, where the assets are, and who is responsible for the assets are foundational steps in establishing an information security asset management policy. Locating data has become more difficult because data has proliferated throughout the organization because of inexpensive local storage, mobile application development, and distributed data collection techniques. Mapping where data resides is a tough task, but necessary.

Laws and regulations are often the source of policy in organizations. There are significant reasons relative to jurisdictional and industry concerns that make understanding the prevailing legal and regulatory mandates important. Regulators around the globe have published standards with many commonalities. Following are some of the common regulatory regimes that formalize the classification and categorization of information:

- **Canada:** Security of Information Act

- **China:** Guarding State Secrets

- **United Kingdom:** Official Secrets Acts (OSA)

- **United States:** NIST Federal Information Processing Standard 199, "Standards for Security Categorization of Federal Information and Information Systems"

- **United States:** NIST Special Publication (SP) 800-60, "Guide for Mapping Types of Information and Information Systems to Security Categories" (this is considered the "how-to" manual for FIPS 199)

- **United States:** Committee on National Security Systems (CNSS) Instruction No. 1253, "Security Categorization and Control Selection for National Security Systems"

- **European Union (EU):** General Data Protection Regulation (GDPR)

- **International healthcare:** HL7 Informative Guidance Release 2, "Healthcare Privacy and Security Classification System (HCS)"

The content of the regulations and laws varies. Each concentrates on one or more aspects of data protection. The UK OSA, for example, is concerned with protection of state secrets and official information, and it informs data classification levels. The EU GDPR strengthens and unifies data protection and informs data flow policy. In the United States, the NIST FIPS 199 can be used for asset classification within the overall risk management process. The best organizational security policy will be developed using the relevant guidance as a foundational source.

Once assets, including data, are classified according to sensitivity, a measure of the impact the loss of that data would have is made. The process of assigning a significance level to the confidentiality, integrity, or availability of data is called categorization. Categories can be as descriptive as high, medium, and low. The categories and classifications can be situational and unique based on organizational factors. Criteria such as industry and variations in acceptable use guidelines will result in categorizations that vary from organization to organization.

TIP The information security asset management policy provides, at a high level, the relevant guidance for acceptable use of data, legal and regulatory considerations, and roles and responsibilities of data users in the organization, for example.

NOTE Review your organization's data use procedures. Does your organization apply sufficiently stringent controls for all types of sensitive information? Some organizations control traditional business concerns or financial information, such as payroll, pricing, or billing rates, and less control for personally identifiable information (PII) or protected health information (PHI). It is appropriate for access to require multiple approval steps, for data sets to be segmented to reduce access, and for data to be available only on a need-to-know basis. Classification schemes depend on the organization.

Asset Classification

Asset classification begins with conducting an inventory of assets and determining the responsible persons, or owners, for the assets. Assets contain data or provide information-handling capabilities. Depending on the organization, examples of electronic types of assets are databases, email, storage media, and endpoint computers. Assets can be inventoried and protected that originate through oral communication, like voice recordings, although they are most commonly stored in digital format. Paper-based records are also assets to be protected. Records or documentation stored in file cabinets, desk drawers, or other physical filing systems can be classified based on sensitivity and value to the organization. You will have responsibility for including these paper assets in your information asset security plan.

Classifying the assets means categorizing and grouping assets by the level of sensitivity. The levels of classification dictate a minimum set of security controls the organization will use to protect the information. Keep in mind, the classification levels may call for protection that exceeds legal and regulatory requirements. A formal data policy is the primary mechanism through which an organization establishes classification levels, and then management can develop controls that provide sufficient protections against specific risks and threats it faces.

Benefits of Classification

Because it provides valuable insight into an environment, classification is a critical first step to better and more secure asset and data management. For a relatively simple process, the benefits are significant. Figure 2.1 depicts the major benefits of classification. The list is not comprehensive, and some organizations will find varying levels of benefit.

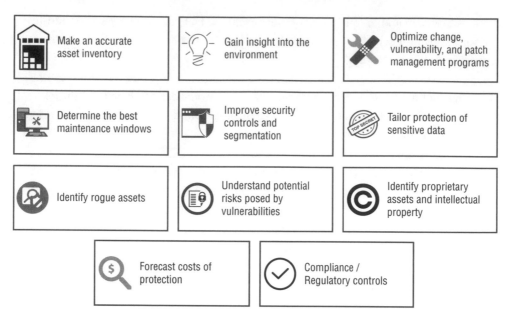

FIGURE 2.1 **General Benefits of Asset Classification**

Qualitative vs. Quantitative Asset Value Analysis

A common way to value assets for classification (and categorization, discussed later in this chapter) is to use qualitative or quantitative risk analysis. Using objective measures and computing a numerical value describes quantitative approaches. This type of value is usually presented in currency, percentages, and specific numbers. Qualitative methodology differs in that measures are based on subjective judgment from assessors and organizational decision-makers. The way these assessments are communicated is in terms like high, medium, and low. The process is equivalent to the general risk management equation used throughout assessment of information risk. The value of the asset is dependent on the likelihood that a vulnerability will be exploited multiplied by the severity of the impact.

TIP Likelihood and probability are both used to describe how likely an event is to occur. Likelihood is relevant to qualitative analysis, and probability relates to quantitative.

Under quantitative analysis, there are several types of equations that can be used. These formulas cover the expected loss for specific security risks and the value of safeguards to reduce the security risks:

- Annual Loss Expectancy (ALE) = Single Loss Expectancy (SLE) × Annual Rate of Occurrence (ARO)

- Single Loss Expectancy = Asset Value × Exposure Factor

- Safeguard Value = (ALE Before − ALE After) − Annual Cost of Countermeasure

To compute the ALE, the first step is to determine the value of the asset (AV). As an example, assume the AV equals $100,000. This helps determine the SLE because SLE equals AV multiplied by exposure factor (EF). EF is the probability the asset loss will occur. EF is expressed as a percentage in this example; if the EF is 30 percent, the SLE is $30,000, as $100,000 × 0.30 = $30,000.

Annualized rate of occurrence (ARO) is the estimated frequency of the threat occurring in one year. To calculate ALE, ARO is multiplied by SLE. So, continuing the example, if SLE is $30,000 and the organization estimates ARO as 50 percent probability, the ALE is $15,000 or ($30,000 × (0.5)).

The organization thinks the vulnerability will be exploited once every two years. To figure out the safeguard value, some related computations are made by taking the ALE results from before the countermeasure was implemented and subtracting the ALE after the countermeasures were implemented. From that result, the annual cost of the counter-measure is subtracted. In the example, a countermeasure that costs more than $15,000 would need increased justification or would not be warranted. There are other consider-ations that may factor into this type of decision. Using a qualitative approach in combina-tion with quantitative measures may provide the justification required.

Qualitative asset risk management uses the same general set of variables to measure risk such as asset value, threat frequency, impact, and safeguard effectiveness, but these elements are now measured in subjective terms such as high or low. The variables may still be expressed as numbers. High may equal 5 and low equals 1, for example. However, these numbers are not treated like numbers in a quantitative approach. If the values of high and low related to likelihood of asset compromise, a high equal to 5 does not indicate 5 times as likely as a low equal to 1. The ordinal nature of numbers is useful in demonstrating the order or rating of the categories comparatively.

There are advantages to using quantitative analysis:

- It is objective and uses real numbers for comparison.
- It is credible and meaningful and easily understood.
- It is aligned with financial considerations and tailored for cost-benefit analysis.

There are several disadvantages to quantitative analysis:

- It can be complex and intensive to calculate.
- It may provide a false sense of accuracy or precision.
- Measures and formulas can be miscalculated; results are not trusted.

Qualitative approaches have the following advantages:

- They are simple to measure and explain.
- They convey the necessary measures to identify the problem.

The disadvantages of qualitative approaches are as follows:

- They are subjective and dependent on the experience and judgment of the analyst.

- The assets can be over- or under-assessed.

- Recommendations are subjective.

- It's hard to track progress.

NOTE Qualitative asset valuation cannot be used to directly justify costs through a cost–benefit risk analysis.

Asset Classification Levels

Assets should be identified and controlled based on their level of sensitivity. This allows similar assets to be grouped according to the value the organization places on the assets. The evaluation criteria can include the types of data the assets handle, the processes the assets accomplish, or both. There is no mandatory formula or nomenclature for asset classification categories. Each organization will have to establish names and sensitivity levels. Table 2.2 shows an example of types of asset classification. This is a notional framework for asset classification to illustrate how a portfolio of assets in an organization can be segmented into criticalities that map to high, medium, and low. The terms *tier* and *significant systems* are used as examples here and are not prescribed by a regulatory authority.

TABLE 2.2 Examples of Asset Classifications

CATEGORIES	ASPECTS	EXAMPLES
Tier 0	Essential to several business units.	Domain controllers
	May handle data that is extremely sensitive.	Databases
		Email servers
	Compromise could have a critical impact on the business's ability to function.	File shares
		Client web servers
	Required to be available 100 percent of the time.	Gateway network devices (firewalls, routers, and network-critical infrastructure)
		Anything else that shuts down business for a day if it breaks or turns off

CATEGORIES	ASPECTS	EXAMPLES
Tier 1	Important but not necessarily critical to the organization. Essential to specific departments but not to the entire business. Compromise of any of these assets would have a moderate impact on the business's ability to function.	Development environments with critical data. Redundant backup systems with critical data. Department file shares. Local network devices (switches, routers, firewalls, and segmentation devices)
Tier 2	Neither essential nor critical to daily operations. These systems are typically only used by a few people or a single individual. The compromise of any of these assets may inconvenience a few people but would not be a major disruption to business processes.	Workstations. Laptops. Mobile phones and tablets. Printers. Desk phones
Significant Systems	Any assets that handle or store data subject to compliance standards. Significant systems may fall into more than one category or may stand alone for categorization, because loss of the system would not disrupt operations, even if it is damaging to the business.	Cardholder data (CHD)—any system that stores, processes, or transmits CHD must align to PCI DSS. Protected health information (PHI)—medical data must be protected per the standards outlined in the Health Insurance Portability and Accountability Act (HIPAA). Financial data—this data may fall under certain privacy requirements outlined in the Financial Industry Regulatory Authority (FINRA). Classified government data (FISMA/FIPS)—for U.S. military and government

DETERMINE AND MAINTAIN INFORMATION AND ASSET OWNERSHIP

Asset ownership is central to proper information security. Within an organization, depending on the mission and the sensitivity levels of data and assets, there may be a data policy and an information asset security management policy. Data that is protected by statute, contract, or other compliance structures must be addressed by the organization's data governance practice. However, a common part of each policy will be assigning responsibility and guidelines for asset ownership. Data owners and data processors will have roles clearly outlined. Data governance, including access, acceptable use, and data retention, must be performed or overseen by the right individuals in the organization.

Asset Management Lifecycle

Figure 2.2 depicts a general asset lifecycle that is helpful in understanding the continuum of phases relevant to information asset ownership. Roles and responsibilities for data owners and custodians are within each phase. The example solution gives companies the ability to track, manage, and report on information assets throughout their entire lifecycle. This can ultimately increase cybersecurity resilience by enhancing the visibility of assets, identifying vulnerable assets, enabling faster response to security alerts, revealing which applications are actually being used, and reducing help desk response times.

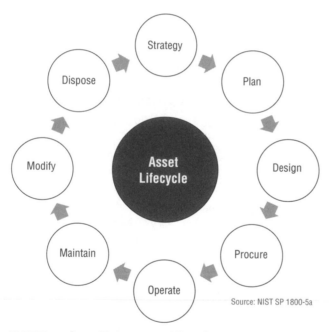

Source: NIST SP 1800-5a

FIGURE 2.2 Asset Management Lifecycle

Important security functions such as incident response, vulnerability management, and configuration control are improved when roles are defined and understood. Three tenets work together to enable the optimum levels of information and asset ownership. When properly implemented, the asset management process helps reduce costs, improve services, and mitigate risk. Activities critical to implementing a formal asset management system include formal assignment of ownership, IT asset management (ITAM), change management, and configuration management.

Formal Assignment of Ownership

Within an organization, the chief executive officer or authorized delegates have formal ownership responsibility. This responsibility includes the authority to represent the organization for the protection and security of the information asset.

Additional responsibilities of asset owners may include the following:

- Keeping the information asset inventory up to date

- Identifying the classification level of the information asset

- Defining and implementing appropriate safeguards to ensure the confidentiality, integrity, and availability of the information asset

- Assessing and monitoring safeguards to ensure compliance and reporting situations of noncompliance

- Authorizing access for those who have a business need for the information

- Ensuring that access is removed from those who no longer have a business need for the information

Information Technology Asset Management

The function of ITAM is to provide accountability for the organization. Drawn from ISO/IEC 19770, ITAM includes the lifecycle view of assets as well as financial concerns for inventory. ISO/IEC 19770 is the data standard for software identification (SWID) tags. SWID tags provide authoritative identifying information for installed software or other licensable items. An accurate and current listing of assets in the organization and who owns them includes hardware and software assets with classification and categorization. When assets are no longer needed by the organization, ITAM guides and supports asset disposition as part of the lifecycle.

Change Management

Organizations must develop policies and procedures to prevent arbitrary and unexpected modifications to the inventory of hardware and software. Change management is the general term for the discipline within an organization to roll out and prioritize changes in a controlled manner that does not adversely impact the production environment or customer expectations. A change is an event that is approved by management, is implemented after mitigating any risks to the production infrastructure to an acceptable level, and provides increased value or capabilities to the organization.

If change management is not handled properly, a variety of issues can arise. For example, significant gaps can gradually emerge between the inventory record and the reality in the environment. The requirement for security personnel to implement antimalware applications to protect each endpoint can become a problem if there are unknown systems documented in the environment.

TIP The Information Technology Infrastructure Library (ITIL) calls for the use of a configuration management database (CMDB) to document the inventory and account for planned deployment of alterations.

Configuration Management

Related to keeping the inventory current, changes in configurations for systems and software must be controlled and documented. Configurations made without direction can lead to problems in other security areas like vulnerability management because hardware and software requirements for upgrades and patching might be unknown and missed.

Many organizations use guides or checklists to accomplish and maintain a secure baseline configuration for their assets. A leading source that is publicly available is the National Checklist Program (NCP), defined by NIST SP 800-70. This is the U.S. government repository for up-to-date and detailed guidance for security configurations.

Some organizations automate much of the baseline security configurations through the metadata available in the NCP and using the Security Content Automation Protocol (SCAP). SCAP enables validated security products to automatically perform configuration checking using NCP checklists.

Software Asset Management

Software asset management (SAM) is a key part of continuous monitoring. The approach described here is intended to support the automation of security functions such as risk-based decision-making, collection of software inventory data, and inventory-based network access control.

SAM, from a security perspective, includes vulnerability scanning and application patching for operating systems, third-party applications, and firmware. Too many firms fail to scan environments, act on vulnerabilities, and keep security patches current, and therefore suffer the consequences. News headlines illustrate failure to remediate known software vulnerabilities appropriately. Take note of the WannaCry virus in May 2017 that exposed flaws in the Windows operating system (OS) or the attack on Apache Struts in the summer of 2017 that took advantage of unpatched third-party software. A sufficient SAM program consists of the following:

- Inventory of applications
- Current list of known vulnerabilities

- Prioritization of each vulnerability by risk level
- Each application patch level
- Actions to patch or apply alternative or compensating controls

The correct approach to SAM can reduce serious disruptive and damaging events such as ransomware, denial of service, or unauthorized access to systems via credential harvesting.

Enterprise patch management is a key part of keeping software assets up to date and secure. The process relies on having a current and complete inventory of the patchable software (applications and operating systems) installed on each host. Without this information, the correct patches cannot be identified, acquired, and installed. This inventory information is also necessary for identifying older versions of installed software so that they can be brought up to date.

Software Licensing

An inventory of software licenses should reside within the asset management system. The inventory can be managed by manual methods like spreadsheets or through automated systems, such as inventory tracking systems. The terms and right to use software are outlined in a license, a legally binding agreement. All software must be legally licensed before it may be installed. If software is used without a license and is discovered during an audit, there can be legal repercussions. Most likely, the unlicensed software use will cause unanticipated increases in software costs. The library of software licenses should be protected with technical controls for access as well as with complementary physical controls, like a safe. Periodic scans should be run to find and remediate unauthorized and unlicensed software.

The security implications of software licensing center around the unknowns of software running illegally on the network. Without proper licensing, manufacturers are likely not providing upgrades and updates, which can increase the chances of the system being compromised. Using NIST SP 800-53 (Rev 4), security professionals should ensure that the required software and associated documentation are in accordance with contract agreements and copyright laws. The controls call for tracking software use to prevent unauthorized copying and distribution.

NOTE   The use of peer-to-peer file sharing technology should be monitored to ensure that the technology is not used to enable unauthorized distribution, display, performance, or reproduction of software to avoid licensing requirements.

Licensing Models

There are several prominent types of licensing models. Each has benefits that are best leveraged in specific operational situations. In other words, the organization should select licensing models based on how the software is going to be used. Vendors of software may offer variations on the major licensing models. The results are many types and permutations of licensing models too numerous to be addressed in this chapter. Keep in mind that the principle function of software licensing is to permit an end user to use the software in a prescribed manner without violating copyright laws. Every new copy of a piece of software that is installed has its own unique license code, regardless of whether it has previously been installed. Various types of licensing models exist, including the following:

- The most commonly used type of license is the end-user license agreement (EULA). This type of license is used for all of the paid-for software and is a legal contract between a software application author or publisher and the user of that application.

- A site license is a method to obtain multiple end-user licenses at one cost. The same piece of software is available to a negotiated number of users (or seats, as the number is sometimes called). The cost of a site license may seem prohibitive, but the advantages of accommodating multiple users, sometimes unlimited users, can be cost-effective over the longer term. Site licenses can help organizations avoid software usage penalties and expensive increases when usage is reviewed by the vendor.

- A subscription software license is a multiple-user or organizational-level license option that generally includes software maintenance, product upgrades, and access to technical and developer support for a negotiated period of time. A benefit of this model is that it reduces the chances of illegitimate copies or unauthorized users in an organization having access. It is more expensive than a per-license option. But if the cost of adjusting licenses at periodic reviews (called the *true-up process*) or fines levied for copyright infringement are considered, subscription licensing is a favorable alternative for purchasers. A security implication for subscriptions is that software currency is enterprise-wide. Legacy software platforms that require particular patching (if patches are developed) or maintenance attention cost time and effort that could be reallocated.

- A perpetual license is like a subscription in that one fee is paid and a negotiated number of users can use the software. There will likely be a term of service that will include upgrades, updates, support, and maintenance from the developer or a representative. However, unlike subscription software licenses, perpetual licenses are valid forever, not for a prescribed period of time. However, vendor support will be limited to a period of time. The other caveat is that the perpetual license usually stipulates a specific version of the software. The terms and conditions for maintenance and upgrades may extend the versioning, but the perpetual license will apply to a certain version of the software. Updates may be provided, but not in perpetuity and not for free.

■ A consumptive license is a negotiated arrangement for an up-front payment for a specified period of time, too. The difference is that the arrangement also includes a pay-as-you-go cost for each use. The volume of use is reviewed periodically. Payment for use could be provided prior to the review, but typically the cost is settled upon review. This version is the most flexible, but it requires the most management from the organization or purchaser, as periodic review must coincide with budget planning and oversight activities.

With the advent of cloud computing, access to software as a service (SaaS) has become a method for organizations to gain the use of applications. There can be one user or multiple users at a time, but the owner of the software provides no access to source code. Application development is limited to presentation layer customization. SaaS, it must be noted, is not a type of software licensing. It is an example of a technology service that should be managed by other service-level agreements. The software access is provided as part of a hosting agreement. That hosting agreement addresses access and authorized use of the software.

NOTE Open-source software is not necessarily free of licensing considerations. Often, security practitioners can examine the source code, while application and system developers are allowed to study, change, and improve the software. However, open-source software does have constraints on how users can use the derivatives of the software.

TIP Freeware is a special type of licensing category that requires no purchase, but the source code and copyrights are retained by the developer.

Software Library

Central to the software library is the approved product list (APL) that the organization maintains. This list contains all the software that is tested and approved for use by authorized individuals. The inventory helps security professionals assess the vulnerability management of the assets as well as assist procurement staff with licensing requirements. According to the Center for Internet Security (CIS) Basic Set of Critical Controls, security professionals must have an inventory of and control of software assets.

The significance of the software library in a security context is that the organization without one does not have control of or access to code updates of software developed internally. This can lead to increased risk of compromise. In this sense the software library is a repository of data and programming code that is used to develop software programs and applications. Within the library are prewritten code, classes, procedures, scripts, configuration data, and more. The software library can be connected to a program to achieve more functionality or to automate a process without writing additional code.

Monitoring and Reporting

From a security perspective, an asset management process must include processes for endpoint and network node monitoring and reporting. Many organizations use automated scanning tools integrated into their reporting environment to ensure that the endpoints and nodes meet the security baselines and patch levels. These tools can often be configured or used in conjunction with dedicated tools to evaluate the software licensing on the endpoints and nodes. The results of the scans can then be compared to the organization's definitive APL and approved pre-coded apps. A guide for implementing a software monitoring and reporting process is NIST SP 800-40r3. This guidance covers identifying which software and versions of software are installed on each host.

There are several measurements that security professionals can use to conduct reporting and monitoring:

- How often are hosts checked for missing updates?

- How often are asset inventories for host applications updated?

- What percentage of software in the environment is not on the APL?

NOTE   Network access control (NAC) is a security asset control process that brings together antivirus, host intrusion prevention, and vulnerability scanning on endpoints and combines them with machine-level authentication to the network to enforce access and authorization controls. In the context of asset security, effective NAC controls can be implemented to ensure that software on endpoints is up to date for patching and licensing concerns are satisfied pre-admission (before access to the network is granted) and post-admission (via a scan of all connected devices).

PROTECT PRIVACY

One way to think about privacy is that it is why we provide security. One part of the security triad, confidentiality, is the provision of privacy. Of course, security is also a method of ensuring information integrity and availability.

Today, individual privacy is a growing global concern. It is helpful to have a general knowledge of the building blocks that led us to the present day, where individual information confidentiality, consent, and control over data collected, stored, and used belonging to data subjects informs security policy and procedures. From a security perspective, it is vital to have a command of the various international regulations dealing with privacy relevant to current regulations.

Cross-Border Privacy and Data Flow Protection

Many countries around the world, especially in Europe and Latin America, have information privacy or data protection laws. In the United States, there is no comprehensive information privacy law, but rather several sectoral or industry-based laws are used. The next section provides a sample of leading privacy regulations that are frameworks to translate expectations of individual privacy into legal standards. Privacy law has an increasingly large domain of issues to try to address, including domestic surveillance, identification systems, social networking sites, video surveillance, DNA databases, and airport body scanners. Technology advances will continue to force privacy regulations to adapt and change at a fast pace in line with the impact of the Internet, the advancements of cryptography, and any other progress in technology that improves privacy.

European Union

As contemporary privacy protection regulation, the European Union (EU) published a comprehensive set of articles and principles for data protection rules in 1995. The central objective of the Data Directive (Directive 95/46 EC) was protection of individuals with regard to the processing of personal data and the limitation of movement of such data. The general principle of the directive was that personal data should not be processed at all, except when certain conditions are met. These conditions fall into three categories: transparency, legitimate purpose, and proportionality. For the EU, the directive is directly attached to privacy and human rights law. For more than two decades, the directive was the prevailing privacy law. Each member of the EU implemented it differently. Advances in technology in an increasingly connected world exposed gaps in how privacy was protected. For these reasons, the EU General Data Protection Regulation (GDPR) was created and adopted in April 2016. The Data Directive be replaced, and GDPR became enforceable on May 25, 2018.

The GDPR is intended to reform the Data Directive to strengthen online privacy rights in a global economic environment. There are some significant changes worth highlighting. The following list is not comprehensive:

- A single set of rules on data protection, valid across the EU. Each EU nation has a national protection authority. However, rules are streamlined under a single market construct to reduce administrative complexity, cost, and burden for compliance.

- Strengthening individuals' rights so that the collection and use of personal data is limited to the minimum necessary.

- Rights to data portability to more easily transfer personal data from one service provider to another.

- The "right to be forgotten" is explicitly recognized. The Data Directive limited the processing of data that causes unwarranted and substantial damage or distress to all personal data from anywhere in the EU when there is no compelling reason for its processing. The GDPR expanded individual rights to allow the subject to demand removal of their information.

- EU rules continue to apply to organizations outside the EU that handle the data of EU citizens, but it has clarified and strengthened data breach notification requirements.

- EU enforcement is increased, with between 2 percent and 4 percent of a business organization's annual revenue at risk of fines and penalties for data protection infractions.

- More effective enforcement of the rules in that police involvement and criminal prosecution are tied to violations of privacy rules.

Under the Data Directive, global companies could achieve safe harbor status. This meant that the EU could determine that a foreign organization had sufficient data protection policy and procedures, and although not directly subject to the Data Directive, the organization voluntarily demonstrated an ability to be compliant with the directive. The U.S. Department of Commerce oversaw the list and required registrants to renew annually. With the advent of GDPR, safe harbor is no longer the standard. Under GDPR, companies have to attest and demonstrate that they meet the high standards of the new guidance. If the EU evaluates that a company's standards and procedures are sufficient, the company could be placed on a list known as the Privacy Shield list.

Safe Harbor Transition to Privacy Shield

The International Safe Harbor Privacy Principles were developed between 1998 and 2000 and were meant to provide a level of assurance that the privacy controls of U.S. organizations were adequate to protect EU citizen data, per EU Data Directive standards. The Safe Harbor provisions allowed self-certification by U.S. companies. The U.S. Department of Commerce developed privacy frameworks to guide compliance and oversaw the program for U.S. interests.

The U.S. control frameworks were deemed adequate in 2000. However, in 2015, the European Commission ruled that a new framework for transatlantic data flows was needed. This action was in response to the U.S. repeatedly failing to follow the directive.

This was true for U.S. entities including the U.S. government. The EU determined that a stricter model was necessary. The prevailing safe harbor agreement was ruled invalid.

NOTE Safe harbor under the Data Directive differs from the concept of safe harbor under U.S. HIPAA. Under U.S. law, if an organization can demonstrate that the risk of unauthorized disclosure of data is not present, a data incident can be considered nonreportable to regulators and affected people. A common example of this is a lost laptop with protected health information stored on it. If the laptop has a verifiable encryption algorithm that is validated by FIPS 140-2, the loss is granted safe harbor, not reportable, because the data is rendered unreadable by unauthorized readers by the encryption. Safe harbor in this context is not impacted by the passing of GDPR.

In 2016, the European Commission and the United States launched a new framework for transatlantic data flows. This new arrangement is called the EU-US Privacy Shield and replaces the International Safe Harbor Agreement. However, the intent is still the same: to enable the transfer of personal data from EU citizens to U.S. commercial organizations. The agreement makes data transfer easier while giving data subjects the privacy protection they expect from their own nations.

Note that the EU-US Privacy Shield designation is specific to the United States. Other data transfer arrangements have been approved by the EU for other countries. There are a few countries that the EU considers to have adequate data protection levels and so data transfers are permitted. The countries that are cleared include Argentina, Canada, Israel, New Zealand, Switzerland, and Uruguay. For countries that are not explicitly approved, adequacy for data protection by those companies in non–EU nations is achieved by the use of standard contract clauses in individual agreements with EU data controllers, called *model clauses*, to meet EU requirements. Another component of compliance for non–EU companies is the use of binding corporate rules that adhere to EU requirements. Binding corporate rules are like a code of conduct for a company and its information protection practices. In general, the privacy protections in place for either a corporation, especially a multinational firm, or an entire nation undergo a process to determine adequacy from the EU before data transfer is approved.

Asia-Pacific Economic Cooperation Cross-Border Privacy Rules

To build trust in the cross-border flow of personal information, the APEC CBPR system was developed by APEC economies with input and assistance from industry and civil society. Currently, there are five participating APEC CBPR countries. Those are the

United States, Mexico, Japan, Canada, and the Republic of Korea. Businesses that agree to participate must adopt the data privacy policies outlined in the APEC CBPR. An independent APEC CBPR Accountability Agent—an entity authorized by the APEC—assesses participating businesses for ongoing compliance. The agent's assessments are enforceable by law. In addition to the five countries already participating, several more are expected to agree to the framework, including the European Commission. The GDPR is being discussed for certification within the APEC CBPR system.

U.S. Data Privacy Laws and Guidelines

In the United States, data privacy is handled as functional concern or regulated within an industry. A typical category of sensitive data is PII. PII is any information that can be used for the purpose of identifying, locating, or contacting any specific individual, either combined with other easily accessible sources or by itself. Government organizations have regulations requiring adequate safeguarding of PII. Commercial organizations may be subject to those regulations, but also to contractual requirements. Some of the most prominent U.S. privacy regulations include the Fair Credit Reporting Act (FCRA), the Gramm-Leach-Bliley Act (GLBA), the Privacy Act, the Children's Online Privacy Protection Act (COPPA), and the Family Educational Rights and Privacy Act (FERPA). Using NIST SP 800-122, some common examples of PII include the following:

- Name, such as full name, maiden name, mother's maiden name, or alias
- Personal identification number, such as Social Security number (SSN), passport number, driver's license number, taxpayer identification number, patient identification number, or financial account or credit card number
- Address information, such as street address or email address
- Asset information, such as Internet Protocol (IP) or Media Access Control (MAC) address or other host-specific persistent static identifier that consistently links to a particular person or small, well-defined group of people
- Telephone numbers, including mobile, business, and personal numbers
- Personal characteristics, including photographic image (especially of face or other distinguishing characteristic), X-rays, fingerprints, or other biometric image or template data (e.g., retina scan, voice signature, facial geometry)
- Information identifying personally owned property, such as vehicle registration number or title number and related information
- Information about an individual that is linked or linkable to one of the previous (e.g., date of birth, place of birth, race, religion, weight, activities, geographical indicators, employment information, medical information, education information, financial information)

This list is broad by design. Some of these identifiers are not considered sensitive by themselves. For example, an address found in a public listing is not considered PII. For information that may be available publicly, like names, addresses, email addresses, and so on, it is important to know how that information was obtained. A set of information termed *nonpublic personal information* (NPI) includes those identifiers that are considered public unless the information was obtained by deriving it in whole or in part using personally identifiable financial information that is not publicly available, such as financial account numbers.

In addition to PII, identifiers can also be composed of a subset of sensitive information defined and regulated by another law. For example, X-ray image information is also PHI and is subject to HIPAA. PHI is personally identifiable data that deals with information related to an individual's medical history, including, but not limited to, information related to health status, healthcare provision, or healthcare payment. Some examples of this include diagnosis codes (ICD-10), date of treatment, images, genetic information, or DNA.

PHI is rather broadly interpreted and includes any sort of medical payment history or records of a patient that can be identified individually and produced or received by healthcare providers, including health plan operators and health clearing houses. PHI may be related to the present, past, or future health of an individual, in either physical or mental terms. PHI may also include the current condition of an individual regarding health. In general, PHI can be utilized for the identification of any specific individual. Additionally, it refers to information that is maintained as well as transmitted in any given form such as electronic, paper, or speech.

In the United States, organizations that handle PHI are subject to HIPAA. Specific sections of the law include a Privacy Rule and a Security Rule to guide organizations on required and addressable (recommended but not mandatory) controls for the proper protection of PHI.

PII and PHI are regulated and of top concern in the United States because of the potential harm that loss, theft, or unauthorized access can have on individuals whose information is compromised. This is a consideration above and beyond the detrimental impact a data breach of PII or PHI can have on an organization in terms of reputational harm, financial costs, and operational loss.

The need to protect the privacy of PII and PHI has become increasingly important. The data can be used to commit crimes and disrupt the lives of individuals. For instance, a stolen medical record can be used to falsify an identity to open credit accounts and obtain medical care in the name of the affected person. In many cases, the affected person does not know their identity is being used to fraudulently obtain credit accounts or medical care until he or she receives inexplicable bills or credit agency calls, or their insurance maximum limits are reached. This impact is particularly true for U.S. people with private health insurance.

The theft of data has been a high-profile news story over the last few years. Uber had the personal data of 57 million drivers and users stolen. Equifax was breached in 2017 and exposed the Social Security numbers, birth dates, and addresses of 143 million people. Between 1 and 3 billion users worldwide were potentially impacted by the data breach of Yahoo in 2013. The ease of committing the crimes, along with how difficult it is to catch cyber criminals, favors the adversary. With the increase in frequency and severity, global regulators have increased guidance, oversight, and enforcement to address privacy protections. Sanctions, fines, and penalties have increased in similar frequency and severity against organizations that fail to exercise due diligence and due care in handling sensitive information, concepts covered later in this chapter. The first step for you as a Certified Information Systems Security Professional (CISSP) in assuring proper information handling is to know the regulations applicable to your industry and jurisdiction and then take steps to align that guidance with organizational policy and procedures.

NOTE   PHI may not have any traditional PII elements within the data set. For instance, the record may not include a Social Security number or a name. However, if multiple health data elements, such as diagnosis, age, gender, and date or treatment provide sufficient information to identify a person, it may be considered PHI and subject to HIPAA.

TIP   Every organization that handles PHI on behalf of a healthcare organization is subject to HIPAA as a *business associate*. However, not every organization that collects, uses, and discards health information is subject to HIPAA. Records related to education may contain health information, but are subject to FERPA.

The Privacy Act of 1974 (U.S.)

Although enacted in 1974, the U.S. Privacy Act continues to play a foundational and relevant role in protecting individual privacy with respect to information collected, used, and stored by the U.S. government. Even though the act is applicable only to U.S. federal government agencies, the Privacy Act certainly has led to later privacy laws and regulations both in the government and in private-sector organizations, even as those regulations had security practices as their emphasis. One example is HIPAA, which protects the privacy and security of information used in healthcare, and another is the FCRA, enforced by the Federal Trade Commission to promote the accuracy, integrity, fairness, and privacy of consumer information.

The Privacy Act protects the creation, use, and maintenance of records that contain personal identifiers such as a name, Social Security number, or other identifying number or symbol. Individuals can seek access to information maintained on them as well as request corrections if something is in error. When someone makes a request, organizations subject to the Privacy Act must provide an accounting of disclosures to the individual to document how the information has been shared. The Privacy Act does not allow disclosure of the sensitive information unless it is under limited permissible uses. Where records are allowed to be shared, the records must be registered in a System of Records Notice (SORN). The register is published in the U.S. Federal Register and posted to the Internet.

Fair Information Practice Principles

The Fair Information Practice Principles (FIPPs) are guidelines authored by the U.S. FTC. These guidelines are not enforceable by law. However, they are widely accepted as a necessary baseline for fair information practice in an electronic marketplace. Organizations that adhere to FIPPs do so through a process of self-regulation in an effort to maintain privacy-friendly, consumer-oriented data collection practices. The principles are categorized as follows:

- **Notice:** Before collecting personal information, organizations should tell consumers and provide awareness about information practices that the business follows. The following information must be explicitly disclosed in the notification:

  - Identification of the entity collecting the data, the uses to which the data will be put, and any potential recipients of the data

  - The nature of the data collected and the means by which it is collected

  - Whether the data requested is provided voluntarily or required

  - The steps taken by the organization to ensure the confidentiality, integrity, and quality of the data

- **Consent:** Consumers should be given choice and consent options to control how their data is used. Usually, consumers express their choice through an opt-in (affirmative consent) or opt-out (affirmative decline) selection. These choices determine whether and how an organization can use the data, especially beyond the initial purpose.

- **Access:** Consumers must be able to participate at some level in the collection of their data. This means that the consumer has the ability to view the data collected as well as verify and contest its accuracy. The consumer must be able to participate in an inexpensive and timely manner.

- **Integrity:** Organizations that gather personal information have an obligation to ensure that it is accurate and secure. One way to maintain the accuracy, and also abide by the access principle, is to have consumers verify the information. Integrity and security are also achieved by limiting access to the information internally and externally as part of this principle.

- **Enforcement:** Although the FIPPs are not law, they can be enforced, and consumers are given methods for redress. There are three means of enforcement of the FIPPs: self-regulation by the information collectors or an appointed regulatory body, private remedies for consumers that give civil causes of action for individuals whose information has been misused to sue violators, and government enforcement that can include civil and criminal penalties levied by the government.

Personal Information Protection and Electronic Documents Act (Canada)

PIPEDA applies to all private-sector organizations in Canada that are federally regulated and use personal information for commercial purposes. PIPEDA does not apply to government agencies or organizations that do not engage in commercial, for-profit activities. It sets out the ground rules for how businesses must handle personal information in the course of their commercial activity. PIPEDA establishes an obligation that any collection, use, or disclosure of personal information must only be for purposes that a reasonable person would deem appropriate given the circumstances. PIPEDA contains 10 fair information principles:

- **Accountability:** An organization is responsible for personal information under its control. It must appoint someone to be accountable for its compliance with these fair information principles.

- **Identifying Purposes:** The purposes for which the personal information is being collected must be identified by the organization before or at the time of collection.

- **Consent:** The knowledge and consent of the individual are required for the collection, use, or disclosure of personal information, except where inappropriate.

- **Limiting Collection:** The collection of personal information must be limited to that which is needed for the purposes identified by the organization. Information must be collected by fair and lawful means.

- **Limiting Use, Disclosure, and Retention:** Unless the individual consents otherwise or it is required by law, personal information can only be used or disclosed for the purposes for which it was collected. Personal information must only be kept as long as required to serve those purposes.

- **Accuracy:** Personal information must be as accurate, complete, and up-to-date as possible to properly satisfy the purposes for which it is to be used.

- **Safeguards:** Personal information must be protected by appropriate security relative to the sensitivity of the information.

- **Openness:** An organization must make detailed information about its policies and practices relating to the management of personal information publicly and readily available.

- **Individual Access:** Upon request, an individual must be informed of the existence, use, and disclosure of their personal information and be given access to that information. An individual shall be able to challenge the accuracy and completeness of the information and have it amended as appropriate.

- **Challenging Compliance:** An individual shall be able to challenge an organization's compliance with the previous principles. Their challenge should be addressed to the person accountable for the organization's compliance with PIPEDA, usually their chief privacy officer.

A variety of circumstances may affect the application of PIPEDA. For example, in some provinces, separate rules that limit the applicability of the federal law apply to municipalities, universities, schools, and hospitals. Similarly, if an entity is doing business exclusively inside Alberta, British Columbia, or Quebec, their respective provincial privacy laws apply. Consequently, applying the appropriate privacy protections to the information processed by an organization in Canada, as in most jurisdictions, requires addressing the unique regulatory environment in which the organization operates.

Nevertheless, PIPEDA has national reach and impact. PIPEDA brings Canada into compliance with the EU Data Directive. Under the new GDPR in the European Union, Canada has a partial adequacy designation with respect to trust in data transfers from the EU to Canada.

TIP An exception to PIPEDA is information collected, used, or stored for the purpose of journalism, art, or literary material.

Data Owners

An important component of understanding privacy principles and data protection is to start with clear roles and responsibilities for the assets. One important role is the data owner. Data owners can have legal rights and complete control over information and can authorize or deny access to that information. Their role in the context of privacy is central. The data owner is the person or group of individuals in an organization responsible and accountable for the data. In most organizations, this responsibility is a senior position, to include a CEO or president of the company, but particular data-related tasks can be delegated. The data owner is where the accountability resides ultimately. The data owner can be held liable for negligence in the event that sensitive data that they own is misused or disclosed in an unauthorized way. The extent of a data owner's responsibility can be established and enforced through legal or regulatory measures. The organization's data policy will outline the manner in which the data owner may use, collect, share, and store data that they own. All data, but especially data with a sensitivity level, must be assigned to an owner.

TIP A data owner sets data use and asset protection rules. In collaboration with information system owners, the data owner will determine the security controls for access and use for data within the system.

NOTE Data owner has synonymous terms used in other guidelines. Consider information owner or steward as interchangeable terms, for instance.

Expectations for the data owner are to provide due care and due diligence. These are primarily legal terms that guide information protection activities.

Due care, in terms of asset management, is using reasonable measures and efforts to protect assets deemed valuable or assigned sensitivity levels. An example of providing due care is keeping and maintaining an accurate asset inventory. Additionally, due care extends to ensuring that all assets are classified appropriately and the classifications are accurate based on the information contained on the asset.

Due diligence is taking all expectable or practical steps to maintain due care. The importance of due care and due diligence is in incident response or data breach investigation. Organizations that demonstrate due care and due diligence may be able to reduce culpability and liability. An example of due diligence begins with an acknowledgment that valuable assets are found throughout an organization and significant effort must be made to account for and assess them. This will allow the organization to properly evaluate risk and protection strategies. Assets are no longer relegated to stationary boundaries. Assets like laptops, thumb drives, and portable devices are mobile. As data moves to the cloud, tangible and intangible assets and, therefore, due diligence extend to the cloud environment too.

Data Controllers

The data controller is the natural or legal person, public authority, agency, or other body that, alone or jointly with others, determines the purposes and means of the processing of personal data. The controller is responsible for adhering to the principles relating to processing personal data. To that end, the controller has to be able to demonstrate compliance with the principles of lawfulness, fairness, transparency, data minimization, accuracy, storage limitation and integrity, and confidentiality of personal data. Data controllers negotiate privacy protections for personal data with data processors via secure contractual terms and assurances, called *data processing agreements*.

Data Processors

The value in data is often in the sharing or exchange of the information between authorized entities. The party responsible for transferring, transmitting, or otherwise sharing data on behalf of a data owner is a data processor. Data processors have a distinct role in the protection of data. In a healthcare setting, data exchange can be important in the safe and proper conduct of patient care, appropriate treatment, managing billing, and other organizational operations. In banking, the data supports business and individual investments as well as creditworthiness. The regulatory focus in GDPR and HIPAA, as examples, reflects the importance of data processing responsibilities.

ASSET SECURITY

2

NOTE   A data processor is not synonymous with a data controller. The key difference is a data processor does not have legal responsibility and accountability for the data, as does a data controller. The processor performs data manipulation on behalf of the data controller. A data controller is an entity that determines the purposes, conditions, and means of processing the personal data. Figure 2.3 depicts the relationship between data processors and data controllers.

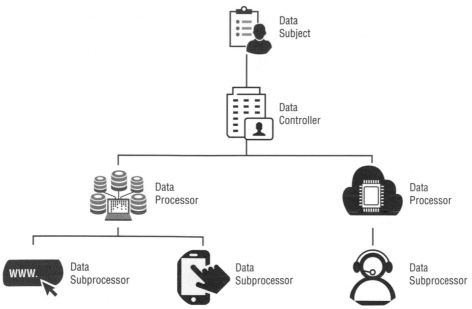

- Data controller determines the need and how the data will be processed.
- Data processor is a separate legal entity processing data for the controller.
    — Cloud providers are generally considered data processors, as are market research firms, payroll companies, accountants.

FIGURE 2.3   Relationship between Data Processor and Data Controller

In some instances, people in organizations play both roles as data processor and data controller. For instance, a human resources firm would have data about their own employees and would be a data controller in this sense. However, if the firm provides outsourced human resource actions for other clients, the human resources firm would be a data processor for the client data, while the individual clients remain the data controllers.

Data Stewards

In the various functional areas of a business such as finance, human resources, sales, or IT, the organization will assign people who are responsible for the formation and execution of policies for the management of data and metadata. These individuals play an important role in the data governance process as subject-matter experts on the categorization of the data, data definitions for its use, and implementing the data governance policies in their area of responsibility. They manage the data quality requirements to ensure fitness of data that is within their business area. Fitness of data includes concerns such as the ability to use the data for its intended purpose in a format that is readable. Data stewards establish internal and external data access requirements for data in their functional area.

Data Custodians

In an organization, the data governance process should include a role for the data custodian. The data custodian role differs from the data steward. Data custodians implement the data delivery process in partnership with the data steward. However, the data custodian is much more concerned with the technologies used in data management and the tools that assist data users with the secure use of the data. There may be one or more people assigned as data custodians.

Data Remanence

Although many popular crime shows on TV depict a fictitious ability to recover any digital data on any medium, it is true that insufficient deletion of data can result in the compromise of the information. Residual data can remain on media if not disposed of properly, and recovery of that data by unauthorized viewers is possible. Data remanence occurs when data destruction efforts were insufficient to prevent the reconstruction of the data.

The underlying principle is that data simply deleted from a hard drive, CD, DVD, USB drive, or backup tape is not sufficiently discarded; in using the deletion command, only the pointers to the data are removed, not the data itself. Data with higher sensitivity classifications, marked as confidential or labeled as PHI, for instance, must follow rigorous destruction methods. The destruction must be certified, and evidence of the destruction/certification must be kept as a proper documentation of the process. A certificate of destruction from the entity that destroyed the data, signed by the persons who oversaw the data destruction, is usually sufficient.

The use of cloud providers has introduced some challenges with respect to data remanence. It takes significant collaboration from the cloud provider to make secure data destruction possible. The cloud user or tenant is not given access to the physical drive, only to a higher-level abstraction like file systems. Techniques such as overwriting file sectors are not possible as they are with on-premises data centers that the organization owns and operates. In SaaS/PaaS (Platform as a Service) environments, access happens only on the data level. In cloud environments, the alternative is to encrypt the data and keep the key outside the cloud environment where the data resides. When the data is no longer needed and the key is deleted, the data is rendered unusable and unreadable. This is not a perfect solution, but because cloud providers allocate resources and cloud users cannot control where the physical assets that house the data reside, overwrite methods are impossible.

The rules and regulations that govern the destruction of data often dictate the level of protection that must be applied to various types of sensitive information. Several U.S. federal laws are potentially applicable to organizations relative to data destruction, including the GLBA, which limits the disclosure and use of customer information and imposes a security rule for financial institutions. HIPAA regulates the handling of customer medical records and information. The FCRA governs the use, disclosure, and disposal of information in reports about consumer credit and credit ratings. The approved European standard BSEN 15713 defines the code of practice for the secure destruction of confidential information. It applies to any organization that collects, transports, and destroys confidential materials. BSEN 15713 can be integrated with other management system standards, most commonly ISO 9001.

The specific requirements of the frameworks and regulations are notable. For example, in the U.S. National Security Agency (NSA) Central Security Service (CSS) Policy Manual 9-12, there is guidance for countermeasures against data remanence. The requirements begin with removing all labels and markings that indicate previous use and classification. After that, the requirements vary depending on the type of medium being used. Some of the requirements include the following:

- Sanitize magnetic tapes and disks by degaussing using an NSA/CSS–evaluated degausser and/or incinerating by burning the material, reducing it to ash. In doing so, the following criteria apply:
  - It is highly recommended to physically damage the hard disk drive by deforming the internal platters prior to release by any means or by using a hard disk drive crusher.

- Hard disks can be degaussed by using a degaussing wand, disassembling the device, and erasing all surfaces of the enclosed platters.
- Disintegrate the hard disk into particles that are nominally 2 millimeter edge-length in size. It is highly recommended to disintegrate hard disk drive storage devices in bulk with other storage devices.
- Shredding of smaller diskettes is allowed using an approved crosscut shredder. Remove the diskette cover and metal hub prior to shredding.

- Optical storage devices including CDs, DVDs, and Blu-ray disks (BDs) can be sanitized in the following ways:
  - The only way BDs can be sanitized is by incinerating the material and reducing it to ash. The other methods listed here do not work for them. Incineration also works for CDs and DVDs.
  - CDs and DVDs can be disintegrated.
  - CDs and DVDs can be shredded.
  - CDs and DVDs can be embossed/knurled by using an approved optical storage device embosser/knurler.
  - CDs can be sanitized by approved grinders. DVDs or BDs cannot be sanitized by grinding.

- For solid-state storage devices, including random access memory (RAM), read-only memory (ROM), Field Programmable Gate Array (FPGA), smart cards, and flash memory, the following methods are acceptable:
  - Disintegrate into particles that are nominally 2 millimeter edge-length in size using an approved disintegrator; it is recommended to do this in bulk with multiple storage devices together.
  - Incinerate the material to ash.
  - Smart cards can be sanitized using strip shredding to a maximum of 2 millimeters or cutting the smart card into strips diagonally at a 45-degree angle, ensuring that the microchip is cut through the center. Also, make sure that the barcode, magnetic strip, and written information are cut into several pieces and the written information is unreadable. Cross-cut shredders are *not* allowed for this shredding.

The requirements of BSEN 15713 are similar and include the following:

- There must be a confidential destruction premises.
- A written contract covering all transactions should exist between the client and the organization; subcontractors must follow the guidelines too.

- Personnel doing this work must be trained, be certified, and have passed a Criminal Records Bureau (CRB) check or Disclosure or Barring Service (DBS) check.

- Confidential material to be collected should remain protected from unauthorized access from the point of collection to complete destruction.

- The trucks that are used to collect and transport protected material have specific requirements, including being box-shaped, having the ability for drivers to communicate to base stations, being lockable, and not being left unattended, and so on.

- In addition to the destruction focus, there is consideration for environmental issues, and recycling is allowed under certain conditions.

- There are prescribed due diligence checks that should be conducted in addition to the stated requirements. These include checking the licenses of drivers, physical checking of trucks and destruction areas, and so on.

There are two general approaches to data destruction. The first approach is to render the actual device containing the media useless. Physical destruction of the media, electromagnetic degaussing, and incineration are common tactics. If the organization intends to repurpose the device after destroying the sensitive data, this approach would be appropriate. If the media is not rewritable, physical destruction is the only method that will ensure the information is destroyed.

The other type of asset disposal is by cleansing or sanitizing the media/drive. The physical media can therefore be reused, but there is no trace of data remanence after the data-wiping action. There are numerous validated processes for this objective.

Asset disposal policy should differentiate between assets being reused within the organization and those to be repurposed outside of the organization. For example, an asset to be reallocated internally may be sufficiently sanitized by a lower level of sanitization (e.g., reformatting or re-imaging the hard drive). This scenario does not preclude the organization from mandating the highest levels of sanitization if the assets are deemed critical or the data is sensitive. Some different tactics to achieve desired levels of security assurance with specific steps and instructions are available in NIST SP 800-88, "Guidelines for Media Sanitization", at `http://nvlpubs.nist.gov/nistpubs/SpecialPublications/NIST.SP.800-88r1.pdf`.

To achieve a level of assurance of adequate asset sanitization, the following techniques can be used:

- **Purging:** This is the indisputable erasing of data from the storage device in such a way that the data may never be recovered. It can be accomplished by overwrite, block erase, and cryptographic erasure, through the use of dedicated, standardized device sanitize commands.

- **Cleansing or clearing:** The organization can use software or hardware products to overwrite storage space on the media with nonsensitive data, using the standard read and write commands for the device.

- **Destruction:** The organization can purge media before submitting it for destruction. There are numerous ways to physically destroy media. Some of the traditional and acceptable methods are drive shredders, pulverization, incineration, and acid.

Examples of specific techniques to achieve the desired level of assurance in sanitization requirements include the following:

- **Zeroing:** This erases data on the disk and overwrites it with all zeros.

- **Degaussing:** This is a process whereby the magnetic media is erased, i.e., returned to its initial blank state through the use of high-powered electromagnets.

- **Overwriting:** Data are written to storage locations that previously held sensitive data. To satisfy the Department of Defense (DoD) clearing requirement, it is sufficient to write any character to all data locations in question. It is typical to use random passes of 0 and 1 combinations, not patterns, to overwrite. The number of times an overwrite must be accomplished depends on storage media, sometimes on its sensitivity, and sometimes on differing organizational requirements.

Data Sovereignty

In relationship to the privacy of sensitive personal information, data sovereignty is becoming a more pressing issue. This is in part because of the increasingly global scope of data transfer for many businesses, the use of digital cloud-based technologies, and more stringent government regulations for citizens (e.g., GDPR). Data sovereignty concerns have to be understood to help data controllers and data processors, for example, have clarity around the location of data, the transfer of the data, and the relevant laws to which the data is subject. Privacy concerns can no longer be managed and constrained within one jurisdiction. This is one reason why information security professionals must have awareness and understanding of laws and regulations enacted by multiple entities around the world. No matter what jurisdiction the company itself is in, it is likely the data will cause it to be subject to multiple sources of data sovereignty.

Data sovereignty refers to legislation that covers information that is subject to the laws of the country in which the information is located or stored. Sovereignty of data laws has an impact that is relevant because of the need to exchange data across jurisdictional boundaries for e-commerce; for example, governmental regulations may differ concerning data privacy, data storage, and data processing. There is no overarching regulatory body like the United Nations to enact one policy that every jurisdiction would have to follow. This is a source of technical and legal challenges when trying to share information across national borders. For example, moving data from an on-premises data center to resources offered by a cloud provider can introduce data sovereignty issues.

By definition, variation in data sovereignty laws includes the reality that some laws are stricter than others. Privacy rules in some jurisdictions like Germany and France dictate that data is stored physically within the country only. Keep in mind that data sovereignty can differ within a country if different government or regulatory entities have the jurisdiction to adapt privacy and security controls. For example, in the United States, some federal government agencies require that their data be stored exclusively within the United States.

One way to address the differing data sovereignty concerns is to employ a hybrid or combination data use model where some data can be stored in a public cloud model and sensitive categories of data are kept on premises. This arrangement is particularly useful if a cloud provider cannot certify that data will be stored with the desired jurisdiction.

The EU's GDPR is a recent example of a data sovereignty law. The EU published the GDPR in May 2016. After a two-year transition period, the GDPR went into effect on May 25, 2018. The GDPR applies to the processing of personal data of all data subjects, including customers, employees, and prospects. The regulation applies to organizations and data subjects in the EU. Noncompliance with the GDPR may result in huge fines, which can be the higher of €20M or 4 percent of the organization's worldwide revenues.

NOTE In 2018, China enacted the Cybersecurity Law to emphasize data protection. In that law, China introduced the concept of cyberspace sovereignty to indicate that each country can govern its Internet environment on its own terms.

Data Localization or Residency

Related to data sovereignty, many jurisdictions or governments have laws that require a citizen's (or resident's) data be collected, processed, or stored inside the country. The data may still be transferred internationally, but it has to originate from the country and can be transferred only after local privacy or data protection laws are met. An example of these conditions is notifying a user how the information will be used and obtaining their consent. This is data localization or residency before the data is exchanged outside of the jurisdiction. In some cases, data localization or residency mandates that data about a nation's citizens or residents must be deleted from foreign systems before being removed from systems in the data subject's nation.

India is a good example of some of the common data localization and residency concerns found in governments of many countries. India has several data localization laws and regulations in place, with more contemplated for near-term implementation. For now, the laws apply only to companies gathering data on Indians and only when the company is located in India. As privacy concerns increase and technology advances, India's government will likely expand requirements to multinational corporations and non-government organizations. There is an intentional skew toward restriction of data flows containing personal information. Approval for data flow depends on the organization satisfying two conditions: the data transfer is necessary, and the data subject has provided consent. That the data transfer is necessary has been hard to enforce, so the only element that can be controlled is data subject consent.

For government data, India has enacted increasingly stringent policies. For instance, a "National Data Sharing and Accessibility Policy" exists that effectively means that government data must be stored in India. In 2014, the Indian government strengthened data residency requirements through a policy that requires all email providers to set up local servers for their India operations. All of the data related to communication between two users in India should remain within the country. In another evolution of policy in 2015, the Indian Department of Electronics and Information Technology issued guidelines that cloud providers seeking accreditation for government contracts would have to store all data in India.

Another prominent example is China's Cybersecurity Law. This law was passed in 2016 and increases the national government's jurisdiction over the business of cybersecurity. All Critical Information Infrastructure (CII) is subject to the law. The government has interest in key industries that maintain data that could pose a national security or public interest risk if damaged or lost. Some of the Chinese businesses that are contemplated by the law are in the industries of energy, finance, transportation, telecommunications, electricity, water, gas, and medical and healthcare. Organizations in these industries must not use network products and services that have not passed the government security examination. The need for a government security exam applies to those products and services obtained from non-Chinese sources for use with CII where the use may affect national security, a condition determined by the government agency.

With the use of a cloud provider, data localization or residency highlights several important considerations, including knowing where your data will reside, the contractual obligations the cloud provider has to support the data collectors' responsibilities, and the transparency of data use and destruction by the cloud provider. Remember, as mentioned, in the cloud data remanence is a large concern. Data localization or residency is another valid reason to mandate that the data controller holds the encryption keys to cloud data stores. If the nation requires international organizations to destroy data before the nation does, deleting the encryption key can be a compensating control to make the personal data unreadable and unusable.

Government and Law Enforcement Access to Data

Since 1986 prevailing U.S. regulations have governed law enforcement's ability to access electronic data. First the Electronic Communications Privacy Act (ECPA) and then the Stored Communications Act (SCA) have stated that when the government subpoenas or provides a court order for information, it must be provided if the information has been stored for more than 180 days. If the data has been stored for less than 180 days, it would take a search warrant for law enforcement or government to obtain access. A search warrant requires a higher standard of probable cause to be met by the government or law enforcement. Without question, the ECPA is extremely out of date. With emerging issues like access to foreign service providers and terrorism, access to information by law enforcement has undergone some significant changes.

On March 23, 2018, the U.S. Congress passed the Clarifying Lawful Overseas Use of Data Act (the CLOUD Act), amending key aspects of U.S. surveillance law and providing a framework for cross-border data access for law enforcement purposes. The act addresses two problems that have been the subject of heated debate for the past five years. First, by amending the SCA, the CLOUD Act clarifies that American law enforcement authorities can compel providers of electronic communication services, such as major email service providers and social media networks, to produce data stored outside the United States. The SCA also establishes new rules facilitating foreign law enforcement access to data stored inside the United States. In short, this new legislation impacts any provider that may receive either U.S. or foreign orders to produce data in furtherance of criminal investigations.

There is significant reluctance with high levels of public visibility to these new powers given to government and law enforcement. Recent cases with international companies with U.S. origin like Apple, Microsoft, and Google have tested the reach of government and law enforcement access to information. These cases also illustrate how technological advancements, particularly the cloud and encryption, are rendering even the most recent legal frameworks outdated. Preserving the balance between public security and individual privacy in the context of law enforcement is a dynamic relationship between the incentives of government, technology companies, and individual consumers.

Government and law enforcement access to information in the United States may have special considerations based on industry. For example, in healthcare, HIPAA broadly defines law enforcement as any government official at any level of government authorized to either investigate or prosecute a violation of the law. As such, HIPAA allows law enforcement personnel to have access to medical information without an individual's permission in a number of ways. Disclosures for law enforcement purposes apply not only to doctors or hospitals but also to health plans, pharmacies, healthcare clearinghouses, and medical research labs, as these entities are subject to HIPAA. To access the information, the police need only provide an administrative subpoena or other written request with no court involvement. The police must include a written statement that the information they want is relevant, material, and limited in scope, and that de-identified information is insufficient.

This issue is not just constrained to U.S. law enforcement or government access to data. Access to data by government and law enforcement is a concern in other countries. For example, in Russia, the Russian privacy regulator, Roskomnadzor, issued an order revising notice protocols for companies that process personal data in Russia. The August 2017 order amended earlier regulations and stipulated that companies must notify Roskomnadzor in advance of personal data processing. The companies have to disclose information on safeguards in place to prevent data breaches. If a company intends to transfer data outside of Russia, the company must make known to which countries the data will be transferred. Russia also mandates data localization. Companies that process personal data of Russian citizens must store the data in Russia.

Another aspect of Russian government access to data is through government surveillance. Russia passed the Yarovaya law, named for one of its authors, Irina Yarovaya. Under the umbrella of counterterrorism and national security protections, it provides an expansion of authority for law enforcement agencies, new requirements for data collection, and mandatory decryption in the telecommunications industry. One such requirement is for telecommunications providers to store the content of voice calls, data, images, and text messages for six months, and the metadata on them (e.g., time, location, and sender and recipients of messages) for three years. Authorities can access this data upon request and without a court order. Telecommunications companies are required to provide communications, metadata, Internet, and any other information necessary as defined by government agencies.

Collection Limitation

The best practices in data protection and privacy begin with establishing governance for collection limitation. This privacy principle, *collection limitation*, is addressed in every major privacy framework. The definition of collection limitation is that a data collector should collect only the information that is necessary for the purpose. Within the concept of collection limitation, the principle of consent is worth noting. Data subjects must be able to have knowledge about or give consent for the data being collected. The purpose of the data collection, meaning how the data will be used and why the data is needed, should be disclosed. The data elements to be collected should be constantly evaluated by the organization to make sure collection is limited to only relevant data and that data is maintained for as long as the data supports a legitimate business need.

There are benefits to the organization for limiting collection. In the event there is a data breach, there will be less unauthorized access. Working with the minimum necessary volumes of data helps the organization efficiently keep data accurate and up to date.

Understanding Data States

Data is a volatile asset. As the use of data changes in an organization, the security controls to protect it must change. Depending on the value of the data, it has to be protected no matter what state it is in. Data can be in storage or at rest on backup tapes, on hard drives, or in the cloud. Data is often in use temporarily by applications and web pages. When data is transferred between users or computing assets, it is considered in motion. Some key methods for protecting data as an asset specifically are encryption and access control, to include proper authorization limits. Encryption prevents data visibility in the event of unauthorized access or theft. Figure 2.4 provides examples for data in the various states.

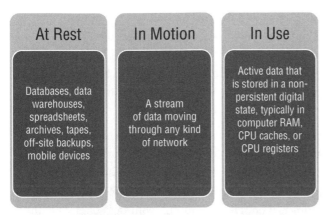

FIGURE 2.4 **Data States and Examples**

NOTE Data protection has evolved over the last several years as initiatives like Big Data have become business imperatives. Big Data is a concept to describe using extremely large sets of data, often sensitive information, and applying complex analytical processes to determine results or meaning. The impacts of Big Data are the same as any data protection, just magnified greatly. You have to account for data storage, collection, privacy, and data sharing.

Data Issues with Emerging Technologies

The emerging themes of emerging technologies present challenges for the proper protection of data. A few of the emerging technologies are cloud computing, the Internet of Things (IoT), machine learning, artificial intelligence (AI), and Big Data. While this chapter does not explore each of these topics in depth, the challenges they present to asset security and protecting the data have some common themes.

- **Volumes of data:** Organizations should ensure that mobile devices and IoT are added to asset inventories. Although this is the right thing to do, the addition of these devices greatly expands an inventory. It is difficult to navigate the sea of data to identify suspicious traffic over the network. There are now multiple infrastructure tiers for storage and computing. Incidents are increasingly hard to identify and alert upon, especially because new compute infrastructures like NoSQL databases have not been thoroughly vetted and are in use. Another issue is the scalability of current encryption capabilities at the large data volumes.

- **Quality of data:** With mobile devices and IoT, the devices that collect, store, and transfer sensitive information also are used for personal reasons and are vulnerable to security risks that could lead to data breaches. Without proper security safeguards, this personal use could jeopardize the quality, security, and confidentiality of the sensitive data.

- **Sharing of data:** This is more accurately defined as the inadvertent sharing of data. IoT, Big Data, and AI are all growing and coming closer to hitting more commercial and mass use cases. With the advent of AI of IoT-like Alexa devices, the ability to process and understand the human voice can lead to collection and transfer of data. AI has reached mainstream adoption. Where this functionality is used in a business context, protections must be put in place.

- **Data accuracy:** Organizations can gather a vast amount of data, analyze it, and generate solutions to the problems they are trying to solve. Because the decisions have to be made in a short amount of time, the organizations also have to have secure technologies and practices to process so much information quickly. Big Data analytics are often performed on samples, not full volumes. Therefore, the results have a greater chance of being inaccurate.

There are some resources that are in various stages of development and maturity that offer guidelines for cybersecurity practices specific to the emerging technologies briefly discussed. Keep in mind that these resources are not limited to asset and data security considerations but applicable to cybersecurity practices in total.

- **NIST Cybersecurity for IoT Program:** Accessible at `https://www.nist.gov/programs-projects/nist-cybersecurity-iot-program`, this program is creating standards, guidelines, and related tools to improve the cybersecurity of connected devices and the environments in which they are deployed.

- **ISO/IEC 27017:2015/ITU-T X.1631:** Information technology—Security techniques—Code of practice for information security controls based on ISO/IEC 27002 for cloud services. This standard provides guidance on the information security aspects of cloud computing, recommending and assisting with the implementation of cloud-specific information security controls, supplementing the guidance in ISO/IEC 27002 and other ISO27k standards.

- **ISO/IEC 27018:2014:** This is tailored for controls and guidelines for implementing measures to protect PII in accordance with the privacy principles in ISO/IEC 29100 for the public cloud computing environment. It establishes commonly accepted control objectives and specifies guidelines based on ISO/IEC 27002. With a focus on PII, it integrates regulatory requirements for the protection of PII.

- **NIST SP 1500-4: NIST Big Data Interoperability Framework: Volume 4, Security and Privacy:** This document is authored by the NIST Big Data Public Working Group (NBD-PWG) and is accessible at `https://nvlpubs .nist.gov/nistpubs/SpecialPublications/NIST.SP.1500-4.pdf`. The group is working to develop consensus on important, fundamental concepts related to Big Data, including privacy and security topics. Within the special publication are security and privacy use cases, proposed security and privacy taxonomies, details of the Security and Privacy Fabric of the NIST Big Data Reference Architecture (NBDRA), and initial mapping of the security and privacy use cases to the NBDRA.

ENSURE APPROPRIATE ASSET RETENTION

The practice of asset retention management dates back to the earliest days of recorded human history, when records were inscribed on mud tablets in Babylon. In fact, the reason historians know of human history is because to some degree proper retention and preservation of records was considered important in those early societies.

Data retention programs serve many purposes. Organizations need to preserve intellectual property. A proper data retention process will support institutional memory. In e-discovery legal or forensic examinations, evidence can be preserved through data retention. In many cases, data retention is an obligation resulting from regulatory and compliance expectations.

The information security professional must address the CIA aspects of information throughout its existence. Absent a data retention process, an organization will experience more incidents of record tampering, data loss, and inappropriate access. Several considerations must be made to establish which types of information should be maintained and for how long. Regulations may establish guidelines based on the category or sensitivity of the data. Examples of information retention regulations include the following:

- HIPAA generally requires healthcare organizations in the United States to maintain records for six years from the date of creation or the date when the information was in effect, whichever is later.

- The PCI DSS provides standards that govern organizations that handle credit card transactions. Organizations should limit cardholder data storage and retention time to that required for business, legal, and/or regulatory purposes. Actual time limits are established per organizational policy.

- In the European Union, the European Court of Justice (ECJ) invalidated EU Data Retention Directive 2006/24/EC and prohibited a blanket law requiring data retention of Internet and telecommunication use by private citizens for a specified period of time. Data collectors must establish organizational policy based on legitimate necessity and limitation of collection. Data must be destroyed when it no longer meets the prerequisites for collection and storage.

Where a regulation or other compliance requirement does not give a specific mandate, organizations must establish asset retention guidelines. These timelines should be relevant to the type of asset (critical, production, etc.) and sensitivity of the data (confidential, public, etc.). Records contain data that is a valuable asset to a business. Asset and data retention is essential for organizations (and society) to protect and preserve records as evidence of actions. An asset management system, including data management, results in a source of information about business activities that can support subsequent activities and business decisions. The process also ensures accountability to present and future stakeholders. Several good references exist for the practice of records management. One is ISO 15489-1:2016, Information and Documentation — Records Management — Part 1: Concepts and Principles. Another is DoD Instruction 5015.02, DoD Records Management Program.

The steps necessary to build a data retention policy are important. The first action is to have a designated person of authority or a steering committee decide what electronic and physical documents the business produces and assign ownership. Next, the person or committee should review relevant state and federal rules on asset and data retention to make sure the policy will align. The team is ready to actually write the policy. A good template of the topics that should comprise the policy is provided below. Once the policy is published in the organization, it is important to train employees on the plan. Continued communication will help ensure success for the processes. On a periodic basis, review the document retention policy and update it as needed.

The list that follows is a general outline to help establish an initial data retention policy. In an organization that already has a data retention policy, this template of steps can be used to review the current policy:

- Document the purpose of the policy.
- Identify who is affected by the policy.
- Identify the types of data and electronic systems covered by the policy.

- Define key terms, especially legal and technical terminology.
- Describe the requirements in detail from the legal, business, and personal perspectives.
- Outline the procedures for ensuring data is properly retained.
- Outline the procedures for ensuring data is properly destroyed.
- Clearly document the litigation exception process and how to respond to discovery requests.
- List the responsibilities of those involved in data retention activities.
- Build a table showing the information type and its corresponding retention period.
- Document the specific duties of a central or corporate data retention team if one exists.

Appendix for additional reference information

The policy should make it clear that during all phases of the data management lifecycle, including destruction, proper secure handling procedures are required.

NOTE   Data retention requirements also apply to security and IT operations audit logs. NIST SP 800-92, "Guide to Computer Security Log Management," offers guidance on log archival, log retention, and log preservation. Data retention requirements are based on factors such as operational need, legal requirements, and, in some cases, a specific incident or event that requires an exception to log management policy.

TIP   Most data should have retention limits, although some data may have permanent value to an organization or society. Keep in mind that indefinite storage may create unnecessary cost, and disclosure of stored data can be required by subpoena in the event of litigation, even if the data is useless to the organization. Unlike data classification where the highest classification is applied to all data in a group as a precautionary best practice, the organization must tailor the data retention length specific to the data sensitivity.

The most important role a security practitioner might have in asset retention is to create and maintain a policy that is informed by and adheres to regulations, meets business objectives, and is understood and followed in the organization. Conducting and documenting training and testing of the policy are important measures of program performance. Users have to be made aware of their responsibilities in maintaining the safeguards during the lifecycle of the asset. Audits should be conducted to assure the organization that the policy and procedures are being followed. A big part of the responsibility is to not dispose of the asset too soon or improperly when the data retention period is exceeded.

Retention of Records

When data is categorized as a collection of related data items documenting a business transaction or satisfying a business need, it is a record. Every business has to establish what it defines as a record. The definition might be established to comply with government regulatory or statutory reporting requirements, to document daily business activities, to document research and development methods, or to preserve the legal rights of the business. Record retention is a balance the security professional must understand. The need of the organization due to regulatory and business requirements to maintain a record have to be assessed and evaluated against the rights of the individual. It is important for security professionals to make sure that the organization understands the different record retention requirements in the organization, record retention requirements are documented in a schedule, and records are maintained according to the schedule and not longer. Unless otherwise mandated by laws and regulations, the organization should not default to the longest required retention period and maintain all records that long. Excessive retention increases risk of data exposure beyond necessary regulatory compliance obligations. The organization should have a periodic review of retained records to reduce volume of both hard- and soft-copy records.

Compliance with record retention requirements is supplemented via active archiving systems. Internationally accepted standards such as ISO 17799 and NIST SP 800-53 r4 provide guidance on information handling and retention requirements over the full lifecycle of information, in some cases extending beyond the disposal of information systems. Archival storage will enable an organization to follow the guidance through a hierarchal storage approach to records management. Some records have to be maintained but are infrequently accessed. Archival helps the organization cost-effectively maintain the information on long-term, slower retrieval systems rather than more expensive, high-speed devices.

Determining Appropriate Records Retention

Security professionals have to stay aware of the various local, national, and international developments that can impact record retention requirements. An example is the emerging enactment and enforcement of the EU GDPR's Article 17, "The Right to Erasure," commonly called "The right to be forgotten." This causes organizations to evaluate previous record retention requirements against the right to be forgotten considerations introduced by Article 17. This provision gives explicit rights to individuals to have their records erased without undue delay. There is an exception for instances where the business or data controller must keep the data for the purposes for which it was collected (e.g., the original business requirement). In this instance, a business requirement can create an exception to regulatory guidance.

There are also regulatory requirements that cause an organization to establish and maintain record retention policies that exceed the internal useful life of the record. An example of this scenario is HIPAA, which requires subject healthcare organizations to maintain documentation related to HIPAA compliance, such as log records pertaining to electronic protected health information (ePHI) review, for six years. While HIPAA mandates a six-year record retention requirement for documentation required to maintain the policies and procedures relevant to HIPAA, U.S. state law generally covers the record retention requirements for patient medical records. See U.S. Code of Federal Regulations (CFR) Section 164.316(b)(1) and 164.316(b)(2)(i) for more detail. The U.S. Department of Health and Human Services (HHS), which has oversight of HIPAA, recommends the six-year record retention minimum in the absence of more specific federal and state-level guidance.

Record retention requirements should also be complemented with de-identification and obfuscation processes. The record retention schedule can include a date when the personal data is no longer needed but other elements are useful for data analytics and trend analysis. This can extend the useful life of the record while protecting the personal information of the individual. Regulatory compliance is met as files are regularly purged and personal data is not retained any longer than is necessary.

Retention of Records in Data Lifecycle

Retention of records in the lifecycle of data is increasingly significant because of the growing volumes of records that a company can maintain and manage due to technology innovations such as digitization, storage file compression, and the cloud. Locating and protecting all of the information in the numerous record storage areas for the organization is a challenge. The security professional must be able to design and implement a records management program to provide ways to identify, maintain, and dispose of company records in a safe, timely, and cost-effective manner.

The use of hierarchical storage management (HSM) is effective as a record storage technique to support a secure lifecycle management process. HSM automatically moves data between high-cost and low-cost storage media. High-speed storage devices like solid-state drive arrays cost more than the slower storage options, such as hard disk drives, optical discs, and magnetic tape drives. Use of high-speed storage is appropriate for frequent retrieval of records and low latency. The bulk of enterprise records do not have a requirement for rapid retrieval, so slower storage devices are appropriate. HSM allows for a copy to be made to faster disk drives when needed. The cache to faster disk storage enables efficiency. The HSM system also supports secure movement of records to slower storage devices according to the organization's record management schedule.

HSM may also be used to support the archiving process, where more robust storage is available for long-term storage. Archiving records is beneficial for records that must be maintained but are rarely used. If an archived record is needed, it is acceptable if retrieval is not immediate. Archiving systems are very cheap for records storage. It is typical to never use archived records after they are saved. The exceptions are in disaster recovery or regulatory requests, namely, audits or subpoenas. An integrated process of active archiving of tiered storage using an HSM system provides the organization with access to records across a virtual file system. The system migrates data between multiple storage systems and media types, including high-speed solid-state drives and relatively slower hard disk drives, magnetic tape, and optical disks. The storage locations can be on site or in the cloud. The result of an active archive implementation is that data can be stored on the most appropriate media type for the given retention and restoration requirements of that data.

Records Retention Best Practices

Each organization must handle and retain records in accordance with applicable laws, directives, policies, regulations, standards, and operational requirements. While the requirements may be different according to geographic jurisdiction or industry-specific considerations, there are several summary-level best practices the security professional can use to model a compliant and effective records management program:

- Maintain records according to the organization's record retention schedule.
- Conduct regular evaluations of the system. There may be triggers to start a review, such as a merger or acquisition. Otherwise, consider a scheduled, periodic review of records in the organization.
- Conduct a review of the actual record retention schedule every other year to make sure the schedule is relevant to business requirements and regulatory requirements.
- Label electronically maintained records.
- Create backup electronic file copies.
- Retain paper copies of records that cannot be accurately or completely transferred to the electronic recordkeeping system.
- Do not keep records longer than is necessary to accomplish the original purpose for which the information was collected.
- Make sure records have valid dates of origin. Movement and use of records can change electronic file dates, but not the date that determines the retention period.
- A reasonable attempt should be made to remove unnecessary electronic records, per the retention schedule, in all identified electronic repositories.

- Maintain information-handling controls over the full lifecycle of information, in some cases extending beyond the disposal of the records.

- Ensure that records remain persistently accessible for the length of the time they are retained according to the frequency with which they are retrieved.

- Deduplicate records to avoid unnecessary storage of multiple copies that increase risk and storage costs.

- Use automated compression utilities and storage tier creation and management.

- Remember to classify and retain emails that are official records. Create an email retention schedule as a subset of the records retention schedule.

- Ensure that records remain accessible for the required retention period by periodically converting and migrating records from media sources, because digital media can degrade or become obsolete over time.

- Securely delete data in accordance with written retention periods and information security and retention policies.

The record retention schedule may be distinct to the organization, but it is foundational to follow best practices to have an effective electronic records retention program. The organization needs to defend its intellectual property rights and provide protection in times of litigation. Appropriate record retention enables organizations to be able to verify the authenticity of the records they keep. As the surge in criticality, value, and volume of digital information continues to grow, records retention is important to prevent the organization from being overwhelmed and records becoming unavailable and unprotected. In sum, while there is no universally applicable records management plan, security professionals need to examine specific requirements at their own enterprises and consider best-practice approaches to best serve the organization.

DETERMINE DATA SECURITY CONTROLS

After assets have been identified and inventoried according to the level of classification, value, and sensitivity, identifying the types and rigor needed for security controls to protect the assets is the next step. There are numerous, proven security controls. With all security controls, the objective is to reduce risk to an acceptable level at a reasonable cost for the organization. Following a proven control design framework best assures a holistic approach to security. The framework also helps organize the process for resource allocation, investment of security spending, and measurement of security preparedness. Security controls help to identify, protect, detect, respond, and recover with respect to security risks to computer systems, data, or another information set. Some proven security control frameworks include the following:

- **ISO/IEC 27001/27002 and ISO/IEC 27018:** A family of standards that provide a systematic approach to formalizing risk management for an information security management system (ISMS) of people, processes, and technology controls. ISO/IEC 27002 includes the catalog of suitable information security controls within the ISMS. ISO/IEC 27018 complements the other frameworks by providing standards for protecting PII in the cloud.

- **NIST SP 800-53/53A:** As mentioned before and as used with NIST 800-37, these are framework documents that inform many other related control standards sources. Although adequate and reasonable for use in commercial organizations, the NIST standards recommend security controls for U.S. federal information systems and organizations. They cover security controls for areas including incident response, access control, ability for disaster recovery, and business continuity. NIST SP 800-53A is used to document and assess security controls for effectiveness.

- **Center for Strategic and International Studies (CSIS) Critical Controls for Effective Cyber Defense:** Referred to as the 20 Critical Controls, this is a document outlining 20 crucial controls that form a risk-based minimum level of information security measures for an organization to implement. The controls are technical in design and focus on high-risk cyber attacks. They are a subset of the comprehensive controls found in other frameworks, most notably NIST SP 800-53/53A.

- **Control Objectives for Information and Related Technologies (COBIT):** Created by the international professional association ISACA, this recommends control objectives for a set of high-level requirements for effective control of each IT process. It subdivides IT into four domains (Plan and Organize, Acquire and Implement, Deliver and Support, and Monitor and Evaluate) and 34 processes.

- **The Committee of Sponsoring Organizations of the Treadway Commission (COSO):** With a view on information security as part of enterprise risk management, COSO originated from the financial industry and assists with integrating strategy and performance within overall enterprise risk management. The five components (Governance and Culture, Strategy and Objective-Setting, Performance, Review and Revision, and Information, Communication, and Reporting) in the updated framework are supported by a set of principles to assess effectiveness.

- **FISMA:** Established to produce several key security standards and guidelines required by congressional legislation. These publications include FIPS 199, FIPS 200, and NIST SPs 800-37, 800-39, 800-53, 800-53A, 800-59, 800-60, and 800-171.

- **Federal Risk and Authorization Management Program (FedRAMP):** This is a U.S. federal government program that provides a standardized approach to security assessment, authorization, and continuous monitoring for cloud products and services.

- **Department of Defense Instruction (DoDI) 8510.01:** This is the Risk Management Framework (RMF) for DoD Information Technology and is meant to be scoped and tailored to DoD organizations with defense missions in the United States.

- **The Australian Government Information Security Manual (ISM):** Used for the risk-based application of information security controls mandatory for government agencies that conduct business under certain provisions outlined in the guide. The guide, however, is encouraged for all other government and commercial businesses. It provides best-practice guidance for making informed risk-based technical and business decisions and implementing strong information security measures. The purpose is to advise users on applying a risk-based approach to protecting their information and systems. The controls are therefore designed to mitigate the most likely threats to Australian government agencies.

- **Information and Communication Technology (ICT) cybersecurity certification:** The EU Commission has developed a common security certification framework for information and communication technology to increase trust and security in products and services that are crucial for the digital marketplace. The framework relies on integration of multiple international standards tailored to the EU organizations.

Technical, Administrative, and Physical Controls

Security control frameworks provide discipline and structure for the organization. They are typically made up of controls that are technical, administrative, and physical. A deeper understanding of each type of control is needed to emphasize the role each plays in securing organizational assets.

- **Technical controls:** The category of controls grouped as technical controls serve to use computer capabilities and automation to implement safeguards. The technical controls defend against misuse or unauthorized access to valuable information. In most organizations, a combination of technical controls is needed to work together to protect, detect, and respond to potential and actual security incidents and events. A few examples of technical controls related to asset management are the use of active and passive asset discovery tools to update the inventory, vulnerability scanning, and monitoring for unauthorized access to assets and data.

- **Administrative controls:** Also known as management controls, administrative controls are the policies, procedures, standards, and guidelines that an organization uses to implement technical and physical controls. The sources of administrative controls can be laws and regulations, industry best practices, and organizational mandates. Administrative controls inform the organization on roles and responsibilities, proper information protection practices, and enforcement actions if controls are not followed.

- **Physical controls:** As information and technology assets transform from paper-based to digital and become more interconnected, physical controls, also referred to as *operational controls*, remain highly important. Controlling physical, human access to information assets is often the least expensive and most effective prevention control we can use. Designing asset protection programs that include guards and receptionists, entry access controls, area lighting and surveillance, closed-circuit television (CCTV), and physical intrusion detection systems provides a layered defense approach.

NOTE Physical, technical, and administrative controls are also defined by their protective purpose. Each type of control can be described as deterrent, preventative, detective, corrective, or recovery. Depending on the control, it may serve multiple functions in the overall security program.

Controls can be prioritized based on risks faced by the organization or specific threats. However, all of the controls work together to provide optimal security. For instance, administrative controls initiate policy and procedures that implement physical controls. Technical controls may implement administrative requirements for access control. Physical controls may be needed to protect the organization's data center, where computing equipment operates to implement technical controls.

Security controls are also designated based on the scope of applicability for the control, the shared nature of the control, and the responsibility for control development, implementation, assessment, and authorization.

Administrative, technical, and physical controls are further designated as common controls, system-specific controls, and hybrid controls. Common controls are those that are inherited by multiple systems. System-specific controls are unique to one system. When one part of the control is common and another part of the control is system-specific, it is a hybrid control. A security professional is expected to understand how security controls work by type and designation, alone and in combination, to provide comprehensive asset security. Table 2.3 summarizes the types and designations of controls.

TABLE 2.3 Types and Purposes of Security Controls

TYPES	DETERRENT	PREVENTATIVE	DETECTIVE	CORRECTIVE	RECOVERY
Administrative (management)	Policies and procedures	Separation of duties	Periodic access reviews	Employee discipline actions	Disaster recovery plan
Physical (operational)	Warning signs	Door locks and badging systems	Surveillance cameras	Fire suppression systems	Disaster recovery site
Technical	Acceptable use banners	Firewalls	SIEM	Vulnerability patches	Backup media

Establishing the Baseline Security

Many variables go into determining the security controls an organization uses and how to evaluate the effectiveness of the controls. The outcome of considering the variables and assessing risk to the organization is a baseline security requirement. That baseline will depend on factoring in all the variables unique to the organization relative to the value and sensitivity of the assets to be protected. It is important and cost-effective to determine the appropriate security controls.

Beginning with a risk assessment, the priority of assets and levels of security required can be designed to achieve a reasonable and tailored information protection approach. Keep in mind that a baseline means a minimum level. Because of the mission of the business and the dynamic changes in the threats and vulnerabilities, it may be more beneficial to an organization to exceed the minimum standards. Of course, some organizations may have a high tolerance for risk where reduction in costs is important. Typically, however, a proactive and defense-in-depth approach is a better risk reduction strategy. Control for the known threats today, but also anticipate and plan for continual increase in threats and in ways to provide defenses.

A security baseline should be understood as a complement to establishing a security framework (covered later in the section "Standards Selection"). Think of the security baseline process as part of the overall risk management process. Using methods and tools, an organization can establish and monitor that minimum (or better) baseline expectations are met and technical configurations are in place. Here are some methods and tools you can use to set baselines:

- Administrative Security Baseline Guides
  - **ISO/IEC 27005:** Guidelines for information security risk management. It supports the general concepts specified in ISO/IEC 27001 and is designed to assist the satisfactory implementation of information security based on a risk management approach.

- **NIST SP 800-30 Rev. 1:** Guidance for conducting risk assessments of federal information systems and organizations. Risk assessments, carried out at all three tiers in the risk management hierarchy, are part of an overall risk management process.

- Technical Security Baseline Guides

  - **Cisco Validated Design Program:** This vendor recommendation is focused on security controls of a network and its devices.

  - **Microsoft Security Compliance Toolkit 1.0:** This is a software tool for the security of Microsoft operating systems and services.

  - **CIS Benchmarks:** This is a set of best practices and requirements for Internet-connected organizations.

  - **DoD Defense Information Systems Agency (DISA) Security Technical Implementation Guides (STIGs):** These military specifications are relevant to many commercial security frameworks to establish a baseline configuration for networks, servers, and computers. Guides are available to reduce vulnerabilities in software, hardware, physical, and logical architectures.

- Physical Security Baseline Guides

  - **Operational Security Standard on Physical Security (Canada):** Source for baseline physical security requirements to counter threats to government employees, assets, and service delivery and to provide consistent safeguarding for the Government of Canada.

  - **Security Physical Safeguards – U.S. Department of Health and Human Services:** Developed to accomplish security baselines for physical protection of healthcare information by outlining reasonable and appropriate safeguards for information systems and related equipment and facilities.

Later, you will understand how security standards or control frameworks can be used to help implement and evaluate the methods and tools described here.

Scoping and Tailoring

Establishing the baseline of security controls begins the scoping and tailoring process. Because every organization has unique factors that impact how it values assets, the threats it faces, and what level of security it can afford, in terms of both resources and business operation impact, refining individual controls is an important role for the security professional. A CISSP has to help build the plan to clarify and limit the general recommendations of guidelines and frameworks to be applicable to the organization.

Scoping and tailoring are not synonymous, but the concepts work together to build the security baseline. Scoping is the process the organization undertakes to consider which security controls apply and what assets they need to protect. Tailoring is the process of modifying the set of controls to meet the specific characteristics and requirements of the organization. As each organization is different, some controls in a framework may not apply. Those controls can be removed from the baseline. Sometimes a security control does apply, but implementation should be altered based on the information asset or information use within the organization. In that case, tailoring the controls is done to eliminate unnecessary requirements or to incorporate compensating controls when needed based on organizational variables. The scoping and tailoring activities must be well documented with appropriate justification. Figure 2.5 illustrates the tailoring process according to best practices, including NIST SP 800-53.

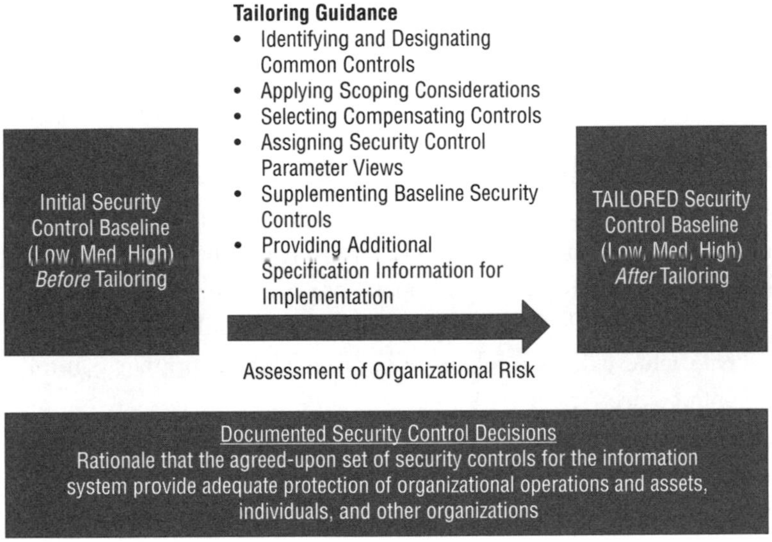

FIGURE 2.5 **Tailoring process**

TIP   Convenience is not a factor for removing or altering security controls. Make sure any changes to baseline requirements are rationalized against operational requirements and are analyzed for impact to risk.

Common Controls

In any enterprise, security controls may safeguard multiple assets. These controls are considered common controls and are typically implemented as part of the organization's control architecture. The security benefits of implementing common controls are inheritable across the assets in scope for the baseline assessment. Effective use of common controls can potentially reduce the overall resource expenditures by organizations. The following are examples of common controls within the types of controls:

- **Physical controls:** The access controls for physical entry are shared by all systems located in a data center. The environmental controls maintain proper conditions and suppression of fire for all computing equipment.

- **Technical controls:** Firewalls, intrusion detection systems, and data loss prevention appliances are types of security devices that provide network boundary defense for all assets. Public key infrastructure (PKI) and network security monitoring are also examples of inheritable technical controls from which all assets benefit.

- **Administrative controls:** Policy for initial and annual information security training applies equally to all users of network and application resources in the organization.

Compensating Security Controls

In some cases, the prescribed or recommended security controls are applicable but cannot be scoped or tailored sufficiently to meet the control objective. When baseline controls have potential to degrade or obstruct business operations or are cost-prohibitive, we have to explore compensating controls. This category of security controls augments the primary control's ability to achieve the control objective or replaces the primary control in order to meet the control objective.

To illustrate this point, segregation of duties for security personnel is a prescribed security control. In some organizations with small security staffs, segregation of duties may be too costly in terms of needing more employees. In this case, a compensating control can be increased collection and review of security activity logs.

TIP Integrating compensating controls into a security baseline requires documentation of why the compensating controls are necessary and how they provide equivalent mitigation of the risk.

Supplementing Security Control Baselines

As a reminder, a security baseline is a minimum set of security controls that are required. You may want to implement additional security controls. Supplemental controls are based on the specific threats or regulatory requirements of an organization or an industry.

Providing Additional Specification Information for Control Implementation

Additional detail may be necessary to fully define the intent of a security control, e.g., directions on how to apply the control in different situations. Organizations may allow additional implementation data per department, business unit, or other subordinate component of the enterprise, but they may not change the intent of the security control or modify the original language in the control.

A resource that highlights supplemental security controls that can be considered is the U.S. National Security Agency Methodology for Adversary Obstruction (`https://www.cdse.edu/documents/cdse/nsa-methodology-for-adversary-obstruction.pdf`).

Standards Selection

The main point in standards selection is to choose a recognized framework or a combination of parts of recognized frameworks to establish the baseline requirements. If a standard is recognized by regulators or security industry entities, that most likely means expert practitioners in the field developed the standards. The following sections cover some U.S. and internationally recognized frameworks.

Leading Security Frameworks

One approach to establishing a security control baseline to start with is to choose an existing framework. The frameworks may have differences in how they focus more on assurance, compliance, or risk management. In general, the use of a framework to establish the security baseline is appropriate to assess and improve the organization's ability to prevent, detect, and respond to cyber attacks. A few examples that can be used in government and private organizations are included here:

- **U.S. Department of Defense Instruction (DoDI): DoDI 8510.01 Risk Management Framework for DoD Information Technology:** (`http://www.esd.whs.mil/Portals/54/Documents/DD/issuances/dodi/851001_2014.pdf`) This directive applies to the DoD information systems and manages the lifecycle cybersecurity risk to all DoD IT. The use of this framework assists DoD security professionals in establishing a baseline and tailoring security controls as it relates to the DoD mission.

- **U.S. National Institute of Standards and Technology Special Publications (NIST SP):** (`http://csrc.nist.gov/groups/SMA/fisma/framework.html`) NIST develops cybersecurity standards, guidelines, tests, and metrics to protect federal information systems.

- **NIST SP 800-37 Risk Management Framework:** Similar to the DoD RMF, the special publications have broader access and applicability to both public and private-sector organizations. Federal government agencies outside of the DoD are subject to the FISMA framework, of which NIST SP 800-37 is a cornerstone directive.

- **U.S. National Security Agency Top Ten Cybersecurity Mitigation Strategies** (`https://apps.nsa.gov/iaarchive/library/ia-guidance/security-tips/nsas-top-ten-cybersecurity-mitigation-strategies.cfm`): The NSA's Top Ten Mitigation Strategies counter a broad range of exploitation techniques used by advanced persistent threat (APT) actors. The NSA's mitigations set priorities for enterprise organizations and required measures to prevent mission impact. The mitigations also build upon the NIST Cybersecurity Framework functions to manage cybersecurity risk and promote a defense-in-depth security posture. The mitigation strategies are ranked by effectiveness against known APT tactics. The strategies are updates to reflect new best practices to mitigate the occurrence of new adversary tactics. The applicability of this framework is to help organizations implement a broader framework, like NIST RMF, and prioritize control effectiveness and any mitigation based on risk (based on the NSA perspectives). While the guidance is most relevant to government and industry with critical infrastructure, it is useful in other organizations attempting to rank order risk mitigations.

- **UK 10 Steps to Cyber Security** (`https://www.ncsc.gov.uk/guidance/10-steps-cyber-security`): The UK National Cyber Security Centre recommendations for cyber protection for business against the majority of cyber attacks. This is an example of a government-published advice document that is meant to help organizations focus on the main threats to reduce the greatest amount of risk. This document is intended for UK organizations and is considered official. It is insufficient alone but is valuable in a portfolio of security controls to make up the baseline control set.

- **International Telecommunications Union-Telecommunications (ITU-T) Standardization Sector** (`https://www.itu.int/en/ITU-T/publications/Pages/recs.aspx`): A specialized agency of the United Nations, it is made up of experts from around the world to develop international standards known as ITU-T Recommendations, which act as defining elements in the global infrastructure of information and communication technologies (ICTs). Standards are critical to the interoperability of ICTs, and whether we exchange voice, video, or data messages, standards enable global communications by ensuring that countries' ICT networks and devices are speaking the same language. International ICT standards avoid costly market battles over preferred technologies, and for companies from emerging markets, they create a level playing field that provides access to new markets. They are an essential aid to developing countries in building their infrastructure and encouraging economic development, and through economies of scale, they can reduce costs for all: manufacturers, operators, and consumers. No participating international country is forced to follow the recommendations, although compliance with the standards is collectively beneficial. Recommendations are neither an implementation specification for systems nor a basis for appraising the conformance of implementations. The recommendations become mandatory when adopted as part of a national law by one of the participatory nations. It is significant to note that ITU-T recommendations are freely available and have identical ISO counterparts.

Security Standards

As an organization approaches scoping and tailoring of security baselines, it may want to supplement or add compensating controls. Security standards or specific control sets are techniques established by expert groups that attempt to protect the cyber environment of a user or organization. There are many sources of security controls that an organization may evaluate and implement. Some examples are provided in the following list.

Instead of using a complete security framework, another reason to use individual controls or standards to build the baseline or add to it is based on the organizational mission or the specific product to be secured. In the case of an electronic health record or customer relationship management system, a more granular, hybrid approach to building a security baseline may be appropriate versus overlaying an existing security framework. Although not an exhaustive list, here are major standards to be aware of:

- **U.S. National Institute of Standards and Technology Special Publications:**

  - **NIST SP 800-53 Rev 4: Security and Privacy Controls for Federal Information Systems and Organizations** (`https://csrc.nist.gov/publications/ detail/sp/800-53`): This is a catalog of security controls for all U.S. federal information systems except those related to national security (e.g., DoD). It is used by organizations to establish the baseline security controls, tailor security controls, and supplement security controls based on worst-case scenario planning and assessment of risk for the organization.

  - **NIST SP 800-53A Rev 4: Assessing Security and Privacy Controls in Federal Information Systems and Organizations: Building Effective Assessment Plans** (`https://csrc.nist.gov/publications/detail/sp/800-53a/rev-4/ final`): Used as a complementary guide, it provides a set of procedures for conducting assessments of security controls and privacy controls employed within U.S. federal information systems and organizations. The assessment procedures, executed at various phases of the system development lifecycle, are consistent with the security and privacy controls in NIST SP 800-53, Revision 4. It is applicable to private-sector organizations too.

- NIST SP 800-60: Guide for Mapping Types of Information and Information Systems to Security Categories (`http://nvlpubs.nist.gov/nistpubs/Legacy/SP/nistspecialpublication800-60v1r1.pdf`): This assists U.S. federal government agencies in categorizing information and information systems. The guide's objective is to facilitate application of appropriate levels of information security according to a range of levels of impact or consequences that might result from the unauthorized disclosure, modification, or use of the information or information system. It can be used by private-sector organizations, although it is not required.

- U.S. NIST Federal Information Processing Standards:
  - FIPS Publication 199: Standards for Security Categorization of Federal Information and Information Systems (`http://nvlpubs.nist.gov/nistpubs/FIPS/NIST.FIPS.199.pdf`): This provides a standard for categorizing U.S. federal information and information systems according to a government agency's level of concern for confidentiality, integrity, and availability and the potential impact on agency assets and operations, should their information and information systems be compromised through unauthorized access, use, disclosure, disruption, modification, or destruction. This is another directive primarily aimed at U.S. government agencies, but it can be applicable and useful for private-sector organizations.

  - FIPS Publication 200: Minimum Security Requirements for Federal Information and Information Systems (`http://nvlpubs.nist.gov/nistpubs/FIPS/NIST.FIPS.200.pdf`): An integral part of the NIST RMF, this standard emphasizes more security during the development, implementation, and operation of more secure information systems. FIPS 200 defines the 17 families of security controls covered under confidentiality, integrity, and availability of U.S. federal information systems and the information processed, stored, and transmitted by those systems.

- U.S. National Checklist Program (`https://nvd.nist.gov/ncp/repository`): The NCP is a repository of publicly available security checklists (or benchmarks) that provide detailed low-level guidance on setting the security configuration of operating systems and applications. Useful for organizations using SCAP tools. SCAP enables validated security products to automatically perform configuration checking using NCP checklists. Established by NIST and defined by NIST SP 800-70, the NCP is valuable in public and private organizations.

- International Organization for Standardization:
  - ISO 27001: Information technology – Security techniques – Information security management systems – Requirements (`https://www.iso.org/isoiec-27001-information-security.html`): This specifies the requirements

for establishing, implementing, maintaining, and continually improving an information security management system within the context of the organization. It also includes requirements for the assessment and treatment of information security risks tailored to the needs of the organization. The requirements set out in ISO/IEC 27001:2013 are generic and are intended to be applicable to all organizations, regardless of type, size, or nature. It is applicable to global organizations independent of national jurisdiction and industry. For example, although not focused on HIPAA, the information security management system framework in ISO 27001 is relevant for use in U.S. healthcare organizations.

- **ISO 27002: Information Technology: Security techniques – Code of practice for information security controls** (`https://www.iso.org/standard/54533.html`): This gives guidelines for organizational information security standards and information security management practices including the selection, implementation, and management of controls, taking into consideration the organization's information security risk environment(s). The code of practice is designed to be used by organizations that intend to select controls within the process of implementing an Information Security Management System based on ISO 27001. It can also be tailored for organizations that want to implement commonly accepted information security controls and develop their own information security management guidelines, but as a modification of the ISO 270001 framework.

- **International Telecommunications Union-Telecommunications Standardization Sector:**

  - **Recommendations X.800 – X.849** (`https://www.itu.int/itu-t/recommendations/index.aspx?ser=X`): The X.800 series of ITU-T Recommendations defines a security baseline against which network operators can assess their network and information security status in terms of readiness and ability to collaborate with other entities to counteract information security threats. This group of recommendations establishes guidelines for implementing system and network security with a focus on telecommunications networks. The security guidelines cover critical activities during the network lifecycle.

  - **Recommendation X.1205** (`https://www.itu.int/itu-t/recommendations/index.aspx?ser=X`): Applicable to international government and private global corporations, the recommendation provides a definition for cybersecurity. It provides a taxonomy of the security threats from an organization point of view. Cybersecurity threats and vulnerabilities, including the most common hacker's tools of the trade, are presented. Threats are discussed at various network layers. Various cybersecurity technologies that are available to remedy the threats are discussed, including routers, firewalls, antivirus protection, intrusion detection systems, intrusion protection systems, secure computing, and auditing and monitoring. It also covers network protection principles, such as defense in depth, and access management with application to cybersecurity. Risk management strategies and techniques are discussed, including the value of training and education in protecting the network. There are also examples for securing various networks included in the documentation.

The best approach is to use a combination of security frameworks and security standards to supplement or provide compensating controls. In this way, the organization can address real threats and vulnerabilities. The security professional is able to scope and tailor the security control program to adequately protect the organization with respect to the business imperative, regulatory requirements, and overall effectiveness. Throughout the process of selecting security frameworks and standards, it is important to address the use of all applicable controls.

ISO 27002 and NIST SP 800-53 provide foundational control standards for the industry worldwide. An illustration of the families of controls that constitute these standards is found in Figure 2.6. This side-by-side comparison demonstrates where the security standards share commonality and differ from each other. The fact that there are gaps underscores the need for the security professional to assess the organizational requirements and implement a comprehensive, properly scoped, and tailored asset protection program that will incorporate multiple sources of security standards.

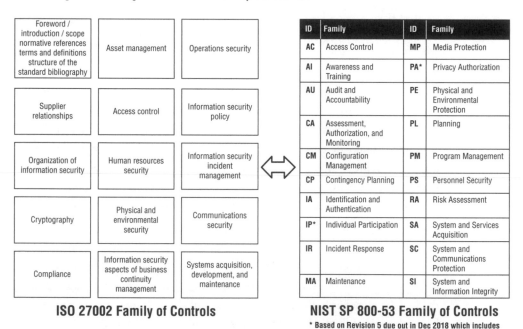

FIGURE 2.6 Side-by-side comparison of ISO 27002 and NIST SP 800-53 Family of Controls

NOTE   The scope of this domain is not to enumerate and evaluate all the control frameworks (or to recommend any one over the others). It is a requirement to be aware of recognized frameworks and how to evaluate the applicability and effectiveness for your organization. You will want to use evaluation criteria such as the following:

- Sensitivity of assets to be protected
- Industry requirements
- Regulatory factors (jurisdiction)
- Cost/benefit
- Organizational controls versus system-specific focus

Other Examples of Security Control Frameworks

In addition to the various examples of standards that you can use to help build an entire security program, other special-purpose or focused frameworks exist to address threats and support resource alignment. While the NIST RMF or ISO 270001/2 frameworks can be effective, scoping and tailoring for business requirements may lead you to a requirement for a more particular set of baseline controls. Some good examples of such resources are described next.

Control Objectives for Information and Related Technology (COBIT)

COBIT is not a primary security framework, but it applies to overall IT risk management. COBIT does contain a body of controls applicable to security. The framework was developed as an IT governance tool by ISACA. The framework is meant to help organizations reduce IT risk much like other security frameworks discussed in this domain.

The Center for Internet Security Critical Security Controls for Effective Cyber Defense

Using actual threat intelligence and reports of cyber attacks, the CIS has created the Critical Security Controls. Organizations can use the controls to focus attention on scoping and tailoring information protection resources on the most common attack patterns. Additional to the threat intelligence, the standards are informed by feedback and contributions from leading security practitioners from government and industry. The CIS Critical Security Controls are a prioritized set of actions to protect an organization and data from known cyber-attack vectors. The CIS framework attempts to focus on the highest actual risks. By accessing the CIS website, you can download the explanatory documentation for each control area listed next can be examined for specific, actionable, and effective specifications an organization can prioritize, implement, and measure for high payoff results.

1. Inventory of Authorized and Unauthorized Devices
2. Inventory of Authorized and Unauthorized Software
3. Secure Configurations for Hardware and Software
4. Continuous Vulnerability Assessment and Remediation
5. Controlled Use of Administrative Privileges
6. Maintenance, Monitoring, and Analysis of Audit Logs
7. Email and Web Browser Protections
8. Malware Defenses
9. Limitation and Control of Network Ports
10. Data Recovery Capability
11. Secure Configurations for Network Devices
12. Boundary Defense
13. Data Protection
14. Controlled Access Based on the Need to Know
15. Wireless Access Control
16. Account Monitoring and Control
17. Security Skills Assessment and Appropriate Training to Fill Gaps
18. Application Software Security
19. Incident Response and Management
20. Penetration Tests and Red Team Exercises

Source: https://www.cisecurity.org/controls/

The Security Content Automation Protocol

SCAP is an automated vulnerability management protocol that provides a structured way to measure compliance with policy for systems. Organizations can use SCAP to automate a process to make sure systems are within configuration standards according to NIST SP 800-53. The SCAP content is informed by the National Vulnerability Database (NVD), authored by the U.S. government. SCAP is designed to perform initial measurement and continuous monitoring of security settings against the established set of security controls.

Cybersecurity Framework

In recent years, the attention has been on asset management in organizations that operate critical infrastructures. Security attacks against organizations that are named in the U.S. Presidential Executive Order 13636, "Improving Critical Infrastructure Cybersecurity," issued on February 12, 2013, may impact the nation's security, economy, and public safety and health at risk. This type of risk is above and beyond financial and reputational risk. Among other directives, the executive order calls for the development of a voluntary risk-based Cybersecurity Framework (CSF).

Developed by the NIST Computer Security Division (CSD) Computer Security Resource Center (CSRC) and made up of standards and guidelines from FISMA, the framework consists of controls found in various NIST SPs. These publications include FIPS 199, FIPS 200, and NIST SPs 800-53, 800-59, and 800-60, 800-160, 800-137, 800-18. Additional security guidance documents that support the project include NIST SPs 800-37, 800-39, 800-171, 800-171A, 800-53A, and NIST Interagency Report 8011. Without question, the framework is a large compilation and combination of current industry standards and best practices provided by government and private-sector security experts. Helping to deliver the message that cybersecurity is not an IT problem (it is a business problem), the framework focuses on using business drivers to guide cybersecurity activities. The risks identified by a security risk analysis are made part of the entire organizational risk management approach.

The CSF was published in January 2017. It is to be customized to the mission and purpose of each organization. Additionally, each organization will have unique risks, threats, vulnerabilities, and risk tolerances. Prioritization of control implementation will have to shape how the framework is utilized.

There are some critical concepts to know about the CSF. The CSF is a voluntary framework. An organization conducts a self-assessment against its selected implementation tier to determine its current state. A tool that can help complete these actions is available at `https://www.nist.gov/cyberframework/csf-reference-tool`.

The Framework Core is based on cybersecurity activities, desired outcomes, and references that are applicable to a broad range of industries. The Core consists of five functions: Identify, Protect, Detect, Respond, and Recover. Each of these functions is further broken down into 22 categories, ultimately identifying 98 outcomes and security controls.

The framework is segmented into *framework implementation tiers* that describe the organization's risk tolerance. The tiers also categorize if the organization is reactive to security or more proactive. The tier an organization positions itself within will be relative to its current risk management practices, threat environment, legal and regulatory requirements, business/mission objectives, and organizational constraints. Tiers can be designed as categories and subcategories.

The other categorization is against a framework profile. The profile comes from the results of the tier categorizations. The profile is the alignment of standards, guidelines, and practices with the Framework Core in a particular implementation scenario. To improve the profile, the organization can set a target profile based on the current profile.

The current state of the CSF has been an evolution from the original intention of improving critical cyber infrastructure to uniting the cybersecurity industry and other stakeholders in a collaborative, engaged model. The CSF is already in version 1.1, with more revisions projected. The process is improving the way organizations can assess their cybersecurity infrastructure in relevant and cost-effective ways. Refer to `https://www.nist.gov/cyberframework/framework` for additional information.

The common theme is that there are many good security frameworks. They all have advantages and disadvantages. Each can be customized to solve specific information security problems. The choice of cybersecurity frameworks depends on the particular variables present in an organization, such as cost, risk tolerance, mission, and legal and regulatory factors. The security practitioner must be able to evaluate the frameworks against organizational requirements and implement the solutions that drive the level of asset security desired.

Data Protection Methods

An organization's data is one of its most highly valued assets. Financial information is central to the business operations of banking institutions, while healthcare information is important to hospitals and medical organizations. Generally speaking, protecting data and assuring confidentiality, integrity, and availability are central to information security practices. There are several general concepts and categories of data protection that should be understood.

Data Backups

A fundamental process in data protection is data backup. Backup data is a second, duplicate copy of the data stored in a different location from the primary data set. There are many reasons for creating backups. Backups help ensure the availability of data and reduce downtime in a variety of ways. For example, if ransomware or some other cyber attack renders data in the production environment unusable, a secure backup ensures that the organization can still operate relatively smoothly. Similarly, when data is lost by inadvertent disposal, having a recoverable backup may save critical business operations or avoid regulatory issues. Data backups are also invaluable in support of audits and investigations.

There are several methods of creating and maintaining backups. Each depends on data sensitivity, information risk, and business requirements.

The location of data backups is also dependent on the assessment of risk and data sensitivity. Data can be backed up off-site on physical media like tapes. There are data backup services online or through cloud service providers.

The Traditional Backup Cycle

Data backups can be processed in a variety of possible iterations. These include full backups, incremental backups, differential backups, and journaling. Most organizations will need to make backups, store data, and restore information from all of these backup types.

Full Backups

Typically, a full backup might be accomplished periodically, such as weekly or monthly, for example. If proper hygiene of full backups is not accomplished, the storage requirements increase, as each copy increases the volume by 100 percent unless the older versions are deleted. Other than making the first full copy of a database, another reason to do a full backup might be in advance of a major system upgrade or migration. The full data backup is a precautionary tactic just in case something goes wrong and data recovery is needed. In the event of production data loss, the full data backup likely results in a gap, depending on the timing of the last full backup. In addition to being the most expensive option, a full backup is the slowest method for backing up data and recovering it into the production environment.

Differential Backups

Once the initial full backup is done, subsequent copies can be made in differential iterations. This is more cost-effective than performing a full backup because only data that has changed since the last full backup is copied. The advantage of a differential backup is that it shortens the restore time compared to a full backup and is less costly to perform. However, if the differential backup is performed too often, the storage requirement builds and may exceed the full backup volume.

Incremental Backups

This type of backup is most cost-effective, as only the data that has changed since the last full or differential backup is stored. Incremental backups can be run ad hoc or more often than differential backups to economize storage space. The main disadvantage is that if a restore is attempted from the incremental backup, the time to restore can be lengthy, as each incremental volume has to be processed.

Journaling

Journal files are created for each update. They record metadata about the transaction and are created during the backup process. It is important to store the journal files separately from the data backups. Both are needed to complete a full restoration from a backup free of data corruption.

Other Backup Approaches

In addition to the traditional methods for creating data backups, there are many other technologies and processes of which the security professional must be aware. As compute and storage environments evolve from on-site data centers to cloud and virtual environments, the choices for backups continue to expand. An organization needs to establish and manage a portfolio of complementary processes and locations for data backup. It is important that the security professional understands the risk of using each solution and the accountability that remains with the organization as traditional backups are augmented by completely outsourced solutions.

Database Mirroring

Using database mirroring, a copy of the information is kept on two different servers, the principal and the mirror. The mirrored copy is a secondary copy and is not active until required. The mirrored copy is consistently synchronized with the principal database. The process assures maximum data availability and improves data recovery in the event there is corruption or loss of data in the primary database.

Snapshots

This technology is a process of making a virtual copy of a set of files, directories, or volumes as they appeared in a particular point in time. Snapshots are not backups. They are point-in-time copies. They lack the metadata that is included when using traditional backup applications. Using snapshots for backups helps storage systems because they do not degrade application performance during the backup process. They are useful for efficiently backing up large amounts of data.

Availability Zones

In cloud computing technology, these designations are isolated locations within geographic regions of the cloud service provider's data center. The choice of locations for availability zones is based on business requirements, which might include regulatory compliance and proximity to customers. The storage of backups replicated in multiple availability zones can decrease latency or protect resources.

Vaulting

An organization can send data off-site to be protected from hardware failures, theft, and other threats. The service can compress and encrypt the data for storage in the remote vault. Data is usually transported off-site using removable storage media such as magnetic tape or optical storage. Data can also be sent electronically via a remote backup service. The locations of data vaults vary. They can be underground in converted mines or decommissioned military sites. They can also be located in free-standing dedicated facilities or in a properly secured location within a building with other tenants.

Physical Media Backup

A couple of common media used for backups are magnetic tape and computer disk. Because the physical media are able to store the data without a connection to network resources, the removable nature allows physical media to be used for transportation of stored data from one location to another. This portability introduces the security risk of losing the assets or having them stolen, for instance, during transfer. Encryption of the data at rest on the media is required to keep the data as secure as possible.

Magnetic backup tapes are usually the most cost-effective, but the retrieval of the data is slower and more complex because of how data is written to the media. Disk-based solutions like external hard drives, network-attached storage, or even DVDs reduce read errors and increase restoration speed. However, several of the options are more expensive than tape backup. A combination of tape and disk media is usually employed in a tiered storage arrangement. Disk storage is used first for data that is required to be restored often. Tape media is used to store data with more long-term storage plans and archiving.

LAN-Free and Server-Free Backup to Disk

Different from local storage options like USB hard drives or connected devices, local area network–free (LAN-free) and server-free options like storage area networks (SANs) are faster and more efficient solutions for large amounts of data. The LAN-free or server-free architecture still requires connection to the devices with databases or media files. This is usually accomplished with the Fibre Channel protocol and media for high-speed data transfer that does not compete with regular network traffic. In most cases, LAN-free or server-free backup is used in tandem with physical media and disk storage in a complete portfolio of secondary data stores.

A SAN is a dedicated high-speed network or subnetwork that interconnects and presents shared pools of storage devices to multiple servers. It moves storage resources off the common user network and reorganizes them. This enables each server to access shared storage as if it were a drive directly attached to the server. SANs are primarily used to enhance storage devices, such as disk arrays and tape libraries, accessible to servers but not other devices on the LAN.

Not to be confused with SANs, network-attached storage (NAS) is file-level computer data storage servers connected to a computer network providing data access to a heterogeneous group of clients. The storage servers are specialized for serving files by their hardware, software, or configuration. They are networked appliances that contain one or more storage drives, often arranged into logical, redundant storage containers. NAS removes the responsibility of file serving from other servers on the network.

Generally speaking, a NAS system uses TCP/IP as the communication protocol. A SAN uses Fibre Channel. Fibre Channel is a high-speed data transfer rate technology, up to 4 Gbps. Fibre Channel is also very flexible. It connects devices over long distances, up to 6 miles when optical fiber is used as the physical medium. Optical fiber is not required for shorter distances, however, because Fibre Channel also works using coaxial cable and ordinary telephone twisted pair.

Data Deduplication

Protecting data includes not storing unneeded data. A type of excess data that organizations struggle with is duplicated data, or redundant data. To reduce the amount of duplicate data, security professionals can implement deduplication processes and use tools to remove duplicate information. This will help data owners and processors efficiently store, back up, or archive only the amount of data required. Duplicate data can be an entire database, a file folder, or subfile data elements, or can be implemented in the storage environment at the block level. Tools can be used to identify duplication of data and automate data deduplication. Figure 2.7 illustrates high-level considerations for the basic functions of deduplication tools. Typically, the environment is scanned and chunks of data are compared. The deduplication happens because the chunks are assigned identifications, compared through computing software, and cryptographic hashing algorithms to detect duplicates. When data is identified and verified as duplicate, the tools insert a pointer or stub and a reference to the location of the primary source of the data. The duplicate data volume is removed, storage requirements are lessened, but awareness remains for where the data can be accessed.

Disaster Recovery Planning

Data availability is often given too little attention in comparison with confidentiality and integrity as security concerns. Business resiliency, continuity of operations, and recovery from disasters are critical responsibilities that rely on data availability even in the event of anthropogenic or natural disasters. Of the anthropogenic variety, disaster recovery is increasingly important in light of cybersecurity attacks aimed at disrupting the business, total destruction of computing assets through ransomware, or theft of all copies of the data. Organizations must have a disaster recovery plan (DRP) in place that outlines backup strategies and prioritization of data recovery for business critical systems.

The plan must be tested periodically to determine whether the plan to restore is actually operational, and personnel should be trained to take the actions required. Although dependent on the industry and regulatory requirements, testing should be performed no less than annually.

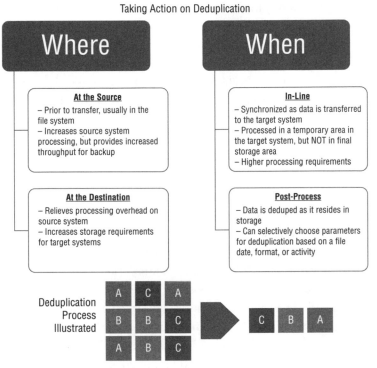

FIGURE 2.7 **Concepts of deduplication**

NOTE Cloud computing solutions have begun to change the way disaster recovery is achieved within organizations. Because cloud service providers configure assets as virtualized computing platforms with redundancy across geographic distances, primarily for high availability, disaster recovery is more of an instantaneous, transparent shifting of computing platforms and data sources invisible to the customer. An organization with assets in the cloud would not require, for instance, an on-premises data center as a recovery site to the cloud platform in which the organization is a tenant.

Disk Mirroring and Storage Replication

Disk mirroring is a technique in which data is written to two duplicate disks simultaneously to ensure continuous availability. A mirrored volume is a complete logical representation of separate volume copies. The same data is written to disk storage on separate areas, or partitions, on the same disk volume to establish fault tolerance. In the event of a disk drive failure, the system can instantly switch to the other disk without any loss of data or service. Disk mirroring is used commonly in online database systems where it's critical that the data be accessible at all times. Disk mirroring provides assurance of data resiliency when one copy of the data is lost or corrupted.

Storage replication differs from disk mirroring in that the second and subsequent backup copies are stored in geographically different locations. It is a managed service in which stored or archived data is duplicated in real time over a SAN. The purpose is the same in terms of data resiliency as part of the overall disaster recovery process. Other terms for this type of service include file replication, data vaulting, data replication, and remote storage replication. The expression can also refer to a program or suite that facilitates such duplication.

The most commonly used type of disk mirroring is in RAID 1 configurations. RAID is short for redundant array of independent disks. RAID storage provides fault tolerance through the use of multiple disks. This improves overall performance and increases storage capacity in a system. In older storage devices, less space was available because they used a single disk.

RAID allows you to mirror the same data redundantly on separate disks in a balanced way. Personal computers do not usually use RAID, but servers often do. The technique RAID uses to spread data over one or more disks in the same array is known as *striping*; RAID also offers the option of reading or writing to more than one disk at the same time to improve performance. The disks in a typical RAID array appear to be a single device, even though the array consists of multiple disks with an increased amount of storage over just a single disk. Although the most common type of disk mirroring is RAID 1, there are many different RAID architectures, called *levels*. RAID levels greater than RAID 0 provide protection against unrecoverable sector read errors, as well as against failures of whole physical drives. The most often-discussed RAID levels include the following:

- **Level 0:** Striped disk array without fault tolerance. Provides data striping (spreading out blocks of each file across multiple disk drives) but no redundancy. This improves performance but does not deliver fault tolerance. If one drive fails, then all data in the array is lost.

- **Level 1:** Mirroring and duplexing. Provides disk mirroring. Level 1 provides twice the read transaction rate of single disks and the same write transaction rate as single disks.

- **Level 2:** Error-correcting coding. Not a typical implementation and rarely used, Level 2 stripes data at the bit level rather than the block level.

- **Level 3:** Bit-interleaved parity. Provides byte-level striping with a dedicated parity disk. Level 3, which cannot service simultaneous multiple requests, also is rarely used.

- **Level 4:** Dedicated parity drive. A commonly used implementation of RAID, Level 4 provides block-level striping (like Level 0) with a parity disk. If a data disk fails, the parity data is used to create a replacement disk. A disadvantage to Level 4 is that the parity disk can create write bottlenecks.

- **Level 5:** Block interleaved distributed parity. Provides data striping at the byte level and also stripe error correction information. This results in excellent performance and good fault tolerance. Level 5 is one of the most popular implementations of RAID.

- **Level 6:** Independent data disks with double parity. Provides block-level striping with parity data distributed across all disks.

- **Level 10:** A stripe of mirrors. Not one of the original RAID levels, multiple RAID 1 mirrors are created, and a RAID 0 stripe is created over these.

There are other nonstandard RAID levels that occur because some devices use more than one level in a hybrid or nested arrangement. Other levels exist as proprietary configurations based on some vendor products.

The type of disk mirroring implementation will depend on the required level of redundancy and performance for the organization. The RAID levels provide a different balance among the goals that the organization has for data: reliability, availability, performance, and capacity.

Data States and Protection

Data exists in a range of states, and some states are more active than others. For example, data can be inactive (at rest), active (in use), or moving from one place to another (in transit). Data must be protected in all of its states, and doing so requires specific approaches.

Data at Rest

Data is considered inactive when it is stored on the cloud, on physical media backups, or on a device such as a laptop, mobile phone, or USB removable drive. The data is "at rest," meaning that there is no active processing or transfer from device to device or across networks. Data at rest can be employed across the entire volume of the hard drive, called *full disk encryption*. A couple of approaches to encrypting the entire hard drive are worth noting.

- The Trusted Platform Module (TPM) is a microcontroller chip integrated into the computer hardware that provides a cryptoprocessor. The cryptographic keys are incorporated in the devices.

- Self-encrypting hard drives (SEDs). With built-in encryption features, the contents of a SED are always encrypted. The encryption key is included but should be stored separately and updated on a regular basis. This approach offers a more user-friendly experience, as the encryption does not impact productivity or performance.

A more granular approach allows encryption to be applied at the individual file level, called *file-level encryption*. Tools for information rights management (IRM) provide a key benefit. File-level encryption is a tailored data protection strategy that may provide additional protection from unauthorized access to a file on a hard drive in the event the full disk is decrypted.

Data in Transit

Data in transit is considered to be at increased risk. Described as data in motion too, data in transit is any data that is actively moving from a point of origin to a destination across networks, including trusted, private networks. The data can also be transferred across untrusted networks through the Internet and to the cloud, as examples. The following are some leading security protocols used to protect data in transit:

- **Web access:** HTTPS
- **File transfer:** FTPS, SFTP, SCP, WebDAV over HTTPS
- **Remote shell:** SSH2 terminal
- **Remote desktop:** radmin, RDP
- **Wireless connection:** WPA2

Link encryption is a method of data in transit security where the traffic is encrypted and decrypted at each network routing point (e.g., network switch, or node through which it passes). This continues until the data arrives at its final destination. The routing information is discovered during the decryption process at each node so the transmission can continue. The message is then reencrypted. Link encryption offers a couple of advantages:

- Less human error because the process of encryption is automatic.
- Traffic analysis tools are circumvented, and attackers are thwarted because a continuous communications link with an unvarying level of traffic maintains the encryption protections.

End-to-end encryption is another data-in-transit method. This type of system of communication ensures that only the sender and recipient can read the message. No eavesdropper can access the cryptographic keys needed to decrypt the conversation. This means that even telecom providers, Internet providers, or the provider of the communication service cannot access the cryptographic keys needed to decrypt the conversation.

Data in Use

While an authenticated user is accessing a database or an application, data is in a volatile state. Active data stored in a nonpersistent state is known as "data in use". The data is typically used in RAM, CPU caches, or CPU registers to perform the transactions and tasks the end user requires. Encryption is not necessarily relevant or a primary control used with data in use, but it can be complementary to other controls. Data in use, presumably by an authorized user, underscores the importance of authentication, authorization, and accounting to control and monitor access to sensitive assets. Once a hacker has stolen valid credentials, many controls like encryption are rendered ineffective because the intruder has access like an insider. These types of issues are discussed further in Chapter 3.

Encryption

Sensitive data at rest and in transit should be protected. The ability to render data unusable to unauthorized individuals in the event the data is lost, stolen, or inadvertently accessed is essential for data protection. One of the mechanisms for accomplishing this is encryption. In doing so, encryption also provides confidentiality. The encryption process must be a central part of the entire layered defense strategy in an organization.

In selecting an encryption methodology, the security professional has to take into account the increased computational overhead of the encryption process and the management of the cryptographic process. It is important to use only widely accepted encryption algorithms and widely accepted implementations, like those found in NIST SP 800-38A, "Recommendation for Block Cipher Modes of Operation: Methods and Techniques" (`https://csrc.nist.gov/publications/detail/sp/800-38a/final`).

Although encryption is a powerful tool, other security controls are still needed to develop an entire baseline set of controls. In many regulatory environments and industry requirements, encryption is a mandatory security control. An organization's security plan must be aware of and aligned with regulatory requirements, industry direction, and encryption capabilities.

NOTE Password use is central to the management of the encryption process, but the two concepts are not synonymous. Encryption relies on password authentication, but it additionally requires the use of a key to decrypt the information, even with a valid login or cracked password.

Public-Key Infrastructure

Public key cryptography, or asymmetric cryptography, gives the framework of standards, protocols, services, and technology to enable security providers to manage and deploy a security system that provides trust. The basic components of public-key infrastructure (PKI) include certification authorities, lists of certificate revocation, and digital certificates. A PKI has to be built to support the basic components and scale the network to the requirements of the organization. Managing of public key cryptography is easily possible on public networks. Without a PKI in place, it is generally not feasible to use public key cryptography on public networks. This is because without a trusted third party issuing certificates, the certificates would not be trusted. In cryptography, X.509 is a standard that defines the format of public key certificates. X.509 certificates are used in many Internet protocols, including TLS/SSL, which is the basis for HTTPS, the secure protocol for browsing the web. They're also used for offline applications, like electronic signatures. An X.509 certificate contains a public key and an identity (a hostname, an organization, or an individual) and is either signed by a certificate authority or self-signed. When a certificate is signed by a trusted certificate authority or validated by other means, someone holding that certificate can rely on the public key it contains to establish secure communications with another party or validate documents digitally signed by the corresponding private key.

NOTE   There are restrictions on cryptography export. Depending on what country or jurisdiction you work in, there may be restrictions placed on what you can obtain and use. Along with evaluating encryption for effectiveness in your business, make sure to evaluate government and trade restrictions as they apply to your choices.

ESTABLISH INFORMATION AND ASSET HANDLING REQUIREMENTS

There are combinations of physical, administrative, and technical controls that assist security professionals in establishing the handling requirements for sensitive information and valued assets. Procedures such as marking, handling, declassification, and storage are used to securely inventory and manage sensitive data, physical media, and computing resources.

Marking and Labeling

Marking is a procedure to place descriptions in plain view directly on the asset that a person can read, indicating distribution limits, handling caveats, and applicable security levels (if any) of the information contained on the asset. Another term for this process is labeling, because the information used to mark the asset is most effective when grouped together and easily accessed on a label or a physical tag affixed to the asset.

TIP   An effective label should contain the title of the protected asset, the data owner, the sensitivity level of the information, the date of encryption, and the retention period.

With a label in plain view, it is much easier to identify the importance of data itself and manage the assets to assure availability, confidentiality, and integrity based on classification levels.

NOTE   Marking and labeling of public data or unclassified information for handling purposes helps to keep security efficient and cost-effective. For example, if an unmarked data asset is found, a handling decision must be made. The best practice is to apply the highest marking or label until the data can be determined as not sensitive or proprietary. Until the situation is resolved, the elevated handling requirements cause more costs for the organization.

Handling

The policies and procedures of an organization provide rules for the handling of each category of information at the appropriate level of sensitivity throughout the lifetime of the asset. Handling rules for information should cover the access, transfer, and storage of sensitive data.

It is important to maintain a consistent process for handling throughout the entire data lifecycle. The use of manual logs to track access to media is useful when automated access tracking is infeasible. Employee awareness and training regarding responsibilities for proper handling of sensitive information is imperative. Training should include warnings about becoming complacent about handling instructions. It is likely that, over time, employees handling even the most restricted information will become complacent, and data loss may be the result. The insider threat of an employee leaving the organization with a thumb drive or accessing sensitive information in a public coffee shop happens when employees become indifferent about policy and procedure.

In cases of assets that are not physical entities, such as data stored on magnetic tape, digital marking is a process to use. Take, for instance, a database or proprietary blueprint for an information system. To mark this type of asset, when the asset is transferred or printed, a digital mark can be used to identify classification that maps to handling procedures. Sometimes the digital marking takes the form of a watermark or a notation in the header or footer of the printout. The mark can also be coded into the metadata of a file for transfer.

TIP   Data loss prevention (DLP) systems are aided by using digital markings, as sensitive information can be more easily identified before it leaks out of an organization.

Declassifying Data

Before an asset is moved toward destruction in the asset management lifecycle, the asset may still have value but is no longer classified at the original level. An organization must have a process to declassify data. When data sensitivity changes from confidential to public, for example, marking, handling, and storage requirements have to be adjusted accordingly. If declassifying does not happen, excessive and costly controls remain in place.

The declassification of assets is a process that requires documentation, the delineation of levels of approval, and integration with asset retention and destruction policies for a comprehensive approach to asset protection. The data owner plays a central role in this process, as they determine the classification level of the data and when it can change. There should be a data governance process within the organization to determine whether there will be a manual review adjustment of data classifications. The organization could opt to automate the process using rules and applications to find and reclassify the data. The rules may be based on the occurrence of a specific date or event as determined by the data owner or the expiration of a maximum time frame.

Methods to declassify assets include altering the data to remove or obfuscate identifying or sensitive elements of the data. A few of these methods are described in the following sections: de-identification, obfuscation, anonymization, and tokenization.

De-identification/Obfuscation/Anonymization

To protect data, particularly when used for testing applications and storing databases, a general control for maintaining confidentiality is to de-identify or anonymize the data. This process involves taking any personally identifying data fields and converting them to masked, obfuscated, encrypted, or tokenized data fields. For instance, the Name data field may change from the actual name to "XXXXX" under a masked process or "53326" under anonymization. Some data fields in a database may remain clear text or the actual values. Fields like address, race, or date of birth may still be useful for analytics even if the personally identifiable information is de-identified. If encryption is used, a re-identification key is required to decrypt the database. No matter what process is used to de-identify the data, guidelines must be followed to keep the data from being easily re-identified by combining data fields or guessing the algorithm used to anonymize the data.

Data Tokenization

Tokenization is a specific form of de-identification that has been around for as long as there have been ciphers. However, it has gained popularity as security threats have changed and technical controls like encryption have become vulnerable because of attacks such as credential thefts. Tokenization is the process of substituting a sensitive data element with a nonsensitive set of characters or numbers. Usually, the token, or the value of the replaced data set, has the same field length as the data that was replaced. The token is not meaningful in relationship to the original data. In other words, unlike encryption, the token cannot be reengineered back to the value in clear text. A lookup table is used as a re-identification key. The original data and re-identification keys are stored securely, separately from the production system and the original data system.

Destruction

If the asset is media or computing equipment, the declassification process will include secure erase or destruction by one of the methods mentioned earlier in this chapter. Corporate policy must address roles and responsibilities for declassifying media. Only after proper secure erasure procedures are followed and validated can the asset be reused. Too often, incomplete asset erasure has led to reuse of assets where sensitive data was remnant or recoverable. In many organizations, the risk of improper secure erase and reuse is too high. In those organizations, destruction of media and computing reuse is the only acceptable declassification final step.

Once an asset is destroyed, documentation of the disposal must be collected and maintained according to organizational information asset security management policy that aligns with regulatory and legal mandates.

Storage

When sensitive information was all paper-based, information storage security was as simple as keeping assets locked up and behind adequate physical barriers. With digital information stored in data centers, on removable hard drives, on mobile phones, and in the cloud, asset storage is complicated. In the digital age, there are too many easy ways for stored data to be stolen, leaked inadvertently because of mismanagement, or accessed by unauthorized individuals through identification credential theft.

A primary consideration for secure asset storage of digital information is encryption. Sensitive data at rest should most likely be encrypted. Depending on the storage solution used, such as NAS or SANs, the additional concern for storage will be the location and safeguarding of encryption keys. The access and authorizations for storage has to be managed by security controls too.

An additional consideration for secure storage is limiting the volume of data retained. Along with data deduplication, making sure to only store data that is needed reduces risk to the organization as well as cost. In terms of risk, limitations on data storage also improve disaster recovery and business continuity because access to data on short notice is more feasible if excess data does not impinge on the overall recovery process.

SUMMARY

In any organization, the most important assets are most likely found in the IT and data inventory. Protection of these assets is incredibly important to security professionals as well as executive leadership, governing boards, and customers of these organizations. Because of the sensitivity and value of these assets, governments and industries across the globe have put legislation and regulation in place to protect them. Along with the loss of revenue or recovery costs if assets are lost or stolen, significant privacy concerns exist when sensitive assets are mismanaged. This chapter covers a great many of the important concepts and guiding principles a security practitioner is expected to know and implement in their daily work. Beginning with constructing asset management policy, the organizational policy must be informed by prevailing law, directives, and best practices but be customized to each organization's mission and unique risk profile. The process for asset management will include multiple stakeholders within the organization, so roles and responsibilities must be clearly documented and people should be trained adequately. In terms of asset recovery and business resiliency, periodic testing of the processes is required.

At the core of asset management are the standards and frameworks that have been developed by industry experts and cohorts of practitioners that should be used to build the asset management program in an organization. The choice of standards or frameworks and the individual security controls put in place to protect confidentiality, integrity, and availability of assets will also differ from one organization to the next. How a security practitioner will scope and tailor asset management controls depends on measuring and evaluating risk based on variables such as legal jurisdiction, industry, and considerations like compensating and alternative controls. Keep in mind, security controls work best when working together, not managed independently. The proper acquisition, inventorying, monitoring, and security management of assets in organizations around the world is a significant undertaking. Information systems are highly interconnected and dependent on each other, information is valuable and requires protection, and the impact of doing it wrong can be disastrous to an organization. Not to mention that unauthorized access to personal information may have a life-changing impact on the affected individuals who suffer from credit problems or the harm of identity theft. Security professionals have to master the proper security management of information through proper marking, storing, handling, and destruction of assets within their organizations to minimize risk and protect the assets.

Security Architecture and Engineering

SECURITY ARCHITECTURE IS THE design and organization of the components, processes, services, and controls appropriate to reduce the security risks associated with a system to an acceptable level. Security engineering is the implementation of that design. The goal of both security architecture and security engineering is first and foremost to protect the confidentiality, integrity, and availability of the systems or business in question. This is generally done by following an industry or governmental accepted enterprise or security architecture methodology.

Before designing security architecture, a comprehensive risk assessment must be conducted so that the security architect has an accurate idea of the risks to be addressed. In Chapter 1, risk management, risk assessment, threat modeling, and other approaches are used when determining the risks to the system. Once properly identified and assessed, each risk must eventually be found acceptable by the organization, either as is or after an action is taken.

What that action is depends on a number of factors, but it generally occurs in one of four ways:

- ❏ **Avoidance**
- ❏ **Transfer (i.e. insurance or contract)**
- ❏ **Reduction (e.g. through security architecture)**
- ❏ **Acceptance**

This is an iterative process. First the initial risk assessment identifies the risks to be reduced through the design of a security architecture to incorporate appropriate security controls. Then an assessment must be made to confirm that the resulting system's risks have been reduced to an acceptable level. This is done in line with the principles outlined below.

It may be that during the security architecture process, the costs associated with certain controls are prohibitive relative to the anticipated benefit of the system. As a result, the decision to reduce certain risks may need to be reconsidered, and those risks treated in another manner, avoided through a system redesign, or the project simply abandoned.

Also, security serves to protect the business. The work of the security architect is to ensure the business and its interests at the very least are protected according to applicable standards and laws, as well as meeting any relevant regulatory compliance needs. At times, the organizational leadership's goal to achieve its objectives may appear to be in conflict with compliance. As an essential technical member of the security team, there is a tendency to concentrate on technical security controls and attempt to address all known security issues or requirements. Security for security's sake, while intellectually satisfying, is a disservice to the organization. We must always remember we first serve as subject matter experts, aware of relevant regulations or laws and capable of ensuring our organization's compliance wherever change is required. As for the organization, the same expertise works together with leadership to advance the goals of the organization securely.

Success in security architecture is much more likely when one is aligned with the business and taking a risk management approach to security architecture.

IMPLEMENT AND MANAGE ENGINEERING PROCESSES USING SECURE DESIGN PRINCIPLES

Selecting security controls and architecting a system so as to reduce the risk is best guided by considering a defined set of secure design principles. Such principles have been proposed over the years, and we shall examine two leading sources:

- Saltzer and Schroeder in their seminal paper "The Protection of Information in Computer Systems" published in 1975 (Proceedings of the IEEE)

- ISO/IEC Technical Standard 19249:2017, "Information technology — Security techniques — Catalogue of architectural and design principles for secure products, systems and applications"

The purpose of incorporating a security architecture into a system is to ensure that the required security properties of the system are enforced, and that attempts to compromise the confidentiality, integrity, or availability of the system or its data are prevented. If an attack cannot be prevented, it must be quickly detected in order to limit the amount of damage done.

This work needs to start at the inception of the system design itself, as security must be part of the system design and not something added later. This is for two primary reasons:

- It is less expensive to incorporate security when the overall functional system design is developed rather than trying to add it on later (which will often require redesign, if not reengineering, of already developed components).

- The need for security controls is not just to prevent the user from performing unauthorized actions, but to prevent components of the system itself from violating security requirements when acting on the user's requests. If security is not intrinsic to the overall design, it is not possible to completely mediate all of the activities which can compromise security.

Examples of the first abound. The case of Equifax getting hacked is a shining example here. Equifax, one of three primary holders of consumer credit data, was hacked in autumn 2017, revealing the personal identifiable information of over 143 million American card holders. In the context of attempting to secure a system after its rollout to production, Equifax's rollout of an external-facing web server was too little, too late. Brian Krebs, a well-known security researcher and journalist, reported that Equifax employees in Argentina managed consumer credit report disputes using an online portal that was protected by the incredibly easy-to-guess password combination of admin/admin.

Fundamental to any security architecture, regardless of the design principles employed, are the basic requirements outlined in 1972 by James Anderson in *Computer Security Technology Planning Study* (USAF):

- Security functions need to be implemented in a manner that prevents their being bypassed, circumvented, or tampered with.

- Security functions need to be invoked whenever necessary to implement the security control.

- Security functions need to be as small as possible so that defects are more likely to be found.

Saltzer and Schroeder's Principles

Two senior members of the IEEE, J.H. Saltzer and M.D. Schroeder, wrote a paper titled "The Protection of Information in Computer Systems." In this tutorial paper, Saltzer and Schroeder write in depth on architectural design and best practice principles for protecting information within information systems. Even though "The Protection of Information in Computer Systems" was published in 1975, this pioneering work is still surprisingly relevant and is often covered in university curriculums on computer science.

Saltzer and Schroeder published a set of eight architectural principles that embody secure systems design, including the following:

- Economy of Mechanism
- Fail Safe Defaults
- Complete Mediation
- Open Design
- Separation of Privilege
- Least Privilege
- Least Common Mechanism
- Psychological Acceptability

Saltzer and Schroeder added two further design principles derived from an analysis of traditional physical security systems. By their own analysis in subsequent publications, these last two principles "apply only imperfectly to computer systems":

- Work Factor
- Compromise Recording

Through many waves of innovation and leaps of technological advancement, many of these principles still hold on as staples of computer security. The following sections explore each of them individually.

Economy of Mechanism

Complexity is the enemy of security. The simpler and smaller the system, the easier it is to design, assess, and test. When the system as a whole cannot be simplified sufficiently, consider partitioning the problem so that the components with the most significant risks are separated and simplified to the extent possible. This is the concept behind a security kernel—a small separate subsystem with the security-critical components that the rest of the system can rely upon.

Information security and cryptography expert Bruce Schneier stated (`https://www.schneier.com/news/archives/2016/04/bruce_schneier_build.html`):

> *Complexity is the worst enemy of security. The more complex you make your system, the less secure it's going to be, because you'll have more vulnerabilities and make more mistakes somewhere in the system. ... The simpler we can make systems, the more secure they are.*

By separating security functionality into small isolated components, the task of carefully reviewing and testing the code for security vulnerabilities can be significantly reduced.

Fail-Safe Defaults

Design security controls so that in the absence of specific configuration settings to the contrary, the default is not to permit the action. Access should be based on permission (e.g. white-listing) not exclusion (e.g. black-listing). This is the principle behind "Deny All" default firewall rules.

The more general concept is fail-safe operation. Design systems so that if an error is detected, the system fails in a deny (or safe) state of higher security.

Complete Mediation

The concept of complete mediation means that every access to every object is checked every time. This means your system must make it possible for the identity and authorization of every request to be authenticated at every step. It matters little if you have a provably correct security kernel for authenticating requests if there are paths that can be exploited to bypass those checks.

It is important to be careful to avoid security compromises due to differences between the time the access authorization is checked and the time of the access itself. For example, in a situation in which access authorization is checked once and then cached, the owner of the object being accessed could change access permissions but the previously cached authorization would continue to be used, resulting in a security compromise.

A more insidious attack is referred to as a time-of-check, time-of-use (TOCTOU) vulnerability. Consider the following pseudo-code on a system that permits symbolic links (i.e. user-created filenames that can refer to another file):

```
if (check_file_permission(file_name, user) == OK)
then
  Perform_file_action(file_name);
```

The attacker creates a file they have permission to access, invokes a system function that contains the above code, and simultaneously runs a program to replace the file with a symbolic link of the same name that points to a protected file they do not have access to.

Should the system run the program between the time of the check_file_permission call and the perform_file_action call, the user will be able to compromise the protected file.

Preventing a TOCTOU attack can be challenging and depends upon support for atomic transactions from the underlying operating system or hardware.

If, for performance reasons, assumptions must be made (such as relying upon the authentication performed by another layer), these assumptions must be documented and carefully reviewed to ensure there is not a path that bypasses the earlier authentication step and presents an unauthenticated request to a service that erroneously assumes it has been validated.

In general, complete mediation means access rights are validated for every attempt to access a resource. If access is not validated or followed through, then any change in access, notably a more restrictive change, is not observed and not enforced, which in turn would lead to unauthorized access.

Open Design

Do not rely solely upon security through obscurity. Security should depend upon keeping keys or passwords secret, not the design of the system. This is not to say that your security architecture should be published publicly—security through obscurity is still security, just that it ought not to be relied upon in and of itself. In the field of cryptography this principle was first associated with the Dutch cryptographer Auguste Kerckhoffs. Kerckhoffs's principle basically states that a cryptographic method ought to be secure even if everything about the system, except the key, is known by the attacker.

In the case of cryptography, the danger of security through obscurity (i.e. using a cryptographic algorithm that is not widely known) is that there is no way to prove a cipher secure. The only way we have confidence that, for example, the Advanced Encryption Standard (AES) algorithm is secure is that all of the details related to its operation and design have been published, enabling researchers around the world to try to find flaws that would enable it to be compromised. Since no significant flaws have been found after many years, we can say that AES is unlikely to be able to be broken using today's technology (or, indeed, the technology anticipated over the next decade or two).

Open design also means taking care to document the assumptions upon which the security of the system relies. Often it is undocumented assumptions that are implicitly relied upon, and which later turn out not to be true, that cause grief. By surfacing and documenting these assumptions, one can take steps to ensure they remain true and can continue to be relied upon.

Separation of Privilege

Separation of privilege requires two (or more) actions, actors, or components to operate in a coordinated manner to perform a security-sensitive operation. This control, adopted from the financial accounting practice, has been a foundational protection against fraud for years. Breaking up a process into multiple steps performed by different individuals (segregation of duties), or requiring two individuals to perform a single operation together (dual control), forces the malicious insider to collude with others to compromise the system. Separation of privilege is more commonly called separation (or segregation) of duties.

Security controls that require the active participation of two individuals are more robust and less susceptible to failure than those that do not. While not every control is suitable for separation of privilege, nor does every risk mandate such security, the redundancy that comes from separation of privilege makes security less likely to be compromised by a single mistake (or rogue actor).

Separation of privilege can also be viewed as a defense-in-depth control: permission for sensitive operations should not depend on a single condition. The concept is more fully discussed in the "Key Management Practices" section.

Least Privilege

Every process, service, or individual ought to operate with only those permissions absolutely necessary to perform the authorized activities and only for as long as necessary and no more. By limiting permissions, one limits the damage that can be done should a mistake, defect, or compromise cause an undesired action to be attempted. Granting permissions based on the principle of least privilege is the implementation of the concept of need-to-know, restricting access and knowledge to only those items necessary for the authorized task.

We see this in practice, for example, with the Linux *sudo* command, which temporarily elevates a user's permission to perform a privileged operation. This allows the user to perform a task requiring additional permissions only for the period of time necessary to perform the task. Properly configured, authorized users may "sudo" as a privileged user (other than root) to perform functions specific to certain services. For example, sudo as "lp" to manage the printer daemon. This is especially valid when it is restricted to privileged accounts related to specific services, but not used to access the root account. The increased security comes from not allowing the user to operate for extended periods with unneeded permissions.

Least Common Mechanism

Minimize the sharing of components between users, especially when the component must be used by all users. Such sharing can give rise to a single point of failure.

Another way of expressing this is to be wary of transitive trust. Transitive trust is the situation in which A trusts B, and B (possibly unknown to A) trusts C, so A ends up trusting C. For example, you conduct online financial transactions with your bank, whom you trust. Your bank needs a website certificate in order to enable secure HTTPS connections, and so selects (trusts) a certificate authority (CA) to provide it. Your security now depends upon the security of that CA because, if compromised, your banking transactions could be compromised by a man-in-the-middle (MitM) attack (more on this in the "Public Key Infrastructure [PKI]" section). You trusted your bank, who trusted the CA — so you end up having to trust the CA without having any direct say in the matter.

Transitive trust is often unavoidable, but in such cases it ought to be identified and evaluated as a risk. Other design practices can then be applied to the circumstance to reduce the risk to acceptable levels (as discussed with open design earlier).

Of course, as with most principles, the applicability of *least common mechanism* is not universal. In the case of access control, for example, it is preferable to have a single well-designed and thoroughly reviewed and tested library to validate access requests than for each subsystem to implement its own access control functions.

Psychological Acceptability

The best security control is of little value if users bypass it, work around it, or ignore it. If the security control's purpose and method is obscure or poorly understood, it is more likely to be either ignored or misused. Security begins and ends with humans, and security controls designed without considering human factors are less likely to be successful.

The security architect has to walk the fine line between too few security controls and too many, such that some are ignored — or worse, actively defeated — by people just trying to get their jobs done.

This principle has also been called the principle of least astonishment — systems ought to operate in a manner which users expect. Commands and configuration options that behave in unexpected ways are more likely to be incorrectly used because some of their effects might not be anticipated by users.

Saltzer and Schroeder have suggested two other controls from the realm of physical security: work factor and compromise recording.

Work Factor

This refers to the degree of effort required to compromise the security control. This means comparing the cost of defeating security with (a) the value of the asset being protected, and (b) the anticipated resources available to the attacker. This is most often considered in the context of encryption and brute-force attacks. For example, if an encryption key is only 16 bits long, the attacker only has 65,536 (6×10^4) different keys to try. A modern computer can try every possible key in a matter of seconds. If the key is 256 bits long, the attacker has 1.2×10^{77} keys to try. The same computer working on this problem will require more time than the universe has been in existence.

Compromise Recording

Sometimes it is better just to record that a security compromise has occurred than to expend the effort to prevent all possible attacks. In situations in which preventative controls are unlikely to be sufficient, consider deploying detective controls so that if security is breached (a) the damage might be able to be contained or limited by prompt incident response and (b) evidence of the perpetrator's identity might be captured. The only thing more damaging than a security breach is an undetected security breach.

Closed circuit TV (CCTV) cameras are an example of a detective control when it comes to physical security. For network security, a network tap with packet capture would be comparable; they don't stop breaches, but can provide invaluable information once a breach has been detected.

This is related to the concept of "assumption of breach." Design your system not only to be secure, but on the assumption it can be breached, and consider mechanisms to ensure that breaches are quickly detected so that the damage can be minimized.

ISO/IEC 19249

In 2017 the International Organization for Standardization (ISO) published its first revision of standard 19249, "Information technology — Security techniques — Catalogue of architectural and design principles for secure products, systems and applications." The aim of ISO 19249 is to describe architectural and design principles to be used to foster the secure development of systems and applications. ISO 19249 specifies five architectural principles and five design principles.

The five architectural principles from ISO/IEC 19249 are:

- Domain separation
- Layering
- Encapsulation
- Redundancy
- Virtualization

The five design principles from ISO/IEC 19249 are:

- Least privilege
- Attack surface minimization
- Centralized parameter validation
- Centralized general security services
- Preparing for error and exception handling

These architectural and design principles build on existing concepts and reflect a number of new approaches to security theory. The following sections examine each of these architectural and design principles.

ISO/IEC 19249 Architectural Principles

In the introductory text of ISO/IEC 19249's architectural principles section, the technical specification describes the primary challenge that all information security professionals know well: finding the difficult balance between security and functionality. The specification proposes that the way to secure any system, project, or application is to first adopt its five architectural principles and then approach the easier challenge of finding the balance between functionality and security for each principle. ISO/IEC 19249's architectural principles are examined in the following five sections.

Domain Separation

A domain is a concept that describes enclosing a group of components together as a common entity. As a common entity, these components, be they resources, data, or applications, can be assigned a common set of security attributes. The principle of domain separation involves:

- Placing components that share similar security attributes, such as privileges and access rights, in a domain. That domain can then be assigned the necessary controls deemed pertinent to its components.
- Only permitting separate domains to communicate over well-defined and (completely) mediated communication channels (e.g., APIs).

In networking, the principle of domain separation can be implemented through network segmentation – putting devices which share similar access privileges on the same distinct network, connected to other network segments using a firewall or other device to mediate access between segments (domains).

Of particular concern are systems in which privileges are not static – situations in which components of a single domain, or entire domains, have privileges and access permissions that can change dynamically. These designs need to be treated particularly carefully to ensure that the appropriate mediations occur and that TOCTOU vulnerabilities are avoided.

Examples where domain separation is used in the real world include the following:

- A network is separated into manageable and logical segments. Network traffic (inter-domain communication) is handled according to policy and routing control, based on the trust level and work flow between segments.

- Data is separated into domains in the context of classification level. Even though data might come from disparate sources, if that data is classified at the same level, the handling and security of that classification level (domain) is accomplished with like security attributes.

Layering

Layering is the hierarchical structuring of a system into different levels of abstraction, with higher levels relying upon services and functions provided by lower levels, and lower levels hiding (or abstracting) details of the underlying implementation from higher levels.

Layering is seen in network protocols, starting with the classic OSI seven-layer model running from physical through to application layers.

In software systems one encounters operating system calls, upon which libraries are built, upon which we build our programs. Within the operating system, higher level functions (such as filesystem functions) are built upon lower level functions (such as block disk I/O functions).

In web applications we see this principle in the *n*-tier architecture illustrated in Figure 3.1.

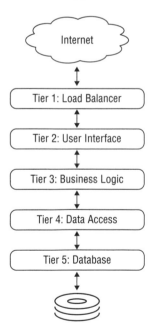

FIGURE 3.1 n-tier architecture

The purpose of layering is to:

- Create the ability to impose specific security policies at each layer
- Simplify functionality so that the correctness of its operation is more easily validated

From a security perspective:

- Higher levels always have the same or less privilege than a lower level.
- If layering to provide security controls, it must not be possible for a higher level to bypass an intermediate level. For example, if a program is able to bypass the filesystem layer and issue direct block-level I/O requests to the underlying disk storage device, then the security policies (i.e. file permissions) enforced by the filesystem layer will be for naught.

Layering and domain separation are related techniques and work well together. A single domain might have multiple layers to assist in structuring functions and validating correctness. Alternatively, different layers might be implemented as different domains. Or a combination of the above might apply.

An example where layering is used in the real world is a filesystem. The lowest layer, access to the raw disk, provides only basic protection to the disk sectors. The next layer might be the virtual or logical partitioning of the disk. Its security assurance would be access to those disk partitions or in the form of certain data integrity or high availability functions. Still, higher layers would be the filesystems as users browse the data, employing advanced access control features.

Encapsulation

Encapsulation is an architectural concept where objects are accessed only through functions which logically separate functions that are abstracted from their underlying object by inclusion or information hiding within higher level objects. The functions might be specific to accessing or changing attributes about that object. The encapsulation functions can define the security policy for that object and mediate all operations on that object. As a whole, those functions act as sort of an agent for the object.

Proper encapsulation requires that all access or manipulation of the encapsulated object must go through the encapsulation functions, and that it is not possible to tamper with the encapsulation of the object or the security attributes (e.g., permissions) of the encapsulation functions.

Device drivers can be considered to use a form of encapsulation in which a simpler and consistent interface is provided that hides the details of a particular device, as well as the differences between similar devices. Forcing interactions to occur through the abstract object increases the assurance that information flows conform to the expected inputs and outputs.

An example where encapsulation is used in the real world is the use of the *setuid bit*. Typically, in Linux or any Unix-like operating system, a file has ownership based on the person who created it. And an application runs based on the person who launched it. But a special mechanism, setuid, allows for a file or object to be set with different privileges. Setting the setuid bit on a file will cause it to open with the permission of whatever account you set it to be. The setuid bit controls access, above and beyond the typical operation. That is an example of encapsulation.

Redundancy

Redundancy is designing a system with replicated components so that the system can continue to operate in spite of errors or excessive load. From a security perspective, redundancy is an architectural principle for addressing possible availability compromises.

In the case of replicated data stores, the particular challenge is to ensure consistency. State changes to one data store must be reliably replicated across all redundant data stores, or the purpose of redundancy is defeated and potential security vulnerabilities created.

For redundancy to work, it must be possible for the overall system to detect errors in one of the replicated subsystems. Once an error is detected, that error may be eliminated or the error triggers a failover to the redundant subsystem. How any particular error is handled depends upon the capabilities of the overall system. In some cases it is sufficient merely to reject the operation and wait for the requester to reissue it (this time on one of the working remaining redundant systems). In other cases, it is necessary to reverse (roll back) intermediate state changes so that when the request is reattempted on a correctly functioning system, the overall system state is consistent.

An example of the first is a load balancer to a website. If it fails, and cannot process a request for a web page, it may be sufficient to fail the request and wait for the user to reload the page.

In a situation in which the request involves, for example, transferring funds from an account at one bank to another, if the funds have been deducted from the first account before the failure occurs, it is necessary to ensure that the deduction is reversed before failing and retrying the request.

Examples where redundancy is used in the real world include the following:

- High availability solutions such as a cluster, where one component or system takes over when its active partner becomes inaccessible
- Having storage in RAID configurations where the data is made redundant and fault tolerant

Virtualization

Virtualization is a form of emulation in which the functionality of one real or simulated device is emulated on a different one. (This is discussed in more detail later in the "Understand Security Capabilities of Information Systems" section.)

More commonly, virtualization is the provision of an environment that functions like a single dedicated computer environment but supports multiple such environments on the same physical hardware. The emulation can operate at the hardware level, in which case we speak of virtual machines, or the operating system level, in which case we speak of containers.

Virtualization is used extensively in the real world to make the most cost-effective use of resources and to scale up or down as business needs require.

ISO/IEC 19249 Design Principles

These design principles are meant to help identify and mitigate risk. Some of these five fundamental ideas can be directly associated with security properties of the target system or project, while others are generally applied.

ISO/IEC 19249 opens its discussion of the design principles by crediting the Saltzer and Schroeder paper mentioned earlier in the chapter. The technical specification follows that citation with the plain fact that, since 1974, "IT products and systems have significantly grown in complexity." Readers will understand that securing functionality requires comparable thought toward architecture and design. Following are the five ISO/IEC 19249 design principles.

Least Privilege

Perhaps the most well-known concept of ISO/IEC 19249's design principles, least privilege is the idea to keep the privileges of an application, user, or process to the minimal level that is necessary to perform the task.

The purpose of this principle is to minimize damage, whether by accident or malicious act. Users should not feel any slight from having privileges reduced, since their liability is also reduced in the case where their own access is used without their authorization. Implementing the principle is not a reflection of distrust, but a safeguard against abuse.

Examples where least privilege is used in the real world include the following:

- A web server has only the privileges permitting access to necessary data.

- Applications do not run at highly privileged levels unless necessary.

- The marketing department of an organization has no access to the finance department's server.

Attack Surface Minimization

A system's attack surface is its services and interfaces that are accessible externally (to the system). Reducing the number of ways the system can be accessed can include disabling or blocking unneeded services and ports, using IP whitelisting to limit access to internal API calls that need not be publicly accessible, and so on.

System hardening, the disabling and/or removal of unneeded services and components, is a form of attack surface minimization. This can involve blocking networking ports, removing system daemons, and otherwise ensuring that the only services and programs that are available are the minimum set necessary for the system to function as required.

Reducing the number of unnecessary open ports and running applications is an obvious approach. But another, less frequently observed strategy for minimizing the attack surface is to reduce the complexity of necessary services. If a service or function of a system is required, perhaps the workflow or operation of that service can be "minimized" by simplifying it.

Examples where attack surface minimization is used in the real world include the following:

- Turning off unnecessary services
- Closing unneeded ports
- Filtering or screening traffic to only the required ports
- Reducing interface access to only administrator/privileged users

Centralized Parameter Validation

As will be discussed later in this chapter in the discussion of common system vulnerabilities, many threats involve systems accepting improper inputs. Since ensuring that parameters are valid is common across all components that process similar types of parameters, using a single library to validate those parameters enables the necessary capability to properly review and test that library.

Full parameter validation is especially important when dealing with user input, or input from systems to which users input data. Invalid or malformed data can be fed to the system, either unwittingly, by inept users, or by malicious attackers.

Examples where centralized parameter validation is used in the real world include the following:

- Validating input data by secure coding practices
- Screening data through an application firewall

Centralized General Security Services

The principle of centralizing security services can be implemented at several levels. At the operating system level, your access control, user authentication and authorization, logging, and key management are all examples of discrete security services that can and should be managed centrally. Simplifying your security services interface instead of managing multiple interfaces is a sensible benefit.

Implementing the principle at an operational or data flow level, one example is having a server dedicated for key management and processing of cryptographic data. The insecure scenario is one system sharing both front-end and cryptographic processing; if the front-end component were compromised, that would greatly raise the vulnerability of the cryptographic material.

The centralized general security services principle is a generalization of the previously discussed centralized parameter validation principle: by implementing commonly used security functions once, it is easier to ensure that the security controls have been properly reviewed and tested. It is also more cost-effective to concentrate one's efforts on validating the correct operation of a few centralized services rather than on myriad implementations of what is essentially the same control.

Examples where centralized security services are used in the real world include the following:

- Centralized access control server
- Centralized cryptographic processing
- Security information and event management

Preparing for Error and Exception Handling

Errors happen. Systems must ensure that errors are detected and appropriate action taken, whether that is to just log the error or to take some action to mitigate the impact of the issue. Errors ought not to leak information, for example, by displaying stack traces or internal information in error reports that might disclose confidential information or provide information useful to an attacker. Systems must be designed to fail safe (as discussed earlier) and to always remain in a secure state, even when errors occur.

Errors can also be indicators of compromise, and detecting and reporting such errors can enable a quick response that limits the scope of the breach.

An example of where error and exception handling is used in the real world is developing applications to properly handle errors and respond with a corresponding action.

Defense in Depth

Defense in depth was first used to describe Roman Empire military tactics in the third and fourth centuries, when the Empire no longer tried to stop all invaders at the border, but instead deployed defenses to defeat attackers on Roman soil. In the context of information security, the U.S. National Security Agency first used the phrase to describe the use of multiple types, locations, and layers of defense combined with the ability to detect and analyze breaches for prompt reaction and mitigation.

By using combinations of security controls, the impact from the failure of any single control can be reduced if not eliminated. Many of the security principles above are types of defense in depth.

Separation of privilege ensures that sensitive operations require the active cooperation of two (or more) individuals. The compromise (e.g. rogue or malicious intent) of one individual is not sufficient to compromise the system.

Domain separation places system components into separate enclaves and enforces security controls on communications between the enclaves, so that the compromise of one enclave does not automatically provide access to other parts of the system.

Layering is another method of separating system components: security controls are placed between the layers, preventing an attacker who has compromised one layer from accessing other layers.

While redundancy is primarily a method of protecting against loss of availability by implemented replicated systems or components that operate in parallel, it is also a way to avoid security single-points-of-failure by replicating security controls serially. This means having overlapping security controls such that the failure or compromise of one does not by itself result in an exposure or compromise. An example would be using Linux iptables to block access to certain ports even though the server is behind a firewall which is configured to block the same ports. Should a configuration change to one control (the firewall or iptables) accidentally remove a *Deny* rule (or add an inappropriate *Allow* rule), the "redundant" control in the iptable or firewall will continue to operate.

Defense in depth is related to the concept of assumption of breach, formulated in the early 2000s by Kirk Bailey, now CISO of the University of Washington. Assumption of breach means managing security on the assumption that one or more security controls have already been compromised. The assumption of breach mindset shifts thinking from being simply focused on defending the perimeter (or perimeters), to a balanced approach of establishing multiple defenses so that the compromise of one does not immediately lead to a successful breach, and of considering detection and mitigation to be as important as defense.

Using Security Principles

When considering the applicability of security controls, realize not every control is appropriate for every situation. You must also consider that some security principles directly conflict with others, making the appropriate choice of the principle to follow a matter of careful consideration and judgment.

For example, Saltzer and Schroeder's principle of least common mechanism indirectly conflicts with ISO 19249's principles of centralized parameter validation and of centralized general security services. Does this mean one or the other of those principles is wrong? Certainly not. There is a time and a place for each.

Saltzer and Schroeder's principle is meant to minimize a single dependency among potential threats, while the ISO 19249 proposes to invest due diligence into building a secure, single dependency rather than depend upon multiple, disparate dependencies where vulnerabilities could also multiply.

To provide a concrete example, Amazon Web Services (AWS) relies upon the security of the hypervisors they use to virtualize servers. A compromise of their hypervisor could lead to a significant breach that affects many of their customers. They put a lot of work into ensuring their hypervisor software is as secure as they can make it. That said, they do not run the exact same hypervisor on every server in every one of their roughly 100 data centers around the world. By having something akin to generic diversity, should a security flaw be discovered in one of their hypervisors, the impact, while potentially large, might still be limited to those data centers using that specific version of the hypervisor. For more on the concern, and what Amazon did about it, see the following resources:

- Issue with Xen hypervisor: `https://arstechnica.com/information-technology/2014/10/security-bug-in-xen-may-have-exposed-amazon-other-cloud-services/`

- Amazon develops its own KVM-based hypervisor: `https://www.theregister.co.uk/2017/11/07/aws_writes_new_kvm_based_hypervisor_to_make_its_cloud_go_faster/`

UNDERSTAND THE FUNDAMENTAL CONCEPTS OF SECURITY MODELS

A model is a hypothetical abstraction of a system, simplified to enable analysis of certain aspects of the system without the complexity and details of the entire system being analyzed. A security model is a model that deals with security policy.

Security models can be formal, intended for mathematical analysis to assist in the verification that a system complies with a specific policy, or they can be informal, serving to illustrate and simplify the assessment of a system without the rigor of a proof.

You will not often hear people say a project can't proceed because it doesn't meet the requirements of the Bell-LaPadula (BLP) model or some other model. The security models, once familiar in name to every schooled security professional for decades, have since been largely relegated to textbooks. But regardless of how old-school these models are, the underlying intent behind their design and purpose is to improve security, and the need to improve security has never been stronger than it is today.

Although these models are not applicable as is to modern information systems, studying them provides a powerful foundation for the security professional. The structured approach of codifying security requirements in a security model can help reduce ambiguity and potential misunderstanding as to what, exactly, a security architecture is trying to accomplish. It distills the essential requirements into clear rules and analyzes the design to ensure that those rules are adhered to at every step in the process. Ensuring that a security architecture conforms to a well-designed security model greatly strenghtens it.

Different Roots, Different Emphasis, Similar Goal

Interestingly, the differences of emphasis between models can be attributed to each model's origin. Security models developed to address the concerns of the military and government emphasize confidentiality as the prime objective. Meanwhile, models designed for commercial entities might focus on the integrity of the data as key to preventing fraud or misleading financial reporting.

NOTE The security professional should have some understanding of the U.S. military's early adoption of computer technology and the development of information systems security practice. The U.S. Department of Defense's theoretical work in computing laid the basis for many of the systems security practices implemented in commercial systems today.

In the military world, all information is tagged with a classification that reflects the sensitivity to disclosure of that information, *e.g.* unclassified, confidential, secret, or top secret. To further reduce the risk of disclosure, the principle of need-to-know is implemented through compartmentalization. An item (or portions of an item) may be assigned to more than one compartment. So, an item's *security level* consists of a classification and a set (possibly empty) of compartments.

The general structure of military information classification is that an individual is not permitted access to an item unless he has clearance at a level equal to or higher than the sensitivity classification of the item and has the need-to-know to have been granted access to every compartment to which the item has been assigned.

The different models have been designed to address specific objectives, be they confidentiality, integrity, or conflicts of interest (segregation of duties). Keep this in mind as you read the following sections that discuss the models. This can guide you in designing your own security model for your specific situation. The end goal is to improve security, with emphasis on the aspect that best suits your needs.

Primer on Common Model Components

In examining security models, it is helpful to understand some concepts common across many security models, particularly finite state machines and lattices.

A finite state machine is a conceptual computer that can be in one of a finite number of states. The computer implements a state transition function that determines the next state, given the current state and the next input, and that can, optionally, produce output. In this model, evaluating the confidentiality-integrity-availability (CIA) properties of each state can ensure the system operates in a secure manner.

A lattice is a finite set with a partial ordering. A partial ordering is a binary relation that is reflexive, anti-symmetric, and transitive that need not apply to all, or any, pairs of items. Reflexive means that each item in the set is related (i.e. equal) to itself. Anti-symmetric means that if a R b, and b R a, then a and b are the same. Transitive means that if a R b, and b R c, then a R c.

To put this in concrete mathematical terms, security levels form a partial ordering. For example,

(Secret, STELLAR WIND) > (CONFIDENTIAL, ∅)

Note, however, (Top Secret, NUCLEAR) and (Secret, GAMMA) have no relative ordering; they are not comparable.

More formally, a security level a dominates security level b, if the classification of a is greater than the classification of b, and the set of compartments of b is a subset of the compartment set of a.

In short, a lattice security model does the following:

- Defines a set of security levels

- Defines a partial ordering of that set

- Assigns every subject (e.g. user or process) and object (e.g. data) a security level

- Defines a set of rules governing the operations a subject can perform on an object based on the relationship between the security levels of the subject and object

Bell-LaPadula Model

One of the first, and the best known, of the lattice security models was published by David Bell and Leonard LaPadula, which specifies the following three rules:

1. **Simple Security Property:** Sometimes referred to as *no read up*, this rule prevents a subject from reading an object at a higher security level.

2. **Star Property:** Sometimes referred to as *no write down*, this rule prevents a subject from writing to an object at a lower security level.

3. **Discretionary-Security Property:** A subject can perform an operation on an object if permitted by the access matrix.

The Simple Security Property rule protects against unauthorized subjects accessing sensitive information that they are not permitted to read. The Star Property rule prevents an authorized subject from breaching security by writing sensitive information to an object at a lower security level.

For a real-world scenario, imagine an intelligence officer in the military who has "Secret" access, a mid-level classification between "Confidential" and "Top Secret." According to the Simple Security Property rule, the officer can only read Secret and Confidential material. According to the Star Property rule, the officer can only write to Top Secret and Secret. The first rule doesn't make unauthorized material accessible to the officer, while the second rule prevents the officer from accidentally revealing unauthorized material to staff with a lower clearance. Figure 3.2 provides a graphical view of these two rules.

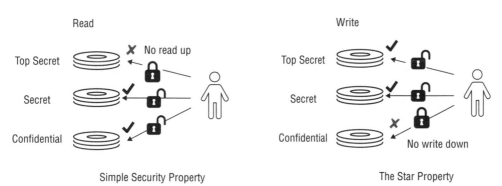

FIGURE 3.2 Simple Security Property and Star Property rules

The Discretionary-Security Property rule is useful when, for example, there are different departments. Let's say our same officer can read Secret and Confidential in one department, but can only read Confidential in other departments. Likewise, other intelligence officers in various departments might have higher clearance levels for their respective areas, but not for all. In this case, the model allows for an access matrix, and the Discretionary-Security Property comes into effect.

An access matrix has a row for each subject and a column for each object, and the element in a cell where a subject row and object column intersect defines what operation (i.e. access), if any, is to be permitted. Table 3.1 provides an example of an access matrix.

TABLE 3.1 An Example Access Matrix

SUBJECTS	OBJECT 1	OBJECT 2
Subject A	Read only	Read/Write
Subject B	No access	Write only (append)

The Discretionary-Security Property operates in conjunction with the other two mandatory access controls. The subject can only access the object if all three properties hold.

There are two other issues that are not well addressed by the BLP model:

- The model focuses on confidentiality, as one would expect from a model developed to meet the requirements of military and government organizations. It does not consider risks to the integrity of information. Protecting the integrity of objects means preventing the unauthorized, possibly malicious, modification of an object. In the commercial world, preventing tampering with financial records, which could facilitate fraud, is more important than maintaining the confidentiality of those records.

- The model does not deal with covert channels. The possibility of performing permitted operations in a manner that reveals confidential information through side channels (e.g. by performing operations in a manner that can be detected by other, less secure, processes—such as consuming bursts of CPU, or forcing abnormal levels of VM paging).

The Biba Integrity Model

To address the integrity issue, Kenneth Biba developed what has become known as the Biba Integrity model which, in a manner similar to the BLP model, posits the following:

- **Simple Integrity Axiom:** Sometimes referred to as *no read down*, this rule prevents compromising the integrity of more secure information from a less secure source.

- **Star Integrity Axiom:** Sometimes referred to as *no write up*, this rule prevents the corruption of more secure information by a less privileged subject.

Figure 3.3 illustrates these concepts.

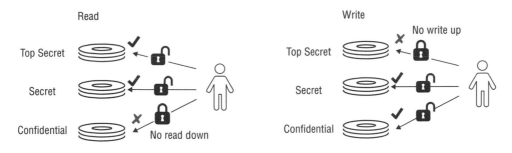

FIGURE 3.3 **Simple Integrity Property and Star Integrity Property**

The Clark-Wilson Model

Clark and Wilson argue that a lattice model, such as the Biba model, is not sufficient to protect the integrity of data. Their proposed approach is to base the security model on two concepts that the commercial world developed to protect against fraud long before computers:

- Well-formed transactions
- Separation of duties

In contrast to the Bell LaPadula and Biba models, which permit a subject to make any changes to an object, if they are permitted to make any (i.e. have write permission), the Clark-Wilson concept of a well-formed transaction is that subjects are constrained to make only those changes which maintain the integrity of the data.

The example from the original paper outlining this model is the handwritten ledger when bookkeepers wrote in ink, and mistakes were corrected by entering a correcting or reversing entry. Signs that the entries in the ledger had been erased (which would be obvious given the use of indelible ink) would be detected as a violation of the ledger's integrity and a possible indication of fraud.

The practice of separation of duties in the commercial world aims to make sure that the accounting record accurately reflects reality.

The Brewer-Nash Model

The Brewer-Nash model was developed to implement an ethical wall security policy. In the commercial world there are regulatory requirements designed to prevent conflicts of interest arising from insider knowledge. These rules require that organizations establish barriers to prevent those with confidential information from being placed in a position where that knowledge could improperly influence their actions.

NOTE In the original Brewer-Nash paper the term "Chinese Wall" was used. This term is deprecated in favor of "ethical wall" or "cone of silence."

For example, a financial analyst working for a bank cannot provide advice for a client company when he has insider knowledge related to another client who is a competitor. Similarly, in countries in which a law firm is permitted to represent adversarial clients, the regulations require an ethical wall to exist between the two legal teams within the same company.

Recall that in the BLP security model, access to data is determined based on attributes of the subject and the object. In contrast to BLP, the Brewer-Nash security model is based on segregation of duties, hence, the visual of erecting an ethical wall. Access to the data must be limited by what data the person is already permitted to access.

The Brewer-Nash model defines a hierarchical model for information:

- Individual pieces of information related to a single company or client are called objects in keeping with BLP's usage.

- All objects related to the same company (or client) are part of what is called a *company data set*.

- All company data sets in the same industry (i.e. that are competitors) are part of what is called a *conflict of interest class*.

The objective of an ethical wall security policy is that people are only permitted to access information (objects) that does not conflict with information they already have access to.

For example, let's say a new financial analyst who has not accessed any information held by his newer employer and therefore, under Brewer-Nash (BN), is free to access any company data set. The analyst already accessed ACME Finance information, and he is free to access information that exists in a different conflict of interest class, say, BETA Chemicals. But if he tries to access an object associated with Ajax Finance, which is in the same conflict of interest class as ACME, the BN security model would bar that access. See Figure 3.4.

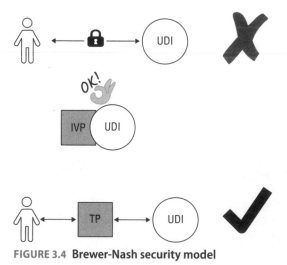

FIGURE 3.4 Brewer-Nash security model

SELECT CONTROLS BASED UPON SYSTEMS SECURITY REQUIREMENTS

Selecting the security controls appropriate for an information system starts with an analysis of the security requirements. The security requirements are determined by:

- An analysis of any regulatory or compliance requirements placed on the system (e.g. regulatory frameworks such as SOX and FISMA in the U.S., the Companies Act in the UK; privacy legislation such as GDPR in the EU or HIPAA in the U.S.; contractual obligations such as Payment Card Industry Data Security Standard (PCI DSS); or voluntary compliance programs such as ISO 27001 certification or SOC 1/2/3 audits)

- An analysis of the threats the system is likely to face (see the "Understand and Apply Threat Modeling Concepts and Methodologies" section in Chapter 1)

- A risk assessment of the system

In some cases, the analysis of both the threats and any applicable regulatory compliance requirements will specify exactly what minimum set of controls is necessary. For example, the organization that processes primary account numbers (PAN) and handles bank card transactions understands their systems must be PCI DSS compliant. In other cases, such as GDPR compliance, the requirements are more nebulous, and the security architect must analyze the threats, risks, and affected stakeholders to determine an appropriate set of controls to implement.

If an organization has not yet adopted a certain framework, it is beneficial to start with an established information security framework such as ISO 27001, NIST SP 800-37 "Risk Management Framework," or the National Institute of Standards and Technology (NIST) Cybersecurity Framework (CSF), ISA624443, or COBIT 5 (to name a few), as this will help ensure that you have considered the full spectrum of controls and that your process is defined, repeatable, and consistent.

There are a few things to understand about these security frameworks:

- They are not mandatory.
- They are not mutually exclusive of each other.
- They are not exhaustive, i.e., they don't cover all security concerns.
- They are not the same as a standard or a control list.

Now let's expand on each of those points.

Frameworks are not mandatory. But as an organization adopts or follows a framework, some of the subsequent documents or steps may involve taking mandatory action. Take for example, a company seeking to secure their systems that process credit card data.

When they act according to a framework prompting them to identify their systems and the risks to those systems, the organization will understand they must adhere to the PCI DSS, not a framework but a compliance standard.

Information security frameworks are not mutually exclusive. Many organizations such as the Cloud Security Alliance, ISACA, and the Unified Compliance Framework have developed mappings between the controls in different frameworks, making it easier to achieve compliance with more than one framework at the same time. This might be necessary, for example, when a specific system must meet PCI DSS requirements, but the organization as a whole has selected, say, ISO 27001 as the framework for its information security management system.

Certainly frameworks are not intended to be completely exhaustive. Frameworks can be specialized in either an industry or scope. Take for example, the NIST CSF, which is widely recognized as a general security framework that is applicable for basically any industry. But the CSF does omit one huge security concern: physical security. No mention of entry points is found in the CSF. Along the same lines, other frameworks can be both comprehensive and specialized for a particular field. The Health Information Trust Alliance (HITRUST) CSF is a comprehensive security framework for the healthcare industry.

Lastly, remember not to confuse a framework with a standard or a control list. Frameworks, control lists, and standards are three different concepts. You will likely find a list of controls in a framework. For example, the set of controls included in the aforementioned HITRUST specifically strives to marry the HITRUST CSF with standards and regulations targeting the healthcare industry. Perhaps the best example is NIST 800-53, which is a list of security controls that is so extensive that it is sometimes confused with being able to stand alone as a framework. It cannot. Similarly, there is a marked difference between frameworks and standards. While a framework is an approach or strategy to take, a standard is a set of quantifiable directions or rules to follow. In most organizations, the standard would logically follow the policy, just as mandatory instructions would follow a decree stating what is mandatory.

What all frameworks have in common is an all-embracing, overarching approach to the task of securing systems. They break that task down into manageable phases or steps. For example, at the highest level, NIST Special Publication 800-37, "Risk Management Framework," breaks down the task of securing a system this way: starts with categorizing the system (based on impact if that system's security were affected), identifying the proper security controls, implementing those controls, assessing their impact, and then monitoring or managing the system. From this breakdown, security controls are the obvious central point involved in securing the system. These controls are the real tangible work performed from adopting a framework. Due to the broad reach and depth of controls, there are whole catalogs or lists available.

Once you have selected your framework, you need to review all of the controls to determine which are appropriate to address the risks you have identified. In some cases, the framework itself will provide guidance. For example, NIST SP800-53 provides three levels of controls, called "Initial Control Baselines," based on the risk assessment. Threat modeling and risk assessment will also provide information on which controls are most important and need to be implemented with higher priority than other controls that address vulnerabilities with a low likelihood and impact. Implementing all of the controls in your selected framework to the same level of depth and maturity is a waste of time, money, and resources. The general objective is to reduce all risks to a level below the organization's risk threshold. This means some controls will have to be thoroughly and completely implemented while others may not be needed at all.

Often, the framework will incorporate a security standard with a minimum set of security controls forming a recommended baseline as a starting point for deployment of systems. Scoping guidance within the baseline identifies the acceptable deviation from control and results in a tailored system deployment that meets the organization's risk tolerance.

As important as making a considered decision on which controls to implement and to what degree, is to have a formal process for making such decisions (from threat modeling and vulnerability assessments, through risk management, to control selection) in which you document the path to your decisions and the information upon which you based your decision. Implementing a defined, repeatable, and industry-accepted approach to selecting controls is one way the organization can demonstrate due care and due diligence in security decision-making.

Of course, selecting controls is just the beginning. You need to:

- Consider the control and how to implement and adapt it to your specific circumstances (the "Plan" phase)
- Implement the control (the "Do" phase)
- Assess the effectiveness of the control (the "Check" phase)
- Remediate the gaps and deficiencies (the "Act" phase)

This Plan-Do-Check-Act cycle (also known as PDCA or the Deming cycle) is, of course, an iterative process. This was explicitly pointed out in ISO 27000:2009, but only implied in later editions. Other frameworks, such as the NIST Risk Management Framework, also leverage the continuous process improvement model to shape the efficiency and effectiveness of the controls environment. See Figure 3.5.

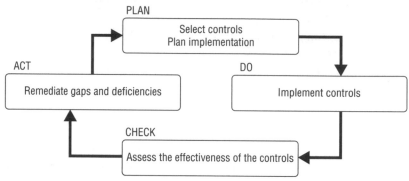

FIGURE 3.5 Plan-Do-Check-Act cycle

On a more frequent basis you need to (re-)assess the effectiveness of your controls, and on a less frequent basis (but still periodically) you need to reexamine your choice of controls. Business objectives change. The threat landscape changes. And your risks change. The set (and level) of controls that were appropriate at one point of time is unlikely to be the same a year or two later. As in all things related to information security, it is certainly not a case of set and forget.

In addition to the periodic review of the control selection, specific events ought to be analyzed to determine if further review is necessary:

- A security incident or breach
- A new or significantly changed threat or threat actor
- A significant change to an information system or infrastructure
- A significant change to the type of information being processed
- A significant change to security governance, the risk management framework, or policies

Frameworks are also updated, and when they are, one needs to consider the changes and adjust as appropriate.

UNDERSTAND SECURITY CAPABILITIES OF INFORMATION SYSTEMS

Not all, but most technical information security controls are based on the hardware security capabilities that support and enable the security primitives upon which more elaborate and sophisticated security controls are implemented. What are "security primitives?" Think of a primitive as a building block, or a tool defined by some type. Often, the word "primitive" is associated with cryptography primitives, but in this case, we're talking about the building blocks of keeping types of hardware security.

Depending on the platform, the types of hardware security primitives will vary. These can include:

- Memory protection
- Virtualization
- Trusted Platform Modules (TPM)
- Cryptographic modules
- Hardware Security Modules (HSM)
- Smartcards

As with all system capabilities, implementing instructions in hardware limits the flexibility of the system. Further, many systems (particularly in the IoT space) do not have the computational horsepower to implement sophisticated security controls while providing an acceptable level of performance. The security professional should be able to identify when tradeoffs between security and performance are being made, and integrate that information into the risk assessment process.

Memory Protection

The basic foundational security control on all systems that permit programs with different levels of security access to run at the same time is memory protection. This feature enables the operating system to load multiple programs into main memory at the same time and prevent one program from referencing memory not specifically assigned to it. If a program attempts to reference a memory address it is not permitted to access, the system blocks the access, suspends the program, and transfers control to the operating system. In most cases, the operating system will terminate the offending program. (See Figure 3.6.)

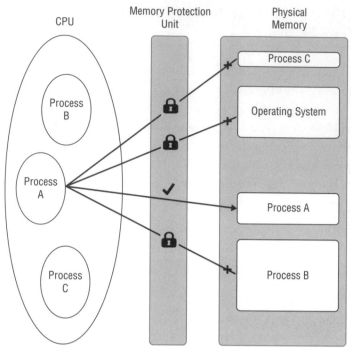

FIGURE 3.6 **Operating System Memory Protection**

A related hardware feature that is required to support memory protection is dual-mode operation. This means the processor can operate in one of (at least) two modes: privileged (or kernel) mode, and unprivileged (or user) mode. The operating system runs in privileged mode, which grants it permission to set up and control the memory protection subsystem. Privileged mode also permits the operating system to execute special privileged instructions that control the processor environment.

Once a program has been loaded into memory and the memory protection is configured to limit that program's access to those areas of memory assigned to it by the operating system, the operating system transfers control to the program and simultaneously transitions to unprivileged mode.

The program runs in unprivileged mode, which limits it to accessing only the specific memory area dictated by the operating system. Should it make an illegal memory reference, attempt to execute a privileged CPU instruction, or use up the time slice granted it by the operating system, control is returned to the operating system (running in privileged mode).

The operating system determines if control has been returned to the OS because of an illegal operation by the user program and decides how to handle the transgression (i.e. returning control to the user program with an error indication or terminating the program).

Another security control, address space layout randomization (ASLR), seeks to mitigate the risks of predictable memory address location. The location in memory for a known instruction becomes a risk when there is a threat of exploiting that location for an attack. For example, a buffer overflow attack requires knowing two things: the exact amount by which to overflow the memory to facilitate executing malicious code and where exactly to send the overflow. ASLR defeats the second item by randomizing the location.

Whatever the approach or specific technical control, the need to protect memory is both fundamental and critical to securing the system.

Potential Weaknesses

Proper memory protection relies upon both the correct operation of the hardware and the correct design of the operating system that uses the underlying memory protection hardware to prevent programs from accessing memory they have not been given permission to access. A defect in either can compromise the security provided by memory protection.

Note that this protection prevents the direct disclosure of memory contents that are blocked from an unauthorized program, but does not necessarily prevent side-channel exploits from revealing information about memory that is protected from access.

Attacks that leverage ineffective isolation and memory protection can have catastrophic effects. As the Meltdown and Spectre exploits in 2018 revealed, flaws in the design of Intel and some other CPU chips permitted clever programming techniques to deduce the contents of memory locations that those programs were not permitted to access directly.

✔ **Meltdown and Spectre**

The roots of how Spectre and Meltdown began date back more than five years before the two famous vulnerabilities were publicly revealed together in January of 2018. Most affected hardware vendors were told six months earlier and, due to the highly speculative nature of the vulnerability, one vendor coined the vulnerability as Spectre.

To understand Spectre and Meltdown, it helps to consider some aspects of how CPUs operate. CPUs sometimes run instructions speculatively, meaning they run instructions out of order in an effort to potentially save time. Sometimes it's worthwhile, and other times it's not. CPUs keep track of those speculative attempts in what's called a Branch History Buffer (BHB).

CONTINUES

Unfortunately, two widespread misperceptions about speculative running and the BHB created a major vulnerability. The first was that when CPUs scanned instructions out of order and acted on them and the speculation turned out to not be worthwhile, the understanding was the CPU's cache memory was then emptied of that effort. That belief was incorrect. The second erroneous perception involved how the BHB works. The addressing of memory locations in the BHB is not absolute (full). Instead the BHB uses only partial addressing to save space. While that could lead to overwriting of multiple memory locations sharing a single BHB position, CPU designers understood it was only addressing speculative execution, so no harm was done if something went awry. Between those two bad assumptions, Spectre and Meltdown are possible.

Understanding that the CPU's cache is not emptied of a bad attempt to do some things in parallel, consider what could be read if you specifically told the CPU to access something secret, such as a password or whether the system was actually a virtual machine. With the BHB addressing being vulnerable to collisions as well, well-designed malware could send sensitive information to the CPU cache and then use a completely different speculative instruction to locate the secret sent earlier. A good explanation can be found at https://ds9a.nl/articles/posts/spectre-meltdown/.

Virtualization

Operating systems provide programs with a set of services to enable them to operate more efficiently (and to be more easily designed and run) than if the program had to run on the computer directly. For example, instead of an application reading and writing disk storage blocks directly, the operating system provides a level of abstraction that manages the details of files and directories. Furthermore, most operating systems also enable multiple programs to run concurrently, with each application able to operate oblivious to the presence of other apps on the same system.

In some sense, an operating system provides a type of virtual computer, a computer that does not exist in reality (i.e. hardware) but which is much easier for applications to use than the physical hardware, and which makes more efficient use of the hardware by sharing it among different programs (see Figure 3.7).

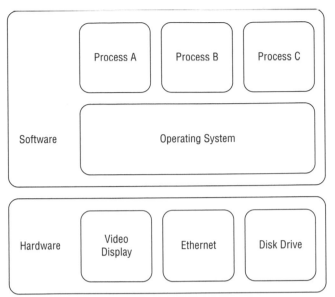

FIGURE 3.7 An operating system efficiently allocates hardware resources between multiple processes

Virtualization takes this concept a step further. Instead of just one operating system enabling multiple application programs running on the same hardware, a hypervisor makes use of a set of specific processor instructions and features to emulate an entire computer. This enables multiple operating systems to run on the same computer, each unaware of and unable (in a properly designed hypervisor) to affect the other operating systems.

There are two types of hypervisors, commonly referred to as Type 1 and Type 2 hypervisors. The primary difference between them is whether an underlying operating system is used to bridge the hardware with the virtual machines. A Type 1 hypervisor is the sole installation, acting as a bridge between hardware components and virtual machines, as illustrated in Figure 3.8. For this reason, Type 1 hypervisors are also called "bare metal" hypervisors. They are commonly found when flexibility and efficiency are most required. This is especially the case when the virtualized servers are running the same or similar services, making the most efficient use of the underlying hardware. In production environments, you are more likely to find virtualized machines sitting on Type 1 hypervisors. With a bit more overhead comes the Type 2 hypervisor, relying on a "host" operating system installed on the hardware. The virtualized machines running within the host OS are then called "guest" machines.

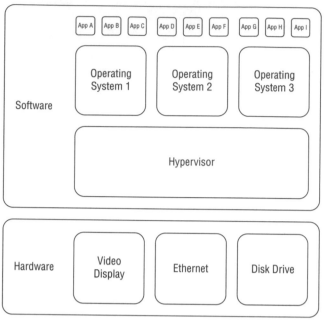

FIGURE 3.8 **Type 1 Hypervisor**

Virtualization is the foundation upon which Infrastructure-as-a-Service (IaaS) cloud providers such as AWS or Google provide virtual machines to different clients who may well end up running on the same physical computer, unknown to each other.

The advantages of virtualization include:

- More efficient use of the underlying hardware (just as operating systems permitted a single computer to be shared by multiple programs and users)

- Dynamic scaling of infrastructure in response to demand

- Additional separation and isolation between programs and applications running on different operating systems (as opposed to running on the same OS) — supporting the security principles of defense in depth and layers of security outlined earlier

Potential Weaknesses

As with memory protection, virtualization depends on the correct operation of both the hardware and the hypervisor. Hardware defects such as Meltdown break the underlying assumption that the hardware will prevent an unauthorized program (and possibly a completely unrelated client) from accessing memory assigned to another program (and client).

Similarly, software defects in hypervisors can improperly permit software running on one virtual machine to access data on a different virtual machine on the same computer. When such defects are discovered, they are usually responsibly disclosed to the largest cloud service providers so that they can be patched before the vulnerability becomes widely known.

There is always the possibility that these unpatched defects in the hardware or hypervisor might be known to a threat actor who is then able to compromise the protections that are supposed to prevent unrelated clients on virtual machines from interacting. To mitigate this risk, some IaaS cloud providers offer dedicated hosts which guarantee that only virtual machines assigned to your account will be permitted to run on the dedicated host.

Secure Cryptoprocessor

The challenge with standard microprocessors is that code running with the highest privilege can access any device and any memory location, meaning that the security of the system depends entirely on the security of all of the software operating at that privilege level. If that software is defective, or can be compromised, then the fundamental security of everything done on that processor becomes suspect.

To address this problem, hardware modules called secure cryptoprocessors have been developed that are resistant to hardware tampering and that have a very limited interface (i.e. attack surface), making it easier to verify the integrity and secure operation of the (limited) code running on the cryptoprocessor.

Cryptoprocessors are used to provide services such as:

- Hardware-based True Random Number Generators (TRNG)
- Secure generation of keys using the embedded TRNG
- Secure storage of keys that are not externally accessible
- Encryption and digital signing using internally secured keys
- High-speed encryption, offloading the main processor from the computational burden of cryptographic operations

Features of cryptoprocessors that enhance their security over standard microprocessors (that could do most of the above in software) can include:

- Tamper detection with automatic destruction of storage in the event of tampering, and a design that makes it very difficult to tamper with the device without leaving obvious traces of the physical compromise. These protections can range from anti-tamper stickers that clearly show attempts to access the device's internal components to secure enclosures that detect unauthorized attempts to open the device and automatically erase or destroy sensitive key material.

- Chip design features such as shield layers to prevent eavesdropping on internal signals using ion probes or other microscopic devices

- A hardware-based cryptographic accelerator (i.e. specialized instructions or logic to increase the performance of standard cryptographic algorithms such as AES, SHA, RSA, ECC, DSA, ECDSA, etc.)

- A trusted boot process that validates the initial boot firmware and operating system load

There are many types of secure cryptoprocessors:

- Proprietary, such as Apple's Secure Enclave Processor (SEP) found in newer iPhones

- Open standard, such as the Trusted Platform Module (TPM) as specified by the ISO/IEC 11889 standard and used in some laptops and servers

- Standalone (e.g. separate standalone device with external communications ports)

- Smartcards

Some of these are discussed further below.

Trusted Platform Module (TPM)

A TPM is a separate processor that provides secure storage and cryptographic services as specified by ISO/IEC 11889 (see Figures 3.9 and 3.10). A TPM can be used by the operating system, processor BIOS, or application (if the OS provides access to the TPM) to provide a number of cryptographic and security services:

- Generate private/public key pairs such that the private key never leaves the TPM in plaintext, substantially increasing the security related to the private key (Public/private keys are discussed further later in this chapter.)

- Digitally sign data using a private key that is stored on the TPM and that never leaves the confines of the TPM, significantly decreasing the possibility that the key can become known by an attacker and used to forge identities and launch man-in-the-middle attacks (Digital signatures are discussed later in this chapter.)

- Encrypt data such that it can only be decrypted using the same TPM

- Verify the state of the machine the TPM is installed on to detect certain forms of tampering (i.e. with the BIOS)

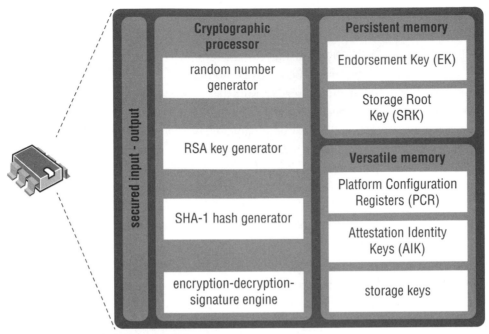

FIGURE 3.9 Trusted Platform Module processes

FIGURE 3.10 Trusted Platform Module hardware

Potential Weaknesses

The Private Endorsement Key (PEK) is a fundamental component of a TPM's security. This key is generated by the TPM manufacturer and burned into the TPM hardware during the manufacturing process. Because of this, the user/system owner depends upon the security of the TPM manufacturer to ensure that the PEK remains confidential.

We also depend on the quality of the TPM manufacturer's processes. In late 2017 it was revealed that a defect in the software library used by Infineon for their line of Smart-cards and TPMs contained a flaw which made it possible to deduce the private key stored internally. As a result, there were millions of cryptographic keys made unreliable and vulnerable. Attackers were able to calculate the private portion of an account holder's key from having access to only the public portion. What happened, unfortunately, is that hackers impersonated legitimate users with the assurance and nonrepudiation provided by having their private keys.

Cryptographic Module

A cryptographic module (see Figure 3.11) is typically a hardware device that implements key generation and other cryptographic functions and is embedded in a larger system.

FIGURE 3.11 A cryptographic module hardware device

The advantages of using a cryptographic module as opposed to obtaining the equivalent functionality from a cryptographic software library include the following:

- By performing critical cryptographic functions on a separate device that is dedicated to that purpose, it is much harder for malware or other software-based attacks to compromise the security of the cryptographic operation.

- By isolating security-sensitive functionality in an isolated device with limited interfaces and attack surfaces, it is easier to provide assurances about the secure operation of the device. It also makes it easier to provide secure functions to larger systems by embedding a cryptographic module within the larger system.

- Increased availability of non-cryptographic dedicated resources.

- Most secure cryptographic modules contain physical security protections including tamper resistance and tamper detection, making it very difficult to compromise the security of the device even if the device has been physically compromised.

- Some cryptographic modules can enforce separation of duties so that certain sensitive operations, such as manipulating key storage, can only be done with the cooperation of two different individuals who authenticate to the cryptographic module separately.

Some government organizations have issued standards related to the security of cryptographic modules and have established evaluation and certification processes so that manufacturers can have the security of their devices validated by an independent third party and users can have confidence in the security that using the module will provide their larger system.

For example, the U.S. government's FIPS 140-2, "Security Requirements for Cryptographic Modules," specifies the requirements for cryptographic hardware and software to meet four different levels of security. It also provides for certification of products to validate they meet the requirements.

Internationally, the "Common Criteria for Information Technology Security Evaluation," documented in the ISO/IEC 15408 standard, provides an alternate set of requirements and certification processes to validate information security products.

Hardware Security Module (HSM)

An HSM (see Figure 3.12) is a type of cryptographic module designed to stand alone as an appliance, and to provide cryptographic services over an externally accessible API (typically over a network or USB connection).

FIGURE 3.12 A standalone appliance cryptographic hardware module

HSMs are frequently found in Certificate Authorities (CAs) that use them to protect their root private keys, and payment processors that use them to protect the symmetric encryption keys used to protect cardholder data. HSMs are also used in many national security applications or other environments where proper management of cryptographic material is critical to the business process. CAs, digital signatures, certificates, and asymmetric/symmetric encryption are discussed later in this chapter.

Smartcard

Smartcards (see Figure 3.13) are credit card–sized cryptographic modules typically used to provide portable secure storage for the purposes of identity management (used for multifactor authentication), secure transport of sensitive information (such as keys between hardware security modules), and payment processing (such as the EMV standard for credit cards).

FIGURE 3.13 A smartcard

Because of the ease with which one can access the internal electronics of a smartcard, a number of hardware-based side-channel attacks have been developed by researchers.

Depending on how poorly or wisely the algorithm was implemented in the chip, side-channel attacks such as a timing attack can reveal valuable information about what's kept secret on the chip. A timing attack is performed like this: the attacker will measure and analyze the exact time period involved for the chip to process any instruction to it. By detecting minute differences in the time needed to complete the instruction, the attacker can infer secret data. Similarly, power analysis attacks can also allow an attacker to make inferences about the data contained in the chip.

ASSESS AND MITIGATE THE VULNERABILITIES OF SECURITY ARCHITECTURES, DESIGNS, AND SOLUTION ELEMENTS

Assessing information security vulnerabilities can be done by inspection or testing. Inspection can be manual, reviewing the design and implementation looking for vulnerabilities, or automated, in which software analyzes the configuration or code. Testing can be white-box, in which the tester knows the details of the system's design and implementation; black-box, in which the tester knows nothing about the internals of the system; or gray-box, in which the tester has some knowledge.

In practice, a combination of some or all of the above methods is usually employed in order to try to reduce the probability that an unidentified (and unmitigated) vulnerability will remain in the system when it is put into production. These activities, combined with threat modeling, increase the level of assurance that the system will operate in a secure manner.

In the case of secure software development, code is usually manually reviewed at least once, sometimes twice: first, a peer review process that requires the approval of a second developer before any code changes or additions can be committed to production; and later, a code inspection of the most sensitive and critical components, conducted by developers unrelated to those who developed the original code, to carefully examine the code looking for vulnerabilities or security defects.

Manual code review is very time-consuming, and must be done by experienced (and therefore valuable) developers. A risk-driven approach to manual code reviews allows the organization to focus on those parts of the code where compromise presents the greatest risk. Such an approach might result in greater attention to authentication, authorization, cryptography, and data sanitization functions.

Once you have analyzed the system and identified the potential vulnerabilities, you need to consider the impact should the vulnerability be exploited by a threat actor, and the likelihood of the vulnerability being exploited.

Different architectures (e.g., distributed vs. centralized) and systems (e.g., databases, servers, applications, etc.) require controls that address the unique security challenges they present, but in all cases the underlying platform (operating system) needs to be secure, which includes ensuring that the underlying system has been appropriately hardened (unnecessary services disabled, unneeded ports blocked, etc.) and updated as part of a vulnerability management process, both discussed in Chapter 7.

Client-Based Systems

A distributed processing environment establishes and uses a client-server relationship across a communications infrastructure. Traditionally, client-server systems implement the application as a standalone program on the client, while newer client-server applications leverage a common browser, and the application is developed within that context. Both approaches remain in widespread use, but evaluating the security posture of applications in either environment requires different skills and techniques.

In a traditional client-server system, client-related vulnerabilities can be grouped into two broad categories: those related to the client application itself, and those related to the system on which the client runs. It matters little how well implemented and configured the client software is if the underlying operating system is vulnerable.

Client software vulnerabilities fall into several categories:

- Vulnerabilities related to communications with the server, such as client software that connects to remote servers but does not take appropriate steps to do the following:
  - Validate the identity of the server
  - Validate or sanitize the data received from the server
  - Prevent eavesdropping of data exchanged with the server
  - Detect tampering with data exchanged with the server
  - Validate commands or code received from the server before executing or taking action based on information received from the server
- Vulnerabilities related to the insecure operation of the client:
  - Storing temporary data on the client system in a manner that is insecure (i.e. accessible to unauthorized users through, for example, direct access to the client device's filesystem)

To address these vulnerabilities, one can consider:

- Using a recognized secure protocol (e.g. TLS) to validate the identity of the server and to prevent eavesdropping of, and tampering with, data communicated with the server

- Using appropriate coding techniques to ensure that the data or commands received from the server are valid and consistent
- Using digital signing to verify executable code received from the server prior to execution

In many cases the client may use software libraries, applets, or applications to process data received from the server. For example, the client may rely upon image display components to permit the viewing of files. These components (e.g. Flash and PDF viewers) will typically be provided by third parties and, as such, will need to be part of a vulnerability management program so that vulnerabilities that are discovered later can be patched in a timely manner.

If the client is a browser, then the browser ought to be configured in accordance with hardening guidelines available for the major web browsers. Similarly, the appropriate steps to protect and patch the underlying system that runs the client software need to be taken. Excellent sources of such guidance for browsers and client operating systems include The Center for Internet Security (CIS) and the Defense Information Systems Agency's Security Technical Implementation Guides (`https://iase.disa.mil/stigs/`).

The client system also needs to be protected from other threats as appropriate, based on the risk assessment and threat modeling. This could include firewalls, physical security controls, full-disk encryption, and so on. See the next section for guidance on operating system hardening.

If the software has been developed specifically for this application, then the appropriate secure software development process as described in Chapter 8 must be employed.

Server-Based Systems

In this section we shall consider the security related to server-based systems other than web servers (which are covered below in the "Assess and Mitigate Vulnerabilities in Web-Based Systems" section).

Server vulnerabilities mirror many of the same vulnerabilities described above, just from the server's perspective.

The server needs to validate the identity of the client and/or the identity of the user of the client. This can be done using a combination of Identity and Access Management (IAM) techniques along with a secure communications protocol such as TLS, using client-side certificates. TLS will also protect the server from eavesdropping and tampering, such as might happen from a MitM attack. The server also must validate all inputs and not assume that simply because the commands and data coming from the client are originating from (and have been validated by) the corresponding client-side software that they are valid and have been sanitized. The client must be considered untrusted, and it must be assumed that the client-end can insert or modify commands or data before being encrypted and transmitted over the secure (e.g. TLS) link. Depending on the nature of the environment, it might be appropriate to protect the server from denial-of-service attacks by using techniques such as rate-limiting, CAPTCHA, and other approaches.

Certainly, a vulnerability management program is needed to ensure that updates and patches are applied in a timely fashion. This holds true regardless of whether the server-side software is developed in-house or is based in part or completely on software obtained from a third party. If the software has been developed specifically for this application, then the appropriate secure software development process must be employed.

This includes ensuring that the server application runs only with the minimum permissions necessary, commonly understood as the "principle of least privilege." If and when privilege escalation is needed, the period during which the server operates with elevated privileges is minimized. Best practices include the server using filesystem ownership and permissions to avoid data leakage, logging appropriate audit info to support SIEM tools, and capturing forensic information to permit analysis of a possible or actual security incident.

Finally, threats to the server itself need to be addressed. This may include physical and environmental threats, threats to the communications infrastructure, and server hardening as per industry recommendations such as those promulgated by the CIS or collected and indexed in NIST's National Checklist Program Repository (`https://nvd.nist.gov/ncp/repository`).

✔ Server Hardening Guidelines

The details of the specific issues that need to be addressed when hardening a specific operating system will vary slightly depending on the OS, but generally involves:

- Installing updates and patches
- Removing or locking unnecessary default accounts
- Changing default account passwords
- Enabling only needed services, protocols, daemons, etc. (conversely, disabling any not needed)
- Enabling logging and auditing
- Implementing only one primary function per server
- Changing default system, filesystem, service, and network configurations as needed to improve security (including full-disk encryption if appropriate)
- Removing (or disabling) unneeded drivers, executables, filesystems, libraries, scripts, services, etc.

Database Systems

Securing database systems is a special case of the more general server-based system security discussed in the previous section. If the database is accessible over a network, then all of the security controls discussed there apply as well as those outlined below. If the database is not network accessible, then there are fewer risks and some server security controls may not be necessary. Database-specific security controls include:

- Only install or enable those components of the database system that are needed for your application.

- Place data stores and log files on non-system partitions.

- Set appropriate filesystem permissions on database directories, data stores, logs, and certificate files.

- Run database service using a dedicated unprivileged account on a dedicated server.

- Disable command history.

- Do not use environment variables, command line, or database configuration files to pass authentication credentials.

- Do not reuse database account names across different applications.

- Disable "anonymous" accounts (if supported by the database).

- Mandate all connections use TLS if access or replication traffic travels over untrusted networks.

- Use unique certificates for each database instance.

- Remove any example or test databases.

- Change all default passwords, ensure all accounts have secure passwords, and consider enabling multifactor or certificate-based authentication (where supported).

- Ensure user account permissions have been assigned using the principle of least privilege. Database privileges can be very complex and interact in unexpected ways — avoid default roles and define those you need with only the permissions needed for each.

- Disable or remove unneeded accounts, especially those with administrative permissions.

- Manage all accounts according to best practices (see Chapter 5).

- Enable logging of sensitive operations and route logs to your log monitoring and alerting system.

- Use *bind* variables where possible to minimize injection attack surfaces.

- Assign unique admin accounts for each administrator (i.e. do not share admin accounts between more than one admin). Carefully consider a role-based approach that supports a least-privilege and separation-of-duties model in which each admin only has those admin permissions necessary to discharge their specific responsibilities. Where possible, ensure that critical operations require the cooperation of two admins.

- Enable logging at a sufficiently detailed level to provide the forensic information needed to identify the cause of events related to security incidents (but ensure logging does not include passwords), and protect the logs from tampering by database admins, either through permissions on the database system itself or by transmitting the log data in real time to a separate secure logging system.

- Consult vendor database documentation for DB-specific security controls (e.g. Oracle supports a control known as "data dictionary protection" which provides an additional level of least-privilege control, restricting certain operations to a subset of those with database admin privileges).

- Consult the CIS's hardening guidelines for the database system being used.

- For databases that are only accessed through application software (e.g. the typical *n*-tier web server application), run the database on private networks only accessible to the business logic servers that need access.

Database encryption deserves special attention. The encryption of data at rest can happen at any (or all) of several different levels:

- At the lowest level, full-disk encryption (FDE) protects all of the data on the storage media, protecting against the physical theft or loss of the drive itself. It provides no protection from threat actors who have logical access to the system, as the operating system or drive itself will decrypt all data that is read from the storage media before it is passed to the application without regard to the identity of the requester (other than the permission to access the file). This can be implemented through firmware (self-encrypting drives) or through the operating system (i.e., Bitlocker).

- Filesystem-level encryption allows the encryption to occur at the filesystem level. This can be done at the volume, directory, or file level, depending on the capabilities of the operating system.

- Transparent data encryption (TDE) protects the data from those who have direct access to the filesystem (i.e. the "root" user), but do not have permission to access the database system and the specific database item. It does not protect against malicious database administrators or attacks, such as SQL injection, that are able to bypass the application-level controls and issue database access commands directly. While TDE provides protection beyond FDE, there are significant vulnerabilities it does not mitigate and so it is not meant to be used alone. Note also that with some database systems, if the attacker can obtain both the operating system image and the TDE-protected database, the unencrypted contents can be extracted. Cell-level encryption (CLE) or application-level encryption (see below) are necessary to protect against threats that TDE does not address.

- CLE encrypts database information at the cell or column level. With this approach, data remains encrypted when read from the database and is only decrypted when requested. It also permits the user to exert very granular control over the cryptographic keys. This additional security and flexibility is not without its drawbacks. Key managements, and handling the decryption/encryption requests can add considerable complexity to the application, and depending on the types of queries (and whether they include CLE-protected data), the performance can be affected, sometimes drastically.

Application-level encryption is a high-level approach that provides protection even if access to the database system is compromised. In this case, the business-logic or application layer is responsible for encrypting the data to be protected before it is passed to the database, and for decrypting it once it has been retrieved. The database itself only sees binary data and does not have any access to the encryption keys. This approach is the most complex, but provides greater security (if properly implemented and managed) than the other approaches. To maximize the benefit of this approach, applications ought to encrypt as early as possible, and decrypt as late as possible. Or to put it another way, handle the encryption/decryption as close to the point of use as possible. For example, if your server-side application has a number of layers (see Figure 3.1), then the cryptographic component ought to be called from the business-logic layer, not the storage management layer. Note, however, that performing the decryption completely externally to the database will make certain database functions unavailable (certain types of search, for example). The decision as to which combination of database encryption approaches to use will be influenced by considerations such as:

- Performance, especially if searches reference data encrypted using CLE
- Backups, which will be protected using TDE or CLE, but not necessarily when using FDE (unless the backup is on another FDE-protected drive)
- Compression as encrypted data does not compress and so the use of encryption may significantly increase the size of backups. Some databases support decrypting the data prior to compression, and then reencrypting so the backup is compressed and encrypted. That may, however, introduce other vulnerabilities in the process.

Cryptographic Systems

As American cryptologist Bruce Schneier famously stated, "All cryptography can eventually be broken—the only question is how much effort is required." The challenge then becomes one of weighing the value of the encrypted information to the attacker against the level of effort required to compromise the cryptographic system. In making this decision, the potential attacker has a number of avenues which can be followed to compromise a cryptographic system. These include:

- Algorithm and protocol weaknesses
- Implementation weakness
- Key management vulnerabilities

As a side note, there are countries that strictly regulate the use of cryptography, and countries that, while permitting the unrestricted *use* of cryptography, regulate the export of cryptographic technology. A detailed discussion of these issues is beyond the scope of this text, but they need to be considered by the security architect who must be familiar with the legislative constraints that apply. See Chapter 1 for more information on legislative compliance issues relevant to information security.

The following sections will explore these vulnerabilities of cryptographic systems, and the "Apply Cryptography" section later in this chapter will examine cryptography further.

Algorithm and Protocol Weaknesses

The first rule in cryptography is never to invent your own cryptographic algorithm. Although technology professionals are generally smart people, it is entirely too common that we become overconfident in our abilities. In 1864, famed cryptographer Charles Babbage wrote, "One of the most singular characteristics of the art of deciphering is the strong conviction possessed by every person, even moderately acquainted with it, that he is able to construct a cipher which nobody else can decipher." This leads to a false sense of security: simply because you have invented a system that you cannot defeat, that does not mean it cannot be defeated by someone else.

Designing a secure cryptographic algorithm or protocol is very difficult, and only those algorithms that have been carefully examined by many experts and have stood the test of time ought to be used. A good pool of cryptographic algorithms with strong potential to be secure are those examined during the open public multiyear competitions to select cryptographic algorithms run by organizations such as NIST. Winners of these contests are carefully examined by cryptographers around the world. Such algorithms are scrutinized to identify any weaknesses or backdoors. Of course, the harsh reality that necessitates much scrutiny is that the threat actors that are most capable and well-funded often position themselves as advocates for secure algorithms. For an example, please see the upcoming sidebar "The Dual Elliptic Curve Deterministic Random Bit Generator (Dual EC DBRG)." As an example of how true peer scrutiny can be done, consider the progress made for symmetric cryptography as the current recommended algorithm (Advanced Encryption Standard or AES) was developed by a group of Belgian cryptographers and subjected to many years of intense scrutiny before being approved.

✔ WEP — A Design Flaw Case Study

Wired Equivalent Privacy (WEP) was the first approach to encryption used for WiFi networks. It had a number of design flaws which made it possible to decrypt most traffic, sometimes after only eavesdropping for a little as 3 minutes. It has been superseded by far more secure protocols (WPA and WPA2) and should not be used.

The primary weakness is that WEP used an initialization vector (IV) that was too short (24 bits). An IV is a number that is used by a stream cipher to ensure that two identical strings encrypted by the same key do not produce the same ciphertext. It is critical that the IV never be reused because if it is, the two messages encrypted with the same IV reveal information about how the data was encrypted. With such a short IV, it is unavoidable that that an IV will be reused given sufficient network traffic.

A second major weakness is a combination of two flaws: the underlying stream cipher that was used, RC4, has known "weak" keys and part of the key is based on the IV (which is transmitted in plaintext). By looking for intercepted packets with certain IVs one could more easily extract the full key.

The net result is that WEP traffic on a busy network can be compromised after eavesdropping for only a few minutes.

Next, realize that as computing power increases and more time is spent analyzing algorithms and protocols, weaknesses in what were previously robust approaches to cryptology will be found. Cryptology never gets stronger; it only gets weaker with the passage of time, so managing cryptologic products through their lifecycle is essential. The examples are myriad. The first symmetric cryptographic algorithm selected by NIST, the Data Encryption Standard (DES), was developed by IBM in the early 1970s, approved in 1977, and publicly broken in 1999. The Secure Hashing Algorithm (SHA-1) was approved in 1996 and deprecated in 2010.

In the future, there is the threat that the performance advances inherent in quantum computing will enable certain cryptographic algorithms currently resistant to brute-force attacks to be compromised. Quantum computing was complete fantasy until only very recently, and it is still mostly science fiction in any sense of practical application. However, the future will arrive quickly, as experts are claiming widespread commercial use could easily happen within the next several years. Given that quantum computing will have the capability to solve problems in seconds, quantum computing poses a significant threat to the sustainability of encryption.

Researchers are working to develop quantum-resistant algorithms. NIST plans to have proposals for post-quantum cryptography standards ready by 2025, and current estimates are that quantum computers capable of compromising today's algorithms will not become available until 2030 at the earliest. There are also European organizations (such as ETSI and the EU's PQCrypto project) working on post-quantum approaches to cryptology.

The story for cryptology protocols is similar. The original protocol to protect HTTPS web traffic was "Secure Sockets Layer" (SSL). The first version was found to be vulnerable and so was not even released publicly. Version 2.0 fixed that problem, was released in 1995, and found to be vulnerable the next year. Its replacement, 3.0, fared slightly better, thought to be secure until the disclosure of the POODLE vulnerability in 2014. The conclusions to be drawn include:

- Cryptology is hard and even the experts get it wrong.

- The cryptographic attack surface includes not only the algorithm, but the people, processes, and technology that implement the cryptographic protections, all of which are potentially vulnerable to attack.

- Cryptanalysis becomes more effective over time, owing to advances in computing, mathematical breakthroughs, and other improvements in cryptanalytic methods.

Because time erodes the security of cryptographic protections, the security architect must consider the lifecycle of the encrypted data when choosing cryptographic methods, particularly in the selection of an appropriate algorithm and key length. An appropriate choice for data that has a lifetime of only one or two years might not be the right choice if the data to be encrypted will remain sensitive for decades. In such a case, applying a compensating control for systems that must archive data for longer periods of time might be to design the system to allow for changing the cryptographic algorithm and re-encrypting the data as required by the risk assessment for the information.

Implementation Weaknesses

Not only is designing a secure cryptographic algorithm or protocol hard, securely implementing an algorithm is no easier. Use industry-standard algorithms, implemented in published libraries. Don't invent or implement algorithms yourself. It might be an interesting intellectual exercise to implement AES-256 or Twofish, but given the number of possible side-channel vulnerabilities, even if your implementation passes all the standard tests (i.e. produces the correct ciphertext given set plaintext), that is no assurance your implementation is not vulnerable.

> ### ✔ Heartbleed — An Implementation Flaw Case Study
>
> Heartbleed was an implementation flaw in the TLS protocol used to secure web traffic (HTTPS). Part of the protocol defined a "heartbeat" packet that contains a text message and a length field. The computer receiving the message is simply to send the message back. The defect was that the size of the message sent back was not based on the actual size of the received heartbeat packet, but on the length parameter sent by the requester. So a malicious actor could send a heartbeat packet containing the message "Hello, world!" but with a length field of, say, 64,000. The reply would contain "Hello, world!" plus the next 63,987 bytes of whatever happened to be in memory beyond that message. That memory could contain the private key used to secure the website, or copies of previous messages containing confidential information. Access to a web server's private keys would enable an attacker to decrypt past and future web traffic, as well as spoof the identity of the website, enabling phishing attacks.
>
> The flaw existed in the widely used library for two years before being reported and patched. At least half a million secure websites were estimated to have been affected, not to mention the hundreds of thousands of devices with an embedded web server used to manage the device. In one example, a curious computer science student used the flaw to exfiltrate 900 social insurance numbers from the Canada Revenue Agency, earning an 18-month conditional sentence in prison for his efforts. Cybersecurity columnist Joseph Steinberg wrote in *Forbes*: "Some might argue that Heartbleed is the worst vulnerability found (at least in terms of its potential impact) since commercial traffic began to flow on the Internet."
>
> More information may be found at `https://heartbleed.com`.

A side-channel attack is the analysis of artifacts related to the implementation of the algorithm, such as the time the algorithm takes to execute, the electrical power consumed by the device running the cryptographic implementation, or the electromagnetic radiation released by the device. More on this can be found in the "Understand Methods of Cryptanalytic Attacks" section.

✔ Enigma — Case Study of a Cryptographic Attack Process

Enigma, the cryptographic machine invented by a German engineer at the end of World War I, was in widespread use by many German government services by World War II. Enigma was a mechanical machine comprised of several rotors which provided the permutations of the key, and a plugboard of resettable electrical connections that provided the substitution and diffusion. For input, Enigma had a keyboard and for output, a lampboard. Effectively, Enigma was a typewriter that operated as a stream cipher for each keystroke.

The machine and cryptographic attacks on it by the British secret agency MI6 were popularized in the Hollywood film *The Imitation Game*. Britain was of course not the only war theater country involved. Poland made the initial foray of cryptographic attacks, particularly against the machine's rotors, reducing the system's cryptographic strength. The French also contributed by way of support and intelligence from German agents, until the French were occupied in 1940. While the Germans did regularly improve upon the machine throughout the war, the Allied Forces eventually broke the cipher and used the intelligence to successfully defeat the Axis Powers.

Defeating side-channel attacks is often difficult since detecting an attack which does not interfere with the operation of the cryptosystem is difficult. The best defense is to use standard cryptographic libraries that have been tested over time for side-channel information leakage.

There are also a number of steps one can take to minimize the possibility of leaking information via side channels, for example (and this is only a partial list of implementation traps lying in wait for the unsuspecting developer):

- Compare secret strings (e.g. keys, plaintext, unhashed passwords) using constant-time comparison routines
- Avoid branching or loop counts that depend upon secret data
- Avoid indexing lookup tables or arrays using secret data
- Use strong (i.e. "cryptographic grade") random number generators

One also needs to be aware that compiler optimizations can change or remove code to introduce side-channel vulnerabilities. The system security requirements need to identify these possible weaknesses and the testing and code validation need to verify they have been adequately addressed.

Vulnerabilities can also be introduced by misusing an otherwise securely implemented sound cryptographic algorithm.

With algorithms that use an IV, the IV must be properly selected to protect the encrypted data stream. Typically this means it must be cryptographically random and unique, and of enough length (i.e. not reused for subsequent messages).

Block ciphers can be used in a number of different modes (discussed later in this chapter), some of which may leak significant information when used with certain types of data. Selecting the correct mode is as important as selecting the block cipher itself.

Key Management Vulnerabilities

The most secure cryptographic algorithm is not going to provide any protection if you use weak keys or treat strong keys insecurely. What is a strong key? A strong key is one that is long and random.

How long should a strong key be? That depends on the algorithm and the duration for which you need to protect the data. Various organizations such as NIST in the U.S., ANSSI in France, or the BSI in the UK provide concrete recommendations such as disallowing the use of 80-bit symmetric keys after 2012, and 112-bit keys after 2030.

How random should a strong key be? Random enough to make it unlikely that an attacker can predict any of the bits of the key. If the mechanism used to generate keys is even somewhat predictable, then the system becomes easier to crack.

This is much more difficult than it seems. Firstly, most (pseudo-)random number generators are designed to produce numbers that appear statistically to be random, which is frequently all that is needed. But passing statistical tests for random distribution is not the same as being unpredictable. Cryptographically secure random number generators need to be both statistically random and unpredictable.

What does it mean to be unpredictable? It means that given a sequence of numbers produced by the algorithm, it is not possible to predict any of the bits of the next number in the sequence.

This is best done using hardware random number generators that are based on some physical property that is truly random. These are found in cryptographic modules embedded on many systems, and in Hardware Security Modules (HSMs) used to manage cryptographic material (see earlier in this chapter). Failing that, one must use a pseudo-random number generator designed for key generation. Guidance on appropriate algorithms may be found in the NIST SP800-90 series of publications, the ISO 18031 standard, and ANSI.

There are a number of vulnerabilities that can be introduced through the incorrect use, storage, and management of cryptographic keys.

Keys should be generated in a manner appropriate for the cryptographic algorithm being used. The proper method to generate a symmetric key is different from a public/private key pair. NIST SP800-133 (Recommendation for Cryptographic Key Generation) provides specific guidance.

Keys should not be reused and should be rotated (replaced) periodically to ensure that the amount of data encrypted using a single key is limited, and the lifetime of data encrypted using a given key is likewise limited.

Symmetric and private keys depend upon confidentiality to be effective. This means great care must be taken with how the keys are stored to reduce the possibility of their becoming known to unauthorized entities. There are a number of approaches to secure key storage, from key management software, to key management services provided by cloud service providers, to dedicated hardware devices that keep the keys stored internally in a tamper-resistant secure device.

Keys that have reached the end of their lifetime (and all properly managed keys ought to have a defined lifetime) must be securely destroyed to prevent their misuse in the future.

Another vulnerability can arise from insider threats. A rogue employee with access to key material can use that access to defeat the security of encrypted material (or enable another to do the same). Dual control or segregation of duties can be employed to ensure that at least two people must be actively involved before any key management operation that might compromise the security of the system can be completed.

The final leg of the CIA triad must also be considered: availability. If the key management system cannot provide access to the key material to authorized processes when required, then access to the encrypted material will be denied, even if the encrypted data is readily accessible.

Key operations must be logged in a manner that ensures accountability and traceability so that should a compromise be suspected, the forensic evidence will be available to analyze the possible breach.

Finally, where possible, key management functions ought to be automated. Manual processes are more prone to error (either of commission or omission), leading to weaknesses in the system that depends upon the keys for security.

Obviously, a key management system needs to be properly designed in the first place before it can be used. The "Key Management Practices" section later in this chapter further discusses the key management lifecycle, including HSMs and various other aspects of key management.

Industrial Control Systems

Industrial control systems (ICSs) are used to automate industrial processes and cover a range of control systems and related sensors. Security in this context concentrates on the integrity and availability aspects of the CIA triad: integrity of the data (e.g. sensor inputs and control setpoints) used by the control system to make control decisions, and availability of the sensor data and the control system itself. (See Figure 3.14.)

FIGURE 3.14 An industrial control system

The importance of this can range from ensuring the proper operation of a building's heating ventilation and air-conditioning systems (HVAC) to the safe production of dangerous chemicals to the reliable distribution of electricity to large areas of the country.

Historically, ICSs communicated using proprietary methods and were not connected to LANs or the Internet, and so security was not a design consideration. Many systems have been attached to IP gateways without much consideration as to the threats such access enables.

There are a number of organizations that provide guidance or regulations related to ICS security:

- ISA/IEC-62443 is a series of standards, technical reports, and related information that define procedures for implementing electronically secure Industrial Automation and Control Systems (IACS).

- The North American Electric Reliability Corporation (NERC) provides a series of guides referred to as the Critical Infrastructure Protection (CIP) standards.

- The European Reference Network for Critical Infrastructure Protection (ERNCIP) is an EU project with similar aims to those of NERC.

- NIST and the UK National Centre for the Protection of National Infrastructure (CPNI). See, for example, NIST publication SP800-82.

The importance of security to critical public infrastructure (such as electrical power distribution, water systems, and other public utilities) has come to the attention of governments because vulnerabilities in such systems are considered prime targets for economic warfare in times of conflict with foreign states.

✔ Ukraine Power Grid Cyber Attack

In the aftermath of Russia's annexation of Crimea in 2014, unknown attackers launched a coordinated and sophisticated attack against three different electrical utilities in Ukraine, taking almost 60 substations offline and disrupting power to more than 230,000 residents. This is the first confirmed successful cyber attack on an electrical power grid.

The compromise appears to have started with a successful spear phishing attack using malicious Word or Excel documents, which enabled the attackers to obtain the information and credentials necessary to access the control systems (which were not protected by two-factor authentication).

Then, in addition to taking control of systems that enabled the attackers to start turning off breakers, they uploaded malicious firmware into various components of the ICS so that even when the utilities regained control of their supervisory control systems, many of the substations would not respond to remote commands and had to be operated manually by technicians dispatched to each site.

Finally, the attackers used a piece of malware called KillDisk to erase essential system files on operator stations.

Although this attack was limited in its impact (the power interruuptions lasted between 1 and 6 hours and affected only about 0.5 percent of the country's population), the analysis showed the attackers had access to the control systems for at least six months prior and could have done a lot more damage if they had wanted. Some suspect this attack was intended to send a message rather than inflict heavy damage.

As a result, compliance with the NERC standards are mandatory in the U.S. and Canada for entities involved in power generation/distribution.

ICS security shares many of the same threats, vulnerabilities, and risks as any information system, and a review of the controls outlined in the standards above shows strong similarities to other information security frameworks.

The challenges specific to industrial control include:

- The difficulty of patching device firmware to address vulnerabilities in the software discovered after placing the device into production in the field

- Failure to change factory-default settings, especially related to access controls and passwords

- The long production lifetime of industrial systems as compared to IT systems

- The reliance on air-gapped networks as a compensating control without proper supervision of network connections

Let's consider each of these in turn.

As has been discussed earlier, patching software (including firmware) to address security defects discovered after the initial release of the software is a critically important aspect of security.

With ICSs, patching can be difficult or impossible:

- With industrial systems operating 24x7x365, it may not be feasible to take an ICS device out of production to update its firmware.

- Similarly, with continuous production being important, the risk of an update breaking something (such as patching the underlying operating system and interfering with the ICS app running on that OS) can be too great (and greater than the perceived risk of running obsolete software).

- Finally, the location of the ICS device in the field may make the simple matter of reaching the device physically to connect a laptop to install the firmware update a significant undertaking.

Obviously, a proper ICS design would accommodate the need to update components, but unfortunately many production systems were installed before there was an understanding of the security vulnerabilities inherent in ICSs. It is to be hoped that future ICS installations will be designed to handle the need to regularly update and replace components without unduly impacting the operation of the industrial processes being controlled.

Many IT departments plan to replace systems every three to five years. Most computer vendors stop supporting devices five to seven years after their first release, and no longer provide patches to address security issues. Most industrial process equipment is designed to operate for 10 to 20 years and longer. Further, the greater reliance on commercial, off-the-shelf operating systems increases the known attack surface for many ICS implementations. The problem is obvious.

If the physical security of the ICS is adequate, then the primary threats are from the Internet. In that case a reasonable and common compensating control is to air-gap the networks used by the industrial control devices. This can provide adequate security if properly enforced, but keeping the air-gapped network safe requires careful diligence and technical controls to prevent foreign equipment from being connected. If external equipment must be connected periodically, say for maintenance purposes, consider using a firewall or proxy between the maintenance laptop and ICS network to provide an additional layer of security.

The classic example of compromising an air-gapped ICS was Stuxnet, which was used to cause considerable damage to Iran's uranium enrichment facility. It has been reported that the air-gapped network was compromised by a virus-infected USB thumb drive being plugged into a computer on the ICS network.

At a minimum, computers used to maintain and manage industrial systems must never be used for any other purpose (or removed from the facility). They must be regularly updated, employ anti-malware protection, and carefully scan any removable media (e.g. USB thumb drives) before being used. See the guidance published by the organizations listed above for more specifics.

If complete isolation from the corporate LAN and the Internet is not an option, then it is essential to limit and screen permitted traffic accessing the ICS network through the use of carefully configured firewalls and network proxies. Consideration ought to be given to further segmenting the ICS network itself to limit the lateral spread of a compromise.

For ICSs that must be remotely accessible, compensating controls such as installing a web-proxy or VPN should be considered to add an additional layer of security on top of whatever access controls are implemented on the ICS itself.

The principle of psychological acceptability of security controls is particularly important. Advocating security awareness among all the technicians and plant operators is critically important. If those personnel burdened with the need to observe security controls understand the importance and rationale associated with those controls, they are less likely to view them as an impediment to their job of running the plant and something to be avoided or circumvented.

Cloud-Based Systems

Cloud-based systems are those based on a pool of network-accessible servers and related resources that can be rapidly and programmatically provisioned and managed.

NIST SP 800-145 and ISO/IEC 17788 define a number of characteristics that distinguish cloud computing:

- **Broad network access:** Resources (physical and virtual) are accessible and managed over the network.

- **Measured service:** Users pay only for the services they use.

- **On-demand self-service:** Users can provision and manage services using automated tools without requiring human interaction.

- **Rapid elasticity and scalability:** Services can be rapidly and automatically scaled up or down to meet demand.

- **Resource pooling and multitenancy:** Physical or virtual resources are aggregated to serve multiple users while keeping their data isolated and inaccessible to other tenants.

There are several service models as shown in Table 3.2.

TABLE 3.2 Cloud Service Models

CLOUD SERVICE MODEL	SERVICE PROVIDED	SERVICE PROVIDER RESPONSIBILITIES	CUSTOMER RESPONSIBILITIES
Software as a Service (SaaS)	Software application accessible to the customer using a browser or API	Provide and manage all infrastructure from server and network hardware to applications software	Provide the client device and manage user-specific configuration settings

CONTINUES

CLOUD SER-VICE MODEL	SERVICE PROVIDED	SERVICE PROVIDER RESPONSIBILITIES	CUSTOMER RESPONSIBILITIES
Platform as a Service (PaaS)	Hosting for customer-provided applications software	Provide and manage all infrastructure from server and network hardware to the libraries and runtime services necessary to run applications	Provide the application and manage the hosting environment
Infrastructure as a Service (IaaS)	Virtual machines enabling customer to run all components from the operating system up to the application	Provide network and server infrastructure to support virtual machines	Provide and manage all components that run on the VM as well as limited aspects of network services

With each service model there is obviously a different division between the components supplied by the cloud service provider and those provided by the customer. This gives rise to the cloud-shared responsibility model as illustrated in Figure 3.15. Security of cloud deployment is shared between the customer and the provider. The cloud service provider is responsible for the security of the cloud, and the customer is responsible for the security in the cloud. This also means that one has to consider the security capabilities and commitments of the provider when assessing the risk of a cloud deployment.

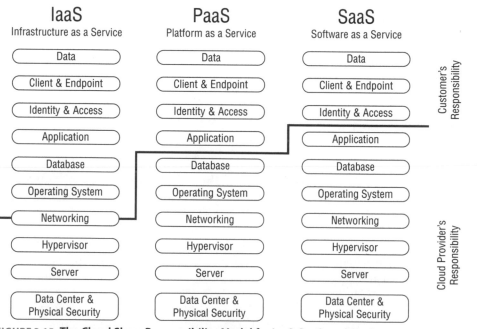

FIGURE 3.15 The Cloud Share Responsibility Model for IaaS, PaaS, and SaaS

In particular, the cloud service provider is exclusively responsible for:

- Physical security
- Environmental security
- Hardware (i.e. the servers and storage devices)
- Networking (i.e. cables, switches, routers, firewalls, and Internet connectivity)

The cloud service provider and the customer share responsibility for:

- **Vulnerability and patch management:** Using Figure 3.15 as a guide to determine which organization is responsible for which activities, the cloud server provider is responsible for patching the software below the responsibility dividing line, the customer above (i.e in the case of SaaS, the customer is only responsible for the computers and browsers used to access the cloud).

- **Configuration management:** The cloud service provider is responsible for the infrastructure, the customer for everything above. Network configuration and security is a special case, as the customer of an IaaS provider typically has configuration control over significant aspects of the network routing and firewalls through APIs and web-based management consoles. As these network controls are a key component of the security of an IaaS cloud deployment, the customer must take great care in ensuring their proper configuration.

- **Training:** Both the cloud provider and customer are responsible for the specific training required for their own personnel.

In the IaaS situation, in which the customer has responsibility for many aspects of network security, providing perimeter and interior security requires a different approach from traditional data center security. In the cloud, the customer rarely has the ability to install actual networking or security devices (such as firewalls, routers, switches, and the like), but instead is given API access to a limited number of firewall and router functions that they can use to control access to their virtual machines. Also, depending on the cloud service provider, access to network traffic, as one might expect in a data center using a network tap or a SPAN (mirror) port, may or may not be available, or might be only available on a sampled basis such as NetFlow or sFlow.

Finally, cloud service can be deployed in a number of ways:

- **Public cloud:** Available to any customer
- **Private cloud:** Used exclusively by a single customer (may be in-house or run by a third party, on-premise or off)
- **Community cloud:** Used exclusively by a small group of customers (may be managed by one or more of the customers, or a third party, on-premise or off)
- **Hybrid cloud:** A combination of two or more of the above deployment models

The deployment model will have a significant effect on the nature of the risk assessment for the cloud deployment. That said, do not assume that private or on-premise cloud deployments are intrinsically more secure than public clouds. The major cloud providers have invested heavily in security, as attested to by their many security audits and certifications, and they can typically provide better security for their clients than those companies can for themselves.

Distributed Systems

A distributed system is a collection of systems designed to appear as a single system to users. Distributed systems are built to achieve a number of objectives, including reliance, performance, and scalability.

Because a distributed system, by definition, involves multiple subsystems, possibly distributed geographically, and interconnected in some manner, the attack surface is much larger than that of a single system.

It is important to model threats to the overall system and identify the relative risks that need to be addressed.

Consider the following:

- The need for encryption and authentication on the connections between the subsystems to ensure attackers cannot intercept, eavesdrop, or spoof communications between subsystems

- The need to protect against denial-of-service attacks against the communications links or the subsystems themselves

- The risks from a lack of homogeneity across subsystems (e.g. different versions and patch levels of operating systems, middleware, and application software; difficulty of maintaining consistent configurations across disparate and distributed systems) and mechanisms to mitigate those risks

- The need to maintain consistency should communications be disrupted (delayed or interrupted) between groups of (normally) connected subsystems (sometimes referred to as the "split-brain" problem)

- The challenge of ensuring comparable security controls in the case of geographically distributed components (e.g. physical, environmental, and personnel)

- The requirements of privacy and data sovereignty regulations that may limit the transfer of personal data across international borders

These risks are not unique to distributed systems, but the nature of distributed systems can make their mitigation much more complex than for non-distributed systems.

Internet of Things

The Internet of Things (IoT) is the name applied to all manner of devices from household appliances to aquariums to video cameras that are able to communicate over the Internet. Estimates are that the number of such devices will reach between 20 and 50 billion by 2020.

The importance of IoT security can be demonstrated through two recent events: the Mirai DDoS attack and the aquarium attack.

The Mirai attack (Figure 3.16) involved a worm that searched for vulnerable IoT devices (typically consumer routers and IP-enabled CCTV cameras), infected them with a copy of the malware, and then waited for instructions from a command and control (C&C) server as to which target to attack with a DDoS attack. In late 2016 this took the *Krebs on Security* blog offline, and later attacked the Dyn DNS service, which in turn seriously impacted many of their customers including GitHub, Twitter, Reddit, Netflix, and Airbnb.

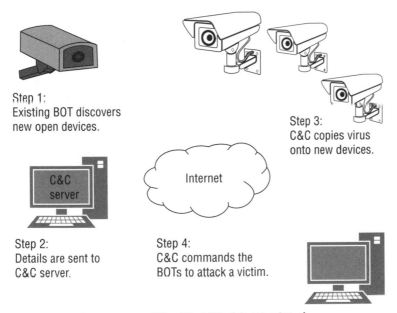

Step 1:
Existing BOT discovers new open devices.

Step 3:
C&C copies virus onto new devices.

Step 2:
Details are sent to C&C server.

Step 4:
C&C commands the BOTs to attack a victim.

FIGURE 3.16 **Components of the Mirai DDoS BotNet Attack**

In 2017 it was reported that threat actors were able to compromise an Internet-enabled fish tank at a casino, and then pivoted from that device to access computers on the same network, exfiltrating 10GB of data before they were detected and shut down.

The proliferation of Internet of Things devices is nothing short of explosive. The ability to physically integrate wireless connectivity into a device can be done cheaply and requires almost no added space in all but the tightest packaging. The ability to codify wireless functionality alongside a device's existing functionality enables connectivity to be added to basically any device. The end result is a dramatic increase in IoT devices in both the personal and corporate worlds. The ability of users to bring devices into their corporate networks creates new risks for those networks, and the organization's leadership appreciates the need for strategy to counteract those risks. Usually, taking necessary action begins with creating or updating policies, and then continues with implementing technical controls such as IoT device segmentation or NAC.

IoT Security from a Manufacturer's Perspective

For a producer of IoT devices, the objective is to market and sell as many of their devices as possible. Manufacturers seek to make money, not to simply "build a better mousetrap" for altruistic purposes. Most products that are made with reasonable care and solve a problem for the customer sell reasonably well.

How well a product sells depends largely on its quality and reputation, regardless of price. And in this day and age of peer reviews, product reputations are readily available for potential customers to read and judge before making a purchase. Shoes and cars known to quickly break down do not get repeat customers. Similarly, IoT products with a reputation of getting exploited and then attacking customers or others do not sell well. Worse yet, exploited products cause liability issues that can cost the company far more than lost sales.

During development you will want to conduct threat modeling to determine the likely vulnerabilities and to ensure that appropriate mitigations are deployed. You are going to want to review the security architecture to determine if the general guidelines outlined earlier in this section have been observed in the design of the firmware.

The development team will need to pay particular attention to secure software development guidelines such as those from OWASP and SANS. And your QA team will need to perform active white- and black-box penetration testing.

Many of the vulnerabilities that have been exploited in IoT devices in the past could have been mitigated through basic security hygiene such as changing default credentials and updating the firmware to patch known vulnerabilities.

Given that, as an IoT product developer, apart from trying to design and develop as secure an IoT device as you can, you need to make implementing the above two security controls as easy as possible. You can make your device the most secure IoT device on the planet, but once it's in your customers' hands, it is out of your control. You need to make it as easy as possible for them to properly secure and maintain the device.

This means that your device ought to refuse to connect to the Internet until the user has changed the default admin credentials. It means that your device ought to update itself automatically (with the consent of the user), and if auto-update has not been enabled, possibly refuse to operate (after sufficient notice) should a patch be available for a high-severity vulnerability being actively exploited in the wild.

While ease-of-use is a key factor in the commercial success of IoT devices, one has to draw the line where ease-of-use is directly connected to ease-of-compromise.

IoT Security from a User's Perspective

As a user of IoT devices, there are steps you can take to mitigate the risks related to devices with poor design or support so that you do not become part of a botnet used to attack others, and your IoT devices are not used as a beachhead from which your other information systems can be attacked.

To start, you can protect yourself (and others that might be a target of your compromised devices) through the same two basic security controls previously mentioned:

- Change default credentials as soon as possible, and before you connect the device to the Internet.

- Keep your device updated with the current firmware release, either by enabling auto-update (if supported by your device) or by periodically checking with the manufacturer's website for firmware updates.

In addition, you can employ security-in-depth through additional controls:

- Do not place IoT devices on the open Internet but behind a firewall so that they are not directly accessible externally.

- Segment your network so that your IoT devices do not have access to other sensitive devices or servers on your internal networks.

- If you have to be able to access your IoT device externally, then at the very least put the device behind a router that does reverse NAT mapping. Recall that reverse NAT provides network address translation, but from an external source to an internal private address. Hence, it is NAT but in reverse. Preferably, put the device behind a proxy that can perform its own user authentication before providing access to the IoT device.

Note, of course, that the router or proxy is also a potential vulnerability and must itself be operated securely: it must be properly configured (change default credentials) and maintained (patched and updated).

Relying on the security of an IoT device is unwise given the history of unpatched vulnerabilities in such devices. By placing the device behind another that acts as an access gateway, one implements security in depth and security layering, requiring the compromise of two different devices before the IoT device can be breached. And if you have properly segmented your network, even the compromise of your IoT devices will have limited impact on the confidentiality and integrity of your information systems (the availability of those systems in the face of an IoT DDoS attack is another matter). In fact, taking network segmentation to the extreme leads to Google's BeyondCorp paradigm: a network in which access to resources is not granted based on network location but by user privileges.

✔ UK Report on Consumer IoT

Many governments have realized the threat IoT poses, not only to their citizens, but to their nations' infrastructures. The UK government published a report in March of 2018 called "Secure by Design: Improving the cyber security of consumer Internet of Things Report" that included a proposed code of practice, the main points of which are listed here:

- No default passwords
- Implement a vulnerability disclosure policy
- Keep software updated
- Securely store credentials and security-sensitive data (and avoid hard-coded credentials)
- Communicate securely
- Minimize exposed attack surfaces
- Ensure software integrity
- Ensure that personal data is protected
- Make systems resilient to outages
- Monitor system telemetry data
- Make it easy for consumers to delete personal data
- Make installation and maintenance of devices easy
- Validate input data

ASSESS AND MITIGATE VULNERABILITIES IN WEB-BASED SYSTEMS

Web-based systems are applications that are accessible using a web browser. Vulnerabilities in web-based systems have been at the root of some of the largest data breaches in recent history such, as Equifax.

This section will speak to vulnerabilities specific to web-based systems. Other issues, such as network security (see Chapter 4) or software vulnerability management and patching (discussed in Chapter 7), can also impact the security of web-based systems.

The definitive references for web security are those published by OWASP and MITRE's Common Weakness Enumeration (CWE). In turn, other organizations use these references to characterize their various reports, such as SANS's 25 Most Dangerous Programming Errors. More detailed information for each of these resources can be found at the following sites:

- **The OWASP 2017 Top 10 List:**
  `https://www.owasp.org/images/7/72/OWASP_Top_10-2017_%28en%29.pdf.pdf`

- **MITRE's Common Weakness Enumerations, version 3.1:**
  `https://cwe.mitre.org/data/`

- **SANS 25 Most Dangerous Programming Errors:**
  `https://www.sans.org/top25-software-errors`

The following sections cover some of the most frequently encountered vulnerabilities. Note that some of these vulnerabilities have applicability outside of the context of web-based systems and are relevant in other contexts and situations.

Injection Vulnerabilities

Injection is when user-supplied content, typically entered into a web form, is not properly checked and sanitized before being processed, enabling the attacker to insert malicious instructions into what is supposed to be data.

The classic example is SQL injection, in which the user's input is combined with an SQL query which is submitted to the database for processing. SQL injection attacks have been implicated in some of the largest security breaches, including an attack in 2009 that obtained the details of 130 million credit and debit cards and at the time was considered by many to be the biggest case of identity theft in American history. It is a sad reflection of the state of our industry that that claim only lasted four years.

Consider the following pseudocode:

```
CustomerInput = request.getParameter("id");
Query = "SELECT * FROM accounts WHERE accountnanme='" + CustomerInput + "'";
```

The intent is that the user enter the name of the account to be queried. But if an attacker enters a string such as:

```
' or '1'='1
```

the SQL statement passed to the database will be

```
SELECT * FROM accounts WHERE custID='' or '1'='1'
```

resulting in the database returning data on all accounts, not just one.

The defense is to never trust any input, carefully check to ensure it contains only valid characters and data, and if it contains any special characters that might be interpreted by the database (or some other downstream component), then those characters must be deleted or properly escaped so they are not interpreted as commands.

Another simple example is a web form that enables the user to enter an IP address to be passed to a shell script to check using `ping`. Imagine a shell script that does no checking of the user's input and simply runs the command:

```
ping -c 10 ${IPAddr}
```

If the user enters

```
8.8.8.8; cat /etc/passwd
```

not only will they get the ping results for Google's DNS service, they will get a list of the password files containing all user names.

In this case the user's input ought to have been checked to ensure it only contained a valid IP address.

Broken Authentication

Authentication is the first defense for most web applications. If the attacker cannot log in as a user, there is often little attack surface accessible. On the flip side, once an attacker can log in as a legitimate user, all bets are off. It is important to understand what vulnerabilities exist regarding authentication.

Vulnerabilities related to authentication can include:

- Plaintext passwords in transit
- Plaintext passwords at rest
- Weak passwords
- Single-factor authentication
- Password guessing
- Man-in-the-browser attack
- Session hijacking

The following sections explore each of these vulnerabilities.

Plaintext Passwords in Transit

If the application permits a user to log in over an HTTP connection (rather than forcing HTTPS and TLS), then the user's password will be communicated in plaintext and at risk from eavesdropping. Web apps should never provide a login screen over HTTP or accept a login over HTTP.

Plaintext Passwords at Rest

If the application stores passwords in plaintext, then should that data store be compromised, all of the account passwords would be accessible to the attacker. While symmetric encryption provides some security, it is considered a far weaker control than using cryptographically secure hashing combined with a unique salt (see the "Cryptographic Methods" section for more information).

Weak Passwords

The main proponent to creating a weak password, besides weak password requirements themselves, is forcing users to regularly change their passwords. That might seem counterintuitive at first, but the perspective on mandating regular password changes has shifted in recent years from being a sensible one to being counterproductive in ensuring a strong password. Forcing users to regularly change passwords often forces users to find the weakest allowable password.

Merely forcing passwords to use a combination of upper and lower case letters, digits, and/or special characters, or forcing passwords to be regularly changed, is no longer considered advisable. Many users who are forced to change their passwords regularly will weaken their authentication in one or more of the following ways:

- Choose a password very similar to the old one
- Choose a password that merely passes the trivial requirements
- Choose a password used elsewhere
- Develop bad habits of writing down passwords
- Forget their password more frequently, losing productivity

What might help in addressing some of these points is for the application to screen new passwords against a list of known "weak" passwords to prevent users from using one.

Single-Factor Authentication

Relying upon passwords alone to protect sensitive information is foolish. Not only do passwords get written down or shared, social engineering and phishing attacks can easily obtain many user passwords.

The best protection from this is (at a minimum) supporting, and (preferably) requiring the user provide to a second authentication factor such as a time-based one-time password.

Note that sending an SMS text message to the user's phone is no longer recommended by NIST (in their publication SP800-63B), as there have been a number of successful exploits against this approach.

Password Guessing

Web systems should detect attempts to brute-force the authentication system by using a bot to try commonly used passwords. This can be done in a number of ways:

- Using a CAPTCHA (Completely Automated Public Turing test to tell Computers and Humans Apart) mechanism to try to detect bots (either for all logins, or after a certain number of login failures)

- Delaying subsequent login attempts after each failure (and increasing the delay with each failure)

- Locking out the account completely (for an extended period of time, until the user reactivates the account by responding to an email message, or until unlocked by an administrator)

Man-in-the-Browser Attack

Users' browsers can be compromised through malware such that the authentication information they enter during the login process is captured and relayed to the attacker. As this eavesdrops on the data before it is sent over the HTTPS link, the encryption protection that comes with TLS is ineffectual.

MitB attacks are usually launched via a Trojan that compromises the victim's browser. These attacks can be mitigated to a certain extent by basic security hygiene:

- Do not install browser extensions or add-ons from untrusted sources.

- Keep your operating system and browser up to date (i.e. patched).

- Install and update anti-malware or endpoint detection and response (EDR) software.

Browsers are adding sandbox or containerization features (e.g. Site Isolation in Chrome) that limit the ability of a website to affect other sessions or websites.

For particularly sensitive web applications, there are other security controls that are more effective but add considerably to the complexity of using the web applications:

- An out-of-band communications channel can be used to confirm the transaction (for example, for a request to wire funds, especially above a certain threshold, or out of the country, the banking application might place a call to the user requiring personal approval of the transaction by speaking to a banking representative to confirm the identity).

- Requiring use of a hardened web browser that is run from a write-protected USB device to access the web app.

Session Hijacking

As users interact with a web application, the app needs to keep track of which requests came from which users. To connect disparate HTTPS requests to a single user, session tokens are used. These are data sent with every request, unique to each user, that identify the origin of the request and tie multiple requests into a single session.

In order to prevent an attacker from masquerading as an authorized user, it is critically important to ensure that the session token remains secret. If the attacker knows the session token, it can be inserted into communications to make the attacker appear to be the authorized user.

Session tokens can be compromised by:

- **Guessing:** Secure session tokens must be generated by a cryptographically secure pseudo-random number generator, making predicting session values highly unlikely.

- **Brute-force:** Secure session tokens must be long enough (at least 128 bits) to make trying every possible session token value infeasible.

Session tokens must also be invalidated when the user successfully logs in (to be replaced with a new session token), and when the user is logged off (either manually or after the session has expired).

Sensitive Data Exposure

The 2017 edition of the OWASP Top Ten Most Critical Web Application Security Risks describes sensitive data exposure as "the most common impactful attack [in recent years]."

Sensitive data exposure is characterized by missing, incorrect, or poorly implemented cryptographic methods (more on this later in this chapter) which might expose sensitive data to attackers. To be clear, sensitive data exposure differs from direct attacks on cryptographic data. Instead, scenarios such as cryptographic keys being accessible and cleartext data being captured are examples of sensitive data exposure.

This vulnerability can take many forms:

- Transmission of sensitive data in the clear (inappropriate use of HTTP instead of HTTPS)

- Lack of appropriate HTTP security headers used to mitigate the possibility of man-in-the-middle attacks, such as HTTP Strict Transport Security (HSTS) and Public-Key-Pins

- Incorrectly configured HTTP headers such as Cross-Origin Resource Sharing (CORS) headers, mistakenly permitting requests from one website to access data associated with another

- Weak (i.e. deprecated) ciphers, or secure ciphers with improperly chosen and managed keys

- Storing user passwords in plaintext, or encrypted using a symmetric cipher, or hashed using an algorithm designed for message integrity checking and not password storage, or without a long and random salt (see the "Cryptographic Methods" section)

XML External Entities

Extensible Markup Language (XML) is a file format frequently used to encode data. There have been a number of vulnerabilities in XML parsers that have enabled threat actors to tamper with, or upload, XML files causing the server to inappropriately disclose sensitive information or malfunction (as a form of a denial-of-service attack).

Mitigations include:

- Using a less complex file format such as JSON

- Ensuring your XML parser library is current (i.e. patched)

- Taking care to properly configure your XML parser and especially to disable security-sensitive options such as XML external entity (XXE) and document type definition (DTD) processing

- Using positive server-side sanitization to validate input and prevent malicious code within XML documents

If these tactics are not possible on the XML server side, other mitigating controls external to the server include the application firewall monitor for XXE attacks.

Broken Access Control

Broken access control occurs when a server does not properly validate every request. This can happen when, for example:

- The server validates the user's access to an admin page, but does not validate the POST or GET from that page. An attacker with knowledge of the POST or GET URL can make the call directly, bypassing the validation.

- The server embeds previously validated and authenticated account or identity information in the POST or GET request (or in cookies sent with the request) that are not validated upon receipt. An attacker who tampers with those parameters can bypass validation.

The obvious mitigation is to always check the identity and authority of the user to perform the requested operation on every request.

It must not be possible for a user, merely by changing parameters or cookies, to change the user's identity or privileges.

Security Misconfiguration

The web or application server's configuration can provide many opportunities for compromise if not carefully reviewed and properly set. For example:

- Default accounts must be disabled.

- Unnecessary features and services must be disabled (e.g. directory listing, status reports).

- Error reports (such as stack traces) may be logged internally but must not be sent to the user because the reports may leak sensitive information.

- Security headers must be enabled and properly configured in order to benefit from their protection (e.g. Content Security Policy, Cross-Origin Resource Sharing, etc.).

Of course, the misconfiguration of files, directories, or accounts is not limited to servers alone. Client machines can be misconfigured as well.

Be careful when upgrading web-server software or components, and be sure to review the release notes carefully as the defaults, parameters, and functionality may change between releases, meaning that a configuration that was secure with one release may not be secure with a subsequent release. For example, a 2017 change to the open-source React JavaScript library caused a company that provided website analytics to hundreds of firms to start collecting user passwords as part of the tracking data. Obviously, this was not the intent of the tracking company but went undetected for almost a year.

Cross-Site Scripting

Cross-site scripting (XSS) occurs when an attacker is able to fool a web application into interpreting data as browser scripting code. XSS is a form of an injection attack but sufficiently prevalent to warrant being discussed separately.

There are several types of XSS attacks, the most common being the stored and the reflected XSS attacks.

In the stored XSS attack, the threat actor manages to store a script in the server's database (e.g. in the user's name field) and then waits for the victim to cause the server to display the database record containing the stored XSS exploit.

In a reflected attack, the threat actor typically will trick the victim into clicking on a carefully crafted link (e.g. in an email or another website) that sends the attacker's malicious script to the target website. If the target website does not properly sanitize the input, and displays it to the victim's browser, the victim's browser will trust the script (as it will appear to have originated from the target website), and the attacker's script can perform malicious acts with the permissions of the user.

The mitigation in both cases is to never trust user input. All input must be carefully screened, preferably using a standard library that will remove or escape components of the input that, if sent back to the browser, would be interpreted as script or code (and not displayed as data).

Not only can XSS vulnerabilities lead to significant security compromises in and of themselves, the existence of an XSS vulnerability can completely defeat common protections against another vulnerability, Cross-Site Request Forgery (CSRF). This vulnerability is discussed in the "Cross-Site Request Forgery" subsection later in this section.

Using Components with Known Vulnerabilities

Keeping an accurate inventory of all the components your web application uses (both client- and server-side) is critically important so that the risks associated with reported vulnerabilities can be quickly assessed, and if necessary, promptly remediated. Consider also using automated vulnerability management tools to scan your web application environment and compare detected packages against a database of known vulnerabilities. Examples of these include MITRE's common vulnerabilities and exposure (CVE) list and NIST's National Vulnerability Database (NVD).

A known (and unpatched) vulnerability in the Apache Struts web application framework is reported to have been the vulnerability that attackers exploited in the massive 2017 Equifax breach of roughly 150 million records, considered by some to be the most expensive data breach in history.

Insufficient Logging and Monitoring

Prevention is important, but assuming all attacks can be prevented is naive and reckless. The responsible and conservative approach is "assumption of breach," first attributed to Kirk Bailey, the CISO at the University of Washington. The idea is to assume you have already been breached and design security controls not only to try to prevent attacks, but also to quickly detect attacks so the damage can be limited and promptly mitigated.

Essential for quick detection is comprehensive logging and carefully tuned alerting that monitors the logged data for events that are indicators of compromise.

Logging must:

- Capture all relevant events (e.g. logins, failed authentication, invalid GET or POST requests, sensitive transactions, etc.)

- Record sufficient details to be able to reconstruct the sequence of actions

- Be centralized so that events across different components and servers can be correlated

- Be immutable so that attackers cannot tamper with the logs and erase evidence of their activity

Monitoring should not only alert on events that are direct indicators of compromise, they should alert when rate limits are exceeded (such as an excessive number of login failures from a single IP) that are indicative of an active attack.

One test of the adequacy of the system's logging and monitoring is to review the logs and alerts generated by an external pen test or vulnerability scan.

Cross-Site Request Forgery

A CSRF attack involves the threat actor fooling the victim into submitting a state-changing request to a site the victim is already logged into.

For example, the attacker sends a phishing message to the victim with an embedded link of the form:

```
https://somebank.com/api/fundsxfer?amt=1500&ToAccount=123456789
```

If the victim is already logged on, then the victim's browser would already have a valid session token and would send the token along with the request to the banking app which would see that it came from a validly logged in user.

There are a number of ways to prevent such attacks, the most common being a CSRF token which is a unique, random value that is embedded in all GET and POST requests in web pages and forms rendered by the web app, such that the application can differentiate between requests that have originated from the user's session and requests that have been crafted by a threat actor.

ASSESS AND MITIGATE VULNERABILITIES IN MOBILE SYSTEMS

Mobile devices are prone to many of the same vulnerabilities as other computing systems, but often to a greater degree. For example, desktop systems are far less vulnerable to being stolen. Another example, the wireless network infrastructure, is far less vulnerable to compromise or tampering. As mobile devices are carried around and made accessible to others, they are far more vulnerable outside the organization's network and physical perimeter.

The likelihood of mobile devices being exploited is also far greater for reasons to be discussed below. Because they are inherently small and portable, mobile devices are far more prone to being lost or stolen. Whereas many employees are happy to use only their company-provided computers for work purposes, almost every employee has a mobile device and wants, at a minimum, to be able to stay in touch with coworkers using email, chat, or other apps.

Security vulnerabilities that arise in the use of mobile systems include the following:

- Weak or missing passwords/PINs
- Lack of multifactor authentication
- Long session lifetime
- Wireless vulnerabilities (Bluetooth and WiFi)
- Mobile malware
- Lack of security software
- Unpatched operating system or browser
- Lack of inherent firewall
- Insecure devices

The following sections discuss each of these vulnerabilities and then explore how Mobile Device Management (MDM) can be used to address vulnerabilities in mobile systems.

Passwords

Mobile users tend to think more about the convenience of using their phone than security, and so either do not enable passwords (on those devices where that is possible) or they use simplistic passwords or PIN codes. Combine a short, simple PIN with the lack of care most users take in protecting the PIN when entering it, and a determined attacker can easily "shoulder surf" from some distance and make a good guess as to what digits were entered to unlock the phone.

This, combined with the long session lifetimes of many mobile applications, means that once an attacker has physically observed the unlock code and stolen the phone, access is possible to whatever apps the user was logged into.

As discussed below, many Mobile Device Management (MDM) packages permit password policies to be enforced, requiring users to select passwords that are less vulnerable to guessing or covert observation. Practicing defense in depth, organizations should employ multiple layers of authentication, e.g., a PIN for device login, then a password for application login.

Multifactor Authentication

Many mobile applications permit users to authenticate using just a username and password. The weaknesses in this approach are discussed later in Chapter 5, as are the benefits of using multifactor authentication (MFA). Note, however, that in many cases the "second" factor is the mobile device itself. In other words, the user, in order to access the application (typically via the Web), has to authenticate using the phone, either by receiving a text message with a secret code, using an MFA app such as Google Authenticator or Authy which generates a time-based one-time login code, or a mobile MFA app such as Duo.

The vulnerability ought to be obvious—if the attacker has your phone, they have your "MFA" device also (and in this context MFA is in scare quotation marks since it no longer is really a second authentication mechanism). It does protect against attackers who attempt to access the mobile app from *their* device, but it does little to protect from the attacker who has stolen a device that is used for MFA.

Session Lifetime

The longer an application waits before requiring a user to reauthenticate, the greater the likelihood of the app being in a "logged in" state when the device is stolen or lost.

There are two parameters that control how long a session lasts before a user has to reauthenticate: session timeout and inactivity timeout. Session timeout determines how long the user can remain logged in without having to reauthenticate, without regard to activity. In other words, what is the maximum period between logging in and being forced to login again? Inactivity timeout terminates the session early should the app not be used for a period of time.

The shorter the timeout period (session or inactivity) is, the greater the likelihood of your users switching to another application or complaining vociferously, or both. These periods must be set somewhere between the user's patience and the application's patience. The challenge is to balance out the two periods within users' frustration.

So, timeout duration is obviously a sensitive balancing act, and one that ought to vary depending on the sensitivity of the data/application and the permissions of the user. For example, a banking application on your phone might have a session timeout occur when the application is closed or the phone is locked. A personal social media account could have a session duration of a week or more and no inactivity timeout (and, in fact, many permit sessions to last months; whether that is wise is another matter). On the other hand, a banking app should have a session timeout measured in hours, with an inactivity timeout of a few minutes.

It would be advisable to consider different timeouts for the same app, depending on the permissions of the user. For example, a human resources app used by employees to look up information on other employees could have a 24-hour session timeout (with no inactivity timeout) when used by an unprivileged user, while an admin or an HR staffer with permission to change information might have a session timeout of one hour and an inactivity period of a few minutes. To reduce the frustration of admins who are mostly using the app in read-only mode, consider allowing them to operate in a reduced-permission mode to obtain the convenience of longer timeouts.

In contrast, consider the scenario with mobile devices, particularly in an organization with a BYOD policy where users are permitted to connect their own devices to the network. In such a scenario, and especially if the organization does not use application wrapping, the risks to the corporate network are considerably higher. Application wrapping is the containerization of a third-party application to empower policies such as activity timeout or session timeout.

Wireless Vulnerabilities

Wireless communications introduces additional attack surfaces.

WiFi can be vulnerable to MitM attacks from rogue access points, not to mention weaknesses in communications protocols (such as WAP) or implementations (such as the 2017 KRACK WiFi vulnerability that enabled attackers to eavesdrop on most Android phones).

Similarly, Bluetooth can be vulnerable as demonstrated by the "BlueBorne" vulnerability discovered by Armis security, also in 2017. This attack enabled threat actors to take over devices and access corporate data without any action required by the user or needing the phone to "pair" with the attacker's device.

Finally, the mobile wireless connection can be compromised by rogue cell towers, cell tower emulators, or cell-site simulators. Given how inexpensive software-defined radio (SDN) is, plus the multitude of proof-of-concepts available from hacker conferences, anyone has the ability to put together a cell-site simulator.

Mobile Malware

Like all computing systems, mobile devices can be compromised by malware. The increased risks from malware in a mobile environment stem from most users' desire to be able to download and install apps on their phones, leading to attacks via a rogue app. In 2018, Trend Micro identified 36 apps in the Google Play store that appeared to be useful utilities but, in fact, installed malware on the users' phones.

Unpatched Operating System or Browser

Like other computing systems, vulnerability management is critically important, with many users owning their own mobile devices but wishing to use them to access company information (the BYOD problem).

The risks include:

- Users not updating their devices
- Users using phones that are no longer supported and therefore no longer receiving security updates

- Mobile device manufacturers and carriers that delay phone updates in order to perform their own compatibility testing. This, of course, leads to an opportunity for attackers to reverse-engineer patches as they are released by the mobile operating system vendor, but before they are made available to customers.

In many cases the security flaws that trigger smartphone manufacturers to issue updates are well publicized, which means the attackers can learn of the flaws and develop exploits. Not patching your phone, or delays in patching, leaves it vulnerable to known attack vectors.

Insecure Devices

Because of the limitations imposed by mobile operating systems (primarily to improve security), some users modify their devices to bypass these controls in order to install apps that can perform functions not permitted normally. This is called "jailbreaking" or "rooting" the device, and significantly reduces the inherent security of the device.

Rooted phones have many more vulnerabilities, and therefore pose an increased risk from malware which can exfiltrate data or record keypresses and thus harvest login credentials. In fact, such applications can be installed on some phones without first requiring root privileges. A variety of keylogging software exists for the market of parents with phone-wielding children and suspicious spouses.

Mobile Device Management

To address many of these issues and to provide additional management and control over mobile devices, one can install MDM agents on mobile phones to provide additional security. These products provide a range of features, including:

- Jailbreak detection
- Vulnerability management (detection and possible resolution)
- Remote lock
- Remote wipe
- Device location
- Data encryption
- Sandboxing
- Anti-malware
- VPN
- Containerization

MDM software gives an organization considerable control over the individual's device and can be used to disclose information many consider private. Consequently, the security office may experience resistance from users when it comes to installing MDM agents on their personally owned devices. In such a case, the security office might opt to use agentless MDMs. If the organization takes the agentless approach, this involves using one or more centralized scanners to regularly scan users' devices. The scan collects mostly diagnostic information as a snapshot, unlike the continuous, performance-monitoring type ability of MDM agents.

Obviously, the organization can just mandate MDM, stating that as a condition of being able to access corporate data (i.e. email and calendar) on users' phones, they must surrender that degree of privacy and control over their devices. Alternatively, a middle ground is to use an MFA app that can check for many (but not all) of the vulnerabilities that could put corporate data at risk, and have the MFA deny access should the phone not comply with corporate policy. An MFA app is far less intrusive, and thus more likely to be accepted, than an MDM agent.

ASSESS AND MITIGATE VULNERABILITIES IN EMBEDDED DEVICES

Embedded systems can be found in a wide range of technologies. Embedded systems are dedicated information processing components embedded in larger mechanical or electrical systems, intended to provide a limited set of functions. The healthcare industry has innovated with embedded systems that provide great benefit to both care providers and patients. One example is the tracking of patients and healthcare staff through a real-time location system (RTLS), fulfilled by active RFID tags and proximity sensors. Another example that truly embraces IoT-capable embedded devices is what's now known as "telehealth" or remote health monitoring. Most helpful for patients who cannot easily travel to a hospital, IoT-capable devices are brought to the patient's home and communicate remotely with healthcare staff.

Assessing the vulnerabilities in an embedded system ought to start with an enumeration of the attack surfaces available, and then examining each. As described in greater detail earlier in this chapter, this examination can be done in a number of ways, including code inspection, threat modeling, and white- or black-box penetration testing.

Generally, these attack surfaces will fall into the following categories:

- User interface (buttons or other methods of user input)
- Physical attacks
- Sensor attacks

- Output attacks
- Processor attacks

User interface attacks involve manipulating the controls of the device in a manner that causes the device to malfunction. This can involve pressing buttons in the wrong order, or in ways not expected or anticipated by the designer (multiple times, multiple buttons at the same time, etc.).

Depending on the nature of the user interface, there may be functions that are restricted and only accessible through special means. This can be as simple as special combinations of button presses to "unlock" administrative or privileged features, or user login processes (which can be vulnerable to all the standard user authentication problems such as default or poorly chosen passwords).

Mitigations for these attacks include careful review of the security-critical parts of the firmware as well as penetration-type testing of the embedded system's UI.

Obviously, pen testing a vending machine takes a slightly different approach than a web app, but the concept is very similar. Consider all of the methods available to send data or commands to the device and then try invalid or unusual data or commands, or sequences of data or commands (both intentionally selected and random, as in fuzzing) in an attempt to get the embedded system to malfunction. Working "hacks" for vending machines are widely available online in the form of odd sequences of button presses that in turn cause a machine to dispense product. Similar to how pen testing a web app is dependent on the underlying language, the vending machine vulnerabilities depend on the underlying programming and thus the button sequences differ per vendor.

Physical attacks involve the compromise of the embedded system's packaging, either to directly compromise the device (i.e. breaking the glass front of a vending machine and grabbing the contents) or to gain access to parts of the embedded system in order to expose other attack surfaces that may be vulnerable (see below). Particularly prone to causing vulnerabilities are the ports or interfaces intended for managing or servicing that machine. A real-world example involves voting machines, where a proof of concept demonstration can be found online as someone defeats the on-screen access control by exploiting the voting machine through its management port.

Defenses for physical attacks can range from increasing the strength of the physical protection (thicker steel container, strong locks, epoxy embedding/soldering of components to make access difficult) to adding forms of tamper detection. Depending on the type of tampering, detection might merely mean building the device so that attempts to physical manipulate it (i.e. by adding a credit card skimmer) are easily apparent or cause the device to take defensive measures (from triggering an alarm, to erasing sensitive memory, to self-destructing).

Sensor attacks involve manipulating, or intercepting data from, the sensors the embedded system uses to detect external conditions that are relevant to its operation. For example, in a vending machine, the coin accepter is a sensor that tells the processor what coins have been deposited. Attacks on the sensor (e.g. using slugs or inserting wires or other thin implements to trip coin detectors) can fool the device into thinking payment has been made and that the product ought to be dispensed.

Much more costly than a vending machine hack are the sensor attacks on keyless entry cars. One well-known example is the viral video feed from an external security camera that shows two men approach a parked and locked Tesla Model S in the homeowner's driveway. A man with a laptop scans close to the home's external walls, hoping to come within distance of the Tesla's keyfob. The other man stands very near the car door with a signal relaying device. By triggering the keyfob, the first thief can relay the signal to his accomplice. The reply attack allows them to unlock the car, and ultimately steal it.

Credit card skimmers and shimmers are forms of sensor attack. A skimmer is when the attacker eavesdrops on the data from the magnetic stripe reader in a credit card terminal. The card's magnetic data might be read by a portable device carried by, for example, a malicious wait server. Or the reading device could be a stationary point-of-sale terminal, where the attacker installed a second sensor to read the same data and record it.

The shimmer also lifts data from bank cards but, unlike a skimmer, the shimmer intercepts data from the card's embedded EMV chip. On bank cards with the EMV chip, the chip is enclosed within the card, but it has familiar gold-plated contacts on the surface to provide conductive touchpoints for when the bank card is inserted at a point-of-sale (POS) reader. The attacker's shimmer is a very thin plastic sleeve or plate, shoved completely inside the POS reader. The shimmer as a plastic sleeve is little more than a surface to hold electrical contacts and a small IC chip for recording the inserted bank card. The shimmer's contacts are placed in a position to be "sandwiched" between the bank card and the legitimate POS reader.

Output attacks involve manipulating the actuators controlled by the embedded system to bypass the controls imposed by the system. Imagine an electric door lock in which the cabling is exposed and so all the attacker need do is strip the insulation and apply the appropriate voltage to cause the door to unlock.

Processor attacks involve compromising the processor directly, through means that can range from connecting directly to the processor or memory chips to carefully removing the tops of integrated circuits and using ion beams to probe the chip to obtain or manipulate information within the processor. Processor attacks are normally preceded by a physical attack to gain access to the processor.

Embedded systems that provide for firmware updates may be vulnerable to accepting rogue firmware. The attacker loads their own version of the firmware (either written from scratch or reverse engineered from code extracted from the device or downloaded from the manufacturer) which causes the device to behave as the attacker desires.

Protection against firmware attacks can include digital signatures to prevent unauthorized firmware from being accepted and executed, and cryptography to protect against reverse engineering of firmware updates.

As with IoT devices, a problem is that it is difficult, if not impossible, to upgrade the software in many embedded systems. This means that vulnerabilities that are discovered after the product has shipped may be difficult or impossible to patch. The result may be the need for compensating controls to mitigate the risk from the unpatched defect or the need to replace the unit entirely.

APPLY CRYPTOGRAPHY

Cryptography is the mathematical manipulation of data so as to protect its confidentiality and/or integrity. Cryptography is arguably one of the most powerful tools in the arsenal of the security architect, yet a tool that can be so easily misapplied, resulting in a false sense of security.

It is hard to think of an aspect of our use of computers that does not touch upon some aspect of cryptography. When you log in to a system, your password is protected using cryptography (at least we hope it is). When you connect to a website using an https: URL, your traffic is protected using cryptography. If you store personally identifiable information (PII) with a responsible service provider, it ought to be protected using cryptography. In short, at every step of the process, cryptography can help secure sensitive information.

In the following sections, we will provide an overview of the various aspects of cryptography that the security architect needs to be familiar with. Earlier, in the section on assessing and mitigating vulnerabilities, we discussed potential weaknesses from the incorrect application of cryptography.

Cryptographic Lifecycle

The cryptographic lifecycle involves algorithm selection, key management, and the management of encrypted data at rest, in transit, and in storage.

Algorithm selection involves a number of choices:

- The type of cryptology appropriate for the purpose (e.g. symmetric, public key, hashing, etc.)
- The specific algorithm (e.g. AES, RSA, SHA, etc.)
- The key length (e.g. AES-256, RSA 2048, SHA512, etc.)
- In the case of symmetric encryption, the operating mode (ECB, CBC, etc.)

Symmetric encryption is best for storing data at rest that has to be recovered (decrypted) before being used. Symmetric encryption is also far more efficient than public key cryptography, and so is appropriate for protecting data in transit. The problem, as explained in detail below, is that for symmetric cryptography to be used for data in transit, both ends of the communications link must have knowledge of the secret key. There are a number of methods for securely exchanging keys over an insecure channel, the most widely used of which uses public key cryptography (also discussed below).

There are some types of data that need to be protected but that do not need to be decrypted. In fact, for security, it is best that some data never be able to be decrypted. For example, to protect the confidentiality of passwords used for user authentication, they obviously have to be encrypted. But there is no need to be able to decrypt them. To verify an entered password against the previously stored password, all one need do is encrypt the entered password and compare the two ciphertexts. In fact, being able to decrypt passwords significantly weakens their security. So, for this purpose we use a one-way encryption function, otherwise known as cryptographic hashing. To be clear, cryptography is not exclusively encryption and decryption. Cryptography uses an algorithm that, regardless of its level of complexity, deals with an input and an output. Cryptographic hashing inputs a string to produce an output, which is generally assumed to be an output of fixed length, regardless of the input length.

Another example is the use of credit card numbers within a billing system. While the system that submits the transaction to the payment processor obviously has to be able to access the account number in plaintext, there are many databases and logs in which the account number needs to be stored. For most of those, it is sufficient to store a cryptographic hash of the account number. This hash can be stored and communicated without significant risk should it be disclosed. Only a very limited number of systems need store the account number using a symmetric cipher which can be decrypted. In this manner, the attack surface is sharply reduced.

Another technique to protecting the primary account number (PAN) is to disassociate the number from the account holder and any information that can identify that account holder. In and of itself, the PAN is like a token. Only when the PAN can be linked to PII does the credit card number become sensitive information. Translation vaults are being used to generate a random token with which the PAN is securely linked. This tokenization process helps separate account numbers from the PII by providing an encrypted relationship between the two.

Having chosen the type of cryptography, one must select the appropriate algorithm. In some cases, the set of algorithms is constrained by protocol standards. For example, if one is using cryptography to protect data in transit, then the standard lists the supported algorithms, and your choice is limited by the standard as well as a desire to remain compatible with as wide a range of browsers as reasonably possible.

Symmetric cryptography is the use of a single key, shared between two or more parties. Symmetric algorithms are broadly divided into block and stream ciphers. As the names imply, block ciphers take a block of data (typically 8, 16, or 32 bytes) at a time. Stream ciphers take either a single bit or single byte at a time. Block ciphers are typically used in bulk encryption, such as with data at rest, while stream ciphers are optimized for encrypting communications links. Stream ciphers frequently have the property of being able to quickly resynchronize in the face of dropped or corrupted bits. Block ciphers in certain chaining modes are unable to resynchronize, and the loss or corruption of the data stream will make the remainder of the transmission unable to be decrypted. It is possible, at the cost of some (or considerable) efficiency to employ a block cipher as a stream cipher and vice versa.

On communications links in which lower levels of the protocol handle error detection and retransmission, block ciphers are typically used (e.g. in TLS and WiFi).

In other cases, such as encrypting data to be stored in a database, one could choose any symmetric block algorithm. In this case, one ought to turn to the guidance provided by national research organizations (such as NIST in the U.S., the National Cyber Security Centre in the UK, or the International Standards Organization). These agencies make recommendations on appropriate algorithms based on an analysis of their relative strengths.

Other considerations include the efficiency of the algorithm. If the code is to be implemented on a system that has limited processing power or will have to encrypt large amounts of data, small differences in algorithm efficiency have a big impact on performance. Consider also that some processors include coded support for certain algorithms. Having support in the processor instruction set for certain algorithms makes their operation much faster than without the processor support. For example, most Intel, AMD, and ARM processors include instructions to speed up the operation of the AES algorithm. One study found an 800 percent speedup from using CPU-accelerated cryptography.

The longer the key, the more secure the cipher. But longer keys mean more processing time. You have to balance the security of long (strong) keys with the impact on system performance. An important consideration is the lifetime of the encrypted data. If the data can be reencrypted periodically (say, every year or two years), then selecting a key that is likely to withstand advances in brute-force attacks over the next two decades is not important. Conversely, if the data is likely to be archived for long periods of time, a longer key may be required. (The details of key management and key lifetimes are discussed at greater length later in this chapter.)

With symmetric block encryption, there are a number of ways to use the algorithm. Figure 3.17 shows the main variants from the simplest, Electronic Code Book (ECB) mode, to the more complex Cipher Block Chaining (CBC) and Cipher Feedback (CFB) modes. These are discussed further in the next section.

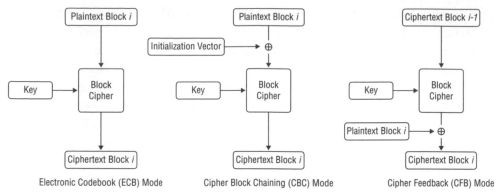

FIGURE 3.17 **Electronic Code Book (ECB), Cipher Block Chaining (CBC), and Cipher Feedback (CFB) block encryption implementations**

One final note, the choices outlined above are only optimal at a point in time. Weaknesses in cryptographic algorithms are discovered, more powerful processors make brute-force attacks more viable, and the development of quantum computing may make certain algorithms obsolete. There have been countless examples in the past of previously considered secure algorithms being deprecated because of advances in cryptanalysis, such as DES, RC4, SHA-11, and others.

Not only do cryptographic keys have finite lifetimes, so do cryptographic algorithms. It is periodically necessary to revisit the choices made to determine if they still provide the security necessary. This also means that systems need to be designed so that changing the cryptographic algorithm can be done with a minimum of disruption.

Cryptographic Methods

There are a number of cryptographic tools available to the security architect to protect the confidentiality and integrity of data, the choice of which depends on the threat being defended against, the nature of the communications, and the sensitivity of the information. See Table 3.3 for cryptographic approaches that can be used for different scenarios.

TABLE 3.3 **Cryptographic Approaches**

USE CASE	TYPE OF CRYPTOGRAPHY
Protect confidentiality of stored data	Symmetric
Protect confidentiality of data in transit	Symmetric (possibly aided by asymmetric)
Verify identity	Public Key Infrastructure
Protect integrity (detect tampering)	Message Authentication Code (Hashing)
Protect passwords	Hashing (with Salt and Pepper)
Protect integrity and confirm providence	Digital Signature

Consider the following different situations:

- Two people (Alice and Bob) wish to communicate confidential information over an insecure channel without unauthorized people being able to eavesdrop on or tamper with the information.

- Alice wishes to send a message to Bob in a manner that Bob has confidence that the message originated with Alice (and not an impostor), and in a manner that Alice cannot later deny having sent the message.

- Bob wishes to store passwords and wants to make sure that the original passwords cannot be obtained even if someone is able to access the file where the passwords are stored, even if the intruder knows the method used to encrypt the passwords.

The following sections will discuss the various categories of cryptographic algorithms and how they can address the situations described above.

Symmetric Ciphers

Symmetric encryption is the most common approach and the one most people think of when speaking of cryptography. Symmetric encryption takes a message (referred to as the plaintext) and an encryption key and produces output (called the ciphertext) that does not reveal any of the information in the original plaintext. The output can be converted back into the original plaintext if a person has the encryption key that was used to perform the original encryption.

The object is to make it difficult for an eavesdropper who does not know the key to extract any information about the original plaintext from the ciphertext. It is also a necessary property of a secure symmetric cipher that an attacker who comes into possession of examples of plaintext and the related ciphertext cannot deduce the key that was used to encrypt the messages (because if the attacker could do so, all other messages encrypted by that key would then be at risk).

For symmetric encryption to work, both the sender and receiver must share the key. In order for the message to remain confidential, the key must be kept secret. For these reasons, symmetric cryptography is sometimes referred to as secret-key or shared-secret encryption.

The basic types of symmetric cryptography include stream ciphers and block ciphers.

A stream cipher is an encryption algorithm that works one character or bit at a time (instead of a block). They are typically used to encrypt serial communication links and cell-phone traffic, and specifically designed to be computationally very efficient so that they can be employed in devices with limited CPU power, or in dedicated hardware or field programmable gate arrays (FPGAs). See Figure 3.18 where the plaintext flows through the cipher function as a stream, out into ciphertext. At the top of Figure 3.18 is the keystream generator, a constant flow of random bits that are generated one bit at a time. The keystream is a necessity for a stream cipher, relying on these random bits to convert plaintext to ciphertext through an XOR function.

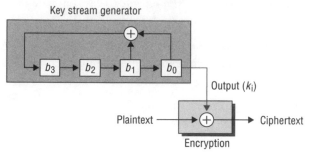

FIGURE 3.18 **Stream cipher encryption algorithm**

Block ciphers use a deterministic algorithm that takes a fixed-sized block of bits (the plaintext) and a key value, and produces an encrypted block (the ciphertext) of the same size as the plaintext block. Different key values will produce different ciphertexts from the same plaintext. See Figure 3.19.

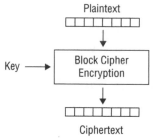

FIGURE 3.19 **Clock cipher encryption algorithm**

Although block ciphers are a useful way of dividing ciphers, it is possible to convert nearly all block ciphers into a stream cipher or vice versa.

Stream Ciphers

An example of a simple and provably unbreakable stream cipher is to take a message of length n (the plaintext) and a truly random string of digits of the same length (the key), and combine them as shown in Figure 3.18 to produce the ciphertext.

American cryptographer Claude Shannon proved in 1949 that if the key is truly random, the same length as the plaintext, and only used once then the system is secure and unbreakable (assuming the key remains secret). This type of encryption is called a one-time pad because the key is used for only one round of encrypting and decrypting. The problem with this approach is that the key must be the same length as the message and cannot be reused, making the method completely impractical except for the shortest of messages or for situations (typically government) in which the cost of securely delivering large amounts of key material can be justified. Developments in quantum cryptography (see below), however, will provide methods of securely delivering large amounts of random data that can be used for one-time pad cryptography.

Practical ciphers use a fixed-length key to encrypt many messages of variable length. As we will see in the section on cryptanalysis, some ciphers can be broken if the attacker comes into possession of enough ciphertexts that have been encrypted with the same key. Changing the key periodically so that the amount of ciphertext produced with each unique key is limited can increase the security of the cipher.

Stream ciphers are divided into two types: synchronous and self-synchronizing.

Synchronous ciphers require the sender and receiver to remain in perfect synchronization in order to decrypt the stream. Should characters (bits) be added or dropped from the stream, the decryption will fail from that point on. The receiver needs to be able to detect the loss of synchronization and either try various offsets to resynchronize, or wait for a distinctive marker inserted by the sender to enable the receiver to resync.

Self-synchronizing stream ciphers, as the name implies, have the property that after at most N characters (N being a property of the particular self-synchronizing stream cipher), the receiver will automatically recover from dropped or added characters in the ciphertext stream. While they can be an obvious advantage in situations in which data can be dropped or added to the ciphertext stream, self-synchronizing ciphers suffer from the problem that should a character be corrupted, the error will propagate, affecting up to the next N characters. With a synchronous cipher, a single-character error in the ciphertext will only result in a single-character error in the decrypted plaintext.

Block Ciphers

Block ciphers process blocks of n bits at a time, using a key of size k. The output of the processed block then becomes the input for the next iteration of the cipher function. The number of iterations that occur is called the "rounds." Table 3.4 provides an overview of block ciphers.

TABLE 3.4 Overview of Block Ciphers

BLOCK CIPHER	BLOCK SIZE (N)	KEY SIZE (K)	ROUNDS
DES	64	56	16
AES-128	128	128	10
AES-192	128	192	12
AES-256	128	256	14

The DES cipher is no longer considered secure because of its short key size, but it introduced the modern age of cryptography and so is historically very important. Because DES was no longer secure, finding its replacement was crucial. Advanced Encryption Standard (AES) was selected after a five-year process to evaluate and select an algorithm from over a dozen candidates.

Most block ciphers, including DES and AES, are built from multiple rounds of mathematical functions, as illustrated in Figure 3.20. While more rounds means greater security, it also slows down the algorithmic process, so the choice is a tradeoff between security and speed.

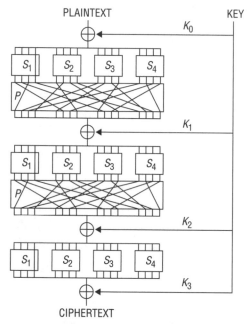

FIGURE 3.20 **Multiple rounds of mathematical functions in block ciphers**

The differences between different block ciphers are in the transformations performed during each round, and the manner in which the encryption key is stretched and then divided to provide a unique key for each round.

There are a couple of standard building blocks used to construct block ciphers, including:

- Substitution or S-boxes (Figure 3.21)
- Permutations or P-boxes (Figure 3.22)

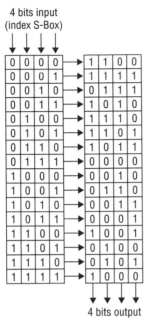

4 bits input (index S-Box)

4 bits output

FIGURE 3.21 **Block cipher with substitution of S-boxes**

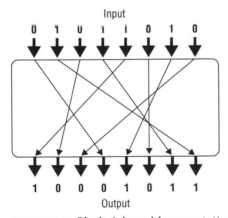

Input

Output

FIGURE 3.22 **Block cipher with permutation of P-boxes**

AES uses multiple rounds of substitutions and permutations, while DES uses a 16-round Feistel network.

Block Cipher Modes of Operation

A block cipher such as AES takes eight bytes of plaintext and produces eight bytes of ciphertext. But what if your message is shorter than eight bytes, or longer than eight bytes, or not a multiple of eight bytes?

To handle messages that are not a multiple of the cipher's block length, one mechanism is to add padding before encryption and remove the padding after encryption. There are many ways to do this, but one approach is to add bytes to the end of the message, each byte containing the count of the number of bytes that have been added (see Figure 3.23). Because the decryption process will examine the last byte of the last block to determine how many padding bytes have been added (and thus need to be removed), if the plaintext is a multiple of the block size, then a final block that just contains padding must be added.

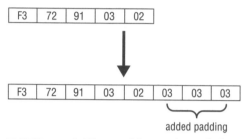

FIGURE 3.23 **Adding padding at the end of a message in a block cipher**

Padding is not without its own risks, such as the Padding Oracle Attack described later in the "Side-Channel Attacks" section.

Once the message has been padded to be an exact multiple of the cipher's block size, it can be encrypted. The easiest, obvious, and least secure method (for longer messages) is the Electronic Code Book (ECB) mode of operation. In this mode, each block of plaintext is processed independently by the cipher. While this may be adequate for messages that are no greater than the block size, it has serious weaknesses for longer messages, as identical blocks of plaintext will produce identical blocks of ciphertext (Figure 3.24).

Original image   Encrypted using ECB mode

FIGURE 3.24 **Electronic Code Book (ECB) padding produces serious weaknesses for longer messages**

Even in situations in which the data to be encrypted is the same or smaller than the block size (e.g. a numeric field in a database), use of ECB may be ill-advised if revealing that different rows of the table have the same value might compromise confidentiality. As a trivial example, if one were to use ECB to encrypt the birthdate field, then one could easily determine all the people in the database born on the same day, and if one could determine the birthdate of one of those individuals, you would know the birthdate of all (with the same encrypted birthdate).

The advantage of ECB, apart from its simplicity, is that encryption can be done in parallel (i.e. divided up across multiple processors), and so can decryption. Consequently, an error in one block does not affect subsequent blocks.

With Cipher Block Chaining (CBC), the first block of data is XORed with a block of random data called the initialization vector (IV). Every subsequent block of plaintext is XORed with the previous block of ciphertext before being encrypted. (See Figure 3.25.)

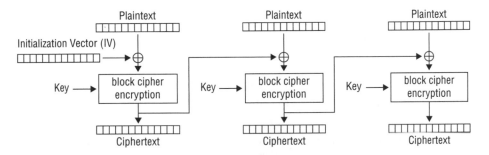

Cipher Block Chaining (CBC) mode encryption

FIGURE 3.25 Cipher Block Chaining (CBC) mode encryption

With CFB mode, the IV is encrypted and then XORed with the first block of the plaintext, producing the first block of ciphertext. Then that block of ciphertext is encrypted, and the result is XORed with the next block of plaintext, producing the next block of ciphertext. (See Figure 3.26.)

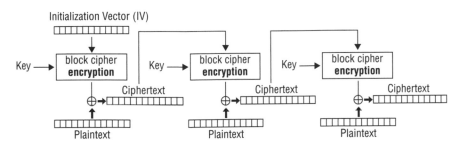

Cipher Feedback (CFB) mode encryption

FIGURE 3.26 Cipher Feedback (CFB) mode encryption

Because with both CBC and CFB the encryption of block P_{n+1} depends on the encryption of block P_n, neither mode is amenable to the parallel encryption of data. Both modes can, however, be decrypted in parallel.

The main differences between CBC and CFB are:

- With CBC, a one-bit change in the IV will result in exactly the same change in the same bit in the first block of decrypted ciphertext. Depending on the application, this could permit an attacker who can tamper with the IV to introduce changes to the first block of the message. This means with CBC it is necessary to ensure the integrity of the IV.

- With CFB, a one-bit change in the IV will result in random errors in the decrypted message, thus this is not a method of effectively tampering with the message.

- With CBC, the decryption of messages requires the use of the block cipher in decryption mode. With CFB, the block cipher is used in the encryption mode for both encryption and decryption, which can result in a simpler implementation.

The problem with both modes is that encryption cannot be parallelized, and random access is complicated by the need to decrypt block C_{n-1} before one can decrypt the desired block Cn.

CTR mode addresses this problem by not using previous blocks of the CBC or CFB in producing the ciphertext. (See Figure 3.27.) By using an IV combined with a counter value, one can both parallelize the encryption process and decrypt a single block of the ciphertext. You'll note that Figure 3.27 includes a nonce value. That unique, randomly generated value is inserted into each block cipher encryption round. Similar to how a random "salt" value is used to ensure different hash values (to prevent comparing to Rainbow tables), a nonce is unique and is intended to prevent replay attacks.

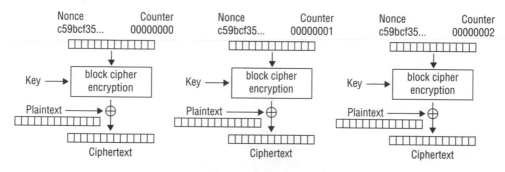

Counter (CTR) mode encryption

FIGURE 3.27 Counter (CTR) mode encryption

With all of the modes other than ECB, you need an IV, which either must be communicated to the receiver, or the message must be prefixed by a throw-away block of data (since decryption of a CBC or CFB stream of data without knowing the IV will only cause problems for the first block).

The IV need not be secret (it can be transmitted in plaintext along with the ciphertext) but it must be unpredictable. If an attacker can predict the next IV that will be used, and is able to launch a chosen plaintext attack, then that may enable launching a dictionary attack on the ciphertext.

Coming back to the overarching concept of symmetric encryption, both block and stream ciphers do what most people envision when thinking of cryptography. They turn intelligible text into an unintelligible representation and vice versa. This functions as a closed box without the need for distinguishing between encryption keys and decryption keys, as is the case with asymmetric algorithms.

Hashing

Hashing is the conversion of a block of data into a much smaller value such that the same block of data will convert to the same value. This enables you to verify the integrity of a message you receive by calculating the hash and comparing it against a hash value provided by the sender. Basic hashing is used to accelerate look-up tables and other search functions. Cryptographic hashing is used to protect passwords or to detect tampering of messages. Hash functions perform multiple rounds of mathematical functions to convert data of any size into a mathematical representation of a fixed size (often 160 or 256 bits).

For password protection, the objective is to store a user's password in a manner that:

- An attacker is unlikely to be able to determine the original password from the hashed value
- An attacker is unlikely to be able to generate a random string of characters that will hash to the same value as the original password (known as a collision)

While necessary conditions for protecting passwords, the above guidelines are not sufficient. Even if the attacker cannot directly deduce the password, just using a cryptographic hash function to convert a password into a shorter fixed-length string leaves the password vulnerable to attack.

Firstly, the attacker can compare the hashed password values to see if the same password has been used by different users (or, if the hash function is widely used, by the same or different users on a different system). This information may be useful in compromising the password.

More seriously, the attacker can construct in advance a table of precomputed hash values from dictionaries and lists of commonly used passwords, and then compare these known hashes with the hash of the unknown password to see if there is a match. This table of precalculated hashes is known as a *rainbow table*.

To stymie these two attack vectors, you generate a random value for each password to be stored, called the salt, and then add the salt to the password before hashing (by concatenating or other mathematical operation). The salt and the hash are then stored. The salt can be stored in plaintext; it need not be secret, just unpredictable and unique for each password.

When the system authenticates the user, it recomputes the hash from the user's input and the stored salt, and if the result matches the stored hash, then we know with a high degree of confidence that the user has entered the same password.

By combining a random unique salt with the password, the stored hash will be different from all other hashes using the same password, making precomputed password hash tables useless and obfuscating the reuse of the same password for different accounts or on different systems.

Another attack vector is the brute-force attack. Once the attacker takes the salt and tries different possible passwords in an attempt to obtain a match, it's more likely the attacker will succeed with matching to hash tables. If the user has chosen a simple or short password, then it matters little which hashing algorithm the security architect has chosen. But if the password is reasonably complex, then the security of the hash will depend on how computationally difficult the hashing algorithm is.

For example, Microsoft used a very simple hashing algorithm in NT LAN Manager (NTLM) and it was possible, using multiple GPU boards, to generate 350 billion password hashes per second, enabling an attacker to try every possible eight-character password in less than seven hours.

LinkedIn used a more secure algorithm, SHA-1, to secure its users' passwords, but when their password database was breached, high-powered password cracking machines using multiple GPUs were able to break 90 percent of the 6.5 million passwords leaked.

The solution is to select a hashing algorithm that takes so much CPU time that even a multi-GPU password cracking system can only try a limited number of guesses. One such example is the bcrypt, a hashing algorithm based on Blowfish. In 2012, research done by Jeremi Gosney found that the same system that can guess 350,000,000,000 NTLM password hashes per second can only attempt 71,000 bcrypt hashes a second. To put that into perspective, an NTLM password that could be cracked in six hours would take 33 centuries to crack if hashed using bcrypt. With processing power increasing exponentially, and with well-funded attackers able to build far more powerful password-cracking systems, we must assume the above cracking speeds have been vastly increased since Gosney's work was published.

By selecting an appropriate cryptographic hash function, the security architect can remain confident that even if the password database is compromised, attackers cannot use that to deduce a password (or equivalent string) that can be used to sign on to the system.

The question then becomes: what *is* an appropriate cryptographic hash function? Appropriate sources of current information on cryptographic algorithms, key and salt lengths, and iteration counts (for password hashing) include the Password Hashing Competition (`https://password-hashing.net/`) and NIST.

Forward Secrecy

An important concept in cryptographic protocol design is that of perfect forward secrecy, also known as forward secrecy. The idea is that the secrecy of past communications will not be compromised, should the long-term keys become known by the attacker. A protocol that has forward secrecy generates unique session keys for every session and then discards them after the session, having generated and shared them in a manner that does not depend upon the long-term keys.

The most well known forward secrecy mechanism is the Diffie-Hellman Key Exchange.

Alice starts by randomly generating two prime numbers, a prime modulus p and a generator g and sends them, in plaintext, to Bob. It does not matter if Mallory is listening.

Alice then generates another random number a which she keeps secret. She then calculates: $A = g^a \bmod p$ and sends that number to Bob. Mallory is still listening.

Bob also generates a random number b which he keeps secret. He then calculates $B = g^b \bmod p$ and sends that to Alice (and perhaps inadvertently to Mallory).

Now comes the magic.

Alice computes the key value $K = B^a \bmod p$.

Bob computes $K = A^b \bmod p$.

The key each has calculated is the same number (see below why) but Mallory, who only knows A, B, g, and p, but not a or b, cannot generate the key.

Alice and Bob then can use any symmetric cipher they choose, with key K, confident that they are the only two who know its value. Furthermore, once they have terminated their communication (session), they discard a, b, A, B, and the key. At that point there is no way for Mallory or anyone else who has recorded the session to decrypt it, even if other keys (private or public) that Alice and Bob may have become known.

Why does the magic work? Due to math.

Alice's key, $B^a \bmod p$ is $g^{ab} \bmod B$ (remember how B was calculated) which is the same as $g^{ba} \bmod B$ (it matters not the order of the exponents) which is the same as $A^b \bmod B$, which is how Bob calculated the key. Voilà. Alice and Bob have the same (secret) key.

Note that this protocol does nothing to authenticate the identities of Alice or Bob, and therefore is vulnerable to a MitM attack. Imagine Mallory, who can intercept and replace every message between Alice and Bob. In this situation, Mallory can generate one secret key with Alice (who thinks she is talking to Bob), and a second key with Bob (who thinks he is talking to Alice), and then decrypt with one key, and reencrypt with the second key every message between Alice and Bob.

To prevent this, an authentication layer is added using public keys (either shared in advance or via PKI, see below) so that Alice knows it's Bob and not Mallory she is negotiating a secret key with.

Asymmetric Encryption (Public Key Crytography)

The problem with symmetric encryption is that both parties to the communication (Alice and Bob in our examples) must each know the secret key used to encrypt the data, and if the encrypted data is to remain confidential, no one else must know or be able to guess the secret key. The difficulties of managing and sharing secret keys can make symmetric encryption prohibitively complex as soon as the number of people involved increases beyond a handful.

If there are n people who need to communicate securely using symmetric cryptography, there must be n $(n$-1$)$ / 2 unique keys, and each person must manage (and arrange to share) n - 1 keys. This is not feasible.

The solution is asymmetric or public key cryptography. The magic of public key cryptography is that instead of having a single secret key that is used to both encrypt and decrypt traffic, you have two keys: a secret private key and a non-secret public key. Data encrypted using a public key cryptography algorithm using one of the keys can only be decrypted using the other key. For example, if Alice encrypts a message to Bob using Bob's public key, only Bob can decrypt it with his private key. Conversely, if Alice encrypts a message using her secret private key, then anyone can decrypt it since Alice's public key is, well, public.

Obviously, encrypting a message with a private key alone does nothing to protect the confidentiality of Alice's message, but it serves a different purpose: it proves that the message originated from Alice (because who else could have produced it?). This, of course, assumes that Alice's private key has remained private. But what if it hasn't? That leads us to the next section on PKI and how public and private keys are managed.

There are a number of public key cryptography algorithms, all based on mathematical functions that are easy to perform in the forward direction but extremely time-consuming to perform in the reverse direction unless a secret is known.

A trapdoor function, as they are called, is one for which computing $f(x)$ is easy, but calculating the inverse function (e.g. determining x if one only knows the value of $f(x)$) is extremely difficult unless one knows the value of a second variable, y.

The most well-known encryption algorithm based on a trapdoor function is the one first published by Ron Rivest, Adi Shamir, and Leonard Adleman. It is called RSA and is based on the difficulty of factoring large integers.

Choose two large primes p and q and compute:

$$n = pq$$

These three numbers are then used to produce the public exponent e and private exponent d. The numbers e and n are made public; e, p, and q are kept secret.

Messages are encrypted with integer modular math on the message using e and n (the public key). Messages are decrypted with similar math but using d (the private key) and n.

The method works because deriving d from n and e is equivalent to finding the two prime factors of n, and if n is a very large semiprime number (i.e. product of two primes of similar size), this is computationally infeasible (at least for non-quantum computers). The largest semiprime factored to date had 232 decimal digits and took 1,500 processor years in 2009. The semiprimes used in RSA have 600 more digits.

Quantum Cryptography

One property of quantum mechanics that lends itself to cryptography is that any attempt to observe or measure a quantum system will disturb it. This provides a basis to transmit a secret encryption key such that if it is intercepted by an eavesdropper, it can be detected. So Alice first sends Bob a secret key using Quantum Key Distribution (QKD) and Bob checks to see if it has been intercepted. If it has, he asks for another key. If it hasn't, he signals Alice to start sending messages encrypted using a symmetric cipher or a one-time pad and the key, knowing that only Alice and he have access to the key and therefore the communications will remain secret.

As this relies upon a fundamental property of nature, it is immune to advances in computing power or more sophisticated cryptanalytic techniques.

Devices that support QKD are on the market but their high cost and restrictions (such as range) currently limit their adoption. This will change as the technology is improved.

Public Key Infrastructure

In the "Asymmetric Encryption (Public Key Crytography)" section, we discussed the concept of public keys, a method for Alice to send to Bob a message only Bob can decrypt, without Alice having to first confidentially share a secret symmetric cryptography key with Bob. For this to work, Alice needs to trust that the public key she is using is really and truly owned by Bob. Obviously she could obtain the public key directly from Bob, but it is not feasible for Alice to directly and securely obtain the public key of every person and organization she wishes to securely communicate with. Public keys solve the problem of everyone having to share unique secret symmetric keys with everyone else (the $n(n-1)/2$ problem described earlier), but unless we have a scalable method of establishing trust, we have merely replaced the problem of sharing $n(n-1)/2$ symmetric keys with a problem of establishing $n(n-1)/2$ trust relationships.

Enter the trusted third party — an intermediary that is trusted by both parties to the asymmetric transaction: Alice, the person claiming ownership of her public key, and Bob, who needs to be sure that the public key Alice claims is hers actually belongs to her (and not to Mallory pretending to be Alice).

The process starts with Alice creating a Certificate Signing Request (CSR). This is a file that contains the details of Alice's identity (name, location, and email address) and her public key. The CSR is signed by Alice using her private key. Requiring the CSR to be signed prevents someone other than the public key owner from requesting a certificate for that key.

Alice sends her public key to a certificate authority (CA), along with such proof of her identity as the CA may require. The CA verifies Alice's identity and then digitally signs her public key and sends back a file (certificate) that includes Alice's public key and the CA's attestation that this key indeed belongs to Alice.

The standard for public key certificates (also known as digital certificates) is X.509, defined by the International Telecommunications Union (ITU). An X.509 certificate contains the following:

- Version Number
- Serial Number
- Signature Algorithm ID
- Issuer (CA) Name
- Validity Period (Not Before, Not After)
- Subject Name
- Subject Public Key (Algorithm, Public Key)
- Key Usage
- Optional Extensions
- Certificate Signature (Algorithm, Signature)

In PKI certificates used for encrypted email, code signing, or digital signatures, the subject of the certificate is an individual or organization. For PKI certificates used to secure TLS (the protocol that protects secure HTTPS browser connections), the subject is the server (e.g. domain name of the website).

For web certificates, the owner of the website generates a public/private key pair and then prepares a key signing request which contains:

- The domain name of the website (with or without wildcards)
- The identity of the website owner
- The public key of the website owner
- A digital signature of the website owner

The certificate is digital proof that the issuing certificate authority (the CA) has certified (to the extent implied by the type of the certificate) that the subject's identity has been verified. By signing the certificate with the issuer's private key, the issuer binds the subject's identity with the subject's public key in a manner that cannot be tampered with and that can only have been produced by the issuer (but see the caveat below).

Who is this certificate authority who bestows certificates? Well, anyone. Alice can be her own CA and can sign her own certificate. These are called self-signed certificates and are useful in situations where trust can be directly established. For example, a company might sign its own website certificates for its internal corporate intranet and configure the browsers on its employees' computers to trust those certificates.

But if Alice wishes to communicate with the larger world, that won't suffice. Commercial CAs have been established that offer the service of verifying identities and signing individual keys and producing digital certificates.

These certificates work because the CAs that produce them have been vetted by the major web browser companies (e.g. Apple, Google, Microsoft, Mozilla, etc.), who have configured their browsers to trust certificates signed by these CAs.

In order for this to be secure, the website owner's private key must remain secret. If an attacker is able to obtain (or guess) that key, then communications with the website can be compromised, either by spoofing the website or by a MitM attack.

Similarly, if the private key used by the CA is compromised, then the attacker can generate a private/public key purporting to be that of the website owner and spoof or MitM the website.

So the security of PKI depends entirely on the secrecy of the private keys — both the participants' keys as well as the CA's keys.

Several methods exist to verify the validity of a certificate prior to its use in a cryptographic session. Every protocol that relies upon PKI includes some check of the certificate to determine if it has been reported as compromised (and therefore no longer to be trusted). There are several methods of validating certificates.

The original approach was for the browser to download a certificate revocation list (CRL) from the CA. Before accepting the certificate (even if it is properly signed), it is checked against the CRL to see whether it has been revoked and, if it has, the user is warned that the communications link is not secure.

Problems with CRLs, not the least of which being their substantial size, led to the development of the Online Certificate Status Protocol (OCSP), defined in RFC 6960, which provides a real-time status of a certificate from the CA, returning either a "Good," "Revoked," or "Unknown" reply from the CA.

At least one browser (e.g. Google Chrome) has decided that problems with both CRLs and OCSP require a different approach, and instead relies upon an internal list of revoked certificates that is updated regularly by Google.

There is one final detail to consider regarding PKI. In order to decrease the possibility of a CA's root private key becoming compromised, it is never used to sign website certificates. It is used to sign a very limited number of subordinate or intermediate certificates, and it is these certificates that are used to sign website certificates. Or, in some cases, subordinate certs can be used to generate third-level subordinate certs, and on and on, creating a certificate chain (see Figure 3.28). Verifying a website requires following the chain from the website's certificate, through any number of subordinate certificates, until reaching the CA's root certificate.

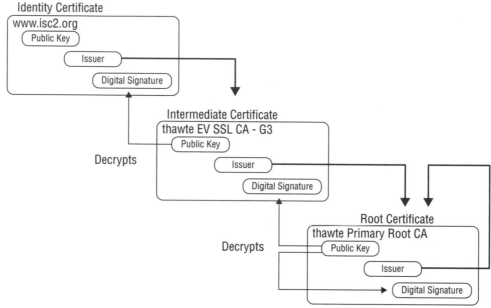

FIGURE 3.28 A certificate chain protects a CA's root private key

Obviously, the need for a chain of trust and CAs complicates the use of public key cryptography considerably. There is a proposed protocol, called DNS-based Authentication of Named Entities (DANE), that would eliminate the need for CAs, but this protocol is not widely supported by browsers and hence has not been adopted by websites.

✔ DigiNotar: When a Trusted CA Is Compromised

In July of 2011, an attacker used DigiNotar's systems to issue a wildcard certificate for Google, allowing an Iranian MitM attack against Google services. Once this issue came to light, DigiNotar discovered quite a few fraudulent certificates for major services.

DigiNotar also found that it wasn't able to ensure that all of the fraudulent certificates were revoked, resulting in Google, Mozilla, and other companies like Apple removing DigiNotar as a trusted CA from their browsers and other products.

The collapse of trust had quite a dire impact for DigiNotar as a CA. The Dutch government, which used DigiNotar as part of their PKIoverheid system, removed DigiNotar's intermediate certificate for the system and replaced untrusted certificates with new ones from trusted alternate providers.

Not long after the issue came to light, DigiNotar declared bankruptcy and shut down. A report released after the bankruptcy showed that DigiNotar's systems were seriously compromised, indicating major security problems for the CA.

DigiNotar is one of the most visible examples of what occurs when a CA is compromised, highlighting how important trust is for a CA and how quickly it can collapse if that trust is lost.

Key Management Practices

Secure use of cryptography depends on keeping symmetric and private keys confidential. Attackers who can obtain or guess a secret key can compromise the confidentiality and integrity of the data protected by that key.

Proper cryptographic key management includes:

- Secure key generation
- Secure key storage and use
- Separation of duties, dual control, and split knowledge
- Timely key rotation and key change
- Key destruction

Secure Key Generation

There are two factors that make for a secure cryptographic key: length and randomness.

Generally, the longer the key, the more difficult it is to attack encrypted messages — but what constitutes a secure key length changes with time as computer power increases and cryptanalysis techniques become more sophisticated. In 1977, the U.S. government selected a symmetric block cipher they dubbed the DES, which was considered secure for non-classified use (e.g. banking, e-commerce, etc.).

In 1999, it was demonstrated that DES-encrypted messages could be cracked in less than 24 hours.

DES used a 56-bit key, now considered wholly inadequate given the capabilities of current computers. The replacement for DES, named the Advanced Encryption Standard (AES), takes a minimum key length of 128 bits, and has variants that use 192 and 256 bits. Estimates are that, using modern computers, a brute-force attack on a 128-bit key would take longer than the age of the universe (~14 billion years) to crack.

The strength of a symmetric key also depends on its being unpredictable (i.e. unguessable). Even if only some of the bits can be guessed, that can significantly reduce the strength of the cipher. Using a mechanism that will generate high-quality (i.e. cryptographically secure) random numbers is essential for key generation. The best method is to use hardware-based true random number generators that rely on physical phenomena known to be truly random. Such devices are embedded in various cryptographic hardware devices such as TPMs and HSMs, discussed earlier, as well as some microprocessors.

Software-based random number generators (RNGs) are very hard to get right. For example, from 2006 until 2008, a defect introduced into the OpenSSL package in the Debian and Ubuntu Linux distributions caused all keys generated to be weak because of a bug in the random number generator (CVE-2008-0166).

Secure Key Storage and Use

Once you have generated a nice long and random key, how do you keep it secret? Obviously the first step is to encrypt your data encryption key (DEK) with another key, the key encryption key (KEK). That solves the problem but creates another: how do you secure your KEK? This depends on the sensitivity of the underlying data being encrypted and the mechanisms that are appropriate for the system you are designing.

An HSM is specifically designed to securely generate and store KEKs and is among the more secure method of protecting keys. HSMs also provide for secure ways of replicating the KEKs between redundant HSMs, and for enforcing controls so that no one individual can use the KEK to decrypt a data encryption key.

For systems that are deployed in the public cloud, the major cloud providers offer cloud implementations of HSM technology. Numerous HSMaaS vendors are also available in the marketplace, often as a service offering in conjunction with other cryptographic functionality such as key escrow and cryptographic acceleration.

For less demanding applications, the approach must be tailored to the specific requirements and risks. One could store the master key in:

- A hardware encrypted USB key
- A password management app
- A secrets management package

Another factor to consider is how your keys are (securely) backed up. Losing access to your keys can cause you to lose access to significant amounts of other data (and backups of that data).

Separation of Duties, Dual Control, and Split Knowledge

Some keys and data are so sensitive that the risk of an insider threat (e.g. rogue employee) is too great to permit a single individual to have access to the key encryption key, the data encryption key, and the encrypted data, or sole access to administrative functions of the HSM.

To review, the three types of controls used to mitigate the risk of a rogue employee are:

- Separation of duties
- Dual control
- Split knowledge

These three concepts are related but different.

Separation of duties (sometimes called segregation of duties) means that certain processes should require at least two different individuals to complete from beginning to end. In the financial world this might involve ensuring that the person who has authority to write checks is not the person who reconciles the bank statements. In the cryptology world, it might dictate that the person with access to the encryption keys does not have access to the encrypted data. Another form of separation of duties is ensuring that the people who administer a system do not have the authority to interfere with the logging system or tamper with the logs.

Dual control means that a specific step in a process requires two or more individuals. In the financial world this would be the requirement that two signatures be present on every check. In the cryptology world it might require that two or more individuals present their credentials to be able to use the key encryption key to decrypt a data encryption key.

For access to a system that supports multifactor authentication, dual control could involve entrusting the password to one individual, and the MFA device to a different individual.

Note that dual control is often incorrectly referred to as the separation of duties. Be aware of the difference and examine the control to determine if it is truly separation of duties or dual control.

Split knowledge is when a key (or password) is split into two or more pieces such that each piece is unusable by itself, and it requires two (or more) pieces be brought together to decrypt the data (or access the system).

For example, a vendor might generate a large key and split it into (say m) multiple pieces. In this model a minimum of n pieces are required to recreate the key encryption key. The numbers n and m are configurable so that one can, for example, split the key into a dozen pieces, but only require any three of the key holders to come together to unlock the key.

Timely Key Rotation and Key Change

Keys should have a limited lifespan. If there is evidence or even suspicion that a key has been compromised, it ought to be rotated as soon as feasible. Even if the confidentiality of the key has been maintained, it ought to be replaced periodically. Further, best practice is to also perform key rotation when essential personnel with access to cryptographic material leave their positions.

Although industry standards vary, current guidance from NIST and the Payment Card Industry (PCI) is to rotate data encryption keys at least annually. In practice the key used to encrypt new data is changed each year, and all of the previously encrypted data is decrypted using the retired key and reencrypted using the new key within the year following the key rotation. Thus, by the end of a year after the key rotation, there is no data encrypted using the retired key, at which time it can be destroyed. In cases in which backups must be maintained for longer than one year, either a process for securely archiving retired keys must be instituted or backups will have to also be reencrypted with the new key.

Why rotate keys?

- To limit the damage should the key be discovered by an attacker

- To limit the amount of data encrypted by the same key (the more data encrypted using the same key, the easier it is to crack the encryption)

- To limit the time available to the attacker to crack the cipher (if none of your data is encrypted with the same key for longer than two years, then any brute-force attack must be able to be completed within two years of the key's being generated)

Key Destruction

Once a key has been retired and it has been determined that there is no data that has been encrypted using that key that will need to be decrypted, then it must be securely destroyed. This involves locating every copy of the key and deleting it in a manner appropriate for the media on which it was stored to ensure that it cannot be recovered.

Depending on the media and the risk of its becoming accessible to unauthorized individuals, this may require overwriting the storage, degaussing of the media, or physical destruction of the media or device containing the media.

Records ought to be kept documenting the locations of the destroyed keys and the means used to ensure secure destruction.

Digital Signatures

Digital signatures use cryptographic techniques to replicate the intent of a signature: authentication (to give the recipient confidence that the message originated with a specific entity), non-repudiation (evidence that the originator did, in fact, compose the message), and integrity (confidence the message has not been altered after it was signed).

The basic process is illustrated in Figure 3.29. The message to be signed is passed through a cryptographically secure hash function which produces a fixed-length output (typically between 160 and 512 bits) called a Message Digest. This hash value is then encrypted using the message author's private key to produce a digital signature. The digital signature is transmitted as an appendix to the message.

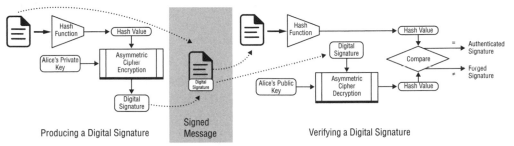

FIGURE 3.29 Producing and verifying a digital signature

When a recipient wishes to verify the document, they compute the Message Digest for the message as received. They then decrypt the digital signature using the author's public key to produce the originator's Message Digest. If the two are identical, then the recipient knows:

1. The message has not been tampered with (i.e. integrity has been preserved).

2. The message has originated with the owner of the public/private key pair (i.e. authentication and non-repudiation).

Note that a digital signature, in and of itself, does not protect the confidentiality of the message. If that is required, the sender must also encrypt the message itself.

Assertion #2 requires that the recipient has sufficient reason to trust that the public key used to verify the digital signature is owned by the originator. This can be done either by direct key sharing (i.e. prior to communicating, the originator provides the recipient with the originator's public key in a secure manner that precludes tampering), or by registering the public key with a CA (as discussed in the section on PKI earlier) who assumes the responsibility of verifying the identity of the originator.

In order to protect the security of digital signatures, it is strongly recommended that the private key used to sign messages only be used for digital signing and not for any other purpose (such as general message encryption).

There are a number of possible vulnerabilities with digital signatures:

- Hash collision
- Private key disclosure
- CA compromise

The security of a digital signature depends upon any changes in the body of the message resulting in a change to the Message Digest. As discussed further in the next section, if the attacker can create two messages that generate the same Message Digest when put through a hashing algorithm (called a hash collision), then the digital signature is no longer reliable.

In order for the recipient to have confidence that a message actually originated with the author, the sender's private key must remain secure, because with access to the key, an attacker can sign any message (including a tampered message), destroying any validity of the digital signature. To mitigate this situation, all PKI models include the concept of a key revocation list that records all keys that have been (or are suspected of having been) compromised or retired.

Finally, checking a message against the sender's public key depends upon knowing the public key is actually the sender's. Usually, this is done by having the owner's identity tied to the public key by a CA, and the recipient of the public key relies upon the trust they place in the CA to trust the public key. But if the CA is compromised, attackers can spoof the identity of a public key and "forge" digital signatures.

Non-Repudiation

Non-repudiation is the ability to prove that a message must have originated from a specific entity. This can be critically important, for example, with contracts or other legal documents, as well as instructions to banks or orders to suppliers. Only with the ability to demonstrate non-repudiation of the received communication can the recipient act on the message with confidence that the originator is accountable for the content of the message.

Non-repudiation is accomplished by the originator's signing the message using a private key known only to the originator, and which the originator commits to protecting. Protecting a private signing key means keeping it confidential and, if the key is compromised, promptly revoking the matching public key.

The primary risk to the non-repudiation property is the disclosure of the originator's private key. As mentioned earlier, if the private key can be obtained (or guessed), an attacker can sign any message and have it accepted as if the owner of the private key sent the message (e.g. "Transfer $100,000 to Bank Account XXX").

To ensure that digital signatures retain non-repudiation even after the compromise of the private key used for signing, one can use a trusted timestamp which proves the message was signed before the time when the private key was compromised. IETF standard RFC 3161 defines the protocol to be used with a Time Stamping Authority (TSA) to provide trusted timestamps. A TSA, like a CA, is a trusted third party that provides assurances. The TSA asserts that a specific datum existed at a point in time, in a manner that the recipient of the timestamp has confidence (if the TSA is trusted) that the assertion is correct and the timestamp has not been, and cannot be, tampered with.

A secondary risk is from weaknesses in the PKI which lead to recipients of the message being fooled into thinking a certain public key is associated with a certain entity, when, in fact, the attacker generated the public key and managed to spoof the identity associated with it. This, for example, is what happened when the DigiNotar CA was compromised and attackers were able to generate public keys purporting to be from Google and other companies. (See the DigiNotar sidebar earlier in this chapter.)

Another approach to non-repudiation is to use a blockchain. Blockchain is a form of a distributed ledger in which records are recorded and linked together, using cryptographic hashes, meaning that to change any record in the blockchain, one must change every subsequent block. Since the blockchain is distributed (i.e. stored by multiple systems), it requires the collusion of a majority of the blockchain participants. For a sufficiently widely (and independently) operated blockchain, this is infeasible. For example, Bitcoin currently (mid-2018) has approximately 12,000 nodes across 100 countries.

Integrity

Cryptographic methods can do more than just protect the confidentiality of messages and help prove the identity of the originator. They can also be used to protect the integrity of messages by detecting tampering.

A hash function is an algorithm that takes a block of data (i.e., a message or file) and computes a derived value such that any change to the data will result in a change to the hash value. Effective hashing functions need additional properties too, as will be seen below.

This function can be used to verify the integrity of the data by comparing the hash value of the original data with the hash value of the data at some later point in time.

Using a cryptographic hash to detect tampering of a message involves the following three steps (as illustrated in Figure 3.30):

1. Generate the hash value (H_1) by applying the hash function to the original block of data or message (M_1).

2. Generate the hash value (H_2) by applying the hash function to the block of data or message (M_2) to be verified.

3. If (H_1) is the same as (H_2), then that indicates that the two messages are likely to be identical and have not been tampered with. As we shall shortly see, however, the key question is "how likely?" What degree of confidence should we have that two messages are identical if their hash values are identical?

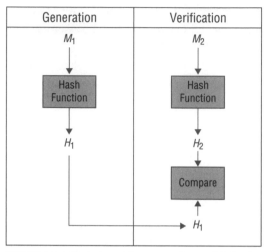

FIGURE 3.30 Steps for using a cryptographic hash to detect tampering of a message
FROM NIST SPECIAL PUBLICATION SP800-175B, GUIDELINE FOR USING CRYPTOGRAPHIC STANDARDS IN THE FEDERAL GOVERNMENT: *CRYPTOGRAPHIC MECHANISMS*

To understand hashing, let's consider a simple example, the checksum. A checksum is a mathematical function that takes a block of data and calculates a number (the checksum) in a manner such that any single change to the block of data will cause the checksum number to change. As the name implies, a checksum is typically calculated by taking the sum of each byte in the message, as an unsigned integer, and ignoring any overflow.

When the primary threat was from noise or other defects in the communications channel, data packets carried a checksum that could be used by the receiving party to determine if the data had been corrupted in transit. The receiving party recalculated the checksum for the packet, compared it with the checksum calculated by the sender and appended to the message, and if they did not match, the recipient would know the message had been received with errors.

In a situation in which the changes to the message are random and not malicious, a simple checksum can be sufficient to protect the integrity of the message. But imagine a situation in which a threat actor wishes to tamper with the message. Instead of an order to transfer $100, the malicious agent wants to change the message to transfer $100,000. Obviously if just the amount field is changed, then the checksum is unlikely to match and his tampering will probably be caught.

That's not a problem for our attacker, however, who understands the algorithm used to calculate the checksum and can further tamper with the message, either by making other changes to the message content so that the checksum remains the same, or by calculating the new checksum and overwriting the original checksum. With either approach, the checksum will validate and the fraudulent message to transfer $100,000 will be accepted as valid.

For example, consider the following transmission, where [0x116c] is the checksum appended to the message by the sender:

`TRANSFER $100.00 TO JANE DOE FOR OFFICE AND MISC EXPENSES IN DECEMBER [0x116c]`

Our attacker wants to send a slightly different message (but copies the checksum from the original message):

`TRANSFER $100,000.00 TO JANE DOE FOR OFFICE AND MISC EXPENSES IN DECEMBER [0x116c]`

The problem is the actual checksum of the new message (0x1228) doesn't match the claimed checksum (0x166c), so his tampering would be detected.

One possible attack would be to make other changes to the message so that the checksum is the same as the original message:

`TRANSFER $100,000.00 TO JANE DOE FOR OFFICE MISC EXPENSES IN DECEMBER7 [0x116c]`

which has the same 0x116c checksum as the original. Alternatively, the attacker could overwrite the checksum that is appended to the message to be the checksum of the message after being tampered with:

`TRANSFER $100,000.00 TO JANE DOE FOR OFFICE AND MISC EXPENSES IN DECEMBER [0x1228]`

Clearly, using a simple checksum and including it in the message is not going to work to detect malicious tampering, but it is useful to help avoid non-malicious errors in transmission or data entry. Checksums are often used to prevent accidental errors for credit card, government ID number, and other types of verification processes. One of the most commonly used algorithms is the Luhn algorithm, which is specified by ISO/IEC 7812-1.

When checksums aren't sufficient, we need a method of verifying message integrity that the attacker cannot easily circumvent. To protect the integrity of data, we need a hashing function sufficiently complex that it is essentially not possible to create a message with the same hash as another message. When two different messages generate the same hash value it is called a collision, so we need a hashing function that makes it almost impossible to create an intentional collision.

In our example above, two factors made it trivial to create a collision:

- The simplicity of the algorithm made it easy to determine what changes need to be made to the modified message to change the hash (checksum) to match the original message's.

- Even if the algorithm had been complex, the shortness of the hash (16 bits) means that, with only 65,536 possible hash values, it would not take long to repeatedly make random changes to the end of the message until one happened upon a collision.

Cryptographically secure hash algorithms must therefore be sufficiently complex that it is not possible to determine what changes need to be made to a message to create a specific hash result, and the length of the hash value (i.e., number of bits) must be sufficiently large to make brute-force attacks computationally infeasible.

One of the organizations responsible for researching and recommending suitable cryptographic algorithms is NIST. Their current guidance (as of 2018) recommends a family of algorithms known as SHA-3 (Secure Hash Algorithm-3). The SHA-3 set of functions includes hashing functions that produce hash values varying in length from 224 to 512 bits.

Using SHA-3 we can compute a hash value that is very difficult to attack by creating an intentional collision — but how do we protect against the attacker simply calculating a new hash value for the changed message and overwriting the original hash? For this, we need to use a cryptographic hash that incorporates a secret key known only to the sender and receiver. The value of the hash depends not only on the contents of the message, but on this secret key.

One method, known as Hash-based Message Authentication Code (HMAC), was developed by Bellare, Canetti, and Krawczyk and formalized in RFC-2104. This algorithm concatenates a secret key (which has been XORed with a string to pad it to a fixed length) and hashes that. It then takes that hash, combines it with the key again, and hashes it a second time, producing the HMAC value (see Figure 3.31). If the attacker changes the message without knowing the secret key K, the HMAC value will not match. This enables the recipient to verify both the integrity and origin (e.g. authentication or non-repudiation) of the message.

Among other uses, HMAC functions are found within the IPsec and TLS protocols. The problem with this, however, is similar to the problem discussed in the context of symmetric encryption. Securely sharing keys between the sender and the receiver can be difficult and cumbersome. What then? Just as the solution to the shared secret problem with symmetric encryption was to use public/private keys and asymmetric encryption, with cryptographic hashes we can encrypt the hash using the sender's private key, which anyone can validate by using the sender's public key, but which no one can spoof without access to the private key. And that is a digital signature (see the earlier "Digital Signatures" section).

HMAC is a less complex method of ensuring message integrity and authentication, but with the overhead of sharing a symmetric cipher key. Digital signatures eliminate the need to share a secret, but require the overhead of PKI. Each has its application.

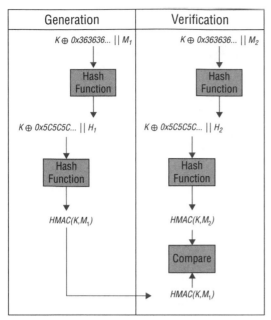

Generation	Verification
$K \oplus 0x363636... \parallel M_1$	$K \oplus 0x363636... \parallel M_2$
Hash Function	Hash Function
$K \oplus 0x5C5C5C... \parallel H_1$	$K \oplus 0x5C5C5C... \parallel H_2$
Hash Function	Hash Function
$HMAC(K,M_1)$	$HMAC(K,M_2)$
	Compare
	$HMAC(K,M_1)$

FIGURE 3.31 Hash-based Message Authentication Code (HMAC) process

Understand Methods of Cryptanalytic Attacks

It is important to understand how cryptography can be attacked so that you understand where vulnerabilities might be found and how the incorrect application of cryptography can result in vulnerabilities. We divide these into attack vectors of interest to security archi-tects, and attack vectors of interest to cryptographers. These are different attack vectors.

As a security architect you will need to understand architectural weaknesses that can be exploited by attackers so that you can ensure that your design avoids or mitigates those risks. But as a security architect, you don't need to worry about subtleties such as related key attacks on symmetric ciphers. This is the concern of cryptographers charged with developing new cryptographic algorithms, or testing existing ciphers. As a security architect your interest is more to follow the news from agencies such as ENISA and NIST who are responsible for making considered recommendations on which algorithms to use (and how), so that should new attack vectors be found by cryptanalysts, you can take their findings into account when you select (or update) the ciphers you are using.

Attack Models

When assessing the strength of a cryptographic system, one starts with the assumption that the attacker knows the algorithm being used. Security by obscurity can provide addi-tional protection (e.g., most military organizations do not willingly disclose their current cryptographic algorithms), but an analysis of a given cryptographic system always starts with the assumption that the algorithm is known.

After that, there are various levels of attack that can be considered, in order of increasing power:

- **Ciphertext-only attack:** The situation in which the attacker only has access to the encrypted traffic (ciphertext). In many cases, some information about the plaintext can be guessed (such as the language of the message, which can lead to knowledge of the character probability distribution or the format of the message, which can give clues to parts of the plaintext). WEP, the original security algorithm for WiFi, is vulnerable to a number of ciphertext-only attacks. By capturing a sufficient number of packets (which typically can be gathered within minutes on a busy network), it is possible to derive the key used in the RC4 stream cipher. It is thought that the 45 million credit cards purloined from the American retail giant T.J. Maxx were obtained by exploiting WEP.

- **Known-plaintext attack:** The situation when the attacker knows some or all of the plaintext of one or more messages (as well as the ciphertext). This frequently happens when parts of the message tend to be fixed (such as protocol headers or other relatively invariant parts of the messages being communicated). An example of a known-plaintext attack is the famous German Enigma cipher machine, which was cracked in large part by relying upon known plaintexts. Many messages contained the same word in the same place, or contained the same text (e.g. "Nothing to report"), making deciphering the messages possible.

- **Chosen-plaintext attack:** The situation in which the attacker is able to submit any plaintext the attacker chooses and obtain the corresponding ciphertext. The classic example of a chosen-plaintext attack occurred during WWII when the U.S. intercepted messages indicating the Japanese were planning an attack on a location known as "AF" in code. The U.S. suspected this might be Midway Island, and to confirm their hypothesis they arranged for a plaintext message to be sent from Midway Island indicating that the island's water purification plant had broken down. When the Japanese intercepted the message and then transmitted a coded message referring to "AF," the U.S. had the confirmation it needed.

- **Chosen-ciphertext attack:** When the attacker is able to submit any ciphertext and obtain the corresponding plaintext. An example of this was the attack on SSL 3.0 developed by Bleichenbacher of Bell Labs, which could obtain the RSA private key of a website after trying between 300,000 and 2 million chosen ciphertexts.

There are ciphers that are secure against weaker attacks (e.g. chosen-plaintext) but not against chosen-ciphertext attacks. There are also attacks that are specific to certain types of encryption.

Attacks Primarily of Interest to Cryptographers

The two main mathematical methods of attacking block ciphers are linear cryptanalysis and differential cryptanalysis.

Linear Cryptanalysis

Linear cryptanalysis was first described by Mitsuru Matsui in 1992. It is a known-plaintext attack that involves a statistical analysis of the operation of the cipher to create linear equations that relate bits in the plaintext, key, and ciphertext.

For example, an examination of the cipher might suggest a linear equation that says the second bit of the plaintext, XORed with the fourth and seventh bits of the ciphertext, equals the fifth bit of the key:

$$P_2 \oplus C_4 \oplus C_7 = K_5$$

With a perfect cipher, the above equation would only be true half of the time. If there is a significant bias (i.e. the equation is true significantly more, or significantly less, than half of the time), then this fact can be used to guess, with probability better than 50 percent, the values of some or all of the bits of the key.

By combining a series of such equations it becomes possible to come up with guesses for the key that are far more likely to be correct than simple random guessing, with the result that finding the key is orders of magnitude faster than a simple exhaustive search.

Differential Cryptanalysis

Differential cryptanalysis is a chosen-plaintext attack that was originally developed by Eli Biham and Adi Shamir in the late 1980s and involves comparing the effect of changing bits in the plaintext on the ciphertext output. By submitting carefully chosen pairs of plaintext and comparing the differences between the plaintext pairs with the differences between the resulting ciphertext pairs, one can make probabilistic statements about the bits in the key, leading to a key search space that can be (for a cipher vulnerable to differential analysis) far smaller than an exhaustive search.

Since the development of these two methods, all newly proposed ciphers are tested exhaustively for resistance to these attacks before being approved for use. The AES has been demonstrated to be resistant to such forms of analysis.

Cryptographic Safety Factor

One of the challenges in selecting an appropriate cipher is that there is no way to mathematically measure the security of a cipher in advance of its compromise. In this regard, the estimation of the work factor of a particular algorithm is precisely that—an estimate. In the selection of the algorithm which became the AES, cryptographer Eli Biham introduced the concept of a safety factor. All modern ciphers are built as a series of rounds, each using a subkey derived from the main key.

Cryptographers typically attempt to break ciphers by first attacking a simplified version of the cipher with a reduced number of rounds. For example, early cryptographic attacks on DES (before it fell to simple brute-force) revealed an attack on eight rounds (the full DES has 16 rounds). With AES-256, there is an attack that works on a simplified version of 10 rounds (the full AES has 14 rounds). This was developed after attacks on six-, seven-, and nine-round versions.

The conclusion is that you can expect the attacks to get better over time and that more and more rounds of a cipher will be able to be cracked.

Biham's safety factor is the ratio of the number of rounds in the cipher, divided by the largest number of rounds that have been successfully attacked so far. While obviously dependent on the level of effort expended by cryptographers trying to undermine a cipher, it is still a useful metric, at least when comparing ciphers that have received sufficient attention from cryptographers.

Using this measure, AES-256 currently has a safety factor of 1.4. Other ciphers, such as Twofish, have greater safety factors, and it was for this reason that the team that developed the Twofish algorithm argued that it ought to have been selected as the AES instead of the algorithm (Rijndael) that was selected.

Attacks of General Interest

In addition to the mathematical analysis of a cipher which aims to detect weaknesses in the algorithm, there are myriad other ways of attacking the use of cryptography which target vulnerabilities in the implementation or use of the cipher. See Figure 3.32.

FIGURE 3.32 Cryptography is vulnerable to human weaknesses and other implementation flaws
SOURCE: XKCD: A WEBCOMIC OF ROMANCE, SARCASM, MATH, AND LANGUAGE (HTTPS://XKCD.COM/538//)

Brute Force

The simplest attack is to try all possible key values until finding the one that works. In the case of a symmetric cipher, this means a known-plaintext attack in which one tries all possible keys until one has decrypted the ciphertext into something that matches the known plaintext. In many cases, full knowledge of the plaintext is not needed. If one knows the general format of the message, or the language of the message, one can check the output of the decryption against certain heuristics to determine if the output is likely to be the original plaintext (i.e. reading the output to see if it makes sense).

If the encryption algorithm uses 64-bit keys, the attacker starts with 00 00 00 00 00 00 00 00$_{16}$ and continues until one reaches FF FF FF FF FF FF FF FF$_{16}$. This can take a while. If your system can decrypt a block of ciphertext and determine if the result is likely to be the desired plaintext in 1 microsecond, going through all possible keys will take roughly 5,800 centuries.

Unfortunately for cryptography, computers get faster every year. In 1998, the Electronic Frontier Foundation (EFF) built a system that could test 90 billion keys per second against the DES cipher, meaning that every possible 56-bit DES key (all 2^{56} or 72,057,594,037,927,936 of them) could be tested in roughly nine days (and, on average, the correct key would be found in half that time).

Obviously, the primary defense against brute-force attacks on symmetric ciphers is key length, which is why the minimum key length for AES is 128 bits. Even if we had a machine a million times faster than the one the EFF built to crack the DES, it would take longer than the universe has been in existence to try every 128-bit key at current processor speeds.

In the case of cryptographically secure hashes (such as are used for securing passwords), the attack scenario assumes one has a dump of the system's password file containing all of the passwords encrypted using a secure hash. The attacker then tries to compare the password hashes with guesses to see which passwords can be determined.

The naive approach is to start with "a" and try every combination up to, say, "ZZZZZZZZZZ." A more sophisticated approach is to have a dictionary of commonly used passwords, typically made up of entries from language dictionaries, combined with combinations of words, letters, and numbers frequently used as passwords (e.g. Password123). After trying all of the entries in a password-cracking word list, the attacker can then start with every possible six-character combination (assuming the system's minimum password length was six), then every seven-character password, etc., until one runs out of patience (or budget).

This is the method used to analyze the 177 million hashes leaked in the 2016 LinkedIn password breach. Roughly 50 million unique passwords, representing more than 85 percent of the passwords in the file, have been cracked.

There are two defenses against such attacks, neither of which was used by LinkedIn at the time:

- Hashing complexity
- Salting

The LinkedIn password file used SHA1, a fast and efficient hashing algorithm. When it comes to protecting passwords, fast and efficient is exactly what one does NOT want. An eight-GPU password cracking system using 2016 technology can test 69 billion SHA1 hashes per second!

When it comes to password hashing, slower is better, much better. One of the currently recommended algorithms is the Password-Based Key Derivation Function 2 (PBKDF2) — using the same eight-GPU engine, one can only generate 10,000 hashes per second (i.e. roughly 7 million times slower).

The counterattack to slow hashing is a precomputed database of hashes. The attacker takes a dictionary of common passwords (hundreds of millions of passwords from past breaches are freely available online) and every possible password up to, say, eight characters, and runs it through the hashing algorithm in advance. When coming into possession of a breached password file, there is no need to lumber through 10,000 hashes per second; if the password hashes are already known, all that is needed is just to look up each hash.

If the storage space it would take to store these hashes is too large, to compress the hashes at the cost of slightly longer lookup times, the technique called rainbow tables can be used.

The defense against stored dictionary or rainbow table attacks is to combine the password with a unique large random number (called the salt), and then store the combined hash of the password and salt. In this manner, one would have to precompute 2^n rainbow tables (if the salt has n bits), so the attack is not feasible.

So the password file contains two fields (in addition to the user's login name and other metadata):

- The salt
- The output of HASH (salt + password)

To be secure the salt must be:

- Long (at least 16 bytes, and preferably 32 or 64 bytes)
- Random (i.e. the output of a *cryptographically secure* pseudo-random number generator)
- Unique (calculate a new salt for every user's password, and a new salt every time the password is changed)

Some go one step further and encrypt the hash using a symmetric cipher, but this is considered to be unnecessary and adds little additional security. In keeping with the nomenclature used in password cryptography, this step is called *pepper*.

Following the defense-in-depth principle outlined at the beginning of this chapter, one should not rely upon a single security mechanism to provide security. In the world of passwords, defense in depth typically means multifactor authentication so that a compromise of a password in and of itself does not lead to the compromise of the access management system.

Man-in-the-Middle Attack

An MitM attack requires that the attacker be able to intercept and relay messages between two parties. For example, Mallory wishes to compromise communications between Alice and Bob. Alice wishes to communicate securely with Bob using public key cryptography. Mallory is our attacker. With that in mind, the following takes place (see Figure 3.33):

1. Alice sends Bob a message requesting Bob's public key
2. Mallory relays the message to Bob.
3. Bob replies with his public key but Mallory intercepts that message and replaces it with Mallory's public key.
4. Alice, thinking she has Bob's public key, uses Mallory's key to encrypt a message (e.g. "Please transfer $10,000 from my account to Acme Company").
5. Mallory intercepts the message, decrypts it (since it was encrypted using her key), tampers with it (e.g. "Please transfer $10,000 from my account to Mallory"), encrypts the tampered message using Bob's key, and sends the message on to Bob.

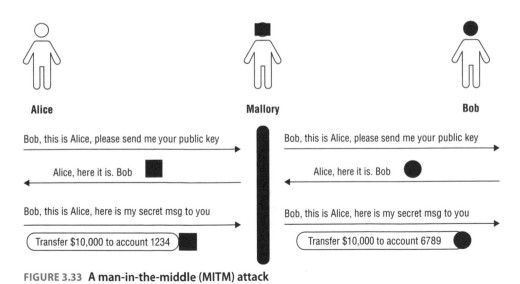

FIGURE 3.33 A man-in-the-middle (MITM) attack

To defend against such attacks, Alice needs to have confidence that the message containing Bob's key actually originated from Bob (and not the MitM attacker, Mallory). In the case of encrypted HTTPS web traffic, this is done by relying upon public key certificates attested to by a CA (as described earlier in the "Public Key Infrastructure" section). But if the CA is compromised, the attacker can circumvent the identity authentication protections of HTTPS.

In 2011, the compromise of the Dutch CA DigiNotar led to successful MitM attacks against an estimated 300,000 Gmail users.

Side-Channel Attacks

Side-channel attacks involve measuring artifacts of the cryptographic process to deduce information to assist with compromising encrypted information. These artifacts can include:

- Timing
- Cache access
- Power consumption
- Electromagnetic emanations
- Error information

The time taken to encrypt or decrypt a block of data can vary depending on the key or plaintext, and a careful analysis of the time taken to encrypt or decrypt the data can reveal information. The time to perform a cryptographic operation can vary for a number of reasons:

- Conditional branches within the code, which can change the time of execution depending on the branches taken, which in turn depend on the value of the key or plaintext
- CPU instructions that take variable time to complete depending on the operands (e.g. multiplication and division)
- Memory access, which can vary depending on where the data is located (type of memory) or the access history (thus affecting the cache and thus the speed of memory access)

Cache attacks typically involve processes running on different virtual machines on the same physical processor. As the VM performing the encryption is timesliced with the VM running the attacker's processes, the attacker can probe the processor's cache to deduce information about the plaintext and the key, and thus compromise the encryption process.

A cache-timing attack was at the heart of the Spectre and Meltdown attacks revealed in 2018 as methods of extracting data from protected regions of a processor's memory (e.g. keys or plaintext messages).

The power consumed by the device performing the cryptographic operation may vary depending on the instructions executed, which in turn depend on the key and data being encrypted. By carefully monitoring the power consumed by the device, it can sometimes be possible to extract information about the key or plaintext.

This type of attack has been most successfully demonstrated against smartcards because of the relative ease with which the device's power consumption can be monitored, but the attack mechanism has wide applicability.

All electronic systems emit electromagnetic radiation, and it is possible to capture this, sometimes at some distance from the device. These radio signals can sometimes be analyzed to reveal information about the data being processed by the device. Early examples of this type of attack involved analyzing the emanations of cryptographic devices which printed the decrypted message on teletypewriters to determine which characters were being printed.

Countermeasures exist, but in some cases they can be very difficult to implement or can exact a considerable performance penalty. In the case of timing attacks, it is necessary to modify the algorithm so that it is isochronous, which is to say it runs in constant time regardless of the key and data being processed.

The difficulty of implementing a secure algorithm that is secure against side-channel attacks is another reason for the edict discussed earlier: do not write your own cryptographic implementation — use a tested and widely used cryptographic library.

Error information provided (or leaked) by decryption software can provide useful information for attackers. In the Padding Oracle Attack, a system that can be sent any number of test messages, and which generates a distinctive error for encrypted messages that are not properly padded, can be used to decrypt messages without knowing the key. The defense is to report generic errors and not to distinguish between padding errors and other errors.

Birthday Attack

A birthday attack is a method of compromising cryptographic hashes, such as those used for digital signatures. The name is derived from the observation that while the odds that anyone in a group of, say, 23 people has a specific date as their birthday is 23:365 or 6 percent, the odds that there are two people in the group of 23 with the same birthday are 1:1 or 50 percent.

Consider the attacker, Mallory, who wishes to produce a bogus will leaving all of Bob's worldly goods to Mallory and that appears to have been digitally signed by Bob. Mallory does not know Bob's secret key so she cannot sign a document. But if she has any signed document from Bob, and can produce a different document which hashes to the same number, she can take the digital signature from the first document, attach it to the second, and it will appear to have been signed by Bob.

But to do this, Mallory would have to generate 2^{n-1} bogus wills (say, by adding superfluous punctuation, white space, etc.) before she is likely to produce a document that hashes to the same n-bit hash (and can therefore be passed off as having been signed by Bob) – in other words, a hashing collision.

Solving for a hashing collision when one does not care what the hash is, just that one has two different documents with the same hash, is like solving the birthday problem. Finding two people with the same birthday is a lot easier than finding one person with a specific birthday.

So if Mallory produces both (a) a huge number of wills that express Bob's real intentions (and which he is willing to sign), and (b) a huge number of wills that express Mallory's evil intent, she need only produce $2^{n/2}$ pairs of wills before she is likely to find a collision. Which is a lot less than 2^{n-1}.

She then gets Bob to digitally sign the real will, and copies the signature to the evil intent version, making it appear to also have been signed by Bob.

Related-Key Attack

A related-key attack is a form of known-ciphertext attack in which the attacker is able to observe the encryption of the same block of data using two keys, neither of which is known to the attacker, but which have a known mathematical relationship.

While it is rare that the attacker can arrange for two mathematically related keys to be used, poor implementations of cryptography can lead to keys being generated that have a known relationship that can be exploited by the attacker. This was the basis for the very successful attack on the WEP security algorithm in the first WiFi standard.

The lessons are twofold: cryptographers need to consider related-key attacks in the design of their ciphers, and security architects need to ensure that the keys they use are well-chosen (by which is meant cryptographically random) and not based on simple mathematical transformations of previously used keys.

Meet-in-the-Middle Attack

A meet-in-the-middle is a known-plaintext attack against block ciphers that perform two or more rounds of encryption. One might think double (or triple) encryption would increase the security in proportion to the combined length of the keys. However, the math behind this doesn't support the increased complexity.

By creating separate lookup tables that capture the intermediate result (i.e., after each round of encryption) of the possible combinations of both plaintext and ciphertext, it is possible to find matches between values that will limit the possible keys that must be tested in order to find the correct key. This attack, which first came to prominence when it was used to defeat the 2DES algorithm, can be applied to a broad range of ciphers.

Unfortunately, chaining together cryptography algorithms by running them multiple times does not add as much additional security as one might think. With 2DES, the total impact of the second run was to increase complexity from 2^{56} to 2^{57}. This has a very small overall impact compared to the work done. The solution to a meet-in-the-middle attack like the one used against 2DES is to do either of the following:

- Add additional rounds of encryption. For example, triple-DES uses three rounds with three different 56-bit keys. While not providing the same security as a 56+56+56 = 168-bit key, it does provide the same as a 112-bit key, which is a lot better than 56 bits.

- Use an algorithm designed to use longer keys. For example, use AES-192 instead of AES-128.

✔ Why 256 Isn't Greater than 128

Normally a longer key is more secure. All else being equal, the longer the key, the larger the key space (number of possible keys) and therefore the longer it will take to brute-force a key. But with AES, it turns out all else is not equal. Owing to problems with the design of AES-256, Alex Biryukov, Orr Dunkelman, Nathan Keller, Dmitry Khovratovich, and Adi Shamir reported in 2009 that there is an attack on AES-256 which requires only 2^{119} time (compared with 2^{128} time for AES-128, or the 2^{256} time one would expect from AES-256). Practically, this does not matter as a 2^{119} time attack is still completely infeasible using any technology available or likely to be available within the next decade or two. These attacks are also related-key attacks, which are impractical in properly implemented systems.

Biryukov et al also found a weakness in AES-192, but that attack takes 2^{176}, not 2^{192} as it ought to, if AES-192 had no flaws, but still much better than AES-128.

Cryptography always gets weaker, not stronger. One needs to monitor the research and recommendations from national institutes, as cryptographic algorithms once deemed sufficient will inevitably be replaced with better algorithms as time passes (and our understanding of cryptology increases).

Replay Attack

A replay attack is one in which the attacker does not decrypt the message. Instead, the attacker merely sends the same encrypted message. The attacker hopes that the recipient will assume that the message originated with the authorized party because the information was encrypted.

Alice is trying to log onto a system over an encrypted link. She encrypts her login name and password and then sends the ciphertext to the server. The server decrypts the message, looks up Alice's password in its authorized user database, verifies the password, and authorizes Alice to access the system.

Mallory is listening on the communications channel and intercepts Alice's message. Mallory cannot decrypt the message but makes a copy. Later, Mallory sends the saved message to the server, and the server accepts the login, thinking it is talking to Alice.

NOTE The classic example of a replay attack is breaking into houses by spoofing the garage door opener remote control unit. Early garage door opener remotes worked by sending a secret number to the garage door opener by radio. Thieves could easily tune into the frequency, record the signal, and then replay the same signal at a later time to open the garage door.

Replay attacks can be prevented by ensuring every message can only be accepted by the recipient once. In other words, there must be a method for the recipient to recognize that a message has been replayed. There are many ways to do this, but they all involve including some variable component in the message that can be used to detect a replayed message.

A simple approach is to include a timestamp so that if a message is replayed at a later time, the server can detect that the message is stale. The problems with this approach are (a) it requires Alice and the server to be synchronized, and (b) it still leaves open a short window in which the attacker could replay the message. Consider, the server receives a message at t_2 with a timestamp of t_1. Even if Alice and the server are perfectly synchronised, t_2 will be later than t_1 by the latency of the communications channel which typically could have considerable variability. To prevent false negatives (i.e. rejecting valid requests), the server will have to accept messages with timestamps within a certain range (i.e. $t_2 - t_1 <$ some window of tolerance). If Bob can capture the message and replay it such that it also arrives at the server within the same window, Bob can still succeed.

The approach used to secure automatic garage door openers is for the remote to generate a different code each time the button is pressed. Each opener generates a unique sequence, and the door opener knows the sequence each of the openers authorized to work ("paired") and keeps track of the last code each remote has used (and therefore the next code that will be accepted). Openers will also "look ahead" in case the remote's button is pressed when out of range of the garage, resulting in the next code the opener receives not being the next number in sequence.

The problem with this approach is that it depends on the sequence of numbers being unpredictable. If the attacker can eavesdrop on a number of messages, and can reverse-engineer the algorithm that generates the sequence, the remote can be spoofed.

A better approach than timestamps (or random sequences) is for the server to generate a random value and send that to Alice before she sends her login credentials, and for

Alice to incorporate the random value into the encrypted message. For example (and see Figure 3.34):

1. Alice asks the server for a login nonce (a number used once, chosen randomly).

2. The server generates a cryptographically secure PRNG (see below for the importance of a CSPRNG), encrypts it, and sends it to Alice.

3. Alice takes the nonce and packages it with her credentials and sends them back to the server.

4. The server decrypts the message and checks that the included nonce matches the one sent to Alice.

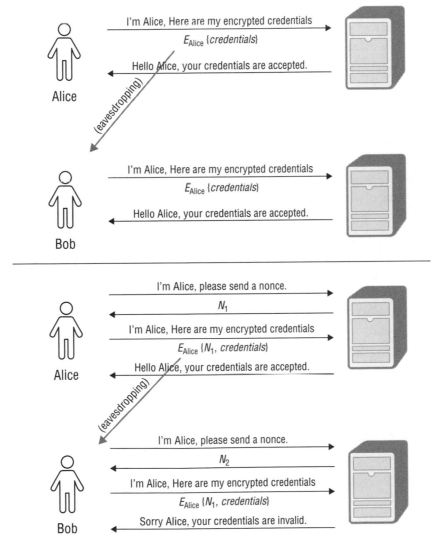

FIGURE 3.34 **Preventing replay attacks with nonce (a number used once, chosen randomly)**

Mallory's replay attack fails (regardless of how quick she is):

1. Mallory asks the server for a login nonce.
2. The server generates a nonce that is different from the nonce sent to Alice.
3. Mallory doesn't have Alice's credentials so cannot use the nonce. Mallory just takes the captured message from Alice and sends it to the server.
4. The server decrypts the message and checks that the included nonce matches the one sent to Mallory. It doesn't and so Mallory's attempt to login as Alice using a replay attack fails.

The nonce is sometimes called a session ID. It is important that the method used by the server to generate the nonce is unpredictable (which is what is meant by CSPRNG). If Mallory can predict a future nonce, she could intercept a login nonce request from Alice, and send Alice a nonce that she knows the server will generate at some point in the future. Mallory then captures Alice's credentials (bundled with her nonce). Mallory does not forward the message to the server, the login appears to Alice to time out, and she tries again (at which time Mallory lets the login proceed as normal). Alice chalks it up to a flaky communications channel and thinks nothing more of it. Mallory waits for the time when she has predicted the server would generate the same nonce she sent to Alice, sends a login request to the server, and when the server replies with the nonce Mallory predicted, Mallory just sends the previously captured message from Alice which contains the nonce. And voilà, Mallory logs in as Alice.

> ## ✔ PRNG vs CPRNG
>
> A pseudo-random number generator is a mathematical algorithm that generates a sequence of numbers which is statistically indistinguishable from an actual random sequence. While useful in many contexts, statistically random does not necessarily mean unpredictable. When it comes to cryptography, predictable random numbers lead to many weaknesses in cryptography. For example, the first version of SSL (used to secure HTTPS communications) was found to use a cryptographically weak PRNG and was thus vulnerable to attacks which could decipher the encrypted data stream.

Differential Fault Analysis (DFA)

Differential fault analysis (DFA) is a cryptographic attack in which faults are induced in the circuitry performing the cryptographic operation in the expectation that the device can be forced to reveal information on its internal state that can be used to deduce the key.

For example, in 2004 Christophe Giraud published an attack on AES-128 implemented on a smartcard. By using a Xenon strobe, and removing the cover of the smartcard processor, his team was able to induce faults in the execution of the algorithm which enabled them, after multiple induced faults, to derive enough information to determine the full key value.

Quantum Cryptanalysis

With recent developments in quantum computing, there has been great interest in the ability of quantum computers to break ciphers considered highly resistant to traditional computing methods.

Symmetric ciphers are relatively resistant to quantum cryptanalysis, with the best algorithm able to reduce the key search for a 128-bit key from 2^{128} to 2^{64}, and a 256-bit key from 2^{256} to 2^{128}. While a 2^{64} key search is within the realm of current technology, 2^{128} is not, and is not likely to be for decades to come, so the solution to defending against quantum cryptography for symmetric ciphers is merely to double the key length.

For asymmetric (i.e. public key) ciphers, the problem is much more difficult. Asymmetric ciphers depend on difficult mathematical problems such as factoring very large integers. Unfortunately, these problems are only hard for classical computers. Using quantum computers, integer factorization becomes much easier.

That said, quantum computers have a long way to go before they can compromise currently used public key algorithms. Consider that when this book was written (mid-2018), the largest integer factored by a quantum computer was 291,311 (e.g. six digits). The integers used in RSA public key systems are recommended to be 2,048 bits in length, or over 600 integer digits.

Digital Rights Management

Digital Rights Management (DRM) is the name applied to technology that permits the owner of intellectual property (documents, music, movies, etc.) to impose technical limits on how copies of that information may be used. There is considerable controversy over how and under what circumstances DRM technology is used, relative to the intellectual property rights of both the content creators and content consumers. Understanding the technical aspects of this technology will help security professionals legally and appropriately implement DRM in their environments.

In the United States the Digital Millennium Copyright Act of 1998 (DMCA) imposes significant penalties on those who would try to reverse engineer or circumvent DRM technologies. (This prohibition also extends to individuals who would attempt to do so for the purposes of conducting security evaluations of the DRM products.) The EU Copyright Directive is similar but imposes even more draconian limitations on circumventing copy protection mechanisms.

DRM uses cryptography to limit the uses that can be made of the information the vendor wishes to control, typically by requiring the use of special software or devices to access the DRM-protected information. The software or device then enforces the limitations on the use of the information, be it the ability to access the information (e.g. satellite video channels) or to copy the information (e.g. eBooks that can be read by the purchaser but not by other people using a different eBook reader or software).

✔ The Debate about DRM

The topic of DRM has been the subject of many debates. One of the most controversial in recent years has been encrypted media extensions (EMEs). EMEs are used to create a communication channel between web browsers and DRM software, allowing the playback of DRM-protected files via HTML5 without media plugins. Since this inserts a proprietary component into an open standards–based software stack and can create barriers to entry to new browsers, as well as creating interoperability issues, organizations like the EFF have protested the creation of the W3C standard that supports it.

DRM proponents argue for tools like this to ensure their ability to protect intellectual property rights. Security practitioners need to be aware of both the benefits of DRM and the implications of implementing it, including the potential for issues with diverse platforms and tools, as well as questions around the lifecycle of DRM-protected data and retrieval in the future.

Some organizations use DRM as a form of Data Loss Prevention (DLP). In this context DRM is sometimes referred to as Enterprise DRM (E-DRM or EDRM) or Information Rights Management (IRM). Sensitive documents can be distributed as encrypted PDF files with prohibitions on printing and copy-and-paste operations. Some forms of document DRM permit the originator of the document to place an expiry date on the document after which it is inaccessible, or to remotely disable further access to the document (viewing the document must be done using software that checks with a central server before decrypting the document for display, and if the originator has marked the document as "virtually shredded" then the software will not be able to download the key needed to decrypt the document, rendering it a blob of useless random bits). This enables organizations to distribute copies of sensitive documents to external users and still exert considerable control over who accesses them. If the document falls into the wrong hands, it is illegible.

Some DRM software intended to control the distribution of documents and files can verify the computer or device being used to access the information, ensuring that only authorized devices are used to process the data. For organizations operating in regulated industries and with legislated requirements to tightly control the distribution and access to classified information, DRM can be a powerful tool to prevent the exfiltration or misuse of corporate data.

These powerful Technical Protection Measures may give rise to privacy risks. If every time a user wishes to read a document the system makes a network connection to determine if the access ought to be permitted, privacy concerns exist.

- What information (intentional or inadvertent) is being collected (e.g. IP address, possibly disclosing the location of the user when reading the document)?
- Has the user given informed consent for this information to be collected and processed?

A successful implementation of an IRM solution requires several steps.

- An appropriate governance model needs to be put in place before the introduction of IRM. The appropriate policies for mandating data classification and the use of IRM must be approved and in place, along with procedures for determining the classification of a data object and the appropriate level of IRM to use (if any) for each classification level. Not all documents need IRM, and a consistent approach for classification is necessary for the proper and efficient use of IRM where required.
- One must evangelize the importance of using IRM for DLP by explaining the risks to the organization of unauthorized access to sensitive data, combined with appropriate training of those expected to classify and encode sensitive documents.
- An analysis of related risks from using IRM has to be conducted, considering:
  - Privacy issues as outlined above
  - Availability issues (What if the IRM server is inaccessible, thus making a document inaccessible at a time when the user must access it to carry out an urgent time-critical task?)

Digital watermarking is a form of DRM in which data is modified in a manner which is not obvious to the casual observer, but which can be used to trace the origin of a copy of that data for the purposes of enforcing copyright, contractual, or legal restrictions on the distribution of the information. For example, a secret document could be digitally watermarked so that if an unauthorized copy were made and leaked to the press, it could be analyzed to determine who leaked the copy (since each authorized copy would have been uniquely watermarked and traceable to the person the document was originally given to). This form of digital watermarking is referred to as fingerprinting. For example, most, if not all, color printers print a "Machine Identification Code" in tiny yellow dots invisible to the naked eye on every page.

Other security objectives that can be achieved through digital watermarking include:

- "Invisibly" marking identity photographs on ID cards or passports to detect tampering (i.e. replacement of the photograph with that of a threat actor trying to thwart access controls)

- Embedding information in documents or photographs to detect tampering (such as changing key parts of the document or "photoshopping" a photograph)

APPLY SECURITY PRINCIPLES TO SITE AND FACILITY DESIGN

The general security principles outlined earlier for information security also have application to site and facility design. The CIA triad applies here and guides our application of security principles to this challenge:

- **Confidentiality and Integrity:** The primary physical threat to confidentiality and integrity is unauthorized access (e.g. intruders and theft).

- **Availability:** In addition to the threat to availability from unauthorized access, availability can also be compromised intentionally or accidentally by a range of events:

  - Environmental events such as fire, floods, storms, or earthquakes

  - Infrastructure events such as power outages, cooling (HVAC) failure, floods (from burst water pipes)

The sections below will outline controls that can be employed to reduce the risk from the above vulnerabilities but as with all risks, the security architect must consider all methods of handling risk: avoid, reduce, transfer, and accept.

One can avoid physical threats by selecting facilities that are unlikely to be vulnerable to certain risks (e.g. locating a data center in an area of known geological stability can effectively eliminate the risk of earthquakes, just as avoiding areas of known tornado and hurricane activity can reduce the risk from meteorological events).

One can reduce threats by implementing the security controls (administrative, technical, and physical) outlined in the sections which follow.

One can transfer many physical risks through insurance (fire, theft, business interruption, etc.) or by contractual means (e.g. contract with a colocation or data center hosting provider to provide a secure site and facility, thus relieving your organization of those responsibilities).

Once one has applied the chosen risk management approaches (avoid, reduce, transfer), then one assesses the residual risk to determine if it is within the organization's risk appetite, or is acceptable to the risk owner. If not, then additional steps must be taken to further reduce the residual risk.

IMPLEMENT SITE AND FACILITY SECURITY CONTROLS

All the thought and effort put into ensuring that the operation of your systems protects the confidentiality, integrity, and availability of your data is for naught if the threat actor can simply walk into your data center and walk out with the disk drives. Designing a data center or engaging the services of a third-party data center requires careful consideration of the risks and appropriate controls to mitigate those risks.

Similarly, the physical and environmental controls protecting your place of work are critical to ensure the security of your information.

In this section we will examine a range of vulnerabilities and outline appropriate mitigations to be considered.

Remember, however, as we pointed out in the beginning of this section, a fundamental principle of security architecture is defense in depth. This means that you must not rely just on physical security to protect physical assets. We must employ other controls so that, to the extent reasonably possible, a failure of a physical security control by itself does not lead to a failure of confidentiality, integrity, or availability.

Physical Access Controls

Because physical access controls can be used in a wide range of situations described below, we'll cover physical access security here.

The objective of physical access controls is to ensure that only authorized individuals have access to the controlled area, and that the physical access controls do not significantly impact the safety of the occupants (e.g. do not impede emergency evacuation in case of fire or other threats to their safety).

Like all controls, physical security controls fall into one of three types:

- Administrative controls
  - Policies and procedures
  - Facility management
  - Personnel screening and management
  - Training (awareness and procedural)

- Maintenance and testing of technical and physical security controls
- Emergency and incident response
- Technical controls
  - CCTV
  - Alarms
  - HVAC
  - Utility power
  - Fire detection and suppression
  - Electronic access systems (e.g. card-access)
  - Environmental monitoring (e.g. flooding, overheating, freezing, humidity)
- Physical controls
  - Facility location and siting
  - Facility construction, fencing, and landscaping
  - Doors, locks, turnstiles, mantraps, lighting
  - Guards and dogs
  - ID cards

A well-designed set of controls creates a layered defense which protects the physical environment. These six layers represent increasingly difficult hurdles for the threat actor to surmount in order to disrupt the physical site. While some controls span levels, the security professional should ensure that controls indeed exist at each level, consistent with the organization's risk assessment processes and taking into account the threat models for the particular physical site:

- Deter
- Detect
- Delay
- Assess
- Respond
- Recover

For example, the obvious presence of CCTV cameras can serve to deter, detect, and assess a particular threat. In a similar way, physical barriers such as bollards, turnstiles, or fences can serve several functions as well:

- They will deter some who will consider the protections too difficult to compromise.

- They will increase the chance of detection by requiring attackers to defeat physical barriers, which is likely to attract attention.

- They will delay compromise by slowing the attacker down while working to get through the physical barrier.

A risk analysis and threat modeling of possible threat vectors against the facility must also consider threats against the security controls themselves. For example, an unprotected card access system can be compromised by an attacker adding a "skimmer" device to copy data from valid access cards, to be used to create fraudulent copies. Placing tamper switches on the card readers, tied to the central alarm system, can mitigate this risk.

Access cards also can be lost or stolen, and they usually have enough identifying information to identify the facility that they provide access to. To prevent purloined credentials from being used to enter restricted areas, consider using a second factor such as a numeric keypad that requires the user to enter a PIN number, or a biometric sensor (e.g. fingerprint, hand geometry, retina, or iris scan).

If access to the higher security zones is mediated by a guard, then the guard should not rely upon the photo on the ID card to verify the person's identity, but instead the electronic ID card is used to access a central database of identity information (photo, height, weight, etc.) as the source of truth.

As mentioned before, security by obscurity is never sufficient in itself, but it is still a form of security. Unless there are compelling reasons to identify high-security areas with signage, putting such work areas behind unmarked doors makes it less likely that an opportunistic threat actor will focus on trying to compromise the security controls for that area.

Finally, one must remember that human safety always trumps security. One must ensure that staff can always safely evacuate all work areas, even in the face of power loss. Electric door locks must either fail open (and automatically unlock in case of a fire alarm), or doors must have crash bars that bypass the electric locking mechanism. Local building codes must obviously be consulted and respected as the final authority on what physical security controls are permitted, and how they must be implemented and operated.

Wiring Closets/Intermediate Distribution Facilities

The vulnerabilities related to networking distribution differ slightly between a data center and an office. In a data center owned and managed for a single company (or cloud-hosting provider), usually the network distribution will be within the same perimeter as the servers themselves, and so the physical and environmental security controls will apply to both. In a colocation facility, different clients will have access to different areas of the facility (to access the equipment owned by or assigned to them for their exclusive use). In this situation the wiring closets are managed by the hosting provider and must not be accessible to clients, as it would permit even authorized clients to access or affect service to other clients. In an office, intermediate distribution facilities need to be protected from both malicious outsiders and insider threats, not to mention environmental risks.

Not all insider threats are malicious — well-meaning staff trying to troubleshoot a networking problem can wreak havoc in a wiring closet. Too often, network switches and other pieces of intermediate distribution equipment are placed in any convenient out-of-the-way location, sharing space with other building infrastructure (e.g. electrical, plumbing, heating, or ventilation). When this is being contemplated, consider the additional risks from environmental impacts (flooding, overheating, or electromagnetic interference from electrical equipment). A small wiring closet full of network switches with poor (or no) ventilation can overheat, at a minimum shortening the life of your equipment, causing random resets, errors, and even total failure in the worst case.

Wiring closets can also be at risk from threats such as burst or leaking pipes that pass through or near the space or overflowing washrooms on the floors above. Again, if the obvious solution (moving the location of the wiring closet) is not an option, one must consider compensating controls — in this case a shield over the top of the equipment to deflect any falling water, and a rack (to keep all equipment and wiring sufficiently high off the floor) to prevent any pooling of water from affecting the equipment.

One must consider not just network infrastructure that you install for your internal purposes, but also cabling for other services (telephone, alarm, electronic door locks, etc.) that may transit spaces outside of your control. How useful are your electronic door locks if the cables powering them are in the suspended ceiling in the hallway outside your office? What good is your alarm going to be if the signal is carried on telephone wires that can be found behind an unlocked panel in the public hallway and easily tampered with?

✔ Telephone Wiring Closets

Telephone cross-connect panels, which connect the main vertical cables in an office building with the individual phone lines on an office floor, are frequently found in public hallways, often unlocked. In other cases, building managers readily unlock the telephone wiring closet when requested by a "technician"; a tool kit and telephone test set hanging off his belt provide a convincing business card.

Server Rooms/Data Centers

Just as with office space, the physical security of your data center can span a wide range of controls. Just as the security of a candy store differs from that of a bank or jeweler, you need to determine the risks in order to ensure you secure, but do not over-secure, your data center.

Security controls need to be selected to address:

- Physical access risks (see the "Implement Site and Facility Security Controls" section)

- HVAC (see the "Utilities and Heating, Ventilation, and Air Conditioning (HVAC)" section)

- Environmental risks (see the "Environmental Issues" section)

- Fire risks (see the "Fire Prevention, Detection, and Suppression" section)

It is not enough to design and build your server room or data center properly, one must also have the proper procedures in place to ensure the data center operates properly. These controls should cover, at a minimum:

- Personnel (background checks, training, access procedures)

- Maintenance

- Logging, monitoring, and alerting

- Control testing and auditing

For example, it is not enough to have a diesel generator to take over should a power outage last longer than the capacity of your uninterruptible power supply (UPS) to carry the load. You must also test and maintain the generator regularly, as well as ensure a sufficient supply of fuel (and attend to the deterioration of that fuel over time).

The art and science of data center design is well understood. Anyone charged with the responsibility of working on such a project (or selecting a vendor to provide hosting or colocation) ought to review the guidance available from organizations such as the following:

- American Society of Heating, Refrigerating and Air-Conditioning Engineers (ASHRAE)

- ANSI / BICSI: ANSI/BICSI 002-2014, Data Center Design and Implementation Best Practices

- Electronic Industries Association and Telecommunications Industries Association (EIA/TIA): ANSI/TIA-942, Telecommunications Infrastructure Standard for Data Centers

- European Union (EU): EN 50600 series of standards

- International Organization for Standardization (ISO): ISO/IEC 30134 series, Information technology – Data centres – Key performance indicators

- Uptime Institute: Tier Standards

These documents cover the entire range of issues that need to be considered. Our treatment here will focus on threats to the CIA triad.

Media Storage Facilities

In addition to the usual threats to confidentiality, integrity, and availability faced by any facility containing information technology equipment, media storage facilities must implement additional environmental controls to ensure that the stored media do not degrade over time (or at least degrade as slowly as can reasonably be provided for).

The specific controls will depend on the media being stored, the manufacturer's recommendations, and the specific threats anticipated, but typically will include:

- Controlled and stable temperature and humidity

- Air filtration and positive air pressure to minimize infiltration by airborne dust and microfine particulate matter or contaminants (such as corrosive fumes and engine exhaust from diesel generators or nearby vehicles)

- Appropriate carpeting or floor covering to minimize static electricity

- Careful siting of the media storage facilities to avoid magnetic fields that might arise from electrical equipment (e.g. transformers or motors)

Other considerations with respect to media storage include the following:

- If the environment of the media storage facility is different (in temperature or humidity) than the production environment in which the tape will be read, then time must be allowed for the tape to acclimate to the different environment before being processed.

- Some tape media needs to be "retensioned" (e.g unspooled and respooled), depending on the tape manufacturer's recommendations (e.g. every three years).

- For longer archival storage it is advisable to read the data from the stored media and rerecord on new media. Again, the tape manufacturer's recommendations ought to be followed with respect to the appropriate frequency (e.g. every six years).

- Appropriate procedures are necessary for the tracking of media that are placed in, and removed from, storage. This may include bar code scanning and separation-of-duties controls requiring two people to sign in and sign out media items.

- Fire detection and suppression systems may need to be installed.

- Proper housekeeping is required to reduce the possibility of fire, and to reduce the fuel available should a fire break out. On a related note, media storage facilities ought to be used only to store media and should not be shared with other general storage.

- Depending on the risk analysis and costs associated with managing on-premise media storage, it may be appropriate to retain the services of an off-site media storage service that will handle the physical security and environmental concerns related to secure long-term storage of media. This can be used for all media, or a portion, in order to provide disaster recovery should the primary media storage facility be damaged by fire or other calamity.

- Appropriate media end-of-life procedures must be enforced to sanitize (e.g. by degaussing magnetic media) and securely destroy media before disposal so that sensitive information cannot be extracted from the media once it leaves the control of the organization.

Evidence Storage

In addition to the security controls appropriate for other facilities (including media storage, should you be storing evidence in the form of magnetic media), evidence storage requires attention to physical controls that can assist in protecting the chain of custody necessary to prove that evidence used in court has not been tampered with or contaminated.

These controls include, at a minimum, a log book that indelibly records every item that has been placed in, or removed from, evidence storage. Additional controls that can increase the confidence in the chain-of-custody log with respect to the evidence storage room include:

- Strict policies surrounding who is permitted access to the evidence storage room, the information that is to be entered into the log, and procedures governing the management of the access keys to the evidence storage room

- CCTV monitoring

- Double locks on the evidence storage room doors, or a locked storage cabinet inside the locked evidence storage room, with separation of duties surrounding the control of the keys, so that two people are required to access the evidence storage

With respect to CCTV monitoring, consideration ought to be given to a system that incorporates motion detection or is linked to door sensors so that the video recording is only performed while people are in the evidence storage room. The reason is that evidence frequently must be kept in storage during long periods while awaiting trial, and continuous CCTV recording will either consume too much storage, or the storage period will be much shorter than the typical time an item of evidence is stored.

Restricted and Work Area Security

Work area security must be designed in response to a risk assessment (including threat modeling) and in accordance with security principles and the appropriate controls to mitigate risk. The considerations to be addressed include least privilege, need-to-know, separation of duties, dual control, defense in depth, and compliance obligations. This is especially important in the context of implementing facility security controls. No other facet of site security controls more directly affects the people of an organization.

Least Privilege and Need-to-Know

Access to restricted and secure areas must be granted only to the extent necessary for individuals to carry out their responsibilities, in accordance with formally approved policies and procedures. Access also must be periodically reviewed to ensure that the justification for access has not changed. Furthermore, detailed auditable records attesting to the above must be maintained.

Separation of Duties and/or Dual Control

Depending on the risk assessment, it may be appropriate to require more than one authenticated staff member to be present in order to obtain access to the secure work area. This can be an administrative control, verified through guard records or CCTV surveillance, or it can be enforced through multiple locks or electronic access controls.

Defense in Depth

The facility ought to be designed with layers of security controls supporting a hierarchy of security levels, from public on the exterior of the building (and possibly including common entrance areas), to low security areas such as reception, all the way to the highest security zones where the most sensitive or high-risk assets or work are located.

Passing from an area of lower security to an area of higher security ought to be obvious to the knowledgeable insider, and must require successfully authenticating with an access control system (be it a receptionist/guard, door lock, card reader, biometric scanner, or other device for identifying the individual transitioning the security boundary). The appropriate rigor and tolerable rate of false positives depend on the security level of the area being protected.

Furthermore, different types of security controls ought to be considered for the higher security zones. For example, in addition to preventive controls such as door locks, detective controls such as CCTV monitoring, corrective controls such as motion detectors and alarms can be used as compensating controls should the primary preventive control (e.g. the door lock) fail or be compromised.

Multifactor authentication techniques are as valuable for physical access as for logical (e.g. login) access. Requiring a user to have an access card as well as enter a PIN to unlock the door to higher security zones protects against loss of the access card and its use by an impostor. Requiring the card (and not the PIN alone) protects against shoulder-surfing by a threat actor observing staff enter their PINs.

Compliance Obligations

Organizations handling government or military classified data will have to institute such security controls as required to meet the obligations of their facility security clearance. The organization responsible for certifying compliance will provide detailed documentation on the controls that are necessary for the level of security clearance being sought, including requirements for:

- Personnel identification
- Guards
- Electronic access control
- Electronic intrusion detection
- CCTV
- Interior access controls

One solution for having confidential discussions is the Sensitive Compartmented Information Facility (SCIF). *SCIF* is a common term among U.S. and British military and governmental agencies with a need for isolated space to preserve confidentiality. Typically, at least a room, if not a secured, hardened building, the SCIF can be temporary or permanent. If you watch any movie where the military leaders are briefing the president on an important and sensitive situation, they are in a SCIF.

GDPR, HIPAA, PCI DSS, and other regulations or contractual obligations may impose security requirements which may affect the design of your physical work area security controls.

For related concerns, see the section "Control Physical and Logical Access to Assets" in Chapter 5.

Utilities and Heating, Ventilation, and Air Conditioning

Power and HVAC are equally important to the reliable operation of your data center. It matters little if you can maintain power to your server racks if your cooling system fails and the room temperature passes 105 degrees F (40° C). As with all aspects of data center design, you start with a risk assessment and then consider the relevant controls that can be used to reduce the risk to an acceptable level. You also need to balance building a single particularly resilient data center versus two geographically separated, less resilient data centers.

Having only sufficient (say N) UPS units to handle the load means some equipment will have to be disconnnected during maintenance.

Having a spare UPS (N+1) and appropriate switching gear means that units can be removed from service for maintenance without disrupting operations. But should a unit be out of service when the power fails, each of the other UPS units is a single point of failure. It also means that the switching gear is a single point of failure.

Having completely redundant UPS systems from separate utility feeds all the way to the rack is referred to as 2N and eliminates any single point of failure.

The degree of redundancy within a single data center is typically characterized by a tier level. The exact requirements for each tier vary somewhat between the different standards but generally provide availability and redundancy similar to what is shown in Table 3.5.

TABLE 3.5 General Data Center Redundancy Tier Levels

TIER LEVEL	AVAILABILITY %	REDUNDANCY
1	99.671	None. Multiple single points of failure
2	99.741	Some. Non-redundant (e.g. N) UPS
3	99.982	N+1 UPS. Able to take equipment out of service for maintenance without affecting operation
4	99.995	2N UPS. No single point of failure, able to automatically compensate for any single failure

Smaller data centers or server rooms without direct and dedicated connections to the power utility's distribution network need to consider who their neighbors (electrically speaking) might be. A server room located near a pump room, air conditioning, or refrigeration compressor, or an industrial facility with large electrical motors might need special power conditioning equipment to remove the interference and voltage spikes introduced into the power circuits by the noisy neighbors.

There are many types of UPS systems which vary in their design and features. Battery UPS systems can differ in a number of important aspects:

- **Load:** The capacity of the unit to deliver a specified level of continuous power
- **Capacity:** The time during which the unit can maintain the load
- **Filtering:** The ability of the unit to isolate the equipment from noise, surges, and other problems with the utility power
- **Reliability:** Some designs trade low cost for reliability

Non-battery UPS systems exist that use large-mass rotating flywheels connected to provide short-term backup. These are appropriate for larger loads (> 200KW) and can provide higher reliability and lower lifetime costs than comparable battery UPS systems.

Typically a UPS is intended only to carry the load during short outages, and for the short time it takes for a backup generator to start and be able to take the full load. So, most data centers or server rooms will need a generator to handle the load, should the power interruption last longer than that which the UPS can handle.

Generators are available in a wide range of capacities and use different fuels (gasoline, diesel, natural gas, and hydrogen). The advantage of natural gas is the elimination of the need to store fuel. The risk is that certain natural disasters can cause both power and gas distribution outages.

Cooling systems must be designed so that there are multiple units with sufficient capacity so that the data center can not only be maintained below the maximum safe operating temperature even in the face of the failure (or maintenance) of one or more units, but also the maximum rate of temperature change is kept within permitted limits (for example, less than 5°C/hour if magnetic tapes are being used, 20°C/hour otherwise), even if a unit is taken out of service for maintenance.

Finally, humidity also needs to be managed. Low humidity leads to increased static electricity, and high humidity can lead to condensation. Both conditions will lead to lower equipment reliability.

With both power (UPS and generator) and HVAC systems, due consideration has to be made for:

- Regularly scheduled maintenance
- Regular testing under full load (of UPS and generators, and backup HVAC equipment if not used in production)
- System fault detection and alerting (and regular tests of those subsystems)
- Periodic checks and audits to ensure all of the above are being properly and regularly performed

Without the above, the risk mitigations from your expensive backup systems might be more imaginary than real.

> ### ✔ Generator Failure Takes Out Major Data Center
>
> In 2008 in downtown Vancouver, a large underground fire destroyed a significant amount of the power infrastructure serving a large area of the business district. Included in this outage was the Vancouver location of a major multinational colocation provider.
>
> The UPS units cut in immediately and functioned as expected. After 10 minutes or so, when the power had not been restored and the UPS battery capacity was draining, the diesel generators fired up, also as expected. The transition from UPS to diesel power was smooth and the servers kept running.
>
> CONTINUES

Roughly 30 minutes later, however, one of the diesel generators carrying the entire load of one of the three floors of the data center failed and stopped. The UPS had recharged slightly, so the servers ran for another 5 minutes — then silence. A thousand servers stopped as if a switch had been flipped.

What happened? It depends on who you talk to. The official announcement claimed that the firefighters' use of water caused a drop in water pressure resulting in generator #7 overheating. Not explained was why generators #1 through #6 continued to work, serving other floors in the office tower.

The other explanation widely discussed at the time was that the generator had overheated because a $30 coolant thermostat had failed. While the generator had been routinely tested every month, the tests had only run for 15 minutes — not long enough to cause the generator's coolant to heat to the point where the thermostat had to function.

Whichever story is true, there are valuable lessons to be learned:

- A generator can be a single point of failure; proper redundancy requires N+1 generators (when N generators can carry the entire load).

- Testing of disaster response plans (DRP) ought to mimic real-life scenarios as closely as possible (e.g. generators that have to run for longer than 15 minutes).

- External dependencies (such as external water pressure) on DRP components need to be identified and assessed.

✔ Sensor Failure Masks Diesel Generator's Fuel Exhaustion

A remote communications tower had been designed to handle most expected power issues. There was a robust UPS unit with a diesel generator. There was a remote monitoring system to report back to the central Network Operations Center (NOC) on the environmental conditions (including power) at the site.

Unfortunately, the loss-of-utility-power sensor malfunctioned, and an extended power outage went unnoticed by the NOC with the result that the generator consumed all of the fuel and the site went dark (which definitely brought the issue to the attention of the NOC).

Obviously, a separate fuel level sensor would have helped, but remote tank level sensors are not cheap and this NOC had managed to determine when the tank needed refilling in the past merely by tracking the number of hours the generator had run (estimate based on the duration of the power outage).

As discussed earlier in the "Industrial Control Systems" section, the system that monitors and manages your HVAC or UPS system can be a vulnerability itself. If an attacker can remotely access your HVAC and disrupt its operation, possibly on a weekend when your data center is not staffed, causing the cooling to be disabled and servers to overheat, that can be just as effective a denial of service as one launched by a 100,000 bots. Similarly, unauthorized remote admin access to your UPS can result, at best, in your UPS being disabled and the next power outage not being mitigated; at worst, a direct power outage triggered by taking the UPS offline.

A variety of industry, national, and international standards cover HVAC, utilities, and environmental systems. These include:

- The Uptime Institute's Data Center design certification tiers assess areas including facility mechanical and electrical systems, as well as environmental and design considerations. Specifications for the tiers can be found at `https://uptimeinstitute.com/resources/`.

- The International Data Center Authority (IDC) provides open standards for data centers, facilities, and infrastructure at `https://www.idc-a.org/data-center-standards`.

- The ASHRAE standards for ventilation, refrigeration, building automation, and a variety of other related topics can be found at `https://www.ashrae.org/technical-resources/standards-and-guidelines`.

Other standards including the LEEDS standard, BICSI-001, and those created by one of the three European standards organizations (CEN, CENELEC, or ETSI) may all be useful or even required in the design of utilities and HVAC systems.

Environmental Issues

Environmental issues that need to be considered include the likelihood of:

- Major storms (hurricanes, lightning, blizzards, ice storms, typhoons, tornadoes, blizzards, etc.)
- Earthquakes
- Floods and tsunamis
- Forest fires
- Internal building risks
- Vermin and wildlife
- Volcanoes

Some vulnerabilities can be mitigated through selecting the appropriate location for the data center, others through building and site design. In fact, areas with specific common threats like earthquakes, floods, tornadoes, or hurricanes, like Japan, California, and others around the world, often have building codes that require new structures to be designed to survive these environmental threats.

Consider not placing any critical infrastructure components in the basement, as they may be prone to flooding (either from external sources such as storms or broken water mains, or internal causes such as burst pipes). Recall that one of the main causes of the Fukushima Daiichi Nuclear Power Station disaster was the flooding of batteries, electrical switching gear, and cooling pumps installed below the level of the reactors.

In the cases of major threats, a decision has to be made as to how resilient to make the data center, as well as which events to accept as beyond the ability of the data center to withstand and which will be handled through a remote backup data center and a disaster recovery plan.

You must also consider that even if you invest the money in a data center that could handle the worst storm or earthquake, like investing in a super-strength link to connect two chains, the ability of the data center depends on external suppliers to continue. If the destruction is widespread, how are you going to get diesel fuel delivered to keep your generators running (or are the natural gas pipelines likely to continue operating)? Or if the storm or earthquake is major, your staff are likely to be concerned about the safety and well-being of their families and homes, and are unlikely to be able to work or even to get to work with roads being impassable.

At some point it makes more sense to invest in your disaster recovery plan than to try to make your data center able to withstand environmental threats that your suppliers and your staff cannot cope with.

As discussed in the "Disaster Recovery and Business Continuity" section in Chapter 6, selecting your alternate data center involves considering the threats that might take out your primary data center to determine if they are likely to affect your alternate too. If the two data centers are too close together, or potentially in the path of the same hurricane, they might not provide the redundancy your DRP depends upon.

Internal building risks include things like: water leaks from burst pipes; condensate from water, sprinkler pipes, or HVAC equipment in the suspended ceiling; and overflowing washroom or kitchen facilities on the floors above.

Mitigations include appropriate routing of pipes within the building relative to equipment, or if moving into an existing building, appropriate location of equipment relative to plumbing. In some circumstances, installing a canopy over some equipment may be the best option.

Vermin and wildlife can do astounding damage to communications cabling and power distribution, either from eating through the insulation or wires themselves, or physically short-circuiting powerlines. Electrical disruptions caused by squirrels are sufficiently common as to warrant an entry in Wikipedia!

Another risk that might be considered to be environmental is an epidemic or pandemic that prevents your employees, or your suppliers' employees, from working, or that places an extra strain on your organization because of service demands triggered by the outbreak of disease.

The analysis must consider the risk level your employees face (obviously those in the healthcare industry or with frequent contact with the public will be more exposed, while those with minimal contact are less likely to be affected).

Mitigations include:

- Monitoring announcements from public health authorities

- Having a sick-leave policy that does not incentivize employees to come to work ill

- Developing a plan to operate with: a reduced workforce; employees working from home; or work shifted to office locations less affected (in the case of larger companies with multiple offices)

✔ Cloud Computing and Availability

Designing to handle environmental issues can often mean ensuring that local environmental issues do not interrupt services or systems. Widespread availability of remote hosting and cloud services has allowed many organizations to move critical services to locations and data centers which aren't threatened by the same environmental concerns. An organization located in a hurricane-prone coastal area may opt to have their alternate operations in an area that isn't likely to be impacted by a weather event.

The same concepts that apply when assessing environmental risks for an on-site facility apply to choosing cloud or third-party hosting, so simply outsourcing to another location doesn't prevent organizations from having to do the work. The advantage is that there is a broader range of choices than a single geographic area may provide, allowing risks to be balanced or influenced in ways that can't be done on site.

The availability increases that highly redundant data centers can provide are impressive, with cloud providers claiming 99.99% or higher availability. That number is only useful if organizations also ensure that they will be able to access cloud providers that are highly available. Redundant network routes and hardware that can stay online through a local or regional disaster are a necessary part of cloud hosting availability designs that can take full advantage of these highly available remote infrastructures.

Fire Prevention, Detection, and Suppression

There are a range of fire suppression technologies that can be deployed to protect technology infrastructure, facilities, and people. The process, as with selecting any set of security controls, is to perform a risk assessment to determine the appropriate mitigation strategy.

As always, human safety is paramount, and any fire safety system must be designed first and foremost to protect the lives and health of those who work in the facility. Enabling occupants to safely exit the building and ensuring that fire suppression systems are unlikely to compromise health or safety are more important than protecting systems and buildings.

Next, one has to balance the costs of:

- Downtime

- Restoration costs

- Fire suppression system costs (capital and ongoing maintenance)

Typically there will be a tradeoff between the first two and the third. In other words, reducing downtime and restoration costs will require a more expensive fire suppression system. Selecting a less expensive approach is likely to increase the time it will take to return the data center to operation after a fire event.

Fire needs three things to start: heat, fuel, and oxygen (more generally, an oxidizing agent). Fire prevention and suppression involves reducing one or more of these three elements such that fire cannot start or be sustained. A more complete model adds the chemical reaction between the fuel and the oxidizing agent, creating the fire "tetrahedron." This model is useful in that some fire suppression systems block the chemical reaction itself rather than reducing one of the three components necessary for that reaction.

Fire safety is subject to many regulations, informed by centuries of experience. It is the realm of trained professionals who ought to be consulted prior to the installation of any fire suppression system. While this section provides the information security professional with general information, it is no substitute for expert advice specific to a given situation.

Most jurisdictions have standards and guidelines for the fire protection systems for IT equipment:

- **Canada and the United States:** NFPA 75 - Standard for the Fire Protection of Information Technology Equipment and NFPA 76 - Fire Protection of Telecommunications Facilities.

- **UK:** *BS 6266:2011*, Fire protection for electronic equipment installations. Code of practice.

- **Germany:** The VdS series of guidelines for fire protection and suppression.

Fire suppression systems work by applying a fire suppressant to the area of the fire, removing one or more of the four components needed to sustain the fire.

The simplest and most widely used system is the wet-pipe water sprinkler system. These systems have water in the pipes at all times, and the sprinkler heads each have valves held closed either by a heat-sensitive glass bulb or a metal link, both designed to release the water at a specific temperature. The advantages of wet-pipe systems include low installation and maintenance costs and relatively high reliability. These systems also only release water through those sprinkler heads closest to the fire, thus limiting water damage. The risk from wet-pipe water sprinklers is the damage that occurs due to accidental release from faulty sprinkler heads or physical damage (hitting a sprinkler head with a rack or ladder while working in the facility).

Dry-pipe systems have, as the name implies, no water in the supply pipes until a sprinkler head is triggered by fire. These are used in warehouses and parking garages exposed to freezing temperature and are not relevant to data centers or most office buildings. The advantage is that the pipes do not contain water, which can freeze and damage the pipes. The disadvantages are increased corrosion and a delay in response time, as the air must be forced out of the sprinkler heads before the water reaches the fire.

Another specialized sprinkler system not usually deployed in data centers or office buildings is the deluge sprinkler. This is a variant of the dry-pipe sprinkler but with open sprinkler heads. Once a fire is detected (using smoke, heat, or manual alarm), a valve opens to let water into the supply pipes and through all sprinkler heads (without regard to the specific location of the fire). These systems are appropriate in certain industrial situations in which a large volume of water is required to prevent the spread of the fire.

Pre-action systems are a combination of one of the previous three types of sprinkler systems (wet-pipe, dry-pipe, or deluge) with a more sophisticated triggering mechanism. A single-interlock pre-action system is a dry-pipe system with pressurized gas in the pipes, in which the activation of a smoke or heat detector causes water to be released into the supply pipes, essentially converting the dry-pipe system to a wet-pipe system. The water, however, is only released if the sprinkler head is triggered. This system sharply reduces the chance of an accidental release of water because should a sprinkler head trigger accidentally, the system will detect a drop in air pressure and set off a trouble alarm but not release any water. A double-interlock pre-action system requires both the activation of a smoke or heat detector and the activation of sprinkler heads before water is released into the supply pipes. This can be an advantage in refrigerated spaces but delays the release of water in the case of an actual fire event.

Proper design of any sprinkler system requires professional advice and continued vigilance to ensure that later developments (such as the addition of suspended cable trays) do not impair the effectiveness of the system. A limitation of sprinklers is that they do not work well in the confined space of a raised floor or suspended ceiling. These require either water mist or clean agent fire suppression systems.

An alternative to standard sprinkler heads that can discharge high quantities of water per minute are water mist sprinklers, which release a much smaller amount of water in the form of microscopic water droplets. These extinguish the fire both through removing heat (as a standard sprinkler does) as well as by displacing oxygen when the mist is converted to steam.

Water, although an extremely effective fire extinguishing agent, can cause damage to sensitive electronics. In situations in which the impact of water damage would be significant, various "clean agent" extinguishants can be used. These have the advantage of causing little or no damage to the equipment being protected. The disadvantage is their much higher installation and ongoing maintenance costs.

The original clean agents included carbon dioxide and halon. Carbon dioxide works primarily by displacing oxygen and additionally by removing heat. Unfortunately, it can cause asphyxiation in concentrations well below that required for fire suppression and so requires pre-discharge alarms to ensure the space about to be flooded with CO_2 is evacuated prior to discharge. Halon gas works by interfering with the chemical reaction (the fourth part of the "fire tetrahedron") and has the advantage of being non-toxic at concentrations well above those needed. This resulted in its widespread use in data centers and other facilities for several decades where sprinklers might cause more damage than a contained fire. Halon, however, is very damaging. In Canada, the Montreal Protocol in 1994 phased out its use.

Newer clean agents that are ozone-friendly have been developed, each with specific advantages. These include HFC-227ea, fluorinated ketone, and various gas mixtures (e.g. argon, nitrogen, and carbon dioxide). These newer clean agents are more environmentally friendly and less toxic than earlier alternatives.

Just as network segmentation can limit the damage of a security breach in one part of the network, physically separating critical communications facilities in a separate room with a two-hour fire wall (literally) from less critical data processing facilities can also limit the damage by preventing a fire (and the water from the fire suppression system) in one area from affecting equipment in another.

Similarly, backup media that must be stored on site can be stored in a separate room or in a fireproof storage vault.

The use of gaseous fire suppression is made more complicated by the need to be able to automatically isolate the affected areas from the normal ventilation and cooling systems so that the HVAC system does not dilute or remove the fire suppression gas.

Fire extinguishers are mandatory, but staff need to be trained in their purpose and proper use. While they may serve to put out very small fires caught in their early stages, they are primarily there to enable staff in the server room to reach an exit should fire block their path. Fires are categorized by the type of fuel:

- **Class A:** Ordinary solid combustibles (e.g. paper, wood, plastic)
- **Class B:** Flammable liquids and gases (e.g. gasoline)
- **Class C:** Energized electrical equipment
- **Class D:** Combustible metals (e.g. lithium metal, but not lithium-ion batteries, which are considered Class B, although water will also work well with Li-ion battery fires)

Fire extinguishers are rated based on the classes of fires they are designed to combat and the amount of extinguishant they contain. A fire extinguisher rated 5BC may be used on Class B or C fires. A 10BC extinguisher would have twice the capacity of a 5BC extinguisher.

Use of the incorrect extinguisher can not only make the fire worse (e.g. using water on a gasoline fire can spread the fuel), it can be a grave safety hazard to the person using the extinguisher (e.g. using water on an electrical fire can result in a risk of electrocution). A person can use a water (e.g. Class A) extinguisher on computer equipment but only if it has been de-energized first.

Training does not end with knowledge of how and when to use the fire extinguishers. All staff who will normally be present in the data center need to be properly trained and rehearsed on how to respond to a fire alarm or fire event.

Make sure they know:

- Where all of the exits are (so they know the closest, and if blocked, the alternates)
- Where all of the fire extinguishers are located as well as how and when to use them (different types of fire extinguishers are appropriate for different types of fires)
- How to disable (or delay the discharge of) the fire suppression system should a false fire detection be suspected
- How to manually trip the fire suppression system (in the case of gaseous suppression and some sprinkler systems) should early signs of fire be detected by staff before the fire detectors are triggered
- Where the fire alarm pull stations or call points are
- How to manually shut off power to the data center

Finally, good housekeeping is an important part of fire suppression. The data center or server room must not be used for storage. Cardboard boxes of computer parts or wooden reels of Cat 5 cabling must be stored in a separate part of the facility. Waste paper receptacles should be outside the facility or, if they must be inside the data center, small and frequently emptied. The less fuel there is available, the less likely there will be a fire, and if there is a fire, less damage will result.

SUMMARY

In discussing security architecture and security engineering, this chapter has taken a path through the third domain of the CISSP Body of Knowledge. The discussion of secure design principles and security models introduced both historical significance and a foundation of understanding of security architecture. Further discussion centered on hardware, from the security capabilities of information systems to securing a variety of platforms.

The majority of the chapter's middle was focused on vulnerability management, namely the process of assessing and mitigating those vulnerabilities. Vulnerability management covered several types of systems and architectures, starting with high-level designs, through web-based systems, then mobile systems and at last, embedded systems.

The chapter ended with cryptography being covered, from the lifecycle, through methods, to various practices and applied uses. And at last, site and facility design was discussed, both how to apply security principles to facility design and their application through several solutions.

Communication and Network Security

THE AIM OF SECURITY programs is to ensure that business will carry on, unimpeded by security threats. Whether the threats are external or internal, technical or human, the myriad risks threatening the organization must be identified and addressed in order to consider the information security program successful.

The success of security programs is measured by the effectiveness and efficiency of security controls and risk management operations. These address the confidentiality, integrity, and availability (CIA) triad. Confidentiality addresses the provision of information to authorized recipients only. Controls to assure data is not tampered with in storage or in transit is the aim of integrity. Availability is a concern for providing the right information to the right recipients at the right time.

In this domain, we will examine various aspects of information security as it relates to the network, interconnections, networked devices, and communication processes that are in the purview of the information security professional.

IMPLEMENT SECURE DESIGN PRINCIPLES IN NETWORK ARCHITECTURES

The scope of this material is to stay aligned with best practices in the secure design of network architectures. There are a variety of emerging ideas and innovative procedures that it may be useful to examine. The reader is encouraged to use supplemental sources and to stay on top of developments in the industry as they evolve. However, the core information regarding communications and network security are found within. The introduction of the concepts begins with secure design principles in network architecture. The previous chapter detailed the five architectural principles and five design principles of ISO/IEC 19249. Additionally, we drew comparisons between the ISO 19249 principles and the fundamental but analogous principles from early academic work on security principles.

To recap briefly, two principles that most directly affect network architecture include domain separation and layering. *Layering* involves designing something in increasingly abstract terms, with each layer offering some aspect of security or assurance. In the context of hosts communicating over a network, the Open Systems Interconnection (OSI) model is the prevailing example. The OSI model is one of increasing abstraction, with each layer making room for varying methods of ensuring security.

Domain separation, as an architectural principle, applies to network secure design. Separating network traffic at the collision domain helps avoid network congestion. Separating network traffic into broadcast domains further inhibits an adversary from sniffing valuable clues to the network topology. Going further, separating a network into segments isolates local network traffic from traveling across routes. This again mitigates the risk of a potential adversary learning about the network design.

The security professional must understand a range of relevant subjects to adequately understand how to implement secure design principles in network architectures. It is necessary to know the OSI model in detail. Similarly, it is important to understand Transmission Control Protocol/Internet Protocol (TCP/IP), in particular IP networking, for comparison. Another significant subject is multilayer protocols where several protocols make up a group, spread across several of the OSI layers. By comparison, converged protocols are where a specialized protocol is grouped with a commonly used protocol. In addition to protocols, networking concepts are significant, beginning with the benefits of virtualized networking, termed *software-defined networks* (SDNs). Wireless networking is also important, including its security implications. Beyond wireless, there are commonly accepted divisions of a network as defined by areas of control, including an intranet, extranet, and the Internet. If a section of an intranet is public-facing yet partially controlled between the Internet and the fully protected intranet, that section is the *demilitarized zone* (DMZ). Lastly, the concept of a virtual local area network (VLAN) is essential, as VLANs form isolated broadcast zones to segment a network. This section and its subsections examine all of these topics.

Although this section introduces you to both the OSI and TCP/IP models, the rest of this chapter focuses on mapping the OSI model to networking/internetworking functions and summarizes the general nature of addressing schemes within the context of the OSI model.

Open Systems Interconnection and Transmission Control Protocol/Internet Protocol Models

We use networking models to reduce complexity, standardize interfaces, assist understanding, promote rapid product development, support interoperability, and facilitate modular engineering. In this way, a series of complex and geographically dispersed networks can be interconnected securely and relatively seamlessly. The prevailing networking models, TCP/IP and OSI, support interoperability and reduce proprietary incompatibilities where there are competing vendor or supplier product lines. Keep in mind that the models are guidelines, not requirements. There may still be some variations among vendors.

TIP Distinguishing between two similar yet different successful models can be challenging. First, this section will explain the specifics of the OSI and TCP/IP models. After that, to help you keep this distinction straight, this chapter endeavors to handle the models in the following ways:

- When discussing layers of a model, the chapter usually refers to the OSI model.
- When discussing protocols, the chapter usually refers to the TCP/IP model.

Open Systems Interconnection Reference Model

The OSI reference model is a conceptual model made up of seven layers that describe information flow from one computing asset to another over a network. Each layer of the OSI model performs or facilitates a specific network function. The layers are arranged in the following bottom to top order:

1. Physical
2. Data Link
3. Network
4. Transport
5. Session
6. Presentation
7. Application

TIP The following mnemonic phrase, where the first letter represents the layer (*A* stands for "Application"), can help in memorizing the names and order of the layers from top to bottom: All People Seem To Need Data Processing.

The purpose of a layered model is to reduce complex tasks or actions into smaller interrelated groups. Each group is applicable to the layer in which it resides. This helps in understanding and troubleshooting protocols, actions, and data based on the separation of the layers. Another benefit is that updates or changes implemented in one layer may not impact all the other layers. If the model was flat, problems would impact the entire system and upgrades could negatively disrupt parts of the system inadvertently. The layers provide important separation.

The specific layers are described in greater detail in the following paragraphs. The OSI model, defined in ISO/IEC 7498-1, is a product of research and collaboration from the International Organization for Standardization (ISO). As the standard has proven reliable, the consensus is that OSI is the primary architectural model in networking and communications.

Figure 4.1 details the seven layers of the OSI reference model.

LAYER	DESCRIPTION	PROTOCOL DATA UNIT (PDU)	Applied Use
Application	— Coding and conversion functions on application layer data — Ensures information sent from one system's application layer is readable at destination system's application layer	Data	HTTP, HTTPS, DICOM, LDAP, MIME, SMTP, FTP, SFTP
Presentation	— Establishes, manages, and terminates communication sessions between presentation layer entities — Communication sessions consist of service requests and service responses between applications on different network devices	Data	In many references, no distinction between Presentation and Application layer protocols & TLS, SSL
Session	— Session management capabilities between hosts — Assists in synchronization, dialog control, and critical operation management — Remembers session information like password verification so a host does not have to repeatedly supply credentials on subsequent access requests	Data	RPC, SMB, SSH, NFS, NetBIOS, H.245, PAP, PPTP, SCP, ZIP
Transport	— Reliable internetwork data transport services transparent to upper layers — Functions include flow control, multiplexing, virtual circuit management, and error checking and recovery	Segment	TCP, UDP, BGP, DCCP, FCP, RDP
Network	— Provides routing and related functions that enable multiple data links to be combined into an internetwork — Uses logical addressing versus physical addressing of devices	Packet	ATM, Routers, IP, IPSec, ICMP, OPSF, IPv4, IPv6, IPX, DDP, SPB
Data Link	— Provides reliable transit of data across a physical network link	Frame	Ethernet, FDDI, Frame Relay, VLAN, MAC, Switches, SPB
Physical	— Bit-level transmission between different devices; electrical or mechanical interfaces; activates, maintains, and deactivates the physical link between communicating network systems	Bits	Volts, PINS, bit-rate, serial or parallel, USB, Ethernet 10Base varieties

FIGURE 4.1 OSI model

Layer 1: Physical Layer

The physical layer defines the electrical, mechanical, procedural, and functional specifications for activating, maintaining, and deactivating the physical link between communicating network systems. The physical layer consists of transmitting raw bits, rather than logical data packets, over a physical link that connects devices across a network. Physical layer specifications relate to electrical signals, optical signals (optical fiber, laser), electromagnetic waves (wireless networks), or sound. Some common physical layer implementations are IEEE 1394 interface, Ethernet physical layer (10BASE-T, 10BASE2, 10BASE5, 100BASE-TX, 100BASE-FX, 100BASE-T, 1000BASE-T, and 1000BASE-SX), DSL, ISDN, and USB. Physical network topologies are defined at this layer.

What sort of attack vectors can you expect to see at the physical layer? Attacks unique to this layer would include passive sniffing, either over the cable or wireless, denying service by cutting the cable, or causing excessive electrical interference. Technical specifics on attacks such as sniffing and interference are discussed later in the chapter. But at the physical layer, thinking of attacks that would cause destruction or denial of service are limited more by imagination than by skill.

Layer 2: Data Link Layer

The data link layer is the second layer in the OSI model, and it transfers data between network nodes on the physical link. This layer encodes bits into packets before transmission and then decodes the packets back into bits. The data link layer is where the protocols for the network specifications are established. Specifically, how devices are to be connected, such as in a bus or a ring topology, are set at this layer. Data link provides reliability because it provides capabilities for synchronization, error control, alerting, and flow control. These services are important because if transmission or packet sequencing fails, errors and alerts are helpful in correcting the problems quickly. Flow control at the data link layer is vital so the devices send and receive data flows at a manageable rate.

There are two sublayers of the data link layer as established by the Institute of Electrical and Electronics Engineers (IEEE) per the IEEE 802 series of specifications. These are the logical link control (LLC) and the media access control (MAC).

The LLC controls packet synchronization, flow control, and error checking. This upper sublayer provides the interface between the MAC sublayer and the network layer. The LLC enables multiplexing protocols as they are transmitted over the MAC layer and demultiplexing the protocols as they are received. LLC also facilitates node-to-node flow control and error management, such as automatic repeat request (ARQ).

The MAC sublayer is the interface between the LLC and the physical layer (layer 1). At this sublayer, there is transmission of data packets to and from the network interface card (NIC) and another remotely shared channel. MAC provides an addressing mechanism and channel access so nodes on a network can communicate with each other. MAC addressing works at the data link layer (layer 2). It is similar to IP addressing except that IP addressing applies to networking and routing performed at the network layer (layer 3). MAC addressing is commonly referred to as *physical addressing*, while IP addressing (performed at the network layer) is referred to *logical addressing*. Network layer addressing is discussed in the next section.

A MAC address is unique and specific to each computing platform. It is a 12-digit hexadecimal number that is 48 bits long. There are two common MAC address formats, MM:MM:MM:SS:SS:SS and MM-MM-MM-SS-SS-SS. The first half of a MAC address, called a *prefix*, contains the ID number of the adapter manufacturer. These IDs are regulated by the IEEE. As an example, the prefixes 00:13:10, 00:25:9C, and 68:7F:74 (plus many others) all belong to Linksys (Cisco Systems). The second half of a MAC address represents the serial number assigned to the adapter by the manufacturer. It is possible for devices from separate manufacturers to have the same device portion, the rightmost 24-bit number. The prefixes will differ to accomplish uniqueness.

An example attack vector unique to the data link layer would include forging the MAC address, otherwise known as *ARP spoofing*. By forging ARP requests or replies, an attacker can fool data link layer switching to redirect network traffic intended for a legitimate host to the attacker's machine. ARP spoofing is also a common precursor to man-in-the-middle (MitM) attacks and session hijacking attacks, both of which are further discussed later in the chapter.

Layer 3: Network Layer

The network layer responds to service requests from the transport layer and issues service requests to the data link layer. At this layer, the logical addressing of devices is necessary to structure the flow of traffic. Data is transferred in the form of packets, which are in an ordered format, along the logical network paths. Proper functions of the network layer include logical connection setup, data forwarding, routing, packet fragmentation, and delivery error reporting. Logical addressing, perhaps more familiar as IP addresses, is a network layer concept.

There are connection-oriented and connectionless network layer protocols. These protocols are differentiated by the point in time that data is transmitted. In connection-oriented protocols, a logical connection is established between two devices before transferring data. Connection-oriented protocols exist at other, higher layers of the OSI model. In connectionless protocols, as soon as a device has data to send to another, it just sends it. In addition to network routing protocols, some additional routing protocols operate at the network layer. These include Border Gateway Protocol (BGP), an Internet interdomain routing protocol; Open Shortest Path First (OSPF), a link-state, interior gateway protocol developed for use in TCP/IP networks; and Routing Information Protocol (RIP), an Internet routing protocol that uses hop count as its metric.

BGP is often thought of as a network layer or transport layer protocol. However, it actually functions on top of TCP, which technically makes it a session layer protocol in the OSI model. Consequently, a security professional might encounter it being discussed at any of these layers.

There are several noteworthy functions that occur at the network layer:

- **Internet Protocol:** When IP was established, it lacked the functionality of ensuring the authenticity and privacy of data through the local area network (LAN) or wide area network (WAN). IP data transmissions, therefore, were susceptible to being intercepted and altered.

- **Addressing:** IP facilitates transmission of data from host to destination IP address, traversing the network until the destination address is located and reached.

- **Host addressing:** Each host has a unique address to provide the location on the Internet. That address is the IP address.

- **Message forwarding:** Gateways or routers are special-purpose devices or hosts on the network that forward data between networks that are segmented, partitioned, or interconnected across the wide area network.

- **Fragmentation:** Packet sizes can be large and complex. The network layer facilitates the subdivision of a data packet into a manageable or allowable size without the loss of data integrity.

- **Internet protocol security (IPSec):** When implemented, secure communications using virtual private networks (VPNs), and encryption is made possible by the set of protocols that provides security for IP.

IPSec uses several security services to accomplish authentication and encryption:

- **Authentication Header (AH):** This authenticates the sender, and it discovers any changes in data during transmission.

- **Encapsulating Security Payload (ESP):** This not only performs authentication for the sender but also encrypts the data being sent.

- **Security Associations (SA):** These provide the bundle of shared security attributes or keys and data that provide the parameters necessary for AH and/or ESP operations.

NOTE Authentication and authorization are related concepts, but they are not the same thing. Authorization is similar to privileges, while authentication deals with verifying an identity. Once a particular user is authenticated as truly being Joe Smith, authorization is what Joe Smith is allowed to do within the system.

There are two modes of IPSec:

- **Transport Mode:** This only encrypts and authenticates the IP payload, which is the data being transmitted in the packet, to ensure a secure channel of communication.

- **Tunnel Mode:** This will encrypt and authenticate the whole IP packet, which includes the data as well as routing information, to form a new IP packet with a new IP header to provide secure communication between two places, i.e., establish a VPN.

Attack vectors particular to the network layer are exploitative efforts specific to how network traffic is routed. A man-in-the-middle attack, involving traffic being redirected to a malicious actor, is an example of an attack at the network layer. Spoofing or forging of a network address is another common form of network layer attack. But provided the attacker has access to the resources, the simplest attack form to execute is the denial of service (DoS), simply overwhelming the target.

A range of protocols functions at the network layer. RIP is an early protocol that is still occasionally used. OSPF is a fast, scalable protocol used in large enterprise networks. The Internet Control Message Protocol (ICMP) is used for troubleshooting and error control purposes. The Internet Group Management Protocol (IGMP) is used to simultaneously transmit video to multiple recipients. The following sections examine more closely how these protocols work at the network layer.

Routing Information Protocol Versions 1 and 2

Assignment of logical addresses to networks requires a mechanism to inform the routers of which networks are directly or indirectly accessible. In the past, manual entries in routing tables created static routes, forcing traffic between two locations to travel on a designated path. As more networks were added, maintaining these tables efficiently required the adoption of standards-based protocols to automatically share this information. The evolution of routing protocols reflects the growth of the Internet in order to address the scope and increasingly complex interconnected infrastructure.

RIP is one of the earliest routing protocols and the first to use the distance and vector routing method. RIP uses the count of hops that a signal makes along the network path. RIP allows a maximum of 15 hops, and, at hop number 16, the distance is considered infinite and the destination unreachable. This constraint limits the size of networks RIP can support, but also is the reason RIP prevents routing loops. RIP implements mechanisms to assure correct routing in the forms of split horizon, route poisoning, and holddown mechanisms.

A RIP router transmits full updates every 30 seconds. When this technology was originated, this was not expected to be a problem. Over time, the volume of routing devices on the network created the potential for high volumes of traffic bursts. The theory was that random implementation of new devices would help to normalize the traffic flow over time.

Because time to converge and scalability issues are prevalent in RIP, it is not the preferred choice in most networking environments. However, RIP is still a viable choice because it is widely supported, is easy to configure, and does not require any parameters, unlike other protocols.

RIP uses the User Datagram Protocol (UDP) as its transport protocol and is assigned the reserved port number 520.

NOTE For support of Internet Protocol Version 6 (IPv6), RIP next generation (RIPng) is an extension of RIPv2. RIPng sends updates on UDP port 521 using the multicast group FF02::9.

Open Shortest Path First (OSPF) Versions 1 and 2

The OSPF protocol is common in large enterprise networks because it provides fast convergence and scalability. Convergence refers to how routing tables get updated. OSPF is a link-state protocol, specifically one of the interior gateway protocols (IGPs) standardized by the Internet Engineering Task Force (IETF). Link-state protocols gather information from nearby routing devices and create a network topology, making the protocol very efficient. OSPF monitors the topology and when it detects a change, it automatically reroutes the topology. Within seconds, OSPF is able to reroute from link failures and create loop-free routing.

OSPF supports Internet Protocol Version 4 (IPv4) and IPv6 networks. The updates for IPv6 are specified as OSPF Version 3. OSPF computes traffic load and seeks to balance it between routes. To do so, several variables are included, such as the round-trip distance in time of a router, data throughput of a link, or link availability and reliability. OSPF encapsulates data directly in IP packets at protocol number 89. It does not use a transport protocol like UDP or TCP.

In a paper titled "Persistent OSPF Attacks" published through Stanford University (by Gabi Nakibly, Alex Kirshon, Dima Gonikman, and Dan Bonch), the researchers share two new attack vectors made available by the OSPF standard. This interesting paper describes how the execution of the attacks relies on eavesdropping, requiring the attacker to be local to a networking device in the path.

NOTE The cost of a route is equal to the sum of all the costs for outbound links between the router and the destination network, plus the OSPF interface cost where link messaging was received. Networking professionals would explain that "cost" is just one routing metric among several others, such as bandwidth, hops, delay, and reliability. But the value set for cost is unique in that it is just an arbitrary value set by the networking administrator to influence the routing calculations done by dynamic and optimizing protocols like OSPF.

Internet Control Message Protocol

The Internet Control Message Protocol (ICMP) message has three fields distinguishing the type and code of the ICMP packet, and those values never change in the header while in transit. They are followed by ICMP-specific information and then the original IP header information. The most common uses for ICMP traffic are manual troubleshooting (the ping utility) and network diagnostics (the traceroute utility) and system-generated error messages during IP transmissions.

The ICMP information is used for troubleshooting and control purposes when there are errors in the IP transmissions. In ICMP utilities, every device forwards an IP packet, and an ICMP message can be subsequently sent to the source address. Using ping and traceroute, for example, the source IP address can ascertain several useful network mapping messages such as Destination Unreachable, Echo Request and Reply (Ping), Redirect, Time Exceeded, and Router Advertisement and Router Solicitation. All are important in the daily operations of security personnel.

Ping and traceroute can also be used by attackers to identify the location of hosts (ping) and, for malicious reasons, to map the network for future attacks of all types (traceroute).

Internet Group Management Protocol

The Internet Group Management Protocol (IGMP) operates at the network layer but is specific to a host or a router within the group. IGMP is the key protocol necessary for doing IP multicast transmissions. Multicast becomes very useful when you have an application needing to perform a one-to-many transmission, such as a video multicast from the CEO to his employees. Likely, an attack on IGMP begins with an attack on the multicast routing software or hardware device itself utilizing IGMP.

Layer 4: Transport Layer

At this layer, there is an end-to-end transport between peer hosts. The transmission is transparent to the upper layers. Some of the functions that happen at the transport layer are flow control, multiplexing, virtual circuit management, and error checking and recovery.

- Flow control manages data transmission and keeps the sending device from overwhelming the processing capability of the receiving device.

- Multiplexing allows several applications to transmit data along a single physical link.

- Virtual circuits are established, maintained, and terminated by the transport layer.

- Error checking involves creating various mechanisms for detecting transmission errors.

- Error recovery resolves errors such as a request that data be retransmitted.

Every security professional should be already aware of these transport layer protocols: UDP and TCP.

The TCP level of the TCP/IP transport protocol is connection-oriented. Before any data is transmitted (and possibly lost), a reliable connection must be established. A three-way handshake is primarily used to create a TCP socket connection. A socket is an endpoint instance. A socket is not just a network port but is an endpoint defined by the combination of the IP address and port. Figure 4.2 illustrates the typical process.

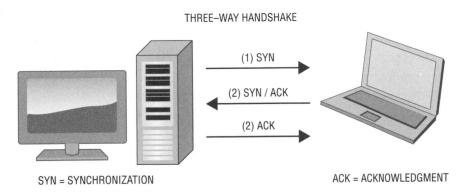

THREE–WAY HANDSHAKE

(1) SYN

(2) SYN / ACK

(2) ACK

SYN = SYNCHRONIZATION   ACK = ACKNOWLEDGMENT

(1) A client node sends a SYN data packet over an IP network to a destination node on the same or an external network. The SYN packet is asking if the destination is open for new connections.

(2) The target node must have open ports that can accept and initiate new connections. When the destination target receives the SYN packet from the client node, it responds and returns a confirmation receipt, specifically the ACK packet or SYN/ACK packet.

(3) The client node receives the SYN/ACK from the destination and responds with an ACK packet.

Upon completion of this process, the connection is created and the host and target can communicate.

FIGURE 4.2 TCP three-way handshake

In contrast with TCP, UDP is a connectionless protocol. UDP also operates at the transport layer (layer 4) of the OSI model. However, it is often referred to as a "best-effort" communications protocol. It offers none of the features of TCP—no error detection or correction, no sequencing, no flow control mechanisms—and does not use a pre-established session. In short, UDP is considered unreliable. However, UDP has low overhead, which permits quick data transmission. The prevailing use of UDP is real-time streaming of audio and video in use cases where the data is considered less essential. Compared to TCP, UDP is lightweight. As a result, the UDP header is fairly simple relative to the TCP header.

Attack vectors unique to the transport layer would include attacks utilizing TCP and UDP. One specific example would be the SYN flood attack that drains a target's network memory resources by continuously initiating TCP-based connections but not allowing them to complete.

TIP   The IP header protocol field value for UDP is 17 (0x11).

Layer 5: Session Layer

The session layer facilitates the logical, persistent connection between peer hosts on a network. The functions include opening, closing, and managing a session efficiently and effectively between end-user application processes. Communication sessions consist of requests and responses that occur between applications. At the session layer, remote procedure calls (RPCs) are the mechanism for application environments to make service requests and service responses between applications on various networked devices. These communications employ several capabilities to be successful:

- **Full-Duplex:** This is when data is sent over a connection between two devices in both directions at the same time. Full-duplex channels can be constructed either as a pair of simplex links or using one channel designed to permit bidirectional simultaneous transmissions. If multiple devices need to be connected using full-duplex mode, many individual links are required because one full-duplex link can only connect two devices.

- **Half-Duplex:** Half-duplex has the capability of sending data in both directions, but only one direction at a time. While this may seem like a step down in capability from full-duplex, it is widely used and successful across single network media such as cable, radio frequency, and Ethernet, as examples. The communications work well when the devices take turns sending and receiving.

- **Simplex Operation:** The communication channel is a one-way street. An example of simplex construction is where a fiber optics run or a network cable as a single strand sends data and another separate channel receives it.

What sorts of attacks target the session layer? This layer and the presentation layer, in particular, aren't popular targets or the "low-hanging fruit" for common attacks. Routing or packet-based attacks are too low on the OSI model. And clearly, application-level attacks are too high, leaving the session and presentation layers at an awkward level of abstraction for identifying vulnerabilities. Still, given the layer's functions, you can hypothesize an attack where authentication to establish a session across the network is compromised.

✔ Border Gateway Protocol (BGP)

To make the Internet work, a core routing protocol standard for an exterior gateway protocol that supports exchange routing and reachability information among routing domains, called *autonomous systems* (AS), on the Internet is required. Border Gateway Protocol (BGP) is that protocol and has been designed and adopted by the IETF. This protocol is relevant to support large, interconnected networks, whether between localized service providers or across multiple Internet service providers (ISPs). It is the most prevalent and scalable of all routing protocols, as it is the routing protocol of the global Internet and private networks of service providers too.

There is a vulnerability inherent in the task of determining the optimal path. The vulnerability is that a network in one region can negatively influence the path that traffic takes far outside that region. Countries with an authoritarian view on controlling network traffic within their borders take advantage of that vulnerability. An example of this happened with China and Russia in 2018, when both countries abused how BGP operates to redirect traffic away from and through their borders. Western countries experienced availability outages for several minutes, while the core Internet routers fought conflicting messages and converged path updates.

BGP operates by choosing the shortest path through the Internet by navigating the least number of ASs along the route. The paths are stored in a Routing Information Base (RIB). Only one route per destination is stored in the routing table, but the RIB is aware of multiple paths to a destination. Each router determines which routes to store from the RIB, and the RIB keeps track of possible routes. When routes are deleted, the RIB silently removes them without notification to peers. RIB entries never time out. BGP functions on top of TCP. Therefore, in the context of OSI model layers, BGP is technically a session layer protocol despite the desire to place it among other networking or transport protocols.

BGP was initially designed to carry Internet reachability information only, but it has expanded in capability to carry routes for Multicast, IPv6, VPNs, and a variety of other data. It is important to note that small corporate networks do not employ BGP.

Layer 6: Presentation Layer

Sometimes referred to as the *syntax layer*, the purpose of the presentation layer is to assure data flow from one application to another application for further processing or display, making sure the data is readable. This is the first layer in the OSI model at which data structure and presentation are evident. At lower levels, data is sent as datagrams and packets. Some examples of the processing done at the presentation layer in the forms of coding and conversion schemes include the common data representation formats or the use of standard image, sound, and video formats, conversion of character representation formats, common data compression schemes, and common data encryption schemes. These functions enable the interchange of application data between different types of computer systems. In short, the presentation layer ensures that formats are converted and presented as needed.

Like the session layer, the presentation layer isn't commonly a target for attackers. This layer is relatively too abstract between the higher and lower layers of the OSI model, not being a target for either routing or packet-based attacks or application-level attacks.

TIP   Compression, encryption, and decryption are all usually handled at the presentation level. Encryption and decryption can be used at other layers with distinct advantages and disadvantages. However, encryption and decryption involve the Secure Sockets Layer (SSL) protocol and more accurately its replacement, Transport Layer Security (TLS). While encryption through SSL is generally done at the presentation layer, SSL/TLS is more complex. Ultimately, the OSI model as a layered stack of abstraction cannot cleanly confine to one layer where TLS functions. But the model places encryption broadly on the presentation layer.

Layer 7: Application Layer

The end user is closest to this layer and interacts with the OSI model directly through a software application. At this abstraction layer, the hosts in a network communicate across specified shared protocols and interface methods. Application layer functions typically include identifying communication partners, determining resource availability, and synchronizing communication.

The Dynamic Host Configuration Protocol (DHCP) works at the application layer. In a TCP/IP network in the OSI model, DHCP is a network management protocol that dynamically assigns an IP address and other network configuration parameters via a special-purpose server to each device on a network. DHCP also ensures that each IP address is unique. This service enables networked nodes to communicate with other IP networks. The DHCP server removes the need for a network administrator or other person to manually assign and reassign IP addresses to endpoints on demand. As DHCP dynamically manages network address assignment, this protocol is actually an application layer protocol.

The computers access the DHCP server through a broadcast message, and the DHCP server dynamically generates and distributes IP addresses and networking parameters automatically from the ISP in an OFFER or DHCPOFFER data packet.

Attacks on DHCP are plentiful and almost simple, given the protocol's nature to trust the perceived source. DHCP can be exploited using a DHCP starvation attack, where forged requests continually request new IP addresses until the allotted pool of addresses is exhausted. Another attack is the DHCP spoof attack, where an untrusted client continues to spread DHCP messages throughout the network.

Attack vectors specific to the application layer are varied. To begin the list, consider the application layer protocols such as Hypertext Transfer Protocol (HTTP), File Transfer Protocol (FTP), Simple Mail Transfer Protocol (SMTP), and Simple Network Management Protocol (SNMP). Attacks like SQL injection or cross-site scripting operate at the application layer. Every attack on the user interface falls into this category. So do HTTP-based attacks such as an HTTP flood or input validation attacks.

4

TIP   HTTP operates at the application layer (layer 7) and is the foundation of the World Wide Web (WWW).

TCP/IP Reference Model

The TCP/IP protocols suite maps to multiple layers. But don't confuse the protocol suite with a reference model of the same name, the four-layer conceptual model known as the TCP/IP model (sometimes also referred to as the DARPA model, named after the U.S. government agency that initially developed TCP/IP). The four layers of the TCP/IP model are Application, Transport, Internet, and Link. These layers are illustrated in order in Figure 4.3.

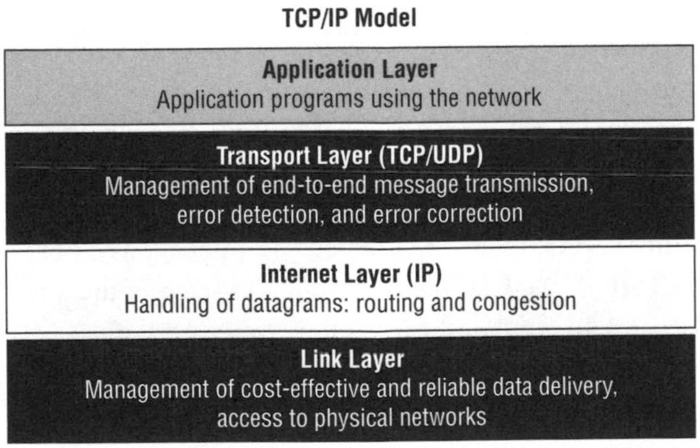

TCP/IP Model

FIGURE 4.3 **TCP/IP reference model**

Each layer in the TCP/IP model corresponds to one or more layers of the seven-layer OSI model. See Figure 4.4. The layers in the TCP/IP protocol suite do not exactly match those in the OSI model, obviously, since one model has more layers than the other model.

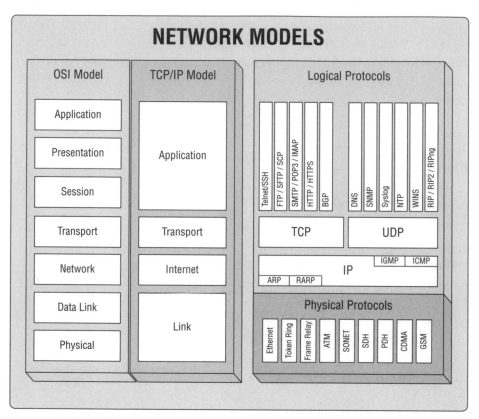

FIGURE 4.4 OSI and TCP/IP block diagram

Link Layer

The link layer is called by several other names, including the network interface layer or the data link layer (and, indeed, the TCP/IP model's link layer includes some of the same functionality as the OSI model's data link layer). Think of it as the physical interface between the host system and the network hardware. The role of this layer is to facilitate TCP/IP data packets across the network transmission channel in a reliable manner. This layer can detect transmission errors. This layer determines how common data link standards like IEEE 802.2 and X.25 format data packets for transmission and routing. The way TCP/IP was designed allows the data format to be independent of the network access method, frame format, and medium that establishes TCP/IP to interconnect across disparate or different networks. It is this independence from any specific network technology that makes TCP/IP scalable to new networking technologies like Asynchronous Transfer Mode (ATM).

NOTE   TCP/IP provides utility and flexibility in LANs traversing the Ethernet, as well as WAN technologies like X.25 and Frame Relay.

There are several important services that the link layer provides:

- **Data Frame:** This is a defined sequence of bits or symbols from a sender that the receiver uses to find the beginning and end of the payload data within the overall stream of other symbols or bits it receives.

- **Checksums:** Data is used within a data frame to manage the integrity of data and allow the receiver to know the data frame was received error-free.

- **Acknowledgment:** This enables reliability in data transmission because a positive acknowledgment is made when data is received. A time-out notice or a negative acknowledgement is received when data is expected but not received.

- **Flow Control:** To maintain traffic and avoid errors due to congestion, the link layer supports buffering data transmissions to regulate fast senders with slow senders.

NOTE   The link layer encompasses the data link and physical layers of the OSI model.

TIP   There are several types of hardware that are associated with the link layer. NICs are typically used with this layer. The NIC is hardware, ranging from a small circuit board to only additional surface layer components added to a motherboard. The NIC provides the physical coupling that interfaces the physical layer media, be it a copper cable, fiber, or a wireless antenna, with the system. Other hardware at this layer would include the various pieces of networking hardware, such as a switch, bridge, or hub. These three differentiate from each other by how they do or do not separate signals between ports. Switches are by far the most common layer hardware in terms of networking.

Internet Layer

Using core protocols like IP, ARP, ICMP, and IGMP, the Internet layer is responsible for addressing, packaging, and routing functions of data packets. Unlike the link layer, the Internet layer does not take advantage of data sequencing and acknowledgment services.

The Internet layer performs several invaluable functions. To transmit packets from host to host, IP selects the next-hop or gateway for outgoing packets across the link layer. It transfers data packets up to the transport layer for incoming packets if the data meets transmission parameters. To that end, the Internet layer helps with error detection and diagnostic capability so data is not transferred in error.

- IP is the principal routable communications protocol responsible for addressing, routing, and the fragmentation and reassembly of data packets.

- ARP resolves addresses like hardware addresses from the Internet layer information to the link layer address.

- ICMP provides diagnostic functions and error reporting when there is an unsuccessful delivery of IP packets.

- IGMP multicast groups or destination computers addressed for simultaneous broadcast are managed by this protocol.

NOTE The TCP/IP Internet layer corresponds to the network layer of the OSI model.

Transport Layer

At the transport layer, services are provided to the application layer for session and datagram communication. You may also hear this layer referred to as the *host-to-host transport layer*. In the TCP/IP model, the transport layer does not make use of the features of the link layer. It assumes an unreliable connection at the link layer. Therefore, at the transport layer, session establishment, packet acknowledgment, and data sequencing are accomplished to enable reliable communications. The core protocols of the transport layer are TCP and UDP.

- TCP communications are segments treated as a sequence of bytes with no record or field boundaries to provide a one-to-one, connection-oriented, reliable communications service. TCP is responsible for ensuring the connection stays reliable and all packets are accounted for. This is done by sequencing and acknowledging each packet sent. This helps with recovery in case packets get lost during transmission.

NOTE Connection-oriented means that hosts can exchange data only after establishing a connection. A connection is established through the acknowledgment service to make sure the destination computer received the data. An acknowledgment (ACK) is sent back for each segment received, and if the ACK is not transmitted in a specified period of time, the sending computer resends the data.

- UDP is a best-effort protocol that provides a one-to-one or one-to-many connectionless, unreliable communications service. There is no assurance of arrival of data or correct sequencing of the packets. If data is not received, there is no attempt at another transmittal because the destination computer does not provide ACK. UDP has usefulness in cases where the data segments are small and TCP overhead is unwanted. In lieu of reliability at the transport layer because of UDP limits, application or upper-layer protocols can accomplish reliable delivery instead.

TIP   UDP is used by services like NetBIOS name service, NetBIOS datagram service, and SNMP.

NOTE   The TCP/IP transport layer encompasses the responsibilities of the OSI transport layer and some of the responsibilities of the OSI session layer.

Application Layer

So that applications can access the services of the other layers of the TCP/IP model, the application layer defines the data exchange protocols used by applications. This is the highest layer in the model, and many application layer protocols exist. New protocols are constantly being developed.

The most widely known application layer protocols are those used for the exchange of user information:

- HTTP is the foundation of file and data transfer on the World Wide Web that comprises and supports websites.

- FTP enables file transfer in the client-server architecture.

- SMTP allows email and associated attachments to be sent and received.

- Telnet is a bidirectional interactive text-oriented communication protocol used to access or log on to networked computers remotely. Telnet has no built-in security, so it should be avoided in use over the public Internet. It is an unsecured terminal emulation protocol.

NOTE   Instead of Telnet, a secure alternative is the Secure Shell (SSH) protocol, which uses encryption to protect data transferred between a client and a server. The categories of data that are encrypted are credentials, commands, output, and file transfers.

Application layer protocols can also be used to manage service on TCP/IP networks:

- DNS resolves a hostname from human-readable language to an IP address. This protocol allows names such as www.isc2.org to be mapped to an IP address.

- RIP is used by routers to exchange routing information on an IP network.

- SNMP is used to manage network devices from a network management console. The network management console collects and exchanges network management information about routers, bridges, and intelligent hubs, for example.

NOTE At the application layer, application programming interfaces APIs like Windows Sockets and NetBIOS provide a standard for TCP/IP applications to access protocol services such as sessions, datagrams, and name resolution. In programming, the API is a description of reusable code to outline expected behavior for how an application calls for and executes a service with another application.

Internet Protocol Networking

IP networking is the main protocol of the Internet. The protocol resides at the OSI model's network layer and the TCP/IP model's Internet layer. For all intents and purposes, IP makes the Internet a reality because the protocol makes it possible to relay datagrams across network boundaries. IP exists in two versions: IPv4, which is currently the main version used, and IPv6, to which Internet-connected devices are expected to evolve. IPv4 uses 32-bit IP addresses, often written as four decimal numbers called *octets*, in the range 0–255, such as 172.16.8.93. Refer to Table 4.1 to see the network classes that subdivide IP addressing.

TABLE 4.1 IPv4 Network Classes

CLASS	RANGE OF FIRST OCTET	NUMBER OF OCTETS FOR NETWORK NUMBER	NUMBER OF HOSTS IN NETWORK
A	1–127	1	16,777,216
B	128–191	2	65,536
C	192–223	3	256
D	224–239	Multicast	
E	240–255	Reserved	

In contrast, IPv6 uses 128 bits portioned into four hexadecimal digits, which are separated by colons for addressing and segmented into two parts: a 64-bit network prefix and a 64-bit interface identifier. An example IPv6 address looks like 2607:f0d0:1002:0051:

0000:0000:0000:0004. The added complexity adds to the number of addresses available for an expanding number of interconnected devices. The scheme intends also to improve network addressing and routing.

Some of the principal benefits of IPv6 over IPv4 include the following:

- **Scoped addresses:** This adds a layer of security and access control for administrators who can group and then deny or allow access to network services, like file servers or printing.

- **Autoconfiguration:** This removes the need for both DHCP and Network Address Translation (NAT).

- **Quality of Service (QoS) priority values:** Based on the content priority, traffic management is conducted according to preset QoS priority values.

The adoption of IPv6 has been slow. Operating systems since about 2000 have had the ability to use IPv6 either natively or via an add-in. IPv6 was developed by the IETF to manage anticipated problem of IPv4 address exhaustion. Adoption hurdles include added cost of some IPv6-capable devices and the fact that IPv4 works well. Decision-makers are reluctant to either make a change for the sake of change itself or make process improvements that provide a minimal financial return on investment. Early adopters of IPv6 are found in private, internal networks in large corporations, research laboratories, and universities.

A basic understanding of the addressing and numbering that define the TCP/IP networking scheme is important. At a basic level, there are three components:

- **MAC address:** This is the permanent address of the hardware device.

- **IP address:** This is the temporary or logical address assigned, corresponding to a unique MAC address.

- **Domain name:** Also called computer name, this is an assigned temporary, human-language convention that corresponds to the IP address.

NOTE Permanent and temporary addresses in the context of MAC and IP addresses can be a bit misleading. MAC addresses are meant to be permanent, but they can be changed via some NICs and modern operating systems. A NIC change is truly a change on the hardware, but the operating system makes the change in memory. However, the operating system change is still effective, and the altered or assigned MAC address overrules the MAC issued by the NIC manufacturer. Additionally, with an increasing reliance on virtualization, the MAC address becomes much less permanent. With every new virtual machine (VM) created, the MAC address often is a new one as well. This can be of special concern when software packages enforce licensing according to the MAC address (which presumed to be a physical asset that wouldn't change no matter how often the client reinstalled the server). IP addresses are changed often by manual intervention or via DHCP services. The IP address can be assigned to be static, but an administrator can change it relatively quickly.

TCP/IP

At this point in the chapter, the term TCP/IP must seem to be a generic concept to define everything—protocols, networking models, and even a synonym for the Internet itself. The concepts behind TCP/IP are central to understanding telecommunications and networking, but there are specific principles and processes that information security professionals must understand in depth. To start, TCP/IP is a set of rules (protocols) that provide a framework or governance for communications that enables interconnection of separate nodes across different network boundaries on the Internet. TCP/IP sets up the way processors package data into data packets, senders transfer the packets, and receivers accept the packets, as well as routing information to the destination.

The acronym TCP/IP often is used to refer to the entire protocol suite, which contains other protocols besides TCP and IP. The transport layer of both the OSI and TCP/IP models is home to UDP in addition to TCP. Similarly, the OSI model's network layer and the TCP/IP model's Internet layer each house the IP, ARP, IGMP, and ICMP protocols. Expanding further is when someone mentions the TCP/IP stack, which likely is referring to protocols and layers above and below the earlier two.

If strictly talking about IP and TCP as individual protocols and not the entire TCP/IP protocol suite, then TCP/IP consists of TCP layered on top of IP to determine the logistics of data in motion and establish virtual circuits. TCP and IP are a longstanding pair of protocols, developed in 1978 by Bob Kahn and Vint Cerf. A description of TCP/IP methodology is that a data stream is split into IP packets that are then reassembled into the data stream at the destination. If the destination does not acknowledge receipt of a packet, TCP/IP supports retransmitting lost packets, a feature performed by TCP. In short, TCP/IP includes the destination and route with the packet while also ensuring the reliability by checking for errors and supporting requests for retransmission.

DNS and domain address resolution are important components that facilitate the ability to scale networking efficiently and effectively. Certainly, the principal reason to enforce addressing is to ensure that networked computers can locate specific machines and tell one computer from another. Another benefit, particularly of domain address resolution, is to enable a naming scheme readable in human language instead of the more machine-like schemes of IP addresses. Humans are more apt to remember www.microsoft.com than 32.100.122.175. The resolution of numerical addresses to human-readable format was more a convenience than a necessity to scale computer adoption and use.

In the TCP header there is some important information contained in areas called *flag fields*. These fields are important because they can contain one or more control bits in the form of an 8-bit flag field. The bits determine the function of that TCP packet and request a specific manner of response from the recipient. Multiple flags can be used in some conditions. In the TCP three-way handshake, for example, both the SYN and ACK flags are set. The bit positions correspond to a control setting per single flag. Each position can be set on with a value of 1 or off with a value of 0. Each of the eight flags is a byte presented in either hex or binary format. A hex presentation of 00010010 is 0x12.

Of that 8-bit flag field, let's specify the last six flags: URG, ACK, PSH, RST, SYN, and FIN. A mnemonic phrase can be helpful, like "Unskilled Attackers Pester Real Security Folks," with the first letter being associated with each of the six TCP flags. In the case mentioned earlier, represented by hex as 0x12, which depicts the initial response of a three-way handshake, the flags set are 000A00S0. In this layout, the fourth and seventh flags are enabled (value is 1). The flag layout can be depicted as one letter per flag, or UAPRSF, as shown in Figure 4.5.

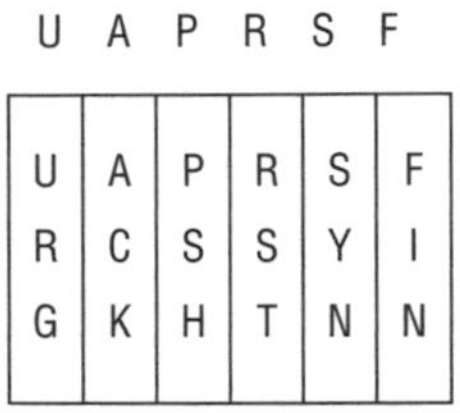

U	A	P	R	S	F
U	A	P	R	S	F
R	C	S	S	Y	I
G	K	H	T	N	N

URG =	Urgent	*Unskilled*
ACK =	Acknowledgment	*Attackers*
PSH =	Push	*Pester*
RST =	Reset	*Real*
SYN =	Syn	*Security*
FIN =	Finished	*Folks*

FIGURE 4.5 TCP flag fields

Network Attacks

Networking protocols were designed long before the necessity of security was fully recognized. Consequently, even today networked hosts remain vulnerable and networked systems fail to implement mitigating controls. Systems that are hardened against attacks that exploit misconfiguration and unnecessary services can still be vulnerable from attacks exploiting network services. Several updates and revisions to networking protocols have been adopted, but weaknesses remain due to security being designed as an afterthought, although progress continues to be made. A recent example is the Google Chrome browser finally adopting support for DNS over TLS (a secured version of the DNS protocol).

The "Open System Interconnection and Transmission Control Protocol/Internet Protocol Models" section earlier in this chapter explored the OSI model and how its layers continue in the abstract from physical to application. It examined where established protocols fall within those layers. The section also touched on what attack vectors exist at each OSI layer to expose some of the vulnerability therein.

By knowing how networked hosts communicate with each other, security professionals can better understand how network attacks can occur and be successful. Armed with that information, the following sections delve into a variety of network attacks.

Distributed Denial-of-Service (DDoS) Attacks

When an attacker does not have the skills or tools for a sophisticated attack, they may use a brute-force attack, which can be just as effective. Simply flooding the targeted system with UDP packets from infected machines has proven successful, especially as the Internet of Things (IoT) devices have been used, unwittingly, to help launch the distributed denial-of-service (DDoS) attacks. A typical DDoS attack consists of a large number of individual machines that are subverted to bombard a target with overwhelming traffic over a short period of time. The individual contribution of any one compromised machine, be it a PC, IoT device, networking hardware, or server, would amount to no damage. But the collective sum creates a crushing amount of traffic to the end target.

TIP To subvert the volumes of machines needed for a DDoS, a botnet is created and used. The botnet is a number of Internet-connected and commandeered computers that communicate in a command and control manner.

Although the term *botnet* has grown in popular media because of the use of the tactic in enlisting IoT devices such as baby monitors, TVs, webcams, and other network-aware wireless devices, botnets were weaponized almost 20 years ago. Medical devices were hacked when the FDA published guidance that any Unix-based machines were to have a standard, known configuration. These certified, special-purpose computing devices became targets because they inherited the weaknesses of the standard configurations. Once hackers discovered vulnerabilities to exploit, the weaknesses were applicable across an entire platform, and a medical device botnet was created. The number and varieties of devices used to create botnets has expanded. In 2016, large numbers of digital recording video (DVR) devices and other Internet-enabled systems were used to create the Mirai botnet. This botnet was used in a series of DDoS attacks against Dyn.com, one of the largest providers of DNS services. This attack disrupted major computing platforms operated by PayPal, Twitter, Reddit, GitHub, Amazon, Netflix, Spotify, and RuneScape. In sum, botnets are enslaving vast numbers of IoT devices and creating highly successful DDoS attacks.

SYN Flooding

In an attempt to overload a system, this type of attack bombards the recipient with an overwhelming number of SYN packets, and the sender or senders do not acknowledge

---

any of the replies. SYN flooding is a form of denial-of-service (DoS) attack, exploiting properties of TCP at the transport layer (layer 4). TCP initiates a connection by sending a SYN packet, which when received and accepted is replied to with a SYN-ACK packet. The SYN flooding DoS attack is executed by sending massive amounts of those SYN packets. The SYN packets accumulate at the recipient system, and the software crashes because it cannot handle the overflow. The attacker attempts to consume enough server resources to make the system unresponsive to legitimate traffic. Some refer to this attack as the half-open attack because of the partial three-way TCP/IP handshake that underlies the attack. Eventually, given enough connection attempts, the capacity of the network card and stack to maintain open connections is exhausted. The attack was imagined decades before it was actually performed. Until the source code and descriptions of the SYN flooding attacks were published in 1996 in the magazines *2600* and *Phrack*, attackers had not executed the attack successfully. That changed when the publicly available information was used in an attack against Panix, a New York ISP, for several days.

Even though these types of attacks have such a long history and the mitigations have been in existence for almost as long, SYN flooding is still a common attack. There are some ways to mitigate a SYN flood vulnerability. A few of the most prevalent approaches are the following:

- **Increasing backlog queue:** This is an allowance or increase of half-open connections a system will sustain. It requires additional memory resources to increase the maximum backlog. Depending on the availability of memory resources, mitigating the SYN flooding threat can degrade system performance. A risk-benefit analysis is required against unwanted denial of service impact and slower performance.

- **Recycling the oldest half-open TCP connection:** This is a first-in, first-out queueing strategy where once the backlog queue limit is reached, the oldest half-open request is overwritten. The benefit is fully establishing legitimate connections faster than the backlog can be filled with malicious SYN packets. However, if the backlog queue is too small or the attack too voluminous, this mitigation can be insufficient.

- **SYN cookies:** The server responds to each connection request, SYN, with a SYN-ACK packet. The SYN request is dropped from the backlog. The port is open to new, hopefully legitimate, new connections. If the initial connection is legitimate, the original sender will send its ACK packet. The initial recipient, which created the SYN cookie, will reconstruct the SYN backlog queue entry. Of course, there will be some limitations as some information about the TCP connection can be lost. This is more advantageous than the full DoS outage.

Smurfing

Smurfing is a historical type of attack dating back to the 1990s that is categorized as a DDoS attack. The name comes from a popular cartoon of the time and represents the concept of an overwhelming number of very small attackers that successfully overtake a larger opponent.

The Internet Control Message Protocol (ICMP) uses ping packets to troubleshoot network connections by determining the reachability of a target host and a single system as the legitimate source. Smurfing exploits the functionality of the ICMP and broadcast subnets configured to magnify ICMP pings that will respond. These misconfigured networks are called *smurf amplifiers*. Using the IP broadcast, attackers send packets spoofing an intended victim source IP. The echo ICMP packet is used because ping checks to see if systems are alive on the network. The result of the broadcast message, especially if exploiting the presence of smurf amplification, is that all the computers on the network will respond to the targeted system. See Figure 4.6 for an illustration of the effect on the targeted system. In a large, distributed network, the volume of responses can overwhelm the target system.

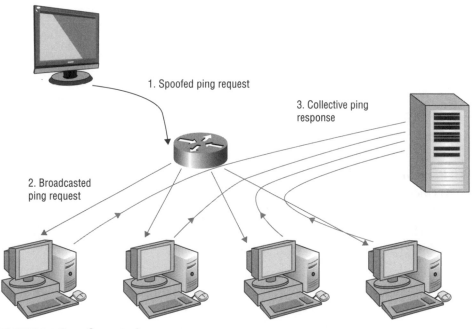

FIGURE 4.6 **Smurfing attack**

Today, techniques exist to mitigate the effects of DDoS attacks. However, the attack method still works well in multiple, effective forms. The famed Mirai attack that crippled several enterprise networks was a form of a DDoS attack, modeled after a smurf attack.

Dozens of companies were affected, including Dyn DNS, GitHub, CNN, Reddit, Visa, HBO, and the BBC.

NOTE Internet Relay Chat (IRC) servers were highly susceptible to these attacks. Script kiddies or younger hackers in general preferred smurf attacks through IRC servers to take down chat rooms.

Today, the smurf attack is uncommon. Preventing an attack involves routine actions that administrators commonly use. External ping requests or broadcasts are typically ignored. The host or router is configured to be nonresponsive, and the requests are not forwarded. The remediation of smurf attacks also had a social component as benevolent actors posted lists of smurf amplifiers. Administrators of systems would notice their IP addresses on the smurf amplifier list and take action to configure the systems correctly. Those administrators that did not would get feedback from business or community users in the network about performance degradation. That pressure persuaded them to take the appropriate actions.

Some of the other commands that are central to creating these types of attacks, like ping and echo, are now commonly blocked. These include sourceroute and traceroute. However, these commands can also be helpful for troubleshooting. There are several specific attacks that are common enough to outline:

- **Ping of death:** Sending a ping packet that violates the Maximum Transmission Unit (MTU) size of 65,536 bytes, causing a crash

- **Ping flooding:** Overwhelming a system with a multitude of pings

- **Teardrop:** A network layer (Layer 3) attack, sending malformed packets to confuse the operating system, which cannot reassemble the packet

- **Buffer overflow:** An attack that overwhelms a specific type of memory on a system—the buffers. Robust input validation in applications prevents this attack.

- **Fraggle:** A type of smurf attack that uses UDP echo packets instead of ICMP packets

DDoS and the Internet of Things (IoT)

As an emerging technology, IoT devices deserve a little more attention in this chapter. From a security perspective, these devices offer a soft target for potential attackers. They are delivered with default settings that are easily guessed or, in fact, publicly well known. Administrative credentials and management access are wide open to Internet-facing interfaces. Attackers can exploit the devices with relatively simple remote access code. What compounds the vulnerabilities is that users do not interact with the devices the same way as they do with office automation or other endpoint computing assets. The default settings are rarely changed, even if the end user has the ability to make changes. Vendors are typically slow to provide upgrades and patches, if they supply post-sale manufacturing support at all. For these reasons, the devices are easy prey, and users often have no idea the devices are being hacked until it is too late.

The volume of IoT devices generates a lot of concern from security professionals. It is estimated that there are already tens of millions of vulnerable IoT devices. That number is growing. The interconnections are usually always on, left unprotected to ingress and egress unlike a typical LAN or WAN, but they enjoy high-speed connections. These variables explain why a botnet of huge groups of commandeered IoT devices presents a serious problem. Common attack sequences consist of compromising the device to send spam or broadcast messages. If spam filters block that attack, a tailored malware insert may be tried, like fast flux, which is a DNS technique to hide spamming attacks. If that does not accomplish the disruption, a brute-force type of DDoS might be launched. Increasingly, well-resourced websites have sufficient bandwidth and can expand capacity above baseline or normal usage levels to withstand most attacks. However, just the threat of launching an attack can be enough to convince website owners to pay a ransom to extortionists to avoid testing the limits of the targeted site's ability to remain responsive.

DDoS and Spam

A working definition of spam is the electronic equivalent of junk mail in the physical world. In most cases, spam is a nuisance but not an attempted cybersecurity attack. However, spam can exist in the context of a DDoS attack. When an attacker sends a command to launch a spam campaign, the end result is an overwhelming volume of traffic. The spam traffic likely originates from a set of malicious botnets, with the outcome being spam. The receiving systems process the messages as legitimate, which is a mistake. The spam bots have spoofed the email addresses, which is a tactic unlike packet-level DDoS.

Normally, an individual spam message is just an unsolicited email message with unwanted advertising, perhaps even seeking to deliver a malicious payload. However, as part of a DDoS attack, spam can be used as an acceptable type of traffic to deliver an onslaught of data. The volume of data to be received could shut down a system or mail gateway.

Man-in-the-Middle Attacks

In a communication where sender and receiver believe they are connected, a MitM attack can be hard to detect and presents a significant threat to unprotected communications. The attacker intercepts the signal and secretly relays and possibly alters the communication before stopping the transmission or allowing the message to reach the intended recipient. Eavesdropping is a specific type of MitM attack. In that scenario, the attacker relays the message to complete the circuit. The entire conversation is overheard, and in some instances controlled, by the attacker, while the sender and receiver think the message is private. Figure 4.7 depicts the general concepts of a MitM attack.

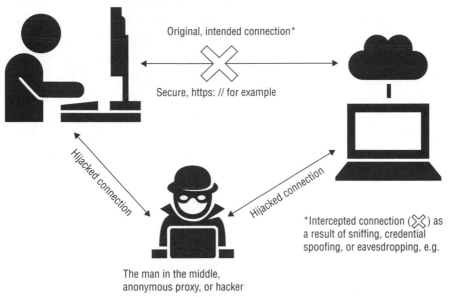

Man-in-the-Middle Attack (MiTM)

Original, intended connection*

Secure, https: // for example

Hijacked connection

Hijacked connection

*Intercepted connection (✗) as a result of sniffing, credential spoofing, or eavesdropping, e.g.

The man in the middle, anonymous proxy, or hacker

FIGURE 4.7 Man-in-the-middle attack

Another type of MitM attack is impersonation. This happens when the attacker circumvents the authentication process and compromises the credentials of one account. The endpoint communicating with the attacker is not aware that the communication is intercepted.

There are two main ways to prevent or detect MitM attacks: authentication and tamper detection. Authentication provides some degree of certainty that a given message has come from a legitimate source. Tamper detection merely shows evidence that a message may have been altered.

- **Authentication:** To prevent MitM attacks, cryptographic protocols are used to authenticate the endpoints or transmission media. One such technique is to employ a TLS server paired with X.509 certificates. The X.509 certificates are used by the mutually trusted certificate authority (CA) to authenticate one or more entities. The message and an exchange of public keys are employed to make the channel secure.

- **Tamper detection:** Another way to detect MitM attacks is through examination of any latency in the transaction above baseline expectations. Response times are checked and normal factors like long calculations of hash functions are accounted for. If a delay is not explained, there may be unwanted, malicious third-party interference in the communication.

Packet Sniffing

Administrators often use packet sniffing tools for legitimate purposes, like troubleshooting. But attackers conduct passive MitM packet sniffing to gain information for adversarial purposes. Any unencrypted protocols are subject to passive attacks where an attacker has been able to place a packet sniffing tool to monitor traffic. The monitoring might be used to determine traffic types and patterns or to map network information. In any case, packet sniffing greatly benefits the attacker in preparing for other types of attacks. Say for example that an attacker using packet sniffing discovers that a company still uses an outdated version of SSL or discovers the IP address of the Active Directory controller. The attacker is now set up to exploit that outdated protocol or server. Packet sniffing can also include actually grabbing packets in transit and attempting to extract useful information from the contents. Contained in some packets are usernames, passwords, IP addresses, credit card numbers, and other valuable payload.

Hijacking Attacks

Hijacking attacks describe many different types of MitM attack. A hijacking attack is any attack that involves the exploitation of a session, which is an established dialogue between devices. Normally a session is managed by a control mechanism such as a cookie or token. An attacker might try to intercept or eavesdrop the session token or cookie. In the case where an attacker has sniffed the cookie or token, the attacker may connect with the server using the legitimate token in parallel with the victim. Or the attacker may intercept the session token to use as well as to send a specially formed packet to the victim to terminate their initial session.

Many websites require authentication and use cookies to remember session tracking information. When the session is terminated as the user logs out, the cookie and credentials are typically cleared. Hijacking a session and stealing the token or cookie while the session is active can provide an attacker with valuable, sensitive information, such as unique details on what site was visited. Even worse, hijacking the session cookie may allow the attacker an opportunity to continue a session, posing as the victim.

TIP Promiscuous mode is a setting that packet sniffers enable to stop a device from discarding or filtering data unintended for it. The packet sniffer can gain access to the additional traffic and data packets that otherwise would have been filtered.

Implications of Multilayer Protocols

TCP/IP is an example of a multilayer protocol, in which dozens of individual protocols are located across the various protocol stack layers. Encapsulation is an important capability and benefit of multilayer protocol schema. In the context of networking

---

communication between two hosts, *encapsulation* means to envelope one protocol's contents as the payload for the subsequent protocol. To illustrate the process of encapsulation, consider a web server to web browser data transfer, which is HTTP-encapsulated in TCP. TCP is encapsulated in IP, and that packet is encapsulated in Ethernet. TCP/IP can also add additional layers of encapsulation. SSL/TLS encryption can be added to the communication to provide additional confidentiality. In turn, a network layer encryption can be achieved using IPSec.

There are instances of TCP/IP encapsulation used for adversarial purposes. Some attack tools can hide or isolate an unauthorized protocol within an authorized one. Using a tool like HTTP tunnel, FTP can be hidden within an HTTP packet to get around egress restrictions.

Attackers can also use multilayer protocol encapsulation to provide an ability to fool interior switching devices to gain access to a VLAN. VLANs are used to isolate network traffic to its own separate broadcast domain. The switch knows what VLAN to place that traffic on according to a tag identifying the VLAN ID. Those tags, per IEEE 802.1Q, encapsulate each packet. Where a VLAN is established through logical addressing, VLAN hopping is an attack using a double-encapsulated IEEE 802.1Q VLAN tag. To be clear, that's one VLAN tag encapsulating a packet already encapsulated with a different VLAN ID. The first VLAN tag is removed by the first switch it encounters. The next switch will inadvertently move traffic according to the second layer VLAN encapsulated tag.

An implication of multilayered protocols is the enablement of particular communication protocols across more ubiquitous transport protocols, chiefly TCP/IP. Probably the most salient examples of that are the industrial control in energy and utility industries using supervisory control and data acquisition (SCADA) systems. SCADA is a control system architecture that uses computers to gather data on processes and send control commands to connected devices that comprise the system. The connected devices, networked data communications, and graphical user interfaces perform high-level process supervisory management. Other peripheral devices, such as programmable logic controllers and discrete proportional integral derivative (PID) controllers, are utilized to regulate plant or machinery. The PID controller, as a basic feedback device, is common in industrial control environments, but its security is solely reliant on external devices or controls. Field sensors and actuators inform automatic processing through the SCADA system. However, manual operator interfaces are part of operations to enable monitoring and the issuing of process commands.

SCADA systems utilize a legacy protocol called Distributed Network Protocol (DNP3). DNP3 is found primarily in the electric and water utility and management industries. Data is transported across various components in industrial control systems like substation computers, remote terminal units (RTUs), and SCADA master stations (control centers). DNP3 is an open and public standard. There are many similarities between DNP3 and the TCP/IP suite, as they are both multilayer protocols that have link and transport functionality in their respective layers.

Ultimately, to provide some connectivity to these SCADA systems over public networks, there is the solution of encapsulating DNP3 over TCP/IP. This encapsulation, while obviously bridging a connection between disparate standards, does introduce great risk. Perhaps the most common exploitation of this risk is through MitM attacks.

Proprietary technologies established the SCADA systems, but recently they have moved to more open and standardized solutions. With the evolution come security concerns. Initially, the systems were designed for decentralized facilities like power, oil, gas pipelines, water distribution, and wastewater collection systems. Connections were not a primary concern as the systems were designed to be open, robust, and easily operated and repaired. Any security was a secondary concern. Increasingly, there have been more connections between SCADA systems, office networks, and the Internet. The interconnectedness has ushered the systems into vulnerabilities like all other IP-based LANs and WANs. Although sensitive personal information is not necessarily the focus of information protection in SCADA systems, the primary concerns with SCADA cybersecurity are system disruption, sensitive configuration information, and national security.

NOTE Another protocol worth noting in industrial control systems is Modbus. It is a de facto standard of application layer protocol. It is used in several variations from plain Modbus to Modbus+ and Modbus/TCP. The protocol enables a Modbus client (or master) to send a request to a Modbus server (or slave) with a function code that specifies the action to be taken and a data field that provides the additional information.

Converged Protocols

Converged protocols differ from encapsulated, multilayer protocols. Converged protocols are what happens when you merge specialty or proprietary protocols with standard protocols, such as TCP/IP suite protocols. With converged protocols, an organization can reduce reliance on distinct, costly proprietary hardware, as well as create variations of performance, depending on which converged protocol is being used.

Some common examples of converged protocols are described here:

- **Fibre Channel over Ethernet (FCoE):** Fibre Channel solutions usually need separate fiber-optic cabling infrastructure to deliver network data-storage options, such as a storage area network (SAN) or network-attached storage (NAS). Fibre Channel is useful because it allows for high-speed file transfers achieving 128 Gbps and today reaching 256 Gbps. Fibre Channel over

Ethernet (FCoE) was developed to facilitate Fibre Channel to work more efficiently, while using less expensive copper cables over Ethernet connections. Using 10 Gbps Ethernet, FCoE uses Ethernet frames to support the Fibre Channel communications.

- **Internet Small Computer System Interface (iSCSI):** iSCSI is often viewed as a low-cost alternative to Fibre Channel. It is also a networking storage standard, but based on IP. It facilitates connection of a remote storage volume over a network as if the device were attached locally. The iSCSI transmits SCSI commands over IP networks and performs like a virtual SATA (or SCSI) cable.

- **Multiprotocol Label Switching (MPLS):** MPLS is a high-throughput, high-performance network technology that directs data across a network based on short path labels rather than longer network addresses. Compared with IP routing processes, which are complex and take a longer time to navigate, MPLS saves significant time. Using encapsulation, MPLS is designed to handle a wide range of protocols. An MPLS network can handle T1/E1, ATM, Frame Relay, synchronous optical networking (SONET), and DSL network technologies, not just TCP/IP and compatible protocols. MPLS is often used to create a virtual dedicated circuit between two stations.

Software-Defined Networks

Software-defined networking is an emerging network administration approach to designing, building, and centrally managing a network. Settings to hardware can be changed through a central management interface. Some of the primary features are flexibility, vendor neutrality, and the use of open standards. In a traditional network construct, routing and switching are primarily in the realm of hardware resources. In many cases, this reality creates a vendor reliance that limits the dynamic ability of an organization to anticipate or even react to change.

Software-defined networking separates hardware and hardware settings at the infrastructure layer from network services and data transmission at the network layer. The configuration is virtualized and managed in a control plane similar to managing virtual hosts through a hypervisor console. Furthermore, this also removes the traditional networking concepts of IP addressing, subnets, routing, and so on, from needing to be programmed into or be deciphered by hosted applications.

Software-defined networking is discussed in more detail later in this chapter in the "Software-Defined Networking" section.

TIP   Network virtualization, with data transmission paths, communication decision trees, and traffic flow control, is a good way to describe software-defined networking.

Wireless Networks

By eliminating the dependency on cabling to the endpoint, wireless technologies have expanded networking capabilities significantly. Deploying a wireless network is relatively easy and has become the preference in many corporate environments. Home networking is made simple by wireless technology. With the IoT devices reaching the market, the demand for wireless capabilities is increasing. The main limitation to wireless networks, or WiFi, is the range of the signal. As this is a security discussion, it is important to balance all the new capabilities with an understanding of the risks that wireless connections present. From there, you can strategize several security approaches to mitigate vulnerabilities. In general terms, the security of wireless transmissions relies on a combination of physical and technical controls, like the implementation of shielded device-use areas and encryption.

Wireless networks face the same vulnerabilities, threats, and risks as any cabled network, but they also have additional security considerations. One of the principal issues with wireless technology is the insecure nature of the technology in the default configuration. For instance, wireless devices are sometimes shipped with a default administrator credential of *admin* for the username and *password* for the password. This is acceptable if the recipient changes the credentials or establishes a multifactor authentication process before the device goes into the production environment. In home settings, end users may not even be aware of this issue. Wireless networks also face an increased risk of MitM types of eavesdropping and packet sniffing using devices that read captured data emanation across electromagnetic signals. Recently, with the proliferation of IoT devices, wireless DDoS attacks have become headline-making attacks of disruption. The configuration weaknesses of wireless connected devices permit attackers to insert malicious bots in things like DVRs, web cameras, intelligent personal assistant devices, and smartphones to create a botnet to send out almost limitless signals to bring down critical services and highly visible web targets.

To be properly prepared to deal with wireless networks, the security practitioner needs to understand the standards and protocols that govern wireless technology. They also need to understand the variety of technologies, techniques, and obstacles involved with securing wireless access points (WAPs) and wireless technology in general. This knowledge is essential in preparing them for adequately understanding how to address wireless attacks. The following sections will examine these topics in more detail.

NOTE   When electrons move, they create emanations and a magnetic field. These data emanations can be picked up by devices that scan for them. Attackers use such devices to capture and re-create these emanations elsewhere to reproduce the electron stream on, for example, the attacker's screen. The obvious result is that your data is exposed to the attacker.

Wireless Standards and Protocols

Wireless network communications are governed by the IEEE 802.11 standard. Evolutions of the standard are published through amendments that document updated versions of the original standard. These are highlighted in Table 4.2, and it should be noted that each version or amendment to the 802.11 standard has offered improved maximum data rates. 802.11x is often used to indicate all of the specific implementations as a collective whole, but that is not preferred over a general reference to 802.11.

TIP   Do not confuse 802.11x with 802.1x, which is an authentication technology and not related to wireless.

TABLE 4.2 802.11 Standard Amendments

STANDARD	FREQUENCY	BANDWIDTH	MODULATION	MAX DATA RATE
802.11	2.4 GHz	20 MHz	DSSS, FHSS	2 Mbps
802.11a	5 GHz	20 MHz	DSSS	54 Mbps
802.11b	2.4 GHz	20 MHz	OFDM	11 Mbps
802.11g	2.4 GHz	20 MHz	OFDM	54 Mbps
802.11n	2.4 GHz and 5 GHz	20 MHz, 40 MHz	OFDM	600 Mbps
802.11 ac	2.4 GHz and 5 GHz	20, 40, 80, 80+80, 160 MHz	OFDM	6.93 Gbps

DSSS: Direct Sequence Spread Spectrum
FHSS: Frequency Hopping Spread Spectrum
OFDM: Orthogonal Frequency Division Multiplexing

Wired Equivalent Privacy (WEP) and WiFi Protected Access (WPA)

The IEEE 802.11 standard defines two methods that wireless clients can use to authenticate to WAPs before normal network communications can occur across the wireless link. These two methods are open system authentication (OSA) and shared key authentication (SKA).

- OSA provides no confidentiality or security because no real authentication is required. Communication happens if the radio signal is strong enough to reach a compatible receiver. All OSA transmissions are unencrypted.

- SKA enforces some form of authentication, and if the authentication isn't provided, the communication is blocked. The 802.11 standard defines one optional technique for SKA known as Wired Equivalent Privacy (WEP), with subsequent amendments to the original 802.11 standard adding WiFi Protected Access (WPA), WPA2, and other technologies.

Wired Equivalent Privacy (WEP) was designed to protect against eavesdropping for wireless communications. The initial aim of WEP was to provide the same level of protection against MitM attacks that wired networks have. WEP implemented encryption of data in wireless transmissions using a Rivest Cipher 4 (RC4) symmetric stream cipher. Message integrity verification is possible because a hash value is used to verify that received packets weren't modified or corrupted while in transit. It also can be configured to prevent unauthorized access. Incidentally, the knowledge or possession of the encryption key helps as a basic form of authentication. Without the key, access to the network itself is denied. WEP is used at the two lowest layers of the OSI model: the data link and physical layers. It therefore does not offer end-to-end security. Over time, WEP has been shown to have weaknesses. For instance, WEP uses static encryption keys, the same key used by every device on a wireless network. It is possible, therefore, that if an eavesdropper intercepted enough encrypted packets, the key could be deduced. In fact, WEP was cracked almost as soon as it was released. It takes less than a minute to hack through WEP protection.

To improve wireless security, a group known as WiFi Alliance developed a new encryption standard called WiFi Protected Access. As a replacement for WEP, WPA could be retrofitted to WEP firmware on wireless NICs designed for WEP already in the computing environment. That feature proved to be more problematic than it was worth. The changes to the WAPs were extensive, and hardware replacement was a better option.

WPA was intended as an interim solution until the IEEE published the promised 802.11i standard. That process lingered for years, so WPA was implemented independent of the 802.11 amendment. The WPA protocol implements the Lightweight Extensible Authentication Protocol (LEAP) and Temporal Key Integrity Protocol (TKIP), which support a per-packet key that dynamically generates a new 128-bit key for each packet. WPA negotiates a unique key set with each host. It improves upon the WEP 64-bit or 128-bit encryption key that had to be manually entered on WAPs and devices and did not change. WPA uses LEAP and TKIP to perform Message Integrity Check, which is designed to prevent an attacker from altering and resending data packets. This replaces the cyclic redundancy check (CRC) that was used by the WEP standard. CRC's main flaw was that it did not provide a sufficiently strong data integrity guarantee for the packets it handled. Researchers have identified a flaw in WPA similar to the weaknesses in WEP. WPA often employs a static yet secret passphrase for authentication. A brute-force attack theoretically can result in a guessed passphrase. The likelihood of a sufficient passphrase (no fewer than 14 characters) succumbing to this attack is very low, but not impossible. Collaterally, the message integrity check hash function can then be exploited to retrieve the keystream from short strings of packets to use for injection attacks or spoofing. Basically, attacks specific to WPA—coWPAtty and a GPU-based cracking tool, to name two—have rendered WPA's security unreliable. Both the LEAP and TKIP encryption options for WPA are now considered crackable using a variety of available and easy to use cracking techniques.

IEEE 802.11i or WPA2

The next evolution was WPA2, which replaced WPA. Originally, it was meant to replace WEP, but as mentioned before, the 802.11i standard lingered, and WPA was implemented independently. This amendment deals with the security issues of the original 802.11 standard. WPA2 is backward compatible to WPA. It provides U.S. government–grade security by implementing the National Institute of Standards and Technology (NIST) FIPS 140-2 compliant AES encryption algorithm and 802.1x-based authentications, and Counter Mode Cipher Block Chaining Message Authentication Code Protocol (CCMP). There are two versions of WPA2: WPA2-Personal and WPA2-Enterprise. WPA2-Personal protects unauthorized network access by utilizing a setup password. WPA2-Enterprise verifies network users through a server using Network Access Control (NAC).

The selection of the name WPA2 is because WPA was already published and in widespread use. However, WPA2 is not the second version of WPA. They are distinct and different. IEEE 802.11i, or WPA2, implemented concepts similar to IPSec to improve encryption and security within the wireless networks. As of 2018, no actual successful compromises have happened to a properly configured, encrypted WPA2 wireless network. That may be more at risk today, though. On October 16, 2017, security researchers disclosed several high-severity vulnerabilities in the WPA2 protocol. There was a proof-of-concept, called KRACK for Key Reinstallation Attacks, to demonstrate that attackers could eavesdrop on WiFi traffic. Devices running the Android, Linux, Apple, Windows, and OpenBSD operating systems, as well as MediaTek Linksys, and other types of devices, are all vulnerable. The good news is that patches have been made available, and no real-world attack was reported.

NOTE   WPA3 is on the way. Announced by WiFi Alliance in January 2018, WPA3 was launched in June 2018. The new standard uses 192-bit encryption and individualized encryption for each user. WPA3 also promises weak password mitigation and simplified setup processes for devices with no human interface.

IEEE 802.1X

Both WPA and WPA2 support the enterprise authentication known as 802.1X/EAP, a standard NAC that is port-based to ensure client access control to network resources. Effectively, 802.1X is a checking system that allows the wireless network to leverage the existing network infrastructure's authentication services. Through the use of 802.1X, other techniques and solutions such as RADIUS, TACACS, certificates, smart cards, token devices, and biometrics can be integrated into wireless networks providing techniques for multifactor authentication.

EAP (Extensible Authentication Protocol)

Extensible Authentication Protocol (EAP) is an authentication framework versus a specific mechanism of authentication. EAP facilitates compatibility with new authentication technologies for existing wireless or point-to-point connection technologies. More than 40 different EAP methods of authentication are widely supported. These include the wireless methods of LEAP, EAP-TLS, EAP-SIM, EAP-AKA, and EAP-TTLS. Two significant EAP methods that bear a closer look are PEAP and LEAP.

TIP   EAP is not an assurance of security. For example, EAP-MD5 and a prerelease EAP known as LEAP are known to be vulnerable.

PEAP (Protected Extensible Authentication Protocol)

Using a TLS tunnel, Protected Extensible Authentication Protocol (PEAP) encapsulates EAP methods to provide authentication and, potentially, encryption. Since EAP was originally designed for use over physically isolated channels and hence assumed secured pathways, EAP is usually not encrypted. So, PEAP can provide encryption for EAP methods.

LEAP (Lightweight Extensible Authentication Protocol)

Lightweight Extensible Authentication Protocol (LEAP) is a Cisco proprietary alternative to TKIP for WPA, but it should not be used. An attack tool known as Asleap was released in 2004 that could exploit the ultimately weak protection provided by LEAP. Use of EAP-TLS is preferred. If LEAP is used, a complex password is an imperative. LEAP served the purpose of addressing deficiencies in TKIP before the advent of 802.11i/ WPA2.

✔ Bluetooth

Although Bluetooth does not actually provide a wireless Ethernet network standard, the technology does support wireless transmissions point to point over a short distance. In general use, the maximum effective distance is about 30 feet. However, there are industrial or advanced versions of Bluetooth that can reach 300 feet. Many types of endpoint devices support Bluetooth, such as mobile phones, laptops, printers, radios, and digital personal assistants, along with an increasing number of other IoT devices.

The benefits of Bluetooth are that it does not require base stations, as it is a direct connection between devices. It also requires very little power, which is good for use with the battery-operated end devices that typically feature Bluetooth.

There are also a few downsides. The transmission speed is slower than the 802.11b wireless standard. It conflicts and interferes with existing 802.11b and 802.11g networks as it uses the 2.4 GHz broadcasting spectrum, causing problems for endpoint devices relying on the transmissions. Another significant downside is Bluetooth's inherent weakness because of its lack of encryption. Using Bluetooth to create a personal area network (PAN) carries security implications, too, since a PAN most likely has vulnerabilities that are not easily identified by corporate sweeps. The reason is that a PAN is a nonroutable section or extension of an existing LAN or WAN, so it is not easily assessed.

TKIP (Temporal Key Integrity Protocol)

TKIP was designed as the replacement for WEP without requiring replacement of legacy wireless hardware. TKIP was implemented into the 802.11 wireless networking standards within the guidelines of WPA. TKIP improvements include a key-mixing function that combines the initialization vector (IV) (i.e., a random number) with the secret root key before using that key with RC4 to perform encryption; a sequence counter is used to prevent packet replay attacks; and a strong message integrity check (MIC) is used.

CCMP (Counter Mode with Cipher Block Chaining Message Authentication Code Protocol)

CCMP was created to replace WEP and TKIP/WPA. CCMP uses Advanced Encryption Standard (AES) with a 128-bit key. CCMP is the preferred standard security protocol of 802.11 wireless networking indicated by 802.11i. To date, no attacks have yet been successful against the AES/CCMP encryption. CCMP is the standard encryption mechanism used in WPA2.

NOTE   The impact that security requirements can have on business and technology is not trivial. For instance, data encryption and filtering, like WPA2 and IPSec VPN, has to be tested and refined to optimal configurations to minimize any performance degradation.

Securing Wireless Access Points

WAPs are the devices within a physical environment that receive signals. Based on access control and required frequency values, these access points permit devices to connect. Even with access controls and frequency settings, a security issue can result from a WAP that has a broadcast beacon that is set too powerfully and sends its beacon far beyond the necessary range. Whether broadcasting the beacon far away is seen as an advantage, say to roaming users, is a decision left to the company. This allows an unwanted wireless device to connect even if the end user is prohibited from accessing the physical area where the WAP is installed. In short, securing the WAP requires attention to proper placement of the device, shielding it, and limiting noise transmission while satisfying customer need to connect.

This section on how to secure WAPs assumes only that the need for wireless access is there, but no action has been taken to create it. Creating wireless access does not start with placing hardware arbitrarily. The first action to take is to conduct a site survey. A site survey is useful for assessing what, if any, wireless access exists currently. It also helps in planning for the future. Once the survey is complete, decisions on where to place wireless access hardware can be made. This section also covers deciding on the correct type of antennas to broadcast from the chosen hardware.

Configuring your access points comes next. Configuration options follow the hardware sections. We first examine how the broadcast channels matter. Then there is discussion on what modes the hardware may be set to, such as whether to centralize the communication or form a type of transmission mesh. Additional consideration is given to how the network is broadcast and labeled, using service set identifiers (SSIDs). Finally, additional methods of securing access are covered, from the low-level filtering of MAC addresses to the higher-level use of captive portals.

Conducting a Site Survey

Site surveys are useful techniques for both identifying rogue access points and defining the placement, configuration, and documentation of access points.

Rogue WAPs are WAPs that are installed on an otherwise secure network without explicit authorization. Sometimes, a rogue access point is implemented by an employee for a perceived access or performance need. More concerning are cases where a malicious attacker installs a rogue access point to try to fool end users to try to connect. Such attacks harvest credentials or help launch DDoS attacks. It is important for security personnel to conduct searches and scans to be on the lookout for these unwanted devices.

A physical walk-through, or site survey, is a way to discover rogue access points in the physical environment. During the site survey, security personnel investigate the presence, strength, and reach of WAPs deployed in an environment, while looking for unsanctioned signals. As the walk-through is conducted, a normal endpoint client with a wireless NIC can be used to simply detect signals. Another approach is to use one of a variety of wireless intrusion detection devices to scan the environment.

Site surveys also provide operational benefits, as the review helps define optimal placement and configuration and generate documentation for access points. Optimal placement and configuration consist of ensuring sufficient signal strength is available at all locations where access is desired. At the same time, where access is not wanted, like in public areas or outside of the facility, the signal availability should be minimized or eliminated. A site survey is useful for evaluating existing wireless network deployments, planning expansion of current deployments, and planning for future deployments.

Determining Wireless Access Placement

Using information determined by site surveys, the WAP locations are finalized. It is not recommended to commit to specific locations until the placements are informed by the walk-through. Conduct the proper testing of configurations and signal strength with multiple WAPs in place. There will most likely be movements and adjustments in this phase. Once an optimal configuration and location pattern is reached, make the locations permanent.

Here are some general considerations for wireless access placement:

- Use a central location.
- Avoid solid physical obstructions.
- Avoid reflective or other flat metal surfaces.
- Avoid the use of electrical equipment (interference).
- Position external omnidirectional antennas pointing vertically.
- Point a directional antenna toward the area of desired use.

An essential consideration for wireless technology is the impact of the environment on the broadcast signal. Wireless signals are impacted by various types of interference, physical and electromagnetic. Distance and obstructions are physical concerns. Electricity and other radio signals can conflict with or impede the effectiveness of the wireless signals. Network administrators will manipulate directional antennas and tune signal strength to accommodate the physical and electromagnetic obstacles to reach the desired areas of access.

A primary security concern for antennas is understanding how the lob pattern extends from the antenna. This is particularly true with directional antennas where the lob reaches far beyond the typical unidirectional antenna in one focused direction while being attenuated in the other directions. Even without special equipment, one can walk concentric circles around an access point and use a mobile device to measure radiation strength.

Antenna Types

The antenna is an integral component in wireless communication systems. The antenna transforms electrical signals into radio waves, and vice versa. Signal transmission requirements and reception quality dictate the choice of antenna from the various kinds available. Standard antennas can be upgraded to signal-boosting, stronger antennas. Some of the most common types of antenna used are as follows:

- The standard straight, pole-dipole, or vertical antenna sends signals in all directions away from the antenna. This radiation pattern is omnidirectional and is the prevalent type of antenna on base stations and endpoint devices.

- Many other types of antennas are directional. Instead of broadcasting in every direction, the signal is focused to one direction. Some examples of directional antennas include the following:
  - **Yagi:** A Yagi antenna is crafted from a straight bar with crossbars to catch specific radio frequencies in the direction of the main bar.
  - **Cantennas:** These are constructed from tubes with one sealed end. They focus along the direction of the open end of the tube.
  - **Panel antennas:** These are flat devices that focus from only one side of the panel.
  - **Parabolic antennas:** These are used to focus signals from very long distances or weak sources.

There are a few key antenna considerations with regard to securing the wireless network. Most importantly, recognize that directional antennas significantly extend the network's reach in one focused direction. This is the case for both receiving and transmitting. Therefore, care must be taken in pointing directional antennas so the network's visibility and vulnerabilities are not cast out too far. For choosing antennas and their placement, bear in mind how the broadcast extends well past walls and through floors, particularly when the organization is in a multitenant building.

Wireless Channels

Wireless signals are subdivided within a frequency range in increments called *channels*. These channels are like the lanes on a road or highway. There are 11 channels in the United States, there are 13 in Europe, and there are 17 in Japan. In the United States, the Federal Communications Commission (FCC) regulates the frequencies and has allocated 11. In the other countries and jurisdictions, the frequencies are regulated by national or the member states' union and explains why there are differences in the number of frequencies.

Normally, a wireless connection is a communication signal between an endpoint client and a WAP. This occurs over a single channel. It is possible to have interference with devices on separate channels when two or more access points are located too closely together or the radio strength of WAPs is too high.

Security professionals should note that channel selection has little to no impact on mitigating wireless risks such as spoofing, jamming, or the visibility of the network. Instead, channels get chosen to minimize the interference between access points or other WiFi networks outside their control.

TIP Configure access points that are located near each other with a maximum channel separation. For instance, for four access points located within close proximity, channel settings could be 1, 11, 1, and 11 if the arrangement was linear, like along a hallway across the length of a building. However, if the building is square and an access point is in each corner, the channel settings may need to be 1, 4, 8, and 11.

Infrastructure Mode and Ad Hoc Mode

When deploying wireless networks, WAPs can be deployed in one of two modes: ad hoc or infrastructure. It is better to deploy the wireless access points configured to use infrastructure mode rather than ad hoc mode to enforce restrictions leveraged through WAPs. Ad hoc mode allows wireless devices to communicate without centralized control. Infrastructure mode prevents the devices or the NICs from interacting directly.

There are four distinct variants of infrastructure mode:

- **Standalone:** A WAP connects multiple wireless clients to each other but not to any wired resources.

- **Wired extension:** The WAP acts as a connection point, or hub, to link the wireless clients to the wired network.

- **Enterprise extended:** Multiple WAPs, all with the same extended service set identifier (ESSID), are used to connect a large physical area to the same wired network. This allows for physical device movement without losing connection to the ESSID.

- **Bridge:** A wireless connection is used to link two wired networks, often used between floors or buildings when running cables or wires is infeasible or inconvenient.

Service Set Identifiers (SSIDs)

Anyone who has connected to a wireless network knows to ask for the network name, the technical term for an SSID. The SSID is that string of characters that identifies the wireless network. The SSID represents the logical wireless network, not the unique access point, as there can be multiple access points to provide coverage for multiple SSIDs.

There are two types of SSID, namely, ESSID and basic service set identifier (BSSID). An ESSID is the name of a wireless network in infrastructure mode when a wireless base station or WAP is used. A BSSID is the name of a wireless network when in ad hoc or peer-to-peer mode. In a scenario where multiple different base stations or WAPs are used in infrastructure mode, the BSSID is the MAC address of the base station hosting the ESSID to differentiate multiple base stations in the overall extended wireless network.

In securing the SSID wireless network, regardless of the types, note that the SSID is comparable to the name of a workgroup. When an endpoint client discovers an SSID, the wireless NIC is configured to communicate with the associated closest or strongest WAP. The SSID has secure access features so that discovery does not necessarily equate to access. There are additional steps before the client can communicate, such as enabling encryption and ensuring that discovered SSIDs are legitimate. With enabling encryption, the client is required to enter a password to permit access. Ensuring the legitimacy of the SSIDs that clients might see requires the organization to periodically monitor for rogue access points.

TIP It is important to reconfigure the SSIDs of new devices before deployment, as many default settings are supplied by the vendor and, therefore, widely and well known.

A step that can be taken to better secure WAPs is to disable the SSID broadcast of the beacon frame. A beacon frame is a special broadcast transmission that the SSID sends regularly from the WAP. Discovery by end user clients occurs as any wireless NIC finds this radio signal. In fact, with a detect and connect NIC feature, the connection can be automatic. Network administrators can disable, or silence, the broadcast. This is recommended as a security best practice. This makes connection a little more difficult, as the end user must know the SSID address to search. Keeping the beacon off and the SSID hidden is not foolproof. Attackers have tools to discover SSID via wireless sniffer technology to capture SSID information used in transmissions between wireless clients and the WAPs, as the SSID is still needed to direct packets. Disabling SSID is a good first step. Hiding the existence of the network is a best practice, but it is not in itself sufficiently strong security. As with all defense in depth and layered security best-practice approaches, not broadcasting the SSID, coupled with using WPA2, will provide a reliable authentication and encryption solution with fewer failed attempts.

Using Captive Portals

Captive portals are authentication safeguards for many wireless networks implemented for public use, such as at hotels, restaurants, bars, airports, libraries, and so on. They are a common practice on wired networks, too. The process is to force a newly connected device to a starting page to establish authorized access. The portal may require input of credentials, payment, or an access code. It is also a good location to publish or provide a link to privacy policies and acceptable use terms and conditions. If end user consent for tracking and information collection is required, the captive portal allows for that as well. Once the end user satisfies the conditions required by the starting page, only then can they communicate across the network.

MAC Filters

A MAC filter is a whitelist or a register of authorized wireless client interface MAC addresses that is used by a WAP. Devices not on the list are blocked. The downsides are that the list is difficult to manage and does not scale to large environments with many changes.

There are two approaches to utilizing MAC filters. In one approach, someone, such as a network security analyst or a security professional tasked with securing wireless access, would determine through asset management what devices are permitted to connect. The other approach would be using a software solution such as intrusion detection. Some access point vendors offer such features, including the ability to detect MAC address spoofing to mitigate the risk of someone forging a known whitelisted MAC.

Wireless Attacks

In spite of increasing attention and capability for securing wireless networks, they are attractive targets for attackers. The types of attacks continue to grow, and many attacks are effective on wired networks as well as wireless ones. Attacks such as packet sniffing, MitM, and password theft are common to both wireless and wired networks and are discussed earlier in the chapter. A few types of attacks focus on wireless networks alone, like signal jamming attacks and a special collection of wireless attacks called *war driving*.

Signal jamming is the malicious activity of overwhelming a WAP to the extent that legitimate traffic can no longer be processed. Even though this is illegal in most places, there are inexpensive jamming products, like a TV jammer, available for sale online.

War driving is a bit of a play on words. The term has roots in a form of attack in the 1980s called *war dialing*, where computers would be used to make large numbers of phone calls searching for modems to exploit. War driving, in contrast, is when someone, usually in a moving vehicle, actively searches for WiFi wireless networks using wireless network scanning tools. These scanning tools and software are readily available and, far too often, free. When a wireless network appears to be present, the attacker uses the tools to interrogate the wireless interface or a wireless detector to locate wireless network signals. Once an attacker knows a wireless network is present, they can use sniffers to gather wireless packets for investigation. The next step in the attack is to discover hidden SSIDs, active IP addresses, valid MAC addresses, and even the authentication mechanism the clients use. MitM attacks may progress or the attackers may conduct advanced attacks with specialized tools, like AirCrack, AirSnort, and WireShark to attempt to break into the connection and gather additional important information. When using no security protocols or older ones, like WEP and WPA, attackers have very little difficulty being successful.

NOTE With the advancement of drones and the ability for private citizens to use them, a newer attack vector known as *war droning* is now a threat. Scanning and cracking activities are accomplished with a drone instead of by a person in a vehicle within proximity of the WAP.

War drivers often share the information they gather. Not all war driving attacks are meant to disrupt or be particularly malicious. It is likely the attackers are trying to simply get Internet access for free. Using the information they obtain from their own tools, they combine data with GPS information about location. Then they publish the information to websites like WiGLE, openBmap, or Geomena. Other people access the maps of various networks to find locations where they can hijack the wireless and access the Internet or conduct additional attacks.

There are no laws that prohibit war driving, although nothing specifically allows it either. Some consider it ethically wrong, but at a high level it is somewhat analogous to neighborhood mapping in the physical world with house numbers and phone numbers publicly listed. In fact, the reporting of war driving information on the Web could be considered an expanded version of what WAPs are meant to do: broadcast. However, as security professionals know, not all WAPs are broadcasting publicly, as they are hidden.

NOTE A real-life example helps underscore the duality of war driving as a potential attack vector, but also sometimes is a reasonable information-sharing act. Google systematically gathered WiFi information through video and mapping functions for its Street View service. The issue was Google's lack of prior notice to the data collection, which created privacy concerns.

Internet, Intranets, and Extranets

Here's a quick primer to distinguish related concepts to bring the previous topics together:

- **Internet:** This is the global interconnection of networks public and private. It combines and connects the TCP/IP transport of data across WANs. The Internet was designed and launched by the U.S. Department of Defense but today is managed and operated by the Internet Corporation for Assigned Names and Numbers (ICANN).

- **Intranet:** This is a type of network that is a diverse range of telecommunications services limited logically to internal users. The intranet runs on a corporate or privately controlled network infrastructure. The principle difference between an intranet and the Internet is that the former is bound by a controlled perimeter. That perimeter might be within a corporate building or might include some off-site or cloud portions. Intranets host organizational websites that are not externally accessible via the World Wide Web.

- **Extranet:** An extranet is a controlled private network that allows access to partners, vendors, and suppliers or an authorized set of customers. The access and information available are typically less controlled than the intranet, but more constrained than a publicly facing website. An extranet is similar to a DMZ because it allows the required level of access without exposing the entire organization's network.

See Figure 4.8 for a comparative list of advantages and disadvantages of hosting an extranet.

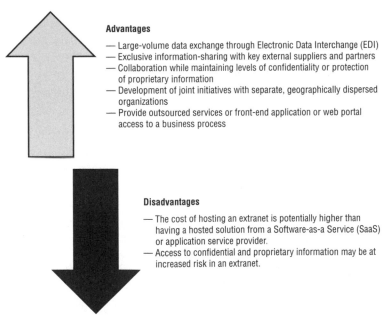

Advantages

— Large-volume data exchange through Electronic Data Interchange (EDI)
— Exclusive information-sharing with key external suppliers and partners
— Collaboration while maintaining levels of confidentiality or protection of proprietary information
— Development of joint initiatives with separate, geographically dispersed organizations
— Provide outsourced services or front-end application or web portal access to a business process

Disadvantages

— The cost of hosting an extranet is potentially higher than having a hosted solution from a Software-as-a Service (SaaS) or application service provider.
— Access to confidential and proprietary information may be at increased risk in an extranet.

FIGURE 4.8 Extranet advantages and disadvantages

Demilitarized Zones

To separate the organizational LANs from the public, untrusted Internet, a perimeter network, called a DMZ, is established. This is a separate physical or logical network segment apart from the organizational intranet or internal network. The goal for a DMZ is primarily security, achieved by limiting access, but it also improves overall network performance. The DMZ is outside of the perimeter corporate firewalls, so precautions and tailored security controls are used to enforce separation and privilege management. The organization's network is behind firewalls, and external network nodes can access only what is exposed in the DMZ.

One of the most common uses of a DMZ is the publicly facing corporate website. Customers and suppliers alike may need access to certain resources, and a group of web servers outside the corporate network can provide the appropriate access in a timely manner. The platform, as a publicly facing asset, is highly likely to be attacked. From a security perspective, the benefit is that the internal corporate network can remain safe if the machines in the DMZ are compromised. At the least, properly designed DMZ segmentation allows the organization some extra time to identify and respond to an attack before the entire organizational network is also infected.

NOTE   The DMZ can be a useful environment to use as a source of testing interconnection through the corporate firewall when troubleshooting problems or developing services.

Virtual LANs

To provide a layered security strategy, organizations will want to create logical segments on the network without expensive and major physical topology changes to the infrastructure. With implementation of internal routers and switches, a number of VLANs can be configured for improved security and networking. On a port-by-port basis, the network administrator can configure the routing devices to group ports and distinguish one group from another to establish the VLANs. This is how multiple logical segments can exist on one physical network. If permitted, communication between VLANs is unfettered. However, a security feature of the design is the ability to configure filtering and blocking for traffic, ports, and protocols that are not allowed. Routing can be provided by an external router or by the internal software of a switch if using a multilayer switch. In summary, VLANs are important in network and security design because they do the following:

- Isolate traffic between network segments. In the event of an attack, the compromise can be contained within a specific VLAN or subset of VLANs.

- Reduce a network's vulnerability to sniffers as VLANs are configured by default to deny routable traffic unless explicitly allowed.

- Protect against broadcast storms or floods of unwanted multicast network traffic.

- Provide a tiering strategy for protection of information assets. Higher-value assets can be grouped and provided maximum levels of safeguarding, while lower value assets can be protected in a more efficient manner.

VLANs are managed through software configuration, which means the devices in the group do not have to be moved physically. The VLAN can be managed centrally efficiently and effectively.

TIP VLANs have similarity to subnets. However, they are different. VLANs are created by configuring routing devices, like switches to allow traffic through ports. Subnets are created by IP address and subnet mask assignments.

SECURE NETWORK COMPONENTS

Society has benefited from the Internet. All of the interconnections, the communication capabilities, the digital transformations, and the speed of sharing information have changed and, in some cases, saved lives. Almost every industry has advanced by exploiting Internet capabilities; healthcare, retail, banking, industrial control, military, government, and telecommunications are all more efficient and effective, to the benefit of the stakeholders of their services and products.

However, with all of the positives, there is a counterbalance of negatives. The Internet also provides a lucrative target for malicious people who have illegal and unethical motives. Assets such as sensitive personal and financial information are accessed by cybercriminals and stolen for resale, identity theft, or to steal money from a person's bank or credit accounts. In the case of critical infrastructure, as in government, healthcare, or industrial control organizations, the objective of the criminal may be to disrupt or deny service to the organization. For security professionals, the impact on information availability of a DDoS attack is just as concerning as the confidentiality and integrity concerns that come from unauthorized data access or information theft. A discussion of how security professionals must balance the pros and cons includes the various architectures, network designs, and networking devices required to protect assets and access to information.

That discussion begins with the typical configuration of a single intranet and extranet network into several interconnecting components or subnetworks (subnets) as segments. There are numerous advantages to segmentation strategies for networks:

- **Performance:** Systems that communicate frequently are grouped together, and others are segmented in groups that communicate less frequently.

- **Reduced communication problems:** Rather than broadcast traffic across an entire network and cause congestion, segmentation can isolate and reduce destination systems to the minimum required.

- **Security:** An unsegmented network is considered flat, meaning that all network devices are accessible across the network. The ability to isolate traffic and enforce access controls on a granular level is made possible by segments. A layered approach is achieved using a combination of switch-based VLANs, routers, or firewalls.

TIP A private LAN or intranet, a DMZ, and an extranet are all types of network segments.

The tools used to accomplish network segmentation include a number of security device categories. These devices are found in all types of networks. You do not need all of the following devices in every network, but one or more types are commonly present. In fact, following a defense in depth approach, it is usually more advantageous to have a full complement of these devices working together at different OSI layers and performing different services. A single device will almost never satisfy every security requirement. That said, improperly used, incorrectly configured, or unmanaged security devices implemented in excess can result in security failure too. You need to analyze requirements and provide tailored risk-based solutions.

A range of network components exists across the spectrum of hardware, software, and services. Using the right ones and making sure they are configured or employed in ways that will increase security is essential. The sections that follow will examine the security considerations of such network components as firewalls, NAT, intrusion detection systems (IDSs), security information and event management (SIEM), hardware devices, transmission media, endpoints, and content distribution networks (CDNs).

Firewalls

A firewall is used to prevent unauthorized data flow from one area of the network to another. The boundary could be between trusted segments and the Internet or between other parts of a private network. In any case, a firewall creates a boundary and is employed to prevent or allow traffic from moving across that boundary.

The capabilities of a firewall can be accomplished with software, hardware, or both. Data coming into and out of the private network or internal segments must pass through the firewall. The firewall examines and inspects each packet and blocks those that do not match specified security criteria. These activities and some other network events are captured on firewall logs. Reviewing and auditing of logs are extremely valuable security tools that security professionals use for incident detection and response, forensic analysis, and improvement of the performance of the security assets.

The term *firewall* is used because the networking versions have a function similar to that of a firewall in a physical structure. A firewall in a building is a barrier meant to prevent or delay the spread of an actual fire. However, unlike a building firewall that suppresses all fire, a firewall in a systems environment is designed to permit approved traffic to transit between two environments.

For the network perimeter, firewalls are considered the first line of protection as part of an overall layered architecture. Elsewhere, firewalls, as noted earlier, are used to establish a boundary for any area and to separate and control traffic flow across that boundary. They are foundational to networking and one of the most prevalent security technologies used to protect information systems and networks. In terms of security due diligence, firewalls are essential. However, firewalls alone are not enough. For instance, they do not provide capabilities for authentication. Other types of devices and techniques are needed to complement firewalls. Without other devices and technologies in the security portfolio, firewalls become a single point of failure.

NOTE The expression "behind the firewall" describes traffic that flows within a subnet. Firewalls govern traffic from one subnet to another and do not protect from malicious data within the subnet.

Firewalls require configuration and human management, which is why security professionals must understand how to best use them. They do not automatically provide benefit. Besides any technical vulnerabilities that may be found, configuration and oversight in firewall management help mitigate the risk of human error and misconfiguration. Security professionals have to configure filtering rules that define permitted traffic. These rules, be they to determine filtering or deny packets, make up the decision process of the firewall. For example, one firewall rule may say, "Drop all inbound packets routed with an internal source address." Also important is how a firewall acts when it fails. If a firewall ceases to operate well, for example, it becomes overwhelmed, then the firewall optimally should fail "closed." This means the firewall should not allow *any* packets through. To make sure the rules remain in place, the firewall must be protected against unauthorized change, and configurations must be kept current over time. Like any other device or endpoint, firewalls have vulnerabilities to be closed or patched, and security professionals also oversee the patching and upgrade procedures.

One of the most important roles of a security professional is to use the activity logs generated by firewalls. The logs should be analyzed for several types of events. Here are a few examples:

- The reboot or restart of a firewall
- Failure to start or a device crashing

- Changes to the firewall configuration file
- A configuration or system error while the firewall is running
- Unusual probes for access on ports
- Unsuccessful logins on devices

TIP   Although the term can be used in other contexts about access control, the list of rules that govern a firewall is usually referred to as the *access control list* (ACL). An ACL contains specifications for authorized ports, protocols, list of permissions, IP addresses, URLs, and other variables to establish acceptable traffic.

Along with where a firewall is positioned, how they process and interrogate data differentiates types of firewalls. The principle of defense in depth applies here too. None of the different types of firewalls is sufficient alone. A combination is preferred.

Along with the variety of traditional firewalls that exist, there is the more recent next-generation firewall. There are also special firewalls such as multihomed and bastion firewalls. The following sections explore each of these, as well as firewall deployment architectures.

Types of Firewalls

There are four basic types of firewalls: static packet filtering firewalls, application level firewalls, stateful inspection firewalls, and circuit level firewalls. The key differentiator between all four firewalls is the OSI model layer at which each operates.

The first, a static packet filtering firewall, is the earliest and the simplest of firewall designs. Also called a *screening router*, the packet filtering firewall is the fastest design. Operating at the OSI model's network layer, it inspects each packet. If a packet breaks the rules put in place, the packet is dropped and/or logged. Able to work most quickly, a packet filtering firewall will mitigate the risk of a particular packet type. This type of firewall offers no authentication mechanism and can be vulnerable to spoofing.

An application level firewall examines packets and network traffic with much more scrutiny than do packet filtering firewalls. Operating at the higher OSI model application layer, an application level firewall seeks to identify what kind of application traffic wants to cross the boundary. Often used as a separator between end users and the external network, the application level firewall functions as a proxy. Deep inspection takes time, making this firewall the slowest of all types.

The stateful inspection firewall is set apart from the key feature that differentiates it from a simple packet filtering firewall: a stateful firewall monitors the state of network connections. This firewall operates at the network and transport layers of the OSI model.

The connection state is based on how TCP operates and how TCP establishes a session through the "three-way handshake" discussed earlier. That state is kept track of, plus other connection attributes, such as destination and source details, are saved temporarily in memory. Over time, these details are used for smartly applying filters.

The circuit level firewall is functionally simple and very efficient, operating most like a stateful inspection firewall. The primary difference is this firewall works only at the session layer of the OSI model. For a circuit level firewall, the only task is to ensure the TCP handshaking is complete. No actual packet is inspected, nor would any individual packet be dropped. Traffic coming through a circuit level firewall will appear as if it originated from the gateway, since the circuit level firewall's big benefit is to verify the session, while masking any details about the protected network.

Those four types of firewalls represent the span from the earliest to the most well-established firewall technology. But there is the next generation firewall, often referred to as the *next-gen firewall* (NGFW). The next generation firewall combines the traditional features of those earlier four with the advanced features of other network-based security devices such as an IDS or IPS. In the context of the OSI model, a next generation firewall operates at multiple levels.

Multihomed Firewalls

This is a general term for firewall or proxy capabilities. Multihomed describes having more than the default two interfaces or NICs providing the boundary. The host uses a set of software-defined rules to determine what traffic can pass between networks it is connected to, minimizing the risk of data being inadvertently exchanged between the two networks.

Bastion Host/Screened Host

A bastion host is so named for its resemblance to the medieval structure used as a first-layer protection guard house at the entry of a castle. In computing, it is a special-purpose type of firewall or host computer positioned logically behind the services of a core network routing device or in a DMZ. That router separates the internal, private network from an untrusted network, which can be the Internet. The terms *bastion hosts* and *screened hosts* are used interchangeably. They are also sometimes referred to as *jump hosts*. They act as a proxy, as the only device reachable from external sources. The bastion host adds a layer of protection by concealing the identities of the internal nodes. A bastion host will have a very limited number of applications, usually only one, to limit the possible impact of host compromise. Most commonly, the application is a proxy server to facilitate services and encapsulate data through the bastion host.

Types of bastion host applications include the following:

- **DNS server:** Like a phone book for the network, translates from its stored directory of domain names to the resolved IP address
- **Email server:** A virtual post office, stores inbound email for local distribution and sends out emails externally over SMTP, for example
- **FTP server:** Allows for the transfer of files over the Internet using an established sender and recipient connection, usually password-protected
- **Proxy server:** A general application that acts as an intermediary between an endpoint device and another server
- **VPN termination point:** An endpoint for a VPN, to extend a private network across a public network
- **Web server:** Processes requests via HTTP, for instance, to transmit data across the World Wide Web

Firewall Deployment Architectures

A screened subnet is a combination of bastion hosts. The basic architecture distinctly separates public and private segments. On the private intranet, the local computers and system are located behind a protective device or application, screening them from public access. On the other segment, public services like web servers and proxy servers are accessible. The subnets are helpful for increased security and can improve performance in data throughput.

In today's complex computing environment, a single firewall in line between the untrusted and the private networks is almost always insufficient. There are some basic implementations for a firewall connected to a router to direct traffic to the Internet. However, it is best practice to eliminate the reliance on a single firewall.

To improve protection and performance among and between subnets and externally to untrusted networks, organizations use multiple firewalls in combination. Figure 4.9 illustrates an example of the hybrid deployment of firewalls at different networking tiers of the private LAN.

The use of a two-tier design introduces the DMZ or an extranet for business-to-business (B2B) purposes. Another purpose is to differentiate between semitrusted partners, such as between a company and its governmental partners. There are two distinct versions of the two-tier model, a multihomed version and a serial version.

The first deployment architecture uses one firewall that has three or more interfaces. In a firewall with multiple interfaces, one of the interfaces leads to the DMZ.

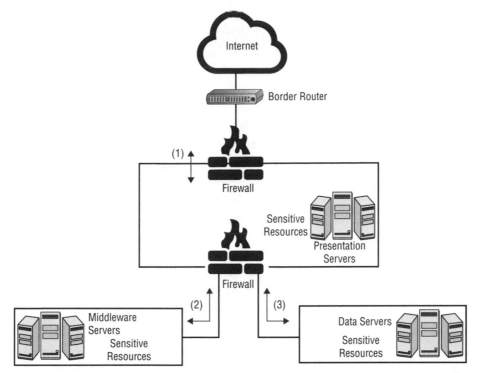

FIGURE 4.9 **Multiple firewall deployment architecture**

The second version consists of two firewall devices in a direct transactional line with each other. In the inline version, the DMZ is between the two serial firewalls. When using the DMZ, information server systems, e.g., web servers, are accessible to authorized external users. Otherwise, the firewall directs authorized traffic to the trusted network based on filtering rules or access control lists.

The most secure and most complex design is a three-tier deployment architecture. In this design, multiple subnets are established between the private network and the Internet through the use of individual firewall devices. As data traverses through each subnet, it meets progressively more stringent filtering rules at each firewall. This increases the chance that only authorized traffic reaches the trusted sources and the most critical assets. Access to the DMZ occurs at the outermost subnet. The first firewall may be a reverse proxy. The systems or data servers that support complex web applications and other transactions operate within the second or middle subnet. The private network is protected directly by the third.

There is a significant operational impact when employing the more complex architectures. The cost of deploying and managing the multiple tiers is a consideration to balance against the value of the assets. With the complexity and significant management requirements, the risk of firewall misconfiguration is something that requires ongoing attention. In this way, the devices that protect the environment become the vulnerability through human error.

Today, these firewall models are not the steadfast solution that they once were. Cloud services have been disruptive to the typical firewall architecture. While firewall models and architectures have been around for years, cloud services are fast becoming common, and corporate dependency on the cloud dictates how protected network traffic moves through the public Internet. One solution is using what Amazon Web Services (AWS) calls *security groups*. AWS security groups (SGs) are a type of firewall instance per virtual private cloud (VPC) or the virtual networking space people using AWS use to define their VMs.

Another approach is offering a firewall as a service (FWaaS), much like cloud service providers offer software as a service (SaaS). With FWaaS, filtering or screening packets are done virtually and off-site. FWaaS obviously requires more than your average trust in the cloud service provider, but its benefits include dedicated management in terms of updates, configuration, and enforcing your agreed-upon rules and policies.

Software-defined networking also presents disruption to traditional firewall architectures. SDN makes managing a network more flexible. This is largely seen as a feature and an advantage for networking engineers. However, SDN also makes maintaining firewall requirements more fluid, which can be a disadvantage. Again, SDN and cloud services have significantly affected how firewall services can be implemented.

Network Address Translation

NAT can be implemented on a variety of different devices such as firewalls, routers, gateways, and proxies. It can be used only on IP networks and operates at the network layer (layer 3). Originally, NAT was designed to extend the use of IPv4, since the pool of available addresses was quickly being exhausted. To that point, NAT is a legacy technology that comes with disadvantages and advantages.

First, consider its advantages. NAT is used to accomplish network and security objectives to hide the identity of internal clients, mask the routable design of your private network, and keep network addressing costs at a minimum by using the fewest public IP addresses possible. An example of how you might find NAT implemented on a perimeter firewall is shown in Figure 4.10. Through NAT processes the organization assigns internal IP addresses, perhaps even a private addressing scheme. The NAT appliance catalogues the addresses and will convert them into public IP addresses for transmission over the Internet. On the internal network, NAT allows for any address to be used, and this does not cause collisions or conflict with public Internet hosts with the same IP addresses. In effect, NAT translates the IP addresses of the internal clients to leased addresses outside the environment. NAT offers numerous benefits, including the following:

- Connection of an entire private network to the Internet using only a single or just a few leased public IP addresses

- Use of private IP addresses (10.0.0.0 to 10.255.255.255) in a private network and retaining the ability to communicate with the Internet as the NAT translates to a public, routable address

- NAT hides the IP addressing scheme and network topography of an internal, private network from the Internet.

- NAT ensures that connections originated from within the internal protected network are allowed back into the network from the Internet.

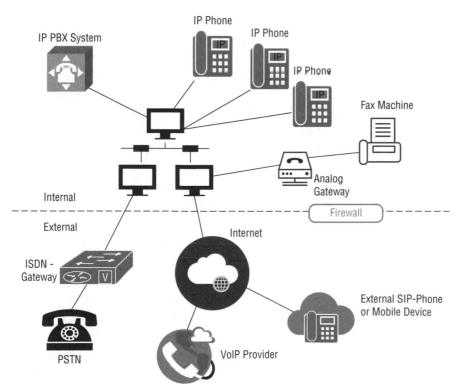

FIGURE 4.10 **NAT implemented on a perimeter firewall**

Public IP addresses are essentially all allocated after the remaining class A (see Table 4.1) addresses were exhausted years ago. This explains the upward trend in the popularity of NAT. Security concerns also favor the use of NAT, which mitigates many intrusion types of attacks. With only roughly 4 billion addresses available in IPv4, the world has simply deployed more devices using IP than there are unique IP addresses available. The fact that early designers of the Internet and TCP/IP reserved a few blocks of addresses for private, unrestricted use is becoming a very good idea. These set-aside IP addresses, known as private IP addresses, are defined in the standard RFC 1918.

Now, consider some of NAT's disadvantages. Again, remember that NAT was developed to help deal with the fact that IPv4 addressing was being exhausted. To that end, NAT was assumed to be a temporary solution. Because it was considered only temporary, the IETF responsible for defining protocol standards didn't pursue creating an in-depth official standard for NAT. In fact, while the IETF recognized the benefits of NAT and published a general specification, they avoided developing a technical specification to discourage NAT's widespread adoption. For that reason alone, the biggest disadvantage to NAT is how inconsistent its implementation in devices is.

A few technical disadvantages of NAT have been recognized, but solutions to those problems were discovered or developed without needing to reinvent NAT. For example, consider how peer-to-peer communication is handled. Without NAT, an initiator communicates with a target. No problem, provided both the initiator and the target have routable addresses. With NAT implemented, an initiator on the Internet seeking to connect with a target behind NAT cannot connect with a nonroutable address. One way to solve this is for the peer-to-peer session to begin "backward," with the target first connecting with the originator for the purpose of discovering NAT in place. Then, once NAT's outside public address is known, the originator can begin a new peer-to-peer session. Services such as Skype, which rely on peer-to-peer or VoIP protocols, needed to create innovative ways to sidestep how NAT would otherwise break their service. Skype, for example, employs "SuperNodes" on public addresses to permit a peer-to-peer connection, even if both the target and the initiator are behind NAT.

Another disadvantage is how IPSec checks integrity. IPSec computes a hash value for the purpose of ensuring the integrity of each packet. That hash value is computed using various parts of the packet, and since NAT changes the packet's values, that hash value is no longer valid. To address this, the technology of NAT-Traversal (NAT-T) was developed. NAT-T ensures that IPSec isn't broken when one or both ends of the IPSec tunnel cross over a NAT device.

Moving from the network layer (layer 3) to the transport layer (layer 4), there is a variation of NAT called *port address translation* (PAT). Whereas NAT maps one internal

IP address to one external IP address, PAT adds an external port number to the mapping of one internal IP address to an external IP address. Thus, PAT can theoretically support 65,536 (2^16) simultaneous communications from internal clients over a single external leased IP address. In contrast to NAT's requirement to lease as many public IP addresses as you want to have for simultaneous communications, PAT allows you to lease fewer IP addresses. With each leased IP address, you get a reasonable 100:1 ratio of internal clients to external leased IP addresses.

Intrusion Detection System

An intrusion detection system (IDS) can be a standalone device or, as is often the case, can exist in the form of additional functionality within a firewall. The main purpose of an IDS is to monitor network traffic and/or compare file hashes. If something is deemed suspicious, the IDS will alert on that traffic. This brings up the primary "weakness" of an IDS: it will alert about suspicious traffic, but an IDS traditionally will not actively act to prevent the threat. Acting to prevent traffic falls under the definition of an intrusion prevention system (IPS).

Another weakness of IDSs is their difficulty to "tune" or customize according to the unique traffic patterns of your network. Invariably, a newly placed IDS will alert unnecessarily on suspect traffic that turns out to be benign. In short, there is a strong tendency to alert on false positives. Similarly, some malicious traffic, positively identified by well-tuned countermeasures, will be missed by the IDS. In that case, the IDS must be adjusted or updated to avoid further false negatives.

IDSs help reduce the blocking of traffic and port access as false positive by efficiently detecting abnormal or undesirable events on the network. As mentioned earlier, IDS functionality is often built into NGFWs, likely labeled as a module. In the scope of secure network components, the relevant concern is how the IDS and firewall might interoperate. The integrated device might additionally provide extensive logging, auditing, and monitoring capabilities. When the abnormal or undesirable traffic is detected, the IDS might then perform a few actions. First, it would alert security personnel. Also, the IDS might put a temporary firewall rule in place.

NOTE Some view false positives as an indicator that should be reduced. That is not always true. Ignoring false positives can result in missing indicators of compromise. Tuning devices to reduce false positives also creates a false sense of security, as rules are relaxed to reduce alerts. In contrast, overly strict rules increase administrative burden as security professionals investigate too many false alarms. Security professionals have to work toward a cost-effective and secure balance based on risk.

Related to IDSs are IPSs. Most consider the distinctions between these systems relatively minor. IPSs are basically extensions of the IDS. Based on the rules in the IDS filter, the IDS monitors the traffic and alerts when the rules are broken. An IPS provides a similar monitoring function but is designed to actually deny access when unwanted or abnormal traffic is detected. A distinction between a firewall and an IPS, which both deny traffic, is that firewalls do not have an ability to interrogate the data packets to identify an attack, but IPS (and IDS) does. Realistically, today's IDS/IPS functionality is almost always part of an integrated device, with fewer commercial products operating exclusively as an IDS or IPS.

Security Information and Event Management

There are a few realities a security professional in an organization should begin to accept:

- Perfect protection of the environment is not possible. Detection and response capabilities are hugely important.

- It is not a question of if the environment will be breached; it is when. And it probably already has been breached.

- The voluminous amount of log data that is available for the substantial number of networked security devices requires machine processing. Manual audit log review for security incidents is impossible.

There are additional compelling reasons for security professionals to seek out innovative tools and technologies to help augment and support the security workforce. One of the best examples of this is SIEM systems. SIEM is a product and a service by which a group of security operators use tools to centralize and interpret logs or events generated by security devices on a network.

Two key factors that make SIEM useful are, first, having an extensive, diverse set of sources and, second, the system's intelligence in correlating between events and information provided by those sources.

The sources can and should vary as much as possible. It's of little value to gather "relatable" information from the same type of source, e.g., several hosts or all the networking gear. A narrow range of source types provides a narrow scope of information and potential insight into the cause (or potential threat). Instead, sources range from endpoint sources such as hosts and applications to middleware applications and network devices, and they include perimeter and boundary sources.

In addition, intelligence in correlating the collected information must be present. Otherwise, any correlation between event and triggered alerts amounts only to a simple "if…then" analysis. To utilize intelligence in event correlation, SIEM needs to have a strong familiarity with the monitored environment. Raw data gathered from disparate sources will be normalized. That is to say, data will be weighed against what value would be expected versus what value should be considered an extreme or outlier piece of data. This is to sift the valuable information from the meaningless.

The tools encompass data inspection tools, machine learning practices, and automated risk evaluations. The security devices include firewalls, IPS/IDS, data loss prevention (DLP), and even endpoint clients. The security devices provide data about machine and user activity that the SIEM analyzes and alerts on in real time. The alerts are acted upon by the SIEM service vendor, specifically by security incident response personnel. The amounts of data are impossible for human or manual processing, as logs are harvested from outputs from a variety of sources. The end goal of SIEM is to reduce signal to noise for the organization's staff. If SIEM operations are not managed internally, the customer organization requires a strong SIEM provider relationship, as these systems are not automatic. Alerts and incidents have to be analyzed for false positives, meaning the SIEM sends an alert that is later determined to not be a security incident. The vendor must communicate to make the SIEM effective and an extension of the information security team.

The SIEM is informed by other streams of security intelligence from outside the organization as well. In some cases, threat intelligence is gained from searching the dark web for instances of data that correlates to previous or potential attacks. For instance, an alert may come from a discussion board containing identifying information about a company or from individuals who are customers of the company. Such alerts might trigger remediation actions, including contacting law enforcement or customers. Or an alert might only be forwarded and archived for later correlation.

Three main languages, Structured Threat Information eXpression (STIX), Cyber Observable Expression (CybOX), and Trusted Automated eXchange of Indicator Information (TAXII), were developed to facilitate information being processed. These languages do not do the processing themselves but instead are standardized specifications. They are not languages in the sense of programming languages but a software developed by a company for security information to be shared, stored, or used to facilitate automation and human-assisted analysis.

Network Security from Hardware Devices

The practice of information security in an organization consists of proficiency with numerous infrastructure and networking components that deliver prevention, detection, and response capabilities. Collaboration with other network architects and engineers will be necessary to implement and operate a defense-in-depth technical control portfolio.

To understand several of the following devices, a working definitions of a few terms may be important. A broadcast domain is a logical division of a computer network, in which all nodes can reach each other by broadcast at the data link layer. The broadcast originates from one system in the group and is sent to all other systems within that group. A collision domain consists of all the devices connected using a shared media where a collision can happen between devices at any time. A data collision occurs if two systems transmit simultaneously, attempting to use the network medium at the same time, with the effect that one or both of the messages may be corrupted.

The operation of network security devices will be impacted by many circumstances of data transfer across media. Security professionals design and manage networks with consideration of forces that help or hinder the signal. Collisions and broadcasts must be managed, as they are significant influencers of data transfer success. With respect to the OSI model, collision domains are divided by using any data link layer (layer 2) or higher device, and broadcast domains are divided by using any network layer (layer 3) or higher device. When a domain is divided, it means that systems on opposite sides of the deployed device are members of different domains.

Repeaters, Concentrators, and Amplifiers

Repeaters, concentrators, and amplifiers operate at the physical layer (layer 1). These simple devices serve to extend the maximum length a signal can travel over a specific media type. They connect network segments that use the same protocol and are used to connect systems that are part of the same collision domain or broadcast domain.

Hubs

Hubs, also known as multiport repeaters, are a physical layer (layer 1) technology. They work only with interconnected systems using the same protocol, in the same domain. They simply repeat inbound traffic over all outbound ports to make the devices act like a single network segment. Because they offer little security-related capability, they are typically prohibited in organizations and are replaced with switches. Hubs are mainly a legacy technology that have little modern use.

TIP   The IEEE 802.3 Ethernet standard expresses disapproval for connecting network segments by repeaters or hubs.

Modems

To support computer communications, a device was needed to convert or modulate the digital information across an analog carrier of the signal. A modulator-demodulator, or modem, operates at the physical layer (layer 1) to support communications across public switched telephone network (PSTN) lines, often referred to as *landlines*. Modems were prevalent from 1960 until the mid-1990s to enable WAN communications and today are widely used in low-bandwidth environments such as building automation, SCADA, and industrial controls environments. In other applications, digital broadband technologies have evolved to replace modems. These include integrated services digital network (ISDN), cable modems, DSL modems, and 802.11 wireless devices. A key improvement in the evolution is the increased bandwidth and throughput modern devices enable. Capabilities like video streaming and teleconferencing are possible because of these advances.

TIP A modem must perform modulation. Therefore, it is a common misnomer to call modern devices such as cable, DSL, ISDN, and wireless connection devices modems. They are actually routers.

Bridges

This technology operates at the data link layer (layer 2). A bridge forwards traffic from one network to another. Unlike repeaters, which just forward received signals, bridges direct signals based on knowledge of MAC addressing. If a network uses the same protocol, a bridge can be used even if the networks differ in topologies, cabling types, and speeds. A buffer is used to store packets, using a store and forward capability until the packets can be released if the networks have differing speeds. Systems on either side of a bridge are part of the same broadcast domain but are in different collision domains. Some bridges use a spanning tree algorithm (STA) to prevent bridges from forwarding traffic in endless loops, which can result in broadcast storms. STAs are an intelligent capability for bridges to prevent looping, establish redundant paths in case of a single bridge failure, uniquely identify bridges, assign bridge priority, and calculate the administrative costs of each pathway.

NOTE Watch for broadcast storms on bridges, which can degrade network bandwidth and performance. The broadcast storms can happen when bridges are forwarding all traffic and become overwhelmed.

Switches

To combat the weaknesses of using hubs, switches are a better choice. A switch is an intelligent hub that operates at primarily the data link layer (layer 2), meaning the switch handles systems on the same broadcast domain, but different collision domains. However, switches with routing capabilities can operate at the network layer (layer 3), providing both are in different broadcast and collision domains.

Able to comprise a level of addressing intelligence for destination systems, switches can discriminate and forward traffic only to the devices that need to receive it. Switches also provide efficient traffic delivery, create separate collision domains, and improve the overall throughput of data where the segments operate on the same protocol.

Switches can create separate broadcast domains when used to create VLANs. The switch segments the network into VLANs, and broadcasts are handled within the VLAN. To permit traffic across VLANs, a router would have to be implemented. Switches cannot accomplish this distribution.

Switches provide security services that other devices cannot. They look deeper into packets and can make granular traffic distribution decisions. By establishing and governing the VLANs, switches help to make it harder for attackers to sniff network traffic. Broadcast and collision information is contained; the valuable network traffic is not continually traveling through the network.

Routers

Routers are network layer (layer 3) devices. A router connects discrete networks using the same protocol, whereby a data packet comes in from one host on the first network, and the router inspects the IP address information in the packet header and determines the destination and best path. The router is able to decide the best logical path for the transmission of packets based on a calculation of speed, hops, preference, and other metrics. A router has programmed routing tables or routing policies. These tables can be statically defined or manually configured. The other way the routing tables can be created and managed is dynamically through adaptive routing. A router has the ability to determine as it processes data how to best forward data. The router can select and use different routes or given destinations based on the up-to-date conditions of the communication pathways within the interconnections. When a temporary outage of a node is present, the router can direct around the failed node and use other paths.

As previously mentioned, there are numerous dynamic routing protocols, including BGP, OSPF, and RIP. It should be noted that static routing and dynamic routing are best used together. Sometimes dynamic routing information fails to be exchanged and static routes are used as a backup. Systems on either side of a router are part of different broadcast domains and different collision domains.

Gateways

An important function of a gateway device is that it connects networks that are using different network protocols. They may be hardware devices or software applications, and they operate at the application layer (layer 7), but arguably also at the presentation layer (layer 6, where formats change). The gateway device transforms the format of one data stream from one network to a compatible format usable by the second network. Because of this functionality, gateways are also called *protocol translators*. Another distinction, gateways connect systems that are on different broadcast and collision domains. There are many types of gateways, including data, mail, application, secure, and Internet.

Proxies

A proxy is a form of gateway that performs as a mediator, filter, caching server, and even address translation server for a network. However, they do not translate across protocols. A proxy performs a function or requests a service on behalf of another system and connects network segments that use the same protocol. A common use of a proxy is to function as a NAT server. NAT provides access to the Internet to private network clients while protecting those clients' identities. When a response is received, the proxy server determines which client it is destined for by reviewing its mappings and then sends the packets on to the client. NAT allows one set of IP addresses to be used for traffic within a private network and another set of IP addresses for outside traffic. Systems on either side of a proxy are part of different broadcast domains and different collision domains.

TIP   Network tarpits, sometimes referred to as *teergrube*, the German word for tarpits, may be found on network technologies like a proxy server. Basically, a tarpit is a service that purposely delays incoming connections to deter spamming and broadcast storms.

LAN Extenders

This is a multilayer switch used to extend network segment beyond the distance limitation specified in the IEEE 802.3 standard for a particular cable type. It can also implemented as a WAN switch, WAN router, repeater, or amplifier.

Wireless Access Points

These operate at the data link layer (layer 2). A wireless router is similar to a wired router in a network in that it also interrogates and determines the pathway and destination for a packet it receives. The wireless router also acts as an access point into the wireless network, or wired network in integrated networks. However, the utility in wireless routers is their ability to allow portable endpoints to access the network, for example, notebooks, laptops, and smartphones. Wireless routers can operate on the 2.4 GHz and 5 GHz bands simultaneously in a multiband configuration and provide data transfer rates of more than 300 Mbps on the 2.4 GHz band and 450 Mbps on the 5 GHz band. WAPs are discussed in detail earlier in the chapter in the "Wireless Networks" section and its subsections.

Multiplexers

These are devices that support a process of integrating multiple analog and digital signals across one shared medium, like a coaxial or fiber-optic cable. The process is a more efficient and cost-effective approach than sending each signal on an independent channel.

Multiplexing is commonly shortened to *muxing*, and a multiplexer device may be called a *mux*. To reverse the process and separate the signals, a device called a *demultiplexer*, sometimes shortened to *demux* or *dux*, performs the reverse process to extract the original channels. With modern technology and cloud usage, multiplexers are not often used today.

Private Branch Exchange (PBX)

Private branch exchange (PBX) is a special-purpose telephone switch that is used as a private telephone network within a company or organization. The PBX can interface with multiple devices. Not long ago, the PBX was always a physical switch, but today most PBX functionality is software-based. Users of the PBX phone system can communicate internally within their company or organization or access external users. The PBX expands capacity for more phones than what would be possible using physical phone lines that use the public switched telephone network (PTSN). Voice data is multiplexed onto a dedicated line connected to other telephone switching devices. The PBX is able to control analog and digital signals using different communication channels like VoIP, ISDN, or Plain Old Telephone Service (POTS). There are several security concerns with PBX implementation that security professionals need to assess. For instance, many PBX implementations still have modems attached to enable dial-up access for services like remote maintenance. Securing PBX implementations is discussed later in the chapter in the "Implement Secure Communication Channels According to Design" section.

Unified Threat Management (UTM)

Unified Threat Management (UTM) is a concept that integrates the functionality described in this chapter in each type of network and security device into a minimum number of multifunction devices. The goal is to move away from numerous devices that provide singular or point solutions to a simplified architecture and management of combination devices. Another benefit is simplified administration of vendor relationships and proprietary interconnections. Some of the earliest adopters of UTM are firewall, IDS, and IPS integrated devices. Next-generation devices and solutions bring together capabilities like web proxy and content filtering, DLP, VPN, and SIEM to name a few. Some security professionals caution against UTM approaches, as they may erode the benefits of a defense in depth security approach.

Cloud Computing

Cloud computing is discussed in greater detail later in this chapter. However, in the context of device operations, cloud computing introduces new opportunities and challenges for security professionals. Cloud service providers offer the delivery of computer processing capabilities as a service rather than as a product. Shared resources, software, and information such as routers, switches, proxies, and gateways are available as a utility that is leased rather than owned.

Cloud offerings designed to replace infrastructure, which used to be only found in a local data center, typically are not found in the cloud. Infrastructure pieces instead are positioned as services, such as firewall as a service (FaaS) or network as a service (NaaS). Organizations can reduce up-front costs of the hardware and software assets used to manage and secure networks. However, a security professional has to remember that using cloud computing resources does not eliminate responsibility for protecting assets shifted to the cloud computing model.

Endpoints

While managing network security with filtering devices such as firewalls and proxies is important, security professionals must also focus on security requirements for the computing endpoints. Endpoints are a general descriptive term for the various access and reporting devices that people use to connect to the internal and external networks. To be clear, an endpoint is simply any end device connected to the network. This can include a PC, a printer, a server, or even a piece of network infrastructure. Protecting the endpoints follows a strategic defense in depth strategy and is referred to as *endpoint security*. If there is a vulnerable endpoint, the risk is high it will be exploited and used to create additional network level damage.

Transmission Media

There is more to securing a network than just implementing the hardware devices and software applications. A security professional must possess an understanding of the physical mediums that connect the various nodes, including cabling, wireless, network topology, and communication models.

LAN Technologies

The most widely used LAN technologies are Ethernet and Wireless LAN using IEEE 802.11. As a security professional, you should concentrate on understanding these. The differences between LAN technologies exist at and below the data link layer.

Ethernet

Ethernet is based on the IEEE 802.3 standard and is the most common LAN technology in use. It is so popular because it allows low-cost network implementation and is easy to understand, implement, and maintain. Ethernet is also applicable and flexible for use in a wide variety of network topologies. It is most commonly deployed with star or bus topologies. Another strength of Ethernet is that it can support two-way, full-duplex communications using twisted-pair cabling. Ethernet operates in two layers of the OSI model, the physical layer and the data link layer. A protocol data unit for Ethernet is a frame.

Ethernet is a shared-media, or broadcast, LAN technology. As a reminder, broadcast and collision domains were introduced and defined earlier in this chapter. As a quick refresher, Ethernet as a broadcast technology allows numerous devices to communicate over the same medium. Ethernet supports collision detection and avoidance native to the attached networking devices. More detail regarding collision management will be discussed later in the section. The design of an Ethernet LAN has network nodes and interconnecting media or links. The network nodes can be of two types:

- **Data Terminal Equipment (DTE):** These are basically the variety of endpoint devices employed to convert user information into signals or reconvert received signals. Examples of DTEs are personal computers, workstations, file servers, or print servers. The DTE can also be a terminal to be used by the end user. It can be the source or destination system.

- **Data Communication Equipment (DCE):** DCEs can be standalone devices such as repeaters, network switches, and routers. These intermediate network devices receive and forward frames across the network. A DCE can be part of a DTE or connected to the DTE. Examples of DCEs include interface cards and modems.

Ethernet is categorized by data transfer rate and distance. Some data rates for operation over optical fibers and twisted-pair cables are as follows:

- **Fast Ethernet:** Fast Ethernet refers to an Ethernet network that can transfer data at a rate of 100 Mbps.

- **Gigabit Ethernet:** Gigabit Ethernet delivers a data rate of 1,000 Mbps (1 Gbps).

- **10 Gigabit Ethernet:** 10 Gigabit Ethernet is the recent generation and delivers a data rate of 10 Gbps (10,000 Mbps). It is generally used for backbones in high-end applications requiring high data rates.

NOTE   Data rates are often measured in megabits per second (Mbps), sometimes represented as Mbits/s. Note that Mbps as a rate differs from megabytes per second (MBps), sometimes represented as Mbytes/s. To convert data rates, know that there are 8 bits per byte and thus 80 Mbps/s is equivalent to 10 MBps.

Wireless LAN

Wireless LAN technology (WiFi) follows the IEEE 802.11 standard and has ushered in a significant amount of mobility and flexibility in networking operations. There are two basic modes of WiFi. In infrastructure mode, mobile access points, like laptops, connect via WAPs or wireless routers with access points. The connections serve as an entry point or bridge to a wired private network or directly to an Internet connection. In ad hoc mode, mobile units transmit directly with each other or in a peer-to-peer interconnection.

TIP   In WiFi network design and implementation, encryption of the signal is important, as the communications are across a more open medium than a wired LAN. The encryption standards and their evolution to the present day are described earlier in this chapter (see WEP, WPA, and WPA2).

LAN Properties and Components

There are various properties and components of LAN technologies that are complementary and should be understood within the context of how the different media configurations work. Of the following examples in this chapter, a security professional can expect to deal with combinations of all on the LAN. Ethernet and WiFi LANs employ a variety of methods, including analog, digital, synchronous, and asynchronous communications and baseband, broadband, broadcast, multicast, and unicast technologies.

Network Cabling

Network cabling describes the connection of devices, hardware, or components via one or more types of physical data transmission media. There are many types that exist, and each has particular specifications and capabilities. Which cabling is used in a network depends on physical and data requirements. Putting the correct network cabling in place is important, as cabling failures are the most common causes of network malfunction. For instance, some types of network cabling have distance or span limitations and may not provide sufficient reach and availability of data across wide geographical areas. The security professional has to plan for length limitations, throughput rates, and connectivity requirements. Lastly, consider the ease with which a potential adversary could wiretap copper network cabling as opposed to glass fiber.

Coaxial Cable

Coaxial cable, also called *coax*, was a popular networking cable type used throughout the 1970s and 1980s. In the early 1990s, its use as a data cable quickly declined because of the popularity and capabilities of twisted-pair wiring (explained in more detail later), but it is still widely employed for analog transmission. Coaxial cable has a center core of copper wire as an inner conductor surrounded by an insulating layer, surrounded by a conducting shield. There are some coaxial cables that have an additional insulating outer sheath or jacket.

Coax enables two-way communications because the center copper core and the braided shielding layer act as two independent conductors. The shielding design of coaxial cable makes it fairly resistant to electromagnetic interference (EMI) and less susceptible to leakage. Coax handles weak signals very well, especially as it can carry a signal over longer distances than twisted pair. For the time period it was most popular, and it supported relatively high bandwidth. Twisted pair is now preferred simply because it is less costly and easier to install. Coaxial cable requires the use of special tools, called *segment terminators*. Twisted-pair cabling does not. Coaxial cable is bulkier and has a larger minimum arc radius than twisted pair. The arc radius is the maximum distance the cable can be bent without damaging the internal conductors. Bending the coax beyond the minimum arc is, however, a relatively common cause of coaxial cabling failures.

Baseband and Broadband Cables

There is a naming convention used to label most network cable technologies, and it follows the pattern XXyyyyZZ. XX represents the maximum speed the cable type offers, such as 10 Mbps for a 10Base2 cable. The next series of letters, yyyy, represents whether it is baseband or broadband cable, such as baseband for a 10Base2 cable. Most networking cables are baseband cables. However, when used in specific configurations, coaxial cable can be used as a broadband connection, such as with cable modems. ZZ either represents the maximum distance the cable can be used or acts as shorthand to represent the technology of the cable, such as the approximately 200 meters for 10Base2 cable (actually 185 meters, but it's rounded up to 200) or T or TX for twisted pair in 10Base-T or 100Base-TX.

EMI is a key security implication when dealing with cabling. As the name implies, EMI is when an electromagnetic field interferes with the object's performance or functionality. The amount of EMI or its impact on the cabling naturally depends on the type of cabling. Table 4.3 shows the important characteristics for the most common network cabling types.

TABLE 4.3 **Important Characteristics for Common Network Cabling Types**

TYPE	MAX SPEED	DISTANCE	DIFFICULTY OF INSTALLATION	SUSCEPTIBILITY TO EMI	COST
10Base2	10 Mbps	185 meters	Medium	Medium	Medium
10Base5	10 Mbps	500 meters	High	Low	High
10Base-T (UTP)	10 Mbps	100 meters	Low	High	Very Low
STP	155 Mbps	100 meters	Medium	Medium	High
100Base-T/100Base-TX	100 Mbps	100 meters	Low	High	Low
1000Base-T	1 Gbps	100 meters	Low	High	Medium
Fiber-optic	2+ Gbps	2+ kilometers	Very high	None	Very high

Twisted Pair

As mentioned, twisted-pair cabling has become a preferred option because it is extremely thin and flexible versus the bulkiness of coaxial cable. All types of twisted pair are made up of four pairs of wires that are twisted around each other and then sheathed in a PVC insulator. There are two types of twisted pair, shielded twisted pair (STP) and unshielded twisted pair (UTP). STP has a metal foil wrapper around the wires underneath the external sheath. The foil provides additional protection from external EMI. UTP lacks the foil around the sheath. UTP is most often used to refer to 10Base-T, 100Base-T, or 1000Base-T, which are now considered outdated and are not used.

UTP and STP are both a collection of small copper wires that are twisted in pairs, which helps to guard against interference from external radio frequencies and electric and magnetic waves. The arrangement also reduces interference between the pairs themselves. The interference is called *crosstalk* and happens when data transmitted over one set of wires is pulled into another set of wires because the electric signal radiates electromagnetic waves that leak through the sheathing. To combat this, each twisted pair is twisted at a different rate, measured in twists per inch. The staggered twists prevent the signal or electromagnetic radiation from escaping from one pair of wires to another pair.

TIP   To decrease the chances of internal and external interference, increase the twists per inch on twisted-pair cabling. This also increases bandwidth and throughput capability.

There are several classes of UTP cabling. The various categories are created through the use of tighter twists of the wire pairs, variations in the quality of the conductor, and variations in the quality of the external shielding.

Twisted pair is not without some drawbacks that must be considered when designing and implementing a cabling architecture:

- The correct category of twisted pair must be used to achieve desired high-throughput networking.
- Exceeding the usable length of cabling, approximately 100 meters, will degrade the signal.
- UTP will be ineffective in environments with significant interference.

Conductors

The reason cabling is built upon copper wiring is because copper is one of the best materials to use for carrying electronic signals. It is also cost-effective and performs well at room temperature. Even though copper can carry signals a far distance, there is some resistance in the metal, so the signal strength does eventually degrade.

Fiber-optic cable provides an alternative to conductor-based network cabling over copper. Fiber-optic cables transmit pulses of light rather than electricity. This gives fiber-optic cable the advantage of being extremely fast and nearly impervious to tapping and interference. Fiber-optic cables can also transmit over a much longer distance before attenuation degrades the signal. The drawbacks are the relative difficultly to install and the initial expense of the line. The security and performance fiber optic offers comes at a steep price.

Plenum Cable

Because regular PVC releases toxic fumes when it burns, many modern building codes require a different material for sheathing network cables. A plenum cable is one that is covered with a special coating that is not toxic when burned. Plenum cable is so named based on its use in air plenums or enclosed spaces in a building. It is typically made up of several fire-retardant plastics, like a low-smoke PVC or a fluorinated ethylene polymer (FEP).

Additional Cabling Considerations

To conclude this section on network cabling, some final thoughts about cabling lengths are useful. While it is true that exceeding the maximum length of a cable type's capabilities will result in a degraded signal, this process of attenuation can be mitigated through the use of repeaters and concentrators. By way of quick review, a repeater connects two separate communications media. When the repeater receives an incoming transmission on one medium, including both signal and noise, it regenerates only the signal and retransmits it across the second medium. A concentrator does the same thing but has more than two ports. There is a limitation that security professionals should appreciate. Using more than four repeaters in a row is discouraged. The 5-4-3 rule has been developed to guide proper use of repeaters and concentrators to maximize cable lengths and remove as many attenuation problems as possible.

The 5-4-3 rule outlines a deployment strategy for repeaters and concentrators in segments arranged in a tree topology with a central hub, or trunk, connecting the segments, like the branches of a tree. In this configuration, between any two nodes on the network, the following must be true:

- There can be a maximum of five segments.
- The segments can be connected by a maximum of four repeaters and concentrators.
- Only three of those five segments can have additional or other user, server, or networking device connections.

TIP The 5-4-3 rule *does not* apply to switched networks or the use of bridges or routers.

Network Topologies

The topology of a computer network is the structure and arrangement of the various nodes and their connections depicted as links between the nodes. The model can be described as a logical or physical design. Logical topology describes how the data flows on the network. Physical topology is the actual placement of the various components of a network. The physical topology is not always the same as the logical topology. The physical topology of networks has four basic variations: ring, bus, star, and mesh.

Ring Topology

In a ring topology, devices are connected, and data packets are transferred in a unidirectional circular loop pattern. The points are connected to make a circle. Figure 4.11 provides a basic illustration. Data is transmitted one system at a time, and if one system is down, the entire network is broken. A digital token is passed around the circle so that a system that needs to send out information can grab it. Only with the token can a system transmit data. When the data is sent, the token goes with the packet. Each system on the ring is watching for the traffic. If a system registers as the intended recipient, it accepts and reads the data. If the system is not the intended recipient, it releases the token and data packet to the circle. The intended recipient releases the token but retains the data packet. The token is once again sent along the ring from system to system, searching for the next node that needs to send data. This topology is seldom used today because it is not scalable to large organizations. However, in smaller networks, ring topology is efficient because a central server is not required to distribute traffic, and the data transfer is relatively fast.

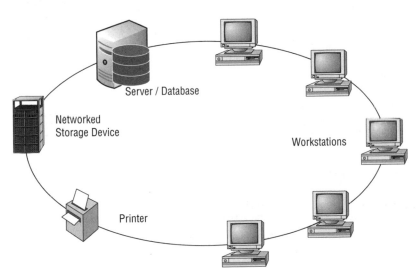

FIGURE 4.11 **A ring topology**

Bus Topology

Each node or system on a bus topology is connected by a single line or backbone cable. Unlike a ring topology, the bus configuration does experience data collisions, as multiple systems can transmit at the same time. The bus topology does have a collision avoidance capability because a system can listen to the cabling to determine whether there is traffic. When a system hears traffic, it waits. When it no longer hears traffic, it releases the data onto the cabling medium. All systems on the bus topology can hear the network traffic. A system that is not intended to be the recipient simply ignores the data. The bus topology, like the ring topology, has a single point of failure. If the bus is disconnected from a segment, the segment is down. However, within the segment, nodes can still reach each other.

The types of bus topology are linear and tree. A basic illustration of each is found in Figure 4.12. A linear bus topology employs a single trunk or main line with all systems directly connected to it, called the *backbone*. The tree topology also has the backbone, but several segments to connected devices span from the backbone like branches on a tree. A bus topology is terminated at both ends of the network. That feature renders the bus topology impractical in modern interconnected networks.

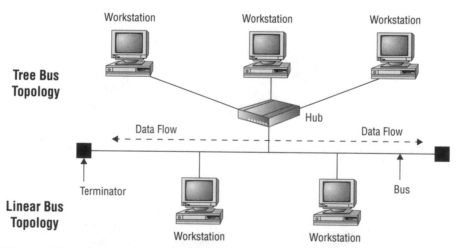

FIGURE 4.12 A linear bus topology and a tree bus topology

Star Topology

In a star topology, the connected devices are attached to a central traffic management device, which is either a hub or a switch. Figure 4.13 shows how a dedicated line is run from each device to the central hub or switch. A benefit of star topology is that there is segment resiliency; if one link goes down, the rest of the network is still functional. Cabling is more efficiently used and damaged cable is easier to detect and remediate.

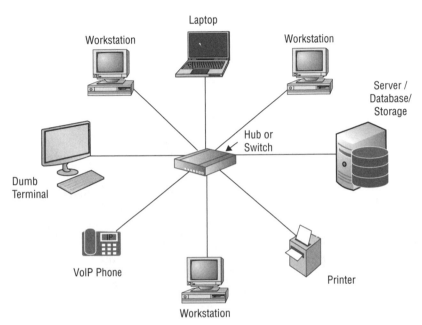

FIGURE 4.13 A star topology

Various logical configurations of a bus or ring topology can result in a star topology. An Ethernet network can be deployed as a physical star because it is based on a bus. The hub or switch device in this case is actually a logical bus connection device. A physical star pattern can be accomplished with a multistation access unit (MAU). An MAU allows for the cable segments to be deployed as a star while internally the device makes logical ring connections.

Mesh Topology

Putting it all together, a mesh topology is the interconnection of all of the systems on a network across a number of individual paths. The concept of a full mesh topology means that every system is connected to every other system. A partial mesh topology stops short of total connection but does connect many systems to many other systems. The key benefit of a mesh topology is the maximum levels of resiliency it provides, as redundant connections prevent failures of the entire network when one segment or device fails. The key disadvantage of a mesh topology is the disproportionate added expense and administrative hassle. This can be best appreciated when seeing Figure 4.14. It's also worth noting that the added cost and administration could lead to a security implication by virtue of resource strain.

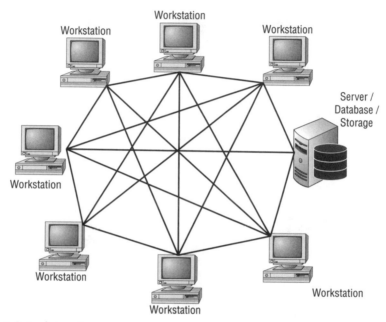

FIGURE 4.14 A mesh topology

Wireless as a Transmission Medium

Signals are transmitted as radio waves across various distances in wireless networks. There are actually a finite number of radio wave frequencies across the wireless spectrum. To minimize interference and conflicting transmissions, the wireless bands must be managed properly. Frequency is a measurement of the number of wave oscillations within a specific time and identified using the unit Hertz (Hz), or oscillations per second. Radio waves have a frequency between 3 Hz and 300 GHz. Different ranges of frequencies have been designated for specific uses, such as AM and FM radio, VHF and UHF television, and so on. Currently, the 900 MHz, 2.4 GHz, and 5 GHz frequencies are most commonly used in wireless products because of their unlicensed categorization. Unlicensed categorization simply means the frequency band is not set aside for a specific transmission, as with AM and FM radio, for example. However, to manage the simultaneous use of the limited radio frequencies, several spectrum-use techniques were developed. These included spread spectrum, frequency-hopping spread spectrum (FHSS), direct sequence spread spectrum (DSSS), and orthogonal frequency-division multiplexing (OFDM).

NOTE   Because the frequencies are unlicensed, WiFi computing devices can experience annoying interference from other wireless devices like garage door openers, baby monitors, and other low-power, nonlicensed transmitters.

The government-regulated nature of frequencies results in a small subsection of frequencies available for use by most devices. In the United States, the FCC regulates the frequencies not directly used by the federal government and its agencies. Those frequencies used by the federal government are controlled by the National Telecommunications and Information Administration (NTIA). Outside the United States, the allocation and use of frequencies for the majority of countries is done by the centralized regulation of the International Telecommunication Union (ITU), which is part of the United Nations.

The biggest reason all available frequencies are not used without control is the desire to avoid interference when saturating adjacent frequency bands. The benefit of having a uniform regulatory approach to spectrum management is avoiding conflicts because of overlap in frequency use across national borders. This is a special concern where nations might share multiple borders in a relatively small area, such as in Europe.

Spread spectrum is a method of communication that transmits across multiple frequencies simultaneously. The message is deconstructed into smaller packets and distributed across multiple frequencies. The packets are not lost and are reconstructed at the destination. The process is considered a parallel communication rather than a serial communication. The following sections describe some examples of spectrum frequency use.

Frequency-Hopping Spread Spectrum (FHSS)

FHSS uses a pseudorandom sequencing of radio signals that the sender and receiver know. This early implementation of spread spectrum rapidly switches a carrier among many frequency channels. The data is transmitted in a series, not in parallel. The frequency changes constantly. One frequency is used at a time, but over time, the entire band of available frequencies is used. The sender and receiver follow a hopping pattern in a synchronized way across the frequencies to communicate. Interference is minimized because reliance on a single frequency is not present.

Direct Sequence Spread Spectrum (DSSS)

With DSSS, the stream of data is divided according to a spreading ratio into small pieces and assigned a frequency channel in a parallel form across the entire spectrum. The data signals are combined with a higher data bit rate at transmission points. DSSS has higher throughput than FHSS. Where interference still causes signal problems, DSSS has a special encoding mechanism known as chipping code that, along with redundancy of signal, enables a receiver to reconstruct any distorted data.

Orthogonal Frequency-Division Multiplexing (OFDM)

OFDM allows for tightly compacted transmissions because of using many closely spaced digital subcarriers. The multicarrier modulation scheme sends signals as perpendicular (orthogonal), which do not cause interference with each other. Ultimately, OFDM requires a smaller frequency set or channel band. It also offers greater data throughput than the other frequency use options.

Cellular Network

Cellular or mobile networks are wireless communications that traverse across cells. The cells are geographically dispersed areas that consist of one or more cell sites or base stations. The cell site or base station is a transceiver fixed to a location. The user of a cell network uses a portable device over a specific set of radio wave frequencies to connect to the cell site and other cellular devices or the Internet. The standard descriptors to differentiate cellular technology refer to the generation when the technology was introduced. This can be confusing. For instance, 1G and 2G mean first- and second-generation, respectively. It does not indicate a specific frequency or signal strength. Table 4.4 provides an overview of these wireless technologies.

TABLE 4.4 Basic Overview of Cellular Wireless Technologies

GENERATION	1G	2G	3G	4G
Encoding	Analog	Digital	Digital	Digital
Timeline	1980 to 1994	1995 to 2001	2002 to 2005	2010 to present
Messaging features	None	Text only	Graphics and formatted text	Full unified messaging
Data support	None (voice only)	Circuit switched (packet switched 2.5G)	Packet switched	Native IPv6
Target date rate	N/A	115-18 Kbps	2 Mbps (10 Mbps in 3.5G)	100 Mbps (moving) 1 Gbps (stationary)

While many cellular technologies are labeled and sold as 4G, they may not actually reach the standards established for 4G by the International Telecommunications Union-Radio communications sector (ITU-R). The ITU-R set the standard for 4G in 2008. In 2010, the group decided that as long as a cellular carrier organization would be able to reach 4G-compliant services in the near future, the company could label the technology as 4G. Standards for 5G have been in development since 2014. However, the 5G network and compatible devices are expected to be commercially available worldwide in 2020. There have been localized deployments, like at the 2018 winter Olympics in South Korea.

A security professional should keep some important considerations in mind when it comes to supporting and securing information sent and received in a cellular wireless network. Since 1G, cellular use is for much more than just voice. Cell phones today, i.e., smartphones, have higher-level computing power to run applications, transmit text, send images, stream video, and store significant amounts of sensitive data. The Global System for Mobile Communications (GSM) standard has been developed and enhanced over time to support the use of text and data in addition to voice. For these reasons, communications that need to be secured will need additional technical controls in place. Cellular transactions are not inherently secure. There are numerous tools available for attackers to intercept wireless transmissions. A common attack scenario uses cell base stations to conduct MitM traffic capture. These attacks can take place whether the cellular connections are to the Internet or just between two or more mobile devices.

Wireless Application Protocol (WAP) Attacks

Many cellular or mobile devices can potentially act as bridges that may be unsecured access into your network. Understanding the way the devices are exploited requires a brief introduction to Wireless Application Protocol (WAP). Where the devices or transmissions are not secure, e.g., access controlled or encrypted, the attacker can hijack the session and gain access to the private network. WAP is not highly prevalent anymore with the advent of smartphones that include full browsers. Instead, as a suite of protocols, WAP should now be considered among other near-obsolete protocols.

Bluetooth (802.15)

Another type of wireless communication network is the Bluetooth, or IEEE 802.15, PANs. These present another area of wireless security concern for security professionals. Many peripheral devices, such as headsets, speakers, mice, and digital personal assistants, interact or interconnect with wired and wireless devices via Bluetooth. The devices connect through a process called *pairing* and transmit on the 2.4 GHz radio frequencies. Pairing is a scanning process where devices search for other compatible devices in close proximity, usually less than 30 feet. If a device is found, the mobile user inputs a PIN or code to complete the pairing. Using a code may reduce accidental or automatic pairings, but it is not necessarily strong security. Many PINs are only four numerical digits and remain 0000, as the default has not been changed. Bluetooth can be intercepted much like other wireless traffic. Bluejacking is the term for the MitM-like attacks on a Bluetooth connection. Bluebugging is an attack that grants hackers remote control over the feature and functions of a Bluetooth device. For a deeper understanding of Bluetooth, particularly its security, consult the standard NIST SP-800-121, currently at rev 2.

Endpoint Security

It is often said within security professional circles that the highest risk to an environment is the end user. The end user is also an effective security control where security awareness and training, incident reporting, and sanction policies are taken seriously and put into effect.

With that in mind, the devices used by people are a security concern. Endpoint security is a significant line of defense, and it is important whether or not the device is attached to a network continuously, like servers, or intermittently, like mobile devices. Keeping infected or suspicious endpoints off the network makes sense. Allowing vulnerable or already corrupted devices access puts the entire networked environment at risk. Concepts like NAC and endpoint security used in tandem with other detection and response techniques are central to good security practices.

A defense in depth approach has always included endpoint security as part of the other layers like firewalls, proxies, centralized virus scanners, and even IDS/IPS/IDP solutions. However, the nature of the attack has changed. An attacker can gain access to valid credentials through social engineering or bypass perimeter security controls through exposed remote access ports. Once the outsider becomes the insider, traditional perimeter and prevention controls are likely to be less effective. Local host firewalls, advanced threat protection applications, multifactor authentication, auditing, and client-based IDS/IPS, among other next-generation endpoint controls, are beneficial.

TIP   Endpoint security should at least consist of keeping antivirus and anti-malware software current and using a host-based firewall correctly configured, a hardened configuration with unneeded services disabled, and a patched operating system.

Mobile Devices

Mobile devices have special implications for security professionals. The small size and increasingly powerful compute and storage power of laptops, tablets, and smartphones make loss or theft of a mobile device a significant risk. The same amount of data that would fill an entire room in terms of physical storage of paper documents uses barely 5 to 10 percent of storage space on a modern laptop. Mobile devices are also easily and quickly lost, unlike the digital devices, like desktop computers or mainframes, that were more difficult to remove from an organization. The devices also present some risk as the launching platform for attacks. Either infected by malware individually or operated as botnets, mobile devices interact with the Internet and are capable of facilitating attacks against corporate and government networks.

The proper security approaches for mobile devices start with guidance that is appropriate for all storage platforms: minimum data retention. If the data is not needed, do not keep it on the mobile device. The minimum data retention is centered around the minimum amount of data necessary for the phone's user. Periodically, remove any data that was once needed but has exceeded the data retention policy. The next step in protecting the data is to use password, biometric, or other available authentication mechanisms to lock the devices when not in use. The other important step is to encrypt data at rest on mobile devices. Some devices, like those that use Apple iOS, have AES-256 level encryption built in. Other platforms have user-enabled encryption or support third-party encryption apps. If sensitive information is going to be used or potentially stored on a mobile device, encryption is at least a best practice and, for many organizations, a regulatory expectation.

For organizations keen on managing mobile devices in a consistent manner, centralized management of mobile devices is key. Additionally, NIST Special Publication 800-124 (currently at rev 1) covers not only management but also aspects of improving secure access and authentication of mobile devices at a higher level. For example, a mobile security professional may reconsider granting access to the internal network by mobile devices solely by credentials. Instead, smartphones, particularly personally owned devices, can be jailbroken or "rooted." Therefore, an organization should consider checking the connecting device's integrity before proceeding to grant full access to the network. To that effect, NIST 800-124 goes into depth on centralized management of mobile device security. NIST SP 800-124r1 covers small form-factor mobile devices, which excludes laptops.

Another technique, growing in popularity in recent years, is the corporation permitting corporate data to be maintained on a Bring Your Own Device (BYOD) device in a "secure container." The corporation requires the container to periodically "phone home" in order to maintain access. In addition, an encryption and security protocol are used to further secure routine access to the container on the device. If the device is offline (does not phone home) to the mother ship for a set period of time (e.g., 30 days), the container is locked, and after another period of time, it is destroyed.

NOTE   To synchronize information from the mobile devices to other storage platforms like external hard drives or desktop computers, mobile devices have USB and Bluetooth connections to transfer data files, documents, music, video, and photos.

The techniques mentioned earlier to secure data, and people's strong preference for their own mobile devices, have made it more worthwhile for corporations to employ BYOD policies. There are several names that refer to the personal ownership of a mobile device. For example, personal mobile device (PMD), personal electronic device or portable electronic device (PED), and personally owned device (POD) are all synonymous. With personal device proliferation, many organizations are using or considering BYOD initiatives. BYOD is a policy and a strategy by which employees are permitted to use their own equipment to perform work responsibilities. There are several options, which include one or more of the following actions:

- Unlimited access for personal devices
- Access only to nonsensitive systems and data
- Access, while preventing local storage of data on personal devices
- Access, but with IT control over personal devices, apps, and stored data

The different options indicate the security implications BYOD has for an organization. Security professionals will need to be able to implement specific security controls to accommodate the increasing popularity of BYOD as a method to control costs and improve employee productivity. Some general technologies to understand related to security are mobile device management (MDM), containerization, app virtualization, and the previously mentioned "secure containerization." These are examples of software solutions and mobile device configurations that help identify, isolate, and layer protection processes on these platforms, while preserving the need for personal privacy. In other words, in an effort to protect corporate sensitive information, it is not always necessary to track or ultimately delete personal information like photos or a personal health record that is not a corporate asset. A few important BYOD policy components are a signed statement from an employee acknowledging the policy and procedures required, and the policy must include permission for the company to remotely wipe a lost or stolen mobile device. Device wipe is the process of using the MDM solution to remotely contact a mobile device and delete or remove all data from the device. Contrast that with corporate-owned, personally enabled (COPE). With COPE, the corporation issues smartphones or mobile devices to the employees but allows the employees to alter them and use them as their own personal devices. The employees are permitted to use them for personal use as well, likely including installing their own applications, such as a game or personal email client.

NOTE Some organizations are taking a hybrid approach to allowing employees to use their own devices. To reduce the risk of unknown device compatibility with security policy and procedures, a choose-your-own-device (CYOD) strategy allows employees to use one or more devices from an approved product list.

Network Access Control (NAC)

NAC as an approach for network security control implements several technologies to limit and meter access to private environments. NAC methodologies are used to unify endpoint security technology (such as antivirus, host intrusion prevention, and vulnerability assessment), user or system authentication, and network security enforcement.

There are several basic goals for the use of NAC:

- Mitigation of non-zero-day attacks
- Authorization, authentication, and accounting of network connections
- Encryption of traffic to the wireless and wired network using protocols for 802.1X such as EAP-TLS, EAP-PEAP or EAP-MSCHAP
- Role-based controls of user, device, application, or security posture post authentication
- Enforcement of network policy to prevent endpoints from access to the network if they lack up-to-date security patches or host intrusion prevention software
- Ability to control access to the network based on device type and user roles
- Identity and access management based on authenticated user identities instead of just blocking IP addresses

When an unauthorized or suspicious device or user attempts to access the network, NAC automatically detects and responds instantly to block access and prevent attacks. This often makes the difference between a contained data incident and a data breach event or some other destructive result. The policies for NAC should be applied consistently for every device that attempts to connect. An effective NAC strategy is defined and continuously improved to better control, filter, prevent, detect, and respond to every internal or external communication. Figure 4.15 illustrates a general view of the NAC components.

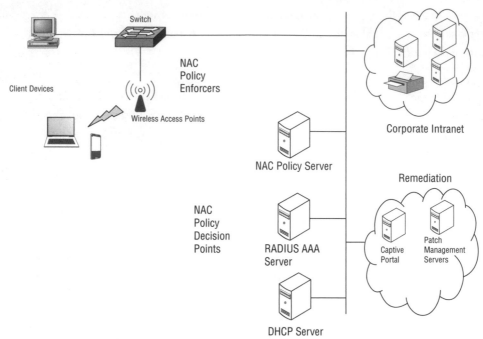

FIGURE 4.15 **Network Access Control**

TIP   802.1X, port-based NAC, is a simple form and just one component in a comprehensive NAC solution.

The following are the significant concepts for NAC that are worth understanding:

- **Pre-admission and post-admission:** In pre-admission, endpoints are inspected for policy compliance before they gain access, e.g., identifying and blocking out-of-date antivirus definitions. In post-admission, network access is granted, but user actions are regulated and decisions to remove access are made based on compliance with network behavior rules.

- **Agent versus agentless:** To make decisions about the endpoints, NAC systems either require a client application on the endpoint to report status upon access attempt or the NAC system can scan remotely and employ inventory techniques to determine access decisions.

TIP   Some software has network access protection agents built in. Microsoft Windows, Linux, and macOS have various capabilities included.

- **Out-of-band versus inline:** Out-of-band devices separate the functions of deciding and enforcing and report to a central console for management. This approach uses (or reuses) existing infrastructure switches, gateways, and firewalls to enforce policy. Some practitioners contend that out-of-band configuration can be disruptive. Inline devices sit in the middle of traffic flow, usually above the access switch level, and decide whether to admit or restrict traffic from each endpoint as it logs in. These can become bottlenecks if they become overloaded.

- **Remediation:** Remediation is necessary to resolve the problem that prevents access, e.g., update the antivirus software. Two different approaches to remediation are:

  - **Quarantine:** The endpoint is restricted to a specific IP network or assigned VLAN that provides users with routed access only to certain hosts and applications, like the patch management and update servers.

  - **Captive portals:** User access to websites is intercepted and redirected to a web application that guides a user through system remediation. Access is limited to the captive portal until remediation is completed.

TIP   Address management techniques like Address Resolution Protocol (ARP) or Neighbor Discovery Protocol (NDP) are used for quarantine processing to reduce administrative overhead of manually managing quarantine VLANs.

Implementing Defense in Depth

Over the course of this chapter's coverage of communication and network security, there have been numerous references to the defense in depth concept. The "Secure Network Components" section discusses the concept in the context of a network device or control. But the security professional needs to consider more aspects of defense in depth when implementing it.

At the risk of almost trivializing defense in depth, a fun way to demonstrate it is to play any "tower defense" game, a popular genre of online games. Tower defense games are all alike in one way: you have a path on which the threats keep coming to attack. Along the path, restricted only by your resources, you place varying kinds of countermeasures and defenses. The theme of the game varies wildly, be it medieval, zombies, or jungle. The threats vary in strength and speed, but they keep coming. The countermeasures vary too, but you keep deploying them. However, you quickly learn that the only winning strategy is to diversify the countermeasures. Eventually, certain threats come that are immune to particular defenses. If you use only one countermeasure, you will be defeated.

Only by using a diversified set of countermeasures can you confidently repel the vast array of threats that come. And that is defense in depth.

In the real world, on a real network, your countermeasures will be both diversified and layered. The diversification provides the ability to detect and repel varying kinds of threats. The layered approach optimizes defense from the anticipated threats at a particular layer while providing some relief for the next layer. This helps shelter countermeasures at subsequent layers from the more external defense and prevent them from being overwhelmed. For example, taking an intrusion detection device that is intended for the most protected subnet and placing it outside the perimeter might result in it being overwhelmed.

One example of a versatile and layered approach to defense in depth would be starting from the external perimeter and moving inward. For instance, you begin with a firewall and NACs and then rely on internal NACs and intrusion prevention or intrusion detection systems. Employing defense in depth does not stop at the network controls but continues with endpoint security and host-based security, such as antivirus, maintaining updates, and access management. Application-layer security controls and restricting access to data would complete the final layer of defense. This is a generalized example of how defense in depth, when layered, can work very well.

Content Distribution Networks

A content distribution network (CDN), also called a *content delivery network*, is a collection of resource services, proxy servers, and data centers that are deployed. The nature of the architecture model is to provide the low latency, high performance, and high availability of content, especially multimedia, e-commerce, and social networking sites across a very large (often national or continental) area. The content is distributed among many data hosts, not centralized in one location. While this positively affects availability, given that content distribution mitigates the impact of any one location going offline, the distribution of content among many hosts can also negatively affect confidentiality. Those businesses concerned with regulatory compliance must also be mindful of how content distribution affects their compliance requirements. Naturally, as data is stored or processed across multiple countries, the CDN must be aware of how local laws affect their business. The design is analogous to physical and logical load balancing that is preferable in other private and public networking implementations. Content is acquired as near to the requesting customer as possible, which results in the lower latency and greater throughput.

NOTE Examples of CDN service providers include Akamai, CloudFlare, Azure CDN, Amazon CloudFront, Verizon, and Level 3 Communications. The fact that many of the examples are cloud service providers is not accidental. The capabilities of cloud computing are often leveraged in a complex CDN, although a CDN does not necessarily have to be in a cloud environment.

The prevailing setup of CDNs is aligned to client-server distribution. Some client-to-client or peer-to-peer (P2P) networks exist. The most widely recognized P2P CDN is BitTorrent. There are significant concerns with P2P systems in that they differ from client-server configurations, where the client does not have to expose internal data to operate. P2P, by definition, requires a level of trust that participants will not abuse their access to other participants' machines/data. Some specific P2P threats to be aware of are as follows:

- **DDoS attacks:** Unlike the traditional TCP SYN-ACK flooding of a server, the P2P network is disrupted when an overwhelming number of search requests are processed.

- **Poisoning of the network:** Inserting useless data that may not be malware, but the superfluous, useless information can degrade performance.

- **Privacy and identity:** Fellow peers may have access to data the sender did not intend, simply because of the nature of the P2P data stream.

- **Fairness in sharing:** The network depends on sharing and contribution, not hoarding or leeching, terms used for those who download content but rarely add content.

IMPLEMENT SECURE COMMUNICATION CHANNELS ACCORDING TO DESIGN

In the previous sections, this chapter provided examples and guidelines to properly analyze, design, implement, and monitor various network protocols, topologies, and infrastructure components. The security of the networked channels is a core competency for security professionals. In this section, the particular aspects and concerns for voice, multimedia collaboration, remote access, data communications, and virtualized networks are addressed.

Secure Voice Communications

Voice communications have largely become integrated with the information technology platform. Digital voice transmissions introduce their own set of vulnerabilities into the system. Authentication is important to stop eavesdroppers from capturing media, identities, patterns, and credentials and possibly using those for subsequent unauthorized connections or other attempts to steal data. Integrity is a concern on two fronts: message and media integrity. The contents of the message, if intercepted, may be changed or reconstructed or the message can be rerouted. The actual media can be hijacked and degraded or the attacker can insert new messages into the media. To protect the data in transit, encryption protocols can be used to encapsulate or even scramble voice traffic. However, as mentioned earlier in this chapter, end-to-end confidentiality cannot be provided in secure voice transmissions, as some portion of all traffic is decrypted to aid in government law enforcement. Although this is not mandated by overt law in the United States, China enacted the Cybersecurity Law in 2017. The Cybersecurity Law requires all network operators to cooperate with the Chinese authorities for spot-checks and "technical support" to allow full access when requested.

Private Branch Exchange (PBX) and Plain Old Telephone Service (POTS)

A discussion on voice communication security starts with the PBX and POTS. PBX is the enterprise-class phone system, as opposed to a residential system. It includes the internal switching network and a controller. The problem with analog PBXs is that they are installed with default access configurations for ports, codes, and control interfaces. If these are not changed by the organization, attackers easily exploit them. An example of a common method of exploiting these poorly configured systems is the massive toll fraud that occurs at the cost of billions of dollars annually. Some of the vulnerabilities, including default configurations, have been remediated as analog PBX has been largely replaced by digital PBX to support VoIP. However, some residual risk remains. The first step toward reducing the risk is identifying the problem. Identifying toll fraud typically comes from the department responsible for examining the phone bills. Once fraudulent calls, particularly those from VoIP services, are identified, you will take steps to remediate. Figuring out how hackers are abusing the digital PBX systems or VoIP systems is difficult without strong vulnerability management on the relevant systems. Understanding the weaknesses in those systems helps identify what may be exploited to initiate the fraudulent calls. Subsequent use of strong policies and training will further minimize abuse by internal employees. Lastly, consider some specialized applications to monitor calls and alert if suspect calls are made.

Considerable risk also remains with modems that are still attached to permit remote maintenance on unmanned services or systems. For example, these might exist in some remote SCADA facility or some other ICS building. Permitting dial-up access through such an obsolete method is beyond irresponsible when discussing the design and implementation of secure communications channels. Locating those modems is done the same way a hacker does it: a war dialer, an application specialized in automated dialing and identifying an answering modem. This can be time-consuming unless only a subset of potential phone numbers is targeted. Once a vulnerable modem is found, it should be replaced with a more modern, secured form of remote access solution.

POTS is still a predominant feature in residential networks and some businesses. It was designed to carry human voice over a bidirectional analog telephone interface. Over a POTS connection, voice communications are vulnerable to interception, eavesdropping, tapping, and other exploitations. Therefore, POTS and PBX security controls rely heavily on physical controls to limit access and protect the equipment. Additional ways to mitigate the risk include segregating network traffic and monitoring the more vulnerable areas. The phone company would be responsible for the security of voice communications between a sender and a recipient. Many alarm systems and out-of-band network links for fax machines, some routers, and other network devices may keep PBX and POTS in organizations for years to come and are a concern for security professionals.

NOTE The PSTN was the collection of analog PBXs and POTS networks, but is now most often digital and consists of all the various telephony networks in aggregate. They are national, regional, or local and provide infrastructure and services for public telecommunication.

Voice over Internet Protocol (VoIP)

VoIP is a method using several technologies to encapsulate voice communications and multimedia sessions over IP networks. VoIP has become a popular and inexpensive way for companies and individuals to operate telephony solution using a TCP/IP network connection.

VoIP technology is not automatically any more secure than analog. It is essentially plain-form communications and is easily intercepted and eavesdropped. With adequate configuration, highly encrypted solutions are possible, and attempts to interfere or wiretap are deterred. Even then, VoIP still requires the attention of security professionals. Hackers have several vectors for VoIP attacks.

- Tools are available to spoof Caller ID, which facilitates vishing (VoIP phishing) or Spam over Internet Telephony (SPIT) attacks.

- The call manager systems and the VoIP phones themselves might be vulnerable to host OS attacks and DoS attacks.

- MitM attacks may succeed by spoofing call managers or endpoint connection transmissions.

- VLAN and VoIP hopping may occur with VoIP phones on the same switches as 802.1X. Hackers can run authentication falsification attempts across channels.

- Unencrypted network traffic may include VoIP, and therefore, decoding VoIP streams is possible.

The remediations for some of these issues center around employing encryption, increased authentication, and robust network infrastructure. As mentioned earlier, some vendors need to employ innovative means to safeguard their own service when protocols or vulnerabilities exist.

Multimedia Collaboration

"The office is wherever you are" is an expression that underscores the impact multimedia collaboration has had on business. Personal well-being has also changed with the introduction of shared video, data, images, and audio platforms. Geographic distances have been bridged by the use of various multimedia-supporting communication solutions. When collaboration is done simultaneously, tools like email, chat, VoIP, video conferencing, use of a whiteboard, online document editing, real-time file exchange, and versioning control, to name a few, can be used efficiently and effectively. Remote meeting technology has transformed the corporate world. With these changes, there are important security effects to address.

Remote Meeting

In this day and age, meetings generally do not require all attendees to be present in order to participate. Many productive meetings are held remotely with participants located in any number of geographically separated areas. To accomplish these remote meetings, several different types of technologies are used. There are hardware solutions like video cameras and VoIP telephony. Of course, it's increasingly common for people's own personal or corporate-issued smartphones to have cameras and microphones capable of teleconferencing. Software helps administer the meetings and allows for interaction between remote parties, like in the use of a shared screen whiteboard. Several terms are used to describe these technologies, such as digital collaboration, virtual meetings, video conferencing, software or application collaboration, shared whiteboard services, and virtual training solutions. Of course, there are more examples. The bottom line is that any service that enables people to communicate, exchange data, collaborate on materials/data/documents, and otherwise perform work tasks together is most likely performing or facilitating a remote meeting. Multimedia remote meeting services have security implications. Because a person is not identified by virtue of being present in a physical meeting room, authentication must be assured in remote meetings. To provide that assurance, there needs to be a form of verification or validation of the attendee's identification, such as when the employee must pre-register for the meeting using a unique password. The transmission of voice, data, or video might need to be protected via encryption. In a physical conference room where everyone is in the same location, voice does not need special protection sender to receiver, except for physical measures like closed doors and soundproofing the walls. To fully capitalize on multimedia collaboration, specifically remote meeting, security concerns must be addressed.

Instant Messaging

Instant messaging (IM) is a collaboration tool that allows for bidirectional, real-time text-based chat between two users connected by the Internet. Initially, the same client software had to be used by each user. In recent applications, JavaScript is more prevalent in IM, and users require only a modern browser. Some IM utilities allow for file transfer, multimedia, voice and video conferencing, screen sharing, remote control, and command scripting. Some forms of IM are based on a peer-to-peer service with direct communications. Other implementations use one or more centralized controlling servers in line. Peer-to-peer IM is vulnerable to several types of attack and potentially unauthorized access to data. However, it is easy to use and set up, which makes it popular in both corporate and personal use. Some of the common ways IM is vulnerable include the following:

- Where IM does not enforce strong authentication, account spoofing can threaten authenticity.

- Without encryption, IM is susceptible to packet sniffing, putting confidentiality at risk.

- File transfer and remote access add to the risk of malicious code deposit, infection, or data exfiltration.

- IM users are often subject to numerous forms of social engineering attacks, such as impersonation or convincing a victim to disclose sensitive information like passwords or classified data.

Internet Relay Chat (IRC) was an early, widely deployed Internet chat system that simply presented text on a screen and left no logs to audit. IRC was a client-server network that did not support encryption and therefore was vulnerable to MitM types of attacks. A range of IM products have existed such as AOL IM, Google Talk, Microsoft MSN Messenger, and XMPP, most of which have been discontinued.

NOTE   IM traffic is sometimes invisible to firewall monitoring, as some IM clients embed traffic within an HTTP packet. Because IM uses ports that are typically open, like ports 80 (HTTPS) and 21 (FTP), blocking ports at the firewall to thwart IM attacks is not effective.

TIP   Spam is an attack vector for IM. When the attack is through IM, it is called SPIM.

Manage Email Security

Securing email effectively is a large part of organizational information protection. Email is widely used and accepted as formal communication or a matter of record. It is one of the most used Internet capabilities. Email infrastructure is predominantly mail-handling servers using SMTP. The servers accept messages from clients, transport those messages to other servers, and deposit them into a user's server-based inbox. The servers communicate with end-user destinations using mail delivery protocols such as Post Office Protocol version 3 (POP3) or Internet Message Access Protocol (IMAP). These protocols permit the clients to pull the email from their server-based inboxes. These protocols are used whether in a corporate LAN or with the plethora of web-based email services.

TIP Many Internet-compatible email systems rely on the X.400 standard for addressing and message handling.

Popular SMTP servers that should be familiar to security professionals are Sendmail for Unix systems and Exchange for Microsoft. As Microsoft gains market share with cloud-based Exchange services, some security implications change. For the purposes of this chapter, understanding the fundamentals of SMTP servers in general is sufficient.

In fact, Sendmail and Exchange are just two of many alternatives. While they are popular in delivering business or private email services, there is growing popularity in using SaaS email solutions, with Gmail for business or Office 365 being two of the more popular email SaaS options. The key factor in deploying and securing SMTP servers is first to ensure that the protocols used provide the same basic functionality and compliance with Internet email standards.

Securing SMTP servers begins with making sure the system is properly configured for strong authentication for both inbound and outbound mail. SMTP is designed to be a mail relay system. This means it relays mail from the sender to the intended recipient. Without proper authentication, the SMTP server is an open relay or an open relay agent. Open relays are vulnerable to attack as they do not authenticate senders before accepting and relaying mail. Therefore, it's important that relays are properly configured and have adequate controls in place.

Spam is a likely outcome, as floods of emails can be sent out because the infrastructure is wide open for piggybacking tactics by attackers. When authentication is present, SMTP attacks are harder to accomplish, but hijacked authenticated accounts do happen.

Email Security Goals

Email is convenient and has transformed communications. However, several security controls have to be implemented to assure the confidentiality, integrity, and availability of email. That is most important at the application level.

At the hardware level, the secure placement of email servers and gateways is critically important, not just for proper functionality but for ensuring the security of the hardware. The basic implementation of email on the Internet does not include the required assurances. Security measures for email should generally accomplish several objectives:

- Secure placement of email servers and gateways on the network
- Ensure nonrepudiation, meaning that the sender is the sender
- Achieve privacy and confidentiality by restricting access through authentication mechanisms; verify the source of messages and delivery
- Classify sensitive content within or attached to messages

Email security should be defined by a policy that is supported by management. That policy should also be shared with employees or end users as part of initial and ongoing security training. Email attacks, such as phishing, remain a common and effective attack method. End users clicking a malicious link or infected attachment is often the first step in a cyber attack. A good email security policy has several main components:

- **Acceptable use:** These are general guidelines for what email can be used for, which may include some personal use. As a business-owned asset, the expectation is that users accomplish business tasks and nothing illegal, immoral, or obscene. Acceptable use policies in general provide guidance on acceptable use of company data. For example, no personally identifiable information (PII) shall be sent via email.

- **Access control:** Access should be restricted to individual inboxes and archives. In some cases, a group email inbox is established with multiple recipients. The user should be prohibited from granting access to other people. How access control is implemented should be described so that users recognize the balance between legitimate access and some level of privacy. At least, access control deters or prevents unauthorized access.

- **Privacy:** Users of a corporate email system are becoming accustomed to having no expectation of privacy.

- **Email backup and retention policies:** Backups and archives are needed for data recovery, legal proceedings, and many audits. Retention rules are important to guide the organization from keeping records that are no longer valuable or needed for legal or regulatory reasons. Excessive record maintenance may lead to security issues of a different kind. Backups can be daily, weekly, or monthly, for example. Retention requirements range from several months of archive to several years. In either case, backup and retention rules must be based on risk, business requirements, and any legal or regulatory guidelines.

Understand Email Security Issues

As noted earlier, basic email services lack significant security measures. To start with, email is not encrypted. The messages are transmitted in cleartext, readable by a sniffing application. Interception and eavesdropping are relatively easy. Some argue that lack of encryption is not the worst of the vulnerabilities. This argument has merit in that most cybersecurity attacks start with a phishing email. Email is an easy and convenient carrier for viruses, worms, Trojan horses, documents with destructive macros, attachments with embedded executable applications, and other malicious code. As almost everyone receives email on a daily basis, the likelihood that one person will fall for the phishing attack is very high.

The nature of the attacks has also become more advanced. The phishing email can deliver malicious attachments and URLs that launch various scripting languages, auto download capabilities, and auto execute features. For a security professional who wants to find a way to block the malicious content, using email sender information as a filter is useless. Attackers can modify the header information while in transit, and there are no built-in integrity checks to identify such tampering. A savvy attacker could go so far as to directly connect to an SMTP port on an email server and deliver email without the normal routing path and security checks. And email does not provide native message integrity checks, so a receiver cannot be sure the message has not been altered. Finally, if the email is not loaded with infected payload to launch an attack, the email itself can be the attack. A flooding of emails to a specific inbox or SMTP server constitutes a DoS attack, often called mail-bombing. The overwhelming number of messages can cripple storage or processing limits or both.

Email Security Solutions

As with all security approaches, a risk versus reward approach must be taken. The cost of implementing and maintaining the security controls should not exceed the value of the information (or the cost of losing it). The security controls should preserve the ability of the business to operate and grow; otherwise, they will be unnecessary, as the business is potentially headed for obsolescence. In terms of email security, an additional consideration to underscore is confidentiality. The message may contain valuable and sensitive information to protect.

There are several techniques that organizations can employ to strengthen the protection of their email communications:

- Use digital signatures to combat impersonation attempts.
- Block suspicious attachments and potentially risky filename extensions (such as .zip and .exe) at the gateway to reduce phishing and similar attacks.

- Employ filters to reduce spam and mailbombing problems.

- Use encryption to prohibit eavesdropping efforts.

- Train users in the importance of and methods for properly recognizing and handling spam or potentially malicious links in email.

- Install, run, and update antivirus and endpoint protection.

There are several protocols, services, and solutions to augment email infrastructure and provide security without an expensive and complete overhaul of the entire Internet-based SMTP infrastructure. Some of these strategies are listed here:

- Secure Multipurpose Internet Mail Extensions (S/MIME)

- MIME Object Security Services (MOSS)

- Privacy Enhanced Mail (PEM)

- DomainKeys Identified Mail (DKIM)

- Pretty Good Privacy (PGP)

- Forced Encryption

S/MIME is an email security standard that uses public key encryption and digital signatures to enable authentication and confidentiality for emails. X.509 digital certificates are used to provide authentication. Public Key Cryptography Standard (PKCS) encryption is used to provide privacy. Two types of messages can be formed using S/MIME:

- **Signed messages:** To provide integrity, sender authentication, and nonrepudiation of the sender

- **Enveloped messages:** To provide integrity, sender authentication, and confidentiality

MOSS is another email security standard that can provide authentication and confidentiality but also enables integrity and nonrepudiation services for email messages. MOSS employs Message Digest 2 (MD2) and MD5 algorithms; Rivest, Shamir, and Adelman (RSA) public key; and Data Encryption Standard (DES) to provide authentication and encryption services.

PEM is an email encryption mechanism that provides authentication, integrity, confidentiality, and nonrepudiation. Like the aforementioned services, PEM also uses RSA, DES, and X.509.

DKIM is a means to assert that valid mail is sent by an organization through verification of domain name identity. This adds a layer of nonrepudiation and authentication that is particularly helpful in identifying and filtering spoofed addresses in emails. Implementing DKIM relies on public keys and digital signing.

PGP is a public-private key system that uses a variety of encryption algorithms to encrypt email messages. PGP encryption can be used to protect files and other digital assets besides email. The first version of PGP used RSA, the second version, International Data Encryption Algorithm (IDEA), but later versions offered a spectrum of algorithm options. PGP encryption can be used to protect files and other digital assets besides email. PGP is not a standard but rather an independently developed product that has wide Internet appeal.

Forcing TLS for email encryption is another method to provide assurance. A few email service providers such as Apple and Google use TLS for @icloud and @gmail, their respective email services. It is not possible to force TLS as a sole option. In fact, RFC 2487 specifies that a public SMTP server must *not* force TLS since its implementation cannot (yet) be made mandatory. However, between email domains for business partners, forcing TLS is a viable option.

NOTE   PGP started off as a free product open for public use. PGP has since been developed into a commercial offering. OpenPGP and GnuPG are open-source products based on PGP that remain in the public domain.

Remote Access

The interconnected computing platforms, the strengths of multimedia collaboration, and the globalization of business are some of the forces that have made decentralized workplace arrangements more common. Telecommuting, or working remotely, occurs when a person separated from the main corporate compute and storage platforms accesses them from another location, such as their personal home, via a laptop. There is also a growing reliance on cloud-hosted resources, where employees on the protected LAN need to remotely access vital infrastructure hosted by a cloud service provider.

When telecommuting or using cloud-based resources, the user might use one of the following access paths:

- Using a modem to dial up directly to a remote access server (an insecure and almost obsolete technology)
- Connecting to a network over the Internet through a VPN
- Connecting to a terminal server system or an access gateway through a thin-client connection

The first two examples use fully capable clients. The connections that are established make the endpoint appear as any other node on the private network. It has all of the permissions and access that it would have if it was physically connected locally on the LAN and inside the perimeter firewall. The user who is remotely accessing terminal services is constrained to the resources made available by the proxy terminal server. The person accessing cloud-hosted systems might use a VPN over public infrastructure. Data cannot traverse outside of the network. Work is conducted inside the private network and not on the device that is connected at the distant end.

NOTE Telecommuting existed before the Internet and multimedia made the practice a business imperative. The term has roots in the original description of telecommuting, which implied the use of telephony to connect workers and customers. Teleconferences over POTS, PTSN, and PBXs with geographically separated individuals conducting business meetings were an example of the first versions of telecommuting.

Remote Access for Telecommuting

For telecommuting to be productive and successful, a person would need to have access to many of the same or comparable resources at a remote location as they would have at the primary office. Access to email, shared storage, and the capability to attend meetings virtually are necessary. Telecommuters use many remote access techniques to establish the required connectivity to the business office network. There are four main types of remote access techniques:

- **Service specific:** If a service such as email via Outlook Web Access (OWA) is needed, a service-specific remote access capability allows users to remotely connect to and use it. Service-specific capabilities are not limited to web-enabled versions of on-premises applications. Terminal service access can be limited to a time and attendance application, for example.

- **Remote control:** Common applications for remote control or remote access are help desk or Tier 1 support and employee training functions. Remote control allows an authorized user to gain remote access to another system and take full control as if they were physically in front of the distant system. There are significant security concerns with remote access. Potential vulnerabilities include brute-force attacks hackers are using to exploit the proprietary Remote Desktop Protocol (RDP) that Windows environments use to enable Windows Remote Desktop and Terminal Server.

- **Screen scraping:** This process provides a virtual application or virtual desktop experience to the distant end computer. In a process known as *screen scraping*, the office target system serves up the information on the screen and presents it to the remote operator. During screen transmission, there are risks of unauthorized disclosure or compromise, so security professionals will want to implement encryption with any screen scraper solutions. A second definition is the technology that automates both the use of a user interface and the transfer of the results.

- **Remote node operation:** Becoming less and less common, remote node operation is another description for modem dial-up access. Through a remote server, a remote client is provided access to other network resources and, in some cases, the Internet.

NOTE   There is another version of screen scraping technology that is not necessarily the same as allowing remote access. However, much as the target system serves up a screen scrape to the distant system, some automated data extraction tools perform a similar feature for easier human interaction. In a search engine like Google, the human data requestor is guided to the relevant screen information based on the search inquiry.

Remote Access Security Management

Organizations that allow for remote access are extending their risk beyond the figurative corporate walls. With the expansion of risk come additional security requirements. The private network can be compromised by remote access attacks. Figure 4.16 illustrates some common areas of increased risk of remote access. There are many security controls that can be put in place, and a few of the most important categories of control are as follows:

- A strong authentication system is required, multifactor authentication is the standard to mitigate credential theft.

- Limit remote access to only those who need it and who routinely use it.

- Implement encryption across the transmission link appropriate to remote connectivity needs to include one or more of these examples: VPNs, SSL, TLS, SSH, and IPSec.

- Understand that a VPN is not a complete security solution. An end user who can authenticate and establish a VPN may be accessing the network with an infected computer or mobile device. As discussed throughout the chapter, endpoint security is also essential. Combinations of security controls are needed to manage and safeguard the remote access workforce.

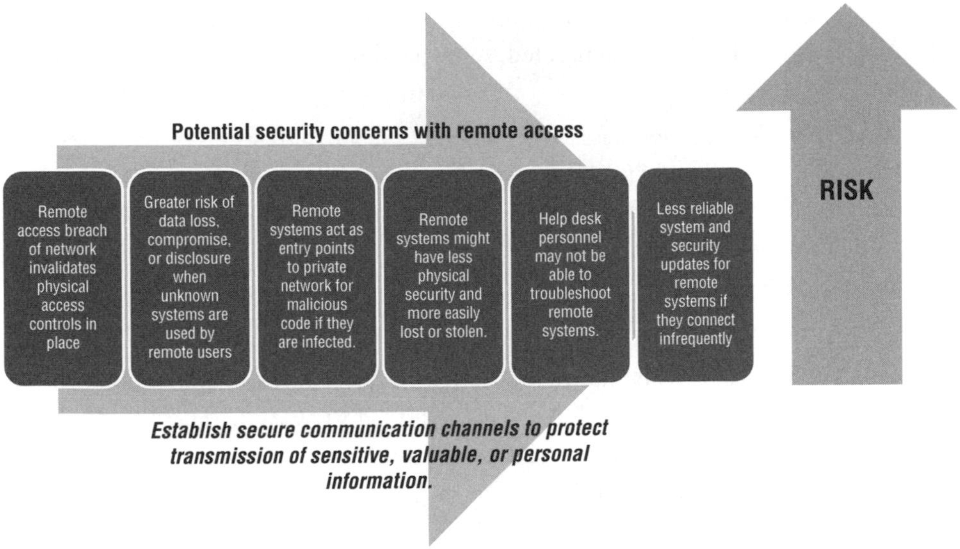

Potential security concerns with remote access

| Remote access breach of network invalidates physical access controls in place | Greater risk of data loss, compromise, or disclosure when unknown systems are used by remote users | Remote systems act as entry points to private network for malicious code if they are infected. | Remote systems might have less physical security and more easily lost or stolen. | Help desk personnel may not be able to troubleshoot remote systems. | Less reliable system and security updates for remote systems if they connect infrequently |

RISK

Establish secure communication channels to protect transmission of sensitive, valuable, or personal information.

FIGURE 4.16 Common areas of increased risk in remote access

Authentication Approaches

Because remote access expands the private network beyond the corporate environment, invalidates many of the physical controls in place, and increases information risk for the organization, taking extra precaution with authentication of remote access users is worth exploring further. There are specific remote access protocols and services that an organization will use to strengthen credential management and permissions for remote clients and users. Most likely, the use of a centralized remote access authentication system should be in place. Some examples of remote authentication protocols are Password Authentication Protocol (PAP), Challenge Handshake Authentication Protocol (CHAP), Extensible Authentication Protocol (EAP, or its extensions PEAP or LEAP), Remote Authentication Dial-In User Service (RADIUS), and Terminal Access Controller Access Control System Plus (TACACS+).

Centralized Remote Authentication Services

Centralized remote authentication services add an extra layer of protection between the remote access clients and the private, internal network. Remote authentication and authorization services using a centralized server are different and separated from the similar services used for network clients locally. This is important because in the event a remote access server is compromised, the entire network's authentication and authorization services are unaffected. A few leading examples are RADIUS and TACACS+.

- **RADIUS:** Dial-up users pass login credentials to a RADIUS server for authentication. This is similar to the process used by domain clients sending login credentials to a domain controller for authentication, although RADIUS is no longer limited to dial-up users.

- **Diameter:** Diameter is essentially the successor to RADIUS. One significant improvement Diameter provides is added reliability.

- **TACACS:** This is an alternative to RADIUS. TACACS is available in three versions: original TACACS, Extended TACACS (XTACACS), and TACACS+. TACACS integrates the authentication and authorization processes. XTACACS keeps the authentication, authorization, and accounting processes separate. TACACS+ improves XTACACS by adding two-factor authentication. TACACS+ is the most current and relevant version of this product line.

Virtual Private Network

A VPN is a communication tunnel through an untrusted network and establishes a secure, point-to-point connection with authentication and protected data traffic. Most VPNs use encryption to protect the encapsulated traffic, but encryption is not necessary for the connection to be considered a VPN.

The most common application of VPNs is to establish secure communications through the Internet between two distant networks. There are other examples and uses of VPNs that should be appreciated

- Inside a private network for added layers of data protection

- Between end-user systems connected to an ISP

- The link between two entire private networks

- Provide security for legacy applications that rely on risky or vulnerable communication protocols or methodologies, especially when communication is across a network

- Provide confidentiality and integrity, but not availability, over insecure or untrusted intermediary networks

Tunneling

The concept of tunneling is fundamental to understanding how VPN works. Tunneling is the network communications process that encapsulates a packet of data with another protocol to protect the initial packet. The encapsulation is what creates the logical illusion of a communications tunnel over the untrusted intermediary network, i.e., the traffic is only visible to the systems on either end of the tunnel. At the ends of the tunnel, the initial protocol packet is encapsulated and de-encapsulated to accomplish communication.

A physical world analogy to help illustrate tunneling is the traditional U.S. postal service. A letter is the initial data protocol. The envelope it is mailed with is the tunneling protocol. The transport through the postal distribution system is the untrusted intermediary network. If all goes well, the letter is received by the intended recipient, and no unauthorized personnel viewed the contents.

In situations where bypassing a firewall, gateway, proxy, or other networking device is warranted, tunneling is used. The authorized data is encapsulated, and the transmission is permitted even though access inside the tunnel is restricted. An advantage of tunneling is that traffic control devices cannot block or drop the communications because they cannot interrogate the packet contents. This can be useful in streamlining important content and connections. However, this capability is also a potential security problem, as security devices meant to protect the private network from malicious content cannot scan the packets as they arrive or leave. This is particularly true if tunneling involves encryption. The sensitive data will maintain confidentiality and integrity. However, again, the data is unreadable by networking devices.

TIP Tunneling can be used to create a routable solution with minimal protocols for non-routable protocols because the nonroutable primary packet is encapsulated by a routing protocol.

The inability of security professionals to monitor the content of traffic within the tunnel is not the only concern with tunneling. There is an increased amount of message overhead when using multiple protocols. Each one probably has its own error detection, error handling, acknowledgment, and session management elements. This adds to complexity and processing time. The tunnel packet is larger in size or length than a normal data packet. This calls for more bandwidth resources that compete with other network resources. Network saturation and bottlenecking can happen quickly. In addition, tunneling is a point-to-point communication mechanism and is not designed to handle broadcast traffic.

How VPNs Work

From understanding tunneling, a better appreciation of how VPN works is possible. A VPN link is possible to connect any network communication connection. This is discussed in the portion of this chapter regarding telecommunications because a VPN can connect a remote access employee client across the Internet to the company private network.

VPNs can also be established over wired cabling connections, wireless connections, a remote access dial-up connection, or a WAN link. The connections are established using in-line VPN devices or appliances added to a network for the purpose of creating and monitoring the VPN tunnels separately from server or client OSs. The logical connection provides services and access much like a direct local connection. The performance differences may be significant because connection speeds may be slower based on constraints of the intermediary network. The protections provided by VPNs are only effective within the tunnel, so when the VPN connects two separate networks, internal network security policies are relevant. Traffic is unprotected within the source network, protected between the border VPN servers, and then unprotected again once it reaches the destination network. The start and end connection points for VPN are on remote access servers or firewalls on the network's border. The key point is that one network may have lower security requirements than the other. The VPN connection does not necessarily mitigate the variation.

The Proliferation of Tunneling

Normal use of Internet services and corporate networks permits daily use of tunneling that is almost transparent to regular end users. There are many common uses. Many websites resolve the connection over a SSL or TLS connection. That is an example of tunneling. The cleartext web communications are tunneled within an SSL or TLS session. With Internet telephony or VoIP systems, voice communication is being encapsulated inside a VoIP protocol.

VPN links provide a cost-effective and secure pathway through the Internet for the connection of two or more separated networks. This efficiency is measured against the higher costs of creating direct or leased point-to-point solutions. Additionally, the VPN links can be connected across multiple ISPs.

Common VPN Protocols

VPNs can be implemented using software or hardware solutions. In either case, there are variations and combinations based on how the tunnel is implemented. There are four common VPN protocols that provide a foundational view of how VPNs are built:

- **PPTP:** Data link layer (layer 2) use on IP networks
- **L2TP:** Data link layer (layer 2) use on any LAN protocol
- **IPSec:** Network layer (layer 3) use on IP networks

Point-to-Point Tunneling Protocol (PPTP)

This was developed from the dial-up protocol called Point-to-Point Protocol (PPP). It encapsulates traffic at the data link layer (layer 2) of the OSI model and is used on IP networks. It encapsulates the PPP packets and creates a point-to-point tunnel connecting two separate systems. PPTP protects the authentication traffic using the same authentication protocols supported by PPP:

- Microsoft Challenge Handshake Authentication Protocol (MS-CHAP)
- CHAP
- PAP
- EAP
- Shiva Password Authentication Protocol (SPAP)

TIP Microsoft used proprietary modifications to develop Microsoft Point-to-Point Encryption (MPPE). This protocol should not be confused with the version of PPTP in the RFC 2637 standard.

NOTE Something to be aware of is that session establishment for PTPP is not encrypted. The authentication process shares the IP addresses of sender and receiver in cleartext. The packets may even contain usernames and hashed passwords, any of which could be intercepted by a MitM attack.

Layer 2 Tunneling Protocol

Layer 2 Tunneling Protocol (L2TP) was derived to create a point-to-point tunnel to connect disparate networks. This protocol does not employ encryption, so it does not provide confidentiality or strong authentication. In conjunction with IPSec, those services are possible. IPSec with L2TP is a common security structure. L2TP also supports TACACS+ and RADIUS. A most recent version, L2TPv3, improves upon security features to include improved encapsulation and the ability to use communication technologies like Frame Relay, Ethernet, and ATM, other than simply PPP over an IP network.

IP Security (IPSec) Protocol

IPSec is both a standalone VPN protocol and the security mechanism for L2TP. It is limited to use with IP traffic. However, it is the most common VPN protocol in use today. IPSec has more of the desired security features like secured authentication, and it enables encrypted data transmission. IPSec has two primary components, or functions:

- **Authentication Header (AH):** Provides authentication, integrity, and nonrepudiation. The primary purpose of the AH is to confirm the origin source of the packet. Also, it ensures the contents of both the header and the payload have not changed. In short, the AH provides integrity.

- **Encapsulating Security Payload (ESP):** Provides encryption to protect the confidentiality of transmitted data, but it can also perform limited authentication. The ESP provides confidentiality and typically encrypts the payload but not the packet header. Following the IP header is the ESP header, which includes a sequence number. After the ESP header is the payload data and then the integrity check. Padding may be included if necessary.

NOTE ESP actually operates at the network layer (layer 3). It has the added flexibility to operate in transport mode or tunnel mode. In transport mode, the IP packet data is encrypted, but the header of the packet is not. In tunnel mode, the entire IP packet is encrypted, and a new header is added to the packet to govern transmission through the tunnel. Each has its own benefits depending on the available network bandwidth and sensitivity of the information.

Data Communications

How a network is designed results in the various communication topologies discussed earlier in the chapter. The decisions to guide choices about which topologies are most appropriate are based on significant variables like cost, data use, protocols supported, fault tolerance, risk, and access to equipment, as examples.

When data is in storage, referred to as *at rest* or in a *static* form, it is easier to secure than when it is in motion or in transit. There are logical and technical controls for access and encryption that are used. Physical controls are important to prevent environmental factors like heat or water from corrupting stored data. Locked storage areas are additional physical controls an organization will want to use. In these ways, data files can be safeguarded to remain confidential, retain their integrity, and be available to authorized users. Security becomes more difficult once data is transmitted by an application or system, especially if the data exits the private network into the Internet.

Telnet

Telnet provides bidirectional, interactive, text-oriented communication over the Internet or within a private network over TCP. It is a client-server protocol that uses port 23 typically. Although it is widely supported, there are serious security concerns with the use of telnet, to include lack of encryption and authentication.

Secure Shell

SSH is a replacement for telnet. The SSH tunnel protects the integrity of communication, preventing session hijacking and other MitM attacks. SSH is also a client-server architecture that is often used to accomplish remote command-line login and remote command execution. Any network service can be secured with SSH. The protocol specification distinguishes between two major versions, referred to as SSH-1 and SSH-2.

TIP   SSH can be used with FTP to encrypt both commands and data to achieve Secure File Transfer Protocol (SFTP).

SOCKS

SOCKS is a protocol used for networking through a proxy server. SOCKSv5 is the current protocol version that also provides authentication. While SOCKS as a protocol does not provide encryption, if the server employing it does, then SOCKS facilitates its use. It can be used with almost any application.

Secure Sockets Layer (SSL) and Transport Layer Security (TLS)

Secure Sockets Layer (SSL) is a session-oriented legacy protocol that can be used to secure web, email, FTP, or even Telnet traffic. SSL is still in broad use despite having known security weaknesses, but it is being replaced by TLS. TLS functions in the same general manner as SSL, but it uses stronger authentication and encryption protocols. Rather than establishing a VPN using IPSec at the network layer and requiring each remote user to have a client installed, SSL or TLS is used to create an on-demand tunnel. Remote users need no client installed, and access to the private network is via a web browser.

SSL and TLS both have the following features:

- Support secure client-server communications across an insecure network while preventing tampering, spoofing, and eavesdropping

- Support one-way authentication using digital certificates

- Support two-way authentication using digital certificates

- Often implemented as the initial payload of a TCP package, allowing it to encapsulate all higher-layer protocol payloads.

- Can be implemented at lower layers, such as the network layer (layer 3) to operate as a VPN. This implementation is known as OpenVPN.

In addition, TLS can be used to encrypt UDP and Session Initiation Protocol (SIP) connections. SSL/TLS encrypted sessions are the preferred mechanism for secure e-commerce.

NOTE X.25 is a rapidly declining technology that once had a significant place in the communication of data. Today, it is important only to recognize as a building block on which modern communication frameworks are built. X.25 is a protocol that supports packet switching. It was designed in an era when users accessed large computers like mainframes with lightweight (dumb) terminals. Its main feature was robust error checking, which also made it very heavy with processing overhead.

Frame Relay

This framework uses packet switching to perform wide area networking, connecting networks operating at physical and data link layers of the digital communication channels. Frame relay has another utility: it often serves to connect LANs with major backbones. It connects separate wide area networks and private network environments with leased lines over T-1 lines. It requires a dedicated connection during the transmission period. Frame relay is sometimes used for video and voice, but it is not best suited for that because it does not provide steady flow transmission.

Frame Relay originated as an extension of ISDN in that frame relay integrates a packet-switched network capability over circuit-switched technology. The technology has become a standalone and cost-effective means of creating a WAN. Devices within the private network performing frame relay services are called *data circuit-terminating equipment* (DCE). Devices that connect to the frame relay DCEs are called *data terminal equipment* (DTE).

TIP Packet-switching technologies use virtual circuits instead of dedicated physical circuits. A virtual circuit is created only when needed, which makes for efficient use of the transmission medium and is extremely cost-effective. The confidentiality of virtual circuits is only as strong as the configuration and implementation. A virtual circuit still means physical circuits are shared among several customers. It is uncommon but very possible that, for example, a misconfigured frame relay can mean one customer's broadcast packets end up within another customer's internal network. The best way to ensure confidentiality is to utilize a VPN to encrypt traffic sent over a shared virtual circuit.

Asynchronous Transfer Mode

This is a high-speed networking standard that can support both voice and data communications. It was designed to integrate telecommunication and computer networks. ATM is normally utilized by Internet service providers on their private long-distance networks. ATM operates mostly at the data link layer (layer 2) and is utilized over either fiber or twisted-pair cable.

ATM is different from other data link technologies, in particular Ethernet. ATM utilizes no routing. It uses special-purpose hardware called ATM switches that establish point-to-point connections between endpoints. Data flows directly from source to destination. Another interesting difference is that Ethernet packets are variable in length. ATM uses asynchronous time-division multiplexing and encodes data into small, fixed-sized cells at 53 bytes each. Forty-eight bytes carry the data payload, and 5 bytes are header information.

The performance of ATM is often expressed in the form of optical carrier (OC) levels, written as "OC-xxx." Performance levels as high as 10 Gbps (OC-192) are technically feasible with ATM. More common performance levels for ATM are 155 Mbps (OC-3) and 622 Mbps (OC-12). ATM traffic has several components to ensure QoS. There are four basic types:

- **Constant bit rate (CBR):** A Peak Cell Rate (PCR) is specified, which is constant.

- **Variable bit rate (VBR):** An average or Sustainable Cell Rate (SCR) is specified, which can peak at a certain level, a PCR, for a maximum interval before being problematic.

- **Available bit rate (ABR):** A minimum guaranteed rate is specified.

- **Unspecified bit rate (UBR):** Traffic is allocated to all remaining transmission capacity.

ATM has design capabilities for a network that must handle both traditional high-throughput data traffic and real-time, low-latency content such as voice and video. ATM operates at the three lowest layers of the OSI model: the network layer, the data link layer, and the physical layer. ATM is a core protocol used over the Synchronous Optical Networking (SONET) and Synchronous Digital Hierarchy (SDH) backbone of the PSTN and ISDN. SONET/SDH are standardized multiplexing protocols that transfer multiple digital bit streams over optical fiber using lasers or light-emitting diodes (LEDs).

ATM provides functionality that is similar to both circuit-switching and packet-switching networks. ATM uses a connection-oriented model in which a virtual circuit must be established between two endpoints before the actual data exchange begins. These virtual circuits may be permanent, i.e., dedicated connections that are usually preconfigured by the service provider, or switched, meaning set up on a per-call basis using signaling and disconnected when the call is terminated.

Multiprotocol Label Switching (MPLS)

We have covered the advantages and strengths of ATM and frame relay. But MPLS seems to capture the benefits of both. Similar to frame relay, MPLS uses labels to direct traffic. While still retaining the speed of ATM, MPLS does so without having to rely on packaging data in cells. In the context of the OSI layers, MPLS is labeled a layer 2.5 protocol, since it operates squarely between the common definitions of data link (layer 2) and the network (layer 3) protocols.

Virtualized Networks

Virtualization technology uses the memory of a single host computer to host one or more operating systems. Almost any operating system can be hosted on any hardware under this construct. The operating system in this scenario is called a *guest* operating system. There can be multiple operating systems running on one hardware host computer, all of which are considered guests. The operating systems, host and guests, can differ on the same virtual machine. Some examples of operating systems that work together well on the same platform are VMware, Microsoft's Virtual PC, Microsoft Virtual Server, Hyper-V with Windows Server 2008, VirtualBox, and Parallels. Other services and applications can be virtualized. Virtualization can be used to host servers, limited user interfaces such as virtual desktops, applications, and more.

To the normal end user, the use of virtualized servers and services, as opposed to physical assets, is indistinguishable. Virtualization has several benefits, which include speed and scalability, resource efficiency to launch individual instances of servers or services on demand, and being able to run the exact operating system versions needed for the particular application.

Virtual environments are resilient in that recovery from damaged, crashed, or corrupted virtual systems is often quick and inexpensive. The virtual system's main hard drive file is replaced with a clean backup version. Then the virtual system is relaunched.

Related to system and data resiliency, virtualization presents security benefits. Backups of the entire system are easier to make and recover than the physical systems. Errors or problems in virtual systems are easily remedied. Developers and system owners can typically tear down and rebuild virtual environments in minutes because of the architecture and technologies. If a virtual system is compromised, the operating system is rarely impacted, and remediation is quick and efficient.

As operating system virtualization has proven effective, virtualization has expanded to encompass other opportunities, such as virtualized networks. A virtualized network or network virtualization is the combination of hardware and software networking components into a single integrated entity. The system that results is managed by software control over all network functions including management, traffic shaping, address assignment, and more. A physical presence at all the hardware locations is no longer needed. A single management console or interface can be used to oversee every aspect of the network.

TIP   Cloud computing is a form of virtualization, and some cloud experts also refer to the host and guest as the *parent* and *child*.

Software-Defined Networking

SDN is an approach to network operation, design, and management that models flexibility and choice. A traditional networking concept is to configure at the device, like on a router or switch. This is complex and requires a lot of administration. Because of training and competency requirements, organizations have to use one vendor or one product line to be proficient and avoid device incompatibility.

Using SDN removes the traditional networking concepts of IP addressing, subnets, routing, and the like from needing to be programmed into or deciphered by hosted applications. It also improves the ability to respond to changes in threats, to adapt quickly to dynamic physical and business conditions, and to take advantage of best available technology.

The purpose of SDN is to separate hardware and hardware-based settings from the network services of data transmission. It splits traditional network traffic into three components categorized as raw data, data transmission method, and data purpose. There are three planes, or layers, of the SDN architecture:

- **Infrastructure layer (data plane):** Network switches and routers and the data itself as well as the process of forwarding data to the appropriate destination

- **Control layer (control plane):** The intelligence in devices that works in true intermediary fashion, determining how traffic should flow based on the status of the infrastructure layer and the requirements specified by the application layer

- **Application layer (application plane):** Network services, utilities, and applications that interface with the control level to specify needs and requirements

Of course, using SDN has security implications along with its benefits. With this architecture being so flexible and scalable, it is not uncommon for SDN to be configured incorrectly. The consequence of misconfiguring SDN leads to the problem's discovery: unexpected flows of network traffic. Traffic intended to be on one area of the network is discovered to be on another part of the network. This issue occurs easily with hardware, but it doesn't with SDN.

Another perceived weakness of SDN is the lack of one common standard or implementation. Again, given its extreme flexibility, the absence of one way of doing things is not a surprise. Still, there are standards. One of the first SDN standards is OpenFlow. OpenFlow started out as a way of defining how the control plane works with the data plane. OpenFlow defines its interaction with the data plane into two separate "directions." OpenFlow works with the switches and routers (whether virtual or physical) through Southbound application programming interfaces (APIs). Along the same lines, OpenFlow works with the network's business logic through Northbound APIs.

Virtual Machine

A VM, also known as the *guest*, is a software program or operating system that emulates the behavior of a self-contained device. It is capable of performing the tasks of running applications and programs as if it were a separate physical computer with a full complement of hard drive, memory, network interfaces, and processing power. In reality, the VM is often just one of multiple guests sharing resources on a physical host.

Hypervisor

The hypervisor or virtual machine monitor (VMM) is a piece of computer software, firmware, or hardware that creates and runs VMs. A host machine would have a hypervisor managing one or more VMs. The hypervisor isolates each operating system and abstracts those from the underlying hardware of the host machine. This facilitates multiple guest operating systems (OSs) running independently on a single host computer simultaneously.

Virtualization has delivered capability, scalability, and cost saving to many organizations that have invested in the technologies:

- There is a significant reduction in the costs of software and hardware, as separate physical servers for each application or operating system are not needed. A single large server host can be virtualized into numerous component VM guests.

- A reduction in actual number of physical servers results in a reduction of energy consumption.

- Security controls are more efficiently implemented and maintained in a reduced inventory of physical assets.

- Installation and configuration management of VMs is more rapid and flexible than that of a physical one.

- Fault tolerance is improved, as an error made inside a VM cannot affect its host system and, therefore, the operating system of the host machine doesn't break — nor should the other guest systems.

- VMs improve resiliency of the computing platforms, as relocation of a VM from one site or host to another is easy.

If the hypervisor runs directly on top of the bare-metal computer, this hypervisor is called a Type 1 hypervisor or simply a *bare-metal* hypervisor. If the hypervisor runs as an application on a host operating system, then it is a Type 2 hypervisor.

Virtual Applications

Applications can be run in a virtual configuration. This means that the application is not installed in the traditional manner. The application operates as it would in traditional implementations on physical servers using dedicated resourcing components. The virtualized application behaves at runtime like it is directly interfacing with the original operating system and all the resources managed by it. However, being virtualized, it is isolated or sandboxed. The isolation makes the application portable and able to operate without the full installation of the original host operating system. The VM containing the application has access to the host operating system.

A type of virtualized application is the virtual desktop interface. That term can refer to at least three different types of technology:

- A remote access tool that grants the user access to a distant computer system by allowing remote viewing and control of the distant desktop's display, keyboard, mouse, and so on

- Encapsulation of multiple applications in a desktop presentation or shell for portability or across operating system operation. This technology offers some of the features and benefits of one platform without requiring users to use multiple computers, manage dual-booting of a system, or virtualize an entire OS platform.

- An extended or expanded desktop larger than the display being used allows the user to employ multiple application layouts, switching between them using keystrokes or mouse movements.

Special consideration should be taken when choosing applications intended to monitor virtual networks. While a traditional network monitor controls traffic on the wire, virtual networks operate in the cloud or virtually. Without hardware to "tap," information passes from VM to VM, making network monitoring a special challenge.

VMs often move across the network unencrypted. This brings another issue unique to virtual networks. If, for example, an administrator was to restore a VM across the network, that VM is transported in the clear. Therefore, that whole system image could be intercepted. The probability is appreciably low, given how infrequently VMs are restored, how large the file is, and how fortunate an attacker's placement of a sniffer would have to be to capture it. Still, the risk exists.

Trojaned Virtual Appliances or Machines

VMs are not impervious to security concerns. One example is Trojaned virtual appliances. This malicious attack refers to infected or prepacked software packages that lure users to download and run them as VMs. It can be a massive security concern for both private and public cloud environments. Trojaned virtual appliances provide hackers an entry point into virtual or cloud environments. The attacker can scan the environment to locate vulnerabilities for exploitation. To protect against these attacks, a security professional should do the following:

- Allow and use only tested and verified VMs from trusted sources.
- Monitor for properly configured hypervisor and other network configurations. Use advanced settings to disable unused functionality.
- Include VM environments within the overall defense in depth architecture behind firewalls, endpoint protection, and intrusion prevention systems, for example. Strict access control to the host, guest, and between guests is also an imperative.

Virtual Machine Jumping or Hyperjumping

Another group of VM vulnerabilities or potential security issues presented by VM environments is VM jumping, which is also called *hyperjumping* or *guest escape*. These attacks happen because of the misconfiguration of the environment, especially the hypervisor. If the VM environment is not configured properly, traffic from one VM can be delivered to other VMs and create added vulnerabilities. Traditional methods or applications intended to monitor networking through hardware links fail to deliver when monitoring virtual networking and VMs. The hypervisor, using APIs common to the VMs, is vulnerable and a common target for attackers.

Access controls and restrictions have to be in place because of the hypervisor's singular reach and control over all the shared resources. In cases where multiple customers are using VMs on a multitenant host, there is the added risk of data leakage. In all cases, VM jumping exploits allow one or more guest VMs to be compromised, and then the attacker has access to other VMs in the shared resources environment.

NOTE The combination and integration of hardware and software resources leads to significant efficiency. However, some argue that the increased integrations have created a loss of visibility for network and security monitors to audit workload over innumerable virtual instances.

Cloud Computing

Cloud computing is a form of Internet-based computing in which a large number of computers are connected in public and private networks to provide a scalable infrastructure for storage, applications, and data. Many of the principles of VM computing make cloud computing an attractive option for organizations.

Cloud computing offers significant advantages, such as the following:

- **Reduced cost:** Expenditures needed to own hardware and software, establishing on-site data centers and requiring energy for power and cooling, are traded for leasing options, often at significantly lower cost.

- **Speed:** Services and infrastructure are available as needed or on demand. Launching a new environment is as easy as a few mouse clicks.

- **Global scale:** In a distributed, worldwide model, leading cloud providers operate at a level that can ensure the delivery of IT resources across the globe with plenty of storage, bandwidth, and computing power within a massive infrastructure. The proficiency for management of the environments, including security, is also on a global scale.

- **Reliability:** Disaster recovery and data backup are built into cloud solutions and tend to be easy and less expensive than an organization operating production data centers with sufficient recovery and backup in house.

NIST Special Publication 800-145 seeks to establish their vision of the traits, or "essential characteristics," of cloud computing. Essential characteristics of cloud computing, per NIST 800-145, are as follows:

- **On-demand service:** This is the ability to turn a service on or off when the customer needs it.

- **Broad access:** This means being able to access those services as needed, wherever needed. There shouldn't be a localized restriction on access.

- **Pooled resources:** The customer is served resources, but those resources are not unique to the customer. Multitenancy requires that resources such as network and storage capacity and CPU processing be combined and shared among customers.

- **Elasticity:** This is similar to on-demand service but refers more to the ability to scale up or down as the customer's needs require.

- **Measured service:** As these services and resources are not delivered free of charge, they need to be monitored and calculated. Those measurements determine actions such as billing and capacity planning.

Cloud Computing Service Models

Cloud computing services are grouped into three categories:

- **SaaS:** This model offers the delivery of software applications and systems with a web portal access point for organizations and end users. The cloud provider manages the entire backend of the system from updates to security patching. Security professionals within the customer organization retain responsibility for access control and oversight of third-party risk management of the cloud service provider. Because SaaS can accessed anywhere, including unsecured, public venues, the risk of credentials being intercepted is higher. Controls most suited to mitigate this risk include two-factor authentication and end-to-end encryption.

- **PaaS:** With PaaS, cloud providers offer an on-demand development environment that can be used to develop and test a software application. Software developers use PaaS to develop mobile or web applications. The organization manages access control, but the provider will keep the platforms up to date with security patching and upgrade installs. Some control over monitoring and auditing is available for customer organizations. However, the primary concern with PaaS is protecting data integrity. As with SaaS, the control to mitigate integrity is encryption.

- **Infrastructure as a service (IaaS):** This model provides leased IT infrastructure as needed. The infrastructure includes servers, VMs, operating systems, storage, network, and so on. The customer organization has a shared responsibility for keeping security patches current and resources upgraded. Access controls, particularly as they relate to the operating systems and applications running on the infrastructure, are also the customer's responsibility. Additional ability to monitor ingress, egress, and intra-environment traffic is also facilitated for customers. The customer must install all the software, including both operating systems and applications. With IaaS, multitenancy is all but guaranteed, and so isolation of resources between tenants is critical. Because of this, the key vulnerability inherent in multitenancy IaaS is the shared technology. As IaaS providers provide infrastructure, some basic parts, like the CPU or GPU, are not designed with isolation in mind. Storage at least can be segmented into logical units to provide low-level isolation. With processing, isolation is more difficult. Controlling this risk comes with employing defense in depth.

Cloud Computing Security Concerns

Several organizations provide guidance regarding the security concerns of cloud computing. The Cloud Security Alliance (CSA) is a not-for-profit organization that offers a controls matrix of security controls. The Cloud Controls Matrix Group is the established body responsible for the control matrix. Another organization that publishes best practices papers on cloud computing is the European Union Agency for Network and Information Security (ENISA). An example of helpful published material from ENISA is their "Security for SMEs." The paper includes a guide and scenario-based tools for small-to-medium-sized enterprises wanting to better appreciate security concerns of cloud computing.

As a security professional, it is important to develop and implement security controls that address the chief concerns and enable organizations to capture the efficiencies and computing power of the cloud. Some of the most prominent of these concerns are the following:

- **Data breaches:** As security controls shift to cloud service providers, ultimate responsibility for data protection does not. Organizations must address the changing nature of required controls. Increased emphasis on maintaining access controls and credential hygiene are typically the sole responsibility of the organization. Data breaches can occur from poorly developed APIs, as data moves in and out of applications and systems. In fact, when a data breach is announced that involves a cloud service provider, the root cause is typically a misconfiguration or failure to protect credentials and privileges that the organization controls.

- **Control of data:** Depending on the industry or country in which an organization operates, many decision-makers are reluctant to use cloud service providers because they perceive a loss of control over the data use, have concern that data is comingled with other data stores using shared resources in the virtualized environments, and anticipate an inability to account for or delete data when they are required to do so. In environments where virtual and physical functions are comingled, you run into the same risks discussed in SDN: a high probability of misconfiguration.

- **Hijacking of accounts:** Related to data breaches, a phishing attack, for instance, may result in obtained user credentials and elevated privileges. The unauthorized access appears as a valid user, causing confusion for security monitoring and alerting. Other types of malicious attacks attempt to harvest valid credentials.

- **Malware injection:** In traditional web portal and website attacks, attackers inject malware scripts to try to cause disruption or break into the backend of the site. In a cloud environment, the attack vector and the objectives are similar. IaaS and PaaS solutions are targets for various malware injection attempts because the customer has the ability to install applications themselves. If an attack is successful, the intruder can compromise the integrity of the sensitive data on the cloud. An administrator can expect the virtual IDS or IPS will detect and alert on malware, but if those systems should fail, the risk of malware injection greatly increases. Defense in depth and redundancy should reduce the risk.

- **Data loss:** Cloud service providers should improve the disaster recovery and resiliency capabilities of an organization. To avoid complete data loss if the cloud provider experiences a natural or man-made disaster, the organization should initially and periodically review the cloud service provider's backup procedures as they relate to physical storage locations, physical access, and physical disasters. Additionally, sometimes a cloud customer wants to leave their current CSP for another, but they can't easily migrate their data. This is known as data loss because of vendor lock-in.

- **Insecure APIs:** APIs offer the ability for organizations to customize portions of their cloud experiences by creating interfaces with the cloud environment. The APIs also impact authentication, provide access, and effect encryption. Programmers and developers have to make sure to implement security controls along with the use of APIs so as not to inadvertently expose the cloud environment.

- **Insufficient due diligence:** While security concerns in the cloud seem to be technical, a large area of vulnerability is in contract or vendor management. The relationship between customer and cloud service provider has a sliding scale of operational and security responsibilities, depending on which cloud model the company is using. Figure 4.17 demonstrates the relationship. Under no model does security responsibility completely leave the customer organization supplying the data. When the responsibility is amplified by obligations based on jurisdiction, industry, or type of data, the company has to take care to perform due diligence. The cloud provider has to perform based on established service level agreements for data availability, vulnerability management, access control for cloud service workforce, and physical controls, to name a few. An additional important security control many cloud providers have to adhere to is data breach notification timelines. In short, the company contracting for cloud services has the responsibility to monitor and measure the cloud services' compliance with these types of contract terms and conditions.

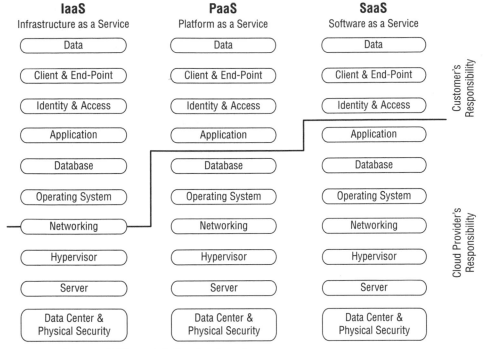

FIGURE 4.17 Responsibility matrix for cloud versions

Controls for Cloud Security

If an organization decides to implement a cloud solution, almost regardless of which model (SaaS, IaaS, or PaaS), the organization must be able to decide whether they can extend their security controls to the cloud solution. Many argue that this approach is impossible, as on-premises controls do not scale to cloud environments. However, general principles such as protection and oversight for access and authentication controls, as an example, are going to remain the customer's job. In other cases, the organization may choose to levy the inherited controls from the cloud provider, like DLP as a service. Some cloud providers and provider solutions do not offer a choice. The organization can use only the security controls provided and administered by the cloud service provider. This is a decision the organization will have to make based on risk tolerance, industry and jurisdiction, and cost.

In general terms, there are some security controls that organizations can expect to maintain no matter which cloud service option is chosen:

- **Access and authorization control:** To provide rigorous oversight to accounts and privileges, access should be limited and controlled. Key management systems can help safeguard tokens and certificates. Developers can be made to use single-use credentials in order to publish software code into production. The bottom line is that the organization is always responsible for who has access and how much authority they are granted.

- **Logging and auditing:** Cloud service providers are probably not going to give customers access to a wide variety of network logs. Even if they provide access or actually deliver the audit logs in a data stream to the organization's SIEM, some of the intelligence and alerts will be the responsibility of the customer to analyze and take action on.

- **Cryptographic key establishment and management:** Whether stored in the cloud or stored on the premises and used in the cloud, the organization will retain the responsibility to properly establish and manage cryptographic keys. Security personnel will develop scanning and auditing processes to attempt to discover improper use or misplacement of security keys outside of sanctioned storage.

- **Incident response:** The organization will not be excused from regulatory or other contractual obligations if the cloud service provider fails to notify or conduct incident response in a timely manner. The organization has to manage this expectation so it can meet the incident response requirements that cannot be delegated to the vendor.

Cloud Access Security Broker (CASB) Technology

A Cloud Access Security Broker (CASB) helps organizations extend on-premises controls or transform controls to the various cloud environments. A CASB does this by acting as a go-between, being a middleman between the cloud customer and the service provider.

Even when the cloud provider does not allow custom solutions for security, a CASB can augment security controls by monitoring for ingress and egress of data and services used in the cloud. A CASB is primarily a software solution that discovers unauthorized attempts at accessing private data. It can also use machine learning to watch human behavior on the network and alert security administrators when abnormal behavior happens and a threat is suspected. CASBs are not strictly only software. A CASB could be an external partner with people operating the service.

In terms of visibility, CASBs provide the first measure of visibility into all the cloud applications being used by an organization, sometimes including unsanctioned use. Regarding unsanctioned use or unauthorized abuse, access and authentication is the responsibility of the customer organization. To assist with that, CASBs may support account maintenance.

CASBs help determine how cloud solutions and services align with the organization's own established workflows. Sometimes an organization cannot overcome the challenge of merging internal processes with potentially useful cloud services. A CASB can, in that scenario, assist with enterprise integration.

CASBs can also provide functionality, such as data security and threat protection. In a manner similar to how SIEM systems use threat intelligence to provide alerting, the CASB draws upon numerous sources to evaluate URLs and services that users attempt to access to provide a risk assessment rating to security personnel. Decisions can be made on whether or not to blacklist (block access) or sanction (allow access) based on the value of the access versus the risk of damage that is incurred. CASBs do this work rapidly. A manual review of logs to glean out the relevant data is impossible if done by a human manually. In short, CASBs offer a single platform for extending or enhancing your security posture for data and assets in the cloud.

SUMMARY

Communication and network security used to be restricted to protecting assets and information within the physical confines of the company. Today, the boundaries of a corporation have changed dramatically. Companies might have workers at home, in coffee shops, or in hotel lobbies. The boundaries of a company extend far beyond its physical buildings, so the structures, transmission methods, transport formats, and security methods used to provide confidentiality, integrity, and availability for transmissions over public and private communications networks and media have changed to accommodate those extended boundaries.

This chapter contains fundamental concepts such as telephony, data communications, the different layers of the OSI model, and transmission media and protocols. Understanding the historical development of communications technology interfaces, interoperability, and high-level approaches to leverage security controls to make everything work together and safeguard information are invaluable for network security professionals.

The nature of communications and network security are always changing. Security professionals need to develop skills in improving and administering remote access, virtualization, and cloud services to enable new business and workplace models. Along with these information technology changes come security challenges and opportunities. One of the foundational concepts that continue to underscore proper security management is that no single solution satisfies all gaps. A security professional has to understand the layered solution approach that describes defense in depth. Access control, authentication, and encryption, for example, work together to extend corporate computing borders, allow employees to work from anywhere, and reduce costs of providing information security. The nature of security attacks will also continue to evolve. In this chapter we discussed several types of attacks, like DDoS, MitM, and phishing, to underscore the importance and the dynamic nature of information security as a profession. As the threats change, so must the approaches to thwarting them.

Identity and Access Management

DOMAIN 5, IDENTITY AND Access Management (IAM), deals with who gets access to what assets at which locations, for how long, and for what purpose. It also addresses ensuring that a person or entity who requests access to an asset actually is who they claim to be. These matters are the essence of IAM.

This chapter discusses the theoretical foundation of these concepts, their historical development, and professional practice today. It also refers you to well-established bodies of practice, standards, and professional organizations and consortia that help all of us advance IAM practice.

This chapter will examine the core aspects of IAM, beginning with the foundational concept of controlling physical and logical access to assets. Then it will delve into the essential practice of managing the identification and authentication of people, devices, and services. Next it will explore integrating identity as a third-party service and implementing and managing authorization mechanisms. Finally, it will discuss managing the identity and access provisioning lifecycle.

As one technical topic after another is explored in this chapter, it will become evident that IAM is involved to some degree in every part of an organization's security arrangements. From basic architecture design to the details of your network defenses, your choices about who can see, use, or alter your organization's assets and services will determine just how effective your security turns out to be.

CONTROL PHYSICAL AND LOGICAL ACCESS TO ASSETS

Everyone has real-life experience with access management, in which a *subject* (you, perhaps) controls access to an *object* (your home, say, or your bank account). Some controls are physical, such as a door lock, a vault, or a detective control such as an alarm. A logical control can be a password that unlocks a folder (or lets you log in), a decryption key, or a list of authorized individuals. Controls can also be a hybrid combination of physical and logical controls, such as the door locks in some modern homes or hotel rooms that require the use of a mobile app to unlock them.

Another factor to consider about the management of physical logical controls is whether the information about those controls should itself be centralized, decentralized, or a hybrid. Think, for example, of the electronic door locks common to hotel rooms these days. To read the key card, the lock has a simple computer inside it. But is the lock's electronic card reader connected, with or without wires, to the front desk, or even to a server at hotel headquarters? In some hotel chains, they are. This makes it easy to change the key code and even make a good guess as to whether the room is occupied at a given moment. Some brands of electronic door, on the other hand, are standalone, requiring someone to physically go to the door and electronically engage it to unlock it, change the code, or download from the lock a record of openings and closings. Each scheme and the many hybrids have pros and cons. One argument for centralized control is economy of scale (in the hotel example, one clerk can set key codes for many rooms). An argument on the side of decentralized control is the potential chaos an attacker could cause if every room in a hotel (or every vault in a museum or bank) were to be unlocked at the same time!

Regardless of whether controls are centralized, the primary purpose when selecting access controls for an asset is to protect the asset's confidentiality, integrity, and/or availability. As a reminder, the three components of the CIA triad are as follows:

- *Confidentiality* is preserving authorized restrictions on information access and disclosure, including means for protecting personal privacy and proprietary information.

- *Integrity* means guarding against improper information modification or destruction and includes ensuring information nonrepudiation and authenticity.
- *Availability* means ensuring timely and reliable access to and use of information by authorized users.

The following sections quickly analyze how each of these three attributes might be at risk if you fail to control access, either physical or logical.

Information

Sound practice requires you to identify and classify the information you need to protect. Identifying what to protect against is part of this. Loss of data confidentiality, integrity, and availability are three different types of loss, and each requires its own type of protection.

For most people, the point of instituting access controls over their information is to protect its confidentiality. Whether dealing with personally identifiable information (PII), such as a bank account number, personal medical data, or the combination to the lock on the server room door at work, the concern generally is information "falling into the wrong hands."

Data integrity can be essential, depending on the context and perspective. However, determining its importance in a given scenario might not always be straightforward. If the job is to protect experimental results relating to, say, nuclear weapons, the nuclear scientists might tell you that their experiments are designed to discover intrinsic characteristics of the physical world. This is critical data to protect from theft, lest nonnuclear states learn shortcuts to making nuclear weapons. But preventing a spy from tampering with the experimental results—changing the reported characteristics of certain fissile material—may seem like a lower priority to the scientists, because repeating well-designed experiments will allow the values to be verified as needed. Data integrity, therefore, may not be the prime concern in this realm.

Similarly, if you are charged with protecting the moment-to-moment figures in the day's stock trading, it is necessary to guard those numbers against all threats so that no one gets an unfair look at the trading strategies of experts. But the data owners might tell you that all stock trades become public very soon after they are completed. Therefore, for stock traders, confidentiality might seem like a lower priority than worrying about whether the markets go down for a few minutes. Similarly, multiple copies of each transaction always exist: a discrepancy between buyer and seller (it happens) tends to be easy to resolve. Availability is the concern here.

There is one final way, often overlooked, in which information itself plays a role in IAM. Careful stewardship of the records of who (or what) requested access to what (or whom) can be the very foundation of sound security. Audit records of all requests and attempts and their outcomes should be protected with care and considered to be at least as sensitive as the most important asset they pertain to. Accountability is an important piece of the management function.

Systems

A system is a collection of hardware, software, algorithms, personnel, policies, budgets, and similar resources that are devoted to accomplishing one or more tasks.

If you are responsible for protecting the information on the system from theft, confidentiality is a significant concern. Similarly, tampering with the chief financial officer's forecast spreadsheets can land the company in terrible trouble. But when dealing with computer systems themselves (and not, say, the data kept on them or produced by them), one phrase that causes serious alarm is "the system is down," which is clearly an availability issue that can result when authentication precautions fail and an intruder is allowed onto the system.

Modern enterprises spend millions or more designing and supporting systems for a wide range of purposes. By the reckoning of some experts, the very definition of a security disaster is that the system is no longer capable of performing the task for which it was acquired—not that it has lost data integrity and not that whatever is secret on it may not stay that way. A true security catastrophe, in this line of thinking, is when the payroll system cannot generate the paychecks, the movie cannot get out over the cable or the airwaves, or a billion users cannot share their opinions on the happenings of the day or photographs of their dinners.

When we are talking about systems and catastrophes, though, we can't restrict ourselves to failures of availability. Some very serious attacks—for example, an attempt to impersonate a trusted system to fake a bank transfer—involve a failure of authenticity. As we discuss later in this chapter, digital certificates are one method of IAM commonly used today to ensure the integrity of system identification.

Confidentiality, too, can relate to systems themselves (in addition to the information they contain). In some circumstances, the very existence of a computer on a network, or a connection to a clandestine subnet, is an important secret to protect. The practice of concealing a system or subnet from unauthorized persons while leaving it available for connection from authorized devices is sometimes called *blackholing*. Authenticating connections into a black-holed system, of course, is a matter for IAM. Digital certificates, simple IP addresses, and other methods are sometimes used for this purpose, as we discuss later.

Whichever system access controls and methods you adopt, you will want to select them based on a carefully considered framework; thereafter, you should implement, monitor, and maintain controls according to accepted best practice. For this purpose, we recommend you investigate adopting an Information Security Management System

(ISMS), a systematic approach to managing sensitive information assets using policies, procedures, guidelines, and associated resources.

Perhaps the best-known ISMS in the world is a set of standards laid out by the International Organization for Standardization (ISO), known as the "27000" family of ISO/IEC standards.

The part of the ISO 27000 series that provides an overview of ISMS concepts and terminology, and pertains specifically to the selection of access controls, is identified (in its latest version) as ISO/IEC 27000:2018, "Information Technology – Security Techniques." ISO, in that document, describes well the many operational, legal, fiscal, and cost-of-opportunity considerations that—among others—should influence your selections. The standard also provides guidance about the administration of controls, including a measurement system used to evaluate performance.

What you will not find—either in ISO standards or in the detailed guidelines available from the National Institute for Standards and Technology in the United States, or NIST (notably Special Publication 800-53, "Recommended Security Controls for Federal Information Systems and Organizations")—is a list of hard requirements, a prescriptive list of "must do's" that relieve you and your organization of the burden of decision. Only in the most tightly regulated industries or governmental do external or even supervising bodies prescribe and require a one-size-fits-all set of controls. As elsewhere in security, you must inventory your assets; evaluate your risks; and then choose, implement, and manage those effective controls best suited to your particular environment and mission.

NOTE The ISO/IEC 27000 family of standards is not distributed free of charge by ISO. The standards are specified in technical documents available for purchase from ISO (see https://www.iso.org/search.html?q=27000) and other distribution channels, such as the American National Standards Institute (see https://webstore.ansi.org/Search/Find?in=1&st=27000%3A2018).

Version 4 of NIST's Special Publication 800-53, "Recommended Security Controls for Federal Information Systems and Organizations,") can be downloaded free of charge at https://csrc.nist.gov/publications/detail/sp/800-53/rev-4/final.

Both the ISO/IEC and NIST (National Institute of Standards and Technology) materials are constantly being reviewed and refined. Be sure to check for updates when procuring these documents.

Devices

Many types of devices exist within a system. Desktop computers, laptops, tablets, keyboards, mice, microphones, speakers, and phones are all devices that people in many organizations use every day. Networks are made up of routers, switches, hubs, servers, and cables (even if these are located at a remote location and accessed through the cloud).

Similarly, archives and storage are made up of discs, tapes, or other hardware (again, even if these are located and accessed remotely). These are all devices.

Just as a significant concern with regard to systems was availability, the availability of the devices that make up those systems ranks as a very high concern as well. Yet, because devices exist in the world of tangible things, you must also worry about how uncontrolled access or damage to the things can interfere with the system.

Uncontrolled access to a disk drive, for example, may allow an adversary to copy the data (which can compromise confidentiality) or to change it undetected (which compromises its integrity). A person could also destroy the device's drive with heat, hyperactivity, or (if direct physical access is gained) even a hammer. If data on such an accessed device hasn't been sufficiently backed up, that poses both an integrity problem and an access problem. Theft of portable devices poses a serious confidentiality concern. Some organizations try to offset the risk of theft by using remote wipe, forced encryption, and similar measures. Such measures are designed to enforce confidentiality, although this is sometimes at the expense of availability if you don't have the right credentials.

Uncontrolled access to a printer may run it out of ink or paper. Similarly, failed access control of almost any device may lead to an exhaustion of its resources. Fortunately, this availability issue is mitigated by the practice of *mobile device management* (MDM), which has grown in response to the difficulty of controlling access to physical devices. We will explore further IAM measures relating to mobile devices throughout this chapter, beginning with our extended view of facilities in the following sections.

Facilities

The security of networks, systems, and physical devices often fundamentally rests on the physical security of the facilities in which those parts of the enterprise reside. Almost all information security measures can be circumvented or overwhelmed if the malefactor has physical access—sustained, unimpeded, unobserved hands-on access—to whatever computer-based asset you are trying to protect.

Measures that protect facilities are sometimes referred to, in the aggregate, as physical access control systems (PACSs). Commonly, the controls include not only physical access control but also visitor management (including logs and badges), intrusion detection, and even video surveillance. In this chapter, which is about IAM, we will focus on the first two of those four topics. We will take up physical access control in this section and cover visitor management in our discussion later of identification cards.

Physical Protection of Classic Facilities

When it comes to the facilities side of IAM, there are some basic security steps you can take. Don't let potential attackers come into physical contact with the computer hardware. Don't let them in the server room. If you can help it, don't let them in the building or even the parking lot. Once your adversary knows where the hardware is and can manipulate that environment or the device itself, your defensive stance is seriously compromised. It is easy to see that, having lost physical control of your facility, the availability, confidentiality, and integrity of your information and other assets are all at risk. Beyond establishing and maintaining good physical barriers and restrictions, also maintain good records of everyone who visits, and attempts to visit, your facilities.

For a large enterprise, many critical assets are kept in data centers and server rooms. The same principle of keeping potential attackers away from the physical hardware applies for large enterprises as well. If you have office buildings filled with cubicles, you need to worry about physical security in those facilities as well. A laptop stolen by a fake job interviewee (which happened to a major credit card company a few years ago) can do a lot of damage if it contains a sensitive database or proprietary algorithms.

Erecting barriers can protect facilities and their contents. Walls are ancient companions to security, as are doors. The selection of the right sort of door lock can add significantly to the physical security of your facility. Here are a few important factors to consider:

- Keypads on doors have been common for decades. They can be quite inexpensive, so long as you do not require them to be connected to a central coordinating service but instead store the numeric passcode locally, right inside the lock.

- Badge-reading door locks are ubiquitous today, typically enabled by either a magnetic credit card–like stripe, or a Radio Frequency ID (RFID) chip embedded in the card (or a hand-carried fob) and read at the door.

- Dual-control door locks add a layer of security by requiring two factors to open them, such as a badge and a passcode.

All electronic door locks raise a policy question, answered perhaps by the fire marshal: when the power goes out, does the door lock fail open or closed? The *time-delayed exit door* raises that question to an urgent level. Many emergency fire exits require a person to push a bar to force the door open (and consequently set off an audible fire alarm). Such emergency exits have saved many lives, but also offer a temptation to some smash-and-grab thieves who are willing to make a run for it. To counter this threat, some facilities may be permitted by their fire departments to install exit doors with a time delay: push on the bar and the alarm will sound, but the door will not open for several seconds. The delay is supposed to give security personnel time to run to the door and take charge. Various additional safety features can be required for such doors, including a fail-safe option that ensures the lock will be disabled if electrical power is lost.

At the entrance and sometimes at checkpoints at the entrances to particularly sensitive areas, many installations with strong physical security incorporate an architectural element known as a *mantrap*, which has the same general layout as a double airlock such as you might see in a science fiction movie or biomedical laboratory. If you live in a region that has very cold winters, you might think of a mantrap as a mudroom with doors on both sides.

Although simple mantraps can be quite effective in controlling traffic, a more advanced design allows security officers to inspect and interview individuals wanting to enter a facility, while maintaining control over traffic flow. In particular, *piggybacking*— entering a facility for which one is unauthorized by following on the heels of someone who is—is tough to pull off through a mantrap. Let's take a look to see why.

A mantrap (see Figure 5.1) consists of two doors on opposite sides of a fully enclosed vestibule or corridor. Suppose you enter a building with a mantrap from the outside. Once you open the door, you see the small corridor in front of you and another door on the opposite side. So long as you hold the front door open, the door on the other side is disabled. Once you close the door behind you, you are in a small room. You may have to wait there while your credentials are examined; in some facilities, the vestibule has the equivalent of a bank teller's window on the side, where you interact with a guard. When you are cleared to leave the mantrap, one door lock is enabled. If all has gone well, it is the door opposite the one you came in from.

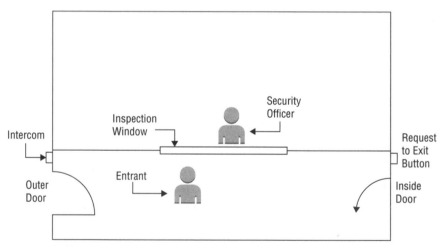

FIGURE 5.1 Mantrap

One subtlety of this sort of entrance is that you should never expect to open the door and find someone else already in the corridor. Once someone enters the vestibule and the door is reclosed, the locks on the outside of both doors are disabled, rendering them inoperable to someone trying to go in, while allowing authorized egress. Similarly, if more than one person enters at once, the second door can be held tight while security enforces a "one at a time" rule.

Extending the "Facilities" View

Although electronic door locks and mantraps can protect the centralized facilities of organizations, the workstations of millions of people exist remotely at outside locations. Our modern view of "facilities" must extend to include them.

When workers at coffee shops, airport hotspots, and various urban hubs make use of your company's networks and systems that are run out of centralized facilities, "remote" locations such as these effectively become extensions of your company's physical offices. Because employees working from home often use wireless devices with a broadcast range that encompasses dozens of neighbors, visitors, and passersby, your design of network access controls must take into account the potential presence of those people on your network. Are these remote workers and random third parties "inside" one of your facilities? Plan—and act—as if they are.

Ultimately, every physical device that a worker uses to connect remotely to the organization's networks and systems is a potential access point that is immersed in an uncontrolled and potentially hostile environment. Your off-site workers and connecting customers will often be involved in human interaction, exposing them to an elevated risk of social engineering, keyboard eavesdropping, video recording of screen content, device theft, and a variety of other attacks.

While these alternate facilities offer you few opportunities for physical controls—employees' homes being an exception, to a degree—the IAM controls you select should aim to control both access to and exploitation of the externally exposed assets. You may not, for example, be able to prevent laptops and mobile phones from falling into the possession of attackers, but the careful deployment of good IAM will prevent or delay attackers from logging in as well as limiting their access to valued resources.

NOTE   Many companies deploy MDM software to limit access to specific networks, applications, and other resources based on time of day, location, identity, and other profile data. There are many advantages to MDM, and the "stolen mobile phone" use case is a great example. (The "your laptop just got taken over because you used an unsecured coffee shop hot spot" is another one.) Properly implemented, MDM can go a long way to address issues raised by today's highly mobile working environment.

Just as the ubiquity of coffee shop computing has forced us security practitioners to expand our view of "office space," cloud computing has forced us to reimagine the data center. Long gone are the days when security designs could count on companies controlling the physical space housing critical data.

When your servers are in the cloud and the physical security of your data is managed by a third-partner provider, IAM issues take on extra importance. Clearly, you will need to ensure that those third-party personnel who service and monitor the hardware you rely on are who you think they are and only have access to the resources you want them to have, at the times and under the conditions you stipulate. Further, since it will sometimes be the case that a competitor or adversary can or will make use of the same commercial cloud provider you use (and might have systems and software housed in the very same facility, even on the same network), it might seem that no physical controls are possible.

That is not so. First, of course, comes isolation. Depending on costs and the actual layout of the cloud provider's data centers, you may be able to maximize (with at least contractual assurance) the distance from potentially hostile systems at which "your" hardware operates. You may also be able to ensure that it is isolated in terms of air conditioning, temperature, air flow, and electrical supplies. You also might (depending again on cost and availability) be able to assert contractual control over personnel, limiting physical access to your hardware to bonded personnel or persons whom you have vetted and approved, or who otherwise meet standards you have specified.

None of those factors will matter much, however, unless you ensure that the physical security of the cloud provider's facilities themselves meets your standards. If circumstances allow, one or more inspection tours by appropriate security staff are certainly called for. At the least, video surveillance and visitor logs, accompanied by strong IAM and access logs, will increase assurance that the facilities side of your cloud operations is well controlled.

Of course, you cannot predict—and you should not assume—which of these measures might be legal in whatever country your data might reside in. For example, privacy rights in the hosting country might preclude the kind of personnel vetting (and surveillance) you would prefer. Be sure to obtain adequate counsel on relevant legal and regulatory issues before signing (also adequately counseled) any cloud computing contracts.

We will turn now from physical and logical access controls to managing the identification and authentication of people, devices, and services.

MANAGE IDENTIFICATION AND AUTHENTICATION OF PEOPLE, DEVICES, AND SERVICES

There are several concepts relating to identity management and access control, often confused, that we must clarify before proceeding. These concepts make up the identity lifecycle, and they are: identity creation, identification, authentication, authorization, and deprovisioning.

A person's identity is, in one sense, who they are. When a person opens a new bank account, creates a new email account, or is hired by a company, the organization creates a formal identity for that person in its system. This often includes defining the specific resources a user needs and determining the type of access to those resources the user may have.

Identification is the process of verifying that a claimed identity is valid. For example, identification occurs when a person supplies a user ID and a system verifies that the user ID is valid. (This step does not prove that the person is who they claim to be, but only that such an identity has been established.)

Authentication is the validation of a provable assertion of an identity. For example, when a person uses a user ID, they are required to provide their password as a way to prove that they actually are the owner of that user ID.

Although authentication proves that a person is who they claim to be, that is not the same as proving they have the right to do whatever they are trying to do. For example, a person might be a validly authenticated member of an organization, but that doesn't necessarily mean they have access to all of that organization's accounting or human resources files. Authorization is the process of determining whether to allow a person to have access to resources.

The final stage of the identity lifecycle is sometimes referred to as *deprovisioning, disabling, revocation*, and other terms, but it generally means ending a person's general access to the system. However, that person's formal identity will often persist within the system for months or years after the person it was created for has no direct need for it. For example, a bank will have archives of a member who closed an account, and an organization will keep records of former employees for taxes, human resources, and regulatory purposes.

NOTE The term *identity proofing* is sometimes used when discussing aspects of the identity lifecycle. This process begins with collecting and verifying information about a person. This information is later used to confirm that a person who has requested an account, a credential, or other special resource is indeed who he or she claims to be. This establishes a reliable relationship that can be trusted electronically between the individual and the resource for purposes of electronic authentication.

Here is an example of the full identity lifecycle: Suppose you go to work at a new job. They enroll you in the personnel system, establishing a new identity for you. They emboss an employee badge for you, maybe with your photograph on it; now you have the means to authenticate as a company employee. But if you want to get into the building using the badge, they will let you in only if you have the authorization to enter that particular building. Authorization defines the specific resources a user needs and determines the type of access to those resources the user may have. When you cease working for that organization, they require that you return the badge to them. We explore this lifecycle in detail later in the "Manage the Identity and Access Provisioning Lifecycle" section.

Identity Management Implementation

Business computing began in the era of mainframe computers. Whether the computer user was an insurance actuarial, a salesperson, or a research scientist, the account management process was often the same. Individuals would be assigned an account on the mainframe linked to their name, and all "timesharing" costs would be charged to their department.

In this highly centralized model, identities and accounts were created and managed by the corporate Management Information Systems (MIS) department. If a researcher did work on more than one project, they might be given a separate account for each project, but often the timesharing costs were recorded on the scientist's main account and "charged back" to a specific project. The percentage of timesharing costs allocated to each department was sometimes a matter for lively debate.

Personal computers entered the work world in the 1980s, decentralizing this account management model. Suddenly, the MIS department (the predecessor to today's IT department) no longer owned all the computers doing the company's business. Salespersons and scientists alike brought in computers and software purchased on their own budgets, made their own accounts for themselves and their colleagues on these computers, and settled into spreadsheet-making.

Few users really want to have to keep track of a separate password for every application they use at work. Similarly, no IT department truly wants to supply you with a separate account for each task you perform at work. The resulting challenge is how to provide authentication for multiple separate applications and services without building an unacceptable burden for users and system administrators. This is the reason *single sign-on* (SSO) became a popular goal for security architects. The idea, simply, is that each user gets a single identity (and a single set of credentials) to use with all software across the enterprise. It becomes the job of the various pieces of software to communicate ("talk to each other"), keeping track of when, whether, and with what degree of assurance the user has been authenticated.

Using SSO is fairly easy. For example, imagine that you log into your bank's website and authenticate so that you can look at your bank account. If your bank now allows you to check a retirement account (or pay down a credit card) without having to log in all over again, it means you selected a bank that uses web browser SSO.

Although SSO seems simple, under the surface there is a lot going on. Those bank services almost certainly were provided by different accounts. In that scenario, how did the credit card service know it was really you making the payment? (You may not care if someone impersonates you to pay down your credit card, but the bank should.) The functioning of SSO is discussed in more detail later in this chapter, but for a brief explanation, what is happening basically is that the bank app, when it was logging you in, relied on an authentication service, which checked your credentials and passed back a thumbs-up sign in the form of a token. When the bank app transferred control to the credit card app, it relayed that token as assurance that you had been properly authenticated.

Many SSO technologies and approaches are available today to implement this chain of trust. We will describe several leading ones here.

As you are evaluating SSO schemes, keep in mind the ever-present risk of centralization: creating a single point of failure. If all of your applications and access to every system rely on the availability of a centralized authentication mechanism, taking the authentication server down will render many files, applications, and services inaccessible that are otherwise still functional. Consider, too, that any service or server holding a centralized aggregation of all credentials will be a prime target of attackers, who—if they can crack your protection scheme—might then be able to impersonate users (and some processes) at will.

Some of the first SSO technologies include the Secure European System for Applications in a Multivendor Environment (SESAME) and Kerberos, a ticket-based system developed at the Massachusetts Institute of Technology (MIT). Kerberos pioneered several elements of session and credential management, and Kerberos authentication protocol version 5 has provided the foundation for several Microsoft Windows authentication elements, including Active Directory. MIT remains involved in Kerberos development and continues to be an active enabling technology, and a Kerberos Consortium contributes to commercially supported versions.

Fast-forwarding to today's business computing environment, the same tension still exists between centralized versus decentralized accounts and identity management. In many (perhaps most) businesses, everyday computing services like email and calendaring are provided by the corporate IT department. This group creates and manages primary corporate computing identities, accounts, and credentials for these services. Can these same accounts and passwords be used when the employee logs into the seemingly countless web-based applications used for timecards, customer management, internal surveys, and so forth? It all depends on the company's identity management implementation.

One modern way the coordination could have been achieved is via Security Assertion Markup Language (SAML) actions. *SAML* (currently at version 2.0) is an open OASIS standard used to exchange authentication and authorization data among cooperating processes or domains. The Organization for the Advancement of Structured Information Standards (OASIS) is a global nonprofit consortium of vendors and other companies, universities, government agencies, and individuals. OASIS has more than two dozen technical standards, either in the field or under development.

SSO can be achieved by using a number of tools based on SAML, OpenID Connect (OIDC), Kerberos, or a similar service to pass information back and forth between cooperating processes needing to authenticate. These mechanisms work via an interprocess communication where coders make use of an application programming interface (API) to enable the software they are working on to exchange data with authentication services.

Regardless of which tool is used, it is important to consider the location, format, and protection of the information. These functions, which must be part of any identity management implementation, are the role of an identity provider (IdP), a service that manages and maintains identity information on the network and can "talk to" the SAML or OIDC service. A SAML service provider will communicate with its IdP in XML.

A related but competing approach would be to use the OpenID protocol and OIDC instead of SAML. OIDC is an implementation of the authorization framework OAuth 2.0, facilitating the communication of attribute and authentication information. One difference is that, whereas SAML specifically relays requests from a website, OIDC can work to effect authentication with either a website or a mobile application as the requester. We will discuss the use of these two authentication and authorization methods in more detail a little later in this chapter.

A third modern mechanism for the exchange of user information for SSO is Service Provisioning Markup Language (SPML), also developed by OASIS. Its primary application is in "federated" environments, a topic that is discussed further later in this chapter.

NOTE   A helpful list of SAML-based products and services can be found at https://en.wikipedia.org/wiki/SAML-based_products_and_services.

Single Factor/Multifactor Authentication

Authentication—the process of proving that a person or system is who they claim to be—has traditionally been based on one or more of three authentication factors:

- **Type I:** Something you know (e.g., a password)
- **Type II:** Something you have (e.g., a smartcard)
- **Type III:** Something you are (e.g., your fingerprint)

Two emerging technologies have recently been coming into greater prominence as authentication factors as well: "something you do" and "somewhere you are."

These factors can be applied alone or in combination. *Single-factor authentication* involves the use of exactly one of these three factors to carry out the authentication process being requested. *Multifactor authentication* helps to ensure that a user is who he or she claims to be via the use of more than one factor to carry out the authentication process being requested. Generally, the more factors used to determine a person's identity, the greater trust you can place on the authentication. Other factors being equal, you might therefore decide to allow users who have completed multifactor authentication access to more sensitive assets than those authenticated by means of a single factor, such as a password.

Something You Know

Everyone who has used a modern computer system is familiar with the first type of authentication factor, "something you know." Two common forms of this authentication factor include passwords and security questions.

Passwords

The media frequently features stories about security disasters caused by weak passwords. Break-ins in which hundreds of thousands (or millions, or hundreds of millions) of passwords and usernames have been captured, compromised, or guessed have become a common phenomenon. The consequences for the people whose identities may no longer be protected can be substantial.

Passwords are by far the most commonly used authentication mechanism. They are just about the weakest, too. There are some methods you can use to get the most out of passwords, but relying on passwords alone as a single authentication factor is poor practice. Here is a short list of bad things that can happen if you do so:

- The user may forget the password.

- The user, if allowed to choose the password, may select a trivial one. Some studies show that the most common password selected by everyday users is "123456." "12345678" is quite popular, too.

- If the password is not trivial, the user may write it down to be able to find it when needed. This in turn means that someone else may find it, too.

- The user may share it with people who are not supposed to know it, which could directly compromise the security of a system—or, at the very least, baffle administrators as to who is to be held accountable for actions enabled by the use of that password.

- Passwords may be written into software or otherwise kept on file on the system the password is supposed to protect.

- Passwords may be guessed, either directly (because an attacker knows something about the user or the system that influences the choice of the password) or via the use of special attack software. The science of guessing passwords has advanced to the point that dedicated password "cracker" hardware can decipher up to 100 million passwords a second in some cases.

Generally, a password should be easy to remember but hard to guess. Even those practitioners who agree with that guideline, however, have yet to achieve a consensus on just what policies and procedures you should deploy to achieve optimal password security. (This lack of a consensus may account for the incredible diversity in password policies you, as a user, have to conform to on the various websites, applications, and services you use every day.) There are some common policies that organizations use to try to strengthen passwords. Many common password guidelines require passwords to be the following:

- Complex. Compose passwords of letters, numbers, special characters, and symbols in as unpredictable a mix as possible.

- Long. Eight characters is a common minimum, but generally, more characters in a password make it harder to guess. A complex 12-character or 15-character password is many orders of magnitude more difficult to guess than an 8-character password of similar complexity. Still greater lengths (some sites today require 32 characters, or even 128) may offer a significant technical barrier to attackers, while raising considerable practical complications.

- Different. Passwords should not be reused from one system to another or from one website to another. Similarly, they should not be recycled or reused on systems where they have previously appeared.

- Nonobvious. Some people try to use something that is easy for them to remember but they believe will be difficult for others to guess, such as the following:

  - Dictionary words

  - Names of relatives, pets, sports teams, movies, and so on

  - Popular expressions

Note that seemingly "nonobvious" passwords are often a lot more obvious than people think. Some people even misspell words or substitute characters for letters (e.g., "3" for "e", "@" for "a"). These practices may frustrate human guessers—and seldom hurt your cause—but will not significantly delay sophisticated cracking software.

Modern operating systems don't store passwords in the plain-text form in which users present them. In fact, passwords are not stored at all.

Here is a simple explanation. When a user first sets a password, the supplied string is fed as input to a hashing function that computes a unique numerical value, called a *hash*. It's the hash, not the password, that is stored. Then, when someone (nominally the same user) supplies a candidate string that purports to be that same password, the authenticating software repeats that hashing function, using the candidate string, and compares the new hash with the stored result. If it's really the password, the hashes will match.

That's just the basic idea. In practice, passwords these days are first combined with an additional secret string known to the system, and that combined string is what's hashed. This practice, known as *salting*, helps stymie attackers who try to guess passwords by building huge dictionaries with millions of possible passwords prehashed. The secret string is known as *salt*, and there are many schemes and algorithms bearing on how best to salt passwords.

One way you can manually construct a long and relatively difficult-to-guess password unlikely to appear in a dictionary is to build a combination of unrelated words, or a phrase. You can then make that password even more difficult to guess by modifying it in some way. A few minutes of thinking will likely turn up novel ways that you can create innovative individualistic passwords for yourself.

An added benefit of this approach is that you may be able to concoct a fairly complex sequence that you nevertheless can reconstruct at will and thus do not need to remember or write down. Ideally, each time that you are required to enter a password for a particular website, you can use this technique to work out what passphrase you would have specified at creation time. Then, supply it again.

- String several words together to make a passphrase. It helps if the phrase is itself novel, but ideally the words will carry enough meaning for you that you can recall it. "Isurehopeitdoesntrain" is a simple example.

- Concatenate words and numbers together. Choose elements that bear no logical relation. Hence, "WorldSeriesBaseball" is far easier to guess than "1Companion2Umbrellas4Beers"; yet the latter may be easy to reconstruct if you can remember that the phrase denotes items that might help you enjoy an out-door sporting event in late October.

- If you are familiar with a "foreign" language (whatever that might be at your facility), mix in words and phrases from that language to add some spice and complexity.

- It will not hurt, and might help, to misspell words, transliterate letters into num-bers, mix in punctuation, reverse strings, and shift numbers up or down. These transformations are unlikely to significantly slow specialized attack software but may confuse human guessers—especially if they have happened to get just a glance at your secret.

Perhaps the best way to avoid the common problem of users picking trivial, easy-to-guess passwords is to provide (and require the use of) an application known as a *password manager*. Such an app will create a strong, hard-to-guess password on behalf of the user whenever they are prompted for one. The password manager will also store all the user's passwords and then provide them automatically and without user intervention when other software asks for a password to be typed.

A person whose passwords are managed in this way does not need to remember them anymore, nor write them down. The passwords can be as long and as complicated as the system and the individual applications will allow. What the user does need to remem-ber is the master password needed to unlock the password manager's repository. (This approach, by the way, is entirely different from the SSO strategy discussed earlier in this chapter. Here, there may be a great many passwords, one for each account; it is simply not necessary for the user to actually remember all of them. SSO obviates the need for a huge collection of passwords in the first place.)

Collecting all or most of a user's passwords in a single repository addresses many important problems long associated with passwords. Be aware, as well, that the deployment of a password manager also makes possible two fairly novel and potentially catastrophic security failures.

The first case, in which all passwords would be compromised, occurs when the central repository for the user's passwords is breached. This can happen either if the master password is guessed by an attacker on the user's system or as a result of a disastrous attack and compromise of the master customer database within the company that sells the password manager. This risk was mentioned earlier in the discussion of SSO schemes in the "Identity Management Implementation" section.

Password managers entail another, much simpler risk, too, which is the possibility that the user might forget the master password. Eventual recovery might be possible, depending on the brand of management software, but some operational disruption would be certain.

A wide variety of password management software is commercially available on every major operating system. In some cases, the function of password management is included as one part of a larger credential management system, incorporating credentials of various types and relating to multiple systems. Credential management systems are described in further detail later in this chapter.

Because passwords are an intrinsically weak authentication mechanism, the quality of your password policies can make a big difference. It is important for a security architect to provide a means for users to make strong passwords and to change them in a timely way. Password managers go a long way toward making these good practices easy.

It is sound practice, then, to make and enforce policies that require users to avail themselves of these tools—to have strong passwords, change them when compromised or expired, and never disclose or share them—or face consequences.

A couple of excellent policies include requiring tools to make strong passwords to be available and enforcing your password rules (whatever they are). Here are a few other candidate policies to consider as part of an authentication strategy.

NOTE For guidance about good password policies, as well as recommendations about sound implementation of password algorithms such as salting, we recommend you study the 2017 password recommendations released by NIST. (See https://pages.nist.gov/800-63-3/sp800-63-3.html.) While they formally apply only to U.S. government systems, they represent decades of hard-won, experience-based knowledge, and when released, they overturned much conventional wisdom. Many of NIST's recommendations are incorporated into this chapter.

- Require passwords to be at least 8 characters (or 12, or more) long. Longer passwords are harder to guess, in roughly exponential proportion to the length increase.

- Allow users to make use of as many characters as possible to build passwords, including all of the printable ASCII table (including the space character), Unicode characters, even emojis.

- Lock out a user after three (or five, etc.) failed login attempts. One problem with this is that some legitimate users will be thwarted in attempts to log in, perhaps at a strategic moment selected by an attacker as part of a denial of service.

Keep in mind that passwords are a weak and outmoded means of authentication and are by no means sufficient as your sole barrier. Require multifactor authentication whenever possible, especially for exceptionally sensitive data (whatever "exceptionally sensitive" means for your environment).

Please note that NIST does not recommend that you require passwords to be changed at regularly scheduled intervals, which has been common practice in some environments for many years. The obvious advantage of this practice is that a password that has been guessed or otherwise compromised will not remain in effect for long. Yet confidence in this practice is on the wane today. (NIST dropped the recommendation in 2017.) Among many practical issues that have arisen over the years, mandating periodic changes can ease the task of attackers, as users find it difficult to produce enough distinct, hard-to-guess passwords over the course of a year. Worse yet, they may be motivated to write passwords down or reuse them by cycling through a familiar set.

Another traditional practice that fell from NIST's recommendations in 2017 has to do with password complexity. While it is important to rule out, where you can, truly trivial selections such as "password" and "123456," there are potential drawbacks to forcing passwords to conform to a specified structure (e.g., begin or end with a digit, and include at least one uppercase character). Taken to extremes, such restrictions (especially if casually chosen by policymakers) may actually make an attacker's guessing easier by reducing the space of potential combinations. At the same time, complexity rules have little chance of defeating modern password crackers, promote a false sense of security, and likely increase the chance that, as with other complications, users write down or otherwise record their passwords for ease of recall.

Security Questions

Passwords are not the only way to use "something you know" for authentication. Most likely, you are already familiar with the most popular alternative, known as *security questions* or *cognitive passwords*.

While the use of security questions rapidly became popular as an easy method of authentication in the days when the World Wide Web was growing to encompass the globe, they have proven to be a weak barrier. Partly because of the popularity of the very social media applications they have helped to proliferate, the answers to many questions are easily guessed (or simply looked up) by attackers. The latest available (2017) guidelines from NIST dropped security questions (and hints) from their list of approved tactics; you should not rely on them, especially as a primary means of authentication.

Here is how they work. Like passwords, security questions are older in practice than computers. Bank managers setting up accounts have been asking for "your mother's maiden name" for a long time. Here are some standard security questions:

- Where did you go to elementary school?

- Where did you meet your significant other?

- What was the model of the first car you drove?

- What was the first name of your best childhood friend?

- What is the middle name of your eldest sibling, or other older relative?

One common use of security questions is that of a backup authentication method. When someone purporting to be a particular user says they have forgotten their account password, for example, a website will often use a mix of these questions to validate the claim before initiating the "change my password" protocol.

Now that more than a billion people have signed up for social media accounts, the use of security questions to authenticate identity is less useful and less safe than it was only a few years ago. Depending upon the precise question asked and the degree to which the candidate user has documented their life online, it may be fairly easy for an attacker to reconstruct the answers to several of these questions.

You might consider answering such questions incorrectly when setting up an account. As long as you can repeat the false answers when required, the cognitive dissonance may have no real-world impact.

Remember, if you are considering the use of security questions in your role as a security architect or software author, you should not place undue reliance on them as a way of validating identity.

Something You Have

The second type of authentication is "something you have." Just as passwords were known in the ancient world, keys have been used since time immemorial as access devices. Even older, perhaps, is the idea of a *pass*: something you can carry with you that you can show to gatekeeper to gain entry.

Such low-tech methods remain in use because they are reliable, inexpensive, and simple to use. Paper passes, unfortunately, are easy to forge these days. And keys, especially, lack versatility, as any security officer who has had to change sets of keys or door locks when an employee left can tell you.

In most modern facilities, badges and smartcards have replaced keys and paper passes. Electronic badge readers have been ubiquitous for decades, reading credentials from a magnetic stripe or chip when the ID is swiped through or waved near the reader.

In the first decade of the 21st century, the U.S. government pursued physical security with a national focus, developing NIST guides and standards relating to PACSs. One of the key outcomes of this focus was the development of smartcards for identification, pursuing several trials and experiments before settling on two workable systems. Today, millions of federal personnel use either common access cards (CACs) or personal identity verification (PIV) cards to authenticate into facilities and computer systems. CACs, for example, are the standard identification means for active duty military personnel in the United States, as well as Department of Defense civilian employees.

NOTE   For more information about the requirements and standards surrounding PACSs and the associated CACs or PIV authentication, see Federal Information Processing Standard Publication 201 (FIPS 201, Parts I and II) developed by the National Institute of Standards and Technology (`https://csrc.nist.gov/publications/detail/fips/201/2/final`).

Because electronic ID cards like the CAC and PIV are intended for mass production and millions of mass-produced cards make an alluring target for attackers, it is critical for researchers and practitioners alike to keep abreast of vulnerability concerns with these and similar devices. For example, an alarming report by two Czech scientists in 2014 about a "highly theoretical" vulnerability in Estonian CAC ID cards led to an investigation identifying a manufacturing error requiring 15 cards to be canceled immediately. After further investigation, the Estonian software was rewritten to compensate for the problem. (For more information, see, for example, `https://news.postimees.ee/4236857/id-card-tip-from-czech-scientists.`) While the fundamental technology appears sound and the cards practical, we can expect many more vulnerabilities and alarms in the future as these hardware-based devices, impossible to perfect and resistant (in their current forms) to patching, proliferate and increase in importance in our careers and our everyday lives.

Another type of portable security device is the *token*. Tokens are electronic devices, small enough and light enough to be carried on a keychain, that display numeric sequences for authentication. The most common type in use today features an LCD display showing a six- to eight-digit number.

These hardware tokens can either supplant or supplement conventional passwords. Used in combination with software running on the system being logged into, the string of digits they display (a personal identification number, or PIN) can be used as a dynamic one-time password. Hardware tokens are used in two different ways, synchronously and asynchronously.

Synchronous dynamic password tokens are time-based, changing to a different number sequence after a specified period of time (say, once a minute). The software on the authenticating system also "knows" the sequence and the timing of changes, and so offers a window to the user during which the number displayed on the token will validate access.

Unlike synchronous dynamic passwords, *asynchronous* dynamic password tokens do not rely on synchronized time. Rather, each side of the login sequence keeps track of a counter, generating the next one-time password by using the same algorithm to produce the same sequence for that count.

In either scheme, the one-time password can optionally be appended or prepended to a conventional password for extra safety, in addition to standing by itself as a second step in authentication.

Although adding "something you have" to the security stack of authentication is generally sound practice, physical items such as smartcards, badges, and tokens can be lost or stolen. Security architectures, policies, and procedures should take this possibility into account and deal with notification and revocation in the wake of such events.

In another variation to consider, tokens can be implemented in software rather than as physical devices. "Soft" tokens these days are most often built as mobile phone applications. They can be made to work identically to "hard" tokens and offer serious advantages: soft tokens cost less and are much easier to patch or update in case a security issue is uncovered. On the downside, bundling an authentication token with an attractive, expensive mobile phone may well increase the chance that the soft token ends up in the wrong hands. Make doubly sure you have your revocation procedures in good shape to be ready if such an eventuality occurs.

Another concept related to soft tokens is that of an *authenticator*. Sometimes used synonymously with "soft token," the term can also refer to a special one-time code sent to a prevetted smartphone. Such authenticators are sometimes invoked in the middle of a login sequence, for example when a login is attempted by a device unfamiliar to the authentication service. In this case, the code, when read from the phone and typed into the login software, provides a separate, out-of-channel means of authenticating the request.

Still more complex authenticator schemes involve a challenge-and-response method, whereby the login sequence displays a "challenge." The user then types the challenge string into an authenticator app on the phone, the app displays a response (often a string of digits), and the user relays the response string back into the challenging software to complete that extra stage of authentication.

Something You Are

Perhaps the surest way of knowing that a person is truly who they claim to be is by comparing physical measurements of the claimant to those recorded in a template. This is the "something you are," *biometric* approach.

As so often happens in security, the concept is not new. Human beings have identified each other by face and by voice for millennia. Footprints have helped to implicate or rule out criminal suspects for centuries.

Types of Biometric Methods

Today, many biometric methods are available to the security architect. They vary widely as to reliability, practicability, and cost.

What may be the simplest biometric method is nevertheless still in use in certain high-security installations, though always in combination with other factors. It is, simply, body weight. While what a person weighs may change often (and by many pounds or kilos) over the course of their employment, weight can nevertheless be a straightforward sanity check of identity. Well-known patterns of periodic loss and gain can be used to help detect anomalies. Measuring body weight is safe, passive, low-tech, and low-key—so much so that if scales are built into the flooring of vestibules or corridors, many authentication candidates may never know that this "scan" has been done (which might be considered unethical or even illegal in some jurisdictions).

The most commonly used biometric technique in the world, today and for the past 100 years, is fingerprinting. A foundation of criminological forensics and a rite of passage for individuals with security clearances, fingerprinting is highly reliable as a means of identification and is quick, safe, and low in cost. With the advent of quick and inexpensive fingerprint scanners that can easily be attached to everyday computer systems, fingerprints have transitioned from paper records to high-tech authentication and will remain a piece of biometric solutions for the foreseeable future.

Palm prints are at least as old as fingerprints as an authentication method and may actually be older. The larger surface area makes possible more detailed differentiation, and palm prints do have some technical advantages over fingerprints. Still, palm prints have never been as popular for everyday authentication. Today, two relatively new technologies have brought the palm back into the mainstream as an authentication element. *Palm vein recognition* is a biometric method that uses near-infrared illumination to see (and record for comparison) *subcutaneous vascular patterns*, which are the pattern of blood vessels beneath the skin that are unique to each individual. Palm scans are fast, passive, and painless. Perhaps because palm vein recognition may seem more invasive, some people placing their hands onto a scanner would prefer the alternate older approaches of palm topography and hand geometry.

In these methods, features of the hand such as finger and palm length and width (and perhaps the ridges of the palm) are scanned, recorded, and compared. In one hand geometry method, you would be asked to place your palm on a flat metal plate. The plate has small round metal stanchions sticking up out of it; they are there to guide your placement so that the stanchions are nestled up against the places where the webbing of your fingers come together (see Figure 5.2). With your palm properly placed, the device can register an image of your hand and develop a set of measurements sufficient to authenticate you in the future.

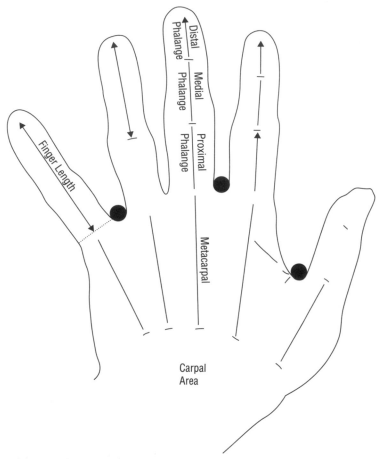

FIGURE 5.2 **Features of the hand**

NOTE The anatomically normal hand is composed of several carpal bones: one metacarpal bone for each finger, attached to the carpal bones, and three phalanges. The proximal phalange attaches to the metacarpal, the medial phalange attaches to the proximal, and the distal phalange is attached to the medial. As you can imagine, looking at the diagram, a properly positioned and anatomically normal hand will yield calculations as to palm width, finger length and width, and the length of several of the phalanges. These measurements form a sound basis for biometric authentication.

Biometric measurements of the eye proceed similarly. The iris is the colorful part of the eye that surrounds the pupil, the dark circle in the middle. Gradations of color and patterns of light and dark are distinctive for any individual. These colors and these patterns persist throughout a lifetime, with little change due to age or illness, making the iris one of the most reliable forms of biometric measurement.

Biometric scans using the retina are even more individualistic than those of the iris. The retina, a thin segment of light-sensitive tissue at the back of the eye, contains both arteries and veins. The structure of the inner retinal vasculature is unique to each human eye, differing even for identical twins. It can be recorded for biometric use by means of infrared light. To acquire a good picture of the back of the eye, it is necessary for the individual being measured to place their eye directly up against a view piece similar to that of a microscope; some people find this experience physically or psychologically uncomfortable. Another drawback of retinal scans is that the appearance of the retina can be affected by diseases of the eye such as glaucoma and cataracts, or even the progression of diseases such as diabetes.

Facial recognition is commonly used as a biometric tool as well. One scheme uses the structure of the face—the positions of the eye sockets, nose, chin, and ears—just as palm geometry maps the hand. Facial layout varies enough from person to person to make facial recognition a fundamental human skill, and it translates to modern computers well.

Similarly, the position of blood vessels and fascia underneath the skin of the face can be discerned by infrared cameras and recorded for biometric comparisons. Because it now can be performed in real time, and from a distance, facial recognition is becoming more and more popular as processor speeds make it increasingly efficient.

Just as facial recognition is becoming more popular as processor speeds increase, so are voice analysis and voice recognition gaining as biometric tools. Comparisons can be done most easily if a special phrase or set of phrases is registered at enrollment time, but as voice recognition technology improves, the cadence of speech and the vocal volume dynamics of particular phonemes make real-time voice recognition more and more feasible.

Signature dynamics can be used for authentication, too. If a special stylus is used, pen pressure can be recorded in addition to the points in the strokes when the writer pauses. Without a special stylus, signature dynamics devolve to more standard graphological analysis, studying the handwriting itself for individualistic characteristics and indications of stress.

Keystroke dynamics can also be used for biometric purposes. In this application, the characteristics of key presses—dwell time, for example, and the pauses between and after certain key combinations—can be recorded and registered as belonging to the legitimate user, for later comparison. As with signature dynamics, keystroke analysis verges on a new dimension of biometric security. It represents, perhaps, "something you do," as opposed to "something you are."

Considerations When Using Biometric Methods

Regardless of the specific technology that is used, biometric techniques all involve the same stages of preparation as any other authentication method. First, the user must be enrolled, and the characteristics that will be used for authentication must be recorded in a registration process. This creates a reference profile to which comparisons can be made. Preparations must be made for the secure storage of reference profiles and their retrieval in a timely way. A method must be available to verify, promptly and within specified accuracy limits, whether a person claiming an identity should be authenticated. A final requirement is a secure method of updating the reference profile when the characteristics to be compared change (due to age or illness, for example) or revoking the reference profile when it is no longer needed, has expired, or can no longer be trusted to be accurate.

Regardless of the authentication method you choose, it is important to understand the degree of accuracy that you can rely upon. The two ways that authentication can fail are known as Type I and Type II. Type I is failure to recognize a legitimate user, a *false rejection*. Type II is erroneous recognition—either by confusing one user with another or by accepting an impostor as a legitimate user. This is a *false acceptance*. To avoid confusing the two types, some security professionals and vendors often refer simply to either "false rejection" or "false acceptance" and don't even refer to authentication failures as being Type I or Type II.

In selecting, tuning, and deploying a biometric method, it is critical to monitor both the types and rates of errors.

The ratio of Type I errors to valid authentications is known as the *false rejection rate* (FRR). If 1,000 attempts to authenticate result in two rejections of legitimate users, the FRR is .002, or .2 percent.

The ratio of Type II errors to valid authentications is known as the *false acceptance rate* (FAR). If, in 1,000 attempts to authenticate, two impostors are erroneously allowed in, the FAR is .002, or .2 percent.

One statistic you will often see cited in vendor material about biometric devices is the *crossover error rate* (CER). See Figure 5.3. (You may sometimes see this statistic referred to as an *equal error rate*, or EER.) This is the number that results when the device is adjusted to provide equal Type I and Type II error rates in your environment. When evaluating biometric systems, check the CERs; other considerations being equal, the device with the lower CER may demonstrate greater intrinsic accuracy.

Your experience in real life will inform you that one can adjust biometric systems, making them more or less sensitive. While the CER is a useful evaluation metric, there is no particular reason it would make an appropriate setting at which to set your biometric threshold when you configure it.

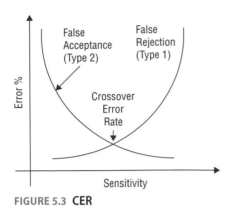

FIGURE 5.3 **CER**

For example, there are certain considerations if you are responsible for a repository of fissile material, guarding the pieces of plutonium that terrorists would need to construct an improvised nuclear bomb. You will want to tune the false acceptance rate on the retinal and palm geometry scanners down just about as far as they will go. Your users, those nuclear scientists and weapon specialists, are used to extreme security and will have planned for entry delays.

If, on the other hand, you are responsible for adjusting the office badge reader at a newspaper office, you will want to consider trying to keep the false rejection rate reasonably low—if only to avoid reading flaming editorials complaining about how security has run amok in modern society.

In selecting a set of biometric tools for authentication, it is certainly important to be aware of the error rates. There is more to be considered, though, besides the accuracy and reproducibility of a potential biometric technique.

First, of course, you want the measurements taken to be unique to an individual. While many (not all—think body weight) biometric tools will succumb to impersonation by an identical twin, uniqueness of the measure is important. After all, depending on the precise nature of the tool, you may find yourself with a degraded reading. Fingerprints can smudge; voice recordings may have a lot of background noise, and poor lighting or infrared interference may cloud a photographic record. A good biometric will have the attribute that the copy to be compared to the registered base will vary minimally and predictably as it degrades in quality.

Consider, too, that it is not only the measurement taken for comparison that may be degraded. Fingers, palms, and faces may be scarred by accident (or, alas, intentionally). Aging, illness, and injury must all be anticipated and compensated for.

Another factor to consider is the accessibility of the part of the body that must be registered. It is not a coincidence that fingers, at the end of our extensible arms, were employed as the first widely used biometric.

Further, one wants biometric measurements to be noninvasive, passive, and safe. Individuals to be vetted will vary in general health; in dexterity; in their ability to see and hear; in their alertness, and the ability to follow instructions; and in their physical and psychological tolerance to being prodded, scanned by various rays, or enclosed in an examination compartment. Many individuals will be concerned about electromagnetic irradiation. Some women to be authenticated by your biometric device may be pregnant at the time or may become pregnant later. All of these individual conditions should be anticipated and respected with due concern for the examined individual's health, well-being, privacy, dignity, and legal rights.

As with all security measures, when selecting a biometric for deployment in your enterprise you must consider the cumulative costs of setting up the system, registering each person, taking each measurement such as a fingerprint, and the storage and retrieval of the candidates' measurements.

Finally, be sure to consider the likelihood and effectiveness of anti-biometric tactics by potential attackers.

If you are using facial recognition, attackers might wear masks.

If you rely on fingerprints, you had better anticipate and test the effectiveness of fake finger casts made out of silicone, rubber, or even ordinary wood glue. Japan's National Institute of Informatics even found that fingerprints can be copied by a digital camera from 10 feet away and then easily reproduced with simple technology. Depending on just how low you need to drive down the false acceptance rate, you might want to select a vendor for fingerprint sensors that can supply "liveness detection," sensing temperature, pulse, and even body capacitance as a means of detecting fake fingers.

In the age of 3D printers, security architects need to think creatively about the technology relied upon by their biometric tools.

Emerging Authentication Technologies

The science of biometric services is constantly advancing. Increased processor speeds, coupled with more compact form factors, are one reason. Each year it becomes possible to pack more algorithmic intelligence into cameras and other sensors. Facial recognition, for example, has leaped forward in recent years—so much so that in the iPhone X, Apple has introduced facial recognition as the chief method for authenticating yourself to your phone, although passwords and fingerprints are still options.

Similarly, behavior-based recognition is improving each year as well. "Something you do"—as represented by signature dynamics, keystroke patterns, and even hand gestures— is growing as a factor in authentication, especially for mobile devices.

Some vendors have gone further, adding another dimension of authentication with "somewhere you are"—that is, location-based authentication. Although location has been dreamt of for decades as a means of assurance, recent advances may make it realistic at last to validate that a person or system truly is where they claim to be. The implications for off-site operation of critical infrastructure in emergencies, if nothing else, would be transformative.

Accountability

Accountability is the attribute of a security architecture that allows individuals and processes to be held responsible for their actions and decisions. It ensures that account management has assurance that only authorized users are accessing the system and using it properly.

In real life, you can hold other people accountable by knowing what they did and being able to prove it. In cyberspace, this translates to monitoring and logging all actions—including requests for access or changes that get turned down—and auditing those actions. This enables you to know who did what and when. These facts must be recorded, protected from unauthorized alteration, and preserved in order for accountability to be possible.

This fact means that if accountability is to be strong, the false acceptance rate of authentication needs to be kept low. You will rarely be successful in enforcing disciplinary penalties against a user if there is substantial doubt about who did what.

One example is how you handle it if someone tries to tamper with log files. Attackers and other malefactors (e.g., embezzlers) will typically attempt to change log files to cover up their wrongdoing. You can take steps to prevent and detect log file tampering.

One approach, useful but often not practical, is to keep the log files on disk drives with physical "write once, read many" (WORM) controls. A more practical (and affordable) option is to send security events in real time to a logging agent protected by separate administrator credentials. Whatever such measures you take to protect against or detect tampering, be aware that anomalous system events such as unexplained restarts could be an attempt to cover or effect a change to log files.

As a top priority, you must protect against the compromise of highly privileged accounts. With sufficient privileges, one can modify log files in a way that is difficult to detect. It may even be possible to alter the "reality" of the computer system itself by introducing subtle yet nefarious changes into the operating system via so-called *rootkits*. Once the very foundation of a system's operation comes under an adversary's control, accountability is hard indeed to recover. (Well-maintained backups may be a saving grace here.)

Session Management

A *session* is a series of exchanges between two entities, perhaps a human user and a web server. *Session management* entails initiating, controlling, maintaining, and terminating the "state" of these exchanges.

The web surfing protocols Hypertext Transfer Protocol (HTTP) and HyperText Transfer Protocol Secure (HTTPS) are conducted statelessly. This means that each request to a web server for information is handled with no knowledge of previous requests. This "stateless" operation was part of the original design of the World Wide Web. However, as the Web exploded in popularity and commercial applications were created for it, the need for some information (like the contents of a virtual shopping cart) to persist through a series of back-and-forth exchanges with a website became apparent.

As the interchange between the user and the site server progresses (the user asks to log in, is challenged for credentials, provides credentials, requests a page, is served a page, and so forth), all knowledge about the previous information exchanged must be preserved as context for the next exchange. This context—state—comprises a *session*.

To pass state information back and forth, a session ID is created, establishing that the user was authenticated. The session ID binds the user's authenticated credentials to the traffic and associated access controls.

The session ID, which can be thought of as a token, will typically expire after a set period (e.g., an hour or a day).

The paradox that stateful exchanges must be conducted via stateless protocols creates fertile ground for many security attacks. If you are ever given the opportunity to design session IDs, try to do it so as not to give away important information, such as the name of the user or the technologies at work inside the browser. Also, make the token value long enough (and otherwise unpredictable enough) so that it cannot effectively be guessed.

One common goal of attackers is to corrupt the state kept by the session manager. In the early days of online shopping carts, for example, it proved possible in some cases to record an "order" for a single item and then add duplicates of that item to the virtual cart without increasing the price calculated by the server.

Another common threat is session hijacking, allowing an impersonator to act in the stead of the authenticated user. Various techniques are used for hijacking, including a simple man-in-the-middle attack (interposing the attacker between the two legitimate ends of the exchange).

Session *sidejacking* can be accomplished by using a packet sniffer (or other eavesdropping technique) to intercept and study the traffic between the two sides. Many sites revert to plain-text exchanges, even in Secure Socket Layer (SSL) sessions, after authentication is complete. The password probably will not be passed in plain text, but the session token (or *cookie*) may be, and this may be enough for impersonation to begin.

Session fixation can be used in cases where the value of a session ID about to begin is known, and fixed. The attacker lies in wait until the session kicks off and then takes the place of the authenticated user in the exchange.

Registration and Proofing of Identity

Deciding who gets access to what in a network or enterprise is just as important as selecting and implementing technical controls such as firewalls or intrusion detection software.

Before any action by a user can be authorized, the person requesting authorization must be authenticated as the user they claim to be. Before they can be authenticated as having the right to an identity, that identity must be created; and the person must be enrolled and associated with that identity in the registration system.

Whether your company supports critical infrastructure (such as the electrical grid) or makes million-dollar movies, if what you have is worth protecting, paying attention to who you bring onto your network makes sense. The person who sets up identities in your organization needs a way to determine whether the person claiming an identity really is who they say they are. Proofing the right to an identity is one of the foundations of all enterprise security.

Suppose you have been assigned the task of validating and proofing applications for the creation of an identity, as for a newly hired employee. (This makes you a credential service provider, or CSP.) You will work through several steps and stages in this task. The first consideration is just how sure you are supposed to be.

Identity Assurance Levels

In this matter of registration and identity proofing, the U.S. government (not surprisingly) has a great deal of experience, and much at stake. NIST is responsible for advising federal agencies how to do this correctly. NIST Special Publication 800-63A, "Digital Identity Guidelines: Enrollment and Identity Proofing Requirements" (`https://doi.org/10.6028/NIST.SP.800-63a`), suggests you consider three "identity assurance levels" (IALs).

- At risk level 1, you as a credential service provider can take "self-asserted" attributes (assertions from the claimant) at face value, neither validated nor verified.

- At risk level 2, you will require evidence that "supports the real-world existence" of the claimed identity and then use that evidence to verify that the claimant has a right to that identity. The evidence could be a state-supplied driver's license, for instance, or a certified copy of a birth certificate.

- At risk level 3, you should require the physical presence of the claimant. They must present themselves to you, and any identifying attributes must be verified by you. This applies to physical measurements, biometric attributes, and other characteristics (such as birth date) that can be established by your validation of original documents.

The next consideration is to determine the level of assurance your organization needs. Evaluate the "bad things that can happen" if you assess the applicant's claim incorrectly. Table 5.1 was adapted from NIST materials and demonstrates the degree to which security measures must ensure confidence to reach one of three identity assurance levels (IALs). You can see that if a threat to personal safety is involved, you should at least require an identity assurance level of 2, even if the likelihood is low. Or if, for example, the chance of civil or criminal violations is high, you probably want to go for the highest assurance level possible.

The values shown in Table 5.1 are, of course, just meant as examples. Each organization needs to make for itself the policy decisions relating to risk and consequence. Our point is that you need to be aware that differing levels of assurance are possible, then think through the risks of failed assurance before deciding on identity proofing policies and processes.

TABLE 5.1 **Sample Identity Assurance Levels**

IMPACT CATEGORIES	IAL1	IAL2	IAL3
Inconvenience, distress, or damage to standing or reputation	Low	Med	High
Financial loss or company liability	Low	Med	High
Harm to company programs or shareholder interests	N/A	Low/Med	High
Unauthorized release of sensitive information	N/A	Low/Med	High
Personal safety	N/A	Low	Med/High
Civil or criminal violations	N/A	Low/Med	High

Adapted from NIST SP 800-63-3 "Digital Identity Guidelines" (https://doi.org/10.6028/NIST.SP.800-63-3).

One factor that has often influenced the decision about what assurance level to use to validate a new hire's identity is the level of position they are applying for. That is the sort of information you can get from the hiring manager, and it often makes sense to apply a higher standard for more sensitive positions. You want to be careful, however, about influencing decisions with derogatory, potentially disqualifying information. Privacy is important.

People who are responsible for inspecting and validating proof of identify are often privy to extremely private information. Some of this material is PII, such as birth date, current address, home telephone number, and so forth. Sometimes other kinds of sensitive information come up during the identity validation process: a criminal background, financial information, or health data (either requested by or enforced against the employee). Each organization needs to have policies in place not only to protect PII but also to ensure that personal secrets that were divulged as part of the proofing process are used only for germane and legal purposes. Protect personal secrets carefully, according to law and policy; gossip has no place in the security office.

Table 5.2 presents the recommendations that the NIST makes to federal agencies as to the strength of evidence needed to achieve each of the three levels of assurance. As in Table 5.1, the three identity assurance levels (IALs) represent gradations of risk.

TABLE 5.2 Sample Identity Proofing Actions

REQUIREMENT	IAL1	IAL2	IAL3
Presence	No requirements	In-person and unsupervised remote.	In-person and supervised remote
Resolution	No requirements	The minimum attributes necessary to accomplish identity resolution Knowledge-based verification may be used for added confidence.	Same as IAL2
Evidence	No identity evidence is collected.	One piece of SUPERIOR or STRONG evidence depending on strength of original proof and validation occurs with issuing source, or Two pieces of STRONG evidence, or One piece of STRONG evidence plus two pieces of FAIR evidence	Two pieces of SUPERIOR evidence, or One piece of SUPERIOR evidence and one piece of STRONG evidence depending on strength of original proof and validation occurs with issuing source, or Two pieces of STRONG evidence plus one piece of FAIR evidence
Validation	No validation	Each piece of evidence must be validated with a process that is able to achieve the same strength as the evidence presented.	Same as IAL2
Verification	No verification	Verified by a process that is able to achieve a strength of STRONG	Verified by a process that is able to achieve a strength of SUPERIOR
Address confirmation	No requirements for address confirmation	Required. Enrollment code sent to any address of record. Notification sent by means different from enrollment code	Required. Notification of proofing to postal address
Biometric collection	No.	Optional	Mandatory

Adapted from NIST SP 800-63a.

There are several subtle points of interest in the sample identity proofing actions provided in Table 5.2. Notice, for example, that for level 2 and level 3 assurance, it is necessary to validate each piece of evidence with a process that is able to achieve the same strength as the evidence. It is poor practice to accept a verbal assurance that the applicant has a college diploma and then give that evidence the same weight as a written diploma itself. That is, if a piece of Strong identity evidence is presented, it is to be validated at a strength of Strong itself.

Note also the level of care to be taken with the collection of biometric evidence. For the lowest level of assurance, none is needed; for level 2, it is optional; for level 3 (the highest degree of assurance), biometric means of verifying identity are mandatory.

These sample recommendations, while official to the U.S. government, may not be appropriate for your organization.

Having explored the sorts of assurance possible or required for proof of identity, we will shift to a related topic of identity assurance, digital certificates.

Digital Certificates

A *digital certificate* is an electronic credential, a document that makes use of modern public key cryptography to provide a means of verifying an identity. It may help to think of a certificate as a driver's license made up of encrypted ones and zeros, bound to an electronically stored identity.

NOTE For details about public key cryptography and how a public key infrastructure (PKI) works, see Chapter 3.

Technically, what the certificate proves is that the particular *public key* included in the certificate is owned by the *subject* of the certificate, which can be a person, an organization, a computer system, or a software application. This ownership is attested to by a certificate authority (CA). A *certificate authority* is an entity trusted by one or more users as an authority that issues, revokes, and manages digital certificates to bind individuals and entities to their public keys.

Like a driver's license, a credential must be created, maintained, and (if necessary) revoked; that is, credentials must be managed.

Various circumstances might invalidate a certificate, such as the following:

- Change of the subject's name (does not always invalidate the certificate, depending on policy and the implementing technology)

- Change of association between the subject and the certificate authority (such as when the subject is an employee leaving the company that acts as the certificate authority)

- Compromise of the private key that corresponds to the public key included in the certificate

In these circumstances, the CA must revoke the certificate. One common way is to put that certificate's serial number on a certificate revocation list (CRL) maintained and made public, perhaps on a website, by the CA.

Checking that a certificate you have received has not been revoked is an important step in verifying it. You can either download the latest CRL from the CA or check directly with the CA in real time using the Online Certificate Status Protocol (OCSP). If the certificate has not been revoked, the digital signature of the certificate authority is authentic, and you trust that CA, then the chain of logic is complete.

Once you have verified a certificate, you may consider the data contained in it as authentic. That choice, like others in our field, is a risk to be balanced. Because digital certificates are such an important part of modern security, it comes as no surprise that attackers have worked hard—and have often succeeded—at discovering and exploiting vulnerabilities associated with certificates. Dozens of flaws with digital certificates have been uncovered over the years.

Some attackers have focused their efforts on certificate authorities. One approach seeks to exploit weaknesses in the domain validation schemes a CA employs to authenticate the applicant for a new certificate. Another is to directly compromise the databases maintained by a certificate authority to cause the issuance of rogue certificates.

The potential use of rogue certificates has afflicted more than one mobile banking application, weakening their defense against man-in-the-middle (MITM) attacks. The MITM risk is that an attacker may intercept an encrypted connection, pose to each side as the other participant, copy the user's banking credentials, and steal their money. Recently, a defensive tactic known as *pinning*—associating a particular host with their expected certificate—has become popular. Pinning, however, fails to solve the problem if the application does not check to see if it is connected to a trusted source (that is, authenticate the hostname) before using the certificate.

Critics have long pointed to cryptographic issues with digital certificates, as well. To make certificates more difficult to subvert, the *hash function* must provide unique values. The ability to generate two different files with identical hash values makes possible a so-called collision attack, diluting the value of the digital signatures used in certificates. NIST warned in 2015 that advances in processing speed had rendered unsafe the use of the popular SHA-1 cryptographic algorithm, and in 2017 Google researchers demonstrated a hash collision attack against SHA-1.

Pure implementation issues not directly due to cryptographic issues have plagued certificate-based security in recent years as well, as the infamous "HeartBleed" and "POODLE" vulnerabilities of 2014 illustrated only too well.

Many of these certificate-based vulnerabilities have been addressed, over the years, with new designs and new implementation versions. Yet as long as clever attackers seek to undermine complex authentication systems, you can never be absolutely certain that a certificate is trustworthy.

The responsible management of digital certificates is so important because they are critical to modern authentication methods. Certificates have so many uses!

For example, a software developer may use a credential scheme to allow their application to log into a database without having to hard-code the username and password into the source code. It is also possible to digitally sign software and patches upon release with credentials so that any tampering with the executable file can be detected. IPSec, a framework of open standards helping to secure communications over the Internet, relies on digital certificates, as do almost all virtual private network (VPN) technologies. Digital certificates also make possible the Secure/Multipurpose Internet Mail Extension (S/MIME) capabilities that can be used to encrypt electronic mail.

The place where the everyday user interacts with digital certificates most often, without question, is when they visit a "secure" website—that is, one with a URL that begins with "HTTPS" and not "HTTP."

When you connect to a website with an address that begins with "HTTPS," you are specifying that you want the browser session to use Transport Layer Security (TLS), a cryptographic protocol that provides communications security between computer networks. (TLS has largely supplanted the earlier protocol SSL, which introduced this capability.)

TLS uses digital certificates. To give you a sense of the complexity of the configuration possibilities, see this section of the NIST guidance:

> *The TLS server shall be configured with one or more public key certificates and the associated private keys. TLS server implementations should support multiple server certificates with their associated private keys to support algorithm and key size agility.*
>
> *There are six options for TLS server certificates that can satisfy the requirement for Approved cryptography: an RSA key encipherment certificate; an RSA signature certificate; an Elliptic Curve Digital Signature Algorithm (ECDSA) signature certificate; a Digital Signature Algorithm (DSA) signature certificate; a Diffie-Hellman certificate; and an ECDH certificate....*
>
> *TLS servers shall be configured with certificates issued by a CA, rather than self-signed certificates. Furthermore, TLS server certificates shall be issued by a CA that publishes revocation information in either a Certificate Revocation List (CRL) [RFC5280] or in Online Certificate Status Protocol (OCSP) [RFC6960] responses.*
>
> NIST Special Publication 800-52, Guidelines for the Selection, Configuration and Use of Transport Layer Security (TLS) Implementations, April 2014 (https://doi.org/10.6028/NIST.SP.800-52r1)

The full details, which extend for several additional pages, are beyond the scope of this chapter. The key concept is that your web browser and the website server use certificates to be sure of the identity of the other side of the transaction.

The most popular design for the content and format of digital certificates is defined by the standard X.509, provided by the Standardization sector of the International Telecommunications Union (ITU-T). Version 1 was defined in 1988, Version 2 in 1993, and Version 3 (the current version) in 1996.

An X.509 certificate consists of three required fields: the `tbscertificate`, the `signatureAlgorithm`, and the `signatureValue`. Here is a quick look at the contents of each:

Inside the `tbscertificate` field, you will find the names of the `subject` and the `issuer`. This field also contains the public key associated with the subject and the "validity period" specifying the `notBefore` and `notAfter` times. The certificate authority generates and inserts a unique `serialNumber` for the certificate, too.

The `signatureAlgorithm` field contains an identifier for the cryptographic algorithm used by the certificate authority to sign the certificate.

The `signatureValue` field contains a digital signature computed for this certificate, encoded as a bit string.

NOTE For more information about the X.509 certificate and its required fields, see RFC 5280, "Internet X.509 Public Key Infrastructure Certificate and Certificate Revocation List (CRL) Profile," from the Internet Engineering Task Force (`https://doi.org/10.17487/RFC5280`).

In addition to specifying the content of X.509 certificates, the standard lays out a certification *path validation algorithm* as well. Digital certificates build and rely upon a chain of trust, and a certificate chain carefully lists for examination each CA in the chain, conveying credence to the certificate.

A certificate can in fact be *self-signed* by the subject. Properly constructed self-signed certificates adhere to the format and satisfy the standard, leaving it up to the recipient to evaluate whether they are trustworthy. Self-certification limits, naturally, the sum of conveyed trust to the subject alone. On the other hand, self-signed certificates do eliminate the potential risk of third parties, which may improperly sign certificates or have themselves been compromised by an attack.

Before leaving the subject of digital certificates, we must tackle the difference between a certificate and a *blockchain*. Blockchains have made cryptocurrencies possible (and increasingly popular) in recent years. They are based on a cryptographic message integrity scheme. A blockchain is a decentralized public record of transactions calculated by distributed computing systems across the Internet. The blockchain uses cryptographic encryption to ensure that any tampering with that record can be detected.

Briefly, the blocks keep batches of valid transactions that are hashed and encoded into something called a *Merkel tree*. Each block holds the cryptographic hash of the previous block. Hence, they are chained together, in a set of continuous links, all the way back to a *genesis block*. This distributed public chain of verifiable blocks ensures the integrity of the blockchain transaction records.

Central to the idea of a digital certificate is a hierarchy of certificate authorities, external entities that are trusted to "certify" the connection between the subject and the data in the certificate. Blockchains are not certificates, because no external entity is performing certification.

Federated Identity Management

Earlier this chapter discussed how SSO helped ordinary users and system administrators keep their sanity. By requiring the user to authenticate just one time with a single account and then use many applications inside an enterprise, SSO eases the authentication burden for all.

In this section, we will discuss two related, but different, approaches to SSO. One is called *federated identity management* (FIM). The other is *delegated identity management* (DIM). In the federated approach to website authentication, users can supply any credentials they want that are compatible with the site and the services behind it. For example, an OpenID account can be used with any service that implements the OpenID service. Delegating an authentication service, on the other hand, transfers responsibility for authentication to a third party. Facebook Connect is an example. If you have ever been offered a chance to "authenticate through Facebook," you have seen delegated authentication in action.

Both approaches allow you to authenticate once and then conduct a session using applications across several cooperating enterprises. A user can log into one enterprise and then be able to employ resources in a second, affiliated network without additional authentication and without applying a second credential.

These two approaches offer a good way to enforce multifactor authentication across many applications. The method scales well and extends cleanly to cloud environments.

One important design element is that these two authentication schemes rely on mutual trust. The user's credentials are stored with an "identity provider" accessible on the connected networks or the cloud. When the user logs into a service (for example, a security as a service application), the service provider puts its trust in the identity provider. These trust relationships mean effectively that the compromise of one significant element of the service chain can lead to the compromise of all connected systems that trust that identity.

One facet of this arrangement amplifies operational security considerably: it is no longer necessary to deauthorize a compromised account or persona non grata user on every individual system or application for which they are authorized. A user can be deauthorized once with immediate effect everywhere on all of the systems using this distributed method.

An implementer of federated identity management has plenty of technical choices. They can use Security Assertion Markup Language (SAML) or even plain XML to transmit authorization messages among partners. Other options include use OAuth, OpenID, and even security tokens or PKI. Various combinations are possible; for example, WS-Federation is an Identity Federation specification developed by a group of companies, part of the Web Services Security framework. WS-Federation has mechanisms for brokering information on identities, identity attributes, and authentication itself.

Using SAML for Federated Identity Management

SAML, a modern open standard defined by the OASIS Committee, was discussed earlier in the "Identity Management Implementation" section. Under federated identity management, XML-based SAML makes use of three *roles* and four primary *components*.

In its simplest application within IAM, SAML provides a formal mechanism and format for one entity to assure a second entity about the identity of a third, usually a human being. These three SAML roles include the following:

- **Identity provider (IdP):** This is the first entity. It makes an assertion about another identity, based on information it has. This information might have just been obtained, say by querying the user for a username/password pair.

- **Service provider (SP):** This entity is the relying party that is being asked to provide its service or resource, based on the assurance provided by the IdP.

- **Subject or principal:** This entity is the subject of the assertion, usually a person, who is in some sense being vouched for.

The four primary components of SAML are:

- **Assertions:** In a SAML assertion, an identity provider makes one or more statements about a subject (also known as the *principal*—usually, a user) that the relying party can use to make access control decisions. The statement vouches for the authentication of the subject (perhaps providing details in an *authentication statement*) and may provide one or more *attribute statements*, describing the subject by means of name-value pairs. The assertion may also specify, in an *authorization decision statement*, conditions under which the principal is permitted to perform certain actions on a given resource.

- **Protocols:** SAML protocols describe how information is to be exchanged between, or consumed by, SAML entities. These rules specify the format and content of several types SAML exchanges, especially queries between entities. For example, SAML version 1.1 provides for queries concerning the kind of authentication, attribute, and authorization information contained in assertions. Additional protocols, added in SAML 2.0, include an Artifact Resolution Protocol, a Name Identifier Management Protocol, and Single Logout Protocol.

- **Bindings:** SAML *bindings* specify how to encapsulate the various SAML protocols in various types of messages. Since SAML 2.0, these bindings have described not only how to include queries in, for example, SOAP envelopes, but also HTTP POST and GET exchanges (among others).

- **Profiles:** SAML bindings, protocols, and assertions can be pulled together to make a *profile*, a set of definitions and instructions for a specified use case. SAML 2.0, for instance, makes available five different profiles for SSO use cases: Enhanced Client or Proxy (ECP), Identity Provider Discovery, Name Identifier Management, Single Logout, and Web Browser SSO. Several other profiles are available in SAML 2.0. There are third-party profiles, too, such as the OASIS WS-Security SAML Token Profile.

SAML assertions themselves do not provide authentication of the user or principal. The next section discusses several methods for achieving this.

NOTE   For more information about SAML, its roles and components, and their formats, see "Security Assertion Markup Language (SAML) V2.0 Technical Overview, OASIS Committee Draft 02," at `https://wiki.oasis-open.org/security/Saml2TechOverview`.

Authentication and Authorization Methods

There are several prominent methods for authentication in use today, ranging from getting a simple username/password pair to the use of multifactor authentication to the most complex of modern centralized methods.

Several older, legacy authentication methods remain in use, including Remote Authentication Dial-in User Service (RADIUS), Lightweight Directory Access Protocol (LDAP), and Microsoft's Active Directory.

RADIUS originated in the early 1990s as a method of authenticating dial-up customers and has seen much use in support of classical remote access. A RADIUS server, when queried by a client supplying candidate login credentials, can reply with either an Access-Accept message, an Access-Reject, or an Access-Challenge. With this lightweight structure, RADIUS can conduct fast and simple authentications when possible or move on to multifactor authentication and even challenge-response dialogs when those are required. RADIUS can also support complications such as the Extensible Authentication Protocol (EAP).

LDAP is a directory service based on the X.500 Directory Access Protocol standard developed by the ITU-T. Designed to take advantage of the IP protocol suite, which evolved after the adoption of the X.500 Directory Access Protocol, LDAP is often compared to an old-fashioned telephone directory. An LDAP server contains information about users in a directory tree, and clients query it to get details. Large enterprises maintain replicated LDAP servers at various points across the enterprise to facilitate a quick response.

Each entry in an LDAP directory tree is a collection of information about an object, pointed to by a unique identifier called a *distinguished name* (DN). The DN represents the complete path in the tree to the desired entry. A set of named component parts called *attributes* hold the data for that entry. Various user attributes are typically stored in LDAP directories, including telephone numbers, physical addresses, postal addresses, and email addresses.

LDAP can also be used to authenticate user credentials by an LDAP command called `bind`. In the simplest case, `bind` checks the entered candidate password against the `userPassword` attribute (receiving either a success code or the error `Invalid credentials`).

Microsoft's ubiquitous Active Directory, developed for Windows domain networks, uses LDAP versions 2 and 3. Active Directory is a proprietary directory service. A server running Active Directory Domain Services (AD DS), called a *domain controller*, authenticates users and authorizes actions, verifying their credentials and defining their access rights. AD DS provide structured hierarchical data storage for users, printers, and services, as well as support for locating and working with those objects.

On a larger, multinetwork or multi-enterprise playing field, Active Directory Federation Services (AD FS) can allow the sharing of information between trusted business partners. AD FS can provide SSO to federated partners just as other federated identity management systems can.

Two more modern protocols, mentioned earlier in this chapter, are commonly used together to provide authentication services. OAuth 2.0 and OIDC offer a related but competing approach to SAML.

OIDC is an implementation of the authorization framework OAuth 2.0, facilitating the communication of attribute and authentication information. Whereas SAML specifically relays requests from a website, OIDC can work to effect authentication with either a website or a mobile application as the requester.

An OIDC authentication sequence requires the selection of an OpenID identify provider. Once the IdP is known, OIDC operates as an authentication layer on top of the

OAuth 2.0 protocol, allowing the relying party to request and receive information about the user from the IdP.

OAuth 2.0 is itself an authorization protocol. Using it, a *client application* can request access to a protected resource from the entity that owns that resource. The request goes to an *authorization server*, which must authenticate the resource owner, validate the request, obtain authorization from the *resource owner*, and then relay an *authorization token* to the *resource server* that hosts the protected resource.

In the OIDC authentication implementation, the relying party (RP) is an OAuth 2.0 application requesting an ID token from an OpenID Connect Provider (OP). The fields in the token will contain data ("claims") about both the user (called the subject, or `sub`, and known by a locally unique identifier) and the timing (both the "issued at" time, or `iat`, and the expiration time, `exp`) of the authentication event. Also, the ID token will contain the issuer identifier (`iss`) of the OP and the client identifier (audience, or `aud`) registered for the RP at the issuer. Additionally, the claims can contain more information about the user, such as `first_name`, `last_name`, and so on.

One way to view this extension of OAuth 2.0 is that OIDC effectively allows an application to request authorization to authenticate a user.

Credential Management Systems

Earlier in this chapter, we explored the idea of using a *password manager* to ease a user's task in creating and remembering complex passwords. We discussed then the pros and cons of storing all of an individual's passwords for a given computer in one central place. It means less work for the user and often results in stronger, more complex passwords. The central storage has special risks, too: the loss or theft of the master password can significantly disrupt the user's work and may open them to impersonation, which can pose a serious threat to network security.

Password managers are one instance of a *credential management system*, in which the same concept of centralization is carried out at an enterprise level (or even a federation of cooperating enterprises). You can use a commercial credential management system (CMS) to create, maintain, and store the following:

- Traditional passwords
- Digital certificates and tokens
- One-time passwords
- Biometric records

A good CMS must do the following:

- Scale well as the enterprise or federation grows
- Handle the needs of devices and users who are on site, remote, mobile, or in the cloud

Just as with any "put all your eggs in one basket" approach, CMSs come with some special challenges and risks. If the security protecting the CMS is compromised, a massive failure may (depending on the exact design of the CMS and other safeguards) be possible via successful impersonation. In any event, an enterprise with a compromised CMS would need to reissue credentials on a massive scale—an expensive, disruptive, and time-consuming process.

Do not let this mostly hypothetical risk of catastrophic failure dissuade you from using such a centralized repository. A well-designed, professional-grade CMS should certainly prove more resistant to attack than the alternative, one or more ad hoc systems spread around a network. Indeed, a CMS may well be the only way to provide sufficient assurance for regulators and boards of directors that credentials are adequately secured.

A useful feature of any CMS is a hardware security module (HSM), a physical device that attaches to a computer system. An HSM protects credentials to a higher degree than any software running on a general-purpose computing system could provide by itself. It can take many physical forms (a PCI plug-in card, a smartcard, or a physically shielded local area network appliance), but all HSMs will feature a specialized processor to provide cryptographic keys and accelerated cryptographic operations.

An HSM thus offers high performance and sophisticated key management, as well as (often) redundant storage for high availability. Perhaps its most important advantage, though, is that it facilitates *separation of duties*. The system administrators who manage the enterprise network, and may have general privileged access to accounts, registers, and directories, can nevertheless be walled off from access to the HSM, administered separately. If no one person has the ability to both manage accounts (including associated privileges) and the accounts' credentials, a single rogue administrator has a much harder time taking total control.

For a complementary perspective on methods and risks pertaining to credential management and further discussion of HSMs, please consult Chapter 3, "Security Architecture and Engineering."

INTEGRATE IDENTITY AS A THIRD-PARTY SERVICE

In implementing identity management services, it is often desirable to integrate identity as a third-party service, engaging an identity provider. We will examine here three scenarios: on-premises implementations, cloud services, and a federated approach. Naturally, these arrangements can be combined in various ways. Any solution must bridge to existing technologies you are already using (e.g., Active Directory) and integrate with your traditionally authenticated applications.

To begin the analysis, consider the traditional security architect's question: what can go wrong?

Before "outsourcing" your identity services, take a careful look at the question of availability. Especially if the bulk of your operations are still on site, introducing a new dependency on the cloud may represent a significant incremental risk. If the mechanisms allowing your users to log into your applications now include vectoring the authentication request to a third party IdP, your business will grind to a halt if that third party is offline.

To manage this risk, try to find a way to avoid making the IdP a single point of failure. Do they offer a high-availability option, perhaps by partnering with a competing service to cover their outages? The peace of mind might be worth the extra cost.

Whether or not you can protect against an outage of your outsourced identity provider, you need to look at the failure scenarios. Presumably, if the IdP is offline, your accounts will fail closed—that is, login attempts will be denied. Does it make sense (is it even possible?) to maintain a core set of on-premises accounts as a backup so that specific administrators will be guaranteed access in case of an IdP outage? Many arrangements are possible; engage the right stakeholders, and choose one.

Another point to keep in mind when considering outsourcing a particular service is your *third-party risk*. If you integrate identity as a third-party service, you are trusting that third party with the identity of your users and their authentication to all the software and data you provide them. A compromise of the identity provider's systems or databases or network could mean giving control to an attacker of the authentication within *your* enterprise. To be diligent, satisfy yourself that the intrinsic enterprise security of the candidate IdP is, at the very least, as strong as that of your own company. Otherwise, you will be simply lowering your security to their level.

On-Premise

If you have already standardized on a traditional technology such as Active Directory or LDAP, you may want to retain that on-premises directory as your master identity source. (However, you might not have a choice. Some of the newer identity schemes and IoT environments are incompatible with legacy environments.)

There are hybrid models to consider. One solution is to use your established methods for employees while managing the identities of contractors and guests via a third-party product. The access given to employees is typically more textured, with many more applications and services involved than for temporary workers. Consider managing identities for the latter with a lightweight modern third-party solution. You want to avoid as many adds, moves, and changes as you can with the more complex services such as Active Directory.

Cloud

Many enterprises today operate either wholly in a cloud environment or with a mix of on-premises and cloud-based operations. In the cloud especially, it is common to implement identity as a service (IDaaS).

IDaaS provides cloud-based services that broker IAM functions to target systems on customers' premises and/or in the cloud. IDaaS is often paired with software as a service (SaaS), implemented as applications in the cloud.

When the movement toward SaaS first began in the late 1990s, authentication was the sticking point, the notable obstacle. As SaaS emerged, it required an enterprise to authorize duplicate accounts (parallel to those already in the enterprise) for its users, on the website of the software service. Maintaining duplicate accounts was troublesome and risky, and the question of who held the passwords (the enterprise or the service company) had no good answer. Using an identity provider in the cloud along with SaaS elegantly resolves this puzzle.

In the identity provider scheme, a user in your organization logs in using an identity from an outside provider, such as Google, Facebook, or Amazon Web Services. That external entity is given permission by your security services to use internal resources on behalf of that validated account. This way, your users can access resources via the cloud without revealing your internal usernames and passwords, or other internal credentials, to third parties in the cloud.

Availability of the identity provider remains a concern, as it always must. Still, will there often be a case when your users want to use cloud software services—which are up—but the cloud-based identity provider is down? Usually, they will both be available; occasionally, they will both be offline due to difficulty in reaching the cloud. The unavailability of the IdP alone should be a rare occurrence.

Federated

To make use of an identity provider across a federated group of partners is a natural extension of the simpler cases. You will need to examine the increased spread of the risks involved, but the business drivers for collaboration are irresistible for most companies in today's environment.

The key is to be able to give access to selected applications and databases—no more. If those services are hosted in the cloud, configured as SaaS, both your employees and your collaborators can use the same IDaaS. If the services to be shared run on your internal, on-premises servers, you will need your servers to receive, accept, and trust incoming directives (typically, SAML assertions) from your collaborator.

IMPLEMENT AND MANAGE AUTHORIZATION MECHANISMS

Suppose that you have the opportunity to devise, from scratch, a scheme for access control to all of the assets for which you are responsible. Not only can you pick the security devices and policies, but you can also decide on the very kinds of attributes that will determine access authority for everyone.

One way to start such a design is to imagine that you—or your avatar—will be queried, moment to moment, for an on-the-spot decision as to who can do what. For this example, suppose you receive the queries via text and respond with your decision the same way.

If the CFO wants to open a forecast spreadsheet, you might see something like this:

`[Date/Timestamp]: User jsmith1 wants to OPEN forecast.xls for WRITE.`

In response, you need to grant or deny access. Your decision will be based on a variety of factors, each of which will be informed by the access control model that you are using.

There are several access control models that exist. The most useful of these include the following:

- Role-based access control (RBAC)

- Rule-based access control (also, ambiguously, RBAC)

- Mandatory access control (MAC) (sometimes known as nondiscretionary access control, or NDAC)

- Discretionary access control (DAC)

- Attribute-based access control (ABAC)

The following sections examine how each model would implement this hypothetical CFO's spreadsheet example.

Role-Based Access Control

RBAC is an access control model that bases the access control authorizations on the roles (or functions) that the user is assigned within an organization.

RBAC has been used in simple forms since the early days of information security. It was formally defined by David Ferraiolo and Rick Kuhn in 1992 and soon became the dominant model for advanced access control. A well-designed and carefully managed RBAC system can dramatically reduce the cost of security administration while providing sound flexible control.

With RBAC, access rules are modeled after the enterprise's structure. Several organizational roles are defined (e.g., manager, software developer, salesperson), and each user is assigned one or more roles. Access rights are then assigned to the roles (not to the individual users) after determining which operations must be accomplished by people in each particular job. The role can be a job description, group membership, or security access level.

In the CFO spreadsheet scenario in our example, a role of "confidential financial analyst" could be assigned to user jsmith1, who would also be assigned a role of (say) "senior manager," sharing that role with other executives. Files similar to forecast.xls would certainly be made available for read and write to the analyst class, while senior managers might only have read access. The organization would need some sort of role for system administrators as well, empowering them to perform backups, and perhaps to read from (but not write to) such files as well.

Notice, by the way, that role conflicts are possible. That is, jsmith1 may have permission to read and write in their role as an analyst, but only reading rights as a senior manager. How to resolve such conflicts is a matter of policy. A permissive system will grant the maximum access of all combined rights, usually permitting any action granted by any of the assigned roles. A restrictive system will grant only the minimum access, the least access of any role assigned to the user.

In this example, therefore, you (or your avatar) would handle the request

```
[Date/Timestamp]: User jsmith1 wants to OPEN forecast.xls for WRITE.
```

by looking up all the roles assigned to jsmith1 and determining, via a policy like the one just described, whether write access is included.

Compared to other access control paradigms, RBAC can reduce employee downtime and simplify account provisioning.

Rule-Based Access Control

RBAC is an access control model that is based on a list of predefined rules that determine what accesses should be granted. It is a simple concept which can result in extremely complex rule lists.

A firewall configuration file is an example of rule-based access.

All traffic presented to the firewall is compared to the rules, one after another. An incoming connection request may be considered first according to its source Internet Protocol address and then according to its IP address destination. If no rule has been triggered yet, the connection request may be filtered according to the particular port sought for a connection. After all the rules and filters have been applied, if no disposition has been determined the default action (if there is one) will be carried out, either a deny or accept.

In the CFO spreadsheet scenario in our example, there would be an access control list (ACL) associated with the file, or perhaps the folder in which the file resides. This ACL will define the types of access (read, write, or read/write, perhaps execute) allowed to each user they want to be able to use the file. Our access control software will consult the ACL associated with the spreadsheet file `forecast.xls` to see whether the user `jsmith1` has `write` access to the file.

Since the acronym RBAC is most often used to denote role-based models, one sometimes sees rule-based access control models referred to as "rule-BAC" (or sometimes RB-RBAC) systems, rather than RBAC.

Mandatory Access Control

This model, often associated with military or government organizations, employs a static and strictly hierarchical approach to controlling resources.

MAC sometimes referred to as *non-discretionary access control (NDAC)*, requires the system itself to manage access controls in accordance with the organization's security policies. The information officer assigns a *security label* to each object or resource. The label names a classification (e.g., Top Secret, Secret, Confidential, or Unclassified) and a category (e.g., management level, department, or project).

End users—often, consumers of the information—have no control over the label settings. The identity administrator assigns each user a clearance and that user can consume information classified at or below that level. For example, a user with a Secret clearance can view documents that are Secret or Confidential but not Top Secret.

The owner or creator of a document sets its classification (we are simplifying here—that may be a specialist's job) but cannot decide which users are authorized. That decision is made by the system itself, depending on whether a particular user's access level rises as high as the document. This model is based on levels and labels, not roles; it is sometimes called a *lattice-based model*. To see how this works, visualize a set of bookshelves in a fancy library, with a ladder giving access to the highest shelves. If you put the most precious books (or facts) on the highest shelves and then control how many steps up the ladder the library's users are allowed to climb, you have implemented a lattice-based access control model.

In the CFO spreadsheet scenario in our example, the access decision will come down to what classification (e.g., Secret) was assigned to `forecast.xls` and whether CFO `jsmith1` has Secret access or better.

Two formal historical methods sometimes associated with MAC are the Biba Integrity Model and the Bell-LaPadula model, both proposed in academic papers in the mid-1970s. Each has had a significant influence on access control theory—so much so that their principles today may sound familiar and simplistic to security practitioners unacquainted with the theoretical underpinnings of modern practice.

In 1973, computer scientists David Bell and Leonard LaPadula proposed a groundbreaking formal model for computer access control. In their model, they divide all entities on a computer system into either subjects or objects. Bell and LaPadula prove mathematically that if their rules for handling of objects by subjects are followed, the confidentiality of the objects will be preserved.

The Biba Integrity Model was proposed by Kenneth Biba in 1975. His model described a set of access control rules designed to preserve the integrity of information. A user with low-level clearance can read higher-level information ("read up"). A user with high-level clearance can write for lower levels of clearance ("write down"). Notice that the latter rule protects the integrity of documents from those unauthorized to change them.

The basic rules are what we described for MAC. Users can create content only at or above their own security level (no "write-down"). Users can view content only at or below their own security level (no "read-up"). They also provided for the use of an access matrix to specify discretionary access control; this facet of the model introduces a taste of DAC, which we discuss next.

Discretionary Access Control

DAC is a paradigm in which the system owner decides who gets access to that computer system. In the case of a file or other data object, it is the owner, creator, or data custodian who defines and controls access (such as reading and writing) to the object.

In the CFO spreadsheet scenario in our example, the file's owner will have created an ACL defining the types of access (e.g., read, write, or read/write, perhaps execute) accorded to each user they wanted to be able to use the file. As in our rule-based example, our access control software will need to consult the ACL associated with the spreadsheet file `forecast.xls` to see whether the user `jsmith1` has `write` access to the file.

Note that DAC allows the individual data owner complete control over the objects they own, even to the extent of granting some users higher levels of access to the object than they would ordinarily have over other similar objects.

Attribute-Based Access Control

ABAC is a relatively new, so-called "next-generation" access control model. It employs a paradigm whereby access rights are granted to users according to policies that combine attributes. For example, access to a given data set or system might only be allowed during "working hours" (however those are defined by the organization). Because it controls access of subject to objects by evaluating rules against the attributes of the subject and object and against the environmental conditions, ABAC is more flexible than the other methods we have discussed. It can be easy to set up but may be complex to manage.

ABAC systems are capable of enforcing both DAC and MAC models. ABAC systems can even be made to adapt as risks change, by expressing the risk values as variable attributes.

In our CFO spreadsheet example, the security office or network administrator might assign to `jsmith1` the attributes of being an officer of the company and a manager in the financial department. The `forecast.xls` file could be assigned attributes showing it to contain sensitive financial records and subject to regulatory control. The system, in comparing the attributes of the user and the file, would (one presumes) conclude that an officer of the company, a manager in the financial department, should be given access to sensitive financial records pertinent to the company's regulatory environment.

The policies with which ABAC operates are written in a structured language called the Extensible Access Control Markup Language (XACML), currently at version 3. One XACML rule for our example might direct the access control system, for example, to "permit managers to access financial data provided they are from the finance department." The language provides a level of contextual awareness difficult to match in earlier access control models.

▶▶ REAL WORLD EXAMPLE:
Desirable Attributes of Authorization Schemes

Whatever access and identity management scheme you select, you will need to ensure that it is the following:

- *Fast in operation.* Logic that is involved in every decision on the network must be crisp. Keep in mind that, usually, simpler principles lead to faster execution

- *Scalable.* Whether you need to control hundreds of assets, or billions, you will want to use the same basic approach. Most enterprises, especially successful ones, grow and change and sprawl and spurt. You do not want your access scheme to hinder growth.

- *Comprehensive.* It is not always possible to subsume all of an enterprise's assets under a single identity or access management scheme. You may not be able to ensure that each employee and consultant and advisor in every department can be given a username and appropriate access regardless of when they join the company and what it is they do. Strive, however, for the minimal number of arrangements and meanings and things to remember that it is possible to achieve in managing assets and identities.

- *Maintainable.* Your organization will change. In a big company, divisions may be added, product groups invented, or an entire business arm may be broken up. Even in a small enterprise, individual contributors will be reassigned, and reporting relationships will change. You want an identity scheme that will power through any such changes and not require that someone change their internal email address or even their username because of a transfer or promotion

- *Adaptable.* Ideally, the same scheme and decision factors should be capable of controlling access on individual computer systems, within a wholly owned data center, in a globe-circling cloud environment, or (more realistically) all of these environments and more, simultaneously.

- *Just (and justifiable).* Authorization decisions need to be justifiable in the eyes of those who are denied as well as those who are granted permission. Arbitrary decisions, or decisions that can reasonably be criticized as discriminatory or frivolous, will at the very least drain energy away from security as they are defended.

- *Comprehensible.* Do not underrate the advantage of being able to explain the reasoning behind the IAM scheme you have selected. Management, vendors, board members or advisors, and many curious and sometimes frustrated employees will want to know how names and access roles are determined and what policy and infrastructure is carrying out access decisions.

MANAGE THE IDENTITY AND ACCESS PROVISIONING LIFECYCLE

The identity lifecycle includes identity creation, identification, authentication, authorization, and deprovisioning. In a simpler sense, these steps can be generalized as provisioning, reviewing, and deprovisioning of identification. An overview of the identity lifecycle was provided earlier in the chapter in the "Manage Identification and Authentication of People, Devices, and Services" section. This section is focused more specifically on aspects of managing the lifecycle, including user access review, system account access review, and the provisioning and deprovisioning of identities.

Access control and identity settings must be kept up to date. People leave the company, and even those who stay change departments or jobs. It is important to review periodically who has access to what and whether the access is still needed.

The need for periodic access review is not just a matter of departmental transfers. Many people go through periods in their lives when they become—perhaps for short periods—less reliable than they might like to be. Whether the cause is a sick child or an ailing marriage, a substance abuse issue or an attitude problem, everyone's loyalty and ability to focus is challenged from time to time. Your policies and processes need to reflect these realities by mandating periodic user and system access reviews. Every person should have the minimum access rights needed for the tasks they are assigned. That access, as well as the person's trustworthiness should be reviewed periodically, to make sure there is still a match between trust and risk.

For much the same reason, access control decisions and provisioning processes must be designed to allocate the minimum amount of access required for the shortest period of time possible. You need to determine precisely what access is needed to accomplish the task for which this person was hired or the system was created. You need to determine whether this system, access, or task is still relevant and necessary. The following sections describe how to do this, concluding with a discussion of how you can ensure that the life-cycle is adequately managed and the implications of failure if you don't.

User Access Review

Whether you control access by enforcing rules or interpreting the various roles of the user, you must periodically review the access privileges accorded to each user (or system or software entity). The period of the review should be set by policy and strictly enforced by well documented processes. Many organizations review the access of each user once per year.

In setting this policy, one must take into account the following:

- Legal constraints, whether statutory or required by regulations
- The frequency with which employees in your enterprise change jobs or change responsibilities within a job
- Generally, the pace of change characteristic to your organization
- The burden that user access reviews place upon the information technology staff and other parts of the company
- The cost, both financial and in lost productivity, of the reviews themselves

Your user access review process should include, at a minimum, the following:

- All of the accounts created for the user, or the accounts to which the user has been granted access
- All of the computers this user can connect to, use, or log into
- All of the databases this user can read from or write to
- All of the applications this user can use
- All of the websites controlled by your enterprise that the user can visit, and whether the user can log in, change things on the site, or merely read from it
- What sorts of data this user can see or change
- The times of day or days of the week all of these things may be done
- The geographical locations—and logical places on the enterprise network or in the cloud—from which all of these things may be done

Many of the most serious computer breaches in history have been the result of access rights left in place after a user changed assignments or left the company. Leftover accounts and no-longer-needed access are like land mines in your network. Defuse them with periodic substantive access review.

System Account Access Review

In addition to conducting a periodic review of access granted to and possible by each user, good practice also requires that you check access from the system point of view as well. Modern computer systems make extensive use of "system" accounts. These are a kind of user account not associated with a human being but rather an automated process. Often used for housekeeping purposes such as backups, disk management, or the general gathering and analysis of monitoring and log data, these accounts usually have elevated privileges that grant access to special devices or system files. Ideally, you would check system by system, for every computer, every security device on your network, and every database—in fact, every technical entity—to see which software and systems can do any of these things:

- Connect
- Read
- Write
- Verify the existence of, or the up/down state or its health
- Start or stop
- Read or change access settings
- Read or change any other configuration settings
- Perform privileged actions, or act as a system administrator

Such checks are time-consuming and in an ordinary network must be automated in order for a comprehensive scan to be practical. As with so many security measures, you may find it necessary to prioritize which systems (and which system accounts) are reviewed.

Provisioning and Deprovisioning

Provisioning is the discrete act by which an identity, with whatever credentials are necessary for authentication, is made available for use. Provisioning is what your company's IT department does when they create an account on the company's computers for you, issue you a laptop or mobile phone, or authorize you to use the enterprise computers.

Conversely, *deprovisioning* is the act of deactivating or decommissioning an identity and associated access. When, for example, you cease to be employed at the company, your accounts may be deactivated, and you will certainly be required to turn back in any phones or computers that had been issued to you.

Further aspects of deprovisioning may include the following:

- Removing you from the list of authorized computer users
- Removing you from any role-related access control lists
- Disabling login accounts
- Disabling email

On that last point many organizations, when an employee leaves, do not remove login accounts and email access right away but rather disable them. The idea is that files and records can stay in one known place for a bit, while the organization figures out how to redistribute the responsibilities of the departed employee. (Your policies should make clear what is to be done, not leaving the decision up to the individual system administrator.)

We began this chapter about IAM by discussing who gets access to what assets in an enterprise. We stepped through the process of establishing an identity, authenticating a user, and determining whether they were authorized for a particular action. It is fitting, then, that we concluded with a discussion about how to remove a user and terminate their access. From beginning to end, the cycle of granting, managing, and removing identities and access authorizations is the essence of IAM.

Auditing and Enforcement

We have laid out here a detailed description of good provisioning practice. But understanding what must be done is not enough. Even a small slip in executing these steps can blow open a gaping hole in your security. Here are a few real-world scenarios you should consider.

Suppose human resources' everyday practices do not ensure that a departing employee's login account is deactivated that same day. That leaves open a back door not only for the departing insider but also for, say, spiteful spouses with whom credentials (or the means to guess or circumvent them) have been shared.

Suppose a manager (acting out of compassion, perhaps, or simply juggling task priorities) fails to ensure that the former employee's laptop, phone, and other equipment is surrendered right away. Well, even if the equipment package does not enable a VPN tunnel straight into the corporate network (enhancing attack chances) and even if emails and files on the devices are somehow inaccessible for the former employee (if they were accessible it would facilitate theft or extortion), the remaining proprietary information on the equipment (employee lists, email addresses, and internal telephone numbers, as well as confidential text messages) can pose a significant security risk. Because even if your former employee is not, prior to surrendering the equipment, motivated to exploit that proprietary information, you might be unlucky enough to be dealing with someone who will make a copy of such potential competitive ammunition, just in case. Many successful enterprise attacks have been based on just such intelligence.

Such dire considerations are not speculations; they are case studies. And to avoid adding your company's mistakes and oversights to the syllabi of leading business schools, you had better engineer compliance to the lifecycle practices we detailed in the previous sections. You can do that with auditing and enforcement.

Auditors can be a real pain. In fact, they ought to be, especially in the critical down-to-earth details of your IAM. As a security professional, do all you can to build and support well-thought-out policies and practices in this area. Then, ask for or arrange or procure the most methodical, unforgiving, clear-eyed, exhaustive (and exhausting) review possible. You might engage disinterested third parties. Alternatively, internal auditing may be your corporate practice. If you are lucky, you may be able to use both. In any case, arranging for repeated thorough professional audits of your IAM is one of the best preventative measures at your disposal.

Keep in mind that managing identities and access is more than making and announcing rules. Being a good manager, you will determine what is needed, make rules as appropriate, arrange for resources, provide training and obtain buy-in, measure performance (auditing is part of this), and then enforce consequences for failure. Whether the failure was in the policies or actions of human resources, the poor execution of technical steps by the information technology team, or a simple oversight by a manager or team member anywhere in the chain of trust, enforcement (and reinforcement, as needed) of best practices can never be skipped.

The final step, of course, is to drive what you have learned from omissions and mistakes back into the workflow so your team (and you) can do a better job next time.

SUMMARY

Controlling who can do what to which object is, it can be fairly argued, the essence of security. Yes, it is possible to imagine a set of protections that make no distinction between friend and foe, block every action, and never allow a peek into whatever records may reside in the database. Such blanket restrictions, however, do not constitute "security" but rather a kind of data prison. A well-secured system is one that is available for the purpose intended by its owner and protects against reasonable threats by measures that do not significantly hamper its intended use. Such protections are impossible without the kinds of IAM techniques discussed here.

Security Assessment and Testing

ORGANIZATIONS NEED TO IDENTIFY and address issues that may put them at risk. To do this, they perform security assessments, risk assessments, and security audits. While they are related, it is important to understand the difference between them.

❏ A *security audit* compares its results against a standard to determine whether the standard is being met. Third-party audits are often required for legal or contractual compliance, but internal auditors are also used by many organizations to provide oversight over their own efforts. Most security audits will determine whether the organization is in compliance with the standard they are auditing against but won't track whether the organization's efforts exceed it.

❏ *Security assessments* are used to determine an organization's security posture. This means that assessors use standards as well as their own knowledge and experience to assess the strength and effectiveness of their security posture. Thus, all security audits are a form of security assessment, but not all security assessments are audits.

❑ *Risk assessments* provide a view of the risks that an organization faces. Many risk assessments categorize risks by probability and impact and include details of findings and potential controls. Since risk is an important element in a comprehensive understanding of an organization's security posture, risk assessments are often included in a security assessment.

Once an organization has completed an assessment or audit, it must prioritize the actions it will take in response. Most assessments and audits provide findings that need to be addressed, and organizations must analyze the gaps and issues based on their knowledge of the organization, its practices, its capabilities, and existing implementations, and then prioritize and plan which they will address and what order they will be handled in. Responses include deploying controls, remediating issues, transferring risk through the purchase of insurance, or documenting and accepting the risk. Each of these responses comes with a cost that needs to be evaluated compared to the improvement in security posture or reduction in security risk that it brings to the organization to make sure that appropriate actions are being taken.

After controls are put into place, they must be tested to ensure the problem is truly resolved. For example, an organization that is notified about a security issue with its website as part of a security assessment will not want to run the website with an insecure configuration, so it will identify possible controls and will select one or more of those controls to implement. Once a solution has been designed, the organization will test the solution, both prior to deploying it to ensure that it provides the security the organization is expecting and on an ongoing basis afterward as part of an ongoing security management effort. Only then can the organization operate with the confidence that the issues have been resolved.

DESIGN AND VALIDATE ASSESSMENT, TEST, AND AUDIT STRATEGIES

Projects require creating a methodology and scope for the project, and security assessment and audit efforts are no different. Management must determine the scope and targets of the assessment, including what systems, services, policies, procedures, and practices will be reviewed, and what standard, framework, or methodology the organization will select or create as the foundation of the assessment.

Commonly used industry frameworks include the following:

- NIST SP 800-53r4, "Assessing Security and Privacy Controls in Federal Information Systems and Organizations"

- NIST SP 800-115, "Technical Guide to Information Security Testing and Assessment"

- ISO 18045, "Information technology – Security techniques – Methodology for IT security evaluation," and the related ISO for controls ISO/IEC 27002, "Information Technology – Security Techniques – Code of practice for information security controls"

- ISO 15408, "Information Technology – Security Techniques – Evaluation criteria for IT security," also known as the Common Criteria

Although National Institute of Standards and Technology (NIST) standards may appear U.S.-centric at first glance, they are used as a reference for organizations throughout the world if there is not another national, international, or contractual standard those organizations must meet. In addition to these broad standards, specific standards like the ISA/IEC 62443 series of standards for industrial automation and control systems may be used where appropriate.

Using a standard methodology or framework allows consistency between assessments, allowing comparisons over time and between groups or divisions. In many cases, organizations will conduct their own internal assessments using industry standards as part of their security operations efforts, and by doing so, they are prepared for third-party or internal audits that are based on those standards.

In addition to choosing the standard and methodology, it is important to understand that audits can be conducted as internal audits using the organization's own staff or as external audits using third-party auditors. In addition, audits of third parties like cloud service providers can be conducted. Third-party audits most often use external auditors, rather than your organization's own staff. You'll find a deeper discussion of each type of audit, as well as its pros and cons, at the end of this chapter as part of the section titled "Conduct or Facilitate Security Audits."

Once the high-level goals and scope have been set and the assessment standard and methodology have been determined, assessors need to determine further details of what they will examine. Detailed scoping questions may include the following:

- What portions of the network and which hosts will be tested?

- Will auditing include a review of user files and logs?

- Is susceptibility of staff to social engineering being tested?

- Are confidentiality, integrity, and availability in scope?

- Are there any privacy concerns regarding the audit and the data it collects?

- Will processes, standards, and documentation be reviewed?

- Are employees and adherence to standards being examined?

- Are third-party service providers, cloud vendors, or other organizations part of the assessment?

Other aspects of security are also important. A complete assessment should include answers to these questions:

- Are architectural designs documented with data flows and other details matching the published design?

- Are things designed securely from the beginning of the design process?

- Is change management practiced?

- Does a configuration management database exist?

- Are assets tracked?

- Are regular vulnerability scans, and maybe even penetration tests, conducted?

- Are policies, procedures, and standards adhered to?

- Is the organization following industry-recognized best practices?

Budget and time constraints can make it impossible to test everything, so management must determine what will be included while balancing their assessment needs against their available resources.

Once the goals, scope, and methodology have been determined, the assessment team must be selected. The team may consist of the company's own staff, or external personnel may be retained. Factors that can aid in determining which option to select can include industry regulations and requirements, budget, goals, scope, and the expertise required for the assessment.

With the team selected, a plan should be created to identify how to meet the assessment's goals in a timely manner and within the budget constraints set forth by management. With the plan in place, the assessment can be conducted. This phase should generate significant documentation on how the assessment target complies or fails to comply with expectations. Any exceptions and noncompliance must be documented. Once the assessment activities are completed, the results can be compiled and reported to management.

Upon receipt of the completed report, management can create an action plan to address the issues found during the audit. For instance, a time frame can be set for installing missing patches and updates on hosts, or a training plan can be created to address process issues identified during the assessment.

Assessment Standards

There are a wide variety of assessment standards and tools available. In some cases, organizations must use a specific assessment methodology or standard due to legal requirements or contractual obligations. When they are not required to make a specific choice, organizations frequently choose one or more as the foundation of their own assessments based on their specific needs and fit to their industry or practices.

SSAE 18

One of the most common auditing standards for service organizations is the Statement on Standards for Attestation Engagements (SSAE), a standard that is overseen by the American Institute of Certified Public Accountants (AICPA). The current version of the SSAE is the SSAE 18, which replaced its predecessor, the SSAE 16, in May of 2017. The SSAE 18 provides Service Organization Control reports called SOC 1, SOC 2, and SOC 3 reports. These reports align to different assessment drivers, coverage, and target audiences as shown in Table 6.1.

TABLE 6.1 **SOC Levels and Applications**

SOC LEVEL	REASON FOR ASSESSMENT	COVERED ITEMS	AUDIT USERS
SOC 1	Audits of financial statements	Internal controls over financial reporting	The client's auditor and controller's office
SOC 2	Governance, risk, and compliance efforts, due diligence	Confidentiality, integrity, and availability, as well as security and privacy controls	Typically shared under nondisclosure agreement (NDA) and also used by regulators and others
SOC 3	Marketing and customer assurance	Confidentiality, integrity, and availability, as well as security and privacy controls	Publicly available

In addition, there are two types of SOC assessment. Type 1 SOC assessments cover a point in time, while Type 2 assessments cover a period of time and assess the effectiveness of the organization's controls. Since Type 1 assessments cover a point in time and do not assess the effectiveness of controls, instead focusing on their design, Type 1 assessments are considered less useful and should not be relied on to provide an accurate view of the organization's ongoing operations.

Assessors and security professionals may still encounter SSAE 16 reports and even older SAS 70 reports. SSAE 18 added requirements around implementation of a third-party vendor management program and a formal annual risk assessment process for all SOC reports, making SSAE 18 particularly desirable if an organization has a strong reliance on third-party vendors or risk assessment information is desired.

SAS 70, the "Statement on Auditing Standards No. 70," was the predecessor to SSAE 16 and was replaced in June 2011. Reports conducted under SAS 70 should be considered dangerously out of date, although they may still be reviewed or available for historical reasons.

ISAE 3402

The Internal Standard on Assurance Engagements (ISAE) number 3402, "Assurance Reports on Controls at a Service Organization," is an international standard for assurance. The ISAE 3402 framework served as the foundation for SSAE 16 and SSAE 18, with additional controls added to the SSAE standard in a number of areas. Like SSAE 16 and 18, ISAE 3402 engagements evaluate control policies and procedures, and they use Type I reports for point-in-time reporting and Type II reports for assessments with evaluation and testing over a period of time.

The Payment Card Industry – Data Security Standard (PCI-DSS) is a set of security standards issued by the Payment Card Industry Security Standards Council (PCI-SSC), a group made up of the major payment card brands. PCI-DSS applies to any organization that transmits or stores cardholder data, making PCI assessments a common requirement for many organizations. PCI assessment requirements are based on the merchant level of the organization, with levels from 1 to 4, as shown in Table 6.2.

TABLE 6.2 PCI-DSS Merchant Levels

MERCHANT LEVEL	DESCRIPTION
1	Any merchant processing more than 6 million transactions per year
2	Any merchant processing 1–6 million transactions per year
3	Any merchant processing 20,000–1 million transactions per year
4	Any merchant processing fewer than 20,000 transactions per year

Compliance requirements, and thus the requirements for assessments, increase as merchants process more transactions, including requirements to use third-party assessors and to use approved vulnerability scanning vendors, as well as providing attestations of compliance.

Cloud Security Alliance

The Cloud Security Alliance (CSA) provides the Security Trust and Assurance Registry (STAR) for security assurance in the cloud. STAR provides three levels: self-assessment, third-party certification, and continuous auditing based on the CSA's Cloud Controls Matrix (CCM), the Consensus Assessments Initiative Questionnaire (CAIQ), and the CSA Code of Conduct for GDPR Compliance.

The CCM is a framework for cloud-specific security controls and provides mappings to major standards and best practices, as well as regulations. The CAIQ leverages the CCM to allow vendor and provider reviews to be conducted by consumers and auditors.

Shared Assessments Tools

Shared Assessments provides licensed tools for risk management assessments via a questionnaire (the Standardized Information Gathering [SIG] questionnaire) and the Standardized Control Assessment (SCA) for performing risk management assessments to validate SIG responses. The Shared Assessments tools focus on cybersecurity, IT, privacy, data security, and business resiliency controls.

The Control Objectives for Information and Related Technologies (COBIT) framework was created by the Information Systems Audit and Control Association (ISACA) to define generic processes for the management of IT. COBIT 5, the current COBIT version, includes a variety of tools, including assurance tools. Organizations that have adopted COBIT as their IT management framework may assess against it as part of their ongoing review or audit processes.

CONDUCT SECURITY CONTROL TESTING

After an organization has selected security controls, it must determine whether a control is effective and efficient. Since controls cover a wide range of types, such as administrative controls, technical controls, and others, testing methods must be chosen that are suited to each control, and some controls may require multiple types of testing to fully validate them.

As an example of a process and technical control, if an organization is using the ISO 27002:13 standard, they might review 8.3.2, disposal of media. The ISO standard's control states that "Media should be disposed of securely when no longer required, using formal procedures," and the implementation guidance for this requirement describes secure shredding and erasure of data as possible options after appropriate procedures have been followed to determine data sensitivity.

The organization may opt to test the assessment procedures by selecting a sample of retired media such as hard drives, SSDs, or backup tapes that represent the types of media that the organization regularly retires from service. It can then check the process that retired the media, if the media was classified properly for handling, and if the media was appropriately wiped or destroyed based on that classification. This requires process, documentation, and technical control testing, all to test a single item from the standard.

Control tests like this are likely to identify problems, and organizations must then choose how to handle the issues they find. Media disposal reviews may find gaps in classification, problems with secure deletion processes, or leakage of media or drives to secondary uses despite sensitive data classifications. Once problems like these are found, an additional control review will need to be conducted to determine whether more controls need to be put in place or whether the existing controls are sufficient if they are properly enforced.

Technical assessment methods, including vulnerability assessment and penetration testing, are also major elements of many security control testing processes. In fact, PCI-DSS requires both a vulnerability scan (requirement 11.2) and a penetration test (requirement 11.3) for compliance.

Vulnerability Assessment

Organizations identify and then categorize and assess their vulnerabilities as part of their ongoing security assessment efforts. To do this, they conduct vulnerability scans that check their assets for known vulnerabilities. Assets include servers, routers, and other hardware devices. In addition, assets also include operating systems and their installed applications and services. Vulnerabilities found on an asset may be exploited, allowing an intruder to gain access to a company's network. Therefore, it's important to identify vulnerabilities and remediate them, but assessing vulnerabilities requires more than scanning and fixing them. In fact, fully assessing vulnerabilities requires an understanding of the vulnerabilities that exist, the likelihood of exploit, and the business drivers and requirements that influence how they are remediated or handled.

As with any security endeavor, this process starts by determining the goals of vulnerability scanning for the organization. Clearly identified goals can help ensure that the scan results are meaningful and have the most impact. If no scanning has previously been done, it is wise to step back and assess the goals prior to initiating a vulnerability scanning program. Obviously, the overarching goal is to reduce the number of unaddressed vulnerabilities in an environment to reduce risk. However, running a vulnerability scan on the entire network would likely be a huge mistake. It could easily result in such a massive amount of data that sorting through the results would take weeks and resolving issues may not be done in a timely manner. Ask some questions to aid in identifying an appropriate scope for your scanning efforts.

- What servers and devices support business-critical functions?
- Which hosts are accessible via the Internet and therefore at greater risk of compromise?
- Where are databases and file repositories with sensitive information?

The answers to these questions can help identify a starting point for your vulnerability identification efforts. However, it is indeed only a starting point. It is foolish to think there are unimportant devices that do not need to be remediated. A variety of entry points into your network exist that you may not think are important, in the traditional sense. However, that unpatched vulnerability may be all an attacker needs to completely compromise your network.

There are several popular tools that can be used for vulnerability scanning, including open source and commercial options. They all share common features. They are automated tools that scan a range of IP addresses or a single host and identify vulnerabilities, missing patches, and other security issues on the targeted hosts. They typically include a severity classification, a brief description, and information regarding patching or remediating the vulnerability. For example, the scan may identify a web server with known weaknesses in its TLS cipher suite. It can classify the ciphers identified by the scan as weak, medium, or strong. Based on the security posture of the organization, the company can then mandate the use of only the strong cipher suites, so those ciphers are no longer utilized. Many of the items found will only be informational, such as the presence of a web server. Critical issues may include a Common Vulnerability Scoring System (CVSS) score, a scoring system created by NIST.

As a best practice in security, vulnerability scans should be conducted regularly, and findings from these scans should be remediated in a timely fashion. Continuous scanning is an increasingly common option, often in partnership with continuous integration and DevOps practices that result in constant changes and upgrades in software and IT infrastructure. A common practice is to scan each change before it is approved for production, after it enters production, and on a recurring basis. With some organizations making hundreds or thousands of changes a day, continuous scanning is a necessity to match that rate of change.

In addition, certain industry regulations, such as PCI-DSS and the Health Insurance Portability and Accountability Act (HIPAA), mandate regular vulnerability scans and prompt remediation of critical vulnerabilities. New assets should also be scanned whenever they are added to the network. Changes, such as the upgrade of an application, installation of a software package, or reconfiguration of a service or firewall, should also require a rescan of the affected asset. In addition, for a vulnerability scanning program to be effective, it is important to have all of these best practices included as corporate policy.

Communication and Planning

Vulnerability scanning tools generate a lot of traffic toward the scan target. Depending on the total number of targets being scanned, this can create issues with traffic load through network devices, such as switches and routers, and the load may also overwhelm a target. Some targets being scanned may also behave erratically after the scan is completed. The target may become unresponsive, or erratic behavior may not manifest until hours after the scan because of application instability or other problems caused by the scanner. In addition to network and service problems, scans can create alerts in system and security management tools, and need to be accounted for or added to exception lists so that they do not create additional work or alerts.

> ## ▶▶ REAL WORLD EXAMPLE:
> ## Scanning Impact
>
> After conducting an enterprise-wide vulnerability scan for a client, targeting their application servers, a third-party security assessment team notified the application owners that testing was complete. The scanning completed around midnight, and the application owners completed testing an hour later. They tested the functionality of their applications and reported that all systems were operational.
>
> Despite this validation, the assessment team received a call the next morning. One of the servers that had passed testing was not responding to client requests any longer. It was rebooted, and everything was back to normal. Further testing revealed that the scanning caused the issue, and the application that became nonresponsive suffered from a memory leak that only became crippling after about six to eight hours passed. Applications may not always respond well to scanning. Ensure that your testing process accounts for this, and closely monitor applications and servers during and for a reasonable time after scanning to ensure functionality.

Planning for all possible contingencies is the best solution to the unexpected impact from scanning. That is easier said than done, of course. When planning the vulnerability scan, determine the route through the network the traffic will take. Which devices in the network will carry the load? This may be a collection of routers and switches. Owners of the devices should be identified, emergency contacts and escalation processes should be documented, and all scanning activity should be coordinated with the owners and customers who may be impacted. This includes determining who may be impacted if one of the network devices fails or suffers from degraded performance during scanning. Quite quickly, the negative impact of the scan can grow. It may be prudent to have someone conduct the actual scan, while another individual coordinates communication for the scan.

Because of these issues, it is important to have a documented and defined process for the vulnerability scan, which includes communication of the testing to any parties that may be impacted by an outage. This includes the server and application owners, management, and customers, as appropriate. A new vulnerability scanning program may begin by scanning a development or test network. As confidence in the settings and process increases, scanning of production servers may begin. Scanning should also initially be conducted during nonproduction times or during a scheduled maintenance window for the organization, if possible. It is also important to ensure that scanning doesn't conflict with maintenance or other activities that might be negatively impacted by the scan, such as backups or patching. In continuous scanning environments, system designs need to account for continuous scanning as part of how maintenance, upgrades, and patching are done.

Scanning certain systems and applications may also have unintended consequences. For example, some scanning tools may complete forms and submit them automatically or add useless information into a back-end database. This is especially common when scanning web applications. Consider preventive measures in these scenarios, for example:

- Identify any systems that have mail forms or back-end databases.
- Redirect the emails or disable email functionality temporarily.
- Back up the database prior to the scan, and restore it after the scan.
- Consider disabling any alerting that triggers text or email alerts to staff for the duration of the scan.

By communicating the plan, informing the appropriate parties, testing, and taking appropriate precautions, vulnerability scanning can be an invaluable resource for improving an organization's overall security.

▶▶ REAL WORLD EXAMPLE:
Scanning Fallout

Scanning is an inexact science, and it pays off to proceed slowly and cautiously. Scan environments during development before they go to production, for instance. Schedule scans for nonproduction time, instead of the middle of the workday. Know that the unexpected inevitably will happen. Older systems running outdated (but still functional)

CONTINUES

applications are especially susceptible to failure from scanning. Such systems sometimes exist in SCADA networks, which often do not have development/nonproduction equipment that can be scanned. Databases can grow in size with useless data from the scanner. Systems can crash from scanning, which can result in frustrated admins who receive hundreds of alert texts in the middle of the night. Following best practices, communicating effectively, and proceeding cautiously can ensure that your vulnerability scanning program is successful.

Part of the planning process should also include the identification of critical systems. In fact, if the company has completed a business continuity plan (BCP) or may have prepared a business impact analysis (BIA), this information may already be available and can be used to identify critical systems. Scanning critical systems may cause outages, so these systems should be handled with the greatest care. Additionally, remediating vulnerabilities on these systems should be the highest priority. If there is no information available from the BCP or BIA, then you can use the following criteria as a starting point for identifying critical servers:

- Supports business critical operations

- Contains sensitive information (such as PCI, HIPAA, PII, or financial information)

- Provides critical network services (such as Domain Name System, Active Directory, or authentication)

Critical servers typically should be scanned and remediated before noncritical servers. Often common sense should prevail. However, ensure that management is aware of the findings, risks, and prioritization of remediation tasks.

Scan Configuration Considerations

Most scans can be configured to scan less aggressively by throttling the rate of packets sent to the target. This can aid in preventing unexpected consequences from a saturated network. Start cautiously by sending traffic at a lower and slower rate, and increase it in subsequent tests. Monitor equipment, including network equipment, the targeted services, and DNS, when significantly changing the test parameters. Don't hesitate to contact the scanning tool's support team to clarify functionality or review settings and features. Ideally, members of the network team and server teams especially should be available while scanning in case of an outage or issue. This can minimize downtime if there's an outage.

Another technique that can help prevent outages when running scans is to disable any potentially unsafe tests. Many scanning tools provide an ability to disable unsafe checks, either by manually deselecting them or by turning off a category of tests that are known to have potential negative impacts. It is important to understand the types of tests that are enabled so that a conscious decision can be made about unsafe tests.

Other typical scanning configuration options include selecting credentialed or non-credentialed scans. A noncredentialed scan sends traffic to the open ports on the server to determine whether vulnerabilities or issues exist. A credentialed scan is a feature that allows the scanning tool to additionally connect to a target and log in with valid credentials to perform testing. The scanning tool must be configured with the credentials needed to log in. Credentialed scans are generally preferable, for several reasons:

- Reduced traffic on the network, by using fewer packets to identify vulnerabilities on the server

- Increased accuracy, by checking for file versions associated with known vulnerabilities

- Improved vulnerability identification, as some issues can be identified only by logging into the server, such as enumerating applied patches to identify missing patches

It is common to have a different set of scan settings for different servers that you are scanning, as a single group of settings is rarely sufficient for most organizations. Organizations may choose to have specific configurations for Linux and Windows servers, workstations, Supervisory Control and Data Acquisition (SCADA) or Industrial Control System (ICS) devices, or applications and servers with known issues that are caused by scans. Crafting scan policies to balance effective, efficient security assessment against resources and time is a key task for security professionals.

When first reviewing scan results, the number of vulnerabilities is often much larger than anticipated, especially for systems that may have older versions of software, such as Java or Flash. It's important to understand how the scanner counts vulnerabilities and the difference between the number of vulnerabilities and the number of fixes that need to be applied. Simply, five vulnerabilities may all be resolved by a single patch.

For example, say an application called Widget v5.0 had a security vulnerability. The scanner will check for Widget v5.0. The issue was theoretically patched in Widget v5.1. Another bug was found, and Widget v5.2 was created, as well as Widget v5.3. Each version had a bug that was patched in the subsequent version. Now, assume the target system is scanned, and it is on Widget v5.0. The vulnerability scanner may indicate the system has three vulnerabilities: one for each version of the application 5.0, 5.1, and 5.2, except for 5.3, which is the latest version.

So, the application has three vulnerabilities; however, one update to version 5.3 will resolve the issues identified in Widget v5.0, 5.1, and 5.2; a single patch brings the application up to date and resolves the three vulnerabilities. Because of the differences in the number of vulnerabilities versus the number of patches needed, it may be preferable to modify the scan settings to help reduce the number of vulnerabilities and the paperwork that each generates. For instance, most scanners allow vulnerability checks to be disabled. A vulnerability scanner could simply disable the checks in the scan configuration for versions lower than the latest, most recent version. So, the scanner would check to see whether Widget v5.3 was installed. If any older versions were installed, the Widget v5.3 vulnerability check would indicate there was a single vulnerability, resolved by updating to Widget v5.3.

Decisions like this must be made with a full understanding of how the organization treats vulnerabilities and patching. If the organization responds promptly to issues such as the discovery of an old version of software and prioritizes it the same way, then a single detection option may be appropriate. If the organization does not respond this way, knowing that there are multiple vulnerabilities, potentially with different exploits and thus different risk levels, may be important to the prioritization process.

While this may not seem worth the trouble for many applications, there are a handful of enterprise applications that update frequently or that commonly have multiple major vulnerabilities found in any given year. A failure to patch these applications can result in large jumps in the number of vulnerabilities on a given machine. Vulnerability checks for applications such as Java, WordPress, and some Adobe applications can benefit from this configuration methodology.

Distributed Scanning

Another consideration arises when considering the path that the vulnerability scanning software will take. To scan an endpoint, the vulnerability scanner may need to send traffic through routers, firewalls, and proxy servers. Any of these devices may impact the results by restricting the traffic sent to the target. In a vulnerability scanning situation, where accurately identifying security gaps is crucial, dropped traffic is simply unacceptable. The scan must identify all issues that are present, and this necessity may be negatively impacted by a firewall rule or proxy server dropping connections. The traffic generated by a scan can appear to be malicious, so interference from intermediary network devices is a common issue, and allowing scanning systems through every security device on a network may be problematic or undesirable, since understanding how the security devices would impact similar traffic can be important.

One solution to address the problem and increase the accuracy of the scan is to set up a distributed scanning environment. This involves setting up scanning agents in each subnet. The agents will receive scanning directives and scanning configuration from a centralized host. The centralized host can schedule scans to begin as needed and automatically send the scan instructions to the appropriate host in the correct subnet. There is no need, with sufficient scanners, to scan through a firewall or proxy server. All scan results are sent to the centralized host to generate reports. The scanning load is also distributed in this model, so the duration of the scans is reduced. It requires more effort (and cost) to set up a distributed scanning environment; however, there are tangible benefits in the long run, including an improved security posture and potentially reduced bandwidth consumption due to having local scanning devices.

Managing Scan Results

Completing a vulnerability scan and analyzing the multitude of vulnerabilities and informational findings can be a daunting task. Handing a vulnerability report to a server administrator with the simple directive to "fix this" can be even more overwhelming for the administrator. Vulnerability scans of multiple hosts can generate hundreds of pages of issues that need remediation. An effective vulnerability scanning program must also consider keeping the remediation task manageable. This can typically be accomplished in a few different ways.

- Prioritize scanning and remediation efforts based on the organization's business impact analysis.
- Use credentialed scans to reduce false positives.
- Assign more staff to the task.
- Reduce the scope of scanned devices.
- Increase the length of time allowed for remediation.
- Use central management and patching tools to allow patching to be done in an automated fashion.

Management will weigh the cost and risks of the approach and decide on the path that best fits their risk appetite. Each approach has pros and cons. Ideally, enough staff can be assigned to the task to complete the most severe issues found on mission-critical servers within an acceptable time frame.

Once the scan has completed, the results should be reviewed for false positives. The results can then be presented to management to determine the action plan for remediation. A general plan should already be in place; however, the results may indicate a need to modify the plan. Several critical issues, for instance, may require immediate attention and prompt remediation. The remediation plan and action items should have the full support of management. Vulnerabilities that cannot be addressed, either because of a lack of a patch or workaround or because of a business requirement, should be formally accepted by management and should be reviewed on a periodic basis to ensure that the underlying reason why it couldn't be addressed has not changed.

Penetration Testing

Penetration testing is another assessment activity similar to vulnerability scanning, but goes further. A vulnerability scan enumerates the issues it finds on a server that present a risk of compromise, and it provides a report of those vulnerabilities but does not work to exploit them. A penetration test may include the same activity as the vulnerability scan to identify potential targets. In addition, the penetration test then continues to attempt to *exploit*, or take advantage of, the discovered vulnerability. For instance, a vulnerability scan may indicate there is an unpatched flaw in the operating system. The flaw allows remote code execution for an attacker. A penetration test takes the information provided from the vulnerability scan and attempts to take advantage of the flaw and remotely execute code. This code may give the penetration tester a remote shell, or command prompt, on the target system. From there, the penetration tester may target other systems, create a user account, gather sensitive information from the server, and scan neighboring hosts for additional targets to compromise.

A penetration test can therefore take a vulnerability report a step further and show the potential real-world impact of missing patches, weak configurations, and bad practices. A penetration test can help identify insufficient operational, administrative, and technical controls in an environment. When the test is complete and the tester provides a final report, the target organization is then able to identify and remediate an actual pathway a malicious actor could take into their network. Few things can test an organization's defenses better than a good penetration test.

Penetration testing should be conducted only with permission from the owners of the system. It isn't ethical to test systems without authorization and may be illegal. Penetration testing without appropriate permission can result in legal action against the tester. Additionally, it is prudent when testing to request a letter or documentation from an organization representative that the tester is permitted to conduct penetration testing activities. The letter (a "get out of jail free card") assures the penetration tester that if they are caught or discovered, they can show the letter, thus proving the legitimacy of the tester's activities.

> ▶▶ **REAL WORLD EXAMPLE:**
> ## The Sacrificial Lamb
>
> Many years ago, a penetration tester was conducting a penetration test for a hospital. They had a wireless network for patients and guests. They had an additional wireless network with a nonbroadcast SSID for hospital staff. They had architected a solution that they felt was highly secure. Once connected to the STAFF network, a laptop user could

then open a VPN connection to the VPN concentrator. Only then would they have access to the corporate network and its resources.

The penetration tester had already obtained the wireless staff network's encryption key and was able to join the network. The next step: scan the network for interesting hosts. A DHCP server and a couple of workstations were the only hosts visible. A vulnerability scan on the DHCP server revealed several open ports, including a web server. The server had also not been patched in some time, as it was susceptible to some older buffer overflow exploits. Within a short time, the penetration tester had full administrative access on the server. This was a good first step, but all of the interesting targets were on the other side of the VPN concentrator. The penetration tester informed one of the security team members of the progress. They were unconcerned, as the server was, in their words, just a "sacrificial lamb," and there wasn't any way the tester would be able to get past their hardened VPN concentrator.

Dumping hashes and passwords from the DHCP server revealed several interesting accounts with weak passwords. The accounts had local administrative access to the server. The same credentials also allowed administrative access on the laptops connected to the network.

With administrative access to the laptops, their local password stores were pilfered. Antivirus was disabled, and a key logger was installed. The VPN connection the laptop had made was disconnected by stopping the background VPN application. When the staff member reconnected, their VPN credentials were captured. The VPN concentrator allowed multiple connections from the same login, so the tester was now in the internal network.

Armed with some local usernames and passwords stored on the laptops on the wireless network, the tester began attempting to authenticate to domain servers. One set of credentials recovered from the laptops—username: Backup, password: CompanyName—looked particularly promising. And it was. The result of the test included access to financial information, patient health records, 70 percent of all staff usernames and passwords, and even the CEO's emails. While there may have been other paths into the network, one "sacrificial lamb" made the work much easier. Never minimize the risk of not patching and maintaining any host in your network, including servers, routers, switches, and even workstations. All hosts need to be patched and properly hardened and secured.

Penetration testing is an effective way to assess the state of an organization's security. A comprehensive penetration test can identify weaknesses in administrative, technical, and detective controls by exploiting configuration issues, cracking weak passwords, and compromising servers undetected. As with any endeavor, however, the skill of the penetration tester or team performing the test can greatly impact the depth and scope of the findings. In addition, the time allotted is also a significant contributing factor. A penetration tester with 20 hours allotted to an assessment will rarely find as many issues as a tester allotted 40 hours. To understand why, it's important to understand the process behind penetration testing.

Penetration testing must be carefully considered by the organization. Vulnerability scanning can be disruptive, as discussed. Penetration testing has an even greater capability to create outages and disruptions. While the risk of an outage is mitigated when the test is conducted by an experienced penetration tester, the risk of an outage can never be eliminated, only reduced. Penetration tests that specifically test the availability of a system through denial-of-service attacks, or that have a known chance of causing services to fail, must be carefully planned and executed with the understanding that an outage may occur. Therefore, management needs to engage the services of a penetration tester fully aware of the risk that accompanies such activities.

Agreeing to which penetration testing standard will be used can be an important part of engagement planning. The Open Web Application Security Project (OWASP) maintains a list of penetration testing methodologies at `https://www.owasp.org/index.php/Penetration_testing_methodologies`.

- The Penetration Testing Execution Standard
- PCI-DSS guides
- The Penetration Testing Framework
- NIST SP800-115
- The Information System Security Assessment Framework
- The Open Source Security Testing Methodology Manual

Other decision points in this process include the scope of the test.

- Which systems will be targeted by the test?
- What level of access, if any, will the testers be granted?
- Will social engineering be permitted as part of the test?
- Will physical security be in scope for the test?
- Are only Internet-facing systems in scope?
- Will LAN or physical access be granted?
- Who will manage the pen test team and handle communication?
- Who will perform the test?

There are a wide variety of individuals and firms offering penetration testing services, and the quality of your results depends on making the right choices. It is important to do your due diligence in retaining someone to perform a penetration test for your organization, including doing the following:

- Obtaining past references
- Performing background checks
- Requesting industry-recognized certifications
- Conducting in-depth interviews

During the interview process, a list of questions should be included, requesting information regarding all aspects of their testing process. Here are some questions to ask:

- What is the firm's approach and process for testing?
- How is your organization's data protected?
- How will communication of sensitive information be protected?
- How is sensitive data collected during the testing process secured?
- At the test's conclusion, how is sensitive data destroyed?
- How will the risk of service disruption be mitigated?
- What are the emergency lines of communication?
- How much of your testing is automated versus manual?
- What tools are used?
- What time frames are available to perform testing?
- When and how are findings reported?
- Do you background check your employees?
- What documentation and logging do you perform while testing?
- What are the rules of engagement?
- What happens when a critical issue is found?

The answers to these questions typically either increase or decrease your comfort level with a prospective penetration tester. You want to confirm that they will handle your data securely and that they have processes in place to handle all the questions you've asked. Any reputable firm should have documented processes, for instance, that indicate how they will handle your data, what actions they take if they find an actual malicious intruder on your network, and how they check for and mitigate the chances of disruption to your organization.

Phases of Penetration Testing

It is helpful to understand the penetration tester's process. Penetration testers may use different names for the phases, but the general concepts are consistent. The typical flow of a penetration test includes the following phases:

Phase 1: Discovery or reconnaissance

Phase 2: Scanning and probing

Phase 3: Exploitation

Phase 4: Post-exploitation

Phase 5: Reporting findings

The Discovery Phase

In the discovery or reconnaissance phase, the pen tester gathers information regarding the target system and network. The information gathered using passive techniques is known as open source intelligence (OSINT). A surprising amount of information can often be found without sending any traffic to the target system or network. This allows the tester to avoid detection and to prioritize targets without interacting with them. For instance, several websites provide valuable information regarding targets. Websites such as the regional Internet registries (RIRs) and others that provide similar lookup services can reveal the public IP ranges assigned to a company. Security search engines like Shodan and Censys can be used to check pre-existing scan data for systems, services, and vulnerabilities. Social network sites, especially those that have a business or professional network component, can reveal vendor equipment and software installed at an organization based on the resumes and profiles of employees who work at the target. WHOIS information regarding domain records may also reveal employee names and contact information. Depending upon the parameters given to the tester, the tester may also use other techniques, such as physically observing the building, employees, and routines of the target. Facilities may be photographed and potential weaknesses documented. The tester may drive around the buildings and campus of the organization with a laptop and a wireless card to identify the wireless network footprint. All these information-gathering techniques can be used by penetration testers as well as malicious attackers to profile your organization without detection by your monitoring systems. The primary goal in this phase is to gather as much information regarding the footprint of the target organization as possible.

The penetration tester may also be given information by the organization. For instance, if the organization has an Internet presence, they may choose to provide the pen tester with the public IP address range. Alternately, a single IP may be all that is provided. Assessments may even grant the pen tester access to a server or to the corporate network, and reconnaissance will begin from that vantage point. This is entirely driven by the objectives of the organization hiring the penetration tester.

The Scanning and Probing Phase

The second phase of the process, scanning or probing, involves using the information gathered in the first phase to identify potential targets and gather more detailed information. Ideally, this is the first phase where the penetration tester actually sends traffic destined for the target network. The goal in this phase is to identify entry points into the network. This may be accomplished in several ways.

- **Ping sweeps:** Pinging an IP or IP range looking for hosts that respond
- **Port scans:** Probing a selection of ports on a target IP for ports in the listening state
- **Banner grabs:** Collecting information provided by a service when connecting to the service port
- **Vulnerability scans:** Using a vulnerability scanner to enumerate vulnerabilities on the target

It is always preferable as a penetration tester to avoid setting off any alerts or alarms on the target system. It is not uncommon for the probes to alert staff of the activity. While this confirms that the monitoring processes are working, it can create barriers for the tester. For instance, the tester's IP address may be temporarily (or permanently) shunned. The tester will have to either change IPs or contact the organization to have the shun action lifted. Therefore, scans and sweeps should not be overly aggressive in their timing and may use other concealment techniques to increase the likelihood of avoiding detection. This is especially important if using a typical vulnerability scanner to identify issues on the target network. A vulnerability scanner generates a significant amount of traffic, and a full scan for all vulnerabilities will almost certainly be detected by the target organization.

After completing this phase, the penetration tester will have a list of systems with potentially vulnerable services. For instance, perhaps an Apache or IIS web server was identified, or FTP, SMTP, DNS, and SSH servers were found, including one or more systems with known vulnerabilities.

The Exploitation Phase

The next phase is the exploitation phase. With the list of potentially exploitable systems and services in hand, exploitation can commence. This can include a variety of methods, including manually executing attacks, running scripts, and executing automated attacks. The goal in this phase is to gain additional access to a system. This may be done by cracking a password, finding a discovered hash in a rainbow table, or using a buffer over-flow to gain system-level access to a target system. Other possibilities include executing SQL injection attacks. The end result is the same: the tester has gained more access than they should have been capable of, and the organization is compromised.

The penetration tester likely has a long list of potential ways to compromise the target at this point. Typically, it is not feasible based on time limitations to try every possible avenue into the system. The penetration tester will use their experience to determine which paths are most likely to yield additional access via a compromised system. This means that while the penetration tester ends up choosing one path into a network, multiple paths may exist but simply were not explored. However, a good penetration tester will include all of the potential and theoretical paths into the network in the report. Even if a vulnerability was not exploited, it can still be investigated and addressed by the organization's technical staff.

Another area of concern that may arise during this phase is the discovery by the penetration tester of indicators of compromise: signs that a malicious intruder has previously gained access to a resource. The penetration tester may even identify an ongoing attack. Prior to beginning the penetration test, it is advisable to document how these situations will be addressed by the organization and the penetration tester. Best practices dictate that indicators of compromise will cause all testing activities to cease, and appropriate personnel will be notified. Management approval must be given to resume testing activities. This is equally true if the penetration tester believes an active attack was uncovered. The penetration test cannot continue until the issue is remediated and resolved.

Often, a penetration tester may identify an open port and then attempt an exploit against the port. In some cases, this may cause the service that has the port open to crash. If the penetration tester is not diligent, they may not realize the service is no longer responding to traffic. This is important because it may create a disruption in services for the organization. A penetration tester should make every effort to ensure that services are not disrupted. If a service has failed, a notification and communication plan should be in place that dictates what actions the penetration tester should take. For instance, it's common to provide the tester with a schedule of on-call personnel to contact in the event anything goes awry. A good, experienced penetration testing firm will ensure they have this information prior to beginning any testing.

The Post-Exploitation Phase

The next phase is the post-exploitation phase. The attack continues in this phase, using information gathered from the prior three phases. However, with successful exploitation in phase 3, the penetration tester has a new perspective. Perhaps a privileged account has been compromised, or the tester has gained access to a server in the demilitarized zone (DMZ). This elevated, additional access gives the tester a new insight into things. It is possible, for instance, that with access to the DMZ server, the tester can launch reconnaissance scans from the DMZ server, initiating the penetration testing phases again. Previously limited by the firewall rules protecting devices in the DMZ, the penetration tester can now scan other DMZ devices from the compromised DMZ server. This new vantage point will then restart the reconnaissance phase as the tester gathers information. The new recon scan may identify additional services and servers that are exploitable, and the cycle of exploitation continues. The process of compromising a server and using that access point to locate and compromise additional targets is often referred to as *pivoting* within the target network. Since this phase can lead to more discoveries, it is common for penetration testers to cycle through scanning, exploitation, and post-exploitation phases multiple times as they gain more access and discover additional targets.

The Reporting Phase

The final phase is the reporting phase. The penetration tester gathers all of their findings and compiles them into one or more reports. Typically, an executive-level report is created. It omits technical detail and focuses on the risk and exposure of the organization. A second report is also created, which includes technical details of value to the organization's technical staff. This second report is used to drive remediation efforts. The penetration testing team meets with both executive and technical staff to discuss the report, testing, outcome, and findings generated during the test.

> ▶▶ **REAL WORLD EXAMPLE:**
> ## The Need for Experience
>
> A penetration testing firm was hired to perform testing at a Fortune 500 company. The testing team decided to check a list of accounts for weak passwords. However, they didn't want to accidentally lock out any accounts. On Windows computers, the command-line utility net accounts will display the workstation's password policy, including two important configuration details.
>
> - ■ **Lockout Threshold:** How many incorrect password attempts will lock out the account
>
> - ■ **Lockout Observation Window:** How long until the failed attempt counter resets to 0
>
> The penetration testing firm saw that the Lockout Observation Window was 30 minutes, and four failed attempts would lock out an account. Selecting what they felt was a conservative number, they configured their script to try a password every 20 minutes.
>
> CONTINUES

This was slow enough that any alerts on failed attempts probably would not be triggered. Additionally, the testers reasoned that one attempt every 20 minutes would allow the counter to reset, and no accounts would be locked out.

The test commenced overnight. The organization's staff arrived at work the next morning to find that numerous service accounts were locked out, and critical batch jobs failed to run as scheduled. The penetration testing team denied responsibility, but all indicators pointed to their script as the culprit. The testers presumed their settings were safe. However, it should have been tested prior to usage because their conclusion was wrong. The logic used by the penetration testers indicated a lack of understanding regarding the Windows settings. The Lockout Observation Window setting indicates the amount of time that must pass with no failed password attempt before the counter will be reset to 0. If there is another failed attempt before the Lockout Observation Window setting elapses, the counter increments by 1. Because the script tested passwords every 20 minutes, 30 minutes never elapsed for the counter to reset. So, after five failed attempts, which took around 80 minutes, the accounts were locked out. The penetration testers did keep excellent documentation of their activities, which is certainly beneficial. The failed login attempts in the security logs corresponded exactly with the timing of their tests and the accounts that were tested.

Lessons like this help to emphasize the need to ensure that anyone conducting testing against an environment is experienced in the art of penetration testing and understands the technical details of the types of systems and software they are testing.

Documentation and Cleanup

A final critical step exists for the penetration tester upon the conclusion of their test—and typically prior to the reporting phase. During the testing, documentation is critical. The penetration tester must log all of their activity, such as the following:

- What servers were targeted
- When traffic to the target was sent, how the target responded, and when it ceased
- Hosts and services that responded
- Results of each phase, such as hosts found and vulnerabilities identified
- Screenshots of banners, login pages, errors, and terminal sessions
- Configuration changes on a target, such as accounts created, services stopped, or tools installed
- Any potential indicators of compromise: signs of a past, or even active, malicious attack

This documentation allows the penetration tester to properly convey their findings and, even more importantly, clean up any remnants from the penetration testing process. It is a failure on the part of the penetration tester to create an account, for example, and leave it on the system.

Testing Types

The type of penetration test being performed can be divided into three separate categories: black-box testing, gray-box testing, and white-box testing. These test types are differentiated by the amount of knowledge and access granted to the tester. In black-box, also called *blind* or *zero knowledge testing*, the tester has no knowledge of the systems being tested. This test creates a situation most like an external malicious actor, who also typically would have no prior knowledge of a target system. The testing in this scenario can take longer, as the tester is starting from scratch, discovering all of the details regarding the system via scanning, probing, and trial and error.

Black-box testing that is done in a way that simulates an actual attack is called *red teaming*. Red team exercises test how well an organization's security designs, responses, policies, and procedures respond to an actual adversary. The defending team, or blue team, is the defending team in security exercises like this. Black-box testing that is performed without prior knowledge of the IT staff and security team for an organization is sometimes called *double blind* or *covert* testing.

On the opposite end of the spectrum is *white-box*, or *full knowledge*, testing, also sometimes known as *covert* testing. As the term implies, the tester is given full knowledge and access to the system. They may even receive application source code to review, if applicable. Where black-box testing is from the outside in, white-box testing is from the inside out. The additional access may allow the testers to uncover more vulnerabilities than in a black-box test. However, this test tends to be less like a real-world scenario and doesn't simulate an actual attack as well as a black-box test. Overt testing is done with the knowledge of the IT and security staff of an organization, which means that penetration testers need to be aware that they may use that knowledge to stop attacks that would otherwise work, potentially making the testing less useful.

In between the two is gray-box testing. As the name implies, it sits somewhere between the other two test types. The penetration tester is given some information regarding the system(s) to be tested. However, it is unlikely they have full access and source code availability. Their access and knowledge sits somewhere between full knowledge and no knowledge at all.

Physical Penetration Testing

Security issues aren't limited to networks and systems. A complete penetration testing effort can involve assessing and testing the physical security of an organization and its facilities. Physical access attacks may target locks, entry access control systems, front-office personnel, security guards, staff behavior, and any other physical security control or mechanism.

Physical penetration testing efforts will frequently leverage social engineering techniques to persuade employees that the penetration tester should be allowed into a secured area or through a locked or access-controlled door. Gaining physical access can result in more danger to the penetration tester, as staff, security guards, and police who discover a penetration tester in areas they are not authorized to be in can respond in unexpected ways. This makes it even more important for physical penetration testers to have well-documented emergency contact procedures and a fully documented letter of permission or "get out of jail free" document.

Log Reviews

Logs are generated by most systems, devices, applications, and other elements of an organization's infrastructure. They can be used to track changes, actions taken by users, service states and performance, and a host of other purposes. These events can indicate security issues and highlight the effectiveness of security controls that are in place. Assessments and audits rely on log artifacts to provide data about past events and changes and to indicate whether there are ongoing security issues, misconfigurations, or abuse issues. Security control testing also relies on logs, including those from security devices and security management systems.

The wide variety of logs, as well as the volume of log entries that can be generated by even a simple infrastructure, means that logs can be challenging to manage. Logs can capture a significant amount of information and quickly become overwhelming in volume. They should be configured with industry best practices in mind, including implementing centralized collection, validation using hashing tools, and automated analysis of logs. Distinct log aggregation systems provide a secure second copy, while allowing centralization and analysis. In many organizations, a properly configured security information and event management (SIEM) system is particularly useful as part of both assessment and audit processes and can help make assessment efforts easier by allowing reporting and searches. Even when centralized logging and log management systems are deployed, security practitioners must strike a balance between capturing useful information and capturing too much information.

NOTE Maintaining log integrity is a critical part of an organization's logging practice. If logs cannot be trusted, then auditing, incident response, and even day-to-day operations are all at risk, since log data is often used in each of those tasks. Thus, organizations need to assess the integrity of their logs as well as their existence, content, and relevance to their purpose.

Logs should have proper permissions set on them, they should be hashed to ensure that they are not changed, a secure copy should be available in a separate secure location if the logs are important or require a high level of integrity, and of course any changes that impact the logs themselves should be logged!

Assessing log integrity involves validating that the logs are being properly captured, that they cannot be changed by unauthorized individuals or accounts, and that changes to the logs are properly recorded and alerted on as appropriate. This means that auditors and security assessors cannot simply stop when they see a log file that contains the information they expect it to. Instead, technical and administrative procedures around the logs themselves need to be validated as part of a complete assessment process.

Assessments and audits need to look at more than just whether logs are captured and their content. In fact, assessments that consider log reviews look at items including the following:

- What logs are captured?
- How is log integrity ensured? Are log entries hashed and validated?
- Are the systems and applications that generate logs properly configured?
- Do logging systems use a centralized time synchronization service?
- How long are logs retained for, and does that retention time period meet legal, business, or contractual requirements?
- How are the logs reviewed, and by whom?
- Is automated reporting or alarming set up and effective?
- Is there ongoing evidence of active log review, such as a sign-off process?
- Are logs rotated or destroyed on a regular basis?
- Who has access to logs?
- Do logs contain sensitive information such as passwords, keys, or data that should not be exposed via logs to avoid data leakage?

Policies and procedures for log management should be documented and aligned to standards. ISO 27001 and ISO 27002 both provide basic guidance on logging, and NIST provides SP 800-92, "Guide to Computer Security Log Management." Since logging is driven by business needs, infrastructure and system design, and the organization's functional and security requirements, specific organizational practices and standards need to be created and their implementation regularly assessed.

Synthetic Transactions

Monitoring frequently needs to involve more than simple log reviews and analysis to provide a comprehensive view of infrastructure and systems. The ability to determine whether a system or application is responding properly to actual transactions, regardless of whether they are simulated or performed by real users, is an important part of a monitoring infrastructure. Understanding how a system or application performs and how that performance impacts users, as well as underlying infrastructure components, is critical to management of systems for organizations that want a view that goes deeper than whether their systems are up or down or under a high or low load. Two major types of transaction monitoring are performed to do this: synthetic transactions and real user monitoring.

Synthetic transactions are actions run against monitored objects to see how the system responds. The transaction may emulate a client connecting to a website and submitting a form or viewing the catalog of items on a web page, which pulls the information from a database. Synthetic transactions can confirm that the system is working as expected and that alerts and monitoring are functioning properly.

Synthetic transactions are commonly used with databases, websites, and applications. They can be automated, which reduces the workload carried by administrators. For instance, synthetic transactions can ensure that the web servers are working properly and responding to client requests. If an error is returned during the transaction, an alert can be generated that notifies responsible personnel. Therefore, instead of a customer complaining that the site is down, IT can proactively respond to the alert and remedy the issue, while impacting fewer customers. Synthetic transactions can also measure response times to issues, allowing staff to proactively respond and remediate slowdowns or mimic user behavior when evaluating newly deployed services, prior to deploying the service to production.

Real user monitoring (RUM) is another method to monitor the environment. Instead of creating automated transactions and interactions with an application, the developer or analyst monitors actual users interacting with the application, gathering information based on actual user activity. Real user monitoring is superior to synthetic transactions when actual user activity is desired. Real people will interact with an application in a variety of ways that synthetic transactions cannot emulate because real user interactions are harder to anticipate. However, RUM can also generate much more information for analysis, much of which is spurious, since it will not be specifically targeted at what the monitoring process is intended to review. This can slow down the analysis process or make it difficult to isolate the cause of performance problems or other issues. In addition, RUM can be a source of privacy concerns because of the collection of user data that may include personally identifiable information, usage patterns, or other details.

Synthetic transactions can emulate certain behaviors on a scheduled basis, including actions that a real user may not perform regularly or predictably. If a rarely used element of an application needs testing and observation, a synthetic transaction is an excellent option, whereas the developer or analyst may have to wait for an extended amount of time to view the transaction when using RUM.

Synthetic transactions can be used for several functions, including the following:

- **Application monitoring:** Is an application responsive, and does it respond to queries and input as expected?

- **Service monitoring:** Is a selected service responding to requests in a timely manner, such as a website or file server?

- **Database monitoring:** Are back-end databases online and responsive?

- **TCP port monitoring:** Are the expected ports for an application or service open, listening, and accepting connections?

- **Network services:** Are the DNS and Dynamic Host Configuration Protocol (DHCP) servers responding to queries? Is the domain controller authenticating users?

By using a blend of synthetic transactions and real user monitoring, the effectiveness of an organization's testing and monitoring strategy can be significantly improved. Downtime can be reduced because staff is alerted more quickly when issues arise. Application availability can be monitored around the clock without human intervention. Compliance with Service-Level Agreements (SLAs) can also be accurately determined. The benefits of using both types of monitoring merits consideration.

Code Review and Testing

When software developers write software, the written software is referred to as *code*. To ensure that flaws in the application do not exist, the code must be reviewed and tested. Failure to both review and test the code can result in flawed software that can be used to gain access to a system without authorization or to conduct other attacks that expose data, provide access, or result in service failures. In fact, poor coding practices can result in SQL injection attacks, cross-site scripting, authentication and session management flaws, buffer overflows, credential theft, and privilege escalation as well as the other flaws described in the Common Weakness Enumeration (`https://cwe.mitre.org/`) and by OWASP Top 10 (`https://www.owasp.org/index.php/Category:OWASP_Top_Ten_Project`).

Code review and testing help ensure the security of the final application. The implementation of security within an application does not begin with the review or the testing phase, however. Security must be built into the application as part of the initial design process and continue to be a focus through the software development lifecycle.

Malicious attackers are experts in identifying and exploiting flaws in applications, as well as weaknesses in interfaces and in the exchange of data between systems. Good programming practices can help reduce and eliminate the number of flaws present in applications and software. There are several different testing and code review techniques that can be employed.

- Automated versus manual testing
- Black-box versus white-box testing
- Dynamic versus static testing

Testing can be conducted with software tools, which automates the examination of the code. This can allow the code to be reviewed quickly. However, an automated tool may miss certain issues. Software developers have different styles, and applications can be increasingly complex. While manual testing may take longer, a skilled manual tester may spot issues that are not evident to the one-size-fits-all automated scanner. Likewise, though, the accuracy and thoroughness of manual testing are highly dependent upon the skill of the individual reviewing the code.

In black-box testing, the testing is performed without any internal knowledge of the workings of the application. For instance, the source code is not available in black-box testing, requiring black-box testing to be conducted by running the application itself. Therefore, black-box testing relies on a skilled individual who can run the application and thoroughly test all aspects of the application, often with the use of a testing tool to help. White-box testing includes more detailed information regarding the inner workings of the application. For instance, source code is often reviewed in white-box testing. This in-depth review can allow the tester to identify coding issues that may be less evident during a black-box test. The accuracy and thoroughness of both test types is dependent upon the skill and knowledge of the tester.

In dynamic testing, the code being tested is actually run. Static testing is the examination of the system without executing the code. It can be done with a set of tools, automatically, or manually. Static testing can be done earlier in the software development phase, prior to the finalized code being ready for execution. This allows identification of flaws sooner in the testing process.

Code security should be considered during the initiation and design phase of application development and should continue throughout the development process. Different testing and review options are used at each stage of the development process.

During the planning and design phase, the overall design of the application can be considered.

- Is the software architecture appropriate and secure for the functions it will provide?
- Will sensitive data be transmitted via the application?
- How will the data be protected?

- Does the design of the application handle data in a way that is compliant with industry regulations, such as PCI?

In addition to considering the architecture, this phase can also consider the different threats to the application and the data it manages.

- How might the application be attacked?
- What is the attack surface for the application, and how can it be reduced?
- How can potential attacks be mitigated or avoided altogether?
- Does the application accept input from untrusted sources?
- Where is input sanitization and validation needed?

During the development phase, when the application code is written, code review can be performed. This can take the shape of static source code analysis and manual code review. In fact, a number of code review processes are commonly used to create secure code, including the following:

- *Pair programming* is an agile software development technique that places two developers at one workstation. One developer writes code, while the other reviews it. Frequent role switches ensure that both developers are coding and reviewing equally and that both are familiar with all of the code.
- *Over-the-shoulder code review* requires one developer to write code while the other watches and reviews the code.
- *Pass-around code reviews* work by sending code to reviewers who check the code at a later date. This is less time-intensive than pair or over-the-shoulder reviews, but also means that developers do not receive immediate feedback.
- *Tool-assisted reviews* rely on a formal or informal tool to ensure that code is reviewed and receives proper sign-off.

Some organizations use a formal code inspection process like Fagan inspection, which uses a multiphase review process to conduct in-depth formal reviews. The downfall of a complex formal code inspection process is that it requires a large amount of time and personnel resources and must be repeated for each new code release or update. This means that an in-depth formal code review process is used only when the business justification for it exists.

In addition to the source code of a program, the compiled source, which creates the executable, can be reviewed. The testing of compiled source code is referred to as static binary analysis and manual binary review. All of these test types observe the code without executing the application. They rely on the tester's experience to identify issues within the code based on their knowledge of secure coding practices.

There are a variety of tools and methods that can be used in software testing. The tester must consider many different factors that can aid in selecting the appropriate tools to test the code.

- Is this a web application, a script, or a compiled executable?

- Does the application have a back-end database?

- Where will the application reside, and what interfaces are available?

- Does the application rely on source code libraries or dynamically import code from a source code repository like GitHub?

- Is version management used for the source code, and how are versions tracked and released?

- What programming language is used? Some tools are designed to work only with specific coding languages and may not provide useful results if used incorrectly.

- Do the results correctly identify issues? Are the results usable and applicable?

- Does the tool efficiently manage system resources?

- Is the tool easy to use and consistent in the results provided?

- Are the tools well supported?

- Do alternate tools with similar capabilities give similar results?

- Is one tool more comprehensive than another?

- Does one tool handle the testing process more gracefully, without crashes or system stability issues?

Just as with any job, selecting the right tool can make all the difference. Selecting the right tool relies on understanding the task at hand, as well as the application and the environment in which it will reside.

Once enough code has been written, the application can be executed. This opens new doors for testing possibilities. A running application can be the target of a manual or automated penetration test, as well as automated vulnerability scanners. All these options provide the ability to identify previously undiscovered vulnerabilities in an application. In addition to the automated nature of these options, they also review significantly more code more quickly than nonautomated testing types. The drawback is that the algorithms used to find errors may not identify issues that an experienced developer and tester might identify.

An automated method that can test in ways that manual tester often cannot is *fuzz testing*. Fuzz testing is another automated approach to testing a running application that uses a *fuzzer*, an application designed to test another application, by sending unexpected data to the application. The tester can then observe how the application responds to receiving the random data from the fuzzer.

Test plans and test cases should be created early in the architecture and design process of an application. The application's testing can be organized into different levels of testing.

- **Unit testing:** Does a particular piece of code properly perform the task it is intended to?

- **Integration testing:** Does the application behave as expected when integrated and communicating with other systems in the environment?

- **System testing:** This ensures that the application provides the required functionality and that the application is trustworthy as deployed in regard to security, privacy, performance, recovery, and usability.

Testing in continuous integration or DevOps environments, like those found in many cloud-centric organizations, now frequently relies on automated build processes that perform regression testing, which ensures that old bugs do not reappear, and test programs, which perform unit, integration, and system testing in an automated fashion before code is deployed.

A comprehensive code testing program, with an emphasis throughout the software development lifecycle, can ensure that developed applications are deployed with minimal vulnerabilities.

As you might imagine, the quality of the results depends highly on the experience of the individual reviewing the code. An inexperienced reviewer may miss many issues. Additionally, reviewers may be more adept at finding certain kinds of mistakes or better at reviewing certain coding languages. Ensure that the appropriate people review the code, and consider outsourcing the task if more experience or expertise is needed than is available within the organization.

Misuse Case Testing

In the context of a software development lifecycle, use cases describe what actors will do and what applications will do in response. Validating that code or an application satisfies the use cases that it was designed for is part of all development processes. This is an example of positive testing, where the desired functionality and behavior is tested to ensure that it works as designed.

Ensuring that applications are secure requires that *negative testing*, or testing that validates what happens when things do not work as expected, is conducted to identify vulnerabilities and coding errors. Thus, to ensure security, misuse cases are also tested to ensure that using an application in ways that it was not intended to be used does not result in unexpected or unintended consequences. Common examples of misuse testing techniques include the following:

- **Required form fields:** The application may require certain fields before a form can be submitted. If the fields are left blank, does the application properly stop the submission and request that the empty field be completed?

- **Data mismatch:** What happens when letters are entered into a ZIP code field? Or symbols are entered into a First Name field?

- **Field limits:** What happens when four or more digits are entered into a form field for a customer's age? Does it truncate the data or reject the entry?

- **Data bounds:** What happens if negative numbers are entered when positive numbers are expected, and vice versa? Does the application properly handle the anomaly, or does it accept the input and yield unexpected results?

- **Unauthenticated pages:** Does a site that requires login allow access to pages without authentication? Can pages be opened directly if the URL is known?

Most use cases simply ensure that the application provides necessary functionality. In contrast, misuse case testing has to test a broader set of possible issues, since invalid inputs, intentional attacks, and many other unexpected behaviors have to be tested for to fully validate the wide range of misuse cases.

Abuse Case Testing

Testing for intentional misuse cases, also known as *abuse cases*, is part of a comprehensive misuse testing effort. Thus, when misuse cases are evaluated, they should also be considered from the point of view of an attacker or malicious insider with a focus on how the system, service, application, or process could be abused.

Abuse cases must be considered at each level of an infrastructure or system, including individual components, how they integrate, and how they are managed and maintained. At each stage, assessors must consider how normal functionality could be misused and how techniques such as providing unexpected input or intentional malicious actions might have an impact.

Since complete coverage for misuse case testing can be extremely time- and resource-intensive, a risk assessment should be performed to determine focus areas. Once focus areas have been determined, abuse case testing emulates common activities of malicious actors who abuse applications by performing actions the application doesn't expect, which can reveal vulnerabilities that may allow system compromise. Exceptional testing for abuse cases may occur during penetration tests, with white-box penetration tests often providing the greatest insight into potential abuse, but conducting thorough abuse case testing can be very expensive.

Since abuse cases are a subset of misuse cases, the differences between them can result in confusion. All abuse cases are misuse cases, but a misuse case becomes an abuse case only when it involves an intentional attempt to misuse the system for malicious purposes.

Test Coverage Analysis

Test coverage analysis refers to identifying how the testing performed relates to the total functionality of the application. When designing the test, are all aspects and functionality of the application thoroughly tested? Is there functionality that cannot easily be tested through the interface? How will such sections of code be tested?

There are four main types of coverage criteria.

- *Branch coverage* ensures that each branch in a control statement has been executed.

- *Condition coverage* requires each Boolean expression to be validated for both true and false conditions.

- *Function coverage* makes sure that every function in the program is called.

- *Statement coverage* validates the execution of every statement in the program.

In addition to these four basic types of coverage criteria, two more advanced types of criteria are often used. The first is *decision coverage*; this validates combinations of function coverage and branch coverage to ensure that every entry and exit point for a program has been tested at least once and that each decision in a program has also been tested at least once. *Parameter coverage* validates that every function that accepts parameters has been tested with common values for the parameter. Other types of coverage, such as *loop coverage, path coverage, and data flow coverage* are used less frequently but may be required for specific testing or validation reasons.

The ratio of tested functionality and code to complete functionality and code equates to the actual test coverage. Ideally, test coverage encompasses 100 percent of a program's code and functionality; however, this is not easy to achieve. When there are gaps in test coverage, undiscovered flaws, such as buffer overflows or logic errors, may be present. When determining what levels of coverage are acceptable, consider factors such as the following:

- Sensitivity of data handled by the application

- Relationship of the application to business-critical processes

- Human safety

The more sensitive the data or the more critical the application, the greater the percentage of test coverage required to maintain acceptable levels of risk. Another factor some may consider important is exposure of the application to the Internet or other exposure risk factors. However, regardless of the zone where the application is deployed, all vulnerabilities present in an application should be fixed. While it is tempting to review public web applications more closely than internal applications, an internal application can still be compromised by a malicious employee, a penetration tester or red team member, or a hacker who has breached the organization's outer defenses.

Interface Testing

When two systems or a user and a system can interact with each other, the exchange of data occurs via an interface. Interfaces allow systems to exchange data with each other, other applications, other systems, and users. Interface testing is used to validate whether systems or components pass data and control information properly. This systematic evaluation of the interface's functionality helps ensure the integrity and possibly the confidentiality and availability of the data and services provided by the application. Interface testing can be conducted by both developers and end users, but penetration testers and security professionals may also perform interface testing as part of their efforts.

Interface testing will typically assess the following:

- If the interface responds as expected
- How the interface handles errors, if it responds to them appropriately
- How the interface deals with unexpected input, or a lack of required input
- What the interface does when there is a connectivity issue
- The security of the interface and the data that it sends through it

Interface testing may require components on both ends of a system to be tested or for multiple elements in an infrastructure to be validated. External interfaces such as APIs, web services, and servers' services are all frequently tested by security professionals to ensure that they are not vulnerable, leaking data, or exposed beyond their designed accessibility. Internal interfaces for programs, operating system kernels and services, and other similar components may also be tested by security professionals, particularly those who develop security tools or who work to defeat malware.

Interface testing is a common part of a typical software development lifecycle (SDLC). In the SDLC, interface testing can ensure user-friendliness within the application. It can also identify issues such as proper error handling in addition to unexpected behaviors. For instance, do transactions maintain their integrity in all circumstances, including an interruption of the transaction? Are errors handled properly, or do they divulge sensitive information?

Server interface testing can also ensure that server to server, server to database, and web application to server communication is performed as expected. Testing should be conducted with a variety of browsers to ensure that each browser performs as expected. Other factors that can cause a test to succeed or fail include the presence of browser plug-ins. Testing should include examining the functionality of the site with and without plug-ins enabled.

Website links should work, and linked documents should be accessible on a variety of operating system platforms. It may be useful to determine whether encryption is necessary based on the contents of the site. Identify whether the copy and paste functions are secure and justifiable from a business perspective. Other elements of the test can answer questions such as these:

- If the website returns an error, does it divulge sensitive information, such as source code, directory listings, or system paths?

- If the application crashes, does it recover gracefully and automatically, or is intervention or a reboot required?

- If a transaction is interrupted, does it gracefully recover?

- Do interruptions cause a loss of data or necessitate a re-creation of work performed?

- Does inactivity log out the user and cancel a transaction?

- Does the system recover the session gracefully after a browser crash?

- Are cookies used, and do they store sensitive information?

Other elements can be tested as well, such as the interface's functionality, performance, usability, intuitiveness, and user satisfaction. Interface testing can ensure the application adheres to security requirements and meets the needs of the organization.

COLLECT SECURITY PROCESS DATA

It is unlikely that a networking and computing environment that was initially configured in 2010 is unchanged today. In fact, it is highly likely that your own network has undergone minor and possibly major changes in the last six months. As technology has advanced and threats to networks have increased, the need to monitor networks has become crucial.

Traditional approaches to security process data collection involved solution-specific logging and data capture, sometimes paired with a central Security Information and Event Management (SIEM) or other security management device. As organizational IT infrastructure and systems have become more complex, security process data has also increased in complexity and scope.

Information security continuous monitoring (ISCM) is a holistic strategy to improve and address security. As with any security initiative, it begins with senior management buy-in. The most effective security programs consistently have upper management support. This creates an environment where the policies, the budget, and the vision for the company all include security as a cornerstone of the company's success. ISCM is designed to align facets of the organization including the people, the processes, and the technologies in place.

An organization needs to do the following:

- Monitor all systems
- Understand threats to the organization
- Assess security controls
- Collect, correlate, and analyze security data
- Communicate security status
- Actively manage risk

This will aid the organization in implementing ISCM. ISCM will help ensure that security controls are effective and that the organization's risk exposure is within acceptable limits.

ICSM standards are increasingly available, and major examples include the following:

- NIST SP800-137, "Information Security Continuous Monitoring (ISCM) for Federal Information Systems and Organizations" (`https://csrc.nist.gov/publications/detail/sp/800-137/final`)
- Cloud Security Alliance STAR level 3 provides continuous monitoring-based certification (`https://cloudsecurityalliance.org/star/continuous/`)
- The FedRAMP Continuous Monitoring Strategy Guide (`https://www.fedramp.gov/assets/resources/documents/CSP_Continuous_Monitoring_Strategy_Guide.pdf`)
- NIST SP 800-37, "Risk Management Framework for Information Systems and Organizations: A System Life Cycle Approach for Security and Privacy" (`https://csrc.nist.gov/publications/detail/sp/800-37/rev-2/draft`), is in draft as of the writing of this book but specifically includes risk management linkages to governance and process.

There are several steps to implementing ISCM as outlined in NIST SP800-137.

- Define the strategy based on the organization's risk tolerance.
- Formally establish an ISCM program by selecting metrics.
- Implement the program and collect the necessary data, ideally via automation.
- Analyze and report findings, and determine the appropriate action.

- Respond to the findings based on the analysis and use standard options, such as risk mitigation, risk transference, risk avoidance, or risk acceptance.

- Plan strategy and programs as needed to continually increase insight and visibility into the organization's information systems.

Depending on the organization and the maturity of the implemented ISCM, it is typically necessary to implement one step of the strategy at a time. ISCM tools pull information from many sources. This data may be integrated with SIEM tools. Ideally this process is automated.

ICSM has become increasingly complex as organizations spread their operations into hosted and cloud environments and as they need to integrate third parties into their data-gathering processes. Successful ICSM now needs to provide methods to interconnect legacy ICSM processes with third-party systems and data feeds.

Account Management

Accounts are the set of credentials used to access a system. Most commonly, people think of user accounts, such as a username and a password, used to log onto a computer. However, in the enterprise, other accounts exist also. Here are some examples:

- Computer accounts used to authenticate and authorize a computer's access to network resources

- Service accounts used by processes running on a system and that can execute commands on a system without the need to log on

- Guest accounts used to allow anonymous access to a resource

- Federated accounts and other third-party accounts that may be provided by identity providers outside of the organization

Since accounts are the core of access to most organizations networks, systems, and services, collecting data on the state of accounts, their usage, and whether they are meeting organization security policy is critical to the ongoing security of the organization.

Account management is fairly complex, but it is easier to understand if you look at it divided into the phases of the account management lifecycle. This can simply be identified as the following phases:

1. Creating accounts

2. Modifying accounts

3. Auditing accounts

4. Deleting accounts

Account management begins with the creation of the account. This is the first phase of the account management lifecycle. Regardless of the type of account that is needed, several things should be considered.

- What is the purpose of the account?
- Who will have the login information for the account?
- Will the account be needed indefinitely or for a shorter, definable time frame?
- Will the account have access to sensitive information?
- How complex and long will the password or passphrase be?
- How will the login information be transmitted to the account's authorized user?
- What's the minimum level of access necessary for the account?

Tracking all of this data is important, as it provides a foundation for assessment, audit, and monitoring of account status and usage. Using central identity management infrastructure, including authorization and authentication systems that have an automated monitoring and audit capability, is key to ensuring this across organizations.

Once an account has been created, modifications to it must be tracked throughout its lifecycle. That includes ensuring that it only has the rights, access, and privileges that are appropriate for the role that it or the account owner needs to perform and that privileges that do not match have been removed. Managing changes to the account, like password changes, tracking requests for additional rights or role changes, and monitoring uses of privileged credentials, are all necessary during the account's life.

The third phase in the lifecycle is the audit phase. This phase is designed to catch any violations of policies and best practices. For instance, when employees move between roles, they may receive new, additional privileges and access for their new roles. However, their old privileges and access may remain intact, instead of being removed. This is typically referred to as *permission creep* or *permission accumulation*. Auditing can identify accounts that are no longer being used. Perhaps a contractor is no longer working for the organization, and the account management team wasn't notified, so the account remains usable in the system. What if an account has been exempted from the password expiration policy and the password has remained unchanged for months or even years? Actively auditing accounts can help identify these risks.

When an account needs to be removed, ensuring that it is removed from all of the systems and services where it may have existed is also a critical step. Attackers often look for unused or unmaintained accounts that they can access, and forgotten accounts belonging to terminated staff members, administrators, or services can all be attractive targets. Monitoring the entire lifecycle, the actions taken by the administrators who manage accounts, and the actions taken by account holders are all important to securing the account management lifecycle.

Management Review and Approval

Security assessment efforts rely on management sponsoring the process and reviewing and approving the results. Management engagement throughout the process is critical to its success. Organizational security is effective only with management support. Ideally, top levels of management are supportive of security initiatives and include security as part of the company's vision. With this level of responsibility, it only makes sense that management must be informed about risk and must have an opportunity to determine whether a risk is acceptable.

Each of the techniques and procedures discussed in this chapter has a role in management's oversight of organizational security. Assessment processes can be used to validate organizational progress toward security goals or to ensure that standards are being met. Internal audits provide a chance to check against specific requirements through the eyes of an auditor rather than the staff members who maintain or use the systems and services. External audits remove internal biases and can provide an unfiltered view of the organization. Finally, assessments of third-party vendors and partners can help management make decisions about business relationships and agreements.

Assessment and audit reports provide a number of key elements that management needs to consider.

- An executive overview that provides a high-level view of the effort, its findings, and recommendations

- A set of detailed findings, typically ranked by priority or severity

- Recommendations for responses, sometimes including a detailed controls mapping and assessment

- Additional appendixes with further data about specifics in the assessment

It is important to present data to management in an easy-to-understand format, including charts and other visualizations that make serious issues easy to identify. Management needs to have a clear understanding of which issues are the most severe, which need immediate attention, and whether there are systemic problems that are part of an underlying issue.

Once the management has reviewed assessment or audit outputs, they must make decisions based on organizational priorities, business needs, and legal and contractual obligations. Ongoing assessments will likely be required to validate the impact of their decisions and the performance of controls and remediations that are implemented based on them.

All action items and decisions from meetings should be documented and assigned responsibility. Any residual risk and the acceptance of any risk should also be documented. Open issues are ideally prioritized, and action items and remediations are assigned deadlines as well.

Key Performance and Risk Indicators

Security metrics can help measure how effective security efforts are. When you want to improve security, you need to determine whether you are making progress. This is accomplished by using key performance indicators (KPIs) to help identify more specifically how security is performing. You also need to know if you're taking risks. Key risk indicators (KRIs) are used to accomplish this.

Both KPIs and KRIs are part of the governance, risk, and compliance (GRC) efforts required to provide security oversight and tracking for an organization. While some metrics and measures are gathered manually, GRC tools are increasingly popular tools for IT and security risk management and oversight.

Key Performance Indicators

Key performance indicators are used to show how the organization is performing based on goals set by leadership, as well as progress toward the goals that have not yet been met. Measuring performance requires an understanding of what meaningful progress is and how it can be measured. Much like any metric, numbers themselves do not have meaning without context that is relevant to the organization and its objectives.

Major industry standards for measuring information security performance include the following:

- NIST SP800-55, "Performance Measurement Guide for Information Security" (`https://nvlpubs.nist.gov/nistpubs/Legacy/SP/nistspecialpublication800-55r1.pdf`)

- ISO 27004, "Information technology – Security techniques – Information security management – Monitoring, measurement, analysis, and evaluation"

- ITIL's information security management module

Several steps are necessary when identifying useful KPIs. For instance, what are the business goals? What data sources provide information regarding the goals? Can the sources of data be used to identify progress toward reaching those goals or indicate the current status in relationship to organization objectives? How frequently should the data be collected? Is the data collection automated or manual? By answering these questions, you'll be better able to identify the KPIs that are useful to your organization. In addition, you'll have a good idea of the task in front of you and the work necessary to accomplish it.

To define useful KPIs, several pieces of information are necessary. You first need to identify the baseline you are starting from and the goals you want to accomplish. Then you can best determine how to achieve those goals.

The baseline—where you are at—is the starting point for developing KPIs. It merely requires taking measurements of the current status. Of course, you must wisely choose which numbers matter. You want to choose factors that indicate the level of security. The KPIs selected should align with the organization's documented goals. In addition, the more readily available the data or the easier it is to collect, the better. Automation is also a key component in being effective. If it takes an inordinate amount of time to gather the data, then the overall effort suffers.

Once the initial data is gathered, the baseline is created. At the next sampling interval, progress toward goals can be evaluated. Analysis of the data can begin. The analysis may be automated, manual, or both, depending on the circumstances. Additional information can also be considered during the analysis, such as external factors that may have influenced the data. For instance, an increase in unresolved calls to the help desk may have been created by issues with an application update. This in turn may indicate that testing for the application update was insufficient. Ensure that all the factors that impact the KPIs are documented. This allows for more accurate conclusions.

The information gathered should be documented. Trends should be observed and analyzed and findings reported to management as appropriate. With this data, determinations can be made regarding budget and resource allocation so that KPIs can show evidence of progress (or the lack thereof) toward organizational goals.

Key Risk Indicators

KPIs measure how well things are being done. KRIs, however, measure the organization's risk and how its risk profile changes. This provides the ability to assess the likelihood of a negative event, as well as assess the risk level of an activity or situation. The risks, if realized, can typically profoundly impact the organization. Therefore, KRIs can strongly impact decision-making by senior-level executives.

Common key risk indicators include the following:

- Vulnerability metrics
- Policy exception rates
- Audit findings that are outstanding or unresolved
- Security incident rates
- Malware infection rates
- Security education and awareness rates
- Measures of the use of unapproved software
- Risk assessment ratings
- Patching compliance
- Account management status and issue rate

KRIs, like KPIs, must be adapted to the organization that will use them and should be both timely and a good fit with the organization's security needs.

Risk also changes over time. The activities of an organization can increase or decrease risk. The resultant KRI should indicate these changes. Management should identify acceptable measurements for any KRI. Any changes in a KRI that result in an unacceptable value should trigger an action on the part of the company. For instance, if the number of unpatched machines with critical vulnerabilities exceeds an agreed-upon percentage, then desktop support staff works after hours to manually patch enough machines to bring the KRIs back into a state of compliance.

Backup Verification Data

It is unlikely that you work at an organization that doesn't perform backups of company data. Backups are an expected part of IT in almost every company. It's also just as unlikely that your organization has never experienced data loss. Whether by an accidental deletion, a failed backup that wasn't discovered, or malware that encrypted information, most people have experienced the consequences of data loss.

The first step in avoiding data loss is identifying the data that is critical to an organization. Once criticality is documented, a backup schedule can be identified, and backups can begin. This is the first half of the process. The second critical portion is ensuring that the backups are functioning property. This involves reviewing the backup logs to ensure that the backups ran without issue. Any issues during the backup process should be investigated and resolved quickly. Problems should be escalated to management so there is an awareness regarding any data that may not have been backed up. Failed backups create risk that upper management must be informed about.

Finally, backups must be tested. Backups should occasionally be restored and tested to ensure that the data is intact and has maintained its integrity. All the hardware needed for the recovery process should be tested and confirmed working. Ideally, use different hardware for the test recovery process. Testing the recovery process ensures that personnel are properly trained and ready for a recovery situation. A backup is useful only if it can be restored. Auditing should review both the process and the execution of backups and backup verification to ensure that the organization minimizes the risk of data loss.

▶▶ REAL WORLD EXAMPLE:
Tape Backups

Few things are more disconcerting than, in the middle of a data recovery situation, realizing there is no viable backup. The backup data can't be read, critical data cannot be restored, and information is lost. It is difficult to account for every situation that might occur. For example, there was a company that was diligent in rotating their tape media in their backup solution. No tape in use was very old. There were written logs that were checked on a nightly basis to ensure backups occurred as expected. A set of backups were stored off-site. After a backup was completed, a small restore was done to verify the information.

But one critical step was missed: the same tape backup drive that performed backups was used for the test restores. However, when that drive failed, a replacement was ordered—and the replacement drive was unable to read any of the backup tapes

CONTINUES

created with the original tape backup drive. Apparently, the heads on the different drives were aligned differently. Data recovery was necessary, adding additional time to the recovery process, which is never a good situation. This could have been avoided by ensuring that the backup media was readable by different physical hardware. Make sure your process accounts for such contingencies.

Training and Awareness

The security landscape is constantly changing. It's a field that requires a dedication to learning. Practices and technologies that were acceptable 20 years ago are now considered insecure. File formats once thought safe have been exploited. Encryption technologies relied upon for wireless communication or secure web transactions have been found to have weaknesses. Issues have even been found in hardware, from Trusted Platform Module (TPM) chips to CPUs, with some issues, such as the Spectre and Meltdown flaws, existing for more than a decade before discovery. A security professional must stay on top of emerging threats to be effective. This creates two important areas all companies should address.

- **Security training:** Teaching people to perform their roles securely
- **Security awareness training:** Educating people about security issues

On the surface, these sound similar; however, they have distinct objectives. For instance, we've discussed aspects of account management and the account management lifecycle. Teaching help-desk employees the processes of secure account creation and password distribution falls into the realm of security training. Employees have job responsibilities, and ensuring their tasks are performed in accordance with established guidelines and best practices falls under security training.

Additionally, emerging threats may pose a risk to the company. Educating employees regarding common attacks, such as phishing attacks and business email compromise, can raise awareness regarding attack methods and educate employees regarding how they can adjust their practices to reduce the risk. Teaching employees the benefits of passphrases over passwords, for instance, can reduce the likelihood of success of password-guessing attacks against your network. Thus, security awareness training that covers each of these items and tracking both its effectiveness and uptake by staff are important parts of security management. In fact, security awareness KPIs are included in NIST SP 800-55, "Performance Measurement Guide for Information Security."

Training activities should be tracked and audited. Identify the security training and security awareness training needed. Ensure that all employees undergo the necessary training. Determine when periodic refresher training may be needed for job tasks. Identify trends that may indicate areas that training can address. Additionally, as the security landscape changes, develop training for employees that raises awareness of threats, bad practices, and behaviors that may increase risk to the organization, such as password sharing. As training is delivered, identify employees who did and did not attend, and offer opportunities to attend an additional session, review a recording of the presentation, or participate in other similar alternatives so that all staff are adequately informed and aware of threats and best practices in mitigating the threats. Many industry regulations, such as PCI-DSS, require training. Therefore, performing training, tracking attendance, and auditing compliance with training are important.

Disaster Recovery and Business Continuity

Disaster recovery (DR) and BCPs are part of an organization's operational controls and need to be considered in any assessment process. Fortunately, standards exist for DR/BCPs as well, including ISO 22301, "Societal security – Business continuity management systems – Requirements" and NIST SP-800-34, "Contingency Planning Guide for Federal Information Systems." COBIT DS4, "Ensure Continuous Service," also addresses disaster recovery and business continuity planning.

Auditing DR plans and BCPs includes asking questions like these:

- Does a DR plan or BCP exist, and is it up to date?
- Is the plan securely stored in an accessible location?
- Are personnel aware of the plan, how to access it, and its contents?
- Are crises identified with an appropriate scale to assess the level of action to take?
- Are critical functions identified?
- Does each critical function have a plan?
- Has the plan been tested?
- Is there a communication plan?
- Are emergency service providers identified?

In addition to these, there are dozens of questions that should be reviewed when assessing a DR plan or BCP. Fortunately, audit organizations like ISACA provide disaster recovery audit toolkits. (See `www.isaca.org/Groups/Professional-English/business-continuity-disaster-recovery-planning/GroupDocuments/DRP%20toolkit_DRP%20and%20BCP%20audit.pdf`.)

IT environments change frequently, and these changes can impact disaster recovery processes. If plans are not maintained regularly, they can quickly become outdated. Other events can also cause the plans to become outdated, such as the following:

- Adoption of new vendors, such as cloud software-as-a-service (SaaS) vendors that remove operational control from the home organization and necessitate understanding their DR plan or BCP and capabilities

- Failure to integrate plan maintenance with change management processes
- Changes and updates to the environment, such as new hardware and applications
- Redesigning or rearchitecting the network, or adding new services
- Department mergers and organization hierarchy changes
- Staff turnover and lack of ongoing training
- Failure to assign responsibility for maintenance tasks (no ownership)
- Plan maintenance does not directly benefit a company's bottom line until disaster strikes

Steps must be taken to counter these issues. An out-of-date plan undermines all the effort that was spent in creating it. Consider implementing countermeasures.

- Integrate plan updates as a required portion of change control processes.
- Ensure all new equipment and applications are deployed through change control processes.
- Make sure all modifications to systems and their architecture also go through change control.
- Assign responsibility and resources to update the plan in the event of mergers and hierarchical changes.
- Require ongoing training and cross training, upon hire as well as annually, at a minimum.
- Assign responsibility for oversight of the plan and its maintenance.
- Regularly review and test the plan.

Assessments must validate both the existence of the plan and its ongoing maintenance and testing. Testing frequency may be dictated by the number of systems being tested. Fortunately, assessing DR plans and BCPs is also a useful way to improve them, as simulated or actual activations as well as walk-through assessments will all provide opportunities for improvement of the plan.

While all systems should be tested at least once a year, an organization may opt to conduct a single large-scale test annually and several tests that are smaller in scope throughout the year. There are several types of tests that can be performed, and the type of test can also be factored in when determining the frequency of testing.

- **Paper or checklist tests:** A copy of the test plan is distributed to team members for review.
- **Structured walkthrough:** Groups review the plan together to identify any omissions or issues with the plan.

- **Simulation or tabletop exercise:** Employees are given a disaster recovery scenario and walk through the actions, communication, and strategy needed to recover, according to the plan.

- **Parallel test:** Recovery processes are put into place, restoring critical systems in a test environment. No disruption to actual production systems is permitted. The ability to replace and restore systems is confirmed.

- **Cutover or full interruption test:** This is the most disruptive test type: production systems are taken offline, and backup systems and processes are tested as replacement systems are brought online to carry the production load.

Each of these testing methods should generate appropriate artifacts based on organizational policies and any audit or assessment requirements that may exist for the organization.

The desired outcome of all these exercises and tests is the same: identify shortcomings in the plans, and document them. Implement changes in the original plan to address any issues that are uncovered. With test types that have a larger scope and impact, consider assigning a point person to collect information regarding issues that arise that will require a plan modification. While the information collected may be minimal during the recovery process, it can be expanded once the process is complete, and this ensures that few, if any, updates to the plan are forgotten during the recovery process.

As you prepare to assess DR plans and BCPs, it may be helpful to consider the lifecycle of the BCP. It is not a static document but must be regularly evaluated. As the company, network, and services change, the systems that support critical processes may change, and the business continuity plan and disaster recovery plan should be updated accordingly. The lifecycle of the BCP is reflected as follows:

- **Phase 1:** Perform a risk analysis.

- **Phase 2:** Perform a business impact analysis.

- **Phase 3:** Create a strategy and develop a plan.

- **Phase 4:** Test, train, and maintain the plan.

Some models for the plan have five phases, by breaking phase 3 into two parts: create a strategy and develop a plan, for instance. Or they break phase 4 into testing and acceptance, and train and maintain. The result, however, is essentially the same.

ANALYZE TEST OUTPUT AND GENERATE REPORT

Security controls, vulnerability scans, penetration tests, and audits—all these activities generate a significant amount of data. Perhaps a few gifted people can review the raw data and draw salient conclusions, but most people need the data presented to them in a meaningful way. This allows them to draw appropriate and correct conclusions about the state of the environment. Generating reports is a critical step in most security endeavors.

One of the first things to consider is the audience for the report. For instance, when reporting on the results of a vulnerability scan, it is important to consider who will review the report. Most executives do not have the time or interest in reviewing the steps required to remediate a buffer overflow on an application server. Likewise, the server administrator who needs to remediate a vulnerability is more interested in the technical details of fixing the issue and less interested in how many vulnerabilities the server had last month.

Often, however, both reports are needed. One approach is to write a single all-encompassing report, which combines all the sections that are applicable to all the audiences. After creating the all-encompassing report, carefully review it, and have it peer reviewed and finalized. Then, determine which sections are needed for each audience. Next, for each audience, remove the unnecessary sections from the all-encompassing report, and save an audience-specific version of the report. This is why the peer review is critical: it is much easier to make a correction on the all-encompassing report prior to creating the audience-specific reports. Any changes to a section after the review will require either re-creation of all the audience reports after correcting the master, which is the safer option, or separate updating of all the audience reports. The likelihood of introducing an error and replicating it is greater, though, when editing all the audience reports.

Some tools will automate report generation; however, automated reports cannot take the place of customized reports for your organization. Your clients will appreciate a report that is designed just for them, as opposed to a one-size-fits-all approach. Take the time to ensure that the report fits the needs of the audience. Additionally, while using templates can speed up the creation of reports and create consistency, you must ensure that all the information included in the report is accurate and relevant to the audience. If too much copying and pasting is used, mistakes can happen, and the validity of the entire report and findings can be called into question.

▶▶ REAL WORLD EXAMPLE:
The Danger of Copy and Paste

After several weeks of penetration testing, the vendor scheduled a meeting to present their report and findings to an organization. The first portion of the presentation went smoothly. The executive summary and high-level review of the findings presented no surprises.

Next came a closer review of the findings. After covering a few findings, one particular finding was a little bit confusing. A server was identified by name, with several missing critical patches. This isn't altogether uncommon in most cases. In this case, however, the server name caused concern: it was not a server on the organization's network, nor was the domain name correct. Based on the domain name, it was quite apparent that this server belonged to another, well-known company in the area. Two more findings were similar.

This incident raised several concerning questions, and the speculation during the meeting was not good:

- Did the vendor accidentally provide the organization information regarding another company's network?
- Did the finding belong to one of the organization's servers and the wrong name was simply left from a prior report?
- Was the organization's confidential information being accidentally shared with other companies?
- Were the findings in the report accurate and complete?
- Did the vendor properly destroy data after an engagement was finished?
- Did all the penetration testers and report writers follow proper procedures?
- Was the report carefully reviewed prior to presentation?

The mistakes caused the validity of the entire report to be called into question. Using the vendor for any additional engagements was a decidedly unwise risk, and their services were no longer utilized. This type of mistake causes significant damage to the reputation of a company. It simply cannot happen, and it is one of the dangers of carelessness when using templates to create reports. Ensure the accuracy of information presented. Have the final draft of the report and findings carefully reviewed. Double- and triple-check everything. The reputation of your organization may be at stake.

Audit reports can take many forms. When presenting the findings, especially to a technical audience, necessary elements include the following:

- Threats and vulnerabilities identified
- Criticality level of the finding
- Exploitation probability
- Exploitation impact
- Remediation steps

This information is typically presented either as a single host and all its associated vulnerabilities or as a particular vulnerability and a list of all its impacted hosts. If the audit identified only a small number of vulnerabilities, then listing a vulnerability and impacted hosts may be acceptable. When many hosts are audited and several vulnerabilities are present, then presenting the findings by host, with all the hosts' vulnerabilities listed, may be preferable. Optionally, both formats can be used and separated into two sections.

- Findings by vulnerability, with associated hosts
- Findings by host, with associated vulnerabilities

It is also not uncommon to find organizations that prefer both. Some staff will find one format more useful than the other, depending on how the information is being used. If an IT staff member is patching a critical vulnerability that was found, they may want to see a list of all hosts impacted by that vulnerability. However, another IT staff member may be patching all issues on a single host at a time before moving to the next server, so having the issues listed by host is ideal.

The report also needs an executive summary. The summary should generally be no longer than one to two pages and accurately summarize the findings. It should be accessible and understandable to senior management. Refrain from technical details and other information that isn't necessary for the audience. The initial paragraph explains the goals and objectives of the audit, as well as summarizing the rest of the executive summary. The following paragraphs of the executive summary can include a high-level overview of the findings. The rest of the summary may identify discovered vulnerabilities based on the type of target, such as summarizing network hardware vulnerabilities in one paragraph, server vulnerabilities in a second paragraph, and workstations in a third paragraph of the summary. In addition, include numbers that reflect the current state of security as uncovered by the audit's findings. How many servers are present with unpatched critical vulnerabilities? How many targets of the audit have no serious vulnerabilities? What are the most critical findings that create the most risk? What is the impact of the vulnerabilities, and how much effort is expected for remediation? Management often seeks the bottom line: what is the cost of fixing the issues, and what is the cost of ignoring them? What is the risk associated with the vulnerabilities found? Ensure that this information is included in your executive summary and that it is easily found in your final report.

CONDUCT OR FACILITATE SECURITY AUDITS

Security professionals often conduct internal security audits and facilitate external audits of their organization. Understanding the benefits and challenges of internal and external audits is crucial that they provide organizational value. At the same time, you may also need to participate in assessments or audits for third parties, such as service providers and business partners. Knowing what types of audit information to request and what standards third parties are likely to have been assessed against can greatly improve the results of these assessments.

Internal Audits

An internal audit is conducted by the staff of an organization. The organization may have an audit person or audit team responsible for performing any audit activities. An advantage that internal auditors have is their familiarity with the environment and the culture. The internal auditor can use their familiarity to ensure that objective goals are met. Unlike external auditors, internal auditors know how the organization works, what issues are likely to exist, and who to work with to obtain all of the information that they need.

The internal knowledge and relationships that the internal auditor brings can also be a weakness. For instance, the relationship between the auditor and fellow employees can result in bias on the part of the auditor. This must be guarded against and is one deciding factor for looking outside of the organization for the auditing team. Additionally, industry regulations may require that an audit be performed by a separate organization to avoid any conflict of interest that might exist with an internal auditor.

In situations where a third-party auditor is required, it is not uncommon for the internal team to perform their own audit, often using the same goals and scope used by the third-party team. For instance, PCI requires third-party auditing and publishes the checklist of items to review. It is prudent for an organization to review the items to be audited and perform their own audit. Issues can be addressed, often before the official PCI audit, and place the organization in better standing. This is a much better approach than simply waiting to see what the auditor will find.

External Audits

In contrast to an internal audit, an external audit retains resources outside of the company to perform the audit as required by laws, regulations, or contractual agreements. There are advantages to this approach. External auditors typically have audited a wide variety of organizations, systems, and processes. This experience helps the auditor know what items and issues to look for, which a less experienced or internal auditor may miss. Additionally, external auditors will generally have no prior relationship to the staff whose systems and processes are being audited. This allows them to identify issues without bias. They are also able to complete their task without knowledge of the politics and culture of an organization, which could bias their findings.

However, there are also cons. External audits can be expensive, depending on their scope. The external audit's primary disadvantage, therefore, is its cost. In addition, while an auditor's lack of knowledge of an organization's politics can be an advantage in some circumstances, it can also be a disadvantage in others. The lack of knowledge regarding an organization can result in additional time being spent learning the organization's structure and potential interdepartmental conflicts of priorities, responsibilities, and communication. A more serious downside is that an auditor's lack of knowledge could lead them to a false positive finding because an organization's unique processes and procedures do not conform to the auditor's previous experience.

External auditors are frequently utilized when performing compliance audits. If an organization is subject to industry regulations, such as PCI or Sarbanes-Oxley, then internal auditors are not an option to attain compliance. While internal auditors can be used to pre-audit and prepare for the audit by identifying deviances from a standard, achieving compliance requires the services of an external auditor. External audits may also require that the auditor has been certified by the regulatory organization. PCI certifies their approved auditors as Qualified Security Assessors (QSAs), and completion of an audit by a QSA is required for certain levels of PCI compliance.

Third-Party Audits

When an organization works with a third-party supplier, vendor, or partner, they may want to perform an assessment or audit of their security practices. Audits performed to standards like the SSAE 18, ISAE 3402, or PCI-DSS are all commonly requested either during initial contract stages or on an ongoing basis from third-party vendors, and SOC 3 reports are specifically designed to be publicly available. In fact, major service providers often post them to their websites, making them easy to check.

When organizations want to understand the details of the security status of a third party, they may request a SOC 2 assessment, which may be released under an NDA. The availability of assessment or audit information to an organization will vary based on the third party's policies. Since audits can expose material weaknesses in the practices of an organization or may provide information that attackers could leverage to attack them, some organizations do not provide a detailed audit report to any third party.

When considering third-party audits and assessments, a few critical questions are important to ask.

- What standards do they assess or audit to?
- What type of audit or assessment reports do they provide automatically?
- What type of audit or assessment reports will they provide upon request or after signing an NDA?
- What is an acceptable level of audit findings or material deficiencies in an assessment?

Third-party service provider assessments can add another layer of complexity if you review where they acquire the services they rely on. A service provider may use multiple other service providers, and those providers may use even more providers. Since contracts are signed between two organizations, you may have little recourse with the downstream partners, but their security may directly impact your data or services.

Integrating Internal and External Audits

Organizations are increasingly operating in a hybrid environment where systems and infrastructure may exist inside of organizational network boundaries and in third-party environments like software-as-a-service providers, cloud infrastructure, or other organizations. This change in design makes it more likely that auditors and assessors will need to assess across these organizational and design boundaries to gain a full view of the organization's security status and compliance efforts.

Fortunately, the common assessment frameworks we discussed earlier in this chapter can be leveraged to ensure that assessments are conducted to the same standard. While third parties may not allow your organization to audit them, validation to the same standard can provide a reasonable level of assurance in many cases. Integration of internal and external audit information can be done through audit management tools using the same framework, making an otherwise difficult task approachable.

Auditing Principles

Regardless of whether an audit is internal, is external, or is a third-party audit, the principles used to conduct an audit are critically important. ISO 19011:2018 describes a number of core principles of auditing that are intended to make an audit effective and to allow organizations to rely on their output. The principles described in ISO 19011:2018 are as follows:

- Integrity
- Fair presentation
- Due professional care
- Confidentiality
- Independence
- Use of an evidence-based approach
- Use of a risk-based approach

Other audit standards may present slightly different guiding principles, but the core elements of these principles will remain for almost any audit an organization conducts due to the importance of providing fair, accurate, and relevant audit results.

Audit Programs

Audit programs are established to ensure that audits are conducted in a consistent manner, with appropriate resources, oversight, and support from management. While individual audits may be useful, one-off audits do not offer the consistency and repeatability that an audit program can, and organizations that are required to perform audits by legal, contractual, or other standards often have to demonstrate audit performance over time.

Implementing and Managing an Audit Program

Audit programs require an objective or objectives to be effective. Security practitioners and auditors must be aware of the objectives of an audit as they implement controls, document how those controls are working, and assess their effectiveness. Audit objectives take into account the risks that the organization faces, compliance with legal and contractual requirements, and management goals and strategies.

An example of the requirements that must be met as part of this can be found in ISO 27002:2017, which outlines the next steps in establishing an audit program, including the following:

- Identifying the roles and responsibilities of the person managing the program, as well as their competence

- Establishing the extent of the program, including the size of the organization, staffing, and sites, as well as the complexity of the organization or systems that are in scope

- Identifying and evaluating risks to the audit program

- Establishing procedures for the audit program

- Identifying resources for the audit program

Once the audit program itself is established, individual audits can be conducted using the guidelines and practices that are part of the program. Individual audits may have more specific scope and objectives or may apply specific criteria based on the reason that they are conducted.

Auditing Techniques and Activities

Audits have a number of stages that may vary from organization to organization, but most share a few common elements: assessment and planning, tool and methodology selection, on-site assessment, control gap analysis, and discussion and reporting. In many cases, an audit will also require the assessment of threats, vulnerabilities, and risks, and an assessment stage may be built into the early stages of the audit if this information hasn't already been prepared by the organization.

Regardless of whether an audit is conducted by internal or external auditors, a number of techniques are commonly used.

- Testing of representative items may be conducted to verify that they match what is expected. For example, change records may be tested to ensure that a change is filed, approved, and tested as required by the organization's change procedures.

- Documentary examination reviews documents and documentation to ensure that they exist and contain the appropriate information.

- Physical examination may be used to validate the existence or state of both controls and physical systems, locations, or other objects. Checking the physical inventory of an organization's systems is a type of physical examination.

- Testing can be used to ensure that responses occur as they are supposed to or that procedures are properly performed.

- Compliance testing tests against compliance requirements and ensures that the controls implemented are effective and reliable.

- Observation techniques are used to review policies and procedures and allow auditors to assess whether they are appropriate, well designed, and in line with industry standards or meet compliance requirements.

Sampling is often part of data review. A sampling rate is selected based on the quantity of data to ensure that a meaningful sample is selected and reviewed, and then a random sample is validated against the audit standard. If issues are discovered, additional samples may be selected, or auditors may choose to review a more significant amount of the data available.

Audit tools may be used to validate configurations or to gather other evidence or data. Auditing techniques that rely on tools must themselves be validated to ensure that the tool is gathering all of the required data and that it does not introduce errors.

Maintaining an Audit Program

Regular recurring audits are an important part of audit programs. A recurring audit will help to verify that issues identified in previous assessments have been remediated and that older problems have not recurred. In addition, a recurring audit provides an opportunity to reassess controls that may have become less useful as the organization or technology has shifted. While organizations typically want to have zero findings, most should identify new issues during periodic audits due to changes. A consistent lack of findings may actually indicate issues with the audit technique, auditors, or the information that is being shared with the auditors.

SUMMARY

Assessing the state of the security of an organization, as well as the success of its security program and operations, requires careful planning. Industry standards for assessments and audits can provide a strong foundation for a security assessment and testing process that includes vulnerability assessments, penetration testing, log reviews, secure coding, and security design. All the elements of an organization's infrastructure, as well as its practices, procedures, and awareness, need to be reviewed and assessed throughout their lifecycle. Whether an organization assesses itself, hires external auditors, or uses third-party audits to ensure that third-party suppliers and partners meet accepted industry standards or specific requirements, conducting security assessments and testing is critical to maintaining a strong security posture.

A critical part of security assessment and testing is collecting the data that you need to validate operational and managerial controls. That means ensuring that training and awareness are measured, that account management practices and procedures are checked, and that disaster recovery and business continuity testing occur. Each security assessment and process should be measured, and key performance and risk indicators need to be associated with the measures that fit the organization's strategic and compliance needs.

Security Operations

SECURITY OPERATIONS ENTAIL A wide breadth of tasks and functions, and the security professional is expected to have a working familiarity with each of them. This can include maintaining a secure environment for business functions and the physical security of a campus and, specifically, the data center. Throughout your career, you will likely have to oversee and participate in incident response activities, which will include conducting investigations, handling material that may be used as evidence in criminal prosecution and/or civil suits, and performing forensic analysis. The Certified Information Systems Security Professional (CISSP) should also be familiar with common tools for mitigating, detecting, and responding to threats and attacks; this includes knowledge of the importance and use of event logging as a means to enhance security efforts. Another facet the security practitioner may have to manage could be how the organization deals with emergencies, including disaster recovery.

There is a common thread running through all aspects of this topic: supporting business functions by incorporating security policy and practices with normal daily activities. This involves maintaining an accurate and detailed asset inventory, tracking the security posture and readiness of information technology (IT) assets through the use of configuration/change management, and ensuring personnel are trained and given adequate support for their own safety and security.

This chapter will address all these aspects of security operations. The practitioner is advised, however, to not see this as a thorough treatment of all these concepts, each of which could be (and has been) the subject of an entire book (or books) by themselves; for each topic that is unfamiliar, you should look at the following content as an introduction only and pursue a more detailed review of related subject matter.

NOTE The countries in which an organization operates each have their own distinct legal systems. Beyond considerations of written laws and regulations, the active functioning of court systems and regulatory bodies often have intricate, myriad applications in the real world that extend far beyond how things are codified in written laws. These factors become even more varied and complex when an organization functions in multiple countries and needs to deal with actual scenarios that directly involve international law and the laws of each respective nation. With that in mind, it is always imperative to get the input of a professional legal team to fully understand the legal scope and ramifications of security operations (and basically all operations and responsibilities beyond security as well).

UNDERSTAND AND SUPPORT INVESTIGATIONS

The purpose of performing investigations is to gather facts so that an informed decision or conclusion can be made or so that an action can be taken with confidence. The output provided by an investigation is a collection of evidence, analysis, and documentation to refer to in the future and to prove that the appropriate level of rigor was taken to arrive at the decision or action taken.

In the world of information systems security, there are many reasons to perform an investigation, and there are many scenarios that may require one, such as in response to a crime, a violation of policy, or a significant IT outage/incident. (An interruption of service or malfunction may indicate something beyond routine equipment failure or user error.) Depending on the purpose of the investigation, they will require different levels of rigor.

What comprises an investigation? So that you understand this, this chapter will discuss these four different facets of the investigation process:

- Evidence collection and handling
- Reporting and documentation

- Investigative techniques

- Digital forensics tools, tactics, and procedures

Evidence Collection and Handling

"Evidence collection and handling" can have a broad range of meaning, much of which is beyond the purview of the CISSP. So, barring things like fingerprints and DNA samples, what types of evidence are applicable? The answer is closely tied to the reasons a CISSP would be involved in an investigation. Organizations need evidence to support criminal prosecution of attackers and malicious insiders, to better manage incidents, and to prove due diligence if and when there is a breach. Evidence also aids in lawsuits brought in civil court. So, digital forensic evidence will fulfill many of these needs and is the most common form we will discuss as information security professionals.

There may be other forms of evidence a CISSP will use, however. Direct evidence is testimony from a witness who personally observed an event. A witness saying "I saw that man walk out with my laptop" is direct evidence.

Some testimony may not be direct evidence. Hearsay evidence is indirect or second-hand evidence. It is not useful in court but could be useful in an internal investigation, because it could lead to the discovery of new facts and more tangible evidence. If during an interview an administrator says, "Joe said Debbie caused the breach," that statement is hearsay and is not useful in law enforcement or court situation. If, however, Debbie wasn't previously on the list to be interviewed, she can be added, and this piece of secondhand information could lead to resolving the incident faster.

Other types of evidence don't come from human testimony but are instead recorded data. This can take the form of hard copy, photographs and video recordings, event and traffic logs, and computer files and memory. Evidence can take physical forms, too, such as objects (damaged or intact), media that contain data evidence, and physical forensic material such as blood, hair, and fingerprints. But what we, as information security professionals, will most likely deal with is evidence from and related to IT assets and data.

There are a number of hurdles to overcome with computer-related investigations. Attorneys, judges, and juries may not have an informed understanding of how IT systems function and how data can be interpreted to reach objective conclusions. It is therefore contingent on practitioners to collect, preserve, and present IT-related evidence in a meaningful and professional manner to provide the court with evidence that is believable and understandable. There are many industry standards related to the capture, collection, and preservation of digital evidence, from recognized standards bodies, government agencies, and vendors. For example, ISO 27037, "Information technology – Security techniques – Guidelines for identification, collection, acquisition and preservation of digital evidence," is designed for just this purpose (`https://www.iso.org/standard/44381.html`).

It behooves the security professional to be familiar with any evidence guidance pertinent to your industry, organization, and jurisdiction.

The following are some general principles to bear in mind when performing digital evidence collection and preservation:

- When collecting digital evidence, the analyst should make copies of the relevant volume or drive. This can be either a logical backup or a bit-level image. A logical backup only copies the directories and files of the volume. This means it's the easier and faster choice, but it doesn't capture deleted files or data remnants in the slack space. A logical backup may also alter the time stamps on a file, which may be relevant to an investigation. A bit-level image, by contrast, copies every sector, byte, and bit, making an exact copy of the entire drive (or other media). This includes deleted files and slack space, making it the necessary choice for material that needs to be submitted as evidence in court. The trade-off is that bit-level images are larger and take more time to perform than a logical backup. There are many tools on the market specifically crafted for the purpose of capturing and collecting digital evidence, such as EnCase, FTKImager, and MacQuisition.

- Copies of data for evidentiary purposes can be complicated in a managed services environment, such as the cloud, because the data owner is often not also the owner of the systems/hardware on which the data resides. In cases that involve managed environments, specific tools and techniques must be used, and collection activities must be supported in the contract between the customer and the service provider.

- Sometimes, a computer's internal memory (RAM) can be relevant in an investigation; for example, a file that is encrypted on a hard drive may be unencrypted when being stored for use by the processor in the computer's RAM. If an investigation requires the RAM from a computer to be acquired, it is imperative that the power to the computer is kept on until the RAM can be copied. Similar to collecting hard drive data, many tools exist to capture RAM, such as The Volatility Framework and Surge Collect.

- Original drives or media should be tagged as such and secured. One copy should be marked as the primary or "best evidence" copy, it should be secured, and no changes should be made to it. Perform all analysis of the data on a separate copy, never the original or the best evidence copy.

- To preserve the integrity of the files and prove that they haven't changed, analysts can use a write blocker and calculate message digests before and after the files were collected and copied. This aids in preventing and detecting unplanned modifications to the data; only intended changes should be made, and these need to be recorded so that the opposing side of a court case can re-create the same actions on the same data and determine whether there is any reason to doubt the outcome of the analysis. These tools and techniques will be covered in the upcoming digital forensics section.

- The chain of custody must be documented for the original or best evidence copy. It must be accompanied by a chain of custody form that covers all of the relevant facts. The form should explain what the evidence is, what machine or system it came from, and a description of the incident or reason for collecting it. It should include the name of the person or people who collected it, the original message digest when it was collected, and the date and time it was collected. A list of all the people who handled it, and when, should be maintained, along with where and when it was moved or stored. If it is a copy of a hard drive, the basic information about the original model, serial number, capacity, and so on should also be noted. Chain of custody documentation will be presented to the court along with the evidence to support the validity of any claims or assertions made about the evidence and what the evidence suggests, and to mitigate any doubts about the validity of the evidence itself or the conclusions drawn from it.

Reporting and Documentation

Evidence will be used to make determinations and decisions. For internal investigations, evidence will be used by management (often for decisions about how to deal with employees who have violated policy or to make changes to the production environment); for court cases (both criminal and civil), evidence will be used by the court to make a judgment. Evidence and documentation provided to management (as noted in the previous section about internal investigations) need only have a professional and understandable format. Evidence provided to a court must meet a much higher standard and requires more extensive documentation for support.

Each step taken to gather evidence and the method(s) should be documented. For digital forensic data, this would include how the file or drive images were created and how the message digests were calculated. The message digest values themselves, before and after, should also be captured. All of this should be documented at the level of detail that another analyst could reproduce the results following the same steps.

In addition to the main report, you may include other supporting documents or appendixes. These should include a list of evidence gathered during the investigation; the chain of custody details for evidence, if applicable; and the contact information of all relevant internal and external parties.

The following are some general concepts related to evidence presented to the court:

- **Be accurate:** The evidence and documentation must not vary, deviate, or conflict with other evidence or contain any errors. Inaccurate evidence can be disputed or dismissed.

- **Be authentic:** Evidence should not deviate from the truth and relevant facts. In addition to harming your side's opportunity for a favorable court decision, inauthentic evidence may be construed as deceiving the court, which is itself a crime.

- **Be complete:** Both sides of a court case will be allowed to review and dispute all evidence provided by the other side; you will be required to share any and all data related to the case, regardless of whether that data supports your side. Even evidence that does not demonstrate your intended outcomes must be shared with the opposing side to give the court an opportunity to make a fair, informed, and objective decision. Furthermore, as with deception, failure to disclose all evidence in a legal matter may have financial and even criminal consequences.

- **Be convincing:** Regardless of the type of court, the purpose of the case is to determine which side's narrative is more believable, as supported by testimony and evidence. You will try to convince the court that your story is more believable, while disputing your opponent's side; the adversary will be doing the same. The evidence you present should support your story, and your story should be reasonably demonstrated by the evidence.

- **Be admissible:** There are many kinds of evidence that are admissible in court and only a few that aren't; some are admissible only after a ruling by the court and discussion/review by opposing counsel (such as expert testimony). Be sure to understand the rules of evidence that are applicable in your jurisdiction to know which evidence will be admissible.

In all matters of evidence, it is absolutely imperative to consult with legal counsel to ensure that your efforts are suitable for the court.

NOTE One of the enduring myths in our industry is the belief that original content will be rendered inadmissible as evidence if it is modified in any way; this is simply not true. Modified content can still be presented to the court; however, it may suffer in terms of believability because doubt is introduced as to the accuracy of the final form of the material and the possibility that the modification created outcomes that the original did not suggest. This is usually overcome with exhaustive, detailed documentation purposefully describing all modifications and analysis processes. Still, the best option remains to use a copy of the original material for analysis purposes and preserve the original in its captured state.

Investigative Techniques

We will briefly explore investigative techniques in this section. To do so, we will begin with common techniques used in criminal investigations and discuss their relation to IT security and the realm of the CISSP. Those techniques are interviewing witnesses, surveillance, and forensics.

We will begin with some basic interview principles.

Choose a private, nonthreatening place for the interview, be respectful of the interviewee's time, and accommodate their schedule to the greatest extent possible. Remove distractions from the room and provide a comfortable seat.

Whenever possible, do not conduct interviews with only two people present (the interviewer and the subject); have at least three people in the room, and, if possible (as allowed by applicable law), record the conversation (and make sure the subject knows it is being recorded). Allow the subject to have an attorney or other representation present. If the interviews will be pertinent to later civil litigation, you may need to consult in-house or outside counsel prior to the interview. Interviews done with the direction of counsel can, in some circumstances, provide a level of protection from having to disclose the interview during subsequent litigation.

Have a list of short, specific questions prepared for the interview, but don't use them right away. Begin with one or two open-ended questions, such as "What can you tell me about what happened?" Once they are comfortable, begin to ask simple, targeted questions regarding the investigation. Avoid yes or no questions early on; they could set the pattern for short answers for all questions. Avoid accusatory questions that seem to place blame, and avoid leading questions that seem to be steering them toward a particular answer.

Proceed through the details of the event or incident you are investigating in chronological order. Stop and make clarifying statements if anything is unclear. Rephrase the question if the interviewee seems to be avoiding answering or is not giving enough detail. Repeat their answer back if it sounds questionable or confusing to either confirm their response or give them a chance to clarify or reword it. Don't be afraid to ask whether there is evidence or witnesses to confirm the statements they make and determine the source of their information. Ask if they observed it directly or if it was learned secondhand.

Give the interviewee plenty of time to answer questions with slight pauses between them. Take detailed notes whenever possible. Finally, ask if there is anything that they feel was left out or if there is anything they want to disclose or clarify before you complete the interview.

Unless you are acting in the capacity of a law enforcement/government agent, at no time can you detain an interview subject or compel them to answer interview questions beyond their role as an employee; an employer/organization may demote or fire the employee if the employee does not cooperate with the interview, or even sue the employee in civil court, but the organization may not use force in any way against the employee. The subject must be allowed to terminate the interview or leave the premises at any time if they choose.

The next technique on our list is surveillance. Surveillance can take many forms: direct human observation, photographic and video capture, audio monitoring, and IT logging (to include usage details, screen captures, browsing history, keystroke capture, etc.), among others.

An organization's legal permissions for surveillance of its employees, customers, visitors, and property vary wildly, depending on jurisdiction. For instance, in the United States, property owners (such as businesses) are completely free to use video monitoring on and around their premises (with very limited exceptions); this even includes harvesting video and photographic information of public spaces that fall outside the owner's control (indeed, all people in the United States are generally free to photograph/record video of anything happening in public). However, in the European Union, employee monitoring is strictly limited, and recording video/photographic images by businesses in public spaces is severely controlled. It is essential that security professionals make themselves extremely familiar with applicable laws and regulations in their jurisdictions prior to implementing any surveillance solutions. Again, it is highly recommended to involve legal counsel in these decisions.

If the organization has reviewed applicable law and decides to implement surveillance solutions, it is extremely important and worthwhile to provide employees and visitors with full notice of surveillance that might capture their activities and to obtain written confirmation of their receipt and understanding of this notice. This should include mention in employment/service contracts, the acceptable use policy, physical signs, and website/browser banners/pop-ups.

The last item in our comparative list of investigative techniques is forensics. For this book the focus is on *digital* forensics, which is a large and complex enough topic that we will cover it separately in the next section.

Digital Forensics Tools, Techniques, and Procedures

The organization needs to designate investigators and analysts with the proper training, expertise, and tools to perform digital forensics. These can be internal employees or contractors, external vendors, or a combination of both. These decisions should take into consideration response time, data classification, and sensitivity.

The forensic team should be made up of people with diverse skillsets, including knowledge of networking principles and protocols, a wide range of security products, and network-based threats and attack vectors. Skillsets should overlap between team members, and cross-training should be encouraged so that no one member is the only person with a particular skill.

Other teams within the organization should be available to support forensic activities. This should have top-down support through policy, and the forensic team should feel enabled to approach members of management, the legal team, human resources, auditors, IT, and physical security staff. Working together, the cross-functional forensic team should have a broad set of skills, capabilities, tools, techniques, and understanding of procedures.

Tools

Digital forensic analysts need an assortment of tools to collect and examine data. Different tools are necessary to be able to collect and examine both volatile and non-volatile data; to capture information from media, software, and hardware; and to craft meaningful reports from all the data collected and created during analysis. There are, for example, many types of file viewers necessary to view files that have different formats, extensions, or compression types. Third-party registry analysis tools provide analysts with new ways to view and navigate registry values and changes. Debugging tools allow analysts to get more details than default reports or logs will include. Decompilers and binary analysis tools allow analysts to look inside executable programs, at the code level, to find anomalies and malicious code. There are dedicated tools to extract data from a database. Analysts also use specialized tools to analyze mobile devices for file changes and to find deleted files and messages.

A drive imaging tool is critical to the forensic process. These come in different forms, such as a dedicated workstation, small appliance, or software, but the function is to make an exact copy of a drive or piece of media. Some versions require the physical removal of the drive or media and attachment to the imaging tool, which is called a *dead copy*. Other imaging tools can interface via transfer cables, FireWire technology, network media, and so on, to capture "live" images or copies, meaning that the image is taken while the device is running.

A write blocker is another valuable tool used in forensic investigation. It can be either an appliance or a software tool. It does just what its names says: it prevents any new data from being written to the drive or media and prevents data from being overwritten during analysis of the drive/media. This is useful to reduce the possibility of introducing unintended modifications to the original data.

It is also useful to have a hashing tool to create digests for integrity purposes. A message digest is the output of a hash function, creating a unique representation of the exact value of a given set of data. If the data changes, even in a minor way (even by one character), the entire digest changes; in this way, an investigator can be sure that the original data collected as evidence is the same data that was analyzed and is the same data provided as evidence to the court and opposing parties. Two common algorithms for creating message digests are Secure Hash Algorithm 1 (SHA-1) and Message Digest 5 (MD5). Many popular forensic tools incorporate automatic hashing/integrity checks.

Network traffic is also an important aspect of digital forensics. Capturing traffic from a sniffer, packet analysis tool, or network threat detection tool provides live session data.

Log files are also a critical element of analyzing the network aspects of a forensic investigation. Log files are found in many locations, including servers, firewalls, intrusion detection systems/intrusion prevention systems, and routers, and can provide significant insight into the events that transpired over networks.

Finally, a video screen capture tool can be valuable for analysis purposes. The ability to capture real-time video can be used to document the steps taken on a forensic workstation, for example. It proves that the analysts are performing the steps they claimed they would perform consistently and in accordance with the written forensic procedures. It can also help with documenting and reporting afterward.

Not all tools are created equal, and there are a wide variety of both open source and commercial tools. It is essential that the selection of tools be made in consultation with the organization's legal counsel, who can provide guidance on which particular tools would provide admissible evidence.

Techniques and Procedures

The previous section addressed the skills and tools the forensic team should have. This section discusses the techniques your team should follow. What are the goals and actions of effective analysts as they proceed through investigations?

- **Start with a standard process:** Analysts should follow a predefined process for collecting data. For example, ISO has standards for the capture, analysis, and interpretation of digital forensic evidence; these include standards 27041, 27042, 27043, and 27050.

- **Define priorities:** An organization has three possible priorities when responding to an incident: returning to normal operations as fast as possible, minimizing damage, and preserving detailed information about what occurred. These priorities are, necessarily, conflicting: a fast recovery will reduce opportunities to collect evidence, taking time to collect evidence may lead to more damage, and so forth. The organization needs to determine in which order to address these priorities, in both the general (what does the policy say?) and specific (what should we do for this incident?).

- **Identify data sources:** Before a team can begin investigating in earnest, analysts need to define what data they are looking for and all possible sources for that data. Consideration needs to be given as to the flow of certain data and all the places where it is stored and processed. Are copies made along the way? Is the data mirrored off-site or to the cloud for backup? What kind of event logs or notifications are triggered in the process? What devices will this data travel through? At this point, the analysts also need to discover the physical location of the components that store and process the data and who the administrators are for those components. Though this will be covered in an upcoming section, logging and monitoring are essential for analysis purposes. If logging and monitoring settings are configured at too low a verbosity, some of the important sources of data for the investigators will be missing. The correct level of detail for log collection needs to be determined long before an investigation needs to take place.

- **Make a plan to collect the data:** The analysts should make a plan addressing how the data will be collected, including the priority and the order in which it should be collected. This should prioritize data of higher value and volatility to avoid the chance that a machine could be turned off or data could be overwritten.

- **Capture volatile data:** Analysts need to be able to gather volatile data, such as data stored in RAM, which will disappear after the device is powered off, or data at high risk of being overwritten or corrupted by new data. There are risks associated with capturing live data, such as file modification during collection, or affecting the service or performance of the machine from which data is being taken. The organization needs to discuss and document in advance whether and when to accept these risks and capture live data. Analysts should be equipped with special tools for gathering live data and understand how each tool might alter the system during collection. The concept of scheduling collection actions based on possible data loss is often referred to as *order of volatility*; the most volatile data should be collected first.

- **Collect nonvolatile data:** As we discussed in the preceding tools section, an imaging tool is used to copy the contents of a drive. If the image is going to be used for a criminal case or disciplinary actions, it should be a bit-level image, not a logical backup, because it includes the slack space and possible data remnants. A write blocker should be employed to protect the image or data from being changed. The method used to shut down the target machine must be discussed and decided in advance. Each operating system (OS) has multiple methods for shutdown, and they have different behaviors and effects on the data.

- **Capture time details:** It is essential to know when files were created, accessed, or last changed. This information must be preserved for the investigation. Based on the OS, the time formats and method for attributing timestamps to files will vary. Going back to the differing uses of bit-level images and logical backups, this is another aspect of digital forensics where a bit-level image must be used in important investigations. This is because bit-level imaging will not alter the timestamps, but logical backup could, for example, change the original date and time the file was created to the date and time the logical backup was performed. The analysts collecting the data need to account for and document inaccuracies in timestamps, such as if the system clock was wrong and/or not connected to a network time source or if they suspect the attacker altered the timestamps. Inaccurate timestamps can hinder the investigation and hurt the credibility of the evidence.

- **Preserve and verify file integrity:** There are many steps and actions that can preserve and verify file integrity. We've already discussed some of them, such as using a write-blocker during the imaging process, calculating and comparing the message digests of drives and files, and using copies of drives or files for analysis, instead of the originals. A chain of custody should be clearly defined in advance and followed closely to preempt any claims of mishandling evidence. This includes using proper chain of custody forms and sealing evidence taken with evidence tape, evidence bags, and other tamper-proofing packaging.

- **Look for deleted or hidden data:** Deleted, overwritten, or hidden files can provide essential clues for an investigation. Deleted files or remnants can often be recovered from slack space using dedicated recovery applications. Files can be found in hidden system folders or folders that an intruder might have created and then marked as "hidden." Actors might also hide files "in plain sight" by changing the file name and/or changing the file extension, such as changing `virusnamehere.exe` to an innocuous and even boring name like `warranty.txt`. Because the name and extension are so easy to change, even for end users with limited permissions, analysts should inspect file headers and not take the extensions at face value.

- **Look at the big picture:** If we take the example of an attacker making a failed attempt to access a server, data about this attack could be captured in many places, such as a firewall traffic log, a server OS event log, or an authentication server log, as well as an intrusion detection system or security information and event management (SIEM) alert. If one action can leave a trail in five places, the analyst must consider this fact in reverse. If the analyst starts working from one or two log entries, are there three or four other places or other pieces of information they haven't seen yet? Would those facts affect how they interpret the few things they currently know? They should seek the other pieces before forming conclusions. Another point to consider is that some monitoring tools operate according to simple rules, such as "event log A + event log B = incident C." In a situation like this, the tool, such as a SIEM tool, is often correct in its conclusion. In an investigation, however, the analyst should verify this type of information. They should look at each event log separately and make their own conclusion about what those things mean together. The logs in this example are more immediate; direct information and the incident alerts from the SIEM tool are derivative and secondhand and have injected an additional layer of inference and decision-making, which may or may not be correct.

- **Make no leaps:** Analysts should use a conservative, fact-based approach in the final analysis and reporting stages. Either there is enough data to draw a given conclusion or there is not and no conclusion can be drawn. The data cannot be "almost conclusive" or "point to" being conclusive.

Forensics in the Cloud

Managed cloud computing services pose several challenges for forensic investigation and analysis. Both the technological implementation of cloud computing and the contractual nature of managed services complicate the investigator's ability to perform the actions and use the tools just described in this section of the book. It is important for the security professional to understand the unique characteristics of cloud computing that can make forensic activities difficult to accomplish.

- **Virtualization:** Cloud computing is typified by the use of virtual machines/containers running on various (and constantly changing) host devices. Often, it is difficult, if not impossible, to know the exact physical machine that any given virtual machine might be "on" at any given moment, and virtual machines, when "shut down," are migrated to other devices for storage, in the form of files. This makes forensic examination and establishing a chain of custody extremely difficult. Proving the state and content of any given virtual machine (or the data on it) takes much more effort and will require a much longer set of logs (thus introducing more doubt to the evidence, and thus the case).

- **Access:** Depending on the vendor, the service model, and the cloud deployment model, the cloud customer may have difficulty acquiring and analyzing evidence for a legal case because the customer may not own the hardware/software on which the customer's data resides and therefore may not have administrative access to those systems and the logging data they contain. Furthermore, all the ancillary sources that often provide useful investigatory data (such as network devices, SIEM solutions, data loss prevention tools, firewalls, IDS/intrusion prevention system [IPS] tools, etc.) may also not be under the customer's control, and access to their data may be extremely restricted.

- **Jurisdiction:** The larger cloud vendors often have data centers geographically spread across state, regional, or international boundaries; users and customers making transactions on the cloud can be located anywhere in the world. This creates many legal and procedural challenges and may significantly affect how evidence is collected and utilized.

- **Tools/techniques:** The technologies and ownership of managed cloud computing may hinder the use of common forensic tools; specific or customized tools may be necessary to capture and analyze digital evidence taken from/existing in the cloud.

Because there are so many variables involved in each of these aspects, it is difficult to dictate a specific approach to cloud forensics. However, some professional and governmental organizations are developing standards for this purpose. For instance, the Cloud Security Alliance, a partner of (ISC)^2, the organization producing this book and the progenitor of the CISSP Common Body of Knowledge (CBK), has created instructions for how to use the ISO forensics standard (ISO 27037) in a cloud environment (`https://cloudsecurityalliance.org/download/mapping-the-forensic-standard-isoiec-27037-to-cloud-computing/`), as well as a capability maturity model for cloud forensics (`https://cloudsecurityalliance.org/download/cloud-forensics-capability-model/`).

Finally, there is one principle that can be recommended regardless of all other variables and conditions in a cloud-managed services arrangement: contractual support for forensics. The cloud vendor and customer should agree explicitly, in writing, as to how incident investigation and evidentiary collection and analysis will be performed and executed, before the managed service commences. Be *sure* to involve legal counsel in the contracting process.

NOTE   Some jurisdictions, such as several American states, require that anyone presenting digital forensic evidence in court must be a licensed private investigator to provide expert testimony. In many courts, an "expert" witness is allowed to make deductions and give opinions about factual evidence that are given significant weight by the court (deductions and opinions by fact witnesses are not and are often inadmissible). Be sure that your forensics efforts comply with local guidance in the courts that have jurisdiction over any case you might be involved in.

UNDERSTAND REQUIREMENTS FOR INVESTIGATION TYPES

In this section, we compare and contrast different investigation types, including administrative, criminal, civil, and regulatory investigations. For each investigation type, we discuss who performs the investigation, the standard for collecting and presenting evidence, and the general differences between the types.

In discussing legal matters, it is important to stress that laws and courts vary significantly across the globe; there are a great many particular distinctions between how law enforcement, courts, lawyers, and judges behave and perform, depending on where you live, where the events leading to the investigation occurred, and other variables. The information presented in this book will be largely based on traditions of adversarial courts and English common law, strictly as an example; however, it is absolutely *essential* that you, as a security practitioner, familiarize yourself with the laws and proceedings relevant to your locale and customers so you can provide adequate, informed service.

There are many forms of law and law enforcement bodies and many ways in which those laws are adjudicated. Here are some examples of different courts:

- **Criminal:** The government prosecutes a person/organization for violating a law to provide for the common safety and security of the public.

- **Civil:** Private entities seek resolution of conflict and compensation for losses.

- **Religious:** An authority figure recognized by practitioners of a given faith interprets the implications of a religious text, makes decisions, and resolves conflicts based on this interpretation.

- **Tribal:** Leaders of a community, recognized by the members of that community, make binding decisions based on their wisdom and authority.

Burden of proof is the requirement that the criminal prosecutor or civil plaintiff/claimant prove the claims they are making against the accused, or defendant. The entity making a claim must demonstrate the truth of that claim, with compelling evidence; the entity defending against the claim, in most modern societies, is presumed innocent or without fault—that is, the court will not recognize the validity of a claim against anyone until that claim is substantiated. The amount and strength of proof required to sway the judgment away from this presumption of innocence or lack of fault differs depending on which kind of claim is being made, for instance, whether the claim is being made by one private party against another or whether the claim is being made by the government against a person or organization (more on this distinction in just a moment). In the U.S. legal system, the two predominant standards of proof that must be met are called *preponderance of the evidence* and *beyond a reasonable doubt*.

Preponderance of the evidence is the lower standard of the two and is used primarily in civil actions. It essentially means that the evidence shows that the defendant is more likely to have caused the damage than not. In other words, the evidence convinced the judge, jury, or ruling body that there was at least a 51 percent chance that the defendant caused the damage.

The second standard, beyond a reasonable doubt, is much harder to prove and is used primarily in criminal actions. It is insufficient for the evidence to merely make the judge or jury *lean* more toward guilt than not. In this case, the evidence has to be so clear and compelling that a "reasonable" person has no doubt or reservation about the defendant's guilt after seeing it.

Administrative

When discussing investigations, for (ISC)² purposes, the term *administrative* will refer to actions constrained to those conducted within a single organization: that is, the organization performs an administrative investigation of itself. Internal investigations are typically performed when the matter involves some violation of organizational policy and does *not* involve any external entities such as law enforcement, investors, third-party suppliers, or attackers.

NOTE It is important to distinguish how the term *administrative* is used in a variety of ways to avoid confusion. For (ISC)², it means an internal investigation. In the United States, *administrative law* refers to a set of laws made by regulatory bodies (such as the Drug Enforcement Agency, the Food and Drug Administration, and the like). For the purposes of the CISSP Body of Knowledge (and the exam), an administrative investigation will *only* refer to an internal investigation.

The organization itself can task anyone to perform activities for administrative investigations. This can include staff and employees within the organization (physical and IT security personnel, auditors, management, etc.) or might involve specialized contractors hired by the organization to perform investigative tasks.

The burden of proof for administrative investigations is the lowest of all investigation types. Management can use whatever criteria they choose to accept/believe evidence.

Punitive measures that may result from administrative investigation determinations include employee termination, loss of privilege, reassignment, and so forth. Management might also choose to change the type of investigation as a result of findings made during the administrative investigation: if the administrative investigation reveals that the parties involved engaged in intentional/malicious or criminal activity, management may escalate to civil actions (lawsuits) or filing criminal charges, both of which would require investigatory actions relevant to those situations.

Despite the low burden of proof required for management to act in an administrative investigation, care should still be taken during the process. Occasionally, evidence gathered during an administrative investigation may lead to or be used in a civil or criminal investigation, as stated earlier. If evidence is mishandled during an administrative investigation, it may compromise the ability to use that evidence in later proceedings. If there is any uncertainty about whether an administrative investigation may ultimately escalate, a discussion of this concern with management or in-house or outside counsel is prudent.

Consider this example of an investigation: The IT department contacts the security office to make a report of an employee misusing the organization's Internet connection to engage in unauthorized file sharing, in direct violation of the organization's policy. The security office makes the situation known to management; management instructs the IT and security departments to gather information about the user's online activity. Personnel in the IT and security departments work together to gather log data about the user's account and machine, and they present this information to management. Management consults with the legal and human resources departments to evaluate courses of action. Management decides to terminate the employee.

This is strictly an administrative investigation.

Criminal

Criminal investigations involve prosecution under criminal laws. The government, at either the local, state, or federal level, prosecutes violations of its laws by imposing fines, incarceration, or, in some extreme cases, even death for offenders. Criminal investigations are conducted by law enforcement organizations, which can include local, state, federal, or even international agencies. While some CISSPs are in law enforcement positions and conduct criminal investigations themselves, most of us will likely be reporting criminal incidents to law enforcement and helping to collect/provide evidence.

For a law enforcement agency to take part in prosecuting a criminal matter, jurisdiction must first be established. Jurisdiction is the legal authority of a governmental body (such as a court or enforcement agency) over a specific matter, often based on geography. With crimes that involve information assets, determining jurisdiction can be complicated and frequently may involve several different government bodies, locales, and laws.

Once jurisdiction has been established, the law enforcement investigator first tries to understand what happened, what damage was done, and what possible range of crimes apply for possible prosecution. In some cases, because of the global nature of IT, a case may be dropped or referred to another law enforcement agency due to a combination of jurisdictional issues, the cost of the investigation versus the scale and impact of the crime, and the likelihood of successful prosecution.

As the investigation progresses, law enforcement begins to understand who the potential suspects might be and what evidence is available, and the investigator must begin to narrow focus to specific laws and statutes. Many countries, provinces, cities, and other jurisdictions have a variety of laws relating to the misuse and abuse of technology.

Typically, criminal courts have the highest legal standard for determining liability/guilt; this is often referred to as evidence that shows that the accused has caused harm beyond a reasonable doubt. With this standard, the overwhelming majority of evidence must show that the defendant is guilty, leaving the court with no other rational conclusion.

The criminal investigator collects evidence until the elements can be proven or until it is clear that they *cannot* be proven. They use investigative techniques, including digital forensics (covered later in this chapter). The investigators may secure media and devices as necessary for evidence.

When gathering evidence, law enforcers may or may not be required to get a court order, allowing the government to access property, devices, and data that are owned by private entities. These court orders may be in the form of warrants or subpoenas; some must be issued by a judge, while others can be issued by any officer of the court (such as a government-commissioned prosecutor).

When a private organization requests law enforcement involvement with or in response to a suspected incident, that organization may give permission to the government to access the property/devices/data, and there is no need for a court order; the organization owns the property/devices/data and therefore can allow access to anyone it chooses. In criminal matters, the security professional in the employ of an organization requesting law enforcement response should *not* try to investigate without guidance from law enforcement personnel. In other words, if you, as a practitioner, suspect a crime has been committed and are going to report this crime to the government, you should suspend investigative activity (beyond containment of immediate damage) until and unless otherwise instructed by the government/agency and immediately escalate the issue to management. It is possible that investigative actions by untrained personnel unfamiliar with legal procedure and the processes for proper evidence collection and handling can taint the evidence and otherwise impede an investigation.

Further, a security professional in the employ of an organization should not unilaterally make the decision to contact law enforcement; this can be a complex decision and should be made in consultation with management and in-house and outside counsel.

Lastly, additional rules apply to security professionals or investigators who are employed by law enforcement and prosecutorial agencies. While a company that owns evidence can simply choose to provide that evidence to law enforcement, stringent rules apply to the collection, handling, and analysis of evidence by law enforcement and the prosecution of employees. Government investigators must be conscious of and understand the legal requirements that apply to them; this will include (among others) whether search warrants are necessary to seize evidence, a stringent adherence to chain of evidence procedures, and the analysis of evidence that does not exceed what is legally permitted in a given situation.

Civil

Civil law governs relations and interactions between private entities. The plaintiff in a civil case sues for compensation for a loss or relief from some type of dispute. As information security practitioners, we may be called on to support our clients when they are either plaintiffs or defendants in civil suits. The following are examples of possible civil actions the security practitioner may be involved in:

- **Organization is plaintiff:** If someone accesses your production environment without authorization and steals data, causing harm to your organization, your organization might sue the perpetrator for damages (restitution for the harm that was caused). You may be called on to oversee collection of evidence (logs from penetrated hosts, intrusion detection systems, and network appliances, for instance) proving the defendant caused the harm. (Note: This may be in *addition* to criminal action against the defendant brought by the government.)

- **Organization is defendant:** If a former employee accuses the organization of creating a hostile work environment, you may have to oversee collection of evidence (such as emails between managers and executives discussing how employees are treated), as well as preventing the destruction of potential evidence (referred to variously as *destruction hold notice*, *preservation notice*, or *litigation hold*, or similar terms) upon request by courts or attorneys.

Unlike criminal law, in civil proceedings, the usual standard of proof is preponderance of the evidence, meaning it is a much lower burden of proof. Preponderance of the evidence is a simple majority of fault/liability: if the plaintiff can prove to the court that the defendant is even 50.1 percent culpable for the damages, the defendant will lose the civil case.

In a civil proceeding, there is no question of guilty versus not guilty but rather liable versus not liable. If the defendant is found liable, they may be ordered to pay for damages, to stop an activity that is harming the plaintiff, or to honor a contract or agreement into which they had previously entered. Unlike criminal sentences, a litigant cannot be jailed or put to death for liability in a civil lawsuit. However, if a civil litigant refuses to obey a court order, it can result in a contempt of court charge, which could eventually lead to jail time.

Because the burden of evidence and stakes involved in losing a civil case are much lower than they are in criminal cases, the level of effort in collecting and processing the evidence is likewise lower. This is *not* to say that evidence in civil cases can be handled in a haphazard or careless manner; due care must still be taken to perform actions in a suitable, professional way. However, in civil cases, investigation and evidence collection will not be performed by badged law enforcement personnel and government agents; instead, it is done by security and IT professionals, such as CISSPs.

Similar to criminal trials, there are rules as to what evidence may be used in a civil trial. Collected evidence that is deemed unreliable may be excluded by a judge presiding over the trial. Care should be taken to retain original copies of evidence collected by an investigator, and chains of evidence should be well documented. Original evidence should never be altered or changed, with very few exceptions, and without direct instructions from counsel who is overseeing an investigation or handling the case. Spoliation of evidence (altering or destruction of the original) can lead to exclusion of evidence in a case or, in some situations, can lead to a separate lawsuit for the damages resulting from the spoliation.

If there is uncertainty about the rules surrounding the collection and handling of evidence for a civil lawsuit, consultation with a digital forensic expert or counsel can be helpful.

Regulatory

Regulatory investigations involve determining whether an organization is compliant with a given regulation. A regulation is a legal requirement set by a government body. Regulations have the force of law; consequently, regulatory investigations are similar to criminal investigations. Regulations are written under the auspices of protecting the average citizen or consumer, protecting the environment, or making an industry safer and more equitable.

NOTE It is important to understand the (ISC)² definition of regulations, as it is used in the CISSP CBK and the exam. A regulation is not a standard, guideline, or suggestion: it is law, established by a government body. For instance, in the United States, the Environmental Protection Agency (EPA) is part of the federal government; the EPA writes regulations concerning activities that may impact the environment (such as handling hazardous/toxic waste, transportation of certain materials, and so forth). EPA regulations have the force of law: anyone violating these regulations may be prosecuted by the government. Conversely, the PCI-DSS is *not* a regulation, as defined by (ISC)²; the PCI-DSS is a contractual standard, affecting only those parties that voluntarily choose to comply with it (i.e., merchants that accept credit card payment).

Government agencies perform regulatory investigations to determine whether sufficient evidence exists to prove some violation of rules or regulations. These agencies have the authority and discretion to decide when to perform investigations. These agencies have their own internal investigators, prosecutors, and courts for their proceedings. Regulators can also demand information from target organizations or utilize audit report data in addition to or instead of performing their own investigations.

The burden of proof for regulatory investigations is the preponderance of the evidence, and the penalties typically involve fines and injunctions. There are, however, instances where regulators call for *referral* to criminal law enforcement that may result in prison time.

Industry Standards

Investigation is a broad term. It certainly implies a range of activities beyond just digital forensics. There are currently many standards/guidelines offered in this realm, some of which are dependent on the jurisdiction or industry in which the organization operates. This section takes a quick look at some of the most common standards and guidelines.

ISO/IEC 27043:2015 recommends procedural steps for conducting security incident investigations. These guidelines cover many incident scenarios from the preparation phase all the way through to the conclusion of the investigation. The scenarios covered include incidents such as data loss or corruption, unauthorized access, and confirmed data breaches.

ISO/IEC 27037:2012 provides guidelines for handling digital evidence. This is covered through a four-step process of identification, collection, acquisition, and preservation. Evidence collection and handling is covered across many types of media and scenarios, including magnetic and optical storage media, mobile devices, camera systems, standard computers, and collecting network traffic data from network devices. This publication also covers chain of custody procedures and how to properly exchange evidence between jurisdictions.

NIST SP 800-86, "Guide to Integrating Forensic Techniques into Incident Response," overlaps significantly in terms of content with the two previous sources. It is the NIST perspective on the digital forensic process. It details how to build a forensic capability within your organization, what that means, and which tools and training your staff will need. The publication also describes how to structure forensic policies, standards, and procedures for your organization and what they should contain. Most importantly, NIST SP 800-86 describes the digital forensic process overall in four phases: collection, examination, analysis, and reporting.

NIST SP 800-101 Revision 1, "Guidelines on Mobile Device Forensics," has a self-explanatory title. It covers the unique requirements for acquiring, preserving, examining, analyzing, and reporting on the digital evidence present on mobile devices. The technical differences associated with mobile devices are discussed, such as differences in memory type and file structure that affect evidence collection. The publication also discusses sensitive areas that may arise when a mobile device is privately owned.

The Scientific Working Group on Digital Evidence (SWGDE) is a consortium based on improving the quality and consistency of digital forensics. They have a library of digital forensic documents available at `https://www.swgde.org/documents`. Because of the granular scope and technical specificity of each document, some of them have become de facto standards in the forensic community. These topics include error mitigation, digital video files, maintaining the integrity of imagery, and digital audio forensics.

The PCI Forensic Investigator (PFI) Program Guide provides specific guidance on how forensic investigators must respond to a security incident involving payment card data. Appendix A defines the steps and processes to perform the investigation. Appendix B specifies the requirements for properly handling and preserving the evidence.

CONDUCT LOGGING AND MONITORING ACTIVITIES

Logging and monitoring activities provide the organization with several critical capabilities. Detecting an attack or an incident while it is happening allows an appropriate response, provides evidence after the fact, and supports the review process following the event. In addition, logging and monitoring contribute to the incident management processes (covered in the "Conduct Incident Management" section).

Several types of monitoring are covered in this section. They include intrusion detection and prevention, SIEM, continuous monitoring, and egress monitoring. Despite their differences, keep the points covered in the following sections in mind as applicable to enable the success of all types of monitoring.

Define Auditable Events

There are many tools that enable logging and monitoring of *events*. An event, according to NIST, is "any observable occurrence in a system or network." Any discrete action on the system can be logged; however, if we log every single event, we create a massive data store of material that may or may not be pertinent, and we make it more difficult to find relevant, actionable information and patterns from the logs. Indeed, we run the risk of creating an overwhelming stockpile of log material that exceeds the transactional data used for business purposes and actually increasing security and privacy concerns as well as associated costs. Most logging tools have configurable options defining which audit details are captured and in what format. To increase the value of logging activities, the organization must decide which events are logged and what data is captured in the log.

Identifying which events to be monitored should be initiated as part of the system design process. This will allow the developers of the system to ensure that the logging system correctly identifies and captures the significant event. Further, implementing the logging requirement early in the development process allows integration of the log information into the testing and operational processes. Some events to consider might include the following:

- Successful and unsuccessful attempts to
    - Log into a system
    - Access data in a specific file or drive
    - Change or turn off a system process or service
    - Change or turn off a security tool (e.g., anti-malware tool) or turn off logging
    - Make system configuration changes in general
    - Copy/export sensitive files
- Uses of elevated privileges/privileged accounts
- Transactions executed in sensitive applications (e.g., related to security, containing financial or privacy data, or intellectual property)

The event logs themselves must have sufficient information to, at a minimum, identify who caused what event to occur at what time. Capturing the subject-object relationship is essential to assigning responsibility and determining causality. These are event log details to consider:

- User IDs
- Time and date of the event in a standardized format
- Device identifier or hostname
- Location of device, if available
- Names of system processes used, or files accessed
- Network addresses and protocols used
- Name of rule or policy which triggered the event log

Logging requirements must address the concerns of a large body of stakeholders to ensure that security concerns and audit and compliance requirements are met. Further, the granularity of the detail of monitoring should take into account the capabilities of the available tools and staff to analyze and correlate the information. Finally, the stakeholders must arrive at a set of auditable events and a rationale for why they are adequate to support investigations of security incidents.

NOTE   It is worth noting that any unscheduled event is, by most academic definitions, an incident. An incident is not inherently dangerous or damaging but should be assessed for the potential for either outcome.

Time

Knowing when something occurs is essential in event correlation and causality. Attackers often attempt to corrupt the timestamps on logs and affect the internal clocks of systems to defeat detection. Further, when the organization is operating across multiple time zones, maintaining accurate time becomes an even greater challenge. Consequently, time services are generally one of the common controls in an organization's architecture to ensure consistent, accurate time across all technology assets. The internal requirements for the method and format of time synchronization should be formally documented for implementation and to satisfy regulatory compliance. This documentation can also be detailed in service-level agreements (SLAs) and contractual requirements.

A common approach to implementing clock synchronization is to start with a master clock, which is tuned to a radio broadcast from a national atomic clock. Network Time Protocol (NTP) or Simple Network Time Protocol (SNTP) is then used to keep all computers, servers, network devices, and appliances in synchronization with the master clock.

The time protocol must be configured on the devices, and depending on the protocol used (123 User Datagram Protocol (UDP) for NTP and SNTP, for example), the corresponding ports must be open on any firewalls and internal access control lists (ACLs) that separate the master clock from the devices.

In the interest of discouraging the use of this UDP port as a possible attack vector, organizations may opt for the use of an internal time synchronization capability, such as a Global Positioning System (GPS) monitor or link to an internal primary clock.

In cloud configurations, where data centers, systems, and users may be spread across many time zones, vendors are addressing this issue by hosting internal timing mechanisms for their customers. For example, the Amazon Web Services approach is explained here: `https://aws.amazon.com/blogs/aws/keeping-time-with-amazon-time-sync-service/`.

Protect Logs

Though event logs provide a form of latent protection by allowing the security office to detect malicious/fraudulent activity as it occurs and investigate it after the fact, logs also introduce several additional security considerations. Logs contain sensitive information that can be used to map and plan attacks against your enterprise. They can reveal weaknesses of your assets, which tools are used to monitor security, and which rules and specific parameters are set to trigger alerts. All of this information can be used to circumvent your security controls.

In aggregate form especially, logs may contain personally identifiable information (PII) and other sensitive information. Logs should be protected at the same level as the most sensitive system from which the log data is collected, as well as adhering to any applicable privacy protection measures.

The loss or corruption of event logs will significantly reduce the value of the logs to your organization. This might disrupt your organization's incident response (IR) process and affect the organization's ability to perform investigations after the fact. According to the Open Web Application Security Project (OWASP), the integrity of the logs must be protected from being edited, deleted, or overwritten. (See `https://www.owasp.org/index.php/Logging_Cheat_Sheet` for more information.)

This level of protection can be achieved through layers of controls. From a physical security perspective, protect the server or storage device where the logs are stored with the same rigor as you would protect the most sensitive system from which it receives log data. From a logical security perspective, deny everyone, including system administrators, permissions to change or delete logs of their own activities. From an availability perspective, ensure that the storage capacity of the drive/directory where logs are stored is adequate to avoid logs being overwritten once it is full. If you run the logs through an analysis or aggregation tool, set up a mirrored copy to be used for that purpose, and leave one set of original logs undisturbed for archival and possible future investigations; also, consider real-time mirroring of event logs to an off-site location.

Lastly, for an additional bit of assurance, for each event you have configured to capture in a log, or at least for each category of event, periodically test your logging by performing the event and verifying that it was captured.

Intrusion Detection and Prevention

Intrusion detection and prevention are two separate but essential concepts. As implemented in systems today, these tools often have overlapping capabilities. Nevertheless, the functions of detection and prevention must be isolated to ensure that the appropriate control technology is implemented.

This distinction is not a semantic exercise. An intrusion detection system (IDS) is a listen-only tool. Its job is to detect network traffic or information system events that violate a rule or policy or match some known malicious behavior. The IDS then sends an alert to administrators and/or analysts, such as in a security operations center (SOC), or sends the alert to a SIEM or similar tool for further analysis. As the name clearly states, an intrusion detection system's job is to detect.

An intrusion prevention system (IPS) is essentially the same tool with the main added capability that once it detects a rule violation or potential malicious behavior, it can also *prevent* it from reaching its intended target. To do so, an IPS must be deployed so it can disrupt the traffic flow between the communicating systems. The detect versus prevent functionality is the main difference between the IDS and the IPS.

NOTE Modern intrusion detection and prevention systems (IDPSs) typically offer both functions, detection and prevention, depending on the settings the owner chooses. It is unlikely that a product currently on the market operates only as an IDS and does not also have IPS functionality. The distinction, at this point in the industry, is almost purely academic.

NIST produced a Special Publication, 800-94, titled "Guide to Intrusion Detection and Prevention Systems (IDPS)," which you can find at `https://csrc.nist.gov/publications/detail/sp/800-94/final`. NIST refers to IDS/IPS together as simply IDPS.

External Threats

The organization should already have a good understanding of the potential external threats that may target the organization, having performed a threat assessment during the risk analysis, to create the business impact analysis. The organization might also consider monitoring the external threat environment; this can include the use of business intelligence services, public and subscription news outlets, and information feeds from industry and government entities that publish exactly this type of content.

To address external threats, an organization needs intrusion detection and prevention capabilities that identify and report suspicious activity, such as a port scan, which is likely a form of reconnaissance and the precursor of an attack. The organization also needs to be able to identify possible incidents and report them to security administrators and incident handlers, as well as create and maintain audit logs that can be used by incident handlers after the fact. Lastly, the organization must define security policies and discern when/whether they have been violated. Similar to the way firewall or proxy rules deny or allow certain traffic, these policies can identify and prevent prohibited functions, ports, protocols, and services.

Internal Threats

To adequately address internal threats, an organization needs sufficient intrusion detection and prevention capabilities. They must deter authorized users from violating internal policies through a credible threat that such activity will be detected. The IDS/IPS capability should monitor, and in some cases prevent, one machine on a subnet from trying to communicate directly with a machine on another subnet. Lastly, an IDS/IPS should provide a countermeasure for privileged users, network users, or system administrators who could otherwise alter audit logs of their own malicious activity.

Considerations and Best Practices

IDS/IPS systems are an essential part of any organization's defense-in-depth strategy and must work in concert with many other security controls and processes. Consider the following points regarding the implementation of IDS/IPS systems and their function and monitoring as security controls:

- Create separate accounts for administrators of the IDS/IPS, and give each user the minimum permissions necessary to perform their duties.

- Harden and secure the components that make up the IDS/IPS. As a security function, the IDS/IPSs need to be afforded extra protection. This is because they will often be primary targets for attackers trying to cover their trail or hide a future attack. Harden and monitor the devices where the IDS/IPS runs. Position them in a highly restricted subnet, where copies of logs and traffic data that the IDS/IPS needs to analyze are fed in, but little other traffic is permitted.

- Use firewall and router ACLs to restrict traffic to the IDS/IPS to that coming from devices that the administrators use in their daily duties. Ensure that remote connections to the IDS/IPS are secure, such as through the use of a physically separated network path or logically separated network path via VLAN, VPN/ encrypted tunnel, TLS, session encryption, and multifactor authentication.

- One essential benefit of an IDS/IPS is that it can help mitigate the insider threat by "watching the watchers." To do this, restrict access to the IDS/IPS and IDS/IPS audit logs from administrators who are granted enhanced privileges on other systems in the enterprise and then configure the IDS/IPS to monitor the audit logs of those other systems. If a privileged insider then tries to change or delete logs of their own actions, the IDS/IPS would trigger an alert.

- Where possible, use dynamic reconfiguration, such as adding a rule to block or redirect a specific IP address that is attacking the network at that moment. Some modern IDS/IPS tools have the ability to do this or to work in tandem with a firewall, router, or other tool to achieve the same effect.

- IDS/IPS systems (or agents of those systems) may be installed on specific client devices, referred to as host-based IDS/IPS (HIDS), or on networking devices, such as routers, switches, etc., referred to as network-based IDS/IPS (NIDS) (obviously the term was originated at a time when IDSs were prevalent). The organization may also opt for installing both types of IDS/IPS components to add greater defense in depth.

- In cloud-based environments, an IDS/IPS may be complicated because of the separate ownership of data (cloud customer) and hardware (cloud provider); the cloud customer may have limited control of or access to the underlying infrastructure and therefore might not be able to install IDS/IPS agents/software. To some degree, this function is being served by products/services referred to as *cloud access security brokers* (CASBs), which incorporate both the detection/prevention capabilities and granular access control and are meant to be placed (physically or logically) between the customer and the provider.

NOTE   Historically, the distinction between IDS/IPS tools and firewalls was delineated by how they operated. Firewalls typically inspected packet headers to determine whether something might be hostile/anomalous, while IDS/IPS would review the entire packet. In today's market, these distinctions are largely blurred, with products/services sold as "next-generation firewalls" or intrusion detection/prevention or data loss prevention tools offering artificial intelligence or machine-learning capabilities, which may or may not inspect headers, packet content, or other data/metadata to enhance security/filtering functions. Currently, the distinction between the various security tools/systems is one of branding and sales, as opposed to function or operation.

Security Information and Event Management

Security information and event management is a vital process and capability, which is related to, but should not be confused with, incident management. The difference between the two is that SIEM is the monitoring of logs and traffic and the correlation of events and alerts that could *potentially* lead to an incident being declared. Once that incident has been declared, incident management begins. Incident management is covered separately in the "Conduct Incident Management" section later in this chapter.

In the early days of cybersecurity, this type of event correlation and management was done in a manual, human-review fashion. It was highly ineffective back then, and because of ever-increasing volumes of data, this process is essentially impossible to achieve today without automated tools.

A SIEM has different capabilities than an IDS/IPS. A SIEM solution provides value by adding additional context to the logs and events captured by other monitoring tools and by performing additional analysis and refinement of data.

As part of its basic function, a SIEM tool accepts the outputs from many sources, including other monitoring tools. These outputs, in the form of log messages and alerts, are analyzed in near–real time and aggregated where possible, so logs that refer to the same event are not mistaken for or treated as separate incidents (which could skew metrics, trigger redundant investigations, etc.).

A SIEM also enriches event logs from one source with contextual details from other sources. For example, an IDS log of one event may only include an IP address, a timestamp, and which rule was violated. At this point, it may look like evidence of a malicious attack. The addition of an Active Directory log with the same timestamp, however, could give more context about the user and/or machine involved and reveal that it was not an attack, but just an accident by an authorized user.

Data stockpiling is another common feature of SIEM solutions. Going back to the previous statements about aggregation and enrichment, a SIEM can use more data points from more sources to create a larger picture with more context. The downside is the resource cost to do this. Consider that a SIEM agent could be installed on every workstation, server, network device, and monitoring device in the enterprise. A large data store is usually needed to capture the resulting flood of logs and alerts generated by so many sources. The solution will require a piece of middleware that acts as a funnel to get all the data from the endpoints into the SIEM. The SIEM will also "clean up" the data by normalizing the records from different sources to the same format, getting rid of duplicates, and performing very rudimentary filtering. Lastly, it can store enough records to provide support for investigations and trend analysis.

After performing the analyses on the logs and alerts, the SIEM sends alerts and reports to administrators, SOC analysts, or the incident management team. It also recommends a prioritization in response to events and incidents, based on contextual data points like how critical the affected systems are or the severity of the attack type.

Like many of the systems that feed data to SIEM solutions (such as firewalls, IDS/IPS tools, data loss prevention tools, etc.), SIEMs can distinguish potential incidents through the use of definitions/signatures, behavioral analysis, and/or pattern matching/historical review/heuristics. These techniques can (and should) be informed by external sources (such as intelligence vendors that can provide attack signatures), internal expertise (your security team), and a baseline sample of normal operations.

NOTE Bear in mind, the term SIEM (like SIM, SEM, and SEIM) does not correlate to a defined, regulated standard for a given type of device; it is a marketing/branding term used by vendors to describe their products. If you buy/deploy a SIEM tool, it may operate in a way and contain a variety of functionalities completely different from another SIEM tool.

Continuous Monitoring

There are multiple definitions of continuous monitoring. The most common argument or confusion in this regard is whether continuous monitoring is a function of IT *operational security* or of IT *security compliance*. The operational security definition says that continuous monitoring is improving your technical security posture through scanning for defects and applying corresponding patches and configuration changes. The security compliance definition says that it is a compliance activity to prove to auditors and executives that specific IT systems continue to operate at an acceptable level of risk. Both are true and valid statements.

Continuous monitoring is the monitoring of security control implementations and security settings that can change or fall out of compliance over time. Continuous monitoring is not only a valuable process both for IT operational security *and* for IT security compliance, but also bridges the gap between the two.

A Continuous Monitoring Program

Implementing a continuous monitoring program in an organization implies a certain level of programmatic maturity. It is not the first step in building a security and compliance program because it relies on many other dependencies, such as policies, procedures, and basic compliance and risk management capabilities. These dependencies are all covered in other chapters in this book, but for this section, suffice it to say that a continuous monitoring program requires some foundational tools and capabilities.

The organization should have a policy that defines continuous monitoring, what the organization's continuous monitoring goals are, and which security framework and control set/control standards will be used. This needs to be complemented by the implementation of a security framework or control catalog to which the monitoring can be tied and from which things like taxonomy and control identifiers can be borrowed. Examples include NIST Risk Management Framework (RMF), ISO 27001/2, COBIT, PCI-DSS, etc.

A monitoring strategy is also necessary. It defines what to monitor and the methods, frequencies, and metrics to use. Finally, an appropriate set of standards and procedures is needed to define how to prioritize, remediate, and report on the discovered findings. Since policy, procedures, and security frameworks are covered in other chapters of this book, we will skip to the monitoring strategy.

Monitoring Strategy

Monitoring strategy is simply a statement of the following, as they pertain to continuous monitoring:

- **Scope:** Which assets is the organization monitoring? Of those assets, for which controls, security settings, or defect types are you monitoring?

- **Methods:** When and where are you performing manual versus automated assessments? When manual assessment is the only option, when and where do you use functional tests versus examination or interview?

- **Frequencies:** Which controls or settings do you need to monitor the most and the least? How does that translate into actual dates on the calendar?

- **Metrics used:** When performing enterprise scans for vulnerabilities or misconfigurations, for example, do you track the number of devices on which a given defect appears? Or do you track how many different defects are present on each device? There are not wrong answers to these questions, but you need to define and apply the metrics consistently, so you can define a baseline and repeat the process to measure progress.

The most common question for this approach is usually, "How do I know which frequencies and methods to use?" Before addressing that, there are some additional continuous monitoring concepts worth reviewing.

Continuous Monitoring Common Misconceptions

There are two common misconceptions about continuous monitoring. One is that *continuous* means "constant." The other is that continuous monitoring *only* includes automated monitoring. It is important to understand each of these misconceptions in order to avoid them.

First, consider what continuous monitoring actually means. Historically, when security compliance activities dictated that certain security control assessments take place at a set frequency, serious operational security practitioners balked at these frequencies as being inadequate and prone to leaving IT systems open to attack for long periods of time between assessments. In a push to make the monitoring and assessment of security controls happen more frequently, they started using the word *continuous* to indicate that the assessments should happen more often. When implementing a continuous monitoring program, the old security snapshot paradigm doesn't go away; it is replaced with a new risk-based frequency (based on several factors, discussed next), which in most cases increases the frequency. Despite the assessments happening more often, they are still performed in discrete increments.

Now consider how automated monitoring is used with continuous monitoring. Vendors that create security scanners and sensors enthusiastically embraced the term *continuous monitoring*. These vendors branded and marketed their products as continuous monitoring solutions, which created a strong perception that continuous monitoring means using automated tools. There are, however, many different types of security controls, security settings, security processes, etc., that can change, fall out of compliance, or break down. They all require monitoring, but only a subset can be monitored or assessed by automated mechanisms. Humans need to manually assess and review the rest of the controls. Table 7.1 shows some examples of each.

TABLE 7.1 Comparison of Automated and Manual Monitoring of Security Controls/Settings

SECURITY CONTROLS/SETTINGS SUITED TO AUTOMATED ASSESSMENT AND MONITORING	SECURITY CONTROLS/SETTINGS SUITED TO MANUAL ASSESSMENT AND MONITORING
Access Enforcement	Access Agreements
Audit Reduction and Reporting	Account Review and Approval
Auditable Events	Change Review and Approval
Component Inventory	Continuity Planning and Exercises
Session Control	Impact Analysis
Configuration Change Control	Maintenance
Identification and Authentication	Personnel Security
Identifier and Authenticator Management	Recovery Planning and Exercises
Incident Management	Removable Media and Storage Protection
Information Flow Enforcement	Risk Assessment
Patch Management	SDLC Practices
Remote Access	Security and Awareness Training
Response to Audit Processing Failures	Security Architecture
Separation of Duties	Security Planning
Unsuccessful Logon Attempts	Security Policies and Procedures
Vulnerability Management	Supply Chain Management
Wireless Access	Vendor and Partner Management

Methods and Frequencies

With these facts in mind, we revisit the question, how do you know the most suitable frequency and methods for continuous monitoring? Methods are relatively easy in that, depending on the control, they are suited to either manual or automated assessment (as per Table 7.1), and either you possess an automated tool to do the assessment or you don't. Determining the frequency, however, is a little more nuanced.

First, to determine the right frequency for monitoring, you have to know some things about your organization.

- **The criticality/sensitivity of your IT systems:** Before you can implement continuous monitoring, you must understand if a specific control or setting is more or less important on a given IT system because of the data stored or processed on that system. The criticality of business processes supported by the system will also be an important factor driving the need for continuous monitoring.

- **The volatility of your security controls:** Assuming your organization has implemented some type of security framework and has some history of control assessment results, you can observe trends in how often the state of the control might change. For example, if a security control assessor checks the text of a security policy, they will likely find that it rarely changes, but in contrast would find that vulnerability scan results could change every few days.

- **The upper bound:** For the most volatile control on your most critical system, how quickly could you repeat an assessment? Could you repeat it every day or every three days? Remember that this frequency must be sustainable and achievable going forward, and also remember that the frequency has to be useful. For example, even if it was possible to run a specific scan twice a day, what is the likelihood that you would find a different result so soon? Is doing twice the work providing twice the value or twice the risk reduction?

- **The lower bound:** For your least volatile control on your least critical system, what is the longest period you could go, based on the regulatory compliance burdens of your organization, before you would be *required* to update your assessment results?

Final Considerations

We have covered all the elements of how and when to monitor, but the obvious gap in the discussion is this: "How do we fix all of the findings and defects uncovered by continuous monitoring?" Most organizations already struggle to find the time and the staff to fix everything. Implementing rigorous continuous monitoring will likely increase the workload through additional monitoring and assessments and a larger backlog of remediation actions.

Newer, better tools and more mature, repeatable processes can relieve some of this problem. Some organizations, however, have budgetary limitations or cultural or regulatory restrictions on their processes. The last best hope in these cases is to find an effective way of scoring and ranking defects. Defects should be prioritized by how much risk they introduce so that even when the staffing is inadequate, the resources that are available are focused on driving the largest amount of risk down in the shortest amount of time.

There are several factors to consider when devising your ranking/prioritization process. First, use predefined scales or methods such as the Common Vulnerability Scoring System (CVSS, published by FIRST [first.org]), the Common Configuration Scoring System (CCSS, published by NIST [`https://nvlpubs.nist.gov/nistpubs/Legacy/IR/nistir7502.pdf`]), or the OWASP Risk Rating Methodology (`https://www.owasp.org/index.php/OWASP_Risk_Rating_Methodology`) scores to assign a risk or impact-based metric to each defect (higher score = higher priority). Asset criticality should be another critical factor in the decision. Consider the criticality of the assets where the defects are found, and place a higher priority on higher criticality assets. Finally, consider the length of exposure—how long a defect has been present (when it was first detected)—when prioritizing between defects that have otherwise similar impact/criticality.

For more information, NIST SP 800-137 addresses continuous monitoring within the context of U.S. government systems (`https://csrc.nist.gov/publications/detail/sp/800-137/final`). Additional sources of interest include a joint effort framework known as CAESARS Frame Extension and DHS Continuous Diagnostics and Mitigation (CDM) Program, as well as ISO 27004, "Security techniques – Information security management – Monitoring, measurement, analysis and evaluation."

Ingress Monitoring

Ingress traffic is any data communication originating from outside the network destined for a host on your internal network. Ingress traffic can be in the form of applications and data accessed on a remote server or any data coming from the Internet.

Monitoring ingress traffic into your networks from less-trusted networks is pivotal to a strong monitoring strategy. Ingress monitoring serves as an organization's first line of defense and should be the first area of focus when designing a security monitoring strategy. Ingress monitoring serves to provide visibility to potential intrusions, help organizations protect their data, and improve network operations. A security practitioner should consider the architecture and classification of the data on the network when designing their ingress monitoring strategy when building any new network.

A strong ingress monitoring strategy provides the following benefits:

- Provides data protection and visibility into inbound communication
- Provides insight into business, network, and security threats

- Allows for aggregation and ease of shipping information to other tools
- Enhances analysis and performance monitoring tools
- Improves the reliability and security of network communications

Ingress monitoring, like all types of monitoring, comes with its own challenges. A focus should be on network telemetry, understanding the flow of network traffic, and being able to detect anomalies and malicious traffic. Common tools used to collect ingress traffic are IDS/IPS systems, network and host-based firewalls, test access point (TAPs), or Switched Port Analyzer (SPAN) ports on networking equipment or configuring monitoring points for cloud-based networks.

Network Visibility

The primary goal of a solid ingress monitoring program is to ensure near 100 percent network visibility in real time and the detection of unauthorized traffic. Typically, ingress monitoring maps IPs, ports, and protocols to include application monitoring and profiling. This level of visibility allows security teams to keep an eye on their corporate networks and allow for proactive IR and detection. It allows for viewing networks trends and setting baselines to what is considered normal and anomalous. It is important to take into consideration virtual and cloud-based network endpoints regarding network visibility so as to not leave blind spots in hybrid networks.

Data Aggregation

Ingress monitoring should provide your tools, such as SEIMs and other monitoring tools, with accurate and timely information. It is important that all monitoring points are synced to the correct time and feed aggregation tools with information in a timely manner to support accurate response to incidents. In particular, with ingress monitoring it is important to make sure you are providing all the necessary information, such as filtering information, ports, or VLAN tags, if part of a virtual environment and if part of load balancing or network concentration points.

Data Filtering

Ingress monitoring will take up a large percentage of your security monitoring tools because of the nature, complexity, and volume. This is true for all log sources but is of more importance in ingress monitoring. The data should be filtered and cleaned for the optimization of security analysis tools. This includes deduplication and stripping of unimportant information. Always consider the outcome when reviewing ingress log sources, as log sources can be modified to monitor applications such as voice over IP (VoIP) or e-commerce. Scalability and flexibility are key when configuring ingress log sources.

Egress Monitoring

Monitoring the environment for attacks from outside the organization is crucial, but so is the practice of reviewing all the possible ways data can leave your organization's control. This is known, in general, as *egress monitoring*.

There are many ways data leaves the organization's control (whether authorized or unauthorized), including but not limited to the following:

- Email
- FTP
- Portable media
- Removal of hardware
- Posted to public-facing website
- Printed
- Image capture

A comprehensive and effective egress monitoring effort should review all possible means for exfiltration of data, determine whether the action is authorized, and respond accordingly (which can include allowing the export of the data when doing so is authorized, alerting management/security personnel, or halting the action).

Current egress monitoring tools are often called DLP, a term that can stand for "data leak protection," "data loss prevention," or any variety of these and similar words. DLP is a marketing and branding term, not a standard nomenclature defined by an agency or industry body. DLP systems have evolved sophisticated capabilities, including extremely sensitive behavior-based and pattern-matching analysis that can be used by management to address potential insider threats.

For DLP systems to function properly, they must be "trained" to recognize baseline data/system/user behavior and operation; this can take a reasonably significant period of time, so DLP tools should not be considered fully effective "out of the box." Furthermore, the administrators "training" the DLP solutions need to be able to create discrete rule sets about the data and normal usage within the environment so that the tools can serve their purpose; this might require coordination and assistance from the DLP vendor. DLP solutions also typically have a data/system discovery component, allowing the tools to locate data within the environment and make determinations about that data's sensitivity and authorized use.

In addition to discovery, DLP solutions are typically responsible for monitoring and enforcement functions. For data monitoring, DLP systems commonly use three types of monitoring tools: database, network traffic, and agents installed on client machines. For enforcement, the organization that deploys a DLP solution is usually capable of customizing the level of response the tool will provide when it detects anomalous/suspect activity; this might take the form of a basic user security awareness reinforcement (the system detects a user trying to send an email with sensitive information and creates a pop-up window the user sees, explaining the situation and requiring the user to verify the action), alerts (sent to the user's supervisor/security personnel/data owner when questionable activity takes place), or prevention (the tool prohibits the action, notifies security personnel, and locks the user's account).

SECURELY PROVISION RESOURCES

Secure provisioning of IT resources has many important elements. Some of these were previously covered, such as architecture in Chapter 3 and supply chain management in Chapter 1. This section addresses asset inventory and configuration management.

Asset Inventory

Any organization needs, as a foundation to its security and compliance programs, effective tools and processes to track its asset inventory. The asset inventory includes all physical and virtual assets, which includes hardware, software, firmware, and more.

Having a current and complete inventory is the absolute bedrock for implementing and monitoring technical security controls.

Robust asset inventory tools and processes will also inform the organization of unauthorized assets. In addition to knowing what to protect, of course we also want to know what doesn't belong, so any unwanted assets can be removed or isolated as soon as possible.

Inventory Tool/System of Record

Because of the size, complexity, and frequency of the task, an organization should use automated tools to assist in creating and maintaining the asset inventory. The tools should have awareness of all assets in the organization's enterprise and the ability to discover new assets introduced to the environment that have not been properly documented in the inventory. This data comes from either an asset management agent or a client installed on each asset or "baked in" to each system image, through integrations with various scanner and sensor tools, or, in the case of hosted or cloud assets, from a data feed or recurring report from the vendor (which may or may not be shared with clients, depending on the contract).

An asset inventory tool should have a way to distinguish authorized devices and applications from unauthorized and the ability to send alerts when the latter are discovered.

The tool should also collect and track individual asset details necessary for reporting, audits, risk management, and incident management. These details need to cover technical specifications, such as the following:

- Hardware
  - Manufacturer
  - Model number
  - Serial number
  - Physical location
  - Number and type of processors
  - Memory size
  - Network interfaces and their MACs and IPs
  - Hostname
  - Hypervisor, operating systems, containers, virtual images running on this device
  - Purchase date, warranty information
  - Last update dates (firmware, hypervisor, etc.)
  - Asset usage metrics
- Software
  - Publisher
  - Version number, service pack/hotfix number
  - License information
  - Purchase date
  - Install date

In addition, operational security details should be collected, such as the type of data stored and processed on the asset, the asset classification and special handling requirements, the business processes or missions it supports, and the owner and administrators and their contact information.

There are, of course, many tools available that do these tasks or portions of these tasks. Most organizations already own many such tools. Consider the following:

- An Active Directory (AD) and Lightweight Directory Access Protocol (LDAP) server can provide a large portion of this information.
- Vulnerability scanners, configuration scanners, and network mapping tools can find and provide basic information about all the hosts in the organization's IP ranges.

- Tools that manage/track software licenses can perform a large portion of this task.

- As was mentioned in the previous section, DLP solutions typically have a discovery capability that can serve this purpose.

For gaps in their available tools, organizations can and do compensate with manual efforts, spreadsheets, and scripting to pull and tabulate asset data. Dedicated asset inventory tools usually provide this functionality and preclude the need for manual data pulls and tool integration.

Regardless of the tool or combination of tools used, there should be one the organization deems authoritative and final so that it can be referenced throughout the organization. The information in this tool needs to be definitive. This is the data source to trust if there is conflict between what other tools are reporting. This should also be the source used for official reports and other data requests, such as part of an audit.

Process Considerations

Now that we've discussed the tools needed, we will discuss inventory management best practices. First, the organization must define the authoritative inventory list or system of record and the frequency with which the inventory should be refreshed or updated. In addition to the regular interval inventory updates, it is also a good practice to manually notify the inventory tool administrator when an asset is installed or removed or when the components are updated/changed in a significant way, just to verify that those changes were captured by the inventory tools.

This can be accomplished in a different way for environments that make heavy use of virtualized components, including managed cloud service implementations. In these cases, use of automated tools to seek out, tabulate, and provision assets is often preferable; popular brands include Puppet, Chef, and Ansible.

For on-premises assets, it is often helpful to augment the inventory process with the use of geolocation information/geotags or the use of Radio-Frequency Identification (RFID) inventory tags. This can increase the speed and accuracy of locating an asset, especially during an incident, when time is critical.

Asset Management

While asset security was discussed in depth in Chapter 3, it is important to restate that proper management of the organization's assets is crucial to the overall security (and business) effort. Operational functions, such as asset inventory, tracking, and maintenance, must be implemented, monitored, and enforced.

Although the CISSP is not expected to know this material in detail, guidance for proper management of physical assets (to include non-IT infrastructure such as power and plumbing utilities) can be found in ISO 55000.

Configuration Management

Configuration management is the sum of the activities used to protect the totality of an IT system by controlling its configurations. This begins with the secure configuration of an IT system when it is first built. Once the system is in the production environment, it needs to be monitored to control any changes to its configuration. The organization also needs a formal process for requesting, reviewing, and approving changes to the approved configuration.

Having a configuration management capability is important for several reasons. First, configuration management has perhaps the largest and most direct impact on an IT system's security posture. In addition, IT vendors' default settings are often unsafe. One simple misconfiguration, such as leaving a guest account open, can bypass all other security controls. Next, even when a system is secured with the right configuration when it is first built, subsequent software installs can undo configuration settings or allow users to change them, intentionally or otherwise. Lastly, configuration management helps with other security domains. In disaster recovery management, for example, having defined configurations for IT components helps you restore your systems to a secure state faster.

Basic Principles

A *configuration item* (CI) is one discrete part of an IT system, like a piece of hardware or software, which has configurable settings or parameters, and should be under formal configuration control. A *baseline configuration* is a defined, desired set of configurations for a specific CI (or combine multiple CIs into an IT system), which has been formally reviewed and approved. A baseline configuration is valid for a given point in time and may need to be adjusted over time as software or hardware versions change, new vulnerabilities are discovered, etc. When the baseline configuration needs to change, it should be done only through predefined change control procedures.

A *configuration management* (CM) plan defines how an organization will manage the configuration of its hardware and software assets. It defines details such as the roles, responsibilities, policies, and procedures that are applicable. A configuration control board (CCB) will manage the CM plan. Under ITIL guidance, this body is called the Change Advisory Board (CAB). As the CCB is comprised of qualified stakeholders from the organization, they will often be the authors, editors, reviewers, and approvers of the organization's configuration policies and procedures. They will also be tasked with applying and enforcing the CM plan and helping technical administrators adhere to and understand the CM plan. Most importantly, the CCB controls and approves changes throughout the lifecycle of the IT systems, which is why they may also be known as the *change* control board.

NOTE This is a common semantic argument: change management versus configuration management. The terms are sometimes confused or used interchangeably, but they are not the same thing. Change involves people, processes, and systems. Configuration deals with electronic systems. IT change management is moving a system from one secure configuration to another. When working with any organization, it is important to ensure that everyone shares the same understanding and usage of these terms.

Tools and Methods

There are many methods and tools for implementing secure configurations and monitoring them. Some of these include manual configuration, configuration scanner tools, change detection tools, and the Security Content Automation Protocol (SCAP). Now take a look at each of these a little more closely.

There are some configurations that must be manually implemented from a guide. An administrator sits, reading the configuration guide and manually making changes, such as changing the key values in the registry in a Windows server.

If you want to check your system's configuration, you can use a configuration scanner tool. This type of tool uses a list of configuration requirements to scan systems, check the systems' registry keys and configuration files for compliance, and report the findings. In recent versions of these tools, the configuration requirements list is populated by Common Configuration Enumerations (CCEs). This is a library of configurations that will be discussed in a moment. The configuration scanner tool provides a snapshot of how compliant each system is at the time of the scan and provides a list of which configurations need to be changed or implemented.

Another useful tool is a configuration change detection tool. It is different than a configuration scanner tool in that instead of asking the IT asset "Are you configured correctly?" it asks "Did your configuration change?" It takes a snapshot of a given system's configurations, presumably after it was configured correctly and securely. Then, if any of the configurations are changed, it sends an alert to one or more relevant security stakeholders. Vendors are adding additional features and capabilities to both scanner tools and change detection tools, blurring the line between the two. Some tools now do both.

When you want to control how your security tools share data, you can use SCAP. SCAP is a way for security tools to share data. It is an XML-based protocol that has many subcomponents called *specifications*. One SCAP specification especially relevant to configuration management is the CCE, which was briefly mentioned earlier. It is a taxonomy for describing configuration requirements, which is essential because of the sheer number of configurations and their nuanced differences.

CCEs are written for, and are grouped by, specific IT products or technology types. The vulnerability equivalent to CCE is Common Vulnerabilities and Exposures (CVE). CVE is more widely adopted than CCE because the vulnerability scanner market is larger and more mature than the configuration scanner market. In fact, some major vulnerability scanning tool vendors have added CCE (configuration) scanning to their traditional CVE (vulnerability) capabilities. Learn more about CCEs at `https://nvd.nist.gov/config/cce/index`.

In addition to other standards and guides, vendors (especially OS vendors) typically publish secure build outlines for their own products and often make tools available for provisioning and monitoring configurations.

UNDERSTAND AND APPLY FOUNDATIONAL SECURITY OPERATIONS CONCEPTS

This section covers security topics that are foundational and applicable across many different security domains. Take, for instance, the concept of least privilege.

In physical security, least privilege might be implemented in such a way that your proximity badge will only get you into the rooms and buildings where you need to be to do your job.

Least privilege for an application may mean that you can see or use only certain tabs, dashboards, buttons, or records within the application that you need to do your job.

Least privilege for development means you can access only the coding tools, repositories, branches, libraries, etc., that you need to perform your job.

In addition to least privilege, this section also covers need to know, separation of duties, privileged account management, job rotation, information lifecycle, and service level agreements.

Need to Know/Least Privilege

Need to know and least privilege are two fundamental concepts that are often conflated and mistaken in practice.

Least privilege is exactly what it sounds like: providing the user with the absolute least amount of access to and control over physical locations, systems, and data that the user needs to perform their specific job function. Users with similar roles will have similar privileges; different user roles will require different permissions. An employee in the human resources office will need access to HR systems and data but will not need marketing data; an employee in the research and development department will need access to research systems and data but will not need access to HR information, and so on.

Need to know, on the other hand, has less to do with a specific user's role and instead concerns the specific project a user is working on or assigned to. For instance, two product testing analysts, working for the same organization, may require the same permissions to the same kinds of systems and data, but if one is working on one project (call it Project

A) and the other is working on another (Project B), they do not each need to know any information about the other project. We often refer to data isolation according to project as being *compartmentalized*. If Alice and Bob both have top secret clearance and they both work for the same organization, are in the same department, and have the same job but they are working on separate projects, then they cannot discuss the projects with each other, cannot share data, and should not, in fact, know anything about projects other than their own. They do not have a need to know about anything other than their own project.

Need to know and least privilege quickly become access control issues at their core. Access control is covered in Chapter 5; however, there are a few access control issues to consider in the context of need to know and least privilege.

You should create tiers of account types or user groups to achieve the granularity necessary to provide least privilege. One generic set of user account permissions for all users would obviously be too permissive for most and too restrictive to a top few. Similarly, create separate domains and/or system images to segregate users with different levels of privilege. With the advent of virtual machines and cloud computing, it is easier than ever to have multiple copies of machine images configured with varying levels of access.

Another consideration is not just whether the organization has granted each user the proper access and permissions for least privilege, but also how the user exercises it. A system administrator should have at least one nonprivileged account to do routine daily work, such as checking email, in addition to one or more privileged accounts to perform system administration. The discipline of using a nonprivileged account at the appropriate time is an extension of the least privilege principle.

Special functions should require privileged accounts to conduct, and those accounts and information systems should be configured to audit, the execution of privileged functions. Some examples of special functions include creating new accounts or changing access settings, audit events, or firewall or IDS rules.

In some cases, applications are installed and configured to run at a higher level of privilege than an end user who may access it has been given. In these cases, the end user is enjoying a temporary higher level of permission than was intended by the organization. This should be considered and prevented where possible.

Separation of Duties and Responsibilities

Separation of duties and responsibilities is a type of security control intended to counter insider threats, whether malicious or accidental. It reduces the potential for deliberate misuse of authorized privileges, as well as the risk of accidental misuse or harm to the organization's assets. Separation of duties and responsibilities targets sensitive tasks, which require special access and capabilities and which could cause serious damage to the organization.

Separation of duties, like all security measures, inhibits productivity and efficiency; applying the concept creates situations that purposefully degrade operational efficiency in return for security.

The classic example is the acquisition process: in the most efficient situation, a manager who wanted to acquire a new asset could find the asset, make payment, and collect the asset. However, to secure the process, most organizations add a step (or multiple steps): the manager who wants the asset creates a purchase order, the purchase order is delivered to the finance office, and the finance officer makes payment to the vendor (in many cases, there are even more offices/personnel involved, depending on the organization, the price of the purchase, and the nature of the asset). While this is inefficient and slows the acquisition process, it allows for additional benefits, such as reduction of asset duplication (the IT department might check the asset inventory before the purchase, determine the organization already owns a similar asset, and can inform the manager that the capability the manager requires already exists so the purchase does not have to be made), operational security (the security office, when reviewing the new asset request as part of the change management process, might notice that the requested asset has critical vulnerabilities and can recommend another vendor with a similar, more secure product), and, most pointedly, fraud prevention (if the manager is allowed to choose the vendor and make the payment without any oversight, the manager is susceptible to inimical motivations, such as bribery/kickbacks, favoritism/nepotism, and personal benefit).

When separation of duties is applied properly, fraud cannot take place without collusion of two or more parties; the manager and the finance officer would have to act in concert to defraud the organization. In forcing collusion, the organization gets the benefit of higher security: there is more likelihood the crime will be detected or reported if there are more people involved.

This means that even in cases where the entire task is actually performed by one person, there is still an additional person/people involved to review, approve, or audit what the first person is doing. This serves as a deterrent to a malicious user and as a second set of eyes to potentially catch accidents that could cause harm.

Here are some examples of how separation of duties can look in practice:

- Employees in the finance department can access a financial application and create and change transaction records, which in turn generate audit logs, but those end users cannot access the audit logs. Inversely, a security administrator who can access the audit logs cannot create or change transactions in the financial application itself.

- A developer who writes code for a software release can't also be a tester for that same release or be the one who approves or moves that release into the production environment. If a developer put a flaw into that code maliciously, it will be intentionally allowed to pass. If the flaw was introduced accidentally or through ignorance or poor training, there is a chance the developer will miss it again in testing. Involving a second person in the testing process allows the organization the opportunity to catch the mistake or malicious flaw.

- An emergency has arisen, and an administrator needs to access a superuser account to perform a sensitive task that is far above their normal level of permissions. Authentication to that account requires a specific hardware token, which must be obtained from the shift lead at the SOC. The SOC lead verifies with the administrator's supervisor and/or verifies that there is an outage, incident ticket, or some other valid reason why the superuser token must be used before issuing it, and the token must be returned when the incident is resolved.

While implementing separation of duties, keep a few additional considerations in mind. First, separation of duties must be well documented in policies and procedures. To complement this, mechanisms for enforcing the separation must be implemented to match the policies and procedures, including access-level authorizations for each task and role. Smaller organizations may have difficulty implementing segregation of duties, but the concept should be applied to the extent possible and logistically practical. Finally, remember that in cases where it is difficult to split the performance of a task, consider compensating controls such as audit trails, monitoring, and management supervision.

Another, similar form of process security is *dual control*. In dual control, two people are required to coordinate the same action to accomplish a specific task. One example familiar from film and television is the military's procedure for launching a nuclear weapon: two officers must each use their own physical key in a launch mechanism simultaneously. This prevents any one person from launching a missile in an unauthorized manner.

A related concept is *two-person integrity*, where no single person is allowed access or control over a location or asset at any time. For instance, a data center might have two-person integrity if it cannot be entered unless two employees present their credentials simultaneously.

Privileged Account Management

Since privileged accounts allow users to perform sensitive functions that could cause grave damage to the organization if misused, whether maliciously or accidentally, issuing privileged access must be rigorously controlled.

Creating and Issuing Privileged Accounts

Privileged access should be issued according to policies and procedures that do the following:

- Define a list of the positions/roles that need privileged access rights and specifically to which information systems and components of each system the access is needed.

- Require unique, identifiable accounts for attribution/nonrepudiation and prohibit the use of shared accounts and generic account names like Administrator.

- Define expiration of privileged access rights wherever possible. Discourage issuing privileged access indefinitely by default, and encourage and enable issuing these rights on an as-needed basis, for the minimum necessary period. All privileged access should necessarily be temporary and renewed only according to operational needs.

- Assign privileged access rights to a separate account from those used for daily activities; each privileged user should also have a nonprivileged account.

- Every privileged access to a data set should be granted/revoked by the data owner.

Protecting Privileged Accounts

Privileged access accounts should be protected according to policies and procedures that do the following:

- Require users to log out of their privileged access accounts when performing any functions that do not require privileged access

- Require the use of multifactor authentication for network access to privileged accounts

- Implement replay-resistant authentication mechanisms for network access to privileged accounts, such as Transport Layer Security (TLS) and challenge-response one-time authenticators

- Use stronger password restrictions than are mandated for regular user accounts; this can include elevated password complexity, more frequent change requirements, and lower threshold for lockout as a result of failed login attempts.

- Employ increased logging and monitoring of privileged activity compared to basic user access

Reviewing and Monitoring Privileged Accounts

Privileged accounts need to be monitored and reviewed regularly. Consider the following:

- Verify that the documentation that maps positions/roles to specific privileged access rights is current and accurate.

- Define a process and mechanism to collect and aggregate the current list of privileged account holders across all platforms.

- Perform a review of current users with privileged access rights:
    - Do their current tasks and skillsets align with the rights they have?
    - For all systems where access is applicable, have they used the privileged access recently? Do they still need privileged access?
    - Based on audit logs, have they used their privileged access account to perform daily tasks that did not require the permission level of the account?

Data owners should review privileged access to all data stores/systems under their purview more frequently than normal user access accounts.

Job Rotation

Job rotation may have benefits such as making employees more well-rounded or keeping them from getting bored at work, but these are not the concerns of the CISSP. From a security perspective, there are many reasons for creating a job rotation policy. These include reducing risks of both insider and external threats, reducing dependence on a single person (who can become a single point of failure), and increasing resiliency for business continuity and disaster recovery (BCDR) purposes.

In practice, job rotation requires cross-training personnel for various positions/tasks within the organization. Typically, this is limited to a particular office/discipline. The various personnel in the security office, for example, might all be trained on the various roles in that office (log analysis, IR, security training, etc.) but are not likely to be trained in other areas of the organization (they will not learn how to perform human resources functions, for instance).

Job rotation mitigates insider threats in several ways. It serves as a deterrent for a potentially malicious insider who is contemplating committing fraud. In cases where separation of duties would necessitate collusion, job rotation disrupts opportunities for collusion. In cases where a malicious insider has found a way to mishandle data or abuse their access, job rotation keeps them from doing long-term damage once they've started. The cross-training aspect of job rotation may also aid the overall security effort by reducing the potential for employees/staff to become dissatisfied and possibly become insider threats; skilled personnel appreciate receiving additional training and challenges of new tasks, and increased training opportunities make those personnel more valuable. Increased morale of skilled personnel reduces costs because of turnover and accentuates loyalty to the organization.

Alternatives to job rotation are forced vacation or leave. The logic here is that if a malicious insider is suppressing alarms, changing or erasing audit logs, or conducting any other activity to cover their tracks or support or assist an attack, this activity should be easier to detect if the suspected insider is suddenly forced to stay away from work. During the period of mandatory vacation, that user's account access should be suspended, and a thorough audit/review of their activity should be performed. This is especially important for those users with privileged access.

Another goal of job rotation is to keep malicious outsiders from being able to learn about your staff over time and trying to target or manipulate them for information or access. Reducing static patterns in personnel taskings and changing access roles repeatedly reduces the opportunity for external actors to subvert particular employees as targets.

Finally, job rotation also greatly improves the resiliency of an organization, essential in successfully executing BCDR actions. During contingency events or disasters, we must assume that some personnel will not be available/capable of performing particular tasks and functions necessary to maintain the organization's critical processes; having other personnel not normally assigned to those functions but trained on how to perform them is a great benefit and vastly increases the likelihood of BCDR response success.

Information Lifecycle

Information has a natural lifecycle. ISO 27002 defines this cycle with five phases: creation, processing, storage, transmission, and deletion/destruction. See Figure 7.1. Security is an important consideration at every phase, but the level of importance can vary, depending on the phase. The formats and media used in the various phases can also affect the security considerations.

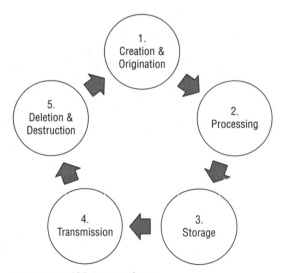

FIGURE 7.1 **ISO 27002 phases**

Consider, for example, design documents for a new product or technology. When those documents/data are new, they are valuable and actionable, especially if a competitor acquires them. Once the product or technology is in production, however, and being sold on the market, those same documents could be near the end of their lifecycle. At this point, one could argue that the documents would do less damage in the hands of a competitor, but they still need to be afforded some level of protection, right up to the moment they are destroyed. In this example, even though the "rush to market" advantage is won, the documents could still contain sensitive data, such as a proprietary production method, which the organization plans to reuse in future products.

There are several important points to take from this example. First, the security impact may vary depending on where the information is in its lifecycle. Next, even though the impact may vary, there can be negative outcomes for the organization at *any* phase. Finally, phase 5, the deletion and destruction phase, is important because destruction of unneeded assets reduces the organization's attack surface. Data at the end of its lifecycle only introduces risk, with little to no benefit.

Between the time that a data asset is created and the time it is destroyed, it may be processed, stored, and transmitted multiple times. Secure processing, storage, and transmission (system hardening, encryption at rest, encryption in transit) are covered in great detail in other sections of this text. See the "Media Management" section for information that is especially relevant to the information lifecycle.

Service Level Agreements

In the modern IT environment, there are many reasons (not the least of which is cost) for an organization to consider contracting with an external service provider to handle regular operational tasks and functions. To create a contract favorable for both parties in this sort of managed services arrangement, everyone involved must clearly understand what is being requested, what is being provided, what the cost is, and who is responsible for what. This is particularly important in what could be considered the most popular current form of managed services: cloud managed services. In the majority of cloud managed service contracts, the cloud provider and customer must determine the expected level of service, and the contract/SLA is the element that gives both parties the confidence to expect defined outcomes: assuring the provider that they will receive payment and assuring the customer that the service will meet the customer's needs.

In these cases, you need a formal agreement that defines the roles and responsibility of each party, explicit to the point where it can be easily understood and measured. The common name for this is the service level agreement. However, depending on the services provided, the agreement can go by other names, like *network services agreement*, *interconnection security agreement*, etc. The SLA is part of the overall contract but deals directly with the quantifiable, discrete elements of service delivery.

These are scenarios where an organization might need an SLA:

- Third-party security services
  - Monitoring/scanning

- Security operations center/response-type services
- Media courier/media disposal
- Physical security

- Hosted/cloud
  - Servers
  - Storage
  - Services
- Interconnecting information systems, especially with data feed/pull/push
- Supply chain scenarios

The SLA portion of the contract vehicle is best limited to those elements of the managed service that are routinely provided as part of continual operational requirements; the SLA is not the optimum place for including contingency requirements (such as BCDR tasks) or for anything that cannot be distilled into a numeric value.

Specific Terms and Metrics

One critical ingredient for an effective SLA is unambiguous terms and metrics that are measurable and understandable. Without this there is no basis for measuring or knowing whether a provider is providing the agreed level of service.

Take the following example from Amazon Web Services (AWS), a well-known cloud service provider. They have a product called Elastic Cloud Compute (EC2), which uses cloud-based servers. If you host your servers in the AWS cloud, your SLA with Amazon is located at `https://aws.amazon.com/ec2/sla/`.

If you read this web page, you can see that it clearly specifies the level of service in terms of server uptime by percentage.

- If your servers enjoy anything above 99.99 percent uptime, AWS has met their SLA.

- If your servers have anywhere between 99.00 and 99.99 percent uptime for the month, you will get a 10 percent discount on the service fee for that period.

- For anything under 99 percent, you will get a 30 percent discount for that month.

This is a good example, not only because the metrics and terms are clear but also because it is clear what happens in the event of noncompliance with the SLA. The contracting manager (in conjunction with the organization's IT department) must determine whether the price reduction would realistically offset the loss in productivity a service outage would cause; if the cost of the outage outweighs the benefit of the rebate/discount, the SLA is insufficient for the customer's needs.

Mechanism for Monitoring Service

It is not enough, however, to understand the terms of the SLA. You also need a mechanism with which to monitor and measure whether the service provided matches the level specified in the SLA.

To continue with the previous example of AWS, visit `https://status.aws.amazon.com/`. You will initially see a dashboard similar to Figure 7.2. The horizontal rows represent the AWS regions. If you look at the corresponding region where your servers are hosted, you can see whether they are having, or have had, any degradation of service or outage.

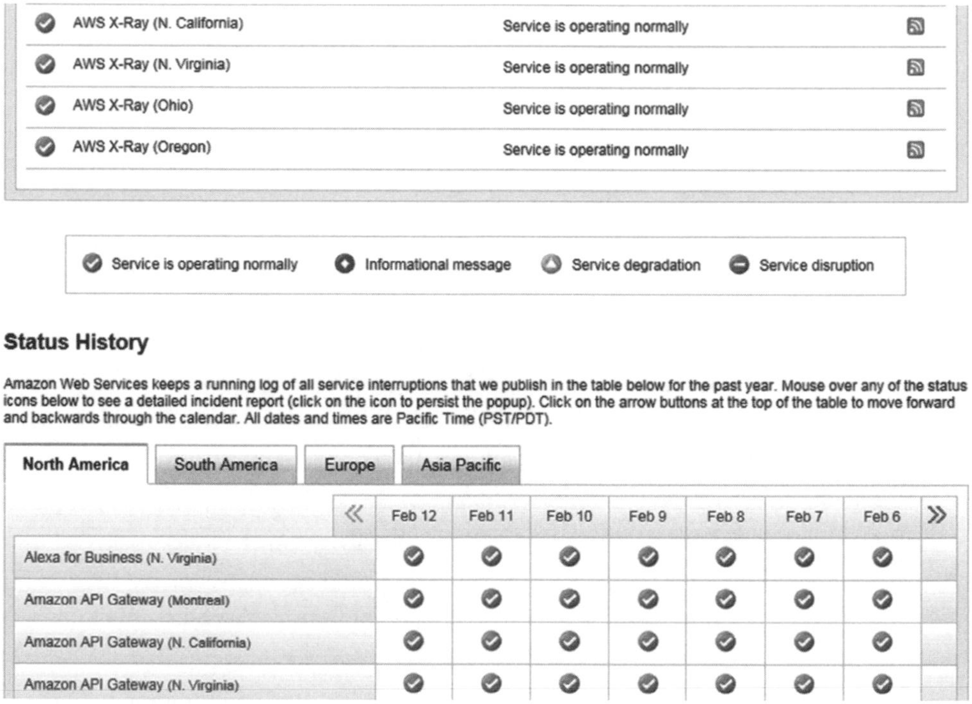

Status History

Amazon Web Services keeps a running log of all service interruptions that we publish in the table below for the past year. Mouse over any of the status icons below to see a detailed incident report (click on the icon to persist the popup). Click on the arrow buttons at the top of the table to move forward and backwards through the calendar. All dates and times are Pacific Time (PST/PDT).

North America	South America	Europe	Asia Pacific						
	«	Feb 12	Feb 11	Feb 10	Feb 9	Feb 8	Feb 7	Feb 6	»
Alexa for Business (N. Virginia)		✓	✓	✓	✓	✓	✓	✓	
Amazon API Gateway (Montreal)		✓	✓	✓	✓	✓	✓	✓	
Amazon API Gateway (N. California)		✓	✓	✓	✓	✓	✓	✓	
Amazon API Gateway (N. Virginia)		✓	✓	✓	✓	✓	✓	✓	

FIGURE 7.2 AWS dashboard

While this dashboard can be used to inform the customer as to the efficacy of the service overall, it might not provide, by itself, the level of assurance the customer desires; the information is necessarily coming from the provider, and the provider has a vested interest in the outcomes of the data (i.e., getting paid) and so is inherently biased. For such SLA elements, the customer may prefer some third-party validation of the service/data to feel confident that the reporting mechanism adequately reflects the actual level of service provided/received.

APPLY RESOURCE PROTECTION TECHNIQUES TO MEDIA

Protection for the organization's resources (hardware, software, personnel, intellectual property, and so on) is discussed thoroughly throughout the book. This section specifically addresses protection measures for media (material that carries data) and how to properly manage media. Managing media includes properly marking, protecting, transporting, sanitizing, and destroying media at the end of its life. The goals for doing these activities, as stated in ISO 27002, are to "prevent unauthorized disclosure, modification, removal or destruction of information stored on media." This goes back to the CIA Triad; the organization doesn't want unauthorized people to see what is on the organization's media, and the organization wants the data stored on media to be accurate and available when needed.

Before covering the methods for properly managing media, it's important to acknowledge that these methods will vary based on the types of media used. The umbrella term of *media* or *information system media* could mean legacy, analog formats, such as hard-copy documents, photos, and microfilm. It could also (more likely) be in reference to a wide range of digital formats, such as external hard drives, floppy disks, diskettes, magnetic tape cassettes, memory cards, flash drives, and optical (CD and DVD-ROM) disks.

Marking

During its lifecycle, media needs to be handled and protected according to the sensitivity of the data stored on it. Once the data assets are classified, the next foundational step in the proper handling of media is marking the media. Mark all information system media in a way that clearly indicates its classification, if it has one, and any limitations as to how it can be handled or distributed.

NOTE Marking media might become complicated, depending on the media used. For instance, it might be possible to include a significant amount of information on the label of a 3.5" floppy disk, but much, much more difficult to put that same information on the label of a USB flash drive that is the size of a thumbnail. The organization's data classification and media marking policies should take this into account to meet the organization's operational and security needs.

Protecting

Consistent with the least privilege and separation of duties concepts we discussed previously, your organization should restrict access to media only to authorized staff who need it for their daily duties, based on their specific roles.

To do this, there must be an element of physical protection and storage that is commensurate with the sensitivity and classification of the data on the media. Here are a few examples, illustrating different levels of protection:

- Backup tapes of audits logs are in a locked desk drawer or cabinet, the key to which is available only to administrators who may need to review the logs.

- Signed hard-copy health insurance forms are in a locked file cabinet in a room restricted to HR staff via proximity-badge access.

- An external hard drive with classified data on it is fully encrypted and is in a locked safe in a protected area, accessible only to users with appropriate security clearance and need to know.

As you can see in the examples, media can be afforded different layers of both physical and logical access control. There are additional measures to consider, based on the sensitivity and criticality of your media. Create redundant copies of critical media to mitigate accidental damage or loss. Use cryptographic mechanisms to ensure confidentiality (example: encryption at rest) and integrity (example: hashes) of the data. To prevent the loss of data because of the degradation of the underlying media over time (magnetic media and film are very susceptible), periodically transfer copies to fresh media. Finally, define formal processes for periodically verifying inventory of media, for formally authorizing users to check media in and out of the media library, and for leaving an audit trail. These processes should be followed until the media is either sanitized or destroyed using approved equipment and methods.

Transport

Your organization needs to have a defined set of procedures for protecting media when it is transported outside of controlled areas. These procedures should define the check in/check out accountability mechanisms used for transport, as well as the documentation requirements of the transportation activities. (Where are these details captured? What format? Which details are required, such as times of transfer and receipt, and so on?)

Any staff or courier transporting media should clearly understand the restrictions applied to the transport (approved travel methods, routes, etc.) as well as special handling and packaging considerations, based on media type, to protect from hazards such as moisture, temperature, and magnetic fields. This also includes when, whether, and how encryption should be used during transport. If any of these transport requirements can be modified, based on the sensitivity of the data and the type of media involved, this should also be specified.

Transport procedures should be clear as to when appointed custodians are necessary, who the approved custodians or couriers are, and how to verify identity if external couriers are used. Consideration should also be given to when and how the responsibilities of the custodian can be transferred to another, as well as specific points of contact to whom the media can be transferred at arrival.

Sanitization and Disposal

The topics of media sanitization and disposal overlap and are interrelated. There is a time in the information lifecycle when certain data is no longer needed, and having this data sitting on media for no reason presents an unacceptable risk. If there is no benefit, why accept even the slightest risk that the media could be compromised? At this time, the media must be sanitized or disposed of. So, what are the differences between the two?

The first difference is the reuse scenario. According to NIST 800-53, media should be sanitized "prior to disposal, release out of organizational control, or release for reuse." Disposal of media doesn't acknowledge a need to reuse the media, but sanitization does.

The next difference is in the methods. The sanitization methods are less physically destructive than disposal methods. For example, sanitizing nondigital media, such as paper documents, is accomplished by removing sensitive pages or entire sections or by redacting or obscuring specific text. In contrast, disposal of paper documents would entail cross-shredding, pulping, or burning the papers entirely. Sanitizing digital media, such as hard drives, would mean overwriting each sector and byte of the drive many times with random characters. Disposal of hard drives, in contrast, entails either degaussing the drive, physically abrading or chemically corroding the surfaces of the disk platters, or breaking the entire drive in a powerful shredder.

NOTE Deguassing does not work on a solid state drive (SSD).

Another slight difference you can see in the NIST verbiage is that sanitization is often a defense-in-depth approach to precede disposal and augment it as a security control. Imagine, for example, a scenario where a hard drive was not effectively destroyed by the organization's normal disposal method or was, for example, intercepted by a curious or malicious person in the chain of custody. Even if the drive wasn't destroyed but had been previously overwritten many times with random characters, it may still be unreadable, and the sanitization is a good mitigation for the failure in the disposal process.

Having discussed the differences, what are the commonalities between sanitization and disposal? Essentially, everything else. The goal of both sanitization and disposal is to ensure that the data previously on the media is not readable or recoverable. They should both happen according to formal processes that review, approve, document, and verify the sanitization/disposal. In both cases, the methods and tools should be commensurate with the data stored on the media. This also includes the removal of external markings and labels.

For both sanitization and disposal, the processes can be adjusted for more stringency or less, depending on the sensitivity of the data on the media. In some cases, also consider that it may be less expensive to apply the more stringent sanitization or disposal method to all media than to spend time separating them.

Both sanitization and disposal use specific tools, whether software tools, grinder, shredder, degausser, etc. These tools need to be periodically tested to ensure they are effective and that the media/remnants cannot be read or restored.

When storing and collecting media *prior* to sanitization or disposal, consider affording additional protection above and beyond normal media classification and marking. If there is a large quantity of nonsensitive information in one place, it can become more sensitive by aggregation.

NOTE It is essential to get verification from the data owners that the record-retention policies are being met and the data is not being destroyed too early.

CONDUCT INCIDENT MANAGEMENT

From an academic perspective, events and incidents are closely related and defined. An *event* is anything that can be measured within your environment, and an *incident* is an unscheduled or out-of-the-ordinary event. However, this definition might not provide sufficient practical description of incidents; the following additional explanation may be used to clarify the point.

A security incident is an event that did the following:

- **Had a negative impact on an IT system:** This is the type of security incident that gets the most attention. The obvious implication is that the affected system is supporting one or more business processes or missions, and *those* are the things that are truly affected by the incident. For example, a worm infecting a dozen machines may delay payroll processing, or a distributed denial-of-service (DDoS) attack keeps customers from performing web transactions.

- *Potentially* **had a negative impact on an IT system:** If your organization's tools and processes have detected events and indicators that suggest there is an incident but it hasn't yet manifested itself as, say, an outage or degradation of service, it is obviously still worth investigating and resolving. There could be impacts that are either not visible without digging or could still be prevented.

- **Violated or presented an imminent threat of violating a security policy or procedure:** Imagine, for example, an insider is using unauthorized software, mishandling privacy data, or doing any number of things that *could* have negative impacts, but just through luck, that negative impact hasn't manifested yet. These are things that are violations of policies and procedures and are worth declaring as an incident *even if nothing happened*. That is because the subsequent investigation and lessons learned will discover gaps where controls, training, and policies could be refined and improved.

An Incident Management Program

The incident management process is addressed in this section as seven steps: detection, response, mitigation, reporting, recovery, remediation, and lessons learned. The organization must perform some preparation and at least possess the foundation of an incident management program before IR activity will be successful.

One of the critical early steps in building an IR capability is to identify any policy or compliance requirements for IR. This will shape the structure, communications, and response activities.

It is crucial to discuss the many incident types and vectors. Incidents can be caused by malfunctions because of design and implementation errors. They can be the result of malicious attacks, either targeted or untargeted, and involve vectors such as email, the Web, or malware. Incidents can also result from improper usage by authorized users or from theft or loss of equipment or media. Some incidents have the potential to become a breach, such as malicious exfiltration of data, or through accidental disclosure of sensitive data (sometimes called a *spill* or *spillage*), while with some incidents, such as a DDoS attack, the concern is a degradation of service. The range of incidents that the organization could face will require a wide range of skills and specialists.

It makes sense that different combinations of response team members can be defined, based on the incident vector or incident type. The same is also true for creating multiple versions of response call trees to use to contact different combinations of people for different incident types.

Policy, Plan, and Procedures

Next, an incident management policy needs to be written, reviewed, and approved by senior management. This policy should give authority to a set of related incident management procedures. There are many existing standards and frameworks for IR that can be used to inform your organization's own policy and approach to incident management. These include (but are not limited to) the following:

- ISO 27035, "Information Security Incident Management"
- NIST SP 800-61, "Computer Security Incident Handling Guide"
- ENISA, "CSIRT Setting Up Guide"
- ISACA, "Incident Management and Response"

The organization also needs an IR plan. Depending on geography or industry, this may also be called an *incident management plan*. The IR plan should define what reportable incidents are and how and to whom to report them. The plan also needs to define the skills, services, and resources needed to coordinate IR and which teams within the organization will provide them. To complement this point, the plan should also specify when and how the various IR stakeholders should contact each other.

Most organizations will form an IR team. The IR team should be an integrated team to facilitate communication and should have the range of skills needed to handle incidents. These skills may include forensic investigation knowledge, developers who can understand custom and potentially malicious code, operational security specialists, and people with the compliance and legal knowledge to know how to recognize and handle a breach.

From a program perspective, the IR plan should provide a set of metrics to measure the performance of the IR capabilities and drive continuous improvement. Lessons learned, taken from iterations of IR testing, exercises, and real incidents, should be captured and incorporated into process improvements in the IR plan and related procedures. When these changes are made to the IR plan, all stakeholders need to be notified and given access to the most current version of the documentation. Lastly, the plan itself should be protected from unauthorized disclosure and modification.

Now that we have discussed the incident management policy and plan, those two documents must flow down and give authority to a set of IR procedures that cover a comprehensive range of incident types. These IR procedures will offer a clear set of steps for handling incidents in moments when stakeholders could be surprised, tired, confused, stressed, and, on top of all these things, when response time is critical. At these moments, the correct responses in the correct sequence can save the organization resources and effort and minimize the impact to the organization and its customers and partners.

The procedures should cover monitoring and detecting information security events and incidents, including criteria for how to declare incidents and breaches; how to assess, escalate, and prioritize them; and how to report them across the organization. Procedures must also exist to address how to document incident management activities, handle forensic evidence, and recovery (when necessary) from an incident, including coordination between internal groups and external third parties.

Tests and Exercises

Once the organization has defined which teams respond to incidents and documented policies, the IR plan, and IR procedures, the next step is to test this IR capability. The IR capabilities should be assessed at regular, defined intervals by performing tests and exercises of the plan and its related procedures. The point here is to determine the overall effectiveness of the organization's incident management capabilities.

The incident test or exercise often uses one or more scenarios, and the response team simulates responding to them using the appropriate checklist. Conversely, the organization may opt for live testing of the IR capability, including a partial interruption of production environment functionality.

> ### ✔ Quasi-Live Testing
>
> One organization's staff were so confident of their ability to respond to incidents and contingencies that they built a tool to continually attack and impinge on their own environment. Netflix, the streaming video provider, has created a set of automated tools, known affectionately as the Simian Army, to purposely present attack-type challenges in their environment. One of these is the Chaos Monkey, which randomly disables Netflix production instances to ensure that Netflix can survive this common type of failure without any customer impact. Not every organization has sufficient confidence in their IR capability to deploy such a tool, but Netflix has made the tool publicly available for those that do. Read more about the Simian Army here: `https://medium.com/netflix-techblog/the-netflix-simian-army-16e57fbab116`.

As the response team works through the appropriate set of checklists and procedures, they make discoveries. Gaps, weaknesses, lack of training, and poor communications will make themselves evident in these exercises. For example, someone on the call tree may have a new mobile telephone number but didn't update it in the documents, or a procedure was written for a certain version of OS or software, but that OS or software has been upgraded since the document was written, affecting some of the procedural steps. Discovering these details is one of the main points of the test/exercise and provides feedback for improvement. There are others benefits as well. The tests/exercises serve as a valuable form of training and often satisfy regulatory and compliance requirements.

Detection

Before the incident management process begins, an incident must be detected. This can happen in many ways. An incident can be detected by an automated tool such as log monitoring, intrusion detection, network monitoring, physical access monitoring, or the use of SIEM tools. Suspected incidents can also be reported by a person or a combination of the previous sources.

In the "Conduct Logging and Monitoring Activities" section earlier in this chapter, we discussed event logs and monitoring tools, which are essential to the subject of incident management. Event logs are typically vast in number, used across many platforms, but often provide only tiny snapshots of information. Through event correlation and analysis, these bits of information are enriched and combined with other sources to form an incident.

Most events are filtered because they do not meet the criteria for response, but a few become true incidents. Let's discuss Figure 7.3 to make this clear. Depending how the level of logging is configured, there can be thousands, or even millions, of harmless events logged for each one that indicates an actual incident. Incidents can also go on to be declared as breaches if, after further investigation, it is confirmed that data was exposed to unauthorized users; for demonstration purposes, Figure 7.3 shows an organization for which only 3 percent of actual incidents results in a breach. Breaches were covered in the "Cyber Crimes and Data Breaches" section of Chapter 1.

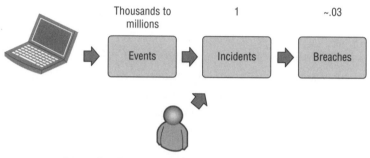

FIGURE 7.3 **Example of an organization's incidents resulting in breaches**

Consider the two examples in Table 7.2. They show how individual events and data from separate machines can be combined to determine whether they indicate a security incident. An event log by itself may seem to give one indication but, when combined with other pieces of context, will point to a different conclusion.

TABLE 7.2 **Aggregate Events to Determine Incidents**

LOOKING AT JUST ONE EVENT LOG	ADDING OTHER CONTEXT	INCIDENT OR NOT?
A server OS event log tells us that Joe logged in and performed a sensitive administrative task at 3:02 a.m. This may seem suspicious by itself.	Active Directory tells us Joe works the third shift and early morning logins are normal.	Not an incident
Jane's laptop OS logs tell us that Jane downloaded a file at 1:26 p.m. This may seem innocuous by itself.	The anti-malware agent installed on Jane's laptop reports a virus at 1:31 p.m.	Incident
	The IDS tells us that connections from Jane's laptop tried unsuccessfully to access five different servers between 1:32 p.m. and 1:50 p.m.	

This aggregation and analysis can be performed automatically by a SIEM or a similar incident management/response tool. Though it will likely be verified by a human in triage later, the initial determination is made using predefined rules about which combinations of events will constitute an incident, without human analysis or intervention.

Conversely, some incidents are reported or discovered by a human with no input from an IDS/IPS, SIEM, or any other monitoring tool. For example, an employee calls the help desk to report that his laptop was likely stolen. He was at a conference and set his laptop down during lunch and moments later noticed it was gone. The help desk tech forwards him to the SOC. The SOC analyst takes details from the employee, such as when and where it happened and what data was on the laptop. In categorizing the event, the SOC analyst determines the potential consequences and raises it to the level of an incident. In cases like this, no event logs, alerts, or machine metrics are needed to know it is an incident.

To enable this human reporting, the organization should require employees and contractors to report suspected incidents within a defined time period, as well as defining how to report them. This information should be regularly disseminated through security training and through policies and procedures. Personnel should be taught to report a wide range of situations, such as suspicious emails, policy violations, human errors, or any suspected mishandling or loss of sensitive data. Hardware or software malfunctions or abnormal system behavior, especially involving security controls, may be an indicator of an attack and should be included as reportable suspected incidents.

The next step is to triage the incidents. This can be performed by different IT security stakeholders, depending on the platform or vector involved, but keep in mind that this is a skilled specialty and is often done by a SOC member or similar on-call security team member who is trained and experienced. It is a best practice to capture the incoming incidents and assign them all to a ticketing system or a similar tracking system to aid with incident metric tracking and incident management program improvement.

The incident tickets or records should go through a triage process, which entails dividing and sorting the incidents based on a few criteria. First, they can be sorted as true, human-verified incidents or just convincing false positives. This is applicable to either incidents reported via reporting devices such as IDS/IPS or SIEM or suspected incidents reported by users that are not actual attacks (generalized spam emails, malfunctioning hardware/software, and so forth).

Next, a cursory determination must be made about the scale and possible impact and whether to activate a full response team. If malware was detected on a noncritical desktop, for example, it could usually be handled by one or two people. In contrast, a major outage or possible privacy breach will not only require a broader spectrum of stakeholders but will also influence how the incident tickets are ranked and prioritized. The IR approach best suited to the organization should be laid out in the policy/procedures.

Response

Once the incident has been declared and triaged, the organization begins to orchestrate response activities. These may vary according to the severity or type of incident, but the important steps begin by activating the appropriate team and following the IR plan and specific response procedures relevant to the current incident. The IR team then begins to investigate the incident and attempts to assess any impact on the organization.

The IR team should begin to collect evidence as soon after the occurrence as possible. This includes the use of both manual methods, such as interviewing the administrators and users of the affected systems, and technical methods, such as digital forensics.

When collecting forensic evidence as part of an IR, careful consideration must be given to preserving and collecting evidence.

Specific processes will differ between organizations, as each organization prioritizes responses in different ways (some are most concerned with halting further penetration of an attack, while others may be most concerned with losing functionality, etc.). Generally, many initial response plans will include such actions as these:

- Disconnect affected hardware from the networked environment; avoid powering down, so data in volatile memory is not lost.

- Gather evidence without modifying original files/data; this often entails making bit-level copies.

- Use integrity checks to ensure copies contain all the data of the original.

- Mark all evidence and make proper documentation of all efforts.

Documentation may not seem dramatic, but it can be one of the most critical parts of the IR process and the easiest part to underestimate and underperform. If the affected organization wants to press charges on a malicious attacker or wants to defend itself against a negligence suit in the case of a breach, the incident investigation data must be clear, complete, accurate, and compelling to be useful in court.

When the IR plan is activated, the incident handlers should begin capturing all the facts about the incident immediately. The medium is not important at first, whether written, computer files, audio, or video recordings, as long as the details are clear and complete. Some of this information will eventually need to be transcribed into incident reports of predefined formats, as well as keeping the incident ticket updated so that stakeholders are informed. Here are the types of details that should be captured:

- A summary of the incident

- Information system events and indicators related to the incident

- Origins of the attack, if applicable

- Observable changes to files or functions of the system

- Details about the malware used, if applicable

- Conversations with the administrator and/or end user of the affected systems

- Every action taken by any member of the IR team, with the time and date

- All notes taken and documents collected in the process, signed and dated

- A list of evidence gathered during the investigation

- Notes, comments, and reactions from incident handlers as they investigate

- Chain of custody details for evidence, if applicable

- Impact assessments

- Current status and next steps to be taken

- Contact information for all relevant internal and external parties

As incident data is gathered and shared, there may be hurdles in communication caused by simple human nature and subjectivity. This can stem from the taxonomy and format of the reporting tools and document templates and differences between the IR team members' training and backgrounds. The organization should agree on one common taxonomy and use it consistently across the entire process. Verizon, the communications company, developed a set of processes for handling incidents internally. One of these, called the Veris Framework, is designed as a set of schemas and taxonomy to share incident data between teams and organizations in a clear, effective, and objective way. Details on the project are shared with the public at `http://veriscommunity.net/`.

The IR team should protect this incident data because it can contain sensitive information about system vulnerabilities, possible criminal activities, or breaches. Evidence should be physically secured. Emails and documents about incidents should be encrypted. The incident document repository or incident ticket/tracking system should be under tight access control. The concepts of access control, least privilege, and need to know are paramount in incident handling.

Mitigation

By the mitigation phase, the organization has summoned the right people and understands enough about the incident and what impact it is having to respond to it. This phase is about containing the incident quickly and stopping it from getting worse. This may involve "quick fixes" that are not the ideal, final solution.

The first step is to try to isolate or contain the incident. This can, for example, mean disabling a user account if it's been highjacked or a trusted user is caught doing something malicious. It could also mean disconnecting or remotely blocking a machine that has malware on it to keep it from spreading and/or blocking the ports on routers and firewalls that the malware uses to attack or spread. Another example is responding to a sensitive information spill via email by temporarily locking the email accounts of the person who sent it *and* the people who have received the data so they can't forward it to anyone else and exacerbate the situation.

The commonality, however, between all these examples is the potential to impact workplace productivity. Security must always balance the three parts of the triad, and in this example, availability may be paramount. Consideration must be given to this topic of how to balance a quick, aggressive response with leaving enough functionality open for people to carry on their work and missions. It is best to have had this conversation before an incident happens. Ideally, business managers and security staff would meet in advance and have a common understanding about the range of mitigation techniques and which are more palatable and less disruptive to the business unit. This should be captured and incorporated into the IR plan and the response procedures.

It is in this mitigation phase where the response team and senior management begin to have enough information to make decisions about operational response actions. They begin to get estimates, for example, whether the system will be down for hours or days. They could also know by this phase which features and functions of the information system are disrupted by the incident and whether any were further affected by the mitigating actions afterward.

At this point, they can decide whether to change their normal operational model temporarily, until the incident is fully resolved. The organization could, for example, fill customer orders over the telephone while their website is down, or perhaps much of the website still works, and only certain sections or pages don't work. Choosing to continue to run in this state is called *graceful degradation*. In another example, the organization could temporarily stand up a new machine (whether real, virtual, or in the cloud) to perform the job of the affected system.

Even when the organization accepts a temporary loss or degradation of service during the mitigation phase, there is still an ongoing push for full (or equivalent) security capabilities. The full restoration of security protection will enable the full restoration of normal business operations to follow.

Reporting

The reporting step is the point in the process where the IR team not only knows enough about the incident to discuss it with some level of confidence, but also may know enough to be *required* to report it (as in a breach). This does not mean, however, that if the IR team discovers critical information in the earlier steps of the process they are required to wait until this step to report it. *Reporting* in terms of incident management can have many connotations. The most significant are reporting incidents to external groups, such as law enforcement, and reporting breaches, but there are other types of internal and external reporting. To avoid confusion, we will briefly cover them all.

Internal Reporting

Internal incident reporting means giving reports within the organization, such as to senior managers and executives, to keep them apprised. In these cases, the need to report should correlate to the severity of the incident. It is not necessary to report every minor incident to the top, especially if it doesn't involve an outage or a breach. This step should not be confused with internal communications between the IR team and any other stakeholders managing the incident, which could (and should) be happening at every step of the process.

This type of reporting is especially important in terms of incident escalation to the level of a disaster. Senior management may decide, upon receiving incident reports, to declare a disaster and enact the BCDR plan.

External Reporting

Members of the IR team will have many different reasons to report incidents to external organizations. None of these includes reporting breaches, which is covered separately in the next section.

There are instances where the organization may be required to externally report incidents, even when they are not breaches. All U.S. federal agencies, for example, are required to report all incidents to the United States Computer Emergency Readiness Team (US-CERT) within specified time frames.

Similar requirements can apply to the private sector. For example, in the retail sector, depending on the payment card brand a merchant accepts (card brands have different policies), there can be requirements to report incidents to the card issuer even before incidents have been confirmed as breaches.

The organization will occasionally need to notify law enforcement of an incident for cases in which the organization wants to prosecute the attackers. The criteria about when and whether to report these incidents should be documented in advance and should take into consideration the impact of the incident and the likelihood of prosecution.

The organization sometimes needs to report an incident to customers or partners, if, for example, the incident and its mitigating actions will impact the level of service defined in an SLA. The decisions about when and whether to make these notifications should be predefined in the procedures. These procedures, especially when they are related to failures to meet the contractual obligations of an SLA, should be reviewed and approved by senior management and your organization's legal team.

The organization can report incidents related to particular vendors or suppliers within the supply chain. In this scenario, imagine an organization using a particular piece of hardware, software, or service provider that is the direct cause of an incident. If it is known that other divisions within the organization or other peer organizations within an industry are using the same component or vendor, the organization may consider reporting this fact to others who can be potentially affected. This is a sensitive subject, and the response should be documented in advance and reviewed and approved by senior management and the organization's legal team.

The organization can report incidents to specific vendors. In this example, if the organization traces an incident to an exploit of a specific software product, they will likely seek out a patch and/or related help text on the vendor's website. If there is no patch available, it may be a "zero-day" exploit, and the affected organization may choose to contact the vendor that makes the product to make sure they are aware of it.

The organization can report an incident to a service provider that caused/allowed the incident. If a service provider is hired to perform a certain security function (boundary protection, IAM, monitoring, etc.) and that function is the primary or even contributory cause for the incident, the organization can notify them of the incident to assist in the response and discuss whether the incident was a violation of an SLA or similar security agreement.

Reporting a Breach

Most countries have federal level breach notification laws for breaches involving PII, as do many state governments. In the United States, there is no federal level breach notification law, but 48 out of 50 states have enacted such a law as of the time this book was written. In the European Union, the General Data Protection Regulation (GDPR) requires breach reporting within 72 hours for incidents involving the PII of EU citizens. Most of these laws are similar because they were partially copied from each other. They follow a similar format where they define to whom the law applies, such as businesses and government organizations, and then define the information types that qualify for protection as personal information, such as Social Security numbers (SSN), account numbers, or names, when combined with other pieces of information. The laws then define the reporting requirements in terms of how long the organization has to report the breach, to whom it must be reported, and by what acceptable methods. Lastly, there are exemptions given (when notification is not necessary). The most common example is when the privacy data is encrypted.

Penalties for not complying with these laws can vary. Criminal charges are possible for knowingly suppressing the fact that a breach happened, but civil cases are much more common.

In summary, as a security professional, how you handle breaches involving PII is quite serious. Depending on the situation, you may face criminal charges, you could be fired, and your organization could be fined. For all these reasons, it is important to understand, based on the countries and states in which your organization operates, which of these notification laws affect your organization. Define a notification process with your legal team and senior management and incorporate it into your IR procedures.

A free and useful resource on national breach notification laws can be found at www.theworldlawgroup.com/wlg/global_data_breach_guide_home.asp.

A list of U.S. state notification laws can be found at the National Conference of State Legislatures site at www.ncsl.org/research/telecommunications-and-information-technology/security-breach-notification-laws.aspx.

Recovery

It is important to point out that not every incident will result in an outage or require any sort of restoration, reconstitution of a system, or "recovery" in any practical sense of the word. For example, you can have incidents that are violations of policies but have little to no negative impact on the organization. In situations like that, there is no applicable recovery step. This section serves to illustrate where in the cycle the recovery step would be performed, if applicable.

Just as in disaster recovery, an incident recovery team with the appropriate skills and training must be identified prior to the incident. The members of the team may overlap with the IR team or may be an entirely separate team. They should follow a set of pre-defined recovery steps, which may already be covered within the IR plan and procedures, or they may be called out in a separate recovery plan. The assembly of this team and the creation of the plan should be done with close consideration given to the criticality of the organization's systems and their business impact analysis (BIA). The conditions under which these recovery plans may be invoked, and the list of people authorized to do so, should also be defined in advance.

When the recovery team responds to an incident, the recovery plan is invoked. They begin to restore services and capabilities incrementally, over time, according to their relative criticality. The recovery may happen in stages, according to predefined intermediate recovery goals and milestones. During this time, some services might continue to operate in a diminished capacity.

Remediation

The remediation phase marks the return from reduced to full functionality. The quick fix in the mitigation can often leave the system with no functionality or partial functionality. The final fix in the remediation phase often coincides with the return to full functionality.

The remediation phase also includes those actions necessary to address damages resulting from the incident. This could be monetary fees/settlements paid to regulators/affected entities or efforts made to assuage/compensate those entities.

Lessons Learned

The final phase of the process is for reviewing everything and seeing how the IR processes could be improved. This may sound a lot like the root-cause analysis we just discussed in the previous step. However, in this phase of the process, the organization should not review the incident itself, but the organization's response to the incident, to determine whether there is some way to improve the IR capability/plan/procedures.

Go through each of the incident management steps and question and critique everything. Every improvement gleaned from this step will reduce the likelihood or impact of future incidents. Metrics should also be gathered where possible to compare to other incidents. Costs and response times for each task are examples of useful incident metrics.

The intent is to illustrate that all parts can and should be questioned and to provide ideas to get started. Most importantly, make sure all of these considerations are incorporated into updated IR procedures, training, and testing. In addition, the sensitive details of specific incidents could be sanitized, and lessons learned can be presented in user awareness training to show end users how to help avoid future incidents.

Third-Party Considerations

Today, with public/private hybrid environments and those that lean heavily on outsourced or third-party services, it is imperative to include them in your incident management program's policies, plans, and procedures. Security teams should be reviewing their third parties as part of their overall risk management strategy; it is also important to make sure they align with your incident management program. This includes pre-incident, during the incident, and post-incident activities.

- **Pre-incident**
  - **Prediction:** Considerations must be made to determine that third parties are providing your incident management program with correct telemetry for their service and, for instance, the partnering organization, with likelihoods of a third-party breach and vulnerability reporting.

  - **Detection:** Does the third party warn of any incidents or take actions to minimize the probability and/or impact of a security incident? This answer can vary greatly with third parties, and it is important to understand how the third party prevents breaches and how they document and provide their customers with security reviews and audits.

- **During the incident**
  - **Response:** An incident may originate with the third party or from within the organization itself. It is therefore important to regularly review contracts and SLAs so that they are meeting the agreed-upon expectations and to regularly test the ability to retrieve data from a third party or escalate requests in a timely manner. In the heat of the moment when responding to an incident, it is important for all processes to function harmoniously, and this includes

any action needed by third parties. Both internal and external team members responsible for responding to incidents and forensically examining evidence on the network or devices should be immediately dispatched to further evaluate the nature and extent of the intrusion.

■ **Post-incident**

    ■ **Recovery and reporting:** Recovery timelines must be in sync with both internal and external parties, as a delay from one could result in damages or fees. A hosting company that fails to recover a database or application could have severe financial impacts to the organization. It is therefore important to develop relationships with the people who receive notifications and how customers are notified. Reporting of vulnerabilities from third parties in a timely manner must take place and be incorporated with internal vulnerability management programs.

    ■ **After action:** The security team should work with third parties to evaluate how an incident may have happened and what steps can be taken to prevent a reoccurrence. The security practitioner should regularly evaluate, address, and verify remediation of weaknesses and deficiencies with the third-party providers.

The involvement of third parties, both upstream and downstream, is vitally important in IR, as they may affect explicit and crucial aspects in the sequence of response actions.

OPERATE AND MAINTAIN DETECTIVE AND PREVENTATIVE MEASURES

The CISSP knows that an effective security program is based on the concept of layered defense or defense in depth. This requires the use of multiple controls to both prevent and detect security breaches or violations of policy. The use of multiple controls (and control types) can reduce the risk of a single point of failure, where the failure or circumvention of one control could lead to an unmitigated incident. For this reason, the deployment of layers of controls is essential to the protection of assets, especially those assets that are critical to business operations or are of most value to an attacker. This may include the choice of tools and technologies used to address the security requirements, including firewalls, encryption, virtual private networks, DLPs, SIEM solutions, and intrusion detection and prevention systems. An effective security program, however, is not based solely on technology. Technology is one essential component of a security program, but without the added elements of administration (management) controls and the securing of the physical and environmental factors, technology is ineffective. Security solutions must include the choice of the correct technology and then surround that technology with oversight, governance, reporting, training, and monitoring. Technology must also be implemented onto a physically secure and reliable foundation.

Throughout the earlier domains of the CISSP CBOK, the groundwork was laid for an effective security program. The identification of risk, including threat modeling, vulnerability identification, and calculation of impact and probability, provided the justification needed to establish a security framework and define the boundaries and objectives of the security program. Examination of cryptography, communications, access control, secure software development, and physical security provided the components of a security program that needed to be designed and built into a working security solution. Now, in the Security Operations domain, the day-to-day operation, maintenance, and oversight of the program takes place.

The security manager will work with IT operations staff to ensure that the controls necessary to support the security requirements are built into a complete and effective security framework according to the design and security strategy.

The security manager plays a crucial role in providing senior management with insight and assurance of the effectiveness of the information security program that was discussed in Chapter 6. The security and IT operations departments must work in concert to determine whether the chosen controls are achieving the desired effect and are working correctly.

In general, detective controls detect an attack as it is occurring or after it has occurred. Techniques used in detection include traffic monitoring, signatures of attack patterns/methods, behavioral analysis, deviations from historic norms, and the like.

Detective controls that utilize behavioral analysis depend on the ability to know what normal behavior of a system or technology is and the user community's use of those tools, thereby noticing any abnormality or deviation from normal activity. Without a "normal" baseline, the control cannot detect abnormal events. Detective controls also require careful and diligent monitoring to enable fast detection of a breach or suspicious activity. This usually entails real-time monitoring by a security operations center.

Preventive measures differ from detective controls in that preventive controls are intended to prohibit attacks or necessarily limit the effect of an attack. These include a wide variety of physical controls (such as fences, walls, and locks), encryption (where an attack cannot acquire data that will be of value to the attacker), access rules/mechanisms, and so forth.

Again, the security and IT operations offices must work in conjunction to select, deploy, maintain, and monitor both preventive and detective controls for the normal operating environment to ensure a robust security program.

White-listing/Black-listing

The rules used to enforce security controls are often based on either of two principles: the principle of allowing everything except that which is expressly denied (*blacklisting*) or the principle of denying everything except that which is expressly permitted (*whitelisting*). Either approach is acceptable, but the choice depends on policy and the approach of management to establishing a security culture. A blacklist could be considered to be more trusting (everything will be allowed except those things that are known to be bad), whereas a whitelist is more restrictive in that nothing is allowed except the actions that are listed. The blacklist/whitelist rules are added to the appropriate devices/tools (routers, firewalls, IDS/IPS tools, etc.) to achieve the desired security approach.

One place to deploy a whitelist is in an untrusted or semitrusted area such as an extranet or Demilitarized Zone (DMZ). A whitelist could list only the processes that are allowed to pass from the extranet into the internal network. Nothing else would be permitted.

A blacklist may be used in a general control by, for example, an Internet service provider that restricts all access to forbidden or illegal sites.

Within the organization, the security manager will verify that the rules in the whitelist or blacklist are documented, subject to a change control process, approved, and reviewed.

Third-Party Security Services

There are many reasons to use third-party security services. An organization may lack an internal core competency of security monitoring/response; a third party that specializes in security will almost certainly have a highly trained staff that is dealing with incidents daily and will be more adept at recognizing, containing, and resolving security problems. The third party may also be monitoring the networks of multiple organizations and will be able to share knowledge about any malicious activity against one organization with their other clients and act to defend against such attacks in a preventative manner.

Third-party providers often have excellent tools at their disposal, especially in the field of data analytics. Being able to amass and analyze vast amounts of data provides knowledge and insight that would not be available to most organizations.

When the security manager proposes to have security and incident handling functions provided by a third party, there are several considerations, both positive and negative, that should be factored into the business case. These considerations include the costs of the service and the level of services to be provided. There are other considerations, such as privacy and a reluctance to allow another organization to have insight into your data. If the third party finds some potentially illegal activity within a client organization, what should they do? Do they notify law enforcement or does the outsourcing organization? If the third party processes the data in another jurisdiction, is there a potential violation of trans-border data controls and regulations? Please note that this chapter does not address the important area of outsourcing development of IT programs and applications, since that area is addressed in the Software Security domain.

Quite often, third-party services can include a bundle of many different but related services such as antispam, anti-malware, incident monitoring, and identity and access management. Using a package of services from a single provider may be cost-effective and easier to manage for the outsourcing organization, but there is the risk of vendor lock-in, where the organization may be vulnerable to any breach of the vendor's systems or processes or the services of the vendor are no longer adequate to meet security requirements.

Once the third-party vendor is selected, the security manager wants to ensure that the terms and conditions in the contract are clearly stated, including performance levels, jurisdiction in case of any legal dispute, response times, and the commitment of the vendor to update and maintain their systems.

The implementation of the contracted services requires the review by the security manager to ensure compliance with the service level agreements and contracted standards of performance. If there is a lack of compliance, the security manager may be in a difficult position. The lack of compliance should be reported to management, but it may well be that management is unwilling to act and thereby risk upsetting the vendor. Documenting the issue is important in case of future disputes or attempts to recover costs.

Problems with third-party security services often arise because of a lack of communication and understanding between the parties of the services to be provided and the expectations of each party. The security manager should ensure that each party understands which services are provided and at what levels of performance. The security manager may also play an essential role as the liaison between the third party and the outsourcing firm, ensuring that issues raised by either party are communicated and responded to in a timely manner. As in all matters regarding contracted services, the organization's legal counsel must definitely be intimately involved in the process.

Whenever an organization contracts for services from external providers, the following elements should be considered:

- Strong contract language protecting both parties.
- Mutual review of security governance to ensure that there is common understanding of goals and approaches.
- Nondisclosure agreements (NDAs), ensuring that data belonging to the client organization is not exploited by the contractor.
- Contractors should provide evidence of errors/omissions insurance and proper bonding when entrusted with the organization's assets.
- Auditing/review of contractors on a regular basis.
- Full approval from regulators in affected industries before outsourcing is implemented.

Honeypots/Honeynets

A *honeypot/honeynet* is a tool that is designed to simulate an operational asset or environment but contains no data or assets of actual value. Ideally, an attacker will be distracted by the honeypot and will waste considerable resources and time trying to compromise a device or environment that has no real value. This allows the operator of the honeypot to learn the tools and approaches used by the attacker and learn how to build a stronger defense against attacks launched on systems of true value.

A honeynet is a type of high interaction honeypot (or honeypots) used to gather information on malicious activity by creating a network of seemingly real services and applications. The attacker may believe that they have found a real network, but in fact it is just a distraction that gathers data about the attacker. Since a honeynet has no real business operations, any activity within a honeynet is malicious.

A security researcher can use the data gathered from a honeynet to learn about attack tools, origins, and techniques. However, there has always been the allegation that a honeynet is a form of invitation, since it is usually public-facing and able to be accessed (with effort) from entities/locations external to the host organization. However, since a honeypot is passive and no activity should be expected on the honeypot, it is doubtful whether this is a valid argument. A more serious concern is that since a honeynet is by its nature an insecure system, there is the risk that an attacker that compromises a honeynet could use it as a platform to launch an attack against the systems or networks of other organizations, making the owner of the honeynet complicit in the attack. For this reason, the security manager should ensure that the IT Operations group, or whoever is responsible for looking after the honeynet, is diligently monitoring both inbound and outbound traffic so that any compromise of the honeynet would be identified and appropriate action taken in a timely manner.

Anti-Malware

Software developed to cause harm to a system is known as *malware*. While a bug or flaw can cause harm, those mistakes are unintentional, usually because of errors in the design or coding of a program. There are many types of malware, and as security researchers get better at identifying and defeating old malware, the malware authors are forced to develop new malware strains and infection vectors.

The security manager should be aware of some of the characteristics of various forms of malware and know how to prevent, detect, and recover from an infection. Malware can take many shapes and forms. The following are some of the more common varieties:

- A virus typically requires a host to infect and cannot spread on its own like a worm. There have been many types of viruses developed over the years, from boot sector infectors and rootkits to file infectors to ones that spread via macro scripts in

Microsoft Office tools. Many types of viruses will attempt to hide their presence or even change their structure to avoid detection.

- A worm usually spreads on its own as a self-contained program that exploits a vulnerability in an operating system or other software. Quite often a worm can spread quickly around the world, taking advantage of unpatched systems.

- A logic bomb is a patient form of malware that can exist on a system for an extended time period waiting for a certain condition to be met before it executes. Some logic bombs have been triggered by a date, others by an event. The challenge with a logic bomb is that it can be difficult to detect, and it may have also infected all the backups while awaiting a time to execute.

- A Trojan horse is a type of malware that appears to be innocent or desirable, such as a picture, movie, or game, but contains a piece of malicious code that will infect the victim's machine when the victim downloads/executes the file.

- Keyloggers may be software tools or pieces of physical hardware. They capture all the keystrokes being entered by the victim, which may include login credentials, passwords, and other sensitive data. Keyloggers are a good example of a type of malware that can be obtained at low cost, often less than USD100. This makes them available to criminals around the world who are interested in breaking into other organizations' systems and networks.

- Zero-day malware takes advantage of previously unidentified vulnerabilities in operational systems/devices/programs. A significant problem with malware is the short time between the identification of a vulnerability and the development of an attack to exploit that vulnerability. In a worst-case scenario, these may even be a *zero-day* attack, where the time between identification and the exploit is hours. Criminals love to find and exploit opportunities for zero-day attacks, and they can be quite dangerous and effective. This makes the job of the IT operations group much more challenging in keeping up with, and deploying, patches rapidly.

- Ransomware is one of the most talked-about forms of malware in use today. Ransomware encrypts files, data, and drives, allowing the attacker to extort the victim in return for access to the keys. Most ransomware can be purchased at low cost and is easily spread through email phishing attacks and infected websites. The challenge is that ransomware can be expensive and difficult to eradicate. If the victim decides not to pay the ransom to obtain the encryption key that was used to encrypt their files (hold them for ransom), they are forced to rebuild their systems from backups—if they have them. Unfortunately, in some cases the criminal does not even provide the key once the ransom is paid, and many organizations that have been victims of ransomware are re-victimized a short time later.

Regardless of the type of malware, its creator needs to use some means to deliver it to devices to attack them. Criminals know that many people will not patch their systems in a timely manner, so they write attacks against problems that should already have been fixed. Infections frequently come from attachments in emails that the recipient opens because they believe it to be a legitimate email from a courier company (for example) notifying them to arrange for delivery of a package.

Some of the most prolific types of attacks are based on robotically controlled networks (*botnets*, for short). These botnets are composed of dozens, hundreds, or even thousands of infected machines that are controlled through a command-and-control server and can be used by the botnet owner in perpetrating various crimes, such as spam, phishing, DDoS attacks, and click fraud. Botnets are often based on installing malware onto a vulnerable machine that will accept orders from the command-and-control server; we often refer to an infected machine used in a botnet as a *zombie* device. These machines may be desktops, laptops, or many Internet of Things (IoT) devices, such as IP cameras or televisions. Botnets have been controlled from Internet Relay Chat (IRC) channels, HTTP bots, and social media accounts.

These botnets have accentuated the ability of amateur attackers to perpetrate larger, more influential attacks without need for personal expertise or capabilities. Some of these botnets may be leased/rented by attackers on a payment-per-attack or time basis, allowing unskilled attackers to decrease the cost per attack, increasing the frequency of attacks, and enhancing the magnitude of attacks.

Malware-type attacks do not have to be technically sophisticated—or even, in fact, malware at all—to be effective. A hoax spreads through social engineering and convinces people that their machine is infected, demanding that they quickly delete a system-critical file or open access for a person masquerading as a technician, who will then proceed to infect their device.

The security manager must take a multifaceted approach to tackling the problem of malware. This will consist of both technical and nontechnical controls that will weave a strong defense against malware-based attacks.

There are a lot of technical controls available to address the threat of malware. Some tools are targeted at a specific problem, such as spam, whereas others will attempt to address many problems through a broad set of controls that may provide both network and host-based defense.

Some malware controls will actively monitor and block suspicious traffic, while other controls will scan systems, hard drives, and networks for resident malware. The security manager should ensure that any technical tools are being implemented correctly and maintained by a skillful and knowledgeable staff who can leverage the benefits of the technology and provide effective protection against attacks.

Technical anti-malware tools often depend on signature files and indicators of known attacks to identify malware. Like firewalls and IDS/IPS solutions, many anti-malware systems can interpret abnormal behavior from a baseline or use rulesets and heuristics to detect attacks.

Configuration management tools should also be utilized to check that every live system in the environment has the current version of all security software, including anti-malware programs.

Beyond the technical tools that the security manager can use, the human factor must also be considered. The administrators who look after the anti-malware system need to be trained, but so does everyone else. There is no better control for malware than security awareness training. Each person must be on the lookout for malware and not become a victim. Teaching people how to detect and prevent social engineering attempts that are often used to deliver malware is an extremely valuable control. Attack detection and avoidance should always be a topic included in regular security awareness and training sessions.

IMPLEMENT AND SUPPORT PATCH AND VULNERABILITY MANAGEMENT

The security manager must ensure that the software, networks, and equipment of the organization are protected against attacks and that known vulnerabilities are patched. While the security manager will rarely be responsible for the operation of the patch management program, it may be the responsibility of the security manager to design and implement it—perhaps based on some of the tools available to manage patching and updates. This must be linked to the asset management process and the configuration management database to ensure that all assets are identified and will be included in any patches that are released.

When a vulnerability assessment or audit has detected an unpatched system, this reveals a fault in the patch management process. While it is important to install the missing patch, the most important matter is to determine why the system was not patched. Something went wrong—all patches should have been applied to each system, and a missing patch indicates a problem in the underlying process. Thorough investigation of the incident may be able to identify the root cause of the problem, and steps should be taken to ensure that this does not happen again.

A patch management program requires oversight to ensure that patches are applied in a timely manner. The security manager should determine the key performance indicator (KPI) for patch management that specifies how quickly a patch will/must be applied to a system from the day that the patch is available until it is deployed. To do this, there needs to be a process for identifying which patches are available from various vendors and then testing the patches to ensure that they will work within the organization's environment.

There is a double-sided risk here. Some patches do not work and, even worse, may disable systems or other business functions. Therefore, some organizations delay the implementation of a patch for a short time until they know whether the patch has caused problems for other organizations that have already deployed it. Even this may not work, however, since the networks and architecture of other organizations may be substantially different from the target environment. Even worse, a delay in deploying the patch may leave the organization vulnerable to an attack that is designed to exploit the vulnerability that was addressed by the patch. In this situation, the organization may be subject to liability for the delay.

When a vendor releases a patch, it provides a source of information for bad actors. The criminal community may reverse engineer the patch to discover the vulnerability that it was meant to address. This allows them to write an exploit to take advantage of that patch that can be used against organizations or individuals who are late in deploying the patch.

Regulations and contractual requirements also influence the scheduling of patches. Some contractual agreements (such as PCI-DSS) may require security patches to be deployed within a set time frame. Insurance policies and vendor warranties may also be void if patches are not applied in a timely manner. The security manager must investigate what regulations or contractual requirements are in place to ensure that the patch management process meets the required time frames.

Once new patches have been identified, the patch management process must involve testing, approving, and scheduling the rollout of the patches. Ideally, it is best to test a patch on an isolated test network first, before scheduling a rollout to the entire organization. The test environment should have sufficient representative samples of all operational systems and devices in the production environment to best estimate the patch's efficacy and impact. Testing should review the potential impact on interoperating systems, as well as standalone/individual units. Patching may affect proprietary systems in ways the vendor/issuer did not anticipate. It is also crucial to perform a backup of the environment before applying a patch to have the capability to roll back to the last known good configuration in case the patch has substantial detrimental effects.

Scheduling the rollout of the patch may also be a challenge because many systems must operate 24 hours per day, and any outage could be expensive and can impact business operations. The patch management process must work together with management to schedule a patch at a convenient time or to roll out patches to different business units in sequence to reduce the risk of total outage.

Vulnerability management is addressed primarily in Chapter 6, "Security Assessment and Testing." However, from an IT Operations perspective, the security manager has to work with the IT department to perform and resolve any issues found during a vulnerability assessment according to the prioritization and severity of the vulnerabilities found.

The vulnerability management process must also mandate resolution for all vulnerabilities detected (even if the resolution is just documenting a "risk accepted" decision); it is surprising how many organizations will perform a second or third vulnerability assessment before they have even fixed the items found in the previous test. Vulnerabilities do not fix themselves, and performing a vulnerability assessment without being committed to fixing what is found just creates an illusion of security management without actually making a difference.

UNDERSTAND AND PARTICIPATE IN CHANGE MANAGEMENT PROCESSES

The importance of and approach to configuration/change management for the organization is described in Chapter 2, as an element of asset protection. As an element of security operations, it is worth restating the crucial role played in the configuration/change management process.

NOTE It is worth mentioning that the terms *configuration management* and *change management* may have confusing or conflicting implications for practitioners, depending on the use of the terms specified by their jurisdiction, industry, and organization. Typically, *configuration management* refers to the establishment, deployment, and maintenance of specific settings/builds/versions of systems/software within an environment, normally to establish known baselines across an enterprise. *Change management* often refers to the review, approval, testing, deployment, and maintenance of modifications to the IT environment, including software, systems, and devices, and their configurations. Many organizations unify these concepts under one effort and have them overseen by a *change management board*, *configuration control board*, or something similar. This effort typically also involves assessing the risk related to changes in the IT environment, evaluating and implementing related controls, and managing the asset inventory to keep it current. For example, the patch process described previously in this chapter is a specific form of change management.

Typically, proposed changes will come from business units or the IT department, and the configuration/change management committee will make determinations as to whether a given change is approved, disapproved, or conditionally approved (subject to successful completion of tests and/or the inclusion of additional controls). The role of the security officer in configuration/change management should involve advising and informing the configuration/change oversight body about potential risks and vulnerabilities associated with proposed changes to the environment, as well as possible controls for mitigation. The security manager might also be involved in creating and/or performing appropriate tests of the proposed changes to determine any effect on the organization's overall security.

NOTE Many standards exist for configuration/change management processes; it behooves the organization to choose an appropriate standard and tailor it as necessary for the organization's purpose, instead of trying to create a wholly new process.

IMPLEMENT RECOVERY STRATEGIES

The organization must have the ability to recover crucial data, operational capabilities, and the functions of the critical processes. These are determined when the organization performs the BIA, as discussed previously.

In performing the BIA, management must declare what the minimum acceptable levels of operation are and still meet contractual and compliance expectations. This is normally expressed as the maximum tolerable downtime (MTD), also sometimes referred to as *maximum allowable downtime* (MAD), and the tolerable level of data loss, or recovery point objective (RPO). Finally, the business must acknowledge the amount of time necessary to recover critical functions, which is the recovery time objective (RTO); the RTO must necessarily be less than the MTD. Collectively, these measures define the level of acceptable risk for the organization. Exceeding those measures is, by definition, a disaster.

Other data gathered during the BIA includes the resource requirements. To continue business operations, what resources would be required: facilities and workspace, equipment, data, personnel, and supply chain?

All of this information enables the organization to decide on recovery options—the plan for how to recover business to an acceptable level within the acceptable timeframe. The speed of recovery necessary to meet the RTO and the data continuity necessary to ensure critical functions (RPO) will dictate which approaches the organization will utilize in recovery operations. The following sections detail some of the techniques and methods for supporting recovery efforts.

Backup Storage Strategies

Having backups of data is critical to prevent the loss of data from user error, equipment failure, ransomware, or disaster. Having backups can make a serious incident much less painful, but when the backups are not up to date or readable, even a minor problem can become a major crisis.

The traditional approach to backups was to take a full backup once a week and store it off site. These backups were often stored on magnetic tape, which is a relatively inexpensive way to store and transport data. These backups were often stored with a third party that operated a secure location and even arranged secure transport between the organization's data processing facility and the off-site storage location. Because these tapes were in the possession of a third party, it was recommended to encrypt the backups using a symmetric algorithm such as Data Encryption Standard (DES) or Advanced Encryption Standard (AES). In the event the organization wanted to retrieve the data, there needed to be a way to ensure that only an authorized person could acquire the tapes and that the encryption keys were available.

Full backups copied everything from the target system, including the operating system, applications (including patches), transaction files, reports, access permissions, configuration files, and databases. This meant that a system could be completely restored from the backup. However, a full backup takes time and may impact production operations and performance while the backup is being created.

The frequency of doing backups depends on several factors, such as the volatility and value of the data. Data that is changing constantly requires more frequent backups than data that is fairly static and unchanging. Another factor is the value of data; some data has a short lifespan and relatively low value, such as weather data, while other data, such as trading data on a stock exchange, has tremendous value and volatility. A weekly backup of stock exchange data would likely not be acceptable.

Some of the options for data backups in between full backups include differential and incremental backups. A differential backup copies everything that has changed since the last full backup. In this case, if a full backup was done on a Saturday, then the differential backups each day would record all changes made since the Saturday backup. On Wednesday, for example, the differential would include all changes made on Sunday, Monday, Tuesday, and Wednesday. If there was an enterprise failure on Thursday, then the organization would need to use two backup sources—the Saturday full backup and the Wednesday differential—to retrieve the most current data.

An incremental backup copies any changes that have occurred since the last backup of any type. In this case, if the full backup was done on Saturday, then the incremental backup on Sunday would copy only the data changed since Saturday, and the incremental backup performed on Monday would record only the data changed on Monday. Each time a file is backed up, the archive bit would be set to show it has been backed up at a certain time.

If the system suffered a catastrophic failure on Thursday, then the administrator would need to restore each backup including the full backup from Saturday and each incremental backup from Sunday through Wednesday.

Many organizations will keep several generations of backups so that if one backup is corrupt, then there are still several other backups that could be used. The problem with this is that older backups will not contain some of the latest changes to data and may result in a higher amount of data loss. There might also be an issue with exceeding regulatory mandates for data retention/destruction.

Some backups may be kept on site. This means that they are readily available in case of a problem, such as accidental deletion, equipment failure, or malware; however, they would not be usable in case of a localized disaster, such as a fire or flood.

Another option is to keep backups nearby, perhaps in another building on the same property or campus. These backups would be good in case of fire but probably not in the event of a hurricane or tornado.

Keeping backups off site should mean that they are available regardless of the type of event that affects the primary data center. The security manager would want to ensure that the backups are stored in a secure location and that they would be available when required, providing 24-hour access and the ability to get to the site in times of crisis.

When a backup is created, it should be checked to validate its integrity. There are many historical examples of backup programs that indicated that backups were being taken but did not actually copy the data properly.

The use of disk drives for backups has greatly increased the value of backups as well as speeded the recovery time. Disk mirroring is when data is written simultaneously onto multiple drives. Ideally, this may also involve the use of multiple disk head controllers to avoid the controller being a single point of failure. This type of backup provides a complete copy of the data so that if one drive fails, the data is still available on the other drive, and there should not be any lost data.

Mirroring may also involve storing data on multiple servers at different geographic locations. In this case, the mirrored drives would still be available in the event of a fire or other catastrophe damaging the primary data center. However, connectivity to geographical disparate sites becomes a dependency for recovery during contingencies; the data may be safe, at a removed distance, but the ability to recover it could be limited by damage to the communications provider (such as during a disaster).

The use of multiple disks and some associated techniques for data recovery are codified by the industry under the term RAID. (RAID used to be an acronym for phrasing such as *redundant array of inexpensive disks* or *redundant array of independent disks*, but it is not solely a term for the mirroring/data protection practice itself.) The CISSP should be familiar with the following RAID types:

- **RAID 0, block-level striping:** Distributes the data across multiple drives. This increases the read and write speed (performance), but it also increases the risk of drive failure, since the loss of any one of the drives will make the data unusable.

- **RAID 1, mirroring:** Copies the data to two or more drives so that the loss of a single drive would not mean the loss of the data.

- **RAID 2, bit-level striping:** Manages bit-level striping with error correction. This is not commercially viable because computational overhead exceeds performance benefits.

- **RAID 3, byte-level striping with parity bits:** Stripes data across multiple drives, and a parity bit is created that would allow the data to be rebuilt in the event of a single drive failure.

- **RAID 4, block-level striping with parity bits:** Stripes data at a block level, and a parity bit is created that would allow the data to be rebuilt in the event of a drive failure.

- **RAID 5, block-level striping with interleaved parity:** Stripes data at a block level, and a parity bit is created and distributed among all drives. This would allow the data to be rebuilt in the event of a drive failure.

- **RAID 6, block-level striping with duplicate interleaved parity:** Stripes data at a block level, and two parity bits are created that are distributed among all drives. This would allow the data to be rebuilt in the event multiple drives fail.

- **RAID 1+0 and 0+1, a combination of mirroring and striping:** Mirrors the stripes or stripes the mirrored data (the order of operations is different). These are the most expensive options, but the best for both performance and reliability.

NOTE It is essential that any data backup plan includes testing that involves an actual recovery of the data from the backup. This is the only method for absolutely ensuring that the backup method is operating successfully and that sufficient data is being captured. Recovery must be performed on a somewhat regular basis (many standards mandate annually) to maintain assurance in the backups.

Recovery Site Strategies

One of the common elements of a recovery plan is the use of an alternate operating site during contingency situations where the primary physical production location is untenable. There are several considerations that go into choosing an alternate location.

Perhaps the first consideration is to ensure that the alternate site will not be affected by the same problem that affected the primary site. The distance between the alternate and primary sites is influenced by the type of crisis expected. A disaster recovery site in case of a localized disaster, such as an office fire, does not have to be too far away, perhaps a mile or less. But in the case of hurricane or flooding, the recovery site should be a considerable distance away. This is quite a challenge for some organizations, as "considerable distance" might result in crossing a jurisdictional or even international border, resulting in additional risks and costs during contingencies.

Consider the types of incidents that could occur and prepare accordingly. Being too far away makes it hard to coordinate and to get employees to the alternate

---

location. In a large-scale disaster such as a flood or tornado, the first priority of many employees is going to be their family and community, and they are not going to be available to support the recovery plan, especially if it requires them to relocate to another city or country.

There are many considerations that should go into the choice of recovery site, in addition to distance. The most obvious must be cost. Different recovery alternatives come with vastly different costs as well, based on the services provided, the size of the hosting organization, and the time frames set up for recovery.

There is also the question of what is available. In some regions, alternate site options may be limited, such as in jurisdictions that place restrictions on outsourcing to a hosting organization in another country or region.

Historically, organizations have approached the use of physical alternate operating sites based on a spectrum of cost, available services, and recovery time. The traditional definitions included "hot," "warm," and "cold" sites, with various standards defining the different levels along the same general lines. A *hot site* was a facility that had the systems, data, and utilities ready for any sort of failover from the primary operating location. A *cold site* was only an empty building ready for occupation by critical personnel who would have to provide those elements during relocation. A *warm site* was typically described as something in between those extremes. It is easy to understand which would be most expensive and which would offer the fastest recovery time.

However, in modern environments, many of these same functions are offered by cloud-managed service providers, with more flexibility and much less cost/maintenance. Some organizations might only use the cloud as an alternate operating site; the organization maintains its own data center for normal operations and switches to the cloud during contingencies (this may or may not include mirroring the data to the cloud or making continual cloud backups on a regular basis, as both off-site storage and in preparation for recovery actions). Some organizations might operate primarily in the cloud and rely on their cloud service provider to ensure backup/recovery capabilities during contingencies. Still other organizations may use one cloud service provider for the primary production environment and have another cloud service provider contracted for contingency backup/recovery situations.

✔ Using the Cloud for Data Backup and Recovery

One of the great benefits of using the cloud as a data backup/recovery option is the flexibility in choosing alternate physical operation sites. Unlike the sunk cost (and

CONTINUES

residual risk) of a fixed hot/warm/cold alternate site that once was the only choice, using the cloud for contingencies allows the organization to relocate personnel and operations to almost any location that has a suitable communication connection and room to work, which could include almost any hotel or conference center. This allows the organization to craft a recovery plan with flexibility to meet the needs of a specific contingency, as opposed to picking one sole location to handle all possible contingencies.

The cost savings and speed of recovery benefits are obvious. If the contingency is local (say, an office fire), the critical operations can be resumed almost immediately at a temporary location in the local area; if the contingency is of greater impact (perhaps a flood), critical operations can be relocated to a facility at sufficient distance to avoid the impact, and, in both cases, as long as client systems are portable (laptops and so forth), the effort necessary to move the production environment and access the organization's current data is negligible. Moreover, there is almost zero risk that the disaster affecting the primary production environment will also impact the alternate site. Since the alternate site is not geographically fixed, the organization can choose any location that is not affected by any given contingency.

Another approach to alternate sites is the use of cooperative agreements with other organizations, allowing one organization to use space in the other's facilities in the event of a contingency situation. These are often structured as a memorandum of understanding or joint operating agreement (legal instruments creating the contractual arrangement). Typically, this method is most suited to organizations in the same local area.

Multiple Processing Sites

One method for ensuring continuity of operations and reducing delay in recovery is to replicate the data from the production environment in several locations simultaneously. This could be accomplished by using a cloud storage solution, using multiple physical storage systems at the primary production facility, copying the data at several physical sites in real time, or employing any combination of these techniques. Typically, disk mirroring is used to write all data to several storage devices/systems constantly.

When implementing this methodology, the organization will be highly dependent on the copying mechanism and the connection between storage locations (usually an ISP or telco). As with all other strategies involving data backups, it is imperative to test the systems on a regular basis by performing restoration from the backup(s) to ensure both the capability and the integrity of the data.

System Resilience, High Availability, Quality of Service, and Fault Tolerance

System resilience is the ability of a system or process to resist failure. The system must be designed to be robust and able to identify imminent failure states and take corrective action. This makes the system tolerant of any faults or component failure.

Some of the ways to build resilience into a system is to build a cluster of servers that balance the workload and automatically manage failures of single elements. Resilience can also be provided through network redundancy, power supply redundancy, hot spares, and duplicated equipment.

Network redundancy is achieved by creating multiple methods of communication so that a failure of one would not isolate the organization. The simplest and most common method of network redundancy is to have more than one network cable available to replicate communications paths.

NOTE Cloud-managed service providers typically design and maintain data centers with a high degree of resiliency to ensure that they are meeting all their customers' SLAs.

IMPLEMENT DISASTER RECOVERY PROCESSES

During the BIA, the organization gathered data used to create BCDR plans. This included determining the RTOs for various systems, products, and services and the RPOs for various datasets. This information was subsequently utilized to craft the appropriate BCDR plan. The security office/department will often be responsible for managing the plans and take a significant role in execution.

The first priority in incident management is to address life safety issues and then gather information about the incident that can be used to do the following:

- Assess the incident
- Notify and escalate
- Triage
- Contain the incident (stop it from spreading)
- Analyze the nature and source of the incident
- Track and document the incident
- Restore to normal

If an incident cannot be resolved within an acceptable timeframe as determined by the BIA, then it is necessary to activate the business continuity plan (BCP). The BCP will focus on recovery of critical business processes according to RTOs. The disaster recovery plan DRP will focus on recovery of the IT services needed to support business operations, products, and services.

The BCP describes the steps necessary for recovery of business products and services in a practical step-by-step process that lists the activities in a simple, easy-to-follow format. Usually a few critical business functions will be recovered first, and then other less critical functions will be recovered according to the priorities documented in the BIA and the availability of resources.

Response

In the event of a contingency situation, the security office is typically an essential element. Security personnel are often tasked with the following:

- Coordinating response actions between the various offices taking part
- Keeping management informed of developments and making recommendations for response actions (including the declaration of disaster and return to normal operations)
- Documenting all actions taken
- Ensuring the safety and well-being of personnel
- Acting as a centralized focal point for communications during the contingency
- Interfacing with external parties (law enforcement, regulators, etc.) as needed (and in conjunction with other subject-matter experts, such as legal counsel and public relations offices)

Security practitioners are often the personnel within the organization most familiar with the BCDR plan, which is understandable, because the security office is usually heavily involved with creating and maintaining the plan and ensuring personnel are trained in the use of the plan. As such, the security office will often be largely responsible for managing response actions, and other participants will consult with the security office for guidance during a contingency.

NOTE   An important role during an incident is that of the scribe. It is important to document all of the actions and decisions made during an incident. This will provide data that can be instrumental in conducting a debriefing session following the incident and ensuring that all data related to the incident is available for examination.

Personnel

In all situations, health and human safety are the paramount concerns. During contingencies, particularly those involving disasters, risks to health and human safety increase

---

dramatically, and all response plans and actions must take this into account; every effort must be made to ensure that people do not suffer harm.

The response plan identifies those critical personnel involved in maintaining business continuity and taking part in recovery actions. These are people who know the critical business processes and have the requisite skills, as well as those with specific knowledge of response procedures. The teams should be built with the diversity of skills that are needed to respond effectively in a crisis. Moreover, each response role must be assigned not only a specific person but an alternate. In contingency situations, it should be assumed that some people will be unable to reach the worksite (whether that is the primary location or an alternate site). This is one of the main reasons why the practice of job rotation discussed earlier in the book is so useful.

There may be many different teams created to deal with different parts of the recovery effort, as well as teams available for different types of situations. The team members need to be trained in how to execute the disaster recovery plan, as well as how to use the tools, preserve evidence for follow-up investigations, and communicate effectively with each other and the business units.

It's worth restating that the first priority in any disaster is the preservation of human life and safety. Evacuation plans should be written and tested; all personnel should be trained and practiced in these procedures. Floor managers should ensure that all personnel in the area have been evacuated safely and assist personnel with disabilities. Staff should move to an identified meeting point where they can be verified against a list of personnel to ensure that everyone was evacuated safely.

When staff have to be relocated to an alternate facility, the organization may need to arrange logistics, including transportation, accommodation, and prepayment of expenses. For planning purposes, it is worth remembering that representatives from the human resources and finance offices may be part of the organization's critical operations and will certainly have a role in BCDR. Even if operations will be maintained at the primary location, personnel may have trouble reaching that facility during disaster situations; the organization must take this into account during planning and execution of response actions.

NOTE The organization may want to plan for relocating the family members of employees and staff during disasters, as well as those essential personnel; it is far more likely that personnel will be willing and able to relocate if they are sure their families are safe.

When an incident has caused injury or loss of life, the organization should ensure that counseling services are available for staff and procedures are in place to communicate with next of kin and keep them informed of any issues related to staff welfare.

Communications

During a crisis, one of the most challenging problems is controlling and managing communications with both internal and external stakeholders. A crisis, by its very nature, fosters rumors, suspicion, and fear. Addressing these problems requires an established communications plan. It is important to have a communications plan that is fast and flexible.

Emergency communications processes should include more than one communications method; during disasters especially, it is quite likely that communications will be either affected by the disaster itself or overwhelmed by the volume of people all trying to contact each other simultaneously.

Communications methods should have at least two functions: push information to personnel and receive it from them. During a contingency, the organization's personnel must be able to receive important instructions/information (such as notice that personnel should not go to the worksite, or that a relocation is taking place); this is particularly important for those personnel with response roles. This type of communication might be active or passive (the difference between reaching each individual by phone or hosting a website that every authorized person can access to get information). Conversely, personnel need some method for contacting the organization during contingencies, if only for confirming they are safe and accounted for. Whichever method is selected, it is imperative that emergency contact information for all personnel is updated and confirmed on a regular basis.

It is essential that the organization have a single voice for communicating with the public; multiple personnel/offices making public reports, even with the best of intentions, may distribute conflicting information, which can result in the public not trusting or understanding the organization's intent. All communications and responses to media requests should be handled by an authorized spokesperson who is trained and knowledgeable about dealing with official communications. All employees should know that any requests from the media should be forwarded to the authorized spokesperson.

Internal communications paths should be established so that various employees and teams know the status of the crisis and so that management is provided with accurate and timely information. Proper handling of the crisis depends on the effectiveness of communications up to senior management and from management to the various recovery teams and affected employees.

Assessment

When a disaster occurs, the response team must identify the nature, source, and impact. This initial assessment will facilitate the recovery efforts through assessing the priority of the incident and identifying the correct response plan to be enacted. The initial assessment should be based on criteria such as the impact on customers, finances, reputation, source, and regulations.

The assessment information should be conveyed to management so that management can best decide the priority of recovery efforts for a given situation.

The criteria for determining extent and cost of a disaster event should be determined prior to a contingency event, as part of the planning effort; these criteria and a guide for performing the assessment should be included in the response plan, along with assessment procedures. The criteria may be based on or informed by internal factors (such as asset valuation performed by asset owners, or the value data included in the BIA) or external drivers (such as SLAs, regulatory audits, insurance valuations, etc.).

Restoration

Incident management plans have the objective to restore operations to normal as quickly as practical following an incident. Depending on the type of crisis, the organization may operate in contingency mode for days or months. The initial recovery may only recover an acceptable (as defined by management) minimal level of service and then expand on that service until the BCP has enabled a sustainable level of service. Eventually, however, the goal is to restore to normal. The resumption of critical business functions is usually referred to as *recovery*, whereas the return to normal is referred to as *restoration*. It can be a challenge, however, to keep data synchronized over the two recovery and restoration sites as the restoration occurs.

The decision to return to normal operating conditions is realistically as fraught with risk as the initial decision to declare a disaster situation. Resuming normal operations (especially at the original primary operating site) too early may put personnel and other assets in danger if the disaster source has not fully dissipated. Conversely, a delay in returning to normal operations might incur additional unnecessary expense, and might incur more losses (such as personnel leaving the organization during the contingency, if they are not paid/utilized during contingency operations). Senior management must have sufficient information to make sound decisions when considering resumption of normal, full operations.

In some disaster situations, returning to the conditions/location of operations prior to the disaster might be impossible. If the primary operating site has been completely destroyed or if returning to the primary site is too expensive, the organization might opt for creating a "new normal," and restore full operations by some other means. This might mean making the alternate operating site the new primary location. It might entail a change in the entire business model; if the organization formerly conducted operations in an on-premise data center but used the cloud for the alternate operating function during the contingency, restoration might take the form of transition to a fully cloud-based operation instead of trying to restore the physical data center.

During restoration, the security professional is concerned with ensuring that security controls are enabled and configured correctly and ensuring the integrity and availability of data, especially as it is moved between recovery sites.

Following restoration, it is extremely valuable to conduct a post-action assessment to review not only the particulars of the contingency itself but how the organization handled it. Conducting an assessment of each incident through careful examination and feedback may highlight weaknesses in the plan that can be addressed and corrected to enable better future results. The end of each incident should trigger a thorough assessment of the following:

- What went well
- What did not go well
- How the staff handled the crisis
- Whether the communications were handled correctly

This review can lead to improvements in the plan that can do the following:

- Improve incident prevention
- Improve incident detection
- Improve incident response
- Highlight areas for training and staff development
- Indicate the need for better tools and technologies

There is a vast difference between "lessons identified" and "lessons learned." When a feedback session identifies areas for improvement, those areas should be acted on to improve the plan. Failure to follow up on lessons identified will lead to disillusionment and frustration on the part of the employees and reluctance to participate in future sessions.

Training and Awareness

Once the BCP and DRP have been written, they must be communicated to the entire staff of the organization. Although some people who have specific responsibilities during a crisis will need more advanced training, everyone should be provided an awareness of the organization's plans and how they should react in a crisis.

At high-risk locations, crisis awareness should be provided to all personnel at the time they enter the site. This will ensure that everyone on the site knows how to recognize an emergency situation and how they should respond. All personnel should be familiarized with safety and occupant evacuation plans at the time of hiring and then provided with annual reminders. These awareness sessions will advise staff on evacuation plans and procedures, specify meeting points, declare who is in charge during a crisis, and advise on how to report a crisis or suspicious activity.

Other personnel may require training in the use of tools or procedures such as chemical suits, system recovery procedures, crowd control, team management, evidence preservation, incident analysis, and damage estimation.

Since staff often change roles within the organization, it can be necessary to retrain staff and reorganize recovery teams on a periodic basis.

Personnel training for BCDR activities should be in concert with plan testing, which is discussed in the following section.

TEST DISASTER RECOVERY PLANS

The primary purpose of a test is to find any problems, weaknesses, or faults in the plans. Tests should be realistic and thorough enough to test all areas of the plans. By creating a test that is realistic, it is possible to simulate some of the stress and abrupt decision-making that would be required in a real crisis. The tests also provide one of the best ways to develop and train staff and familiarize them with the plans and provide an appreciation of how their roles integrate with the roles and activities of other team members.

The best approach is to start with simple tests and then progress to more comprehensive tests once the initial flaws in the plans have been identified and fixed.

Tests are inherently risky. For instance, a test may cause an actual business interruption and create a real crisis. Therefore, tests should be carefully planned to avoid causing business interruption. This might include performing tests at a time that would have minimal impact on normal business operations. Every test should also have a "stop code" that, if declared, immediately ends the test. This code could be used to signal the end of the test or declare that a situation has arisen that is a real disaster and that the alarms and alerts being communicated are part of the management of a real crisis and not just a test. Another risk of testing is unrealistic results. If the test does not include sufficient coverage of potential situations or if participation is inadequate, personnel may not be prepared for actual contingencies.

Tests should consider adding in "interrupts" or unexpected factors that will change the flow of the test to see whether staff can respond in a flexible manner and adapt to changing circumstances.

Conducting tests also makes other staff aware of the business continuity practices and creates assurance for management that the plans would work in a real crisis. For this reason, it is recommended that the audit team oversee the tests and provide independent feedback on the test results, effectiveness of personnel, test thoroughness, and lessons learned.

Tests may also include vendors and outside parties such as the fire department. By working with outside agencies, it can be determined if the plans would have the support

7

SECURITY OPERATIONS

and correct interaction with outside agencies so that the team knows that critical supplies will be provided as per the plan, and to ensure that the organization will be able to coordinate with emergency personnel in a crisis.

Tests should also be arranged to train alternate staff and account for situations where primary personnel will not be available.

Depending on the regulatory environment the organization operates in, there may be requirements for an organization to conduct tests at a certain frequency and report on the results of the tests.

At the completion of every test, a debriefing session should be held to review the results of the test and examine ways to improve the plans and mentor staff. The results of the test should be compared against the initial objectives. The examination of the plans following a test should also involve the auditors and the business units to ensure that the plans are aligned with the business priorities and strategy. Debriefing can be conducted immediately after the test in what is sometimes known as a *hot debrief*, when the activities of the test are still fresh in everyone's mind, but this can also run the risk of some of the tension and stress of the test affecting a person's response and perception. A debrief at a later data (preferably within a week) may allow the participants more time to reflect and analyze the test and thereby provide more detailed, objective feedback. This can be done through a survey or a formal workshop.

There is a distinction between a test and an exercise. As stated in ISO 22301:2012, "A test is a unique type of exercise which incorporates an expectation of a pass/fail component within the goal or objectives of the exercise being planned." Certain frameworks require testing. However, to build resilience, all plans require exercises.

Read-Through/Tabletop

The most basic level of BCDR testing is a simple read-through of the plan. This review should be done by the manager or liaison from each business unit and the emergency planner coordinator on (at least) an annual basis to ensure the plan is up-to-date and reflects business priorities. Each manager should be required to review and approve the plan for their department and provide updates where required.

The manager of each business unit should verify contact information, validate priorities and key personnel, and verify that all of their staff is familiar with the business continuity procedures.

The tabletop exercise accentuates the read-through. The response participants (those with roles in crisis management/response) meet together, along with a moderator, and role-play a response to a simulated contingency situation, using the response plan as a guide/resource. This is the least expensive/intrusive form of test/exercise and is used to validate the utility of the plan and familiarize participants with their respective roles.

Walk-Through

A walk-through builds on the concept of the tabletop/read-through, adding the simulation of response activities at actual locations where response actions will be performed. In a tabletop exercise, a participant might say, "I go to the wire closet and flip a switch," whereas, in a walk-through, the participant will actually go to the wire closet, point to the switch, and say, "I flip this switch." The action, at this level of exercise, is only simulated, but the locations are mapped to the activity, and participants are familiarized with specific areas and hardware.

In some cases, a test like this may be based on an actual scenario to test the response process and create a realistic setting for the test to be conducted in. A test like this may follow the actual timelines of the scenario or jump ahead to a later point in the scenario to test specific conditions or activities.

Simulation

The most common simulation test that people are familiar with is to do a fire alarm test. This tests the alarm system, the evacuation plan, and the role of floor managers and ensures that staff are able to evacuate according to anticipated timelines. A simulation should minimize the impact on business and not cause a full interruption (a fire alarm test may still leave some appointed staff at their positions).

A simulation is often based on a real-life scenario where staff need to ensure that they are prepared to deal with the situation in an organized manner. This is sometimes known as a preparedness test.

Parallel

Parallel tests are useful and usually involve fully duplicated systems or operational locations. For example, an organization that has a mirrored hot site may run that site in parallel to the primary location once a month, or an organization with a subscription to a commercial hot site may load their data onto the hot site and run their operation at that site once or twice per year. This allows the systems and operations to be tested at the recovery site without impacting normal business operations, which continue to operate at the normal or primary location. Another example is restoring data backup media in a test environment to determine whether the backup can be accessed in a specific time frame (whether the media is on site or off site), whether the restoration procedures are sufficiently detailed and clear, and whether the backup data is complete and accurate.

This type of test often finds errors that are not easy to find during other types of tests. Examples of this include access permissions set incorrectly, missing files, incorrect configurations, outdated or unpatched applications, and licensing issues.

Full Interruption

A full interruption test presents the highest level of risk to an organization. It is designed to test the plan or a portion of the plan in a live scenario and requires the participation of many team members. This type of test may inject an intentional failure into the process to ensure that staff and recovery systems operate correctly. An example of this is where a telecom company is required to demonstrate to regulators that the telephone system can continue to operate in the absence of commercial power. For this test, the telecom company has to cut over to batteries and diesel backups for several hours once per year. Such tests always introduce a level of stress and uncertainty, since it is common that some part of the failover process will not operate correctly on the day of the test. It is noteworthy that the telcos will do a parallel test of their power backups monthly but a full interruption only once per year. A full interruption test should be conducted only when other, less risky tests have been completed and only with the approval of senior management.

PARTICIPATE IN BUSINESS CONTINUITY PLANNING AND EXERCISES

Security professionals may not play a core role on the actual recovery or restoration teams but will play a key role in ensuring that the security of physical facilities, systems, and data is maintained during a crisis. This can include the need for increasing physical security protection to prevent looting or theft, the need for compensating controls to address missing separation of duties, and the need for ensuring the safety of personnel.

For this reason, security professionals may play more of an observer role in regard to business continuity exercises. This is like the role often played by internal audits during planning and exercises.

However, it is extremely important to have the participation of security and audit team members during the actual planning. This will ensure that security concerns are identified and addressed during the design and writing of the plans and that security is prepared to support recovery operations.

BCDR plans are quickly outdated or need review because of the following reasons:

- Changes in staff
- Changes in business processes
- Changes in technology
- Changes in business priorities
- Regulations
- Results of past incidents

- Audit recommendations
- Results of tests/exercises

For this reason, the maintenance of BCDR plans is a never-ending process that requires review of the plans at least annually, or more frequently in a fast-changing environment. To ensure that BCPs are updated, the change control process should require that BCDR issues be identified prior to initiating a change in the environment. The business continuity team is one of the key stakeholders in the change management process. Integrating BCDR requirements into change requests will provide the business continuity professionals with notice of pending changes to systems and operations and enable them to make updates to the plans that would be in effect at the time of the organizational change.

During a crisis all members of the BCDR team must be working from the same version of the plan. This requires a version control process to manage and coordinate changes to the plans and the distribution of new or updated plans. The plan must be available to essential stakeholders during a crisis. This may require the off-site and electronic storage of the plans and the ability of staff to obtain or access a copy of the plan.

BCDR planning is a fundamental factor in ensuring the resilience and survival of an organization. Incidents will happen, but through well-designed controls, effective monitoring and detection, rapid response and containment, and coordinated plans, the organization can increase its likelihood of survival even in the event of a major crisis. Business continuity depends on understanding the priorities and strategies of the organization and the creation of plans that management will trust, depend on, and follow in a crisis. A crisis is also the opportunity to improve business functions and IT infrastructure. Preparation and team development are keys to success in the majority of cases.

IMPLEMENT AND MANAGE PHYSICAL SECURITY

While physical security management should typically be tasked to personnel specifically trained and experienced in that field, information security professionals should understand basic physical security fundamentals. This section offers a brief distillation of relevant physical security topics, such as access control and data center protection.

Physical Access Control

One tenet worth restating is that any other protections within an environment can be overcome if an antagonist can get physical access to the systems/data. Access control is therefore crucial to truly protect assets. Refer to Chapter 5 for the bulk of the discussion of logical access controls, but in this section we address the physical aspects of access control.

Layered defense is a necessary component of physical security, both in terms of the location of the assets and in the use of various types of controls. For location, layers can be perceived as controls implemented at various distances from assets: the approach to the property, the perimeter of the property, the entrance to the facility, and internal access controls. For types of controls, the layers are as described previously (preventive, deterrent, detective, compensating, recovery, directive, and corrective) and include the implementation methods (administrative, technical, and physical). This section will address the latter (types) as applied to the former (distance).

Property Approach

Consideration should be given to areas outside the property belonging to/under the control of the organization.

- Visual line of sight, depending on the sensitivity of the organization's operations. Line of sight might be obscured by limiting windows in construction, covering windows in sensitive areas, obstructing views with landscaping/formation, or other means.

- Vehicular approach, including roads and driveways leading toward the property/facilities. For secure facilities, these should deter a straight approach to disallow a driver to build up excessive speed and should include obstacles with bollards, barriers, or retractable tire spikes.

Perimeter

At the outer boundary of the property, security controls can be implemented for access control.

- **Fences/walls:** While generally seen as deterrent/preventive controls, fences/walls can also be combined with additional mechanisms to offer detection capabilities.

- **Cameras:** Cameras serve a deterrent purpose but can be combined with monitoring capabilities (such as guards watching a video feed or motion sensors) for detection functions.

- **Buried lines:** While these serve no deterrent function, underground sensors can be used for intrusion detection within the border of a property.

- **Access control points:** Guard stations or gates can be staffed or equipped with additional mechanisms (card readers, cameras, turnstiles, etc.).

- **Patrols:** Guards (human or canine) can provide deterrent, detective, corrective, and recovery controls.

- **Motion sensors:** There are a variety of technologies that support the organization's ability to surveil the perimeter and any area outside the facilities, including the cameras and buried lines, as well as microwave, laser, acoustic, and infrared systems.

- **Lighting:** Well-lit areas serve both deterrent and detective purposes. Continual maintenance of all lighting sources is crucial, as a burned-out or broken bulb can defeat any security benefit the light might provide.

Parking

The most dangerous workplace location is the site where vehicles and pedestrians meet. It is imperative to include sufficient lighting, signage, and conditions (width of right-of-way, crosswalks, etc.) to minimize the possibility of threats to human health and safety. Monitoring is also useful, as parking areas are often locations that are accessible to the public and have been frequently used to stage criminal activity (workplace violence, robbery, rape, murder, etc.).

If the parking structure allows for entry to the facility, this entry should be equipped with access controls, and all entryways should feed to a single reception point within the facility.

Generators and fuel storage, as well as utility access (power lines, water/sewer pipes, etc.), should be protected from vehicular traffic, either with distance or with additional physical obstructions. There must be sufficient access for fuel delivery traffic, but this should be severely limited to reduce risk.

Facility Entrance

In addition to the other entrance controls already mentioned, the entry to the facility might include the following:

- **Reception staff:** This includes guards or administrative personnel who observe people entering and leaving the facility.

- **Logging:** This may be as technologically rudimentary as a sign-in book or combined with sophisticated badging/monitoring capabilities.

- **Flow control:** Turnstiles or other mechanisms ensure that only one person at a time can pass, typically only after presenting a credential (such as a badge or biometric element).

Internal Access Controls

In addition to the other access control elements used for maintaining physical control of the workplace environment listed elsewhere in the book, the security practitioner should be familiar with the following:

- **Safes:** Secure containers that can offer protection from unauthorized access, fire, water damage, and, in some cases, chemical contaminants. Both the safe itself and the lock on the safe should be rated by a standards body for specific criteria, according to the particular needs of the organization.

- **Secure processing areas:** Specific areas within the workplace that are set aside, both administratively, technically, and physically, from the rest of the production environment. These are typified by secure entryways, severe limitations on personnel access, hardened structures (walls, no windows, etc.), and electromagnetic shielding. In the U.S. government sphere, these are referred to as *sensitive compartmented information facilities* (SCIFs), and the term has taken on a wider general use.

The Data Center

As the focal point of the data assets of the organization, the data center is in particular need of protection within the property/facility. The data center also has some specific requirements that make it somewhat different than the rest of the production environment. In addition to the other access controls placed on secure areas within the workplace (discussed earlier in this chapter and Chapter 5), security of the data center should include consideration of the following factors:

- **Ambient temperature:** IT components generally function better in relatively cold conditions; if the area is too hot, the machines will not function optimally. However, if the area is too cold, it will cause discomfort for personnel.

- **Humidity:** An interior atmosphere that is too dry will increase the potential for electrostatic discharge. An atmosphere that is too damp will increase the potential for development of mold, mildew, and insects.

Standards for maintaining a desirable range of data center environmental conditions should be used to establish targets. One such reference is the ASHRAE Technical Committee 9.9 thermal guidelines for data centers; see `http://ecoinfo.cnrs.fr/IMG/pdf/ ashrae_2011_thermal_guidelines_data_center.pdf`.

The data center should also be designed, constructed, and equipped for resiliency, such that it is resistant to unplanned outages from human error/attack, system/component failure, or natural effects. This is typically accomplished by including a great deal of redundancy within the data center. The use of design standards to achieve a significant level of robustness and resiliency is highly recommended.

The Uptime Institute publishes a multi-tier standard for use by data center owners in determining and demonstrating their particular requirements and capabilities ("Data Center Site Infrastructure Tier Standard: Topology"; see `https://uptimeinstitute.com/ tiers`). The tiers range in purpose and requirements from basic data centers that might be used for archiving or occasional data storage to facilities that support life-critical processes. The CISSP should have a cursory knowledge of the four-tier levels and their descriptions. (For more information, see `https://journal.uptimeinstitute.com/explaining-uptime-institutes-tier-classification-system/`).

The standard is free for review/guidance; certification against the standard is, however, performed only by the Uptime Institute and requires payment.

Organizations that receive Uptime Institute tier certification for their data centers can be listed in the Institute's online register: `https://uptimeinstitute.com/TierCertification/allCertifications.php?page=1&ipp=All`.

Finally, fire poses a significant, common risk to data centers because of the high potential for occurrence and because of the disproportionately heavy impact a data center fire would have on the organization. Material related to fire suppression can be found in Chapter 3.

ADDRESS PERSONNEL SAFETY AND SECURITY CONCERNS

As stated previously, health and human safety are the paramount concerns of any security program. This book has included a great deal of information on this topic, including several different aspects found in the preceding chapters. This section will address two specific safety elements not contained elsewhere: personnel security while traveling and the use of duress codes.

Travel

When an employee has to travel for work, the organization has an obligation to ensure their safety. This can include extra medical coverage, insurance, and having defined emergency procedures. Employees should be aware of the risks associated with where they are going and both local emergency contact information and a means to contact the organization. Employees should be booked with a reputable travel agency and into facilities that are known to practice appropriate security. Employees should be warned about visiting public areas or being in the vicinity of demonstrations or unrest. Registering with the consulate or embassy of the employee's country of citizenship can assist in the event of problems.

In some cases, the employee should be provided a security escort or host who can look after the employee and assist when required. Regular contact should be maintained, and the employee should register their itinerary with their employer prior to departure. When driving in a foreign country, it may be advisable to hire the services of a local driver or guide.

Duress

When an employee is under duress, they may be forced to do something that they did not want to do. For example, when a person is a victim of a robbery, they are under duress and must cooperate with the thief or risk injury. Employees should be trained in how to handle a stressful situation and what to do when under duress. This may include having code words to alert others in the vicinity to a dangerous situation. When forced to open a combination (on a vault, for example), the employee may enter a duress code that would open the vault but still signal that the employee is being threatened and under duress.

Employees in high-security/risk roles and those traveling away from the workplace should also be trained in the use of verbal duress codes to covertly communicate when they are being threatened or acting against their will. Employees in contact with these personnel should be trained to recognize duress codes and the appropriate process for reporting receipt of a duress signal. Duress codes should typically be something easy to remember, not common in normal speech, but not so discordant as to immediately be recognized by antagonists when the code is transmitted. Duress codes should be changed at regular intervals, but older duress codes that are no longer current should also be treated as suitable for communicating emergencies, in the event an employee has forgotten the current code while in a stressful situation.

When an employee has been subject to duress, the organization should provide sufficient and specific support to the employee and allow them time to recover.

SUMMARY

The security practitioner is heavily involved in the organization's business processes and functions, in almost all areas. As security always has some deleterious effect on operations, these trade-offs of cost/benefit must always be considered, negotiated among the business units, and finally decided by management. The security officer must understand the business needs of the organization, as well as the comprehensive topics across all disciplines of the security field.

DOMAIN 8

Software Development Security

SOFTWARE DEVELOPMENT SECURITY IS a security discipline covering a variety of concerns. These concerns span the security of the development environment, software and component security, application security, and the secure development lifecycle. It is a necessary and essential part of an organization's overall security strategy. The world we live in has become a place that, more often than not, runs on software. Unfortunately, software contains vulnerabilities that present a variety of significant risks.

Software applications are increasingly becoming the vector of choice for attackers. As vendors harden their operating systems, the application stack, often developed by less security-aware developers, provides a broad attack surface for potential compromise. Securing something as pervasive and essential as software is a multilayered and multifaceted discipline. Software development security is about more than just the code.

This chapter is about software development security. It provides a comprehensive exposition of software development security. It describes how to integrate security into the software development lifecycle (SDLC). Securing the software development environment with necessary security controls is discussed. This chapter discusses ways to assess the effectiveness of software security, of software developed both in-house and elsewhere. Finally, this chapter goes through secure coding guidelines and standards.

UNDERSTAND AND INTEGRATE SECURITY IN THE SOFTWARE DEVELOPMENT LIFECYCLE

Software programs are fundamentally products of developers' thoughts. Consequently, it is necessary to formally assess and verify these thought products for their quality, their fidelity to their intended design and purpose, and their level of security in both composition and use.

To ensure these properties of quality and security, a variety of approaches exist. Different software development methodologies have evolved to achieve intentionally better outcomes, but with mixed results. Maturity models can be used to assess and compare the capability or maturity of processes important to an organization's success, including those related to the security of its software. After the development process, the front line of security is where software is put to use in operations and maintenance. Change management is another important aspect of the SDLC, since it is critical to the secure evolution of the software.

Ultimately, because software is an intellectual creation, the best and most secure practices of software development are found in how groups of contributors collaborate as an integrated product team.

Development Methodologies

Development methodologies involve and are informed by several different topics. First, the SDLC is a process-oriented approach to development. The SDLC answers how, at an organizational level, software development is done. Software development standards and practices are used to build security into the SDLC. Knowledge of the variety of different software language concepts provides the security practitioner with an informed perspective on the security of the software being built. This informed perspective is essential in understanding software security patterns and frameworks. A key success factor in software security is to use what works, and thus it is important for the security practitioner to know and understand these concepts.

Beyond the conceptual information just discussed, there are also a few topics that are important for the security practitioner to be aware of regarding how they influence aspects of a development methodology's security. These topics are distributed computing, artificial intelligence, and mobile applications and their ecosystems. All of these topics are explored in the following sections.

Software Development Lifecycle

The SDLC is a formalized model of the phases through which software progresses in the entirety of its lifespan. An SDLC describes stages that an organization uses in software management, from its initiation to the disposal of software. The exact details of an SDLC will differ from organization to organization. An organization will often choose an SDLC that meets its software development requirements.

Common SDLC phases are initiation, requirements, architecture, design, development, testing and validation, release and maintenance, and disposal.

Initiation

The initiation phase involves project conception and development of the business case. It is in the initiation phase that the viability of the software project is determined.

Requirements

In the requirements phase, the customer's requirements for working software are captured and documented. The requirements phase includes the gathering and documentation of overall system requirements as well, including the functional and nonfunctional requirements. Security requirements are gathered and documented in this phase.

Architecture

Although sometimes skipped or often combined with the design phase, the architecture phase is the time to build security into the architecture requirements of both the software development environment and the application to be built. The architecture should also align with the organization's architectural strategy. The architecture phase is your first line of defense in determining the technical security posture of the software application. On an architectural level, this phase offers the opportunity to conduct threat modeling to identify threats to the application, to apply security principles and controls to mitigate those threats, and to satisfy other security and nonfunctional requirements.

Design

In the design phase, the customer, application, and security requirements are translated into designs that ultimately can become working software. The design phase is the opportunity to build security into the software's blueprints. Threat modeling and abuse cases can be used to determine what needs to be protected in the application and then, after designs are made, to validate or improve the design and its selection of patterns and structures to mitigate these threats. Vulnerabilities found and fixed in the design phase are multiple times more cost-saving than remediation performed at later phases.

Development

The development phase is when the software's architecture and designs are translated into working software implemented in code. There are a number of essential practices to follow for security in the development phase. One is to follow the secure coding practices and conventions of your organization. Comprehensive testing should be used to verify and maintain an evolving baseline of correct functionality and security during ongoing development. Use frameworks, libraries, and patterns from trusted sources to enhance the security features and functionality of your application. Integrated development environments (IDEs) automate many of these features, making their use more natural in a developer's workflow.

Testing and Validation

The testing and validation phase formally amplifies the quality control measures utilized in the development phase. This phase employs comprehensive automated and manual testing and evaluation to determine whether the software meets its functional and nonfunctional requirements. Nonfunctional requirements are those that define the architectural and security qualities of the system being built, such as availability, scalability, maintainability, and the security control environment, to name a few. During this phase, comprehensive security testing is done, which commonly includes penetration testing, static and dynamic code testing, and customer acceptance testing. Preproduction testing prior to release is performed to determine the application's fitness for deployment to its production environment.

Release and Maintenance

After the software is deemed fit for use, the release and maintenance phase is when it goes into production. The security control requirements for releasing an application to production are much higher than those required to secure the development and test environments. Production releases are typically controlled ceremonies. During production deployment, an application must be protected from internal abuse, tampering, and mistakes as well as the potential abuses coming from the untrusted external environment. Maintenance covers ongoing bug fixes and future development.

Disposal

When the software reaches the end of its useful life, it is subject to the disposal phase. There are a number of key information security concerns in the disposal phase.

NIST SP 800-64 outlines the key security activities for this phase as follows:

- A transition plan for the software
- Archiving of critical information
- Sanitization of media
- Disposal of hardware and software

Software Development Methodologies

Software development methodologies are the conventional means and methods by which software is produced. How software is developed has a direct impact on how security is addressed in the development process. It is important for a security practitioner to be familiar with these methodologies to know when and how to engage to improve the security of each process.

Build and Fix

The build and fix software development method is also known as the *ad hoc model*. The SDLC of the build and fix method can be summed up by the following:

1. The software developer creates the first version of the program with a limited specification and design.
2. The software developer may sketch out a functional or technical design based on the needs of the customer.
3. From this initial product, the software is repeatedly modified until it satisfies the customer.

The build and fix method is arguably the simplest and least disciplined means of developing software. Where the real software development coding activities are concerned, build and fix can be considered hacking.

Nevertheless, the build and fix method may be useful for small software development where product quality is not important. For instance, build and fix can be used to explore and learn new software frameworks or technology quickly. Ordinary scripts, such as nondestructive utilities, written by experienced programmers could be created quickly by this method.

However, perhaps with exceptions for unimportant or trivial development, it is not a recommended software development practice. More often than not it leads to programs lacking in design quality, haphazard software construction, and customer dissatisfaction.

Moreover, if design is lacking, software security will be, too. The build and fix method is the least secure coding method because little or no attention is paid to secure coding methods, defensive programming, security controls, or the like. Poor design, haphazard development, and a lack of attention to secure coding practices become at best a software equivalent time bomb. The best practice is to discourage the use of build and fix.

Despite the undesirable outcomes, this method is one that many software developers use in their day-to-day practice. It is a method that can hide in a larger methodology when the disciplines of the larger methodology break down. When a waterfall process is driven by bureaucracy and its architecture and design artifacts are disregarded, software developers resort to ad hoc programming. When agile disciplines are not followed, software developers fall back on ad hoc programming.

Here are some things to watch out for when developers may have fallen back to a more build and fix method:

- No automated tests or a decrease in the number of them

- No testing code coverage or a widening gap in test code coverage

- Increased number of reported defects

- No team communication

- Increased customer dissatisfaction

Waterfall Method

The waterfall method provides a sequential, noniterative flow of software lifecycle phases through which software is constructed. Moreover, as progress through this model flows from high level to low, this one-way downward flow conceptually resembles a waterfall.

As Figure 8.1 shows, the waterfall model typically consists of the following phases:

- Requirements

- Design

- Implementation

- Testing

- Deployment

- Maintenance

However, there are variations on this model.

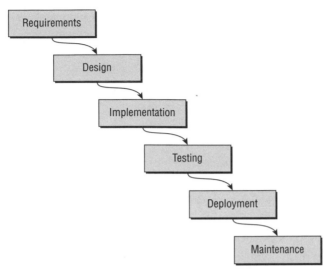

FIGURE 8.1 **The Waterfall Model**

The conclusion of each phase comes with a set of expectations that capture the activities of that phase. The system and software requirements phase activities are typically captured in requirements documents. The analysis ends with a refinement of requirements, with use cases, early models, schema definitions, and sometimes prototypes. The design phase refines the products of the analysis phase leading up to the development of overall software architecture as well as subsystem designs. The coding phase then takes that output and translates it into working software. Testing efforts discover flaws and defects that are to be resolved before the operations phase, which is when the software is deployed to production.

In theory, if one were to have full knowledge of every aspect of a project, the customer's needs and requirements, and the architecture and design that met those needs and was descriptive enough to translate into secure, bug-free code, then a hierarchical model like waterfall is perfect.

Some would argue that the waterfall method is superior for developing secure software, as more time is spent up front to discover all of the security requirements. This argument maintains that the concentration of efforts for each phase results in better requirements, designs, and secure bug-free code. These expectations are just not the case for many reasons, however.

It is not possible to know everything up front. Nor is it possible to know all of the vulnerabilities and threats to the software that is to be built.

The customer may not know what they want and will change their mind. With customer changes come changes to some aspect of the software. If the project team is lucky, then it is a change in the requirements phase, but often it is a change after the customer has the working software. When code changes come late in the process, they can introduce flaws or bugs that can lead to vulnerabilities.

Market awareness will change the features of the product. In this case, market awareness has two meanings. First, if the software is to be a commercial product, the sooner it gets tested by the market, the sooner it can be determined whether it will be successful or not.

Frontloading design effort takes away from software development and testing time. Formal definitions of waterfall have the phases' durations at set percentages of the project plan. Experience shows that these phases do not fit neatly into their time allocation buckets, and when requirements, analysis, and design take too much time, there's not enough time to do the actual work of creating and testing working software.

Long-duration discrete phases support bureaucracy, not communication. Overwrought process and bureaucracy are a pernicious drain on the viability and quality of a software project. When each phase creates its own set of artifacts for its purposes, often the needed communication between analysts, architects, risk management, developers, and quality assurance staff is lost.

The waterfall method is not good for software development with incomplete knowledge of what to build or where the requirements may change. It is not good for software development that is on tight timelines.

The main disadvantage of the waterfall method is its inability to adapt to new project information. It leads to a false sense of project schedule confidence because of how it cleanly maps to project planning, but does little to account for the changes that may come from the customer, market forces, or project capabilities.

Possible security advantages of the waterfall method come from the prescribed intensive activities to discover requirements and create designs, both of which are opportunities to include security concerns. Of course, this assumes that security is integrated into the methodology's processes.

Incremental Method

The incremental build model is characterized by a series of small, incremental development projects (see Figure 8.2). The structure of the incremental model begins with determining the business and system requirements. These are evaluated and prioritized at a high level to proceed with priority-based development. Subsequently, small development cycles are pursued, each working through design, development, testing, and implementation, toward the end of producing a small piece of the overall program. The intention of these incremental efforts is to lead up to the development of the complete system.

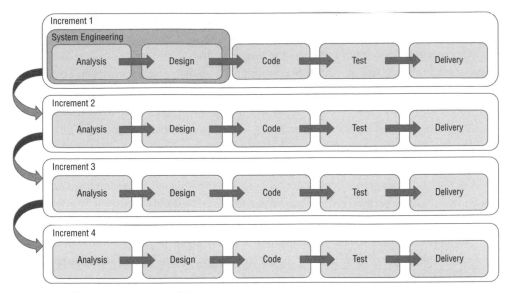

FIGURE 8.2 **The incremental model**

The incremental method is sometimes characterized as a repetitive mini-waterfall model, and it also shares a similarity with agile methods. Development is done in smaller, focused efforts. The software developed in each cycle is based on its importance and priority to the project. Customer feedback on what is being built is desired and welcomed. It is useful for projects that need a flexible scope.

There are drawbacks to the incremental model. Because it consists of a series of small development efforts leading up to completing the whole, a complete understanding of the ultimate product is needed. Having a complete picture of a project is not always a reasonable expectation. Furthermore, unless there is rigorous design discipline, the small incremental pieces may potentially lead to a fractured software architecture with each increment being a force that influences the overall architecture.

A security advantage of the incremental method is that the code delivered in each increment is smaller and more accessible to test and review.

Since each increment involves design, development, and testing, there's a risk that this method may miss a coherent security strategy for the product. The security professional should know how to introduce security requirements into the increments, leveraging the organization's security architecture and common controls.

Spiral Method

The spiral method is a model of progressive software development that repeatedly passes through phases of planning, risk analysis, engineering, and evaluation. The risk analysis phase considers risks to the project. The risk analysis phase is an improvement over other methods that don't take risk aspects as seriously.

It is considered a spiral model because progress through the model sweeps around and outward through the quadrants of planning, risk analysis, engineering, and evaluation repeatedly.

The spiral model is useful for projects that are complex, high risk, and expensive because of its repeated discipline of revisiting the four fundamental aspects of software development. The spiral model, by design, should catch changes or problems with each visit to each of its four phases.

The spiral model differs from waterfall because it revisits its phases repeatedly, thus allowing it to discover and be more responsive to project risks and changes. It is therefore considered an iterative model.

The spiral model is not the best choice for smaller projects because of the overhead of its repeated phases. It is an expensive model to support because of the expertise required to participate in each phase.

As security risk analysis can be incorporated into the spiral model's risk analysis phase, it has security advantages of discovering and adapting to risks and changes.

Cleanroom

The cleanroom model of software engineering is based on producing software with a certifiable level of reliability by avoiding software defects. It uses formal development practices and exhaustive inspection to achieve this goal. The objective of this approach is zero-defect software.

The cleanroom model assumes that more time spent in up-front software quality activities saves time spent in the later phases, such as testing and bug fixing. Quality is achieved through design, rather than testing and remediation.

An organization using cleanroom must have in place systematic design methods, formal inspection procedures, documented requirements in a natural language, developer-performed unit testing, configuration management of software after its release to the independent test organization, and ad hoc functional testing.

Essential characteristics of the cleanroom process are an incremental development lifecycle and independent quality assessment through statistical testing. Cleanroom can be used with waterfall, incremental, or spiral models to produce software of arbitrary size and complexity.

Stages of the cleanroom model are a formal specification, incremental development, structured programming, statistical verification, and statistical testing of the system. Project management decisions, such as the decision to stop testing and release the product, are based on objective information from the cleanroom's statistical measurement approach.

Disadvantages of the cleanroom model are the costs of the disciplined, requirements-intensive mathematical approach that may be too much overhead or creatively stifling for an organization. This is not a method that suits projects that need flexibility.

On the other hand, for organizations that require formal methods, the cleanroom can build in security and risk considerations early and reduce defects by early detection.

The cleanroom process is supported by Technical Report CMU/SEI-96-TR-022 ESC-TR-96-022: Cleanroom Software Engineering Reference Model Version 1.0.

Joint Application Development

Joint application development (JAD) is a methodology that involves the client or end user in the design and development of an application. The client or end user participates in collaborative workshops called JAD sessions.

The JAD model assumes that customer satisfaction at each stage is the most important objective.

JAD is used in projects that have the following characteristics:

- Involve many groups of users whose responsibilities cross traditional department or division boundaries

- Are considered critical to the future success of the organization

- Involve willing users

- Are first-time projects for the organization

- Have a troubled project history or relationship between the systems and user organizations

The structure of the JAD model includes phases such as planning/definition, preparation, design sessions, and finalization.

The JAD approach leads to shorter development lifecycles and greater client satisfaction because it draws users and information systems analysts together to jointly design systems in facilitated group sessions.

The JAD model is not efficient when requirements are to be finalized before moving on. Requirements are frequently changing with each JAD session. Other challenges are preparation costs, expertise requirements, and communication management.

The customer's early and ongoing involvement can improve software bug/vulnerability discovery, which reduces future project costs of quality assurance and defect management.

Rapid Application Development

The rapid application development (RAD) model is an iterative model that is based on prototyping. The RAD approach to software development de-emphasizes planning for the sake of development and producing working prototypes.

RAD was a response to the perceived deficiencies of waterfall processes. RAD emphasizes working software and user feedback over strict planning and requirements recording. The RAD model is used to deliver projects in shorter timeframes. Success with RAD requires having the users and budget to test prototypes thoroughly.

The RAD model works well for certain types of projects. RAD works well for projects with a focused scope, where the business objectives are well defined and narrow. The RAD model is useful for quickly generating working software and making measurable progress, rapid and constant user feedback, early systems integration, and adaptability.

The RAD model is not good for projects where the business objectives are obscure or broad. RAD also does not work well when there are many stakeholders involved in project decisions.

Agile

Agile is an iterative customer-value-centric approach to project management and software development. Agile helps teams deliver value to their customers faster and with fewer headaches. Unlike heavyweight, up-front planning approaches where software is released in "big bang" launches, an agile team delivers working software in small and manageable increments.

Agile emphasizes high-quality communication, technical discipline, and iterative development. Requirements and solutions evolve together through the collaborative efforts of self-organizing cross-functional teams. This collaboration prioritizes delivering the highest-value and highest-risk features through working software. Agile compresses the waterfall phases into a disciplined workflow process that is repeated in time-boxed, iterative intervals. Working software is repeatedly produced through these iterations until the product is completed or the project stops.

This section will explore various facets of the agile methodology.

Agile Manifesto and Principles

The Agile Manifesto, also called the Manifesto for Agile Software Development, is a formal proclamation of values and principles to guide an iterative and people-centric approach to software development. The manifesto prioritizes collaboration, interaction, software functionality, and responding to change, while still recognizing the importance of documentation, contracts, planning, and processes.

The principles behind the Agile Manifesto, commonly referred to as the 12 agile principles, are a set of guiding concepts that support project teams in implementing agile projects. Agile principles allow people to accommodate changing requirements throughout the development process, ensuring frequent delivery of working software. Attention to technical detail and design can enhance the security of the software.

Security practitioners generally want a solid design before building a product begins, thorough documentation, and accurate risk assessment. Some security professionals are skeptical that the agile methodology has ramifications for software development security, particularly due to automation, emphasis on testing, the focus on good builds, and continuous integration and deployment. However, many dedicated and experienced agile professionals work hard to establish security as a core competency in the organization's application of the 12 agile principles.

✔ Principles behind the Agile Manifesto

According to `http://agilemanifesto.org/principles.html`, the Manifesto for Agile Development states the following 12 principles:

- Our highest priority is to satisfy the customer through early and continuous deployment of valuable software.

- Welcome changing requirements, even late in development. Agile processes harness change for the customer's competitive advantage.

- Deliver working software frequently, from a couple of weeks to a couple of months, with a preference to the shorter timescale.

- Businesspeople and developers must work together daily throughout the project.

- Build projects around motivated individuals. Give them the environment and support they need and trust them to get the job done.

- The most efficient and effective method of conveying information to and within a development team is face-to-face conversation.

- Working software is the primary measure of progress.

- Agile processes promote sustainable development. The sponsors, developers, and users should be able to maintain a constant pace indefinitely.

- Continuous attention to technical excellence and good design enhances agility.

- Simplicity—the art of maximizing the amount of work not done—is essential.

- The best architectures, requirements, and designs emerge from self-organizing teams.

- At regular intervals, the team reflects on how to become more effective and then tunes and adjusts its behavior accordingly.

8

SOFTWARE DEVELOPMENT SECURITY

Automation

A good rule of thumb with automation is that if you perform a task more than three times, consider automating it. Many tasks and processes are involved in producing quality functional software. Automation enables consistent and thorough processing. Automation is a cornerstone process enabler. The more tasks and processes are automated, the less their burden is on the developer, the more consistent their execution becomes, and the less likely mistakes will occur. Reducing human error goes a long way to reducing security vulnerabilities. The less human involvement in software development is, the greater the control over the process is.

Automation integrates security into the development process. Security testing and scanning can be automated. Automation makes security testing and scanning a routine process. It enables a routine delivery of actionable results for the developers to respond.

Emphasis on Testing

Agile development recognizes that testing is not a separate phase but an integral part of software development, along with coding. Testing and coding are done incrementally and interactively, building up each feature until it provides enough value to release to production.

As one of its core values, agile embraces change. However, every code change is a new potential bug or vulnerability. The most effective way to prevent this is by thorough software testing. Agile processes use many types of testing, such as unit, functional, integration, and regression. Security testing and scanning are part of agile testing.

Testing promotes agility and production speed. When automated, testing continually validates the functional and security states of an application as new code is produced. Automation allows continuous regression testing to determine if the current code has created bugs or vulnerabilities. This helps maintain a predictable quality of the product's working software and code.

Agile Lava Lamp, aka Focus on Good Builds

Working software is a core agile value. Automated comprehensive testing is a core agile practice. Tests should verify the working software. When developers check code that causes tests to fail or the software build process to break, it is important to fix the problem before proceeding. A conspicuous signal can be set up in the office to show the build's status. This signal is sometimes referred to as the *agile lava lamp*.

This focus on maintaining good builds is essential to maintaining the speed of delivery. A good build is one that was produced that has passed all of the quality and security checks and has been verified as good to use. A good build supports the agile directives for frequent delivery of working software, continuous attention to technical excellence, and good design. A good build is produced by testing to validate its security. This process is automated.

When security testing and verification are built into the build process, the agile lava lamp, or its equivalent, becomes a form of automated secure software assurance.

Continuous Integration/Continuous Deployment (CI/CD)

Continuous integration (CI) is the practice of merging all developer working copies to a shared mainline. CI involves integrating early and often to minimize code incompatibilities. CI aims to reduce rework and thus reduce project cost and time.

Agile teams, because they are producing working code each iteration, need to avoid the time and effort involved with diff resolution and debugging sessions that often occur at the end of long integration cycles. And, the more programmers who work on the code, the more problematic this is. Furthermore, agile teams routinely deliver working software with a progressive number of features completed. CI supports these development process requirements.

Continuous deployment (CD) extends continuous integration by deploying the products of CI into a production environment. This method requires a high degree of maturity in automation in quality assurance and security testing. CD significantly removes human controls from deploying production software. Because of this, it may not be compatible with an SDLC that is subject to regulatory restrictions.

Agile Methodology Practices

These are some of the more popular agile methodology practices:

- Dynamic systems development method (DSDM)
- Scrum
- Extreme programming (XP)
- Test-driven development (TDD)
- Lean software development
- Minimum viable product (MVP)

DYNAMIC SYSTEMS DEVELOPMENT METHOD

DSDM is an organized, commonsense process focused on delivering business solutions quickly and efficiently. It is an iterative, incremental approach that is primarily based on the rapid application development methodology. DSDM focuses on the delivery of the business solution, rather than just team activity. It takes steps to ensure the feasibility and business sense of a project before it is created.

SCRUM

Scrum is a framework through which people can employ various techniques to solve complex problems and continuously and incrementally deliver valuable products. The Scrum framework uses an empirical process to use a team's and its customers' experiences as a driver to make decisions for change to or improvement of a product, workflow, team, or the like. Scrum takes an iterative and incremental approach to optimize processes and outcomes and control risk.

The scrum team participates in scrum ceremonies to continually make progress toward its goals. The scrum team consists of three roles: the scrum master, the product owner, and the development team. Scrum teams self-organize and have cross-functional capabilities. Cybersecurity governance and security engineering roles can add their expertise to a scrum team's cross-functional capabilities.

Scrum is designed to work with smaller teams with no more than 10 members. If the number of members increases, multiple teams can work on the same project. The scrum of scrums is a technique to operate scrum at scale, with multiple teams working on the same product; it allows them to discuss progress on their interdependencies and focus on how to coordinate delivering software, especially on areas of overlap and integration.

The scrum framework has the following events:

- **Sprint:** The sprint is time-boxed project time. The sprint is when development work is done to create working software. Sprint planning, daily scrum, sprint review, and sprint retrospective are also part of the sprint. A sprint can range from one week to one month. Any changes to the sprint's goals or conditions are avoided if possible. Sprints contain project risks of development to the time period of the sprint, which should not be more than one month.

- **Sprint planning:** Sprint planning is when the work is chosen, goals for the sprint are agreed upon by the team, and the team organizes to achieve the goals.

- **Daily scrum:** The daily scrum is the daily event of the sprint when the team reviews sprint goal progress and impediments and plans development until the next daily scrum.

- **Sprint review:** The sprint review is conducted at the end of the sprint and reconciles the new work done on the product backlog.

- **Sprint retrospective:** The sprint retrospective is conducted at the end of the sprint, and it is a time for the sprint team to conduct a critical but friendly self-analysis to find opportunities to improve.

Scrum also includes what it calls *artifacts*, which are the product backlog, sprint backlog, and the increment. The product backlog is the most comprehensive set of requirements for a product as possible at the time. The product backlog is an ordered list of product features and requirements. Ordering is based on the priority and the project risk that the feature presents. The sprint backlog consists of highest-priority/highest-risk features picked from the product backlog to deliver in the sprint as the increment. The increment is the working software that is produced based on implementing the sprint backlog.

The definition of "done" is important in scrum because it is necessary for the whole team to have an understanding of the conditions required of a unit of working software to be present for it to be complete. Security engineering features, security controls, security testing and scanning activities, and similar security concerns can be added to the definition of "done" to establish baseline security requirements for working software delivery.

As an empirical framework, scrum accommodates security concerns well. As mentioned previously, the definition of "done" can be enhanced with requirements for security engineering, controls, scanning, and testing.

The scrum team should have a security-trained resource to maintain team awareness of security concerns and topics related to the product and to work with developers to mitigate risks present in the application by use of secure coding techniques and resources.

Sprint planning can include threat modeling and abuse case activities to identify threats and attackers. Security requirements are formed around these threats and attackers and the protection needs of the product. The development team can organize their efforts to produce secure code around these security requirements. Daily scrums can include monitoring the progress toward implementing secure code as a peer to the feature development. Sprint reviews can include security testing and scanning results review.

EXTREME PROGRAMMING (XP)

Extreme programming (XP) is an agile software development framework that aims for high software quality and responsiveness to changing customer requirements. XP is the most specific of the agile frameworks regarding appropriate engineering practices for software development. XP was created by Kent Beck during his work on the Chrysler Comprehensive Compensation System (C3) payroll project.

XP advocates the paired programming experience in which two programmers work together. XP asserts that the code quality improves beyond the additional cost of the paired programmer. XP focuses on frequent "releases" in short development cycles, which is intended to improve productivity and introduce checkpoints at which new customer requirements can be adopted. XP plays a "planning game" every iteration in which both release planning and iteration planning are conducted. XP relies on continuous integration and test-driven development to routinely produce working software.

XP is really about bringing efficiency in the coding process and providing customers with maximum value. XP can be summed up by its components, listed here:

- **Planning games:** Quickly determine the scope of the next iteration by taking into consideration business priorities and estimates.

- **Small releases:** Deliver quickly and early by having short iterations, first creating a minimum marketable feature and releasing new versions based on feedback.

- **Metaphors:** Guide development using a simple shared story to eliminate technical talk.

- **Simple design:** Have a just-enough design policy (i.e., the exact specifications just for that story). Extra complexity is removed once discovered.

- **Testing:** Develop test cases first, then code to test cases, and then automate test cases.

- **Pair programming:** Have two developers working on one story, where one drives and the other navigates, with them continuously switching roles.

- **Refactoring:** Restructure complex/poor structured code without affecting behavior. This aims to remove duplication, simplify, or add flexibility.

- **Collective code ownership:** Anyone works on any code to avoid knowledge silos, which results in high-quality code.

- **Continuous integration:** Automate builds and tests so the system is checked every time a task is completed.

- **40-hour workweek:** Have no overtime to enable long-term productivity and predictable results.

- **On-site customer/whole team:** Have a product owner/business/real-life user on the team to answer questions.

- **Coding standards:** Strictly adhere to code standards with rules that emphasize communication through code.

XP's emphasis on pair programming and extensive code review, as well as unit testing of all code, improves security outcomes by improving code quality. Defects are caught and fixed sooner. As a security practitioner, you should further improve security outcomes by partnering with the developers to educate them on common application security issues, sharing Open Web Application Security Project (OWASP) security guidelines for the languages and frameworks they use. An emphasis on code simplicity and clarity improves the understandability, which improves the software's security.

XP strictly adheres to code standards with rules that emphasize communication through code. Code is more important than design in XP, and that may be a problem.

Good design improves quality and reduces bugs and security vulnerabilities in software applications.

However, in XP projects, the defect documentation is not always good. Lack of defect documentation may lead to the occurrence of similar bugs in the future.

TEST-DRIVEN DEVELOPMENT (TDD)

Test-driven development (TDD) is a software development process where code-level testing, also known as *unit testing*, guides software design and implementation. It is based on the repetition of an extremely short development cycle: write a test, run tests, write code, run tests until it passes, refactor, then repeat.

TDD has the following steps:

1. Add a test.
2. Run all tests and see if the new test fails.
3. Write the code.
4. Run all the tests.
5. Refactor the code.

This cycle of writing the test first, running the test, and then writing the code may seem strange at first glance. How do you know what test to write when you haven't written the code yet? TDD uses unit tests as stepping stones for incremental design. Similar to how the requirements drive software design, by this philosophy the requirements drive the test design, which then acts as an incremental target state for small units of code to achieve.

When followed correctly, the benefits of TDD are significant. Throughout the development process, all code will have tests and will be tested. The body of tests created for TDD are run each time new tests and code are developed, acting like an incremental regression test. Contemplate the implications of this through a security lens. All code changes made with TDD are tested both for their own functionality as well as for the functionality of the whole codebase of which they are a part. This naturally leads to fewer flaws and defects in the software.

Tests can be added to verify code-level security controls. These security control tests and the results of their execution can be used as material for contributing to a security control verification process. By providing evidence of code-level control verification, TDD can benefit organizations with regulatory and compliance requirements for controls.

Because each code change in TDD is small, incremental, and tested, developers can produce higher-quality software code more quickly. TDD can help developers find defects, bugs, and vulnerabilities much earlier than they otherwise would. Despite the additional testing code to be written, TDD has a positive impact on development velocity.

TDD requires discipline, however. TDD requires up-front time and effort investments in additional test code writing, which can make development feel slow. Oversimplification of design can lead to significant refactoring requirements.

Tests become part of the maintenance overhead of a project. Poorly written tests, for example ones that include hard-coded error strings or are themselves prone to failure, are expensive to maintain. Tests need to be routinely evaluated for their correctness.

If the software design changes rapidly, you'll need to keep adding and changing your tests. You could end up wasting a lot of time writing tests for features that are quickly dropped.

TDD is designed to work with small to large organizations. Exercising TDD on large, challenging systems requires a modular architecture, distinct components with published interfaces, and disciplined system layering with maximization of platform independence. These proven practices yield increased testability and facilitate the application of build and test automation.

TDD is a method that is sure to improve code quality. It requires up-front investment and discipline and doesn't necessarily work for every type of project, but it is a methodology that can improve the quality and security of an organization's software development practice.

LEAN SOFTWARE DEVELOPMENT

Building commercial software is an experience that is based on best guesses and one that is riddled with expensive mistakes. Agile methodologies were presented to improve this situation through empirical and adaptive means. One significant source of expensive mistakes in software development is waste. Building the wrong thing, basing the build on the wrong requirements, or producing something the market does not need or want are all wastes. Low-quality software engineering, done in haste or incompletely, is waste. Overlooking security as a necessary product capability is a waste that brings unknown future consequences and damages. Waste in software development needs to be eliminated. This is where lean software development works.

Lean software development has its roots in the lean manufacturing principles and practices of the Toyota Manufacturing Process. The principles and practices of the Toyota Manufacturing Process are based on eliminating three kinds of deterrents to an efficient production system: overburden, inconsistency, and waste.

Eliminating overburden is achieved by a realistic standardization of the workflow. Inconsistency in this system is eliminated by a "just-in-time" pull system for parts that stops manufacturing to fix defects in the process at the time of discovery. Waste is eliminated by recognizing it by type and efficiently dealing with it.

The waste of making defective products perhaps is the most harmful waste in software development. Not engineering security into the product is by outcome creating a defective product. Lean manufacturing principles and practices inspired lean software development to fix these wastes. Lean software development is an adaptation of that process with its principles and practices.

The lean software development principles are as follows:

- Eliminate waste.
- Amplify learning.
- Decide as late as possible.
- Deliver as quickly as possible.
- Empower the team.
- Build integrity in.
- See the whole.

Lean thinking has to be understood well by all members of a project before implementing in a concrete, real-life situation. "Think big, act small, fail fast, learn rapidly" are slogans that summarize lean principles along the whole software development process. Only when all of the lean principles are implemented together, combined with strong "common sense" concerning the working environment and an emphasis on security, is there a basis for success in software development.

Success in lean software development depends on the team's discipline and practices. A great deal of responsibility and flexibility is given over to the team. The team must strive for technical and security excellence to achieve secure working software development. As a security professional, you need to focus the team on building the necessary security capabilities into the product.

MINIMUM VIABLE PRODUCT (MVP)

Minimum viable product (MVP) is a product and development style that produces just enough features to satisfy early customers and enough to provide feedback for directing future product development. The primary driver of MVP is to learn and adapt a product to meet market needs through small and incremental hypothesis testing and feedback on your product without fully developing it. This gets the right product feature set to market faster and cheaper, or not at all if the MVP shows no market interest. The process reduces wastes of time, money, and development effort on undesirable features. MVP is an iterative, data-driven approach that relies on many of the facilities of agile methods to produce, test, validate, and direct the minimum viable product.

Security must be a consideration in MVP. Security controls and secure coding practice may be overlooked in MVP for the sake of delivering customer-oriented features. As a security professional, it is crucial that you identify and communicate the necessary secure coding practices, security frameworks, and controls required for a safe and secure MVP. Don't let MVP become "minimum viable functionality" without security.

When keeping security in mind as part of MVP, the MVP process becomes a security advantage. One of the MVP process's security advantages is the adaptability it encourages. If there is an error or some development that does not meet a market need, it can be corrected quickly and at any time in the project.

Standards and Practices

A security professional should be familiar with the standards and practices that apply to securing the SDLC. There is a range of SDLC standards, each with its own set of phases. Because of the variety of standards and their differences, there are a couple of things you should keep in mind. First, in relationship to the CISSP, you should know the vendor-neutral standards. As a security professional, you should know the general lifecycle phases that cover complete, end-to-end security of the SDLC. For this, consider using the standards guidance that best meets the needs of your organization.

The following sections explore ISO/IEC and NIST standards, as well as the process of the Microsoft Security Development Lifecycle (SDL).

ISO/IEC 27034:2011+, "Information Technology – Security Techniques – Application Security"

The ISO/IEC standards offer the security practitioner guidance on many aspects of information security. This standard, "ISO/IEC 27034:2011+ Information technology – Security techniques – Application security," describes how to integrate application security into an SDLC. It presents a process-oriented approach intended to work generally with any SDLC methodology.

This standard has seven parts, each one addressing a particular aspect of application security. Part 1 of this standard, "Information technology – Security techniques – Application security – Overview and concepts," sets the foundation for the standard and defines its overall use as general guidance for application security. Application security is described as a process that can be used to select, set, and manage controls to manage application risks. It defines terms and describes concepts, principles, and processes for subsequent parts of the standard.

Part 2 of this standard, "Information technology – Security techniques – Application security – Organization normative framework," proposes a structure to maintain and orchestrate the elements of application security in a manner that enables an organization to best adapt it to their needs. This Organization Normative Framework (ONF) describes the processes required for application security and the relationships among these security processes. It is a guide for an organization to create and manage its own ONF. Its structure is best suited for organizations with a need for a more formalized application security management.

Part 3 of this standard, "Information technology – Security techniques – Application security – Application security management process," describes an application security management process that uses the ONF to tailor security management for specific applications.

Part 4 of this standard is titled "ISO/IEC 27034-4 – Information technology – Security techniques – Application security – Application security validation (draft)." When this draft is complete, it will describe a validation and certification process for application security. The standard defines a concept called *levels of trust* to describe an application's risk and control profile. In a validation and certification process, an application level of trust can be used to measure and compare an application's risk and control requirements against an application's actual risk and control profile as determined by an audit.

Part 5 of this standard, "ISO/IEC 27034-5:2017 – Information technology – Security techniques – Application security – Protocols and application security control data structure," defines a data structure known as the Application Security Control (ASC). The ASC data structure serves as a basis for the description and communication of application security control components. This section also describes the Application Security Life Cycle Reference Model.

Part 6 of this standard, "ISO/IEC 27034-6:2016 – Information technology – Security techniques – Application security – Case studies," gives examples on how to use Application Security Controls in the software development process.

Part 7 of this standard, "ISO/IEC 27034-7:2018 – Information technology – Security techniques – Application security – Assurance prediction framework," focuses on a framework to determine what the standard calls the *security predictability* of an application based on various security-impacting aspects related to its realization and usage.

For more information on ISO/IEC 27034:2011+, "Information technology – Security techniques – Application security," see `http://iso27001security.com/html/27034.html`.

ISO/IEC JTC 1/SC7, "Software and Systems Engineering Standards"

The SC7 is a standards subcommittee of the ISO/IEC Joint Technical Committee (JTC) whose focus is on software and systems engineering standards. The ISO/IEC JTC SC7 software and systems engineering standards are an integrated set of software and systems engineering standards that focus on process models and practices to support the full lifecycle of a system. As such, the SC7 set of standards can be considered a reference shelf of standards guidance for software and systems engineering. Some of the standards of interest to software security practitioners included in the SC7 domain are ISO/IEC ISO/IEC 12207, "Systems and software engineering – Software lifecycle processes," 15288:2015,

"Systems and Software Engineering – System Life Cycle Processes," as well ISO/IEC TR 15504 "Information technology – Process assessment."

ISO 12207-2017

ISO/IEC/IEEE 12207:2017, "Systems and software engineering – Software lifecycle processes," establishes a common framework for software lifecycle processes. It applies to the full lifecycle of a software system. ISO 12207:2017 provides processes that can be used for defining, controlling, and improving software lifecycle processes within an organization or a project. It can be used by itself or in conjunction with ISO/IEC/IEEE 15288. It describes how to align the activities of participants of the SDLC, including developers, managers, architects, project management, and quality assurance. One of its main goals is to make possible effective communication among these stakeholders. Management and software lifecycle process leadership may refer to this standard for guidance on a framework of processes for a comprehensive organizational software development capability. The security practitioner would use this standard to frame the necessary security activities for each lifecycle, supporting, and organizational process.

ISO/IEC/IEEE 12207:2017 has three process groups:

- **Primary lifecycle processes:** Acquisition, Supply, Development, Operation, Maintenance, and Destruction

- **Supporting lifecycle processes:** Audit Process, Configuration Management, Joint Review Process, Documentation Process, Quality Assurance Process, Problem Solving Process, Verification Process, and Validation Process

- **Organizational processes:** Management Process, Infrastructure Management, Improvement Process, and Training Process

ISO/IEC/IEEE 15288:2015

ISO/IEC/IEEE 15288:2015, "Systems and Software Engineering – System Life Cycle Processes," is an international standard that establishes a common framework of processes that describe the lifecycle of systems. This framework defines its processes by four different categories: technical, project, agreement, and enterprise. Management and systems process leadership would use this standard as a reference for a (or the) common systems engineering process framework. This standard can be used with ISO/IEC/IEEE 12207:2017, as software lifecycle processes are components of the system engineering lifecycle. A security practitioner would use this standard to understand the process lifecycle of developing complex systems as well as a reference to identify necessary security activities throughout the systems engineering lifecycle.

ISO/IEC TR 15504

ISO/IEC TR 15504, "Information technology – Process assessment," is a set of standards that serve to describe a reference model for maturity models. This standard can be used as a reference to create or validate a maturity model used to evaluate the software and systems engineering lifecycle processes. The security practitioner can use it as a reference to ensure that consideration of the security activities are included in the capability and maturity assessment of security processes.

NIST SP800-64 Revision 2

NIST Special Publication 800-64, "Revision 2: Security Considerations in the System Development Life Cycle," is a standard intended to guide the introduction of essential security services into the established system development lifecycle. Although this is a U.S. federal government standard, use of this special publication guidance has many benefits to any organization.

The standard establishes a baseline understanding of cybersecurity and the system development lifecycle. It uses a typical SDLC that includes five phases: initiation, development/acquisition, implementation/assessment, operations/maintenance, and disposal. It describes the major security activities and control gates that apply in general as well as to each SDLC phase.

NIST SP800-64 Revision 2 describes controls, processes, people, and other considerations that help integrate security into each phase of the SDLC. Security controls are assumed to align with the NIST SP800-53 standard. Included in this guidance are the roles and responsibilities of whom to involve in securing each phase.

The "Additional Security Considerations" section of the standard highlights security considerations for development scenarios, such as service-oriented architectures and virtualization, for which the approach to security integration varies somewhat from that of traditional system development efforts.

NIST SP800-64 Revision 2 recommends addressing security vulnerabilities early to lower costs and improve security posture. It also directs attention to areas where security services and strategies can be reused to improve security coverage and reduce development costs. The standard addresses the engineering challenges caused by mandatory security controls. Adding a security emphasis throughout the SDLC improves systems interoperability and integration that would otherwise be hampered by securing systems at various system levels. Comprehensive documentation of security decisions made during development, as well as other phases, improves security integration in the SDLC. Adding security to the SDLC ultimately improves organization and customer confidence.

To read the standard, see `https://doi.org/10.6028/NIST.SP.800-64r2`.

Microsoft Security Development Lifecycle

The Microsoft SDL is a software development process that helps developers build more secure software and address security compliance requirements while reducing development cost. It prescribes best practices, processes, standards, security activities, and tools in an approach to implement an SDL program.

The SDL is intended for use by a variety of different organizations of different sizes and capabilities. It includes an optimization model to guide SDL adoption and practice maturity improvements. Security roles and responsibilities are outlined.

The SDL is designed to apply to a standard development lifecycle as well as to an agile approach. It maps security activities to software development phases. The software development phases covered by the SDL are training, requirements, design, implementation, verification, release, and response.

The SDL has 17 mandatory SDL activities that are required practice to prove compliance with the program. These practices are grouped by how they apply to different software development phases. Each practice consists of references, materials, and training to support its focus. Guidance is given on when to apply each practice to either a traditional SDLC phase or an aspect of an agile practice. Agile methodology is further discussed in the "Software Development Methodologies" section of this chapter.

Microsoft SDL practices per phase are shown in Table 8.1.

TABLE 8.1 Microsoft Secure Development Lifecycle Practices per Phase

PHASE	SDL ACTIVITY
Training	
	1. Core Security Training
Requirements	
	2. Establish Security and Privacy Requirements
	3. Create Quality Gates/Bug Bars
	4. Perform Security and Privacy Risk Assessments
Design	
	5. Establish Design Requirements
	6. Attack Surface Analysis/Reduction
	7. Use Threat Modeling

PHASE	SDL ACTIVITY
Implementation	
	8. Use Approved Tools
	9. Deprecate Unsafe Functions
	10. Perform Static Analysis
Verification	
	11. Perform Dynamic Analysis
	12. Fuzz Testing
	13. Attack Surface Review
Release	
	14. Create an Incident Response Plan
	15. Conduct Final Security Review
	16. Certify Release and Archive
Response	
	17. Execute Incident Response Plan

The SDL also recommends optional security practices whose performance should be considered with critical security software. Some examples of these optional practices are manual code reviews, penetration testing, and vulnerability analysis of related software.

The standard has an Application Security Verification Process. Having a systematic SDLC security practice is one thing, proving that it is being followed is much better. Microsoft's SDL includes requirements and direction to verify that the SDL is being performed in its Application Security Verification Process. This process describes the processes and actors, the data collection, and supportive elements to verify that the SDL is being followed.

Microsoft's SDL is useful for addressing compliance requirements with a proactive and future proofing approach designed to address ever-changing regulations. Adherence to the program lowers the total cost of development as well. Finding and fixing vulnerabilities early, for instance in the design phase, is significantly more cost-effective than doing the same during the testing phase.

For more information about the SDL, see `https://www.microsoft.com/en-us/sdl`.

Software Language Concepts

Programming languages are the means by which correlated sets of instructions are written to produce programs that can be executed by a computer. Programming language grammar consists of symbols that describe different data types, methods to create and manipulate data, and logical structures that can control the flow of execution of the program.

Language Types

There are two types of software languages: compiled and interpreted. Each language type has security implications for the software that it is used to produce.

Compiled

Compiled languages are those where the program instructions are translated into a form that is directly interpretable by the machine. A program called a compiler does this translation. An advantage of compiled languages is that the compiler is typically optimized for the target hardware. And because of this translation into a machine code, compiled languages typically execute faster than interpreted languages.

Compiled languages have many features that support security. The compilation process checks the program structure for correctness. A security type system can be employed at compile time to enforce information flows to verify or report violations of confidentiality or integrity. It is possible to generate a certificate during compilation as a form of proof that the source code was compiled following a set of rules that satisfies a security policy.

Interpreted

An interpreted programming language is one where most of its code is executed directly without first having to compile it into machine-language instructions. Many developers favor interpreted languages for how quickly they can be used to write programs. Many are easy to learn and powerful.

There are potential security trade-offs with the speed and facility that come with using an interpreted language. Interpreted languages do not come with the up-front benefits of program correctness, type checking, and security policy verification that compiled languages do. Securing interpreted languages requires layering extra efforts to the development done in the interpreted language, including automated and comprehensive testing, scanning, security testing, and code reviews. These practices are all part of the security of software development; however, interpreted languages increase the necessity of their use. However, even with the best testing, there's no guarantee that the low-level language aspects are correctly aligned without checking.

Type Checking

Regardless of the language used, all programs deal with data, and they generally distinguish data by categorizing it into different types. Each data type has formats, memory sizes, and conversion rules. All data types are not the same. For instance, an integer and a "string" are two different data types. These two data types have different underlying memory structures that require a translation when converting or comparing between them.

Type checking is the process of verifying and enforcing constraints of data types. Type safety is the aspect of type checking that prohibits data stored in incompatible data types from being transferred from one data type to the other. Even assigning similar data types needs to be checked if their sizes do not match; after all, variables do have to live in memory. Trying to store a 4-byte field (long integer) into a 2-byte field (short integer) simply will not fit into the memory allocated, and it will overflow the space.

Type checking can occur either at compile time or at runtime. Type checking that happens at compile time is known as *static type checking*. Type checking that occurs at runtime is known as *dynamic type checking*.

- Static type checking is when a programming language knows the data type of variables at compile time. The data type can be either specified in code or derived by type inference. Static type checking is done by the compiler, and therefore bugs related to incompatible data types can be caught in the compile stage.

- Dynamic type checking determines the data type based on the runtime values of variables and not by any specified data type.

Some languages have type ambiguity. Some scripting languages interpret the value null, 0, and the empty string, all as being false. This is a potential cause of logic or program errors.

Language Generations

Computer languages have come a long way since the early 1940s and the first general-purpose digital electronic computer, the Electronic Numerical Integrator and Computer (ENIAC). There are five generations of computer languages:

- **1GL:** This first-generation language is machine code. Machine code is a binary series of ones and zeros that the machine would read and run directly. Because it was machine code, it was specific to the computer and couldn't be ported to other computers. Machine code is complicated to edit and update. The code was installed on the computer via punch cards, punch tape, or by setting switches.

- **2GL:** Assembly language is the second-generation programming language (2GL). Mnemonic labels in place of binary machine instructions made assembly more accessible for the programmer to use.

- **3GL:** Third-generation programming languages (3GL) are the general-purpose programming languages that developers use. 3GLs introduce conditional statements, looping structures, expanded label naming, structures, and classes. Third-generation programming languages are significantly more useful and powerful for the programmer. Another 3GL improvement is that the code became machine independent. Interpreters and compilers stepped into the role of translating 3GLs into machine code. They also enabled structured programming and object-oriented programming. Examples of 3GLs are Fortran, COBOL, C, C++, and Java.

- **4GL:** Fourth-generation languages (4GL) are designed to build specific programs. 4GLs are considered to be a subset of domain-specific languages, which are computer languages that are specialized to a particular domain. Some examples of the domains that 4GLs inhabit are database management, web development, GUI development, and report generation. Examples of 4GLs are the Structured Query Language (SQL), ColdFusion Markup Language (CFML), XML User Interface Language (XUL), and Oracle Reports.

- **5GL:** A fifth-generation programming language (5GL) is designed to solve problems independent of the programmer providing the logic. Fifth-generation languages execute and solve problems based on information provided them. 5GLs are mainly used in artificial intelligence research. Prolog is an example of a 5GL.

The higher the level of a language the greater its level of abstraction and the more complex its systems interactions. Understanding the level of language can be useful when considering code review and similar security-related concerns.

Programming Paradigms

Different styles of programming give programmers a variety of different strategies and tools to solve the problems for which they write the code. It is important for a security professional to be familiar with these paradigms to be able to infer the security benefits or the impact of its use.

- **Imperative:** Imperative programming is a paradigm that describes how a program operates. It does this by using an explicit sequence of statements that update the state of a program. Program correctness, or how well the program executes its logic to satisfy its purpose, depends upon the sequence of its code. In the imperative programming paradigm, security comes in both the correctness of logic and how secure coding patterns and idioms are insinuated in the program's logical flow.

- **Procedural:** Procedural programming languages group common logic together in functions, enhancing their modularity and cohesiveness. Programs then access that functionality using procedure calls. Security in the procedural paradigm is similar to imperative programming in that the structure and how security is embedded in the software structure are important. Of particular concern in procedural programming is how well the software logic is decomposed into functions. How this is done is beyond the scope of this book, but the specificity of logic and the number of lines of code in the functions affects its inherent risk to the overall program by affecting the complexity, maintainability, and defect likelihood within its code.

- **Declarative:** Declarative programming describes what a program should do and not how it should do it. Declarative languages such as Prolog or SQL let the programmer code by specifying the desired result. Although declarative programming removes the details of how the result is obtained, that does not mean it is without security considerations. Input validation and sanitization is a security concern that should be layered onto the declarative programming environment.

- **Logic:** Logic programming is also known as rule based and is a paradigm based on specifying a set of facts and rules in a knowledge base. An engine infers the answers based on the outcome of the relationships between the facts and rules. Security in the logic programming environment should concentrate on input validation and sanitization as well as minimizing program defects. However, another security consideration is the languages that implement logic programming. These languages weren't necessarily created for general-purpose commercial use.

- **Symbolic:** Symbolic programming is a paradigm in which the program can manipulate its own source code to create new functions and logic, giving it advantages in expressivity. Symbolic languages are powerful in their ability to rewrite themselves. Security in the symbolic programming environment should concentrate on input validation and sanitization as well as minimizing program defects.

- **Object-oriented:** Object-oriented programming abstractly models the environment and software requirements into separate objects that communicate with each other. Objects maintain an encapsulated internal state that is hidden from the external environment. Because encapsulation hides the internal state of a program from the environment, it is not always evident what effect changes to the internal state have on the program correctness. Testing the internal state is challenging because it is not directly accessible to test from the environment external to the object. One positive aspect of object-oriented programming is that objects have rules that can be used to enhance security. For example, a rule could be used to limit specific transformations of data.

- **Functional:** Functional programming is a declarative type of programming paradigm based on composing pure function calls. Pure functions are those that always return the same value for the same input. Unlike object-oriented programming, functional programming avoids maintaining a shared state and mutable data. These, along with other qualities, make functional programming more predictable and easier to test than other methodologies. These qualities of functional programming support secure software. Predictable and testable software is more likely to be secure software.

- **Aspect-oriented:** Aspect-oriented programming separates business functionality from other types of software concerns such as logging, authorization, data validity, and transactions. These separate, nonbusiness-related software concerns are known as *cross-cutting concerns*. These cross-cutting concerns can then be applied transparently as a layer to the business functionality software in a process often referred to as *weaving*. Being able to separate out such important but nonbusiness functionality makes for cleaner and more maintainable code, which supports the software's security. Furthermore, as cross-cutting concerns, security controls can be applied or "woven" into the business functionality without significant changes to the code.

- **Concurrent:** Concurrent programming is a paradigm where a number of computations are carried out concurrently and not sequentially. Security concerns with this paradigm mainly come from failures in managing the interactions and shared contention for resources that are a product of multiple concurrent computations that can lead to availability and integrity issues.

- **Multiparadigm:** Multiparadigm languages have features of more than one programming paradigm. Languages such as these can combine object-oriented programming with functional programming to meet different software challenges. Security in multiparadigm languages combines the security concerns of the paradigms mixed together.

Software Patterns and Frameworks

Good designers know not to create from first principles. Good designers create designs from existing structures that have solved many of the functional and security problems.

A pattern is an abstract design solution to a recurring problem. The concept of software patterns comes from observed recurrences of problems found in developing software and a consistency in the solutions to these problems. The problems we mention here are not those of chasing down bugs or of original designs but those that are part of nearly every software product: the problems of creating data structures, managing programming behavior, enforcing correct procedures, and the like. Common solutions have been discovered to solve these problems.

A pattern is a design description of a solution to a repeated problem in a particular context. A pattern's context is a description of the situation to which the pattern can be applied to solve the problems that define its existence. A pattern's context describes the various participants, their goals, and their limitations and constraints to achieving their goals.

The concept of a pattern is not limited to the software design level. It can exist at the software architecture or even enterprise architecture level. Two key elements make a design a pattern: the reusability of the design and the general applicability of the design to similar contexts.

Software frameworks often implement one or more software patterns for general use. A software framework is a software implementation of patterns. As patterns are abstract reusable solutions, frameworks can be used in creating the code for a solution to a software problem.

Design Patterns

A design pattern is a reusable solution developed to solve a particular common problem. A design pattern is not a completed design but rather a template or written document that can be applied to solving a recurring problem during the process.

Before diving into the different types of design patterns, let's review some concepts that are essential to understanding the topic. The topic of design patterns had primarily come through the object-oriented paradigm of design and programming software systems. Object orientation models program structures on what would be analogous to what one would find in the real world. Programs are composed of different structures, with each structure having its own data and behaviors that are defined for a specific purpose and use in the program.

Program structures in this paradigm are referred to as either classes or objects. A class is the template of a program structure. At a high level, it can be considered to be a program structure's blueprint. As a blueprint or template, a class is meant to become something to be used in a program. To use a class in a program, it becomes an object. An object is a class that has memory allocated to it and data. This process of creating an object from a class is called *instantiation*.

Multithreaded programming and *concurrency* are other concepts to refresh before jumping into design patterns. Concurrency is when program code can execute multiple and distinct lines of logic simultaneously. To achieve concurrency, a program can use a concept of a "thread" of program logic. A thread in a program is both a program structure and facility to execute logic independently of the main execution of a program. Software that uses multiple threads is known as multithreaded programming, and it is a complex design and program resource management task. This is where design patterns come in as a way to reduce complexity and make repeatable the solutions to common design challenges.

There are four families of software design patterns:

- Creational patterns are for class instantiation. Types of creational patterns include Abstract Factory, Builder, Factory Method, Prototype, and Singleton.

- Structural patterns define relationships between objects or classes and include Adapter, Bridge, Composite, Decorator, Facade, Flyweight, and Proxy Patterns.

- Behavioral patterns define how classes and objects communicate. Types of behavioral patterns include Chain of Responsibility, Command, Interpreter, Iterator, Mediator, Memento, State, Strategy, Template Method, and Visitor.

- Concurrency patterns solve the common design challenges in multithreaded programming. Some examples of the concurrency patterns are Active Object, Balking, Proactor, and Reactor, as well as others.

Because of their emphasis on good design, all design patterns have a security impact. Software design patterns can aid in improving confidentiality, integrity, and availability.

For more sources of software design patterns, refer to the Portland Pattern Repository (http://c2.com/ppr/) and the Hillside Group (www.hillside.net/). The Hillside Group sponsors an annual Pattern Languages of Programs conference.

Security Patterns

A security software pattern is a solution to a recurring security problem that occurs in a specific security context presented in a generic formula. Software security patterns describe designs for the purpose of achieving a security goal. Security patterns are an effective means of collecting, describing, and communicating software security design concepts. The reference and use of security design patterns provide building blocks for secure software designs. Security software patterns help to:

- Reduce attack surface area

- Create secure settings by default

- Provide least privilege to users to carry out their job functions

- Establish controls in depth

- Ensure applications remain in a secure state if they fail

- Separate the duties of users

The growth of security patterns interest and development came about in the late 1990s, with a significant expansion in the 2000s. The Jul/Aug 2007 *IEEE Software Special Issue on Software Patterns* featured an article by Munawar Hafiz, Paul Adamczyk, and Ralph Johnson called "Organizing Security Patterns" that collected and classified the body of existing security patterns. The article describes how security patterns can be aligned with the context of target applications, organized by STRIDE threat model categories, and with pattern language examples describing relationships among multiple security patterns working together.

This material organizes patterns around here are three areas of concern: application, the application's perimeter, and those related to the exterior environment. Application-oriented patterns are known as *core patterns*, as they apply to the core of the application. Application perimeter patterns are concerned with security issues at trust boundaries between the application and other trust environments. Exterior security patterns cover security concerns surrounding the application domain and perimeter.

Some examples of security patterns organized in this system are demonstrated in Tables 8.2 through 8.4. As you can see, not every category has a security pattern. For a more exhaustive list of patterns, see Munawar Hafiz's Security Pattern Catalog (`http://www.munawarhafiz.com/securitypatterncatalog/index.php`).

TABLE 8.2 Core Application Security Pattern Concerns

SPOOFING	TAMPERING	REPUDIATION	INFORMATION DISCLOSURE	DOS	ESCALATION OF PRIVILEGE	MULTIPURPOSE
	Checkpointed System	Audit Interceptor	Container Managed Security	DoS Safety	Compartmentalization	Multilevel Security
	chroot Jail	Secure Logger	Exception Shielding	Small Processes	Controlled Virtual Address Space	Server Sandbox
	Safe Data Structure		Directed Session			

TABLE 8.3 Application Perimeter Security Pattern Concerns

SPOOFING	TAMPERING	REPUDIATION	INFORMATION DISCLOSURE	DOS	ESCALATION OF PRIVILEGE	MULTIPURPOSE
Authentication Enforcer	Intercepting Validator		Authorization Enforcer	DoS Safety		Policy Enforcement Point
Account Lockout	Message Inspector		Role-Based Access Control	Small Processes		Single Access Point

TABLE 8.4 **External Security Pattern Concerns**

SPOOFING	TAMPERING	REPUDIATION	INFORMATION DISCLOSURE	DOS	ESCALATION OF PRIVILEGE	MULTIPURPOSE
Assertion Builder			Anonymity Set			Demilitarized zone (DMZ)
Single Sign-On (SSO)			Cover Traffic			Front Door
Intercepting Web Agent						

A discussion about software security patterns is not complete without mentioning cloud application security patterns. Cloud design patterns have been produced by a variety of sources, both vendor neutral and for and by the leading public cloud service providers.

Good patterns solve common problems in a context, and true to form, many of the cloud application pattern catalogs are organized around the typical challenges of cloud development. Like the common design patterns, cloud patterns can have a positive impact on security because their use improves the confidentiality, integrity, and availability of cloud applications.

CloudPatterns.org (`www.cloudpatterns.org`) is a vendor-neutral cloud technology and patterns resource published on the Web. It has organized a pattern catalog into the following categories:

- Sharing, Scalability, and Elasticity
- Reliability, Resiliency, and Recovery
- Data Management and Storage Device Patterns
- Virtual Server and Hypervisor Connectivity and Management Patterns
- Monitoring, Provisioning, and Administration Patterns
- Cloud Service and Storage Security Patterns
- Network Security, Identity and Access Management, and Trust Assurance Patterns

CloudPatterns.org also defines compound cloud patterns. Compound cloud patterns are higher level, meta-cloud patterns that are composed of a number of more granular cloud patterns. Compound cloud patterns describe large-scale patterns such as the composition of the private cloud or a public cloud, among many other similarly sized cloud concerns such as software as a service, platform as a service, and infrastructure as a service. Compound cloud patterns also describes functional, behavioral, and compositional patterns of clouds such as elasticity, bursting, multitenancy, and workload management, to name a few.

For additional resources for cloud application and design patterns, see the sites of AWS (`http://en.clouddesignpattern.org/index.php/Main_Page`) and Microsoft (`https://docs.microsoft.com/en-us/azure/architecture/patterns/`).

Model View Controller

The Model View Controller (MVC) pattern is an example of an intersection of both a design pattern and a security pattern. It is used in languages such as Java, C#, C++, Ruby, and Python. Some of the most popular software frameworks to implement the MVC pattern are Java Struts, Spring MVC, Ruby on Rails, and Python Django. MVC is a popular software architectural pattern used for the development of web applications.

MVC divides an application into three layers: the model, the view, and the controller. The model separates the application's representation and storage of data. The view controls the presentation of data. The controller encapsulates and directs the business logic of data. It also serves as a bridge between the model and the view.

MVC is a security pattern for many reasons. MVC's layering of presentation, logic, and data allows for the implementation of appropriate security controls and security patterns at each layer. Authentication, account lockout, and session management can be managed at the view layer. Access control can be enforced at the controller layer. Data inspection and sanitization, encryption, and access control can be enforced at the model layer. Additionally, cross-cutting security concerns such as secure error handling, secure logging, and communication can be implemented and contained at each layer.

MVC promotes good design practices that lead to higher-quality software implementations. MVC promotes cohesion, where program functionality is grouped into structures by similarity. Design implementations such as these improve software maintainability, reduce complexity, and promote code reuse, thus reducing the likelihood of software defects. MVC also promotes good design through low coupling of modules of code. Low coupling means that the software modules that make up the program are relatively independent of each other. Modular independence makes the development and maintenance of a module less likely to have an impact on other modules.

Software Languages and Frameworks

Software frameworks are code platforms that contain generic code for developers to adapt and use. Software frameworks by their design are the implementation of one or more security or design patterns in its code. As such, software frameworks provide the code already composed that makes up these security and design patterns for the developers to customize and use. Developers often use application programming interfaces (APIs) to access a framework's libraries when they develop software. A software framework increases the efficiency and productivity during new software development. Because software frameworks are implementations of software security and design patterns, their use improves the quality, robustness, and reliability of new software development.

Software frameworks are most useful in providing the code that software developers need that offers most of the solution that they are looking to build. They save developers the time and effort of having to write the basic plumbing code essential to a good application.

Web application security is a common framework theme. Many frameworks such as Struts, Django, and Rails offer input validation, secure sessions support, XSS protection, and so forth. Software frameworks also offer communications facilities such as HTTP/S support, endpoint configuration, software patterns implementation, messaging, logging facilities, user interface development, and security features that are essential to the composition of an application.

Java

Since the mid-1990s, the Java language has been a popular language for business and academia. Java has had many features since its beginning, such as security, cryptography, graphical user interface, database connectivity, distributed computing, and multiprocessing capabilities. The Java language improves upon the security of other third-generation languages that had come before it.

Java has a robust error and exception handling framework. This framework handles buffer overflow problems, null pointer references, and many other code-related issues that otherwise would become security vulnerabilities.

Oracle provides the Secure Coding Guidelines for Java Standard Edition (www.oracle.com/technetwork/java/seccodeguide-139067.html).

These are a few of the many popular Java implementations:

- **Java Enterprise Edition:** Java Enterprise Edition is commonly used to develop e-commerce, information systems, or large-scale applications development. Java Enterprise Edition's security model is both declarative and programmatic. Declarative security applies security layers to the application defined in project configuration or annotations on the source code. Programmatic security is writing security statements into the business logic code. The Java Enterprise Edition's security vulnerabilities mainly consist of the classic vulnerabilities to which most applications are susceptible, the OWASP Top Ten. Vulnerabilities in the Java Runtime Environment affect the security of the Java Enterprise Edition.

- **Struts:** Struts is a free open-source framework for creating Java-based web applications, managed by the Apache Software Federation. It is an implementation of the MVC architecture pattern. The OWASP has organized the security features of Struts along the lines of the MVC pattern (`https://www.owasp.org/index.php/Struts`).

- **Spring:** Spring is an open-source development framework that offers extensive infrastructure support for building high-performing Java applications efficiently and quickly and is sponsored and maintained by Pivotal Software. Spring's base platform has a number of security-promoting features. Spring's model of dependency injection promotes good design through loose coupling of components. This improves code quality and therefore potentially reduces software flaws and vulnerabilities. Spring's Aspect Oriented Programming enables flexibility in the application of security to code. Spring's design allows easy security testing of your code. The Spring Security project adds many security features (`https://projects.spring.io/spring-security/`):

  - A comprehensive security architecture
  - Extensive authentication and authorization support
  - Web security features
  - Method-level access control
  - Protection against many attacks
  - Integration with the Spring MVC framework

.NET

Microsoft .NET, first released in 2002, is a free, open-source platform for building applications. Although it is a cross-platform framework, it runs primarily on the Windows operating system. It is a common development platform. The .NET framework has features for software development security.

.NET's code access security (CAS) prevents code from being executed beyond its allowed permissions level on a machine. Evidence-based security determines the type of permissions to be allowed before any code is executed at runtime. For example, the verified identity of the software publisher can be used as a source of evidence. Role-based security utilizes the principles of authorization and authentication to determine the users to be allowed or denied access to system resources.

Although routinely updated by Microsoft, the .NET framework has a history of security vulnerabilities. The latest versions of the frameworks with better security features may not be available in older versions of Windows. Also, .NET code can be prone to reverse engineering, and a wide variety of tools work within the .NET environment to obfuscate the code and provide cryptographic protections and other methods to defeat this sort of attack.

The OWASP .NET Security Cheat Sheet (`https://www.owasp.org/index.php/ .NET_Security_Cheat_Sheet`) is a handy set of security references covering the .NET framework including data access, encryption, and other general security topics. It also has guidance for ASP.NET MVC, Windows forms, and Windows Communication Foundation (WCF).

Microsoft's published security guidance (`https://docs.microsoft.com/en-us/ dotnet/standard/security/`) comprehensively covers .NET as a platform and framework. It covers fundamental security concepts such as language type safety and authentication and authorization. It also focuses on role-based security aspects, the .NET cryptographic model, Windows Identity and .NET, and secure coding guidelines for both managed and unmanaged code.

Managed code runs inside the .NET Common Language Runtime (CLR). Code created outside of the .NET CLR, such as a library based on Win32 C++, is unmanaged code. The .NET CLR does not have control over the execution of unmanaged code, particularly its memory management. It exposes the system to any potential flaws or risks that may exist in the unmanaged code.

.NET applications are susceptible to common security vulnerabilities such as SQL injection and cross-site scripting. Some security vulnerabilities to prevent include the following:

- Code injection
- Command injection
- Connection string injection
- LDAP injection
- Resource injection
- Second order SQL injection
- UTF-7 cross-site scripting
- Path injection

A detailed explanation of these vulnerabilities is beyond the scope of this text. Vulnerabilities for Microsoft.net can be found in the Microsoft.net framework security section of the common vulnerabilities and exposures (CVE) database (`https://www.cvedetails.com/ vulnerability-list/vendor_id-26/product_id-2002/Microsoft-.net-Framework.html`).

Personal Home Page

Personal Home Page (PHP) is a server-side scripting language that was implemented in the C language in 1994. Although originally designed for web development, it also can be used as a general-purpose language. The language is sponsored and maintained by Zend Technologies.

The PHP user communities foster a development culture for developers to embrace secure development practices. Some PHP frameworks protect web applications from the common security vulnerabilities, such as SQL injection and cross-site scripting, and offer error and exception handling support.

PHP has security vulnerabilities that the security professional should be aware of, one being how it supports unsafe implicit data conversions. When using PHP to develop large applications with sensitive security requirements, be aware of its vulnerabilities and compensate for them. As a security professional, you should focus on best practices to identify and reduce web application security issues when presented with PHP use.

For more information, see OWASP's PHP Security Cheat Sheet (`https://www.owasp` `.org/index.php/PHP_Security_Cheat_Sheet`).

Python

Python is an interpreted, multiparadigm, general-purpose programming language, first released in 1991 and still widely used. Python and its frameworks are supported by a community of dedicated developers who take security vulnerabilities seriously and promptly institute proactive countermeasures. Python frameworks have several built-in security features that make them difficult to compromise.

Python's design philosophy makes it a good choice as a secure programming language. Python emphasizes simplicity, readability, consistency, and good design. Because Python is an interpreted language, comprehensive testing is a cornerstone to discovering flaws in Python development.

Mature Python-powered web frameworks have built-in security features such as HTTPS support, template systems, and models that secure, validate, and sanitize data. A security professional has two main responsibilities in this regard. First, ensure that Python frameworks with security features are being used for your organization's Python-based software. Second, make sure these frameworks' configuration settings and security features are implemented in a manner that meets the risk and control requirements for the application software of which it is a part. Although research into the frameworks and auditing the software can take you far toward these ends, consider partnering with the software developers and architects to comprehensively achieve these objectives.

Ruby

The Ruby language is an interpreted, open-source, object-oriented general-purpose language developed in the mid-1990s. It is a popular programming language, with many developers favoring its dynamic and highly expressive nature. The web application framework Ruby on Rails brought the language into a mainstream development consciousness.

Ruby frameworks have features that support software development security. They have built-in features for safeguarding applications from input validation weaknesses and other web-based attacks. Ruby supports meta-programming, where security practices can be injected into code. Ruby's syntax is favored by many developers to create clean, uncluttered, and secure code. Security information on the Ruby language, including common vulnerabilities and exposures, can be found at `https://www.ruby-lang.org/en/security/`.

One popular example of Ruby is Ruby on Rails. Released in 2005, Ruby on Rails is a Ruby-based web application framework that is designed for developers to create database-driven applications.

Ruby on Rails prevents SQL injection attacks with a built-in feature for escaping specific harmful SQL characters.

Ruby on Rails provides helper methods that offer protection against cross-site scripting attacks. It has conventions for implementing security, and it is an extensible framework allowing integrations with third-party features to enhance the application's security.

The OWASP has a cheat sheet of Ruby on Rails security vulnerabilities at `https://www.owasp.org/index.php/Ruby_on_Rails_Cheatsheet`.

JavaScript

JavaScript is an interpreted, high-level, weakly typed, multiparadigm programming language. Despite its name, it is a completely different language from Java. Along with HTML and CSS, JavaScript is one of the three core languages of the web browser. Despite that it is best known as a browser scripting language, JavaScript has found a place in nonbrowser environments, such as the language of choice for Node.js.

JavaScript has a number of vulnerabilities. Common JavaScript vulnerabilities relate to its use on the client side. JavaScript can be susceptible to cross-site scripting and cross-site request forgery.

There are two significant factors contributing to JavaScript vulnerabilities. The first is that it is an essential and interpreted language in the browser, and thus the implementations may vary. The second and even more significant factor contributing to JavaScript vulnerabilities is the poor management of libraries used by JavaScript frameworks.

Two areas that a security practitioner should focus their attention on when evaluating JavaScript frameworks are the following:

- At least one library contains a known vulnerability.

- The library packages used are out of date with the current release, possibly on the order of years behind.

These are significant issues for many web applications that use JavaScript frameworks.

JavaScript vulnerability reporting is not organized as that of other languages is. There is no single consistent source of documenting JavaScript libraries' vulnerabilities or their effects.

Also, when you consider that the proliferation of newer JavaScript frameworks may not have been sufficiently tested for security weaknesses, with their code visible as opensource, these frameworks can be targets for security attacks, and thus it is a best practice to exercise caution and thoroughly evaluate JavaScript libraries prior to their use.

JavaScript can be disabled on the client side.

One popular example of JavaScript is Node.js. The Node.js framework was released in 2009 as a runtime environment for running JavaScript code on the server side. It is a single-threaded, event-driven, nonblocking Input/Output (IO) that allows for simultaneous handling of requests that results in great scalability. Node.js on the server shares similar structures with client-side code, both being JavaScript, which makes it easier to integrate security practices into web applications. An emphasis on JavaScript on both the client side and the server side brings with it the advantages of a concentration of language expertise as well as shared language productivity and security tooling. These combined factors improve secure coding practices. The code can be deployed quickly as well, allowing for faster bug and vulnerability fixes. This speed of responsibility is an effective risk management technique.

Node.js has security vulnerabilities. In October 2017, nodejs.org reported a high severity denial-of-service vulnerability due to changes in one of its dependencies. Fortunately, Node.js vulnerabilities are reported as CVEs and are hosted by MITRE at `https://www.cvedetails.com/vulnerability-list/vendor_id-12113/product_id-30764/`.

For information on how to report a Node.js security vulnerability or how to be informed of Node.js vulnerabilities, see `https://nodejs.org/en/security/`.

Becoming and staying informed about Node.js security vulnerabilities is half of the picture to securely using the framework. It is just as important to make sure that you are keeping its libraries up to date, particularly when the Node.js reference material tells you to do so.

The functionality of the Node.js framework consists of software libraries known as *packages*. These packages are installed and managed via the Node Package Manager, more commonly known as *npm*. A significant Node.js security concern is that npm can be exploited for malware distribution. When using npm, make sure that the npm library name is correct, inspect the source code, and install it safely with `–ignore-scripts`.

Include a security source code inspection of the code in the Node.js packages your organization uses. Not all Node.js package source code meets secure coding standards, so the packages are a source of vulnerabilities in applications that use them.

Distributed Computing

Distributed computing typically refers to the concept of a network of independent computers collaborating to achieve a specific objective. Distributed computing is often used by scientific research projects, education projects, and resource-intensive industrial applications. Distributed computing is an architectural strategy that defines standalone functionality and methods that can be accessed separately over communication channels. In this regard, distributed computing architectures allow what would otherwise be a monolithic system to be broken into separately managed and collaborating parts.

Separately managed units of functionality typically hosted on individual servers that are accessed over a network present some common threats to this distributed computing environment. These will be covered in this section.

Furthermore, this section on distributed computing provides an overview of common distributed computing frameworks that you may come across as a security professional. These include remote procedure calls (RPC), the Common Object Request Broker Architecture (CORBA), and the Component Object Model (COM) and Distributed Component Object Model (DCOM).

Finally, this section looks at currently significant distributed computing architectural methods. Service-oriented architecture (SOA), web services, and microservices are all described in detail.

Common Threats to a Distributed Computing Environment

Distributed computing's security vulnerabilities are inherent in the nature of its interconnectedness. One vulnerable system can propagate vulnerability into the entire environment. It is important to understand this when evaluating the security of a distributed computing environment.

Common threats to control in a distributed computing environment are as follows:

- Unauthorized user access
- User masquerading as another user
- Client masquerading
- Bypassing security controls
- Eavesdropping on communications
- Tampering with data being communicated between participating systems
- Lack of accountability

Remote Procedure Call

A *remote procedure call* (RPC) is a protocol used to exchange data between computers connected to a network.

RPC-connected systems can be susceptible to client spoofing and remote code execution attacks. Because RPC systems expose procedure calls over a network, they are susceptible to buffer overflow and input validation attacks just like any network exposed functionality. The networked nature of RPC makes port scans and operating system information preferred sources of information for RPC attacks.

Sun Microsystems developed Secure RPC to make using RPC more secure. It uses public key cryptography to secure RPC. There are a few drawbacks to Secure RPC, however. Although Secure RPC authenticates the user, the responsibility for data confidentiality and integrity is on the Secure RPC user.

Common Object Request Broker Architecture

The Common Object Request Broker Architecture (CORBA) is a specification that allows computer applications on a network to exchange data with one another regardless of their native platforms and programming languages. CORBA is an object-oriented model. Systems that use CORBA do not need to be object-oriented, however. CORBA allows for objects to be distributed across different address spaces and interact with each other by message passing. CORBA can be used as the backbone to develop a distributed object application.

The Object Management Group (OMG) developed CORBA. The CORBA specification is an ISO standard: ISO/IEC 19500-2:2012.

The main points of the CORBA standard are the following:

- Interface Definition Language (IDL) is used to define interfaces for language- and location-independent distributed objects.

- Internet Inter-ORB Protocol (IIOP) enables language- and location-independent distributed object communication over the Internet.

- Object Request Broker (ORB) is the middleware that facilitates the distributed objects' communication.

CORBA is a mature and stable architectural specification. This maturity directs comprehensive security specifications for the development of secure and robust applications in varied platforms and environments.

As a language-independent platform, CORBA does not limit developers to any particular software language and thus allows them to choose CORBA-supported languages based on criteria of the functional and security fitness that the language would offer their application clients.

CORBA security defines three levels of participation:

- **Security unaware:** The CORBA specification does not require the distributed object system developer to do anything to use the security features that the CORBA middleware provides except for what would be required of them to configure for its normal use.

- **Security policy controlling:** The application directs but does not enforce the CORBA middleware's use of specific security policies.

- **Security policy enforcing:** This is when the application not only directs and relies upon the CORBA middleware in security policies but actively enforces those security policies itself.

Java Remote Method Invocation

Java Remote Method Invocation (Java RMI) is a Java language framework for distributed computing based on a proxy architecture. With RMI, a client application can invoke methods on a remote server through a proxy.

Although REST and JSON over HTTP have eclipsed the use of Java RMI, it is mentioned here because it may still be found in legacy code.

Java RMI security should consider the risks to the client and to the service. Compromise of client information confidentiality is a risk. The service may send confidential information about the service to the client. Java RMI service can be subject to denial-of-service attacks.

Much of Java RMI's security is based on the security of the Java language environment. Following secure coding guidelines for Java will take you far in securing a Java RMI program. Securing Java RMI should focus on securing the communications between the client, the proxy, and the server. Beyond that, trust in the server and the clients must be established. Server authentication should be employed to establish trust in the server. The clients should be authenticated, and an authorization mechanism should be employed for the clients. Authentication of both the service and the client can be done by the proxy.

Component Object Model and Distributed Component Object Model

The Component Object Model (COM) is Microsoft's invention to advance reusable object-oriented software. COM was one of the first software models of component integration that allowed binary reuse of components.

To understand the significance of this, it is important to understand how COM compares to pre-COM programming. Creating a program is a process that involves writing software code and using existing software libraries and components. Before technologies like COM, creating the binary executable program included compiling the written code and including the existing software libraries and component's binary code. This process tightly coupled the libraries and code in the program. Consider this for a moment: in the pre-COM world, whenever a new version of a library was released, perhaps because of a security patch, the whole program would have to be reassembled and released again. COM allows programs to use libraries and components without having to rebuild the program with the libraries included.

COM works by using object-oriented components that have a state and communicate via messages. These components are identified by a globally unique ID (GUID). The underlying security mechanisms of COM rely on authentication to verify a caller's identity and authorization of the right to execute specific functionality. This is encapsulated in a security context that establishes the means by which confidentiality, integrity, and authentication are enforced among the interacting components.

A means of attacking COM that security professionals should be aware of is compromising the Windows Registry. The Windows Registry establishes references to COM objects. By compromising the Windows Registry, references to COM objects can be hijacked to refer to an attacker's component instead of the actual component.

The Distributed Component Object Model (DCOM) is a proprietary Microsoft technology that enables software component interaction across a network. It extends RPC to allow efficient placement of components on a network. These capabilities make DCOM a preferred foundation for distributed component applications built upon the Windows 2000 platform.

Service-Oriented Architecture

Service-oriented architecture (SOA) is a method of network-based software design that provides business logic to its consumers via services.

A service is remotely callable business logic. Software programs can call or update services independent of other program modules. Services are developed, maintained, and deployed separately from the programs that consume them. A set of services can become the basis of a larger software application.

Service-oriented architecture is a vendor- and technology-neutral design style, where the enabling feature of web services is the standardization of communication message format. This neutrality is a benefit that allows services to be consumed over the network independent of the choice of calling language.

Service-oriented architecture is used for the following:

- Dynamic web applications (Web 2.0)
- Maintainability
- Loose coupling
- Integration of external vendors' business logic
- Public cloud interaction

Service-oriented architectures, in a general sense, cover a number of different types of remote call-based software designs, such as web services, Microservices, event-driven architectures, and Web 2.0.

Two of the main protocols that support SOA are Simple Object Access Protocol (SOAP) and Representational State Transfer (REST). SOAP is an XML-based language that is designed to promote extensibility, such as security and addressability extensions, language and protocol neutrality, and programming model independence. REST is based on the interaction patterns of HTTP. It is a stateless approach whose strengths lie in its simplicity and convention.

Service-oriented architectures are susceptible to a variety of attacks, including network-based attacks, message interception, man-in-the-middle attacks, session hijacking, and impersonation.

The OASIS body of standards supports web services (`www.opengroup.org/standards/soa`).

Web Services

Web services are generally subject to the same threats that are common to websites, such as the following:

- Denial-of-service attacks
- Man-in-the-middle attacks
- SQL injection
- Buffer overflow
- Improper error handling

However, web services also can be attacked by threats specific to their design and architecture, such as SOAP-based web services attacks and XML bombs.

SOAP-Based Web Services Attacks

SOAP-based web services use a Web Services Description Language (WSDL) file to describe the endpoints and operations of that service. This information in the WSDL can be used in reconnaissance for an attack on the web service. Often access to this WSDL file is exposed without restriction over the network. Restrict access to the WSDL and use encryption to protect the web services information from leaking into the wrong hands.

XML Bombs

An XML bomb, also known as an *exponential entity expansion XML bomb attack*, is when specific XML entity patterns exponentially expand when evaluated with the malicious intent of consuming all of the parser's resources to cause a denial-of-service attack.

A common form of this type of attack is known as the *billion laughs attack*. In the billion laughs attack, the malicious code expands a series of entity references that ultimately end by referring to text, such as *lol*, *ha*, or the like; when parsed, they expand to a large number of that text whose expansion exceeds the capacity of the XML parser with the laugh text.

Depending on the XML parser you are using, the following countermeasures to an XML bomb may be available:

- Setting limits on individual parser memory allocation

- Lazy expansion of entities only when they are used, which may at best serve as a delay

- Setting limits on entity expansion

- Turning off entity expansion

- Setting limits on the number of characters that entities can expand to

Microservices

Microservices are a popular form of service-oriented architecture that focus on delivering specific-purpose business capabilities as independently deployed services. Microservices are small and focused software with minimal dependencies that have fast and short development times. Typically, they come with an immutable architecture. Microservices have a minimal commitment to specific technologies or software stacks. The orchestration of multiple microservices can be complex.

With more microservices comes more complexity. Because each microservices endpoint is a specific delivery of business capability, each would have its own deployment, access management, and security concerns. Each of these concerns comes with challenges particular to it.

Evaluating the security of a microservices architecture requires taking a layered approach. The reason for this is that a microservices architecture is an information technology ecosystem in and of itself. Authentication and authorization from callers to services and transitively carrying the authentication/authorization (AuthN/AuthZ) across services is a necessary aspect of evaluating a microservices architecture. Evaluating the network security is another layer of a complete approach to microservices security. The microservices endpoints should not be exposed to public networks, particularly not the Internet. Check to make sure that there is an intermediary API that fields and filters all public calls to the microservices and that the microservices are in a controlled isolation from public networks. A firewall should enforce granular access control to each of the microservices' endpoints. Because of the fine divisions of services and proliferation of security control, overall service availability becomes a material concern, and performance metrics and monitoring become part of the security evaluation. And as with any information technology, it is important to ensure that best-practice security guidelines are being followed, such as application security scanning, proactive vulnerability and patch management, good cryptographic practices, logging, monitoring, and alerting. Be sure to consider how these best practices apply to the specifics of the microservices architecture that you are responsible for evaluating.

Microservices can come in two communication flavors: synchronous and asynchronous.

Synchronous microservices respond to their requests in turn and typically use the HTTP or HTTPS protocol. When there's dependency on synchronous microservices, that means the calling service is blocked from further execution until it receives the response. Synchronous services do not scale well, and the wait time for responses may cause errors or other undesirable conditions that additional logic would have to be written to compensate.

Asynchronous microservices architecture decouples from the dependency on service responses. Asynchronous services typically use queues as a communication medium and use the Advanced Message Queuing Protocol (AMQP) for asynchronous communication. Although this decoupling is not complete, handling the circumstances of underperforming or unreliable services can be solved on an architectural level in addition to a code logic level. With asynchronous services, more services can be added and attached to a queue to scale up the responsibility and performance of the dependencies.

Regardless of whether microservices are synchronous or asynchronous, two significant areas of consideration are deployment and access management.

Deployment Options

Microservices can be deployed either in a container framework or in a cloud-based serverless framework.

SOFTWARE CONTAINERS

Based on their design imperatives, containers and microservices go together well. A container is a lightweight, standalone infrastructure stack. It is designed to contain exactly everything required to host specific software and no more. Software containers provide a complete runtime environment for the software they host. Containers are a smaller application deployment solution than hosting the software on a virtual machine. Containers bundle the application, a runtime, its dependencies, libraries, binaries, settings, and anything that an application needs to run. Once the application is packaged in a container, it is separate from its surroundings and can be deployed on any supportive platform, irrespective of the underlying infrastructure. Some common container solutions are Docker, BSD Jails, LXC, Windows Server Containers, and Hyper-V Containers.

Docker is a popular container system. The Docker project's activity, contributions, and specifications, as well as its technology's ease of use, make it popular. Some solutions that secure Docker are Twistlock and Docker Bench for Security.

Because a container environment consolidates what was once a variety of runtime environments onto one platform, it potentially introduces risks by putting everything in one place. Containers share a host environment. Containers thus share a kernel with the other containers in the container environment as well as with the host. The host must be hardened, patched, and secured to mitigate risks to all of the software running in the containers it supports. Container privilege escalation is a concern as well. If by a mistake or malicious action a container is allowed to run with root privileges, it exposes the whole container environment to the consequences of root actions. Containers share resources in the container environment. Anytime there is a situation of shared resources, there also is a potential to abuse access to these resources. This means that a container could consume or control shared resources to the point of starving other containers, leading to a denial-of-service compromise of the software hosted in the other containers.

With this information, controls can be put in place to mitigate the risks of the exploits that can happen to containers, and with that we can discuss the security advantages that software containers offer. Software containers address many of the risks that accompany the modern operational software environment. This standardization of runtime environment, libraries, configurations, and software makes for consistent, fast deployments. Moreover, being self-contained executable environments that run on supportive environments, each container isolates its software from the surrounding infrastructure. This formula of just-enough, complete, lightweight, isolated software exactly supports microservices' minimalist design requirements.

The microservices container deployment pipeline is structured as follows:

1. Microservices code is committed to a source code repository.

2. The commitment triggers the deployment orchestration pipeline, which includes the following:

   a. Building the code

   b. Running tests

   c. Packaging the application into the container

   d. Uploading the container to a registry

3. From this point, the container can be taken into a quality assurance (QA) workflow for formal assessment.

4. After passing quality assurance, this same container could then advance through other steps, ultimately to production.

In this scenario, securing microservices amounts to securing the service code against the threats afflicting web services as well as securing the container.

SERVERLESS COMPUTING

Serverless computing is another good fit for microservices deployment. Serverless computing platforms such as Amazon Web Service's Lambda and Microsoft's Azure Cloud Functions are becoming popular methods for software deployment. Hosting software in a serverless computing environment removes much of the overhead of managing the operational environment, as the cloud service provider assumes much of that responsibility.

Securing a cloud-based serverless operational environment requires attention to the separation of security responsibilities between the cloud consumer and the cloud services provider. The cloud services provider, such as AWS or Azure, has the responsibility for securing their cloud services environment. This responsibility extends up to the point where the customer has control over their code and its deployment. With the public cloud service provider managing their security responsibilities, it allows the microservices developer to focus on their service's security.

To this extent, the cloud consumer needs to know what their own responsibilities are in terms of securing the virtual network, their cloud identity and access management, and other cloud-based controls.

Serverless computing is a great fit for microservices because of its constraints. Serverless computing is stateless. It mandates a top limit execution time. Serverless computing platforms also limit code size. These constraints are aligned with good microservices.

An important consideration regarding using microservices is that they are typically a stateless computing environment, or they should be. A "state" is a snapshot of information that describes a microservice's process configuration and data at a point in time. Microservices are intended to be stateless because of their design imperatives to be fast and scalable, all with ease of code deployment.

Keeping a state of a program is often important to its functionality. Keeping a state in a microservice is an additional overhead that would break from the microservice design philosophy of doing just one thing. If a state needs to be maintained in a microservice, it should be kept outside of each microservice, perhaps in a state management service.

Again, because microservices offer a specific business capacity through a service, they typically are used in concert with other microservices. That said, the time it takes for each microservice to complete execution adds to the clock time of the composite functionality of all orchestrated services. Microservices need to have quick execution times. Stateless computing platforms by design support this constraint.

Another important consideration when using a serverless computing platform is that they limit the code size that can be deployed. A microservice's code base is a collection of specific purpose code and libraries for the delivery of the microservice's business capabilities and nothing more. Read the previous line one more time. Code size limitations work in the microservice developer's favor in this case. Smaller code sizes are helpful to security as well. A small code base is easier to review and maintain, thus making security review and management easier. Smaller code sizes naturally narrow the microservice's functional scope, making it easier to contain, monitor, and control it, which enhances its security control environment.

Microservices Access Management

Authentication and access management are significant issues for microservices. Because of their performance requirements, microservices should not be burdened by client authentication. Similarly, microservices should be only minimally burdened by authorization concerns. OAuth 2.0 is often used to mediate access to microservices. In this case, the third party is the client calling the microservices. The client would request access through an OAuth 2.0 authorization server. If client authorization is successful, then the authorization server would create an access token for the client to access the microservices.

A challenge exists in deprovisioning fine-grained access to the microservices with this strategy, however. If changes in access to specific microservices need to be imposed for a particular client, the burden of these changes rests on the OAuth 2.0 authorization server. Be sure to control the environment between the communicating parties, as this potentially could expose a time of check/time of use vulnerability if left uncontrolled.

An API gateway is a pattern useful for managing client access to microservices. An API Gateway pattern acts as a facade that offers a number of features required for microservices access management:

- A single-entry point for clients of the microservices
- An authentication and authorization point for the microservices
- Service discovery
- Management of client sessions
- Single point of event logging
- Data inspection and validation
- It also can cache frequently used data

Good security for microservices should be based on a defense-in-depth approach. This practice should consider the security at the boundary, in the services environment, in the services platform, and of the code.

Security at the boundary should consist of strong network boundary controls. When using public cloud services, it can help to also look at other cloud services that can improve the security of a microservices-based architecture. Public cloud service providers have to defend themselves against web-scale attacks, and typically these types of services they offer have built-in durability.

Leading cloud service providers offer services such as a content delivery network (CDN), web application firewall (WAF), and API Gateway services. A cloud CDN is typically built to withstand and mitigate the effects of Internet-based distributed volumetric attacks. A CDN can be used as a means to offload serving static and semi-dynamic data, allowing the cloud-based microservices to concentrate on providing business functional value. A web application firewall cloud service can stand as a front line of web application defense for your microservices, with it handling the security heavy lifting of protecting against common threats such as those described in the OWASP Top Ten. A cloud API gateway service provides scalability, monitoring, and security features that can integrate with a cloud function as a service-based microservice. Leading cloud service providers offer a number of services that can be a useful and important front line of defense for your public cloud-enabled microservices framework and a great start to your defense-in-depth strategy.

Securing your network is also important. Segment your microservices by risk or data value classifications. In this segmentation strategy, ensure that stronger, more comprehensive controls are applied to the higher-value services. There are specific types of firewalls that are designed for microservices. Project Calico (`https://www.projectcalico.org/`) is a firewall that offers policy-based microsegmentation that could apply to each microservice in your ecosystem.

Once inside the perimeter, securing the services environment involves identity and access management and secure APIs.

Artificial Intelligence

Artificial intelligence (AI) is a broad topic covering automated capabilities of learning, problem-solving, reasoning, interpreting complex data, game playing, speech recognition, social intelligence, and perception.

These are some of the areas of information systems security in which AI has been used:

- Incident response
- Cognitive algorithms to recognize malware behaviors
- Automated defense based on autonomous learning security systems
- Assistive technology

AI and Security

AI is not without security concerns. Common security concerns include social engineering, the unpredictability of AI, and enhanced malware. Each of these is explored next.

AI and Social Engineering

One example of AI social engineering is the Microsoft chatbot "Tay." Tay is a machine-learning Twitter social intelligence bot that was designed to adapt its conversational style based on social training. Within 24 hours of public deployment, Tay was trained by repetitive interaction with abusive users' Tweets to spit back hate speech, effectively becoming a troll based on modeled behavior. This form of abuse might be considered a form of "social engineering" of an AI program.

As more socially intelligent machine entities enter widespread use, this form of attack will be a weapon in the arsenal of cyber-psychological warfare. Such choice of vocabulary was obviously not the intention of Tay's designers. Although this was not a direct security issue with Tay, the features of AI were exploited by users. To confront the threat of social engineering to AI-based social programs, the issues of unpredictability and enhanced malware need to be addressed.

Securing socially intelligent learning agents requires developing and following a plan that will lead toward the general end state behavioral outcomes of the agent. This plan breaks from a pure learning experience, but given the example of what happened to the intelligent agent Tay, it is a necessary and worthwhile constraint.

A socially intelligent learning agent secure development management plan includes the following steps:

1. Determine the agent's behavioral outcomes.

2. Develop a training set oriented toward behavioral outcomes.

3. Train the agent on the curated training set to seed the initial language dictionary and behaviors.

4. Develop a blacklist of languages and language patterns to block the agent's exposure to the blacklisted items.

5. Develop a training set to train the agent on the proper handling of the blacklisted languages and language patterns.

6. Develop a testing protocol to verify the agent's behavioral outcomes and properly handle blacklisted languages and language patterns.

7. Evaluate the agent via the testing protocol.

8. Based on test assessment outcomes, return to steps 1–7 to adjust the agent's behavior to align it with the desired outcomes.

9. Upon deployment, continuously monitor the agent's social interaction to detect and block blacklisted languages and language patterns from being exposed to the agent's learning.

10. Routinely evaluate the agent based on the testing protocol, revisiting the guidance of step 8.

Unpredictability

Because of the complexities in AI's logic and learning, the outcome of an AI-based system may not be predictable. It is tough to determine what it will do. When such AI-based systems are in charge of systems whose malfunctions would have a severe human impact, such unpredictability can exact an inconceivably high cost.

Controlling the behaviors of a system that is unpredictable is challenging. Classically, the best options for controlling unpredictable systems are to set up guidelines of acceptable behavior, to monitor for behaviors that occur outside of these guidelines, and then to take corrective action upon such detection.

This can be implemented by developing a supervisory control layer that evaluates all of the AI-based system's outputs and selectively inhibits, prohibits, or modifies the AI system's outputs from causing undesirable behaviors. Think of this as being similar to a firewall for the commands coming out of the AI system. This supervisory control layer must operate independently of the AI system in order to have executive control over it, and never vice versa. A fail-safe or fail-secure approach, depending upon the nature and criticality of the system, is necessary to secure AI-based systems from unpredictable outcomes of the performance of the system.

Enhanced Malware

Just as AI systems can be used to learn and adapt to malware threats, they can be used to enhance the threat potential of malware. "Intelligent" malware could manifest a threat to systems and society in a myriad of ways. Socially enhanced malware could impersonate trusted colleagues or friends to obtain sensitive information or lead individuals into situations of peril. Intelligent malware agents could coordinate reconnaissance and attack efforts to target high-value or high-impact assets. These high-impact targets could be critical infrastructure, hospital equipment, or corporate assets.

Expert Systems

An expert system is a form of AI whose purpose is to model a human expert's decision-making process. Expert systems have a knowledge base of facts and rules of an information domain. To make "decisions," an expert system uses an inference engine to apply rules to known facts in the knowledge base to arrive at new facts. Expert systems focus on the "what," not the "how."

Popular expert system platforms are:

- CLIPS, the "C" Language Integrated Production System (`www.clipsrules.net/`)
- Jess, the Java expert system shell (`https://herzberg.ca.sandia.gov/`)
- JBoss Drools (`www.drools.org/`)
- PyKE, the Python knowledge engine (`http://pyke.sourceforge.net/`)

Expert systems are arguably the first successful form of AI having many applications. They have been used in medical diagnosis, genetic engineering, credit authorization, fraud detection, chemical analysis, and more.

Some examples of how expert systems are used for security are in risk management decision-making, cybersecurity attack detection and intervention, and vulnerability scanning.

Expert systems are well suited to assist in risk management decision-making. Although empirical methods are employed, the line on practical project risk management ends with human expertise. Ultimately a human expert makes risk management decisions based on an assessment of facts, their knowledge and experience, guidelines, education, training, and best guesses. When this knowledge is used to create an expert system, it can reveal risks faster than a human could.

Expert systems can also be used against cyber attacks. An expert system's rules and fact base can know many different types of attacks. An expert system can detect the symptoms of a cyber attack. By comparing the symptoms and attack features against its rules and fact base, it can aid in identifying the specific attack and present countermeasures for the attack. Identifying attacks is difficult. Thus, an expert system can help identify and resolve cyber attacks.

An expert system can be helpful with vulnerability scanning when its knowledge base has detailed knowledge and rules about the IT environment and its vulnerabilities.

Neural Networks

An artificial neural network is a computing system based on biological neural networks. These systems can "learn" by exposure to examples. Neural nets have the following learning paradigms: supervised learning, like being taught by a teacher, and unsupervised learning, where they are just fed data.

Perhaps the most significant security vulnerability of neural networks is how they can be spoofed. Neural networks trained by supervised learning methods to recognize specific patterns and environmental features are particularly susceptible to spoofing. Because of the specificity of their training and how these neural networks use their pattern recognition algorithms to identify the objects they are trained to recognize, small changes imposed on these objects can change how the neural network identifies them.

To understand how this is a security issue, imagine how a neural network may be used by autonomous vehicles to recognize control signs in its environment. Neural networks trained like this could be used to recognize and respond to the features of an unknown environment. A stop sign would be an example of such a feature. Encountering a stop sign is normally not a big deal. It is easy for a human to recognize. However, change the face of the stop sign, by vandalism or possibly by the application of a few stickers added to its face, and the neural network interprets the defaced stop sign differently.

A stop sign changed to any other type of sign is implicitly a risk in many ways and poses a potentially serious risk to life and safety.

Mobile Apps and Their Ecosystem

A mobile application is a type of application software designed to run on a mobile device, such as a smartphone or tablet computer. Mobile apps generally run in a sandbox environment on the mobile device. Two common mobile ecosystems are Apple's iOS mobile operating system and Android. Regardless of a mobile device, it is important to secure it. Two ways to do this are at the code level and at the human behavioral level.

iPhone and Apple's iOS Mobile Operating System

The iPhone is a line of smartphones designed and marketed by Apple that was first released on June 29, 2007. They run Apple's iOS mobile operating system. The iPhone was an advancement in mobile computing. It standardized the touchscreen keyboard. It merged a phone with a digital media player. It has an Internet browser. It has a vibrant ecosystem of applications ("apps") that run on the phone.

Android

Android is a mobile operating system developed by Google. Android is based on a modified Linux kernel and other open-source software. Android was designed mainly for touchscreen mobile devices such as smartphones and tablets. Android was first released commercially in September 2008. Ongoing Android development is by Google and the Open Handset Alliance.

Android has a security model that supports an ecosystem of applications and devices built based on the Android platform. Android has multilayered security designed to support an open platform while still protecting all users of the platform.

Mobile Code

Mobile code is any program, application, or content capable of movement while embedded in an email, document, or website. Some examples of mobile code include Java Applets, client-side scripts (JavaScript, VBScript), ActiveX controls, dynamic email, viruses, Trojan horses, and worms. Mobile code is often termed *executable content, remote code,* and *active capsules.*

There are two categories of mobile code security: attacks against the remote host on which the program is executed, as with malicious applets or ActiveX programs, and attacks due to the subversion of the mobile code and its data by the remote execution environment. Preventing each type of attack requires protecting system resources and data. Controlling mobile code becomes an issue of enforcing isolation controls around the component.

A sandbox is one of the most effective means of controlling mobile code. It is a protected and restrictive runtime environment for mobile code. Sandbox restrictions include limitations on networking, memory, system access, and storage. Sandboxes often grant access control explicitly. Much of a sandbox's security is in configuring to restrict mobile code's access to system resources, and it is often a situation controlled by the sandbox's system administrator.

Securing Mobile Devices

There are several recommended practices to protect mobile devices from being hacked and to improve their security. It is important to ensure that all members of an organization understand and embrace the following principles:

- Be careful on public Wi-Fi networks.
- Don't compromise security, which includes not jailbreaking your device.
- Be prepared to track and lock your device.
- Delete messages from people you don't know.
- Do not open random emails or links.
- Practice safe browsing.
- Keep software updated.
- Be careful of what you install.
- Conceal or disable lock screen notifications.
- Avoid public chargers.

✔ Jailbreaking

Jailbreaking is a process of privilege escalation for removing software restrictions imposed by mobile devices. Restrictions in the mobile phone environment exist for your own protection and to maintain the overall quality of apps. Apps run in a protected environment, a sandbox, on the phone. However, the restrictions and security protections of a sandbox can be circumvented by jailbreaking. Jailbreaking is risky. It makes the device more vulnerable to attack.

Maturity Models

Developing software that is secure, reliable, and usable is challenging. Developing this software on schedule and within budget is yet even more challenging. How can an organization improve its software development performance? How does a customer determine that an organization will perform as needed within a project plan to develop software? Just like anything an organization undertakes, software development is made up of a set of processes, practices, and goals. These processes, practices, and goals can be appraised to determine areas for improvement. Such an appraisal requires a model.

A maturity model is a tool for process improvement. Sometimes referred to as a *capability maturity model*, a maturity model is used to evaluate areas of capability or performance and to point out specific areas of improvement. Maturity is a yardstick by which an organization's processes and practices may be evaluated. The more formalized, managed, and evolving the processes and practices, the more mature they are.

A maturity model can be used for different purposes. A maturity model can be used as a standard by which an organization may evaluate its processes. Its results can be used to benchmark an organization's processes. This benchmark can be used to compare how the organization rates against expectations as well as how the business compares with competitors within an industry. Maturity models can be used as a framework to envision the future and as such can be a source of information for the development of improvement plans.

A maturity model is a simple tool. It can look like a scorecard. It uses specific criteria and measurements to determine the maturity or capability of a system, process, or organization. Maturity models are used to both point out areas of weakness and identify areas for improvement.

A maturity model can be used to evaluate many different types of things. A maturity model can show how "green" an organization is. A maturity model can be used to score how well your company complies with privacy regulations. A maturity model can provide insights into an organization's software development practices. It can measure the effectiveness of a security program.

Each aspect is evaluated against sets of goals and conditions that each indicate an evolutionary plateau of successful performance and maturity.

The Institute of Internal Auditors' *Practice Guide: Selecting, Using, and Creating Maturity Models: A Tool for Assurance and Consulting Engagements Recommended Guidance* states that a maturity model can provide the following (`https://na.theiia.org/standards-guidance/recommended-guidance/practice-guides/Pages/Selecting-Using-and-Creating-Maturity-Models-a-Tool-for-Assurance-and-Consulting-Engagements.aspx`):

- A framework for envisioning the future, the desired state, and the development of improvement plans

- Benchmarks for the organization to compare its processes internally or externally

- A mechanism to provide insight into the improvement path from an immature to a mature process

- A disciplined method that is easy for management to understand and implement

Similarly, a maturity model assessment's results have different uses for its various consumers. Consumers of a maturity model are auditors, consultants, management, and risk management. Auditors use a maturity model as a structured tool to assess the current state of capabilities and process the maturity of an aspect of an organization.

Maturity Model Structures and Definitions

To understand how a maturity model works and how it measures, evaluates, and can be used as an assessment tool, it is useful to understand its parts. A maturity model consists of model domains, levels, criteria, and targets.

Model Domains

Model domains in a maturity model represent the essential aspects of what management wants to assess. Each model domain supports the model's measurement outcomes. Some of the fundamental aspects that are represented by model domains in a maturity model include an organization's software development risk management, secure coding, configuration management, and analysis and resolution of defects. In the Capability Maturity Model Integration (CMMI), a model domain is known as a *process area*.

Levels

A maturity level is a well-defined plateau that represents an evolutionary state of achievement of a mature process. Layers are meant to offer an accessible understanding of the states of maturity of the model. Levels define an incremental scale for measuring the maturity of an organization's software process and for evaluating its software process capability. An example of levels in a maturity model are the five levels of the CMMI: initial, repeatable, defined, managed, and optimizing.

Criteria

Each model domain is evaluated against criteria that precisely define the state, conditions, and outcomes that are required to achieve a particular level. These criteria glue together the various model domains with a level. Because each model domain is different, the criteria that establish maturity may not be directly comparable with another model domain's level criteria. For instance, a model domain such as "risk management process" has criteria that it has to meet to be at an "initial" level of maturity. Another model domain, configuration management, has "initial" criteria as well. These are at the same level but define the particular goals and activities at that state. The criteria for these model domains are not interchangeable.

Targets

A target is the desired maturity level for each model domain of the maturity model. A good target satisfies the process quality requirements and the risk appetite of the organization. Across the board, one would think that for all model domains their improvement goals should be set to a high level. Aiming for highest-level targets is not necessarily an ideal state, however. Cost, time, and outcome are factors when setting targets as improvement goals. Cost/benefit analysis should be done before setting targets. In many cases, an appropriate target is to establish an industry peer–level target. Other organizations may have the constraint of "coming from behind" where achieving the next level is sufficient. Targets may be target state visionary goals. Targets represent the ideal state of maturity that is set as a goal to achieve.

Selecting a Maturity Model

Maturity models vary. They are typically purpose built. They are constructed to evaluate a specific aspect of an organization, such as its software development practice, security program, or compliance program. The maturity model should be selected based on the specific need. Management, such as a CISO, may need visibility into the effectiveness of the security program. An auditor would want a maturity model tailored to the type of audit and organization. The organization receives a level rating that indicates where it fits according to the selected maturity model. Who provides the level rating depends on the model. For example, if it is CMMI, ISACA is involved. For the NIST Cybersecurity Framework, a capability model is built in. The model's results give direction about how the current state of process management impacts the organizational culture.

Even when using the right maturity model, you should be aware that a certain level of subjectivity is involved. Use the information with caution when assuring management that a process is appropriately controlled based on a maturity model assessment.

The pitfall of selecting the wrong maturity model is that process improvements may not work. You can change to a different maturity model even after already using one, but it is costly and should be avoided. Instead, more effort should be put into selecting the best model and tailoring it to your organization's specific needs.

Building a Maturity Model

Why would you want to build a maturity model? As a security professional you may need to evaluate aspects of your organization's secure software development practices for the purpose of finding areas that need improvement. Management may need to see a formal representation of these results to justify areas where they might apply funding for improvement. Perhaps the enterprise security architecture team needs to establish and track the adoption of security architecture practices and patterns across the development teams. A maturity model is a useful tool to achieve each of these goals and presents the status of each concern in a consistent and overall relatable way.

When you can't find a maturity model that meets the organization's or management's needs, you can create one. Alternatively, if a maturity model already exists that meets the process area requirements, it may need customization to meet specific organizational or management needs. Either way, an understanding of a maturity model's purpose, content, and structure is needed to understand how to effectively create or modify one. The Institute for Internal Auditors describes the steps to building a maturity model as follows:

1. Determine the model's purpose.
2. Determine the model domains.
3. Determine the levels.
4. Set model domain–level expectations.
5. Set domain targets.
6. Assess maturity level.
7. Discover what the model missed.
8. Report on model results.
9. Revisit the model routinely.

Each step is examined in the following sections. To illustrate the utility of a maturity model in security assessment, the sections also consider an example of the step in the development of a maturity model oriented to the specific purpose of evaluating, road-mapping, and tracking an organization's migration to adopt DevSecOps practices.

Determine the Model's Purpose

The maturity model sets objectives the organization intends to meet. Asking questions is helpful to discover a maturity model's purpose. What does the model need to assess? What does management need to know? What business processes are involved? What is the scope of the assessment? Are any specialized process knowledge, tools, techniques, or skills subject to assessment?

A maturity model can be used to improve the security of an organization's software development practices. One example could be to develop or customize a maturity model to evaluate, road map, and track an organization's migration to adopt DevSecOps practices and move away from a traditional waterfall lifecycle of deployment.

Determine the Model Domains

A maturity model's purpose drives its content and structure. Model domains are the subject areas of the maturity model. They make up the parts of the maturity model's purpose.

They are also the subject areas that are evaluated by the maturity model. In the CMMI, these model domains are referred to as *process areas* because the CMMI is focused on process improvement. The states of these model domains directly impact the overall maturity model score.

To use the model, pick the aspects that are necessary to evaluate to determine its level of maturity. These aspects include the model domains.

With respect to domain selection and security, let's continue with our example from the "Determine the Model's Purpose" section to measure the adoption of a DevSecOps practice in a software development organization. The selection of domains needs to reflect the areas of activity and process in a DevSecOps practice. These areas might include the security engagement process, emphasizing up-front security, automation, developer security responsibilities, defect resolution, security testing, configuration management, pipeline patching and hardening, and feature deployment rate. While these might constitute the domains of such a maturity model, this is by no means an exhaustive list. Take care to ensure that the list of domains that are used is comprehensive, as the right selection of model domains determines the success or failure of a maturity model.

Determine the Levels

Levels define the degrees of maturity in the model. Levels are used to describe the maturity of the overall subject matter as well as of each model domain. A good scale of levels should naturally represent the full potential range of maturity of the model domains. The lowest level normally represents an initial state. Initial state characteristics are an absence of controls and low process discipline. The highest level is when a process exhibits an optimized, best-practice execution. The levels between these bounds are then metered proportionally.

As an organization moves up in levels of maturity, the predictability, effectiveness, and control of an organization's software processes improve.

Select levels that best describe the maturity of the subject matter. Start by mapping by purpose. Does the model evaluate an organizational program containing multiple process areas? It might make sense to choose levels like initial, repeatable, defined, managed, and optimizing. Does the model take into consideration the maturity level of the security program components? Descriptors such as nonexistent, reactive, managed and proactive can be used to measure these components. Maturity model levels should make sense to the organization as a whole so that its results are within everyone's understanding. A shared understanding makes collaborative efforts more effective.

Keep in mind that each domain, or process area, of the model has some of its meaning defined at each level. Levels can be levels of refinement of a domain. It is best to determine levels based on the purpose of the model and accurately with its model domains in mind.

Now consider an example of the levels in the DevSecOps maturity model discussed in the previous "Determine the Model's Purpose" and "Determine the Model Domains" sections. To define the levels, let's take a closer look at a few of the domains we had identified for the purpose of finding common ground among them. For this example and for simplicity's sake, let's pick three domains to use for the assessment: automation, developer security responsibilities, and security testing.

With the domains picked, the simplest first approach is to identify levels in this model that represent the extremes of maturity. The level at one extreme is "not performed" and the level at the other extreme is "optimizing," where not performed is the least mature and optimizing means the best possible outcome. These extremes frame the subsequent level discovery.

Next, determine what levels exist between these extremes. To do this, it's useful to consider what it would take to be at an optimizing level and work backward from there. For instance, to optimize each of the domains we're examining, first the processes of each domain should be defined.

The next step would be to take this ordered set of levels and evaluate each domain against it to see whether they fit. The goal of this step is to keep the levels that work for all domains or remove a level if it doesn't and to refine what remains to fit all of the domains' needs. When refining this list, you may have a target number of levels to meet.

Once defined, the processes defined at each level should be repeatable. After that, considerations should be addressed regarding how they are managed, how resilient these processes are, and whether feedback is collected and used for improvement. This brainstorming activity yields an ordered set of potential maturity levels that may fit the needs of the model.

Following this exercise to its conclusion defines the maturity levels and their criteria for use. Use this criteria as guidance to then conduct a structured assessment of the DevSecOps processes to determine the maturity level of the DevSecOps practice. This information and the structured assessment results can be presented to stakeholders and management for them to identify specific areas to improve or to invest in.

Set Model Domain-Level Expectations

Each level defines a new level of achievement. Maturity model levels have qualifying criteria that the target of assessment must meet to achieve that level. The maturity assessment criteria for each model domain will be different per level compared to other model domains. Each domain is different. The maturity level evaluation of each domain is specific to its nature. In-depth research or facilitated conversation with subject-matter experts can help with model development.

As an example, consider a maturity model that evaluates a security program that has software configuration management and vulnerability management domains and has maturity levels of nonexistent, reactive, managed, and proactive. Each of these domains would have different maturity level criteria. Defining the criteria for "nonexistent" may be similar between the two. The criteria for "managed" would be very different. "Managed" configuration management is different than "managed" vulnerability management. Nonetheless, the maturity level is still "managed."

Set Domain Targets

A target is the desired maturity level for each domain. A realistic target level is based on the current state and the investment value and cost to achieve the target level. A cost-benefit analysis and assessment of an organization's risk appetite should be done to calibrate what level a target should be.

For instance, a target for software development improvement may be to be at the maturity level known as "managed." In this respect, one requirement describing that level is for the software development environment to have "automated, comprehensive testing."

Assess Maturity Level

Test-drive the model. Use analytical techniques to evaluate models to see the results they produce. Line up subject-matter experts to size up the model domains, levels, criteria, and results. Is the model accurate? Is it comprehensive? Are the levels right? These are some of the types of questions to ask after running the model subsequent times for refinement.

Set a baseline. The results of the maturity model runs can be used to set a baseline. This baseline can be used for subsequent improvements both in the process/system and in the model.

Discover What the Model Missed

The results of the model runs may be missing data. There may be a need for adjustments in the model. The model may not have everything it needs to achieve its objectives. Review the model and its results with subject-matter experts who would know about the model. Have them provide feedback to improve the model. Model domains may be added, modified, or deleted. Levels may change. Model domains' criteria may change.

Report on Model Results

A detailed report should be given to management on the results relevant to their needs and objectives. Additional narrative on the development, use, and detailed results of running the maturity model should be stored and accessible. Be sure to include a description of the model and references where to find more extensive information on the model in the report to management as well.

Revisit the Model Routinely

If the model that was developed is one that will be used again, it is a good practice to revisit the model on a routine basis. Returning to evaluate the model is a control activity that can keep it current and accurate. It is an opportunity to make it fit with the current reality of the system/processes it evaluates. However, be aware that changing the maturity model levels or their components' criteria can require having to reconcile with past model results. When the model's methods are changed, so are its measurements. Revisit the model regularly to improve it.

Capability Maturity Model (CMM)

The Capability Maturity Model (CMM) is a framework built to describe guidelines to refine and mature an organization's software development process. It is based on a previous U.S. Department of Defense process maturity framework that was built to assess the process capability and maturity of software contractors for the purpose of awarding contracts. The Software Engineering Institute (SEI) formalized this process maturity framework into the CMM. As the CMM had been used over time, the industry's needs of a capability maturity model had exceeded the original CMM's definition. The CMM then evolved into the Capability Maturity Model Integration (CMMI) framework.

Capability Maturity Model Integration (CMMI)

CMMI is a process-level improvement program created to integrate an assessment and process improvement guidelines for separate organizational functions. The CMMI Institute, a subsidiary of ISACA (`https://cmmiinstitute.com/cmmi`), sets process improvement goals and priorities and provides a point of reference for appraising current processes. The CMMI framework is oriented toward what processes should be implemented rather than how the processes should be implemented. It describes the procedures, principles, and practices that are part of software development process maturity. The CMMI addresses the different phases of the SDLC, including requirements analysis, design, development, integration, installation, operations, and maintenance.

The CMMI framework addresses these areas of interest:

- **Product and service development:** CMMI for Development (CMMI-DEV) concentrates on product development and engineering.

- **Service establishment, management:** CMMI for Services (CMMI-SVC) covers the best practices and key capabilities of service management.

- **Product and service acquisition:** CMMI for Acquisition (CMMI-ACQ) focuses on responsible acquisition practices.

- **People management:** People Capability Maturity Model (PCMM) has key capabilities and best practices to improve people management.

These areas of interest are capability maturity models in their own right. The CMMI integrates these areas of concern under the common framework of the CMMI. Each specialized model consists of the core process areas defined in the CMMI framework.

The CMMI provides a detailed elaboration of what is meant by maturity at each level of the CMM. It is a guide that can be used for software process improvement, software process assessments, and software capability evaluations.

Representation

The CMMI has two approaches to process improvement called *representations*. The CMMI has two types of representations: continuous and staged. Continuous representation evaluates "capability levels." Staged representation evaluates "maturity levels." Both capability levels and maturity levels provide a way to improve the processes of an organization and measure how well organizations can and do improve their processes.

The selection of the type of representation or emphasis on capability or maturity that is needed from an organizational perspective depends upon its development or improvement goals. Similarly, this applies to the security goals of an organization, as will be explored in the following "Continuous" and "Staged" sections.

Continuous

The CMMI continuous representation focuses on a specific process area. Continuous representation uses the term *capability levels* to relate to an organization's process improvement achievement for individual process areas. Continuous representation is for when an organization focuses on specific processes to improve. An organization can choose the processes to improve based on their business objectives and risk mitigation needs.

Continuous representation can be used to focus on evaluating or improving an organization's security processes within their overall SDLC processes. Furthermore, a continuous representation can home in on improving specific security capabilities within the security processes, such as the development and usage of security architecture patterns in the secure SDLC.

Staged

CMMI staged representation provides a means to measure the maturity level of an organization. A staged representation is a predefined road map for organizational improvement, which then translates into maturity. It provides a sequence of process improvements, with each serving as a foundation for the next. Maturity levels describe this progress along the improvement road map. A maturity level is a definite evolutionary step toward achieving improved organizational processes. CMMI staged representation allows comparisons within and between organizations by the use of maturity levels. It can serve as a basis for comparing the maturity of different projects or organizations.

In this way, a staged representation can be used to measure the maturity of an organization's information security management system against competitors or industry reference points. In a similar fashion, it may also be used to compare the secure SDLC against a reference to measure its maturity.

Levels

Levels in the CMMI describe the degrees of progress along the evolutionary paths of capability or maturity. The CMMI levels for process areas, also known as *continuous representation*, are capability levels. The CMMI levels for maturity, known as *staged representation*, are maturity levels.

Capability Levels

The capability levels for continuous representation are Incomplete, Performed, Managed, and Defined. These levels represent an organization's process improvement achievement in an individual process area.

- Incomplete, also known as level zero, indicates a process that is either not performed or partially performed.

- Performed, also known as capability level 1, represents a process that is performed and that accomplishes its specific goals.

- Managed, also known as capability level 2, represents a performed process that accomplishes its specific goals and that has been instituted by the organization to ensure that the process maintains its performance levels. Characteristics of a managed process are that it is planned and executed according to policy. Processes at this level are monitored, controlled, reviewed, and evaluated for adherence to its process description. These disciplines help to maintain the process effectiveness during times of stress.

- Defined, also known as capability level 3, is a more rigorously defined managed process. Level 3 processes are more consistent than those at the managed level because they are based on the organization's set of standard processes and are tailored to suit a particular project or organizational unit.

Maturity Levels

Maturity levels describe an organization's process improvement achievements across multiple process areas. The maturity levels for the staged representation are Initial, Managed, Defined, Qualitatively Managed, and Optimizing.

- Initial, also known as maturity level 1, describes an organization whose processes are ad hoc or chaotic. Despite this, work gets done, but the work is likely over budget and behind schedule.

- Managed, or maturity level 2, indicates that processes at this level are planned and executed according to organizational policy, and the management has visibility on work products at defined points.

- Defined, or maturity level 3, relates to processes that are described in standards, procedures, and methods. Maturity level 3 processes are rigorously defined.

- Qualitatively managed, or maturity level 4, is when an organization uses quantitative objectives for quality and process performance as project management criteria. Statistical techniques are employed to improve the process performance predictability at level 4. Formal measurements are key at this level.

- Optimizing, or maturity level 5, collects data from multiple projects to improve organizational performance as a whole. Level 5 emphasizes continuous improvements through quantitative and statistical methods as well as by responding to changing business needs and technology.

Building Security in Maturity Model (BSIMM)

The Building Security in Maturity Model (BSIMM) is a descriptive, software security–focused maturity model based on actual software security initiatives. It is available under the Creative Commons license. It documents what organizations have actually done, not what security experts would prescribe should be done. The BSIMM is built from hundreds of assessments of real-world security programs. It is regularly updated to reflect actual practices in real software security initiatives. When changes are made to the BSIMM, it is based on observed changes in software development practices and the BSIMM reflects it.

Using a model that describes real software security experiences with data collected from a variety of organizations is powerful. As an evidence-based model, it describes what is being done in industry and what works for organizations for their software security programs. The BSIMM is a source of empirically based guidance and ideas for an organization to use to meet their needs.

Software Assurance Maturity Model (SAMM)

The Software Assurance Maturity Model (SAMM) is a framework to help organizations formulate and implement a security software strategy that is tailored to the specific risks facing the organization. Unlike the BSIMM, the SAMM is a prescriptive framework. The OWASP created and maintains the SAMM.

The SAMM can be used to:

- Evaluate an organization's existing software security practices
- Build a balanced software security assurance program in well-defined iterations
- Demonstrate concrete improvements to a security assurance program
- Define and measure security-related activities throughout an organization

It provides a framework for creating and growing a software security initiative. For a software security program to be successful, security has to be built in; it cannot be bolted on after the fact.

SAMM Business Functions and Objectives

The structure of the SAMM is based on four business functions. These functions are governance, construction, verification, and operations. For each of these business functions, the SAMM defines three security practices. For each security practice, SAMM defines three maturity levels as objectives.

Governance

The governance function describes how an organization manages its software development activities. The three security practices of the governance function are strategy and metrics, policy and compliance, and education and guidance. Strategy and metrics direct and measure an organization's security strategy. Policy and compliance involve setting up an organizational security, compliance, and audit control framework. Education and guidance deliver software development security training.

Construction

The construction function focuses on the activities and processes of creating software. The three security practices of the construction function are threat assessment, security requirements, and secure architecture. Threat assessment is focused on identifying and characterizing potential attacks against an organization's software. Information gained from threat assessments is used to improve risk management. Security requirements involve adding security requirements into the software development process. The secure architecture practice is based on promoting secure by default designs and maintaining the security qualities in controlled use of technologies and frameworks.

Verification

The verification function centers on the activities and processes that an organization uses to test and evaluate software to verify its quality, functionality, safety, and security. The verification function's three security practices are design review, implementation review, and security testing. The design review practice focuses on design artifact inspection to ensure built-in security supports and conforms to the organization's security policies, standards, and expectations. Implementation review concerns assessment of source code to discover vulnerabilities and associated mitigation activities. Security testing examines running software for vulnerabilities and other security issues and sets security standards for software releases.

Operations

Operations function consists of the processes and activities that an organization uses to manage software releases. The three security practices of the operations function are issue management, environment hardening, and operational enablement. Issue management involves managing both internal and external issues to support the security assurance program and minimize exposures. The environmental hardening practice relates to enhancing the security posture of deployed software by implementing controls on its operating environment. The operational enablement practice involves securely and correctly configuring, deploying, and running an organization's software.

SAMM Maturity Levels

The SAMM has a maturity level of zero, which represents a starting point. Level 0 indicates that the practice it represents is incomplete.

The three SAMM maturity levels are as follows:

1. Initial understanding and ad hoc performance of security practice

2. Improved security practice efficiency and effectiveness

3. Security practice mastery at scale

Each maturity level for each security practice has objectives that the security practice must meet and activities that must be performed to achieve that level. Objectives and activities are specifically associated with the security practice and level. They represent the minimum state and conditions that a security practice must present to be at that level of maturity.

To illustrate the differences in objectives and activities among security practices and maturity levels, Tables 8.5 and 8.6 compare the governance function's strategy and metrics security practice against the construction function's threat assessment security practice.

TABLE 8.5 Governance Function's Strategy and Metrics Security Practice

GOVERNANCE	LEVEL 1: SM 1	LEVEL 2: SM 2	LEVEL 3: SM 3
Objectives	Establish a unified strategic road map for software security within the organization.	Measure relative value of data and software assets and choose risk tolerance.	Align security expenditure with relevant business indicators and asset value.
Activities	A. Estimate overall business risk profile. B. Build and maintain assurance program road map.	A. Classify data and applications based on business risk. B. Establish and measure per-classification security goals.	A. Conduct periodic industry-wide cost comparisons. B. Collect metrics for historic security spend.

TABLE 8.6 Construction Function's Strategy and Metrics Security Practice

CONSTRUCTION	LEVEL 1: TA 1	LEVEL 2: TA 2	LEVEL 3: TA 3
Objectives	Identify and understand high-level threats to the organization and individual projects.	Increase accuracy of threat assessment and improve granularity of per-project understanding.	Concretely align compensating controls to each threat against internal and third-party software.
Activities	A. Build and maintain application-specific threat models. B. Develop attacker profile from software architecture.	A. Build and maintain abuse-case models per project. B. Adopt a weighting system for measurement of threats.	A. Explicitly evaluate risk from third-party components. B. Elaborate threat models with compensating controls.

The Software Assurance Maturity Model: A Guide to Building Security into Software Development, Version 1.5 provides the descriptions of objectives, activities, and the like that are shown in Tables 8.5 and 8.6.

These two tables are examples of how two different business functions' security practices have the same three maturity levels but have different objectives and activities.

For more information on the SAMM, see *The Software Assurance Maturity Model: A Guide to Building Security into Software Development*, Version 1.5 (`https://www.owasp.org/images/6/6f/SAMM_Core_V1-5_FINAL.pdf`).

Maturity Model Summary

Maturity models are useful in determining the level of competency and effectiveness of an organization in its practices. Maturity models are particularly well suited for understanding an organization's software development capability and maturity. Maturity models apply well to an organization's security practices and, as you've seen from the BSIMM and SAMM earlier, particularly to how security is applied to software development practices.

Maturity models are assessment tools, however. Like most assessment tools, they are a point-in-time understanding of the environment of their concern. Software development security extends well beyond static snapshots. The real test of software development security comes when the software is running and in its operations and maintenance.

Operations and Maintenance

Software enters the operation and maintenance phase after the testing and verification activities have been completed.

The software serves its intended purpose while in the operation and maintenance phase. However, to keep the software running well (and securely) in the production environment, there is more effort necessary. Organizational challenges around the operational environment include ensuring continuity, handling incidents, recovering from problems, implementing changes, and detecting and fixing bugs, flaws, and vulnerabilities. However, controlling the operational environment is not like controlling the software development environment. Operational problems require operational solutions.

Operational solutions focus on controlling access, inputs, and variability. Visibility of the software and its environment is a significant component of this control. Logging and monitoring are essential for operational information. The many moving parts in an operational environment require many security measures. Operational security measures were discussed at length throughout Chapter 7, so this section will focus more on maintenance concerns.

Maintenance functions are a natural part of operations. The maintenance routine includes a schedule of risk analysis, patch management, upgrades or replacements of software and its dependencies as needed, an encryption key and certificate rotation, log rotation, snapshots and backups of data, and similar functions.

Maintenance functions can impact the routine functionality and service capabilities of running software. Organizations should advertise set periods of time when maintenance functions are to take place to inform the application users of when they may experience service interruptions.

Major changes to an application, its environment, or configuration, such as platform changes, significant functionality changes, framework upgrades, or the like, may cause the application to be subject to another certification and accreditation effort.

Moreover, it is likely that these changes will negatively impact its security features or functionality. At a minimum, the software should go through regression testing and a controlled release to maintain expected functionality, security, and compliance.

Two significant security aspects of maintenance are secure bug fixes and automated application and IT infrastructure configuration. The following two sections will explore those topics.

Secure Bug Fixes

Secure bug fixing is based on four essential factors. First, there need to be clear criteria for secure code development, with a test development strategy to verify new functionality and the security of newly developed code. Next, there needs to be a set of tests that, when run, verify baseline functional, nonfunctional, and, in particular, security expectations of the software. Third, it is necessary to have the best possible understanding of the bug, including the code related to the bug, its software environment, and the situations and conditions for its presentation, as well as its functional and security requirements. Finally, the secure bug fix process needs to proceed in a cycle of development and testing that ultimately results in the bug being fixed and all valid tests passing.

The criteria for secure code development exist in the implementation of a secure SDLC, secure coding standards, software security testing, and software security education, discussed throughout this section and elsewhere in the Common Body of Knowledge (CBK). These processes and standards contribute to establishing methods for how to develop and verify secure and properly functioning code.

The tests developed to verify the baseline functional, nonfunctional, and security expectations of the code developed or modified to achieve the bug fix contribute to and become a part of the set of tests used to verify the functionality and security of the software. Apart from the tests written to verify the bug fix, the other existing tests, when run, should indicate if the software's functionality or security qualities have changed in a manner that is not expected. Unexpected changes like this are known as *regressions* from the software baseline. Running tests to find unexpected and undesirable changes like this is known as *regression testing*.

Regression testing is used to verify the consistency of the code base and should be performed prior to the release of bug fixes. These tests include unit tests, functional tests, integration tests, and security tests. Automating regression testing is a best practice, as it reduces variance and the potential for human error. Vulnerability scanning, penetration testing, and similar tests can also be added to this process to improve the regression testing process. In a secure software build workflow process such as a continuous integration or continuous deployment pipeline, the bug fix code would be evaluated by all of the tests until deployment. A test failure is a build failure. The new version of the software should not be deployed until all of the tests pass, proving not only that the bug was fixed but also that the software did not regress.

Naturally, the better the tests are and the better test coverage is, the better the accuracy and precision of the software's future performance will be to meet all expectations. It is important to make sure that all of the necessary tests are run and that no important tests are "commented out" by the developers to make the process complete successfully. A routine security audit of the automation infrastructure and workflows is necessary to help ensure the comprehensiveness of security and other testing.

With the software testing and verification solidly in place, it is necessary to have as complete as possible an understanding of the situations and conditions in which the bug presents itself. The developers who will work to fix the bug should make an effort to understand the code related to the bug. They should also know its software environment, the situations and conditions for its presentation, and its functional and security requirements. This is so the bug can be re-created to diagnose and fix the problem.

Then the development to fix the problem commences. The ultimate goal is to get to a state where the bug is fixed and the software's set of tests is incrementally improved to verify the bug fix when they are run.

Automated Application and IT Infrastructure Configuration

Application and IT infrastructure configuration automation software exists to benefit the software security development lifecycle. It does so by reducing errors and shortening the time necessary for infrastructure configuration management and application deployment.

Such software also routinely checks the configuration of the target node. If it detects that a change has been made that does not match the intended configuration, it can reset the situation to its baseline. Several configurations are typically monitored for this purpose. These include operating system state configurations such as running or stopped services, files such as data and code files, and changes to the application binaries. An automated configuration management framework is a powerful tool.

Common infrastructure automation software includes Chef, Ansible, and Puppet. These tools translate the many steps of setting up a system environment into sets of instructions. This form of infrastructure automation can be used to set up on-demand environments for needs such as an instant test environment. This instant test environment can then become part of a rapid software remediation process.

Change Management

The only constant in software development is change, and this is what makes change management so important. There are many reasons for making changes in software. The process of planned software development is itself a series of changes. The customer may alter requirements, necessitating changes to the code. The development team making advances producing new releases or upgrades are considered changes. Unexpected problems crop up, such as the need to fix bugs in the software, and these are changes as well. Enhancements and patches are causes for change as well.

Change management must be a controlled process. Its activities must be visible to the team and management. All changes are ultimately authorized by management, whether directly or implicitly by the overall development process. All changes are durably recorded and tracked. An audit trail should be maintained for all changes. Changes are communicated to stakeholders and interested parties. Changes, once implemented, are verified and documented, and all of the code accessory to the changes is stored, protected, and managed in source code management (SCM).

With the change management process come a number of ceremonies that you as a security practitioner should know. When making changes to software code that is controlled by a change management process, a developer would "check out" and "check in" code from and to a source code repository. A source code repository is a configuration management system that manages versions of software code that are generated by changes to the software. To "check out" code is when a developer reserves code from the repository for the purposes of changing it. Once these changes are made, the developer would then check the code back into the repository, and it becomes a new version of the software in the repository. This process continues as the software evolves in functionality, quality, and stability. Once the accumulated software changes bring the software to the desired level of functionality, quality, or stability, changes to that version of the software will often be prohibited, effectively "freezing" the code from further changes. These ceremonies of check out, check in, and code freezing are fundamental to understanding the software change management process.

The consequences of poor change management are breaking functionality, security instability, wasting development resources, and increased cost.

Change Management Best Practices

Good change management practice begins with a clear and accurate documentation of changes. Changes to any aspect of the software should be recorded, and an audit trail should be maintained. A ticketing system is recommended for documenting changes.

A cardinal rule of proper change management is that code is never changed directly in production. Instead, the developer makes and tests changes in their environment until they are sufficient, and then the change products go to QA for testing. Once QA has verified that the changes are adequate and secure, the code is then deployed to production.

Another rule of proper change management is that there should always be a rollback plan in case the change is not successful.

The following are some additional change management practices:

- Clearly and accurately document changes with the use of a ticketing system.
- Never make untested changes directly in production.
- Test and verify in a lower environment and then promote.
- Always have a backup/back out plan in case change is not successful.

These practices and rules apply to the changes related to patch management as well.

Obviously, change management will proceed more smoothly if the software was properly configured in the first place. Configuration management is discussed later in this chapter in the section "Configuration Management as an Aspect of Secure Coding."

Change Management Workflow

Change management is a formal process. A high-level formal change management process can be as follows:

1. Identify and characterize the need for the change.
2. Make a formal request for change by submitting a ticket for the change request.
3. Assess the change request.
4. Approve the changes and associated development activities.
5. Implement the change request in a repeated routine of code changes and testing until the change requirements are sufficiently completed.
6. QA tests and verifies that the change is sufficient.
7. Promote the code to the next deployment stage, which could be production.
8. Report changes to management for their review.

Emergency Change Management Process

The organization should have an emergency change management process for when there are severe problems in production that need to be resolved quickly. This dire situation involves having an emergency path to a quick resolution that has an abbreviated but sufficient analysis activity and a streamlined approval process. The change request associated with the emergency change management process should have a high priority to its ticket. This ticket remains in a high-priority state until the problem is fixed sufficiently to rectify the situation in production. This ticket should then have its priority reduced. However, it should also remain open until the emergency situation is fully understood and resolved.

If the changes are significant enough, the system should be recertified and reaccredited.

The change management practice, its processes, and the change request that flow through it should be routinely audited to ensure the process is performing effectively and that all of the changes made under its purview are necessary, appropriate, and comply with security policy.

Integrated Product Team

An integrated product team (IPT) is a multitalented group of people from different disciplines responsible for delivering a product. IPTs are formed to tackle complicated projects with challenging requirements or to increase the quality and velocity of product creation or both.

Structure and Interactions

The integrated product team came about to ensure that all of the required roles, skills, knowledge, and personnel resources were either assembled on the team or readily available to the team to make product development, or software development, more efficient and effective.

IPTs commonly consist of software developers, quality assurance staff, product management, project management, and designers. Each specialty brings a unique focus, input, and decision-making to the software development process. Representation from all essential functional areas of the project should be included on an IPT. Each IPT member has decision-making influence over the product.

Formally, the integrated product team comes from integrated product and process development. However, the concept of an integrated product team has a place in other methodologies such as Agile and DevOps, too.

Integrated Product and Process Development

The integrated product team came from an initiative called Integrated Product and Process Development (IPPD). IPPD is a management technique that came out of industry to improve competitiveness and customer satisfaction. It is driven by the customer's needs. It integrates software development activities, from requirements gathering and analysis to support, to optimize the overall software development process.

IPPD tenets provide insight into its purpose and practice. According to NPD Solutions, the key tenets of IPPD are as follows (`www.npd-solutions.com/ippdtenets .html`):

- Customer focus
- Concurrent development of products and processes
- Early and continuous lifecycle planning
- Maximize flexibility for optimization and use of contractor unique approaches

- Encourage robust design and improved process capability
- Event-driven scheduling
- Multidisciplinary teamwork
- Empowerment
- Seamless management tools
- Proactive identification and management of risk

All in all, these tenets describe a product development and team management style that focuses on customer needs and quality, one that is responsive to real-world situations and proactive in the identification and management of risk.

Agile Teams

An Agile team is a form of integrated product team. Clear and effective communication is the cornerstone of Agile methodology, and development concepts, techniques, and ideas are integrated within the team's dynamic. The Agile team management and communication patterns connect them with other teams, expertise, and entities in an organization for necessary information flow and access to these resources as needed.

On the surface, an Agile team resembles the composition of members that you would see on any software development team, regardless of methodology. An Agile team is different, however, in that it places responsibility and decision-making capabilities on the members of the team. Agile teams are small in size, and they put much of the responsibility of product delivery on their members. Software developers, being the makers of the product, have a say in the direction and management of a project. Moreover, this authority extends to team members whose roles commit them to the process. Software developers are by their efforts committed to the process, whereas supporting or accessory participants are only just involved.

Like the integrated product teams formed out of the IPPD, Agile teams exist to produce high-value working software on a frequent, routine basis.

DevOps

With a focus on agility, automation, rapid development, and frequent delivery of working software, new working styles emerged. These forces coalesce development with automation and aspects of system administration and operations. This integration of disciplines and technology has come to be known as DevOps.

DevOps breaks down the wall between developers and operations. DevOps enables continuous integration and continuous deployment. DevOps accelerates software delivery and increases software quality and security.

Many of the DevOps practices, such as process automation, emphasis on testing, and frequent deployments, are similar to those used in agile and iterative methodologies. The distinction between the two is that DevOps is an implementation of these practices and that this implementation can be used within the practice framework of the various methodologies.

DevOps workflow operates much like an assembly line, and the driving force is to build quality into both the process and the software it produces. A complete DevOps assembly line is a specialized automated orchestration of software development and quality assurance activities. This automation of critical activities such as building, testing, and packaging provides many competitive benefits to an organization.

According to the 2017 State of DevOps report put out by the company Puppet, some significant benefits of a high-performance DevOps practice are a 5 times lower change failure rate, 96 times faster mean time to recover (MTTR) from downtime, and 440 times faster lead time from commit to deploy. These results equate to rapid software throughput and production as well as significant gains in stability. (For the full report, see `https://puppet.com/resources/whitepaper/state-of-devops-report.`)

These forces directly impact software development security. Software-based vulnerabilities can be identified and fixed by the development team. These vulnerability fixes can then be rapidly deployed to production. The DevOps continuous workflow verifies the quality, and security assurance tests rapidly deploy the updates into production. The responsiveness and comprehensiveness of testing make the DevOps workflow a great boon to software security.

Security governance is particularly important when establishing DevOps in an organization. Because of its multidisciplinary set of responsibilities, it is possible to grant the DevOps role too many privileges. DevOps role entitlements must be carefully controlled. When adopting DevOps, it is important to be aware not to create toxic combinations of role entitlements. The security principles of least privilege and separation of duties should be at the fore of DevOps role-entitlement designations. DevOps's access to deployment environments should be limited to development, with restrictions on access to the test and production environments. The ability for DevOps to affect the operations environment, particularly a cloud environment that is closely associated with DevOps, should be controlled. Where DevOps requires the ability to create user identities, it should be limited in the privileges that it can grant those identities. Where DevOps can change the infrastructure configuration, these changes should be carefully reviewed before promoting the changes to higher deployment environments. With proper security governance and design of the DevOps role and workflows, however, the DevOps discipline naturally points to building security into the software development process.

DevSecOps

DevSecOps (www.devsecops.org/) is the merging of security with DevOps. It takes the DevOps role, automation infrastructure, and workflows and builds in security techniques and continuous attention to security.

DevSecOps is best summed up by the words of its manifesto, which describes how DevSecOps continually learns how security practitioners can contribute with less friction. DevSecOps seeks to innovate to ensure data security and privacy. It seeks to make security and compliance available as services. DevSecOps seeks to open new paths to promote security. In doing so, it proactively engages in security activities with the software. It actively seeks to find security issues and to partner with the organization to resolve them effectively and permanently.

DevSecOps provides a set of values that include an excellent summary understanding of what drives DevSecOps. These values also set the expectations that one should have when working with DevSecOps in an organization. The DevSecOps values are as follows:

- **Leaning in** over always saying "no"
- **Data and security science** over fear, uncertainty, and doubt
- **Open contribution and collaboration** over security-only requirements
- **Consumable security services with APIs** over mandated security controls and paperwork
- **Business-driven security scores** over rubber stamp security
- **Red and blue team exploit testing** over relying on scans and theoretical vulnerabilities
- **24/7 proactive security monitoring** over reacting after being informed of an incident
- **Shared threat intelligence** over keeping info to ourselves
- **Compliance operations** over clipboards and checklists

Working with these values builds security into software development while also supporting the realization of responsive product adjustment, high quality, and rapid product delivery. DevSecOps is a significant improvement in the meeting of security with software development.

IDENTIFY AND APPLY SECURITY CONTROLS IN DEVELOPMENT ENVIRONMENTS

A primary security goal in the control design of a development environment is to develop secure code. A security practitioner should be familiar with the essential elements of a software development environment and their security implications on protecting source code and assets. A security practitioner should understand how the source code, assets, and environment are managed and controlled as they move through the SDLC.

This section will describe key aspects of the software environment, then will describe how configuration management is an important aspect of secure coding, and then finally will explain how to secure source code repositories.

Security of the Software Environment

So far, the discussion of software development security has covered the SDLC, operations and maintenance, change management, and maturity models. This overview has demonstrated the impact and importance of each topic to software development security. Here, we discuss the security of the software environment.

There are a number of topics related to the security of the software environment. This section focuses on the security considerations with programming languages, secure use of open-source software, database management systems, and security considerations of deployment environments.

Programming Languages Security

When it comes to the security of programming languages, not all languages are created equal. Nor are the security skills of the software writers who use these languages. Security with respect to programming languages needs to consider both the language used and the skills capacity of those who use it.

There are various ways to evaluate these aspects of security in the use of a programming language. It is possible to collect metrics on the total number of vulnerabilities for applications written in various languages. Furthermore, the impact of developers' security skills on the capability to reduce these vulnerabilities can be measured. The security vendor Veracode analyzed more than 1.5 trillion lines of code from hundreds of thousands of web and mobile applications and in 2015 published some remarkable key findings in their "State of Software Security Report" (`http://intersog.com/blog/programming-languages-vulnerabilities-2015/`). Here are two salient points in the findings:

- Web scripting language-based applications have significantly more cross-site scripting and SQL injection vulnerabilities than Java and .NET-based applications. The choice of programming language has a bearing on OWASP Top Ten pass rates.

- Software development team e-learning demonstrated a 30 percent improvement in vulnerability fix rates over companies that did not provide software security training.

To determine a programming language's security, it should be looked at from the perspectives of language design and developer fluency. Both of these topics are examined more closely in the next two sections. Regardless of the language that is used, a related concern is whether secure practices are followed in coding and configuring the software. Those topics are explored later in this chapter in the sections "Configuration Management as an Aspect of Secure Coding" and "Secure Coding Practices."

Language Design

Software languages vary in the security of their design. Software languages are human artifacts created for different purposes. Some languages are designed to work with computer systems at a low level, accessing memory, hard disks, and networking. Other languages are designed for higher-level specific purposes such as rapid web development or logic programming. Because of the variety of reasons languages are created, the emphasis on the security of a language varies as well.

The base C language is a good example. As a system-level language, the C language is powerful in how it accesses computer system resources. However, this power comes with a security cost as the language is vulnerable to buffer overruns, null pointer errors, segmentation faults, and other memory-related errors. Because of the level of access the C language has to the computer system, security in the C language strongly depends upon the security knowledge and proficiency of the software writer.

Another language is the Personal Home Page (PHP) language. PHP is designed as a scripting language specifically for rapid development of database-driven web pages with quick and convenient database access. And, as its name implies, PHP is a language designed primarily by individual creators. PHP is written in C, so it can inherit the security vulnerabilities from an insecure implementation of its parent language. However, the security concerns that emerge in PHP are more oriented toward its purpose as a rapid data-driven web development language. These are mainly related to the OWASP Top Ten Most Critical Web Application Security Risks. Similar to the C language, security in PHP language strongly depends upon the security knowledge and proficiency of the software writer as well.

Contrasted with the previous two examples, the Ada language, a language designed for military, avionics, and real-time systems, was designed with an emphasis on safety and security. The safety and security required by the types of software programs in these domains set high standards for the Ada language.

Many of the design features of the Ada language support a secure software implementation. Ada encourages a modular program structure that supports security by minimizing defects through good design and encouraging reuse, readability, and maintainability. This is an important aspect of Ada, since it is specifically designed to be the software language of large and complex systems. Systems that are large and complex need to be broken down into manageable sets of functionality that can be developed, tested, and verified independently by different teams and then integrated into the product system as a whole when ready for release.

Good software design is important in minimizing flaws that lead to security vulnerabilities. Also, correct use of language syntax minimizes defect-causing vulnerabilities and thus security vulnerabilities. The Ada language has syntax checking, which ensures that programs written in it are correct. Ada's strong type checking detects and prevents common software errors such as mismatched types and range violations. These types of issues have significant safety and security consequences in systems with high consequences to compromise or failure. Furthermore, Ada has built-in detection and protection against buffer overflow, null pointers, and array access errors, which are typical areas that attackers seek to exploit in software programs.

Java is another language that is designed with security built in. The Java Virtual Machine has a security manager that checks the validity and security of the byte codes of Java programs prior to execution. It has mature security libraries that support necessary security capabilities such as authentication and authorization, cryptography, secure communication, public key infrastructure, and more. It also has many security frameworks that are designed to support secure program development in Java.

As you've seen from the discussion of these languages, there are a number of considerations when evaluating the security of a programming language. One consideration is the amount of access to the computer system resources that the language offers the software developer. Another is the extent to which security is designed into the language or is being imposed upon the software by secure coding practices, frameworks, testing, and verification. Further considerations include the design purpose of the language and whether it supports secure implementations. The following are different security aspects of a programming language that you should use to evaluate the security of a programming language:

- Syntax checking
- Safe typing
- Safe pointers
- Safe architecture
- Safe paradigm implementation (e.g., object-oriented, function-oriented)
- Safe object construction
- Memory management, garbage collection, invalid access protections
- Safe and managed error and exception handling
- Safe startup
- Safe communication

- Safe concurrency, deadlock detection, and resolution
- Security patterns and frameworks
- Secure execution environment (e.g., a security manager)
- Developers' security expertise

Developer Fluency

Many of the security vulnerabilities in software programs can be avoided by improving a developer's expertise in the limitations, capabilities, and secure usage of the languages they use. Educating software development teams on security significantly improves their vulnerability fix rate. The foundation of security quality is established in software developers knowing how to implement security in the language that is being used. Ultimately, it is the programmer and not the language they use who is responsible for the secure operation of their code. Make sure that your developers and engineers fully understand the security features, patterns, and frameworks of the programming languages they use to develop your software.

Open-Source Software (OSS)

Open-source software (OSS) is computer software whose source code has been made publicly available. Some OSS is completely in the public domain, meaning that anyone can change it and use it for any purpose. Other OSS comes with a license that limits to varying degrees the rights to change and distribute the software.

Ever since the early days of software development, programmers would share software to learn from each other, get work done, and advance the field of computing. Academia still often collaborates in software development. Notable examples are Donald Knuth with the TeX typesetting system and Richard Stallman with the GNU operating system.

Several considerations of OSS include its provenance, benefits, community, and security concerns and approaches.

Software of Unknown Provenance

The concept of *software of unknown provenance* is a significant security concern that should be a priority consideration when selecting or using OSS. Software of unknown provenance describes software that has not been developed with a known software development methodology and thus has uncertain security. Some OSS projects can fall into this area of concern because of the open and voluntary contributions to the project's software development. Be wary of OSS that does not follow a software development process. Be sure to verify that there is acceptable quality, feature, and security governance of open-source projects.

Benefits of Open-Source Software

Without OSS, we might not have the World Wide Web as it is today. Linux, Apache, PHP, and Java frameworks are a few technologies that enabled the Web to grow quickly. Being able to use OSS for free gave businesses an on-ramp to doing e-commerce on the Web and provided software engineers with opportunities in the marketplace. Businesses offered models of support for OSS, and the open-source projects continuously responded to pressures to improve. Overall, the accessibility and free functionality made OSS a popular and attractive choice as a foundation on which to grow online business during the early days of the Web as well as today.

OSS development has culminated in a range of possible benefits including flexibility, community, variety, licensing options, low cost, and potentially even security.

Flexibility

A common concern with proprietary software is "commercial lock-in." Commercial lock-in is when a customer is locked in to having to use a vendor's software because of a dependency on that software for critical parts of their business. Vendor lock-in means having to accept a software feature set dictated by the vendor and delivered on their schedule.

This is where OSS is different. A developer can modify OSS to meet their specific functional needs. Open the source, change the code, assure that it works and is safe and secure, and then use it.

Community

It is easy to recognize the knowledge, sharing, and passion of the community of people involved in OSS projects. Open-source contributors code for free. They need some specific functionality from software. They're motivated to exercise or demonstrate their skills. Freedom and choice are fundamental to these individuals, and they want their software to be used. Documentation for OSS varies, since most developers focus on code instead of records. However, documentation and support do exist in forums, wikis, newsgroups, and chats for every popular open-source project.

Variety

The open-source phenomenon encourages participation and contribution as well as software consumption. A software developer can demonstrate their talents by contributing to open-source projects. Or they can create their own open-source project. There are many open-source projects that meet a wide variety of software needs. That is the benefit of an active, passionate, smart community of developers who are free to create software to solve many needs. The variety can be overwhelming, but services such as `https://www.openhub.net/` can help you find the open-source software you need.

Licenses

A consideration to take seriously is the license option that comes with the OSS you choose. Make sure the license that covers the OSS you choose is one that fits with your software needs. Not all open-source licenses allow for the code they cover to be freely used within other software, regardless of commercial interest or lack of it. Consult with `https://blog.codinghorror.com/pick-a-license-any-license/` for some food for thought concerning open-source licenses. Refer to `https://opensource.org/licenses/category` for more information on specific licenses.

Cost

OSS is (mostly) free. The source code is free. The expertise to understand, modify, and use it is not. Many OSS products come with optional paid commercial support.

Security

Compared with commercial closed source code, whose bugs and vulnerabilities resolutions depend upon the resources of its parent organization, OSS has the eyes of the world on it to use it and hypothetically to report bugs, find vulnerabilities, improve upon it, and provide quality assurance. Yet, on the other hand, some believe that open-source transparency is a security paradox because the vulnerabilities are sometimes tragically overlooked and are open to the public.

To Trust the Herd or to Not Trust the Herd

A significant concern about OSS built by communities of developers is that access to the source code is also open to hackers and malicious users. Following this logic, one could assume that OSS is less secure than proprietary applications.

Beyond being exposed to the world, another security concern is that the open-source community may not be as focused to issue critical software patches as vulnerabilities emerge.

Some IT stakeholders distrust OSS because of its apparent lack of discipline and rapid change. These biases come from the early days of the open-source renaissance, when the coordinated efforts of the communities were immature. What was to become the most popular web server in the world, the Apache web server, was so named because it was "a patchy server."

However, what can be viewed as weakness, in this case, can also be viewed as a strength. OSS is a significant part of most commercial IT infrastructures. Perhaps Kerckhoffs's principle of transparency of an encryption system applies to the security of open-source software? Only if someone verifies the OSS for you.

Openness combined with the open-source value proposition has attracted commercial resources and support. A famous example of this is Red Hat Linux. Red Hat pioneered the open-source business model. Red Hat offers the Linux operating system for free, but it charges customers for maintenance, support, and installation. This business model makes sense for complicated OSS like Linux. As the open-source business model evolved, so did the depth of commercial involvement in the assurance and security of the software.

Your organization doesn't have to rely upon commercial support, but expertise in the OSS you use is required to manage it. Regardless if you choose community, commercial, or organizational expertise, the best recommendation to ensure the safety and security of your OSS choices is to practice care, caution, and diligence in validating its security.

How to Secure Open-Source Software

The SANS Institute provides guidelines to secure OSS implementations in its "Security Concerns in Using Open Source Software for Enterprise Requirements" (found at `https://www.sans.org/reading-room/whitepapers/awareness/security-concerns-open-source-software-enterprise-requirements-1305`).

- **Security policy:** A well-documented and comprehensive security policy is needed to guide an organization to realize the real benefits of the use of OSS. This security policy should provide guidelines on the selection, installation, security requirements, and maintenance of open-source. It should explain the scope and the basic guiding principle (a policy statement) and define the roles and responsibilities without any ambiguities. It is the basis of secure OSS use.

- **Evaluation:** All OSS should be thoroughly evaluated before its use by an organization. Don't take the security assurances of the open-source project for granted. A technical evaluation of functionality, integration, and security should be done for verification. Seek out trusted sources to provide use and risk information to determine whether an open-source product falls within the acceptable risk of the organization. Furthermore, conduct a CVE search against the OSS for security awareness.

- **Avoid ad hoc installations:** Do not allow administrators or users to download or install any unsanctioned OSS to critical environments. All OSS to be installed and used in an enterprise environment should be sanctioned by the organization. Sanctioned OSS has been thoroughly evaluated and found to be acceptable for use. It has a formal installation process, and the organization actively manages it. Management of sanctioned open-source includes security and patch management.

- **Download OSS only from trusted sites:** Only choose reputable and trusted sites to download OSS. Trusted commercial entities that support OSS are good sources.

- **Prefer source code to binaries wherever possible:** Most OSS comes in both source code and binary package formats. Trust the source code over the binaries. The binaries may not have been compiled by the source code. Verify the source code by verifying it against the MD5 checksums that should be provided with it.

- **Scan for vulnerabilities:** It is important to conduct vulnerability scans on the OSS.

- **Disable unwanted services:** When preparing the OSS for any use, disable any unnecessary services or functionality options that are not required for it to satisfy your requirements. A rule of thumb, in this case, is to follow a "deny by default if not explicitly permitted" model.

- **Have a defense-in-depth strategy:** Always follow a defense-in-depth strategy to ensure the secure use of OSS. Taking a layered security approach not only protects the OSS from abuse but also protects your environment from the OSS. Make sure that you have a robust defense strategy in place.

- **Install and forget model is very dangerous:** OSS maintenance and operations must be audited periodically and conducted like any commercial software. The individuals in your organization's open-source management program should subscribe to respected open-source security mailing lists. A patch management program should cover it. Software upgrades should be maintained current, provided they have been tested and verified to be safe for production use.

- **Training and documentation are important:** Training and education are essential for effective OSS security management. OSS often requires intensive technical expertise. An open-source training and education program should exist. It should be periodically audited and updated as well.

- **Consider OSS in DR and BC plans:** Your organization's disaster recovery and business continuity plans should be updated to account for the dependency on the deployed open-source products. To successfully implement security and trust in the OSS your organization relies upon for its business, you should have an OSS program to ensure informed and secure selection, use, modification, and maintenance of software. This program would closely follow but extend software assurance guidelines to include the following:

- Requirements analysis, to establish the actual needs

- Acceptance criteria, for a formal evaluation to accept a selection

- Competitive analysis, to sort out the best selections from many

- Functional evaluations, to evaluate if software functionality satisfies needs

- Architectural evaluations, to ensure that the software satisfies necessary qualities such as scalability and integration

- Security evaluations, to gain information on the state of vulnerabilities and exposures of software, as well as availability of security patches

- Security testing, to conduct security tests to discover and become familiar with the risk profile of the OSS

- Secure procurement, to find a trustable source of software source code or binaries

- Commercial support, to find trustable and reputable commercial entities to provide support, product information, patches, upgrades, and so on

- Education, to educate information technology staff on OSS, from use, to code, to configuration, to security

Databases and DBMSs

A database is a structured collection of data held in a computer system. This structured collection of data provides information in a model form to an information system that is meaningful for its use. An example model form of database information could be, in the case of a structured SQL database, a table of user data for a program to use.

A database management system (DBMS) is a software application that manages databases and provides an interface to users to interact with its databases. A DBMS allows for the definition, creation, querying, update, and administration of databases.

A database is strongly associated with the DBMS that created it. Standards such as SQL provide some degree of interoperability between DBMSs. Protocols such as Open Database Connectivity (ODBC) or Java Database Connectivity (JDBC) allow applications to use DBMS functionality.

DBMS functionality falls into four main classifications:

- Data definition, which allows for the creation, modification, and removal of database definitions

- Update, which facilitates the insertion, modification, and deletion of the actual data

- Retrieval, which provides information in a form that is usable to the calling environment

- Administration, which facilitates the registering and monitoring users, enforces data security, monitors performance, maintains data integrity, manages concurrency control, and provides recovery of information in the case of an unexpected system failure

Capabilities

A DBMS provides a data definition language (DDL), a data manipulation language (DML), and a data dictionary.

The data definition language, also known as the data description language, is used to create and modify database objects in a database. These database objects subject to the DDL between varying DBMS models, but for instance, in the relational database model, these objects would include views, schemas, tables, indexes, and so on.

The data dictionary contains a database's metadata. It is a collection of information about the database, such as data ownership, data description, relationships to other data, origin, usage, and format. Because of this metadata, it is a critical aspect of the DBMS and typically used only by database administrators.

The data manipulation language allows users to manipulate data in a database. DML typically facilitates inserting data into database tables, retrieving data from database tables, deleting data from existing tables and modifying data. SQL is the best known DML.

Database Transactions and ACID

Operations performed on the database through the DBMS interface are defined by a control structure called a *transaction*. A transaction is a sequence of operations such as insert, update, or delete that a DBMS executes as a single logical unit of work against a database. Thus, a transaction is a general representation of any independent change made to a database. A valid transaction must exhibit atomicity, consistency, isolation, and durability, which are commonly referred to together as ACID.

The ACID characteristics are necessary for reliable data management. When a database possesses these characteristics, it is considered to be ACID-compliant. Why are these characteristics essential to reliable data management? Let's examine each of the ACID characteristics in more detail.

Atomicity is a requirement that all data modifications must be "all or nothing." When a transaction is executed against a database, either all or none of the transaction's constituent operations will be committed to the database. With atomicity, there are no partial changes. If one part of the transaction fails, the entire transaction fails. Atomicity holds in the presence of deadlocks, software failure, hardware failures, and application failures.

Consistency is the requirement that a database transaction must only change its subject data in ways that are valid according to all defined rules, constraints, cascades, and triggers, and that the representation of data in the database is uniform per transaction where every read has the data from the most recent write.

Isolation requires that multiple simultaneous transactions do not impact each other's execution and individual end state. The DBMS manages multiple simultaneous transactions against a database. Isolation only ensures that transactions will not interfere with each other and not the order in which transactions will execute.

Durability ensures that all transactions committed to the database are recorded, persistent, and stable. Database backups and transaction logs are used to ensure that no transactions are lost.

Database Normalization

Central to the use of a DBMS is how it organizes the data that it maintains. This concept is known as *database normalization*. Database normalization comes from the relational database model and describes how formally the data is organized against criteria of standard structures known as *normal forms*. These normal forms define requirements for data to be primarily referenced, nonduplicative, and independent of other data.

The main objectives of normalization are to reduce data duplication and improve data integrity.

You may already be familiar with the structures that the normalization process uses to organize data to achieve these goals. Data is organized into what is known as a *schema* of tables, with each table representing a collection of related data. Columns and rows organize data in tables. Columns distinguish separate data attributes that are associated with the others in the table. A row associates these attributes into a logical grouping of data known as a *set*.

The concept of a key is used to distinguish these sets of data and rows (or data rows), and thus reduces data duplication. Keys are data elements, often unique among their group, that are used to both identify and look up rows of data. There are different types of keys; however, for the purposes of this discussion, the most common types of keys are primary keys and foreign keys. A *primary key* is the unique data attribute that identifies the row. *Foreign keys* are used to maintain references, known as *relations*, between the data in rows of one table and the data in rows of another table.

Relating data among tables in this fashion also reduces data duplication because the relation allows for each of the data elements represented in tables throughout the schema to be associated and meaningfully referenced with other data without necessarily having to duplicate the data to make these connections. Here is where we return the discussion to normal forms.

The normal forms of how data is structured formalize how data is organized to reduce data duplication and improve data integrity.

A variety of normal forms have been defined. The most commonly used of these normal forms are unnormalized, first normal form, second normal form, and third normal form. Unnormalized data does not have any relationships with other tables and often has redundant data and multiple data elements grouped into single columns. This actually can provide an advantage in that queries to the data are simpler and thus may be faster compared against querying more normalized data. Fast queries are an advantage when serving data on an Internet scale of demand. NoSQL databases often are based upon or more directly support the unnormalized normal form, which is why they are popular in web-scale applications. The downside is that the absence of relationships with other tables can lead to data redundancy and a lack of data integrity.

The first normal form creates separate tables for related data. The first normal form requires data attributes to have an atomic value. Requiring an atomic value for each data attribute means that groups of data cannot be stored into an attribute. The first normal form uses primary keys to identify sets of data. The advantage is that the first normal form reduces data duplication.

The second normal form extends the first normal form by making all nonkey data attributes dependent upon the primary key. The second normal form improves how data is grouped, but in complex schemas, with multiple related data sets, it does not eliminate the potential for relationships between data attributes that are linked together by nonprimary keys. This type of relationship is known as a *transitive dependency*. The third normal form removes transitive dependencies.

The third normal form extends the second normal form by requiring that subsets of column data in what was second normal form that could be identified by a unique attribute are separated out into their own tables.

How does this relate to security? Of the CIA triad, the degree to which data is normalized impacts its integrity and availability. Normalization structures control how data is accessed and modified and thus improves data integrity by improving its consistency and enforces the atomicity of its representation. The degree of normalization impacts data availability, however, because it increases the complexity of queries to access and manipulate data as well as increases the complexity of modifying the data. These consequences impact the speed of data retrieval and updates, which, when there is a high volume of requests for data and application response times are critical to success, can have a negative impact on the availability characteristics of the application.

Database Models

A relational database model with its table-based format is a common database management system. This is not the only type of database, however. There are many more database models. A database model defines the logical database structure and essentially determines the manner in which data is stored, organized, and manipulated.

Common logical data models for databases include the following:

- Network model
- Graph
- Object model
- NoSQL
- Relational model

Physical data models can differ as well. Examples of different types of physical database models include inverted indexes and flat files.

Network

The network database model represents its data as a graph in which object types are nodes and relationship types are arcs. This graph model is a flexible way of expressing objects and their relationships because it doesn't restrict data relationships in a strict hierarchy or lattice.

Charles Bachman invented the network model. Its standard specification was published by the Conference on Data Systems Languages (CODASYL) Consortium, ultimately becoming an ISO specification.

One of the leading benefits of the network model is that it allows a natural modeling of relationships between entities while maintaining a hierarchical structure.

Graph

The graph database model extended the network model to break from the constraints of a hierarchy to allow a more fluid and human-centric way of thinking. A graph database model uses graph structures to represent data. Nodes in the graph represent data entities. Nodes can hold any number of attributes, or properties. Labels can be applied to nodes to add metadata such as constraint or index information. Relationships are semantically significant directed connections between two nodes in the graph. Such a relationship between nodes could be "Sally" (the first node, a person) "is employed by" (a directed relationship) "Big Security Consulting Company" (the second node, a company).

A graph database with these structures and associations allows for the user to ask meaningful questions to search the data in the form of semantic queries, such as "Where is Sally employed?" or "Who does the Big Security Consulting Company employ?" Imagine what it would take to do this in a relational model. For those of you who know SQL, this is much more efficient and straightforward than composing a JOIN method. All nodes in a graph database have connections. Therefore, there are no orphan nodes in a graph database. Graph native databases can access nodes and relationships in constant time and traverse millions of connections per second per core.

Because graph databases excel in qualitative directed relationships among entity data, they are well suited for representing and querying complex data environments such as cybersecurity data. MITRE's platform for exchanging cyber-threat intelligence, the Structured Threat Information Expression (STIX), was developed to provide collaborative threat analysis, automated threat detection, and response capabilities. STIX version 2.x uses graph database technology as core architecture to deliver these capabilities.

For more information on STIX, see `https://docs.google.com/document/d/1yvqWaPPnPW-2NiVCLqzRszcx91ffMowfT5MmE9Nsy_w/edit#heading=h.8bbhgdisbmt`. A widely used graph database is Neo4J. For more information on Neo4J, see `https://neo4j.com/`.

Object

An object database represents information in the form of objects as used in object-oriented programming. Object-oriented database management systems (OODBMSs), otherwise referred to as ODBMS (Object Database Management System), combine database capabilities with object-oriented programming language capabilities. The benefit of an OODBMS is how it allows object-oriented programmers to directly use the OODBMS to store and retrieve objects and their state without having to use a translation and mapping layer such as what they use with relational databases. Having the same model of data representation makes integration of the database and programming language more fluid and allows the programmer to maintain consistency within one environment.

The following are popular object-oriented databases:

- InterSystems Caché
- Versant Object Database
- ObjectStore
- Matisse

NoSQL

NoSQL databases make up a database family whose focus is on the challenges of web-scale and massive data sets where flexibility, speed, and scale are important. Whereas you will soon see that relational model databases have a static, structured data representation, NoSQL databases are much more flexible on what data is stored in the database.

The NoSQL model has four common models of data storage, which are document databases, key-value stores, wide-column stores, and graph databases.

Document databases hold data as JSON-formatted documents. The structure of the data in these documents typically does not need to be specified in advance. Popular NoSQL document databases are CouchDB and MongoDB. It is also becoming more popular to use open-source search engine frameworks, such as Elastic Search, as NoSQL type databases.

Key-value stores keep data in the database accessible via key values. The data stored can range from simple integers to JSON documents. A popular NoSQL key-value store is Redis.

Wide-column stores store data in columns instead of rows. The advantage of a NoSQL column-oriented database is that this type of storage can increase the speed of queries because it can skip over nonrelevant data that otherwise would come with a query on a relational row-based model. A popular NoSQL wide column-based database is Cassandra.

Relational Databases

The relational database model is the most popularly used database model. It is based on the relational model of data proposed by E. F. Codd in 1970. A relational DBMS manages relational model databases.

In a relational model, all data has an inherent structure. This structure is known as a *schema*, and it is a formal definition of how data will be composed in the database. The schema organizes data into one or more tables, known as *relations*, of columns and rows. Rows in this model are also known as *records* or *tuples*. Columns in the relational model are called *attributes*. Each table is intended to represent one *entity type*. An entity type represents a thing, such as a customer or product item. Each row represents an entity instance, with the columns of the row representing values attributed to that instance.

A unique key identifies each row in a table. Rows in a table can be associated with rows in other tables. Such a relationship is made by adding a column for the unique key of the associated row, also known as a *foreign key*. These relationships are a logical connection between different tables, based on the data relationships and interactions between the tables.

Popular relational DBMSs are Oracle Database, Microsoft SQL Server, MySQL, and PostgreSQL, among others.

DBMS Threats and Vulnerabilities

Databases contain and provide access to vast amounts of information. They are naturally subject to a number of threats and vulnerabilities. The following are some such threats and vulnerabilities to be aware of:

- **Default, blank, and weak username/password:** Default, blank, and weak login credentials should not exist in databases.

- **SQL injection:** Failure to sanitize inputs can result in exposure to potential SQL injections with the possibility of allowing attackers to achieve privileged access to the database. Preferred use of prepared statements, along with input validation and sanitization, go far to prevent this from happening. A prepared statement is functionality provided by a DBMS that allows for parameterized repeated reuse of a SQL statement.

- **Extensive user and group privileges:** Unmanaged user and group privileges is a problem. Instead, groups or roles should be used to administer privileges to users by associating users with their proper group or role. It is not advisable to assign users direct rights.

- **Unnecessarily enabled database features:** Database products can come with enabled features that an organization doesn't need. Disabling or uninstalling unused and unnecessary services reduces the attack surface.

- **Broken configuration management:** Databases offer many configurations to optimize performance or enhance functionality. While these configurations could be useful, they can also be unsafe. Evaluate all database configurations that could be enabled by default or turned on for someone's convenience.

- **Buffer overflows:** Like any software that accepts input from the external environment, databases can be subject to buffer overflow vulnerabilities such as flooding an input with excessive characters. Examine inputs. Sanitize and validate inputs. Keep your database software and security patches up to date.

- **Privilege escalation:** Beware that some database vulnerabilities allow attackers to escalate privileges to gain administrator rights.

- **Denial-of-service attack:** SQL Slammer showed how attackers exploit DBMS vulnerabilities to take down database servers by a denial-of-service attack. Ironically, a patch existed at the time that addressed this vulnerability. Keep your database software and security patches up to date.

- **Unpatched databases:** Don't unnecessarily expose your critical data assets to vulnerabilities that can be fixed by patching. Keep your database software and security patches up to date.

- **Unencrypted sensitive data at rest and in motion:** Protect sensitive data with proper encryption. All connections to the database should be encrypted.

Securing the Database Management System

Consider the following best practices and internal controls when formulating a security matrix for your DBMSs:

- Routinely assess and address DBMS vulnerabilities.
- Place DBMS in secure network zone.
- Check and sanitize all inputs.
- Secure DBMS endpoints.
- Manage user access rights with emphasis on enforcing least privilege.
- Remove inactive users.
- Prefer SQL prepared statements.
- Avoid building SQL statements with string concatenation.
- Classify all sensitive data.
- Monitor, detect, prevent, and alert on unauthorized SQL and big data transactions.
- Block malicious web requests.
- Automate DBMS auditing.
- Routinely create secure snapshots and backups of databases.
- Encrypt databases.

Deployment Environments

A *deployment environment* is a general term that describes a relatively isolated information systems environment that is dedicated to the requirements and hosting of particular classes of applications and services. While the specific types of deployment environments can vary between organizations, the standard deployment environments are known as Development, Integration, Test, Staging, and Production. Each standard deployment has its level of trust and security. The level of trust is at its lowest starting with the development environment and progresses to the highest level of trust in the production environment. Access control, services, tools, and source code are aligned with each production environment.

Software changes are made in the development environment. This environment is typically a developer's workstation. As such, this environment has the lowest level of trust, with the trust being only that which can be placed on an individual developer. Typically, the development environment is logically limited to its version control branch. The developer works on a copy of this branch. Formal code reviews may be conducted on the code associated with this environment. They typically have control over their environment with the ability to download and run the software. The developer is responsible for code quality, safety, security, and integration at this level. This freedom makes this environment untrusted.

The integration environment is one where the collective developers' changes are combined and compiled together. The integration environment is used to verify code quality, safety, security, and integration. This environment is one where the code is evaluated against a battery of tests including unit testing, integration tests, functional tests, and often security code scans, as well as other code quality measures. Any code quality failures in the integration deployment environment usually are and should be treated as a sign to the development teams to "stop and fix" the problem(s) before committing any more code to version control.

The test deployment environment is the next stage of quality control where various automated quality measures and tests are complemented by human-directed quality activities. This environment is also the next step up in scope and size of data complexity and assessment rigor. Data sets mirror production, but as they are sanitized for test purposes, they are used to simulate a real-world (production) environment. Load and performance testing is conducted at this level.

The staging environment is used to test all installation, configuration, and migration scripts and procedures before they are applied to the production environment. This evaluation verifies the reliability of these factors before promotion to production.

The production environment is when the software goes live. This is where the actual value of the collective software development activities is realized. This is the most protected environment and as such is the most trusted environment. Access to the production environment should be strictly on a needful, least privileged basis and should be strongly enforced. Furthermore, data held in the production environment can be highly sensitive or valuable, or have classification restrictions, and should be protected as such.

Secure Code Promotion

After code has been written by the developers and is complete enough to be tested, it should be tested in a different software environment than the one in which it was developed. The code should be delivered to the test environment in a form similar to how it would be deployed to production. The control over the test environment should be more intensive. Advancing code from a lower environment to a higher environment like this is known as *code promotion*.

Promoting code from development to integration, integration to test, test to staging, and staging to production comes with more stringent code quality, code safety, and software security and security control environment requirements. Promoting code from one deployment environment to the next should be done only to the next immediate level up. Skipping a level, such as going from the development environment to production, is both poor form and bad security practice. Each deployment environment has a specific software quality and security control purpose. When a deployment environment is skipped over in a code promotion, critical testing and verification activities can be missed that might lead to bugs or security vulnerabilities. It also means that your development process lacks maturity.

The code promotion workflow does not have to be slow or cumbersome. Automating the build, verification, quality assurance, and security testing accelerates this process. Automation such as this takes more up-front investment in standing up the workflow process automation and writing the tests, but these investments pay off by building security into the software development environment. This is also known as "shifting security left."

Security Issues with Deployment Environments

Security control is intensified with the progression from a development environment to a production environment. This is because of the type of data used in each environment and the increasingly greater confidentiality, integrity, and availability requirements. This progression of deployment environments goes from least trusted/least secured to most trusted and most secured. As the trust and security requirements increase, so do the following control requirements: access control and privileged access control, logging, monitoring, security event management, configuration management, change management, and data protection.

These are some of the control areas that intensify with the increasing level of trust and security of the environment:

- **More rigorous access control:** Access control shall adhere to the least privilege model and be implemented commensurate with the requirements of the environment.

- **Privileged access management:** Baseline access control in higher environments is privileged to access and should be limited by least privilege. The entitlements considered privileged in lower environments is highly privileged in higher environments.

- **Logging, monitoring, and security event management:** Logging, monitoring, and security event management control requirements intensify in higher deployment environments. Higher environments that have significant risk exposure require security event management.

- **Configuration and change management:** The control over the state of the software and its environment and the process by which the state of every aspect is managed increases with the trust and security requirements of the environment to which they apply.

- **Secrets management:** Secrets in this context are the configuration and environment variables that are required to deploy the software and set up aspects of its environment. Some examples of secrets are database connection and credential information, services credentials, and service or application secret keys. Keeping these variables in source code is a serious security mistake because doing so could lead to a potential sensitive data exposure. Secrets should be securely held and managed outside of the source code. Many of these variables are specific to the deployment environment. As the trust and security levels of the environment increase, so do the protection requirements for these variables. These configuration and environment variables, when associated with higher deployment environments, become secrets. It is essential to the security of the deployment environments that these variables be managed as secrets. These variables must be strictly maintained by a "need to know," least privilege access control and data protection that is commensurate with the trust and security of the environment with which they are associated.

- **Encryption key management:** As the security and trust levels increase by environment, so shall the encryption and key management requirements.

See FIPS 140-2, "Security Requirements for Cryptographic Modules" (`https://csrc.nist.gov/Projects/Cryptographic-Module-Validation-Program/Standards`) and the OWASP Key Management Cheat Sheet (`https://www.owasp.org/index.php/Key_Management_Cheat_Sheet`) for insights on aligning these requirements.

Configuration Management as an Aspect of Secure Coding

Configuration management is an aspect of secure coding. A security professional needs to understand what configuration management is, what its essential properties are, and how it works within secure coding.

In particular, configuration management is a fundamental aspect of secure coding in the following ways:

- Maintaining a durable configuration history

- Providing a foundation for a secure coding environment

- Creating secure baselines

It has been said that software programming is the only art form that fights back. Software solutions are complex human artifacts. Many different parts compose a software solution, which can be many files from many different sources. Variety like this creates complexity in software solution management. In addition to this variety, the very nature of software is to change.

Software evolves as business needs evolve and change. As the elements that compose a software solution change, the software solution's functionality, side effects, and configuration change. Software development is a practice in managing multiple moving targets.

Configuration management is the means to have knowledge and control over the artifacts and their state that compose a software solution. Configuration management captures and documents the current state of the software, libraries, frameworks, operating systems, patching, hardware, including versions, patch levels, configurations, documentation, and all the elements that make up a software-based solution. This is necessary for the correct and secure functionality of the solution.

The basic building blocks of software configuration management are the following:

- **Configuration item:** A configuration item is the atom of configuration management. Configuration items are things such as software source code files, requirements documents, or program resources such as image or video files, and software libraries. A configuration item is an individual element that is part of the configuration of items of a software system. A configuration item must be uniquely identified to be distinct from other configuration items. A configuration item is subject to change with changes to the software system. A collection of configuration items make up a baseline.

- **Baseline:** A baseline is an immutable set of configuration items that have immutable states. A baseline may have the properties of being associated with workflows, workload environments, conditions of approval, or qualitative states such as security. As such, a baseline is an identified configuration and is thus a special version.

- **Version:** A version is a concept that describes the immutable state of a configuration item, a set of configuration items, and a baseline. A version is associated with a change set. When a change set is applied to a previous version of a baseline, it creates a new version of that baseline. Versions are typically identified by labels.

- **Change set:** A change set is group of related changes to configuration items that have been changed, and it is the basis of how changes to the software system are controlled. Change sets are subject to code review, quality assurance, testing, verification, and acceptance measures.

- **Branch:** A branch in configuration management terms has two definitions. The first one is that a branch identifies a set of versioned configuration items that are being developed in parallel to the main configuration. Second, to branch is a verb where a set of configuration items are copied off for parallel development. A *main* branch, or *trunk*, is the base configuration from which all other branches are derived.

Note that while some of these terms have specific definitions in other contexts, they are being described in the context of their role as building blocks of software configuration management. These building blocks form the essential conceptual basis of configuration management. A version control system materializes these concepts for practical use. A version control system, also known as *source code version control* or *revision control*, is a software tool that organizes, manages, and documents the changes to configuration items.

The chief aim of configuration management of software is to maintain visibility and control over all of the elements that compose a software system. A change to any of the configuration items can introduce a bug or flaw to the software. Uncontrolled changes can ultimately lead to potentially exploitable vulnerabilities in the software. A change control process manages ongoing differences in the software code and configuration.

In this sense, configuration management also relates to the larger discipline of change management. Change management is discussed earlier in the chapter in the section "Change Management."

Security of Code Repositories

Source code repositories are the backbone of secure software development. Considering the human and intellectual capital invested in source code, most likely it is among an organization's most valuable assets.

A source code repository persistently stores uniquely identifiable versions of software source code. It also enables developers to make parallel changes to source code files in a separate branch and then merge the changes into the original or other branches of the software configuration.

Protection of Source Code

Confidentiality, integrity, and availability all come into consideration when determining the best method to protect your source code. One way to protect the confidentiality and integrity of your source code is to limit the ability to copy it to portable devices such as a laptop and instead have developers mount the version-controlled source code from a central server. It is easier to manage security on a centralized server rather than multiple computers. A centralized version control system (CVCS) works this way. If availability is the most important aspect, then a distributed version control system, DVCS, may be a better choice. Nonetheless, each system needs to be considered holistically, taking into account your organization's overall security policies, standards, and controls.

However, when limiting access to source code, there still is the human factor to consider. If someone can read source code in a CVCS, they can distribute that code widely. A DVCS typically has more capabilities for controlling code workflow.

All modifications to the code in your source code repository must be accounted for, including who committed the change, when the change was committed, and a reason for the change. This is so easy to do with today's technology that it's almost more difficult not to have change tracking in place. If you use Git or Mercurial or any modestly usable source control system, you get change tracking, and you rely on it heavily.

Security Challenges in Use of Code Repositories

When using source code repositories, you must consider the security challenges, threat sources, and best practices that such use involves.

- Internal threats including actors such as disgruntled employees, careless actors, contractors
- External threats such as hackers
- Ransomware
- Denial of service
- Disclosure or theft of sensitive data or intellectual property
- Destruction of sensitive data or intellectual property

When discussing the security challenges related to source code repositories, it is necessary to take it from two perspectives: security *of* the repository and security *in* the repository.

Security of the Repository

Defense in depth should be the essential strategy employed when securing a source code repository. This strategy consists of layered security measures and, in this case, specific attention toward protecting file data assets. While there are many control layers you can consider in securing your source code repository, some of the most important are the following:

- Network security
- Communications security
- Authentication and authorization
- Anti-malware
- File integrity checking
- Filesystem and backups

Network Security

Any means that an attacker can use to get access to protected assets must be secured, and therefore network security is a must when securing source code repositories. Network security controls to secure source code repositories at a minimum should include firewalls, data loss prevention systems (DLPs), and intrusion detection systems (IDSs) or intrusion prevention systems (IPSs).

Communications Security

Following network security, the security of communications on the network is necessary as well. Ensure that all communication between endpoints and the source code repository are protected. Depending upon the communication layer, different protocols will apply, such as HTTPS, TLS, SSH, or IPSec. By using these protocols, you can protect your communicating channel from unauthorized access by attackers. As with any other asset, source code needs to be accessible as well as have adequate protections around that accessibility.

Authentication and Authorization

Access to source code repositories should be based on the least privilege model. Each user's ability to view, create, modify, and delete items in the repository must also follow the least privilege entitlement model. The capacity to deprovision and remove user access to the source code repository upon termination or change in the role should be immediate.

Anti-malware

Protection from ransomware is a primary concern when protecting source code in a source code repository. Anti-malware should be used at different points in the network and on the source code repository hosts to defend against ransomware and to prevent the source code from being infected with malware. Keeping the anti-malware program signatures current is critical to securing your source code repository.

File Integrity Checking

File integrity checking is a line of defense that can detect whether an attacker modifies any file on a system. File integrity checking is typically done by checksum comparisons of selected files on the system. Use file integrity checking on a continuous basis to alert your incident response team of any changes to the operating system or the source control software environment as soon as possible to protect the system.

Filesystem and Backups

Because you are protecting your source code assets, filesystem security and backup management are necessary. The backup strategy you choose should align with your high availability and disaster recovery requirements, including disaster recovery from ransomware. However, the organization should pay particular attention to backup durability, redundancy, and recovery because, depending upon your operations and intellectual property situation, your source code repository may hold assets critical to your business.

Security in the Repository

The other half of source code repository security is to secure access to what it holds, maintains, and controls. This securing access is also known as security in the repository. To ensure the protection of objects managed by the repository, access control and sensitive code segregation should be used.

Access Control

Just as access control secures access to the source code repository software and its files, access control is vital to securing the assets managed by it. Limiting who can view, add, modify, and delete objects in your source code repository is a necessary part of the security in the repository.

The two types of access control limits used in code repositories for ensuring the security of its contents: software and code access limitations.

Software access limitations are constraints placed on a user's access to the source code repository software. Use the principle of least privilege when granting access to the software. Enforce access to objects based on your organization's policies on data classification and access. Best practice would be to constrain the user's connection to the source code repository within a session.

A user session's concurrency and duration should both be limited to meet your organization's security policies. If no such statements of limitations exist, then set these to reasonable values. Restrict the number of concurrent user connections allowed to an amount that would be necessary and reasonable for a developer to do their work. Restrict the session timeout to expire upon idle after 15 minutes. If possible, limit the access to the software by IP address range or geolocation.

A source code repository's central security capability is to protect the confidentiality of the objects that it contains. The principle of least privilege should govern access to these objects. Each source code repository's access control model may differ from others. However, user constraints on the abilities to view, add, modify, delete access to files, objects, directories, or repositories should be enforced.

Sensitive Code Segregation

All code is not created equal. Depending upon your organization's asset management and data classification policies, the code maintained by the source code repository can possess a sensitivity that requires more control over its protection. Code segregation protects important code from both unauthorized access and commingling with code of lesser classification or importance. The segregation of higher value code should have stronger security controls protecting it. Strong authentication and encryption can be useful in this situation.

Furthermore, properly implemented code segregation reduces the chances of third parties gaining access to the code. As a rule, third parties should not be given complete access to your organization's source code. Third parties should only get specific access to that code which they need to do their work.

ASSESS THE EFFECTIVENESS OF SOFTWARE SECURITY

Unless software security is measured, it cannot be managed. Event logging and audit and risk analysis and mitigation are two key capabilities to assess the effectiveness of software security. The process of logging and auditing the stream of events and changes that occur in the software environment achieves two goals. The first is to assess that the controls in the environment and application are operating correctly and are effectively based upon the expected event history. The second is to find evidence of any unauthorized activities. This works in a complementary fashion with risk analysis and mitigation, as logging and audit functions provide evidence of activities that can be used by the risk analysis process to determine areas of vulnerability or potential concern. Risk analysis and mitigation follows with activities to assess risks and controls in the software environment and to identify where attention should be applied to appropriately control the risks discovered by its process. The specific software-related concerns will be called out when discussing these capabilities.

Logging and Auditing of Changes

Visibility is key to controlling software development security. Logging and auditing are critical capabilities for visibility into software development security. Logging and auditing of changes are processes that capture and compare what actually happened in the stream of events occurring in the software environment against what was expected to happen.

Any change to the software development environment, whether intentional or accidental, can have a negative impact on its security posture. For instance, a software change may be related to feature development, or it could be an introduction of malware. All changes that occur within the software development should be visible, known, and approved. Thus, an essential key to managing changes in the software development environment is to be able to see all of the changes. A mature security program emphasizes logging and audit capabilities for security response and management.

Overview of Concepts

There are several important core logging and auditing concepts, including logging, accountability, nonrepudiation, and auditing.

Logging

Keeping a record of all events that have occurred in a software system is necessary for the assessment of its security. Logging events as they occur in a uniquely distinguishable manner makes a history that can be viewed and analyzed later. Such an audit trail can be used later to review the ordered sequence of events in the software environment. Auditors rely upon these logs to analyze events for significance and sequences that contribute to the overall health picture of software development security.

Accountability

Knowing who or what is responsible for events that occurred in a software environment is a cornerstone capability for a software environment's security. This "who did what and when" information is essential for nonrepudiation and traceability of actors and their actions.

Nonrepudiation

Nonrepudiation is the indisputable association of a unique individual with actions that they committed. Nonrepudiation is a quality of record that prevents an entity from denying that they did something.

Auditing

Auditing a software environment for security purposes focuses on examining management and security controls to determine whether they are sufficiently protecting assets, maintaining data integrity, and operating effectively to achieve the organization's goals or objectives. Auditing also may seek to determine whether an organization's policies, standards, and processes are followed by examining the logs that reflect the events in the software system.

Purpose of Logging and Auditing

Logging and auditing are key capabilities to securing the software development environment. They provide security through detective and reactive control over the activities conducted in the software development environment.

Logging provides an authoritative record of activities and events in a system. Event log data has many important uses in the enterprise. Event logging data provides insights into information systems' operational status. Event logging can be fed to a security information and event management (SIEM) system to monitor, correlate, analyze, and alert on security incidents that occur in the software development environment.

Audits are used to discover information on operational effectiveness as well as to provide evidence related to an organization's compliance with administrative and legal regulations. It can confirm for management that the business is functioning well and is prepared to meet potential challenges.

The security capabilities of logging and auditing work together to address specific concerns in the software development environment. These concerns include error and exception management, SCM, operational environment logging, and responding to security posture changes in the software development environment. Furthermore, you'll see how SIEM, forensics, Payment Card Industry (PCI) Standards, the Health Insurance Portability and Accountability Act of 1996 (HIPAA), the Minimal Acceptable Risk Standard for Exchanges (MARS-E), and the HIPAA Omnibus Final Rule influence logging and auditing requirements.

Error and Exception Management

Error and exception management is the process of appropriately handling problem situations in running software. Errors and exceptions need to be treated with care. When an error or exception occurs, it can reveal sensitive information about the program and its data, information that can be off-putting to a customer and useful to a hacker. Error and exception management should provide guidance on how these events should be presented to the user, how they should be logged, and how the program should recover from them.

Situations like these require specialized processing to handle the error or exception. Exceptions or errors alter the program's expected logic path. The software environment captures and signals that an exception or error has occurred. This generates an execution stack trace. Exception or error messages are generated. All of these side effects need to be managed as you do not want the user, or particularly an attacker, to see any of these side effects.

Exceptions and errors have different impacts on the system. Some exceptions are easily recoverable situations that do not affect the running state or integrity of the program. Other exceptions and errors can be severe enough to make a program crash. These different layers of consequence should be handled in a tiered approach. Several levels of application logging are typically used to indicate the severity of an exception or error. These levels are listed in order of decreasing severity:

- **FATAL:** FATAL is when there is a problem with the program or service that is severe enough to require its termination. In FATAL situations one should construct meticulous procedures to manage data preservation as well as to deallocate resources. Bear in mind that FATAL cases usually call for administrator attention regardless of time of day.

- **ERROR:** An ERROR is a problem for an operation but not for the overall program or service. ERRORs require either a direct user or administrator intervention to resolve the issue.

- **WARN:** WARN is for events that may cause unusual application behavior but where the program has compensated for the event. An example is retrying an operation after a timeout.

- **INFO:** Any useful information about the system to be logged, not necessarily exceptions or errors, such as starting/stopping, startup or shutdown milestones, or the like.

- **DEBUG:** DEBUG should be reserved for development purposes where there is a need to emit debugging information for the developer to improve the code.

- **TRACE:** TRACE should be reserved for development purposes where there is a need to trace into a part of a function's execution.

Good secure programming practice uses these standard logging severity labels to indicate how the exception or error should be handled, logged, and in all respects treated. These logging levels should thus have specialized handling per severity that includes switches for their activation as well as channels to where their event stream goes. Higher severity events should be durably logged as well as fed to an operational logging system or a SIEM system, depending upon if the event type has a security impact.

Source Code Management

SCM is a business and technical process that controls the record, management, sharing, and versioning of source code. It is a vital system that enables developers to work together on the same development project whether they are in the same room or a continent away.

SCM logging tracks modifications to the code. This logging provides accountability and change history. It identifies who made changes, the time of changes, what changes were made, and a comment by the submitter describing the purpose for the changes. It traces development modifications back to change control requests. It helps resolve conflicts when merging contributions from multiple sources. Changes can be audited for security purposes.

SCM includes several core features:

- **Source code accountability:** Source code accountability is a primary feature of an SCM tool, tracking down who changed/wrote what line of code. Accountability traces all changes made back to the original developers who committed the changes so that when problematic code or configurations are identified, they can be traced to the exact person responsible for the change.

- **Source code integrity:** The goal of software development is to develop applications that satisfy customers' requirements. Logging of activities related to the code provides an audit trail that describes code changes at various points in its lifespan.

This logged record of changes can, in a review, reveal program modifications that either converge or diverge from requirements.

■ **Verification:** Verification is the process of ensuring the completeness and correctness of the code. Source code management logging supports verification by establishing a record of software development changes. It records evidence of the baseline version of the verified software.

Operational Environment Logging

Logging captures events that occur in the operational environment. Foremost in securing an operational environment is to define authorized and unauthorized activities in the operational environment, because this draws the line between a securely controlled environment or whether the events that occur are authorized. With this understanding, events relating to changes in the operational environment can then be sorted into events that are supportive of the security of the environment and those that compromise the security of the environment. Events that relate to the security of the operational environment come from a number of different sources. The software running in the environment generates security-significant events. The monitoring and oversight security controls set in place to protect the software environment are important to ensure the continued and proper operation of these controls. Logging the events related to performance metrics provides a view into the software's availability and insight into denial-of-service attacks on the software and its operational environment. An operational environment's security is based on its consistency with a secure baseline configuration. Any changes in the operational environment should thus be logged. When the cloud is the operational environment, its dynamic nature, when not properly controlled, makes it susceptible to changes that requires thorough logging and audit.

Detecting Authorized and Unauthorized Changes

The key distinction between a secure operational environment and an insecure one is to define what is allowed to change and what is not allowed to change. Controlling all changes to any aspect of the software development environment is one of the most effective ways to support security. Changes of this nature include but are not exclusive to software code changes, application or service configuration changes, infrastructure configuration changes, access controls, and the like. Identify the events that reveal changes to the status or configuration of your environment. Log these changes. Use this record as a source to a SIEM and for auditing purposes.

Running Software

Software running in a production environment is the front line of cybersecurity. It is the digital face of a business. It is the gatekeeper to data access. It is often the choice target for cyber attacks. Event logging in live software is necessary to record and catch both normal events, such as ordinary logins, and exceptional events, which are events outside of its expected running states, to detect situations that will hurt the running software, such as attacks or stress factors that exceed its design. Error and exception management, security event monitoring, and performance issues are three key areas to keep track of with software.

Security Oversight

Logging events that have a security impact support security oversight of running software. An example of an event with a security impact is multiple login attempts, which may indicate unauthorized access attempts. Attempts to input dangerous values into the system is another example. The visibility and recording of these types of events make them actionable security intelligence.

Performance Management

Performance in the operational environment should be maintained at a service level that satisfies customers. Performance metrics of applications and the environment should be logged to maintain control over their service levels. The various application performance metrics include response times, concurrent sessions, memory consumption, network bandwidth used, open file handles, and the like. The acceptable ranges of an application's performance metrics should be known. Deviations from these tolerances can indicate abuse of the software and similarly abuse of the operational environment. Logging and audit provide up-front as well as retrospective insights into the situations that affect a software environment's performance, as well as how to better control it.

Configuration Changes

The software development environment's configuration is the basis of its security. This configuration includes the infrastructure as well as the applications it hosts. All configuration changes should be traced to an approved requirement for the change. Logging supports visibility, awareness, and alerting of changes in the software development environment's configuration. Auditing supports efforts to assess and improve the software development environment's compliance requirements.

Cloud Environment Changes

Use of the cloud is attractive because of its on-demand self-service and rapid elasticity. These qualities make the cloud environment configuration dynamic and changeable. Due to the fluid nature of cloud environments, meticulous logging and monitoring of those systems should be considered a primary requirement in securing the use of cloud.

Securely managing the cloud's dynamic environment is one of the most significant challenges that traditional businesses face when migrating to the cloud. Comprehensively logging events in a cloud environment is a critical piece to solving that problem.

These different types of cloud events should be categorized by severity and impact. Changes to the cloud's security control environment would be deemed to be critical. Identity and access management changes are ones to watch closely as well, because changes like this can lead to toxic entitlements and shadow access in the cloud environment. All changes to the cloud environment should be logged according to your organization's security requirements and handled with the appropriate care and intervention.

Changes in Security Posture

An organization's security posture is based on its security policies, standards, guidelines, and procedures. Security controls are used to meet these organizational security objectives. Information on the activities, operations, and performance of security controls via events provides insight into their effectiveness at achieving these security objectives. Security control–related events often are the basis for security incident response activities. Furthermore, this information can be used in an audit to verify the proper functioning and effectiveness of the security controls. Logging information on the security control environment is key to maintaining an effective security posture.

Security Incident Response

Security-related event logs can be sent to the SIEM system. The SIEM system analyzes and correlates security events to discover and respond to security situations. A potential response to an identified security event may be the application of corrective controls deployed to remedy the situation immediately.

Security event logs are used in audit situations to learn more about the security environment. They can be evaluated to discover a more effective countermeasures configuration. Security event logs can also serve as the basis for law enforcement or legal activity.

Security Control Verification

Security controls need to be routinely tested for their appropriateness and operational effectiveness. Verification confirms that a security control is performing as expected. Logging a security control's event information keeps a record of insights into its fitness and effectiveness. An audit process can use this log of security control data as evidence to evaluate whether the security control has been situated in place correctly and is operating effectively.

SIEM

SIEM is a means of security management that provides real-time information on security events. The real-time feed comes from event logs generated by applications, services, and network hardware as well as other sources. The SIEM system aggregates and correlates this data to determine appropriate actions to be taken. Correlated event data can provide a clearer picture of an incident and its context. A SIEM's actions on this information may be to generate an alert, log the event, and potentially trigger compensating security controls to contain and halt the further unfolding of the incident.

Forensics

Forensics is the scientific process of collecting, analyzing, and presenting evidence. Computer forensics is the recovery and investigation of material found in digital devices, specifically in computers and digital storage media. This evidence is often related to computer crime.

Logging is a necessary part of digital forensics, as it serves as a source of record for forensic evidence. A vital point for forensics investigators is that evidence must be collected in a way that is legally admissible in a court case. If an intrusion leads to a court case, the organization with thorough and comprehensive event logging and the computer forensics capability to procure those logs will be at a distinct advantage when compelled to present evidence. A security professional needs to consider the influence and context of existing laws of evidence when implementing a logging strategy and solution as part of the security of the software environment.

PCI

The Payment Card Industry Data Security Standard (PCI DSS) is maintained by the Payment Card Industry Security Standards Council. This group was created in 2004 by MasterCard, Visa, Discover, JCB, and American Express to establish a universal platform to prevent fraud when credit card information is being transmitted. Compliance with PCI is to adhere to the set of PCI policies and procedures. PCI DSS compliance is required by all card brands.

Effective daily log monitoring is a requirement to comply with PCI standards. For more information, see the PCI Security Standards Council's "Information Supplement: Effective Daily Log Monitoring" (`https://www.pcisecuritystandards.org/documents/Effective-Daily-Log-Monitoring-Guidance.pdf`).

HIPAA

HIPAA is U.S. legislation that provides data privacy and security provisions for safeguarding medical information. The law has emerged into greater prominence in recent years with the proliferation of health data breaches caused by cyber attacks and ransomware attacks on health insurers and providers.

Security Metrics' article "What are HIPAA Compliant System Logs" states that HIPAA requires you to keep event, audit, and access logs on each of your systems for a total of six years. The security practitioner should be aware of HIPAA requirements for logging and log monitoring. For more information, see `http://blog.securitymetrics .com/2015/02/hipaa-compliant-system-logs.html`.

MARS-E

MARS-E version 2.0 provides security guidance that supports the mandates of the Patient Protection and Affordable Care Act of 2010 and the Department of Health and Human Services (HHS). All marketplaces and exchanges that are Affordable Care Act administering entities must use
this information to secure their information systems. MARS-E 2.0 is composed of four documents: "Volume I: Harmonized Security and Privacy Framework," "Volume II: Minimum Acceptable Risk Standards for Exchanges," "Volume III: Catalog of Minimum Acceptable Risk Security and Privacy Controls for Exchanges," and "Volume IV: ACA Administering Entity System Security Plan." Volumes II and III describe minimum acceptable risk standards and security controls applicable to information systems. For more information on MARS-E, see as a starting point the following informational bulletin: `https://www.medicaid.gov/federal-policy-guidance/downloads/ cib-09-23-2015.pdf`. To read Volume II, see `https://www.cms.gov/CCIIO/Resources/ Regulations-and-Guidance/Downloads/2-MARS-E-v2-0-Minimum-Acceptable-Risk- Standards-for-Exchanges-11102015.pdf`. To read Volume III, see `https://www.cms .gov/CCIIO/Resources/Regulations-and-Guidance/Downloads/3-MARS-E-v2-0- Catalog-of-Security-and-Privacy-Controls-11102015.pdf`.

Omnibus

The HIPAA Omnibus Final Rule, put into effect in 2013 by the U.S. Department of Health and Human Services, was instituted to modify the HIPAA to provide patients with more flexibility and control over their personal health information and strengthen the existing HIPAA privacy and security protections of health information. For information on the HIPAA Omnibus Final Rule, see `https://www.govinfo.gov/content/pkg/ FR-2013-01-25/pdf/2013-01073.pdf`.

Logging Best Practices

While Chapter 6 covers this topic in a good amount of detail, this section emphasizes effective software security logging management by first referencing NIST SP 800-92, the "Guide to Computer Security Log Management," as a basis for good log management practices and then by directing the security practitioner to industry best-practice guidance in the "OWASP Logging Cheat Sheet."

Logging management is essential for visibility and security intelligence of critical systems, applications, and data stores. Without logging, there is no visibility. This data can be used as a measurement tool to evaluate issue responsivity, security controls evaluation, and supporting regulatory compliance. This report examines this goal from a security operations and auditing perspective.

Pervasive logging management increases the effectiveness and efficiency of many aspects, from application and system troubleshooting to intrusion detection system tuning and forensics investigations. A best practices approach to logging comes in layers.

To implement a comprehensive and effective application logging strategy, follow these steps:

1. Define your purpose for logging and include security in that purpose.

2. Decide what to log based on the purpose defined in the previous step, select the sources that meet the criteria, and identify those that don't.

3. Select a logging framework that meets your purpose and integrates with your chosen computer languages and software frameworks. An example of this would be the choice of Log4j for the Java language. See: `https://logging.apache.org/log4j/2.x/manual/index.html for more information on Log4j.`

4. Centralize your log collection.

5. Standardize the log data set captured by the log formatting templates for each log source.

6. Standardize on short log messages.

7. Format the structure of data in logs to allow machines and humans to read the data more efficiently.

8. Add unique identifiers.

There are several resources that provide best practices, such as those provided by NIST and OWASP, as the following sections describe.

NIST SP 800-92

NIST SP 800-92, "Guide to Computer Security Log Management," is a U.S. federal government standard that provides practical enterprise guidance on effective log management practices. The standard is available at `https://nvlpubs.nist.gov/nistpubs/Legacy/SP/nistspecialpublication800-92.pdf`. This standard provides an overview of the following:

- What to log
- Why logging is necessary

- Challenges in log management
- Log protection
- Log analysis
- Recommendations to meet log management challenges

OWASP Logging Cheat Sheet

The OWASP Logging Cheat Sheet (available at `https://www.owasp.org/index.php/Logging_Cheat_Sheet`) provides guidance on building application logging mechanisms, with an emphasis on security logging. This Logging Cheat Sheet is meant to be used to overcome the frequent problem that application event logging is overlooked or insufficient for comprehensive security.

Logging should be consistent across the enterprise, using industry standards where possible. Application logging should similarly be consistent in coverage and format to that of the enterprise. The purpose of enterprise-wide logging is so that the universe of events logged can be collected, managed, correlated, and analyzed by a variety of logging and SIEM systems. When the logging is consistent and normalized, its data becomes useful for informing an organization on how well its security program is performing and where to make investments.

The OWASP Logging Cheat Sheet is an excellent reference that defines the purpose for logging and provides guidance on design, implementation and testing, and deployment and operation guidance where both sections effectively read like a checklist of things to cover when implementing an application logging strategy.

Auditing and Software Development Security

Audits are an important tool to ensure the security and quality of every aspect of the software development process. Audits provide visibility into the various aspects of software development, enabling opportunities to improve and, perhaps more importantly, prevent failure.

Auditing software development can bring visibility into inventory and management of project risks and security risks, requirements, design, definition of and adherence to SDLC processes, project management, quality management and testing of software solutions, development quality and management, the inventory of third-party and component off-the-shelf software used in solutions, the quality of management and record keeping, and the costs and budget of software development. These aspects are important to be aware of in the software development process because each is an aspect that can lead to success or failure of projects, as well as the overall security of the solutions under scrutiny and the organizations that use them.

An audit can help you know whether your software development environment complies with your organization's security policies and guidance as well as how well it complies with laws and applicable regulations.

Furthermore, a software development audit can validate that an organization is following the regulatory requirements as well as the security policies, standards, guidelines, and procedures that it is required to adhere to, as well as to evaluate the effectiveness of controls they have implemented to enforce this adherence.

An audit, however, is a broad function in an organization, and its scope can vary greatly. Within the scope of software development, the audit function can be applied in three dimensions: the SDLC, application auditing, and the code review function.

Software Development Lifecycle Auditing

Auditing the SDLC provides an opportunity to conduct both broad and in-depth audit assessments on different focal points of software technology and management during the process.

At a high level, the SDLC consists of the following phases:

1. Requirements

2. Design

3. Implementation

4. Verification

5. Maintenance

6. Disposal

The audit objectives and evidence are different in each phase. The audit evidence changes as the related artifacts change. Use the artifacts of the phase for analysis. An analysis of the artifacts at each phase may provide information that can sufficiently describe continuity of policy, requirements, development, verification, and maintenance activities to prove an organization's adherence to its compliance requirements.

An audit has a different focus at different phases. In the requirements phase, adherence to regulatory and policy requirements can be proved by documentation review. This same audit focus at the implementation phase, however, may require various software assessments and code-level reviews. Consider how the SDLC phase affects an audit's agenda and focus.

Requirements Phase Auditing

Auditing the requirements phase evaluates the comprehensiveness, detail, and correctness of the requirements. At this phase, the artifacts subject to audit would be the business case, project charter documents, and system and software requirements specification. Security requirements at this phase should at least indicate a classification of the data subject to the solution, potential risk exposures, and conceptual security protection.

Design Phase Auditing

Design phase auditing evaluates how well the system's organization, architecture, and design meet the stated security, functional, and other nonfunctional requirements in the dimensions of the roles, processes, and structural composition of the solution. Artifacts to be evaluated at this level are solution architectural blueprints or specifications, system and software design specifications, system process specifications, and use cases as well as a variety of design models. Security auditing at the design phase evaluates a number of aspects of how security is treated in the solution design. It examines how architectural security principles are satisfied by the solution design. The audit process looks for how secure design patterns and structures are incorporated in the design. Actors, interactions, and use cases are scrutinized, and process designs are evaluated.

Implementation Phase Auditing

Auditing the implementation phase evaluates the process of building the software solution as well as the software itself. The process artifacts include, among others, secure coding standards, security design patterns, and implementation models. These artifacts guide how and what software is to be written. The software code is also an artifact subject to audit.

The software code of a solution is developed in the implementation phase. As such, it is an artifact subject to an audit of this phase. The software code as an artifact is unlike the requirements and design artifacts. Software code first and foremost is an artifact that has real consequences for the security of the solution. A design artifact does not expose a vulnerability, at least not the narrative of the design document, but the source code does. Software source code also is a large artifact in terms of quantity of artifact to consume. Source code is more changeable than requirements and design artifacts too. This is where auditing source code is different than the requirements or design artifacts audit. Its state of completion may be unfinished or developing. As a matter of fact, the earlier security is embedded into the SDLC processes, the more likely that an audit of the implementation phase will be conducted on artifacts that are snapshots in time of their finished state.

To understand what this means, take, for instance, the source code and unit tests of the solution under audit in the implementation phase. These artifacts are subject to an audit review to reveal compliance with secure coding standards, software security controls implementation, secure design pattern implementation, unit test coverage, and the code change correspondence with change control tickets.

Change control tickets provide particular insight in the implementation audit. Change control tickets demonstrate adherence to a change control and software configuration management process. The quality of and adherence to change management and configuration management processes fundamentally impact the security of software solutions. The reason for this is because these processes control how the implementation satisfies the design and requirements, including the security. Analysis of the change control tickets will reveal adherence to these processes.

Verification Phase Auditing

Verification phase auditing involves evaluating test plans, the testing code, and the test result reports. At this phase, the audit is mostly concerned with verifying that the developed software meets the stated requirements. The results of testing security requirements are evaluated at this phase.

Maintenance Phase Auditing

The maintenance phase relates to the operations and maintenance of the software solution in a running state. Auditing this phase puts a heavy emphasis on log analysis. The software solution logs are audited for evidence that the software and its security controls are functioning properly. Operations manuals are subject to audit in this phase with an emphasis on evidence of security operations. Security and routine patch management procedures and records are subject to this audit phase. User manuals are also examined for description of the secure use of software.

Disposal Phase Auditing

The disposal phase artifacts subject to audit relate to the secure decommissioning and disposal of the software and its data. There should be documentation that states the retention period required by law or regulatory requirements of software code, program binaries, and program data. Other artifacts of this phase include certificates of secure disposal of data, as well as records of decommissioning and disposal. These records can be logs recording the disposal events.

✔ Continuous Integration/Continuous Deployment Environments

Continuous integration/continuous deployment (CI/CD) has emerged from agile and automation practices to enable an automated continuous workflow that supports secure

CONTINUES

software delivery. CI/CD pipelines have automated many of the software assessment and testing processes. Before automation, the software assessment and testing processes were often left undone or manually triggered. By automating quality and security assessments checks into its systematic workflow, a CI/CD pipeline produces more secure software. This automation is complemented by comprehensive activity logging in the CI/CD pipeline. This logging supports its audit-ability.

Activity logging of standard CI/CD workflows shows repeated series of similar events throughout time. The CI/CD pipelines automate a consistent set of activities, so similar sequences of events are typically repeated over time. When variances in their workflow show up, they should be investigated to determine whether there is a threat.

The security of the CI/CD processes relies directly upon the security of its supporting infrastructure. An audit can evaluate the CI/CD infrastructure's security posture to determine its compliance with an organization's required regulations, policies, and security guidance.

Application Auditing

Application audits discover whether an application adequately protects its data and determine the existence and effectiveness of controls. The level of control expected for a particular application depends upon the degree of risk involved in the incorrect or unauthorized processing of its data. At a minimum it would include an information security assessment. This should contain a statement of the data classification of the data in the application.

Design aspects of the application are audited. An application audit seeks to discover the presence of any software weakness that may exist based upon the nature of the application. The Common Weakness Enumeration or OWASP Top Ten resources are used for this evaluation. Armed with this information, an application audit investigates the application's potential vulnerabilities and risks. A risk assessment is part of the information security assessment, revealing the security controls necessary and appropriate for the application. Following this, a detailed description of the security control environment as well as the placement and functionality of the controls is a part of the audit.

An application audit dives deeper into the software's security design and implementation. Adherence to secure coding practices and standards are examined. It evaluates the software's use of secure and approved design patterns and structures. The material aspects of the application are audited as well to determine that the versions of software languages, libraries, components, and software frameworks that comprise the application are safe and secure to use as approved by the organization or industry best practices.

An application audit should, at a minimum, determine the existence of controls in the following areas:

- Administration
- Inputs, processing, outputs
- Logical security
- Disaster recovery plan
- Change management
- User support
- Third-party services

Code Review

As much an activity of quality assurance as audit, a code review is a systematic examination of software source code by subject-matter experts. In the context of an audit, it is an activity whose focus is to evaluate the quality and security of source code. Code reviews identify design flaws or logic errors and areas for improvement. A security code review extends a code review by looking for potential security vulnerabilities in the software code. Reviews can be conducted in various forms, such as pair programming, informal walkthroughs, and formal inspections. By reviewing the software code for flaws, errors, and security concerns, code reviews offer a deep dive into how the written software code complies with an organization's regulatory and policy compliance.

Risk Analysis and Mitigation

This section looks at risk analysis and mitigation through the lens of software security. A risk is the likelihood that a vulnerability will be exploited by a threat agent that compromises or damages an asset with a resulting business impact. Risk analysis is an effort to identify vulnerabilities and their related threats, assess the potential costs of exploitation, and determine appropriate and cost-effective security controls. Risk management concepts have been thoroughly covered in Chapter 1 of this book. However, there are particular elements of risk analysis and mitigation that apply specifically to software development.

Risk Analysis Goals and Approach

Risk analysis seeks a clear and realistic understanding of risks and the best way to handle these risks that meets an organization's risk tolerance and requirements. It is an exercise to make security purposeful, responsive, and cost-effective by prioritizing risks and handling them effectively.

Risk Analysis Goals

The following are four goals of risk analysis:

- Identify the assets to protect
- Identify the assets' vulnerabilities and related threats
- Provide realistic information on the probability and impact to an organization of a risk's occurrence
- Determine the best way to handle the risk based on a cost-benefit analysis of different ways to manage the risk

Realizing these goals better align the organization's security program with its business objectives.

When to Do Risk Analysis

Software risk analysis is optimally conducted at a few stages in the development process. The first time a risk analysis of software is best conducted is after requirements have been gathered. The requirements should provide important information and insight about the risk level of the software.

The software requirements should declare the classification of the data that the software will hold or process. The information and technical security requirements should be documented. The requirements should also provide insight into the importance of the software to the business model, the software's intended usage, and its service level requirements. These requirements provide good initial material to use when assessing the potential risks that the software may expose. From this initial analysis, security engineering and architecture have some evidence for controls selection to mitigate the risks identified by the assessment of the software requirements.

The next time a risk analysis should be conducted is after the architecture and designs have been created. Software architecture and designs should manifest the risk mitigation strategies and controls that emerged from the earlier risk analysis effort. Risk mitigation controls should be built into the software architecture and design. Building in security up front like this pushes security to the early stages of software's lifecycle as opposed to bolting on security after the application has been built. In addition to verifying the security aspects of the architecture and design, an analysis of this material should be conducted to identify potentially exploitable vulnerabilities introduced by design flaws. Discovering flaws at this time is preferred over finding them after the bulk of the software code has been written. From this aspect of the software risk assessment, the architecture and designs can be improved.

The architecture and design risk analysis is also a good time to develop automation and testing to validate the improved architecture and design mitigation strategies.

Designing automation and testing toward this end builds into the software development process tests that, if testing is integrated in the development process, quite possibly could continuously assess the effectiveness of the software environment.

Layered Approach

Risks to information technology systems exist in layers. In a software development environment, these layers resemble the layers of a security defense-in-depth strategy and continue through the application architecture to its implementation and component dependencies.

The best approach is to conduct a risk analysis on each layer of an organization's defense-in-depth security strategy. Identifying the risks, impacts, costs, potential safeguards, or management at the perimeter alone is not enough to improve the security of the software environment.

A risk analysis of the information technology environment, including the communication and data facilities and computing infrastructure, should be done. Notwithstanding the information technology environment, it is essential to analyze the risks of the applications within the environment as well. When analyzing software applications, each tier of a software application's architecture should be evaluated for potential risks and risk management solutions.

Taking this approach, let's examine a typical four-tier web application consisting of a client tier, web tier, application tier, and data tier.

Applying risk analysis practices and principles at each tier of an application, you can collect useful information about its security design. Just framing an application risk analysis by its architectural tiers can reveal a variety of useful information such as the following:

- The types of threats present in each tier

- Different types of vulnerabilities to software components

- Impact on the business if risk were to occur

The potential threats vary per tier. In the frame of the client tier, client session management and its exploitation by external attackers is a threat. Denial of service is a real threat to the web tier. Data theft by internal threat agents is a possible threat in the application's data tier. These are just some examples of threats. A thorough examination of each tier should reveal more of their particular threats.

Software Risk Factors

Software presents a set of different types of risks to consider. These risks are the risks related to the software's data, the risk of using new technology, software and system architecture change risks, risks inherent to code modification, and risks associated with usage. These risk factors should be part of a software risk analysis.

Data Risks

Software's main function is to maintain, present, and manipulate data. Data classification directly impacts the risk assessed for software. Highly classified data is an attractive target to an attacker. The impact of highly classified data exposure elevates the risk to which the software is exposed. A security practitioner should always use the data classification as a metric in a software risk analysis. The data classification should also influence the selection and intensity of controls to be applied to the software.

The type of data can subject the software to regulatory or legal compliance requirements. As part of a software risk assessment, the security practitioner should discover whether the type of data comes with any regulatory or legal compliance requirements. These compliance requirements can mandate the use of a set of controls or may restrict where the data can exist.

New Technology Risks

The choice to use new technology often is seen as an advantage. New technology may offer more efficient or effective solution components or advancements in how to solve business or technical problems. However, with the potential benefits of new technology come potential risks stemming from the novelty of the technology, the lack of subject-matter experience with it, or insufficient supportability. With new technology comes new problems, including many that have not yet been discovered. New technology may not be stable. By being new it is likely that the technology has not been used enough in a variety of real-world scenarios to have sufficiently revealed its weaknesses. Similarly, the technology may not have been around long enough for the security community to discover its flaws. A risk assessment evaluating software that uses new technology should consider these unknowns that elevate the risk.

Software and System Architecture Changes

Changes to software or system architecture have a significant impact on the risk level in a software risk analysis. A change to the software architecture, such as migrating a monolithic application to a microservices model, changes the risk and control requirements by adding new vulnerabilities and threat vectors. This change may also compromise existing controls. Controls applied to mitigate risk exposures in the previous architecture may no longer apply to the new architecture. Metaphorically speaking, old controls may be protecting doors that no longer exist.

Like changes to the software architecture, a change to the system architecture that supports the software also increases software risk. Too often, software lacks sufficient security controls written into its code to protect itself. The software control environment is the protection that it gets from the system architecture. Changing the system architecture changes the software's risk exposure.

Code Modification Risks

Not all change is good, and with respect to software code, changes should be considered a risky business. Code modification in this context is a broad label that includes developing code, bug fixing, refactoring, and maintenance activities. Next to production usage, code modification is the second most frequent interaction with the software. And every time code is modified, it potentially opens a weakness or flaw. This frequency of exposure due to potential weaknesses or flaws increases the software risk exposure. A security practitioner should know that active development requires a risk analysis and mitigation strategy that emphasizes a secure SDLC, secure coding standards and practices, and comprehensive security reviews and testing.

Usage Risks

The best way to secure software is to not use it. Software is exposed to a variety of risks by being exposed to its users. As the number of users increases, so does the risk exposure. As the variety of users increases, so does the risk exposure. These risks come in the form of the variety of actions that the users do with the system. Accepting input from the user, accepting different kinds of input, and the extent to which the software validates and sanitizes the input all affect the degree of usage risk. How the software is to be used and how that usage requires the software to be accessed influences its risk level. If the software is to serve customers via the Internet, it is exposed to a higher likelihood of attack as it opens its input to the world.

Risk Analysis Methodologies

Knowing different risk analysis approaches is essential for a security professional. A number of different risk management methodologies exist. These methodologies overlap in the fundamentals of risk analysis: vulnerability identification, threats association, and risk calculations. However, each approach has its useful distinctions that serve a specific type of risk analysis the best or may be better suited to an organization's needs. Furthermore, knowing different risk analysis approaches enables a security professional to have more choices of techniques to use.

NIST SP 800-30, "Risk Management Guide for Information Technology Systems"

NIST SP 800-30 is a U.S. federal government standard known as the "Risk Management Guide for Information Technology Systems." Its focus is on information technology threats and their relationship with information security risks. It defines a risk assessment process through a sequence of activities that frame a rational risk analysis approach.

The NIST SP 800-30 risk assessment activities are as follows:

- System characterization
- Threat identification
- Vulnerability identification
- Control analysis
- Likelihood determination
- Impact analysis
- Risk determination
- Control recommendations
- Results documentation

OCTAVE

OCTAVE stands for Operationally Critical Threat, Asset, and Vulnerability Evaluation. OCTAVE is a framework for identifying and managing information security risks created by the Carnegie Mellon University's Software Engineering Institute (SEI). OCTAVE relies on staff knowledge of the organization and the information security risks it faces.

OCTAVE is a comprehensive approach that occurs in three incrementally related phases:

- **Phase 1:** Build enterprise-wide security requirements
- **Phase 2:** Identify infrastructure vulnerabilities
- **Phase 3:** Determine security risk management strategy

The OCTAVE methodology is suited to assess an organization on an enterprise level consisting of all of its applications, systems, and related business processes.

SEI provides "Operationally Critical Threat, Asset, and Vulnerability Evaluation (OCTAVE) Framework, Version 1.0" at `https://resources.sei.cmu.edu/asset_files/TechnicalReport/1999_005_001_16769.pdf`.

OCTAVE Allegro

OCTAVE Allegro is a variant that is designed for an organization to assess information security risks but within time, staff, and resource constraints. Whereas the OCTAVE methodology is comprehensive, OCTAVE Allegro streamlines, improves, and focuses risk assessment activities. It streamlines data collection and threat identification, and it has improved the asset focus, analysis capabilities, and risk mitigation guidance.

The OCTAVE Allegro methodology consists of the following steps:

1. Establish risk measurement criteria.
2. Develop an information asset profile.

3. Identify information asset containers.

4. Identify areas of concern.

5. Identify threat scenarios.

6. Identify risks.

7. Analyze risks.

8. Select a mitigation approach.

SEI provides "Introducing OCTAVE Allegro: Improving the Information Security Risk Assessment Process" at `https://resources.sei.cmu.edu/asset_files/TechnicalReport/2007_005_001_14885.pdf`.

ISO/IEC 27005

ISO/IEC 27005:2008, "Information Technology – Security Techniques – Information Security Risk Management," is an international standard for risk management practices within the context of an information security management system (ISMS). It is a general approach to risk management including, in addition to information systems' security, the broader concerns of an ISMS.

Failure Modes and Effect Analysis (FMEA)

Failure Modes and Effect Analysis (FMEA) is a structured and systematic process to determine failures and the effects of those failures. It was first developed to evaluate the potential failures in products. However, it is also useful in finding failures in systems. FMEA is useful in determining major failure modes; however, it is limited in its ability to comprehensively represent a landscape of vulnerabilities.

Fault Tree Analysis

Fault tree analysis is a top-down failure analysis approach that deductively analyzes failure events in a system. It is a tree structure that uses Boolean logic as a framework to associate contributory or causal failure events in the tree structure. The main branches of the tree can be general categories of threats such as Internet threats, network threats, software threats, physical threats, personnel threats, and so on. All of the failures and threats that can occur in a system should be populated in the tree. Branches of threats can be assessed for their validity and associations and then pruned as needed where their material does not apply. A tree of valid system faults and threats is a useful tool to analyze software failure events.

Risk Analysis Limitations

Risk analysis strives to achieve accuracy, but at best it is an exercise in approaching reality. There is no complete inventory of real vulnerabilities that exist in any given system. If such an inventory did exist, it would be overwhelming in the volume of information it contains. The same knowledge limitations exist in knowing all of the potential threats to those vulnerabilities. Last, there is no crystal ball to show precisely when risks will be realized or the magnitude of impact wrought by the realization. Risk analysis is a "best-effort" methodology to discover risks and safeguard against or manage the consequences of their realization.

Risk Analysis Approaches

There are two approaches for analyzing risk. Quantitative risk analysis examines risks that can be measured numerically or monetarily. Qualitative risk analysis considers risks based on their likelihood, impact, and severity. Each approach has its strengths.

Quantitative Risk Analysis

The purpose of quantitative risk analysis is to assign numeric or monetary values to all elements of the risk analysis process. Quantitative risk analysis takes a scientific and mathematical approach to the process. Quantitative risk analysis is done to get an empirical handle on the process.

Each element of the risk analysis process—asset values, threat frequency, likelihood, the degree of vulnerability, impact damage, safeguard costs and effectiveness, and the degree of uncertainty—is subject to the quantitative risk analysis equations.

Theoretically, when the risks are mathematically and financially understood, then cost-benefit analysis can be done for their optimal management, safeguards selection, or disposition. The total risk can also be accurately calculated. With the total risk quantified, then the *residual risk* can be determined after safeguards have been selected and the risk they offset has been determined.

Quantitative risk analysis deals with these core concepts:

- **Asset value (AV):** The value of an asset to an organization. This value's tally includes its current value as well other costs such as maintenance costs, operational costs, and protection costs, along with other financial considerations.

- **Exposure factor (EF):** The exposure factor is the potential percentage of asset loss, ranging from 0 to 100 percent, caused by the realization of an identified threat.

- **Single loss expectancy (SLE):** This is the percentage loss of value to an asset expected from the realization of a risk.

- **Annualized rate of occurrence (ARO):** The annualized rate of occurrence is the probability that a risk will occur within a year.

- **Annual loss expectancy (ALE):** The annual loss expectancy is the percentage loss of value to an asset expected from the realization of risk over a year. The ALE is the value that a quantitative analysis seeks to find.

The rule of thumb in quantitative analysis countermeasures selection is that the cost of the safeguards should not exceed the expected damage costs to the asset. How to get to this point, however, is by following the equation's steps.

Quantitative Risk Analysis Equation

The most common quantitative risk analysis equation is ALE = SLE × ARO. This equation is frequently used because it calculates the value of the ALE in financial terms. An ALE fits well within annual cybersecurity budgets. Knowing this amount then becomes the annual budgetary yardstick for how much to spend on safeguarding the assets.

Quantitative Risk Analysis Calculation

At a high level, the process of quantitative risk analysis is as follows:

1. Gather information and establish AVs, vulnerabilities, and their threats.

2. Determine the EF.

3. Calculate the SLE.

4. Calculate the ARO.

5. Calculate the ALE.

Information Gathering

There is a significant amount of prework that is necessary to gather enough information to perform a quantitative risk analysis. The assets subject to analysis must be identified. The value of each asset needs to be determined to a reasonable degree of accuracy. The vulnerabilities and their associated threats need to be listed. The probability, or likelihood, of these threats being exploited needs to be determined. The damage outcome, the impact, needs to be calculated. This information can be determined by conducting a risk assessment and vulnerability study.

Part of this information-gathering process should be to gather information to determine values for the constituent parts of the quantitative analysis equation: the AV, the EF, and the ARO.

A scope statement is used to set expectations for management and the threat analysis team. The scope statement should clearly communicate the following:

- Exactly what is to be evaluated

- The type of risk analysis that will be performed

- What the expected results should be

Determining the Exposure Factor (EF)

The EF is how likely it is that a risk will be realized on an asset. The EF depends upon the desirability, ease of access, and durability of the asset. Calculating the EF requires tailoring for the specific asset. The "SANS Quantitative Analysis Step by Step" provides a reference formula for what to consider in this calculation.

Considerations suggested in this formulation may include modifications for the presence of a firewall, backups, countermeasures, detection capabilities, or the rate of attack, among other considerations.

As a simplified example, let's consider the EF of a data center to the realization of the risk of a severe flood. The EF, as a percentage of damage resultant of a realized risk, that we are considering in this particular risk analysis is exposure to damage during a severe flood.

Many factors are needed to arrive at a real EF; however, for the sake of our simplified example we will conclude the EF to be 20 percent.

Calculating the Single Loss Expectancy (SLE)

Calculate SLE based on AV and EF. The SLE is determined by multiplying the AV times the EF, as follows:

$$SLE = AV \times EF$$

Continuing the data center flooding example from earlier, let's calculate the SLE of this data center. Assume that in the information gathering phase the data center's value as an asset was established at $10,000,000.00.

So, with the EF being 20 percent, you have the following SLE equation:

$$SLE = \$10,000,000.00 \times 0.20, \text{ or } \$2,000,000.00$$

Calculating the Annualized Rate of Occurrence

The ARO is the value of the estimated frequency of a specific threat taking place within a 12-month time frame. The ARO value determination differs per type of asset. For instance, if insurance data suggests that severe flooding is likely to affect the data center once every 125 years, then the ARO is $1/125 = 0.008$.

Insurance data is a common source of ARO information. Insurance reports on risk realization can be good references for ARO data. The mean time to failure of components can also be used as a factor to determine an ARO.

The range of ARO values can reflect any number from zero times a year to multiple times within a year or to single occurrences within a period of time that can be many years.

Calculating the Annual Loss Expectancy (ALE)

Calculate the annual loss expectancy based on the SLE times the ARO. The equation is ALE = SLE × ARO.

Continuing with our data center flooding risk analysis example, you have the following values so far:

- AV: $10,000,000.00
- EF = 0.20
- SLE = $2,000,000.00
- ARO = 0.008

The ALE is SLE × ARO, or the following:

ALE = $16,000.00 = $2,000,000.00 × 0.008

This ALE value can then be used to justify the expense of countermeasures to safeguard against the loss or damage of the risk. So, for the simplified example, the organization that owns this data center can justify spending $16,000.00 per year to protect it from severe flood damage.

Uncertainty

Where do the values for risk analysis come from? They come from historical data, industry experience, and, many times, best guesses. These data sources are a generalization, but their example is not too far off from the truth. Because the data is often obtained by best effort or best guess methods, there is a degree of uncertainty that comes with it. Be aware of taking into account this uncertainty of the data subject to risk analysis calculations.

Expectations and Results

The expectations and results of quantitative risk analysis are the following:

- Monetary values assigned to assets
- An exhaustive list of possible and significant threats
- A probability of occurrence is associated with each threat
- Risk countermeasure recommendations

Qualitative Risk Analysis

Qualitative risk analysis is another method that can be used. It does not assign monetary or numeric values to the aspects or consequences of analysis. It takes a scenario-based approach to examine the various potential risks. In each scenario, it ranks threat significance and consequences and the effectiveness of potential countermeasures. So, instead of assigning dollar amounts to risks based on the outcome of an equation, it ranks risks based on ratings of likelihood, impact, and severity.

Typical qualitative risk rankings are, in order of increasing severity, "low, medium, and high" or "green, yellow, and red." Qualitative risk rating systems like these relate risk criticalities in a natural order for easy understanding.

The decision-making basis of qualitative risk analysis is rooted in opinions and professional expertise. The experiences of the risk analysis team as well as of members of the organization are the means by which threats, their likelihood of occurrence, and the choices of how to manage the risk are made. This approach walks through different scenarios of risk possibilities and ranks the seriousness of threats. Following the risk possibility assessment, countermeasures are evaluated for their applicability to these threats.

Gathering this type of information requires techniques oriented toward sorting opinions and expert knowledge. Some examples of qualitative data gathering techniques are surveys, questionnaires, focus groups, storyboarding, brainstorming, and interviews. These techniques are meant to get the highest-quality opinions on the various risks' dispositions and the most effective means to handle them.

Another technique used with qualitative risk analysis is the Delphi technique. This technique gets a group consensus on particular threats while avoiding the individuals having to agree verbally, thus removing the effects of peer pressure persuading the opinions of any particular group member. It iteratively processes individuals' anonymous inputs to provide feedback to the group for further input until the resulting group opinion converges on agreement on cost, loss values, or likelihood.

The likelihood impact matrix is a tool to help with prioritizing qualitative risks. It shows where risk fall in a range of criticality from insignificant to severe, based on their likelihood and impact. See Table 8.7.

TABLE 8.7 Qualitative Risk Analysis Likelihood Impact Matrix

LIKELIHOOD	INSIGNIFICANT IMPACT	MINOR IMPACT	MODERATE IMPACT	MAJOR IMPACT	SEVERE IMPACT
Highly likely	M	H	H	E	E
Likely	M	M	H	H	E
Possible	L	M	M	H	E
Unlikely	L	M	M	M	H
Rare	L	L	M	M	H

The likelihood is the probability that a risk will occur. This value is used within the context of the assessment, so its exact meaning should be a shared understanding of the analysis team. It certainly should take into account the period that the risk analysis is using. A common likelihood rating system is rare, unlikely, possible, likely, highly likely. Each likelihood should encompass a range of values. Likelihood may be based on occurrences per year or percentage of probability.

The impact is the damage that a risk causes when realized. This value is used within the context of the assessment, so its exact meaning should be a shared understanding of the analysis team. A common impact rating system is insignificant, minor, moderate, major, severe. For risk analysis calculations, it is recommended to assign a number to each rank in the system you choose. Numbering the ranks allows for numerical analysis of risks. Each impact should encompass a range of values. Impact may be based on financial costs, service downtime, or a combination of the two.

A risk tolerance line sometimes is drawn on the probability impact matrix. The risk tolerance line is the upper limit of risk criticality that your organization will tolerate. Any risks that exist above that line must have mitigations or be approved for an exception.

Choice of Method

There are several considerations when choosing between the quantitative and qualitative methods. The qualitative method is best when subject-matter expertise is high and awareness of relative measures is appropriate. The qualitative approach is not suitable for when financial data is needed for cost-benefit analysis, however. The values produced in qualitative analysis are highly subjective and opinion based.

Quantitative methods are suitable for when financial data is needed for cost-benefit analysis. If the threat, likelihood, financial, and other information required for the analysis is available, this method supports an annual security budget. More work is involved in information gathering in this method. This method's calculations can be complicated as well. Sometimes information needed for the calculations is just not available.

Often a hybrid approach is taken where each method is used to the extent it supports parts of the overall risk assessment.

Risk Mitigation

The cost of selecting countermeasures to safeguard an asset should not exceed the value of the asset. Risk mitigation is the second half of risk analysis. After the probable risk cost estimation has been done, the emphasis turns toward how to manage the risk. At this point, a cost-benefit analysis is done to guide the next steps.

Security Control Value Calculation

The rule of thumb for selecting a security control is that it should not cost more than the asset it protects. It doesn't make business sense to pay more to protect an asset than it is worth. So, how is the value of a security control determined? The value of the security control is the net reduction of loss it brings to the organization by its function. How is this different from the ALE? It goes beyond the reduction to the ALE by the reduced risk to add back the annual cost of the security control. It costs money to save money, so the total savings of the reduced ALE is adjusted to add back the cost of the security control. This adjusted amount reflects the real expense to the organization of the risk and cost of the control.

The next consideration is how the value of the security control is calculated. A cost-benefit analysis compares the calculated expected financial cost of the realized risk's impact on the assets versus the cost to safeguard those assets. Here is where quantitative risk analysis is useful. Quantitative risk analysis describes risk in measurable metrics and monetary values. These values can be used in a cost-benefit analysis to estimate the value of a security control to the organization.

Using the quantitative approach to estimate the value of a security control on an annual basis, a cost-benefit analysis calculates the reduction of risk-related ALE provided by the security control, less the annual cost of the security control. The equation looks like this:

(Amount of risk reduced by security control) = (ALE before security control) – (ALE after security control)

(Security control value) = (Risk reduced by ALE) – (Annual cost of the security control)

To illustrate a cost-benefit analysis of a security control, now you will evaluate the value of a DDoS mitigation solution for a company's e-commerce website.

In this example, the company's revenue exclusively comes from sales generated from its e-commerce site. This company had been affected by DDoS attacks in the past, causing it to conduct a detailed quantitative risk analysis to determine the cost of this type of attack and the best approach to mitigate the problem.

The quantitative risk analysis determined that the ALE with the combined losses of revenue, remedial operational costs, and the loss of customers from DDoS attacks over a year's time was about $10,000. After selecting a DDoS mitigation solution as a safeguard, the ALE was reduced to $2,000. The annual cost for the DDoS mitigation solution safeguard is $3,500.

- ALE before applying DDoS mitigation security control: $10,000.00
- ALE after applying DDoS mitigation security control: $2,000.00
- Annual cost of DDoS mitigation security control: $3,500.00

Plugging these values into the cost-benefit calculation gives the results shown in Table 8.8.

TABLE 8.8 **Cost-Benefit Calculation**

DESCRIPTION	VALUES
ALE without security control (ALE)	$10,000
ALE with security control (ALE $_{sc}$)	$2,000
ALE reduced by security control (ALE $_{reduced}$) This is the difference in the ALE between no security control and with security control expressed in dollar amounts.	$ALE_{reduced} = ALE - ALE_{sc}$ $8,000 = 10,000 - 2,000$
Annual cost of the DDoS mitigation security control solution (Cost $_{sc}$)	$3,500
Value of security control (Value $_{sc}$) The dollar amount of the loss, reduced by applying the safeguard, minus the cost of the safeguard	$Value_{sc} = ALE_{reduced} - Cost_{sc}$ $4,500 = 8,000 - 3,500$

As you can see from the calculation in Table 8.8, there is more to the equation than just the reduction of the ALE. Let's examine the steps of the calculation more closely. After applying the security control, the dollar amount of the expected annual loss is reduced from $10,000 to $2,000. This amounts to an $8,000 reduction of ALE. This $8,000 of reduced loss to an organization is realized by the security control. The cost of the security control is factored into calculating the total cost reduction resulting from the reduced risk.

Factoring in this cost adjusts the value of the "total savings" realized by the organization. This total savings is the value that the security control brings to an organization. How is this the value of the security control? First, recall that the organization by its ALE calculation was losing $10,000 per year. After implementing the security control, this ALE was reduced to $2,000. This means that the company still expects to lose $2,000 per year due to residual risk. Add to this the annual cost of the security control, $3,500, which brings the total expense of the ALE + security control costs to $5,500 per year. Compared to the original ALE of $10,000, this results in a net savings, or value, to the organization of $4,500. This is the value of the security control.

Security Control Costs

Security controls come with a price, but how much do they cost? Is it just the purchase price? Should support costs be considered? The answer is that a security control's price is always more than its purchase price. When calculating the cost of a countermeasure for a cost-benefit analysis, you should always consider its full cost, which is made up of a number of accessory costs that should be considered:

- Product costs
- Professional services costs
- Design/planning cost
- Implementation cost
- Testing/evaluation cost
- Training costs
- Cost for compatibility with other safeguards
- Maintenance costs
- Operating and support costs
- Cost impact on staff productivity
- Subscription costs

These additional costs are but a sample of additional, "hidden" costs of the safeguards that are purchased. As a security professional, you should understand that the price of a safeguard is always more than the purchase price and that it is important not to spend more to protect an asset than what the asset is worth.

Evaluating Security Controls

The goal of countermeasure selection is to find those countermeasures that reduce the costs of a risk event by more than the cost to use the countermeasures. This goal was explained by the countermeasure value calculations earlier.

The overall qualities of a countermeasure should also be evaluated to determine its fitness and usability by the organization within its operating environment. The following are some qualities to consider when evaluating countermeasures:

- Ease of use
- Testability
- Least privilege defaults
- Configurability
- Administrative functionality
- Auditing functionality
- Maintainability
- Understandability and usage of output

Residual Risk

There will always be some risk that exists for an organization even after implementation of safeguards or countermeasures to reduce the risk. The risk that remains after the implementation of countermeasures is known as the residual risk.

It is important to understand a few concepts first to understand residual risk. Residual risk calculations are based on the knowledge of the total risk that an organization faces before the implementation of safeguards and countermeasures. Safeguards, proactive security controls, countermeasures, and reactive security controls all are applied to reduce risk. These security controls reduce the total risk to the extent by which they diminish the potential for threat realization. Security controls can also reduce the impact of a risk exploitation, such as when a firewall block is put in place after a workstation is found to contain malware. A *control gap* is where security controls do not cover the potential for threat realization. Therefore, to understand residual risk, it is necessary to know that it is based on these two variables, the security controls' risk reduction capability and the gap in protection that remains after the security controls' implementation.

Total Risk Equation

The equation to calculate total risk is a multiplication of the affected assets' value, their vulnerabilities, and their associated threats as follows:

Total risk = Threats × Vulnerability × AV

Residual Risk Equation

There are two equations to calculate residual risk, as mentioned earlier. The first residual risk calculation takes into account the amount of risk reduction realized by the implementation of selected security controls, as such:

Residual risk = Total risk – Security controls (also known as countermeasures)

Alternatively, residual risk is calculated as the product of the unprotected portion of the total risk, also known as the security controls gap:

Residual risk = Total risk × Controls gap

Risk Treatment

There are four different ways an organization can treat risks: reduction, transfer, avoidance, or acceptance. Here are some examples of risk treatment applied to the software development environment:

- **Risk reduction:** Risk reduction, also known as *risk mitigation*, is the process of reducing the risk to the point where it is acceptable to the organization. Typically, implementing security controls reduces risk. In the software development environment, risk is reduced by applying and enforcing controls with examples such as following secure SDLC processes, enforcing secure coding guidelines, using automated and comprehensive testing (including automated security testing), and imposing a strict separation of software development, deployment, and data environments.

- **Risk transfer:** Risk transfer is when risk is legally assigned to a third party. With respect to software development, risk transfer is often done by outsourcing a project to a third party. This is typically thought of as a cost-savings tactic, but it also can reduce the security risks related to software development. A third-party development organization can have more expertise in secure software development. It may also have more mature secure SDLC processes. Transferring the software development in this case places the risks of the software project on a more mature organization that is more capable in producing secure software.

- **Risk avoidance:** Risk avoidance is when an organization chooses to deflect or terminate situations that cause a risk. Avoiding security risk in a software development project can be done in many ways. One way is to reduce the number of features to be developed to allow more development attention to a smaller set of features to release. This makes room for improved code quality and testing. This also gives the software developers the opportunity to learn better ways to write secure software. Another motivation is to remove software features and functionality that have an unacceptable level of vulnerability exposure.

- **Risk acceptance:** Risk acceptance is the assumption of risk. Risk acceptance is necessary because it is impossible to reduce risk levels to zero. There will always be an element of security risk in software development and its artifacts. How does an organization accept these risks? First there needs to be an understanding of the level of risk and the potential consequences and cost of the damage. A software risk assessment supports this discovery. Among many things, a software risk assessment should take into account the software's data classification to get a good understanding of the risk impact. Another software security risk that is often hidden behind notions of "progress" and delivery is the risk of haste. Skipping steps in the secure SDLC, rushing software construction, and weak testing can cause or allow flaws, defects, and insufficiencies in software security controls to manifest. When conducting a risk review for risk acceptance purposes, be sure to incorporate compliance checklists of secure SDLC processes and practices in your risk assessment criteria. As a security professional you should beware of accepting a risk that is not fully understood.

ASSESS THE SECURITY IMPACT OF ACQUIRED SOFTWARE

Making significant purchases requires a thorough quality assessment. With acquired software, it is almost impossible for an organization to know the full scope of its safety, quality, and security for a number of reasons.

Acquired Software Types

When an organization acquires software, it also acquires the risks inherent in or related to that software. When an organization acquires software, it also acquires the product of the skills and habits of the developers. It receives the management effectiveness, or lack thereof, of the company or community that developed it. It might inherit malware in its envelope.

There are different types of software. Some software is commercial off-the-shelf software. Other software is provided by a vendor. OSS is another type. Even if an organization develops software internally, it often requires libraries and packages developed externally for necessary functionality. Even after an organization assesses the software products that it already uses, the products require updates and patches. These are all sources of acquired software. And if one organization acquires another one, the acquisition may come with all these forms of software. That's why it's important to assess acquired software.

Commercial Off-the-Shelf (COTS) Software

Commercial off-the-shelf (COTS) software is software that is ready made and available to the public for sale. It can be purchased outright with a license or leased. It may come with vendor support.

An advantage of COTS is that it can immediately fulfill a business or technical need at a low cost. The downside of COTS is that it can come with vulnerabilities, and some can affect the organization's information systems once installed and used. Vulnerabilities can exist in COTS because the source code is a black box and the best COTS evaluation options often include using the software in the production environment.

According to the United States Computer Emergency Response Team (US-CERT), security concerns of COTS software include the following:

- COTS software is an attractive attack target because of organizational dependency on them as well as their high profile in the marketplace.

- It is difficult to verify the security of COTS products because they are black boxes to their customers.

- The COTS software vendors have limited liability as designated by the end-user license agreement (EULA) that the user must agree with prior to software use.

- COTS is typically designed without consideration for your specific security control requirements. While this is not universally true, COTS products are usually developed to be standalone products.

Furthermore, the US-CERT, in its article "Security Considerations in Managing COTS Software" (`https://www.us-cert.gov/bsi/articles/best-practices/legacy-systems/security-considerations-in-managing-cots-software`), offers guidance to consider on how to mitigate the risk of COTS software use. This guidance serves as good reference material for developing a framework for COTS assessment. Some of the suggestions they make in the section "Mitigating Risk" are the following:

- Identify the COTS components.

- Understand what counts in terms of acceptable risk with COTS.

- Get as much security information as you can from the COTS vendor, including results from vendor security scans and CVE information.

- Operate a secure computing infrastructure.

- Control access to the COTS software.

- Engage with the user community and security community.

- Test the software, particularly testing by fault injection.

- Look for ISO- or CMMI-certified vendors.

- Understand how the COTS software operates.

This is not their complete list of suggestions but is instead a set to consider for when you develop your COTS product assessment.

Outsourced Development

Outsourced development is when your organization contracts with an outside vendor to build software for your organization. The organization has very little day-to-day control over the software development practice. Mostly, any control the customer has is based on contracts and a review schedule.

Outsourced development can be done in a foreign country, which is sometimes also referred to as *offshoring*. On the other hand, outsourced development can also be done in the same country but in an area where the expense of development would be less than at the originating market.

Two significant benefits of outsourcing software development are cost savings on production and decreased need to manage internal technical staff. Each of these outsourcing forms poses interesting challenges, not least of which can be time zone differences and jurisdictional conflicts of interest. The further away you are from the software, the less control you have. Your organization won't be absolved of all production costs, either. There still may be the expenses of management, design, testing, and deployment.

When your software is developed by entities that you do not have direct supervision over, these are major concerns:

- Embedded malware
- Design or coding flaws exposing software vulnerabilities
- Disclosure of software or sensitive data
- Unauthorized back door mechanisms
- Security verification of outsourcing vendor
- Establishment and compliance with security metrics and service level agreement

Open-Source Software

There are many benefits to OSS. First, OSS is often free or more affordable than commercial software. Depending on the software, it can also offer flexibility to modify the program source code to meet your needs. Open-source is typically supported by an active community of developers. And it's (arguably) secure.

On the other hand, the downsides of OSS include its complexity, the fact that it often requires technical expertise and a thorough evaluation process, and that it is (potentially) insecure. (There are two sides to the security/insecurity argument, each with its own merits.)

Security risks to OSS come in the following forms and should be key factors in your assessment of the OSS:

- Lack of sufficient evaluation
- Spurious open-source code
- Lack of sponsorship
- Vulnerabilities

The following sections examine these open-source security risks more closely.

Sufficient Evaluation

Because OSS is typically complex software developed by multiple people from around the world of varying skills and its development is usually not managed like commercial software, it is essential to critically evaluate it because it may not have the same level of security management and quality assurance as commercial software.

One of the ways to evaluate the safety and security of open-source code is to look at the project repository. The prerequisite for this activity is to have technical and security experts on hand to conduct this evaluation. Furthermore, it is useful to have a plan.

Many open-source projects are hosted on publicly viewable project sites such as GitHub. GitHub is now to OSS hosting, sharing, and configuration management as Java is to the language of OSS. You can get a lot of information on an open-source project hosted on GitHub from the project page. Among a number of things that you'll find on a GitHub project page, you'll find the issues with the project, the source code, and the people who contribute to it.

In a project's list of issues, you can see the number that are open and closed. You can also view each issue's narrative and subscribe to any activity on the issue.

You can view and download, or pull, the source code of the project. In GitHub, the project's modules or subsystems are typically hosted in separate repositories. This organization tells something about the project management and design quality, as modularity is a means for quality in both areas. Within the code itself, GitHub also provides a volumetric breakdown of the languages that the project uses. It's good to know which languages make up the project. In the code, look for test code. You can see the number of commits to the project and the number of branches. For more detailed assurance, you can even do your own code review.

You can see the project's contributors. GitHub shows the people who've contributed to the project. You can see where they claim to reside. Often the contributors will share their blogs, websites, or other affiliations. You can see other projects to which they contribute. Getting into the details, you can evaluate their activities with various projects, from the perspectives of contributions per day over the past year to the actual code changes they made per contribution.

Ensure Source Code Integrity

Throughout this book, you've seen examples of the various means by which information systems and communications can be compromised. OSS code and distribution are subject to many of these vulnerabilities. It isn't that much of a stretch for even an amateur hacker to embed malware into a modified version of the open-source distribution. Don't blindly trust the download distribution of OSS.

At a minimum, verify the integrity of the OSS distribution with the supplied MD5 checksum. Better yet, get the open-source distributions from trusted and authenticated sources and then verify its integrity with the MD5 checksum. Make sure you are using an authentic version of the OSS. When using open-source libraries, it is important to maintain a local repository that in-house development projects use for builds. A process for monitoring those libraries for security updates will need to be established to ensure updates are performed and pulled in to projects accordingly.

Ensure Commercial Support and Sponsorship

Popular OSS these days is typically supported by contributions from its community and sponsors from industry. As an example, the Internet Systems Consortium (ISC) is a not-for-profit organization that maintains a number of Internet standards, as well as technologies such as BIND, DHCP, and NNN. ISC is supported by individual and corporate sponsors. The Apache Software Foundation is a self-attested "cornerstone of the open-source software ecosystem." IBM has sponsored a number of open-source projects. Red Hat pioneered the sponsorship of Linux.

Sponsorship is a benefit to open-source projects because it offers both technical resources and expertise, as well as management and financial support. Sponsorship impacts the safety and security of open-source projects by improving the overall technical quality of the projects, including security maintenance. Furthermore, by selecting trustworthy, reputable, commercial support vendors to support your open-source journey, you increase the assurance that the software they provide and support will further approach your safety and security needs.

Check for Vulnerabilities

Like any software product, OSS is not without its vulnerabilities. Good stewardship of an open-source program at your organization should involve awareness and management of existing vulnerabilities as well as continuous education of future security impacting information.

OSS vulnerabilities exist for a number of reasons. The software code could be based on bad design. The quality of code could be poor. Secure and defensive coding may not have been a priority in the OSS's code development. The developers may not have either the knowledge or the interest to write secure code. The OSS's project management may not know or think to include secure software processes and practices into its SDLC. Project management may effectively not exist. Each of these factors can cause vulnerabilities as OSS is created, packaged, and distributed.

An effective strategy for checking for vulnerabilities recognizes how vulnerabilities get introduced into software. Since vulnerabilities can result from code design, development, and quality management issues, an effective strategy to check for vulnerabilities is to conduct routine code reviews on the open-source code to identify vulnerabilities. The concept of code review has been covered earlier in this chapter. Code review is a great technique for discovering vulnerabilities, but it is very labor and time intensive. This limits its ability to cover the code base. Assessing all of the code vulnerabilities is essential for improving the success of the effort. Automated code scanning techniques are effective for discovering vulnerabilities across volumes of a code base. Common types of automated code coverage are static application security testing (SAST) and dynamic application security testing (DAST). Automated code scanning techniques are covered elsewhere in this chapter.

Staying informed of the vulnerabilities in OSS is important. Industry and vendor guidance and the user community are great sources of open-source vulnerability information. The security documentation of open-source projects is another valuable resource for information on the security vulnerabilities of the open software programs and libraries that your organization uses. For instance, each Apache Software Foundation project has a security page that discusses the state of open and closed vulnerabilities in the releases of its software. The Red Hat Customer Portal provides searchable security advisories and common vulnerabilities for the projects that it manages. It also provides a Security Labs section for its subscribers containing information and tools to help its customers secure their software.

The CVE dictionary of vulnerabilities is a helpful reference for discovering potential vulnerabilities in OSS. Because of the number of evolving vulnerabilities and the rigor with which CVEs process them, these resources do not cover all of the vulnerabilities that exist. Even so, CVE searches can provide a substantial volume of information, so it is best to be as specific as possible in querying them to find the most useful results for your security program needs. The CVE is discussed in more detail in the "Security Weaknesses and Vulnerabilities at the Source-Code Level" section of this chapter. It is a searchable database of common vulnerabilities in software, including OSS. See `http://cve.mitre.org` and `https://www.cvedetails.com` to take a closer look at and use the CVE.

As open-source packages, modules, and libraries are produced, any vulnerabilities that exist within them are carried forward into the software that uses them. As open-source projects are composed of many of these constituents, most vulnerabilities exist in the software's dependencies, including the libraries, packages, and modules that it incorporates into its packaging or workflow to deliver functionality.

Modules, Libraries, and Packages

Modules, libraries, and packages are collections of preassembled software with common functionality. They are made available for general use in other programs and comprise the most common form in which OSS functionality is included for use by programs.

The terms *module*, *library*, and *package* are often used interchangeably to refer to the concept of a piece of included software. However, there are distinctions between them. A module typically describes a grouping of reusable code often associated with the Python programming language. A library in the context of software is a collection of reusable functionality. This reusable functionality can be associated with software programs but also with operating systems. A package similarly has multiple common meanings as well.

In the context of Python programming, it can refer to a collection of modules. On the other hand, a package also refers to the units of software that can be deployed onto some Linux operating systems.

Modules, libraries, and packages are often overlooked in the security evaluation of software. Conventional software security evaluation is thorough and includes a number of different approaches to conducting assessments. SAST evaluates source code. DAST evaluates the code execution. Software testing can be driven interactively. Human experts examine software in code reviews. All of these approaches are thorough and comprehensive. However, there is a gap in the verification that one can trust the safety and security of these artifacts.

Modules, libraries, and packages as binary objects may not be subject to scans. The best a code review can accomplish is to evaluate their external aspects. Libraries and packages could contain malware hidden from testable functionality. How can you trust libraries and packages?

There are several things to consider with libraries and packages:

- Verification of the security software supply chain that produced the software
- Verification of trustworthiness of vendor
- Integrity and authenticity of all libraries and packages
- Black-box security assessment of libraries and packages
- Obtaining original source code for libraries and packages instead of binaries and treating as OSS
- Source security scanning and testing if source code is available

Software Updates and Patches

Software updates and patches could be considered an aspect of the first three categories of commercial off-the-shelf, outsourced development, or OSS; however, they are called out here because they deserve special attention with respect to the particular care required to address their safety and security assessment.

A cornerstone piece of guidance on how to improve software development security is to ensure that you keep your systems and software, from BIOS to applications, up to date and properly patched. Nonetheless, updating and patching do not come without their own concerns and consequences. The downside to updates and patches are that they can be malware infection vectors or could be defective and disrupt your business services or software environment.

In many respects, software updates and patches are the same as modules, libraries, and packages, as often the former come in the form of the latter and fundamentally it's all essentially unknown code. Thus, the security considerations for software updates and patches are the same as for software modules, libraries, and packages. Consult the previous section for these concerns.

Software with Company Acquisition

When an organization merges with or acquires another organization, software comes with the deal. The acquired company most likely will have a variety of different types of software. In a merger or acquisition transition, it is important to treat all of the software brought in with the situation the same as any other software acquired from a third party. Protecting against potentially dangerous code needs to be part of the transition proceedings.

Another concern when one organization acquires another is that the new organization comes with its existing array of supply chains, customers, and partners and all of their software. Some (or all) of those parties might not have the same security focus or diligence for their software as your organization does. In such circumstances, business pressures to maintain existing systems, software, and configurations can potentially be problematic. It is important for the security professional to be aware of these factors and to address them with the appropriate parties.

Software Acquisition Process

Regardless of the number of ways to acquire software, at a high level, the software acquisition process applies to all and consists of four stages, which are planning, contracting or procurement, implementation and acceptance, and follow-on. As a security practitioner, you should be aware of the steps in the software acquisition process and what security challenges each step poses. You should also be familiar with industry standards that pertain to the process and how each standard solves the security challenges for different situations related to the process, such as the impact it has in public versus private organizations, open-source versus commercial software, and any specific situations that your organization may face.

Planning

The planning process is indispensable because it clarifies and directs the real needs, options, solutions, risks, and vetting criteria into forms that translate into action. The planning phase consists of the following:

- Determining the need for the software or service to be acquired
- Identifying alternative solutions to acquiring software
- Identifying risks associated with acquiring software
- Developing clear requirements for the software or service
- Defining an acquisition strategy

- Defining evaluation and acceptance criteria
- Defining an evaluation and acceptance plan
- Identifying alternative options or vendors based on requirements, criteria, and plans

Contracting or Procurement

The contracting or procurement phase of the acquisition process is essentially a selection process. Depending upon the type of acquisition, it can follow one of two branches: contracting or procurement. Contracting is used if the software acquisition is to be an outsourced development project. Procurement is used if the software acquisition is either COTS or OSS. Some people wonder why something that is freely downloadable needs to be procured, which is an understandable question. OSS is procured because it must be carefully selected, preferably from a trusted source.

The security practitioner should understand that the procurement process can vary by organization or type of organization. Public organizations such as governmental organizations often have a formal open evaluation process that works to remove preferential bias from product or service selection and determine their selection based on established nondiscriminatory and needs-based constraints. Private-sector company procurement processes are generally driven more by time pressures and specific quality outcomes more so than public organizations. The procurement process varies around the world, influenced by laws and regulations of the governing bodies that cover the participating parties.

Contracting

Contracting applies to outsourced development. The steps involved in the contracting phase generally follow:

1. Evaluating and selecting a set of vendors from those that were identified in the planning phase

2. Creating and issuing a request for proposal or solicitation to the vendors, which includes but is not limited to the following:

   - Statement of work
   - Technical requirements
   - Terms and conditions
   - Timeline
   - Points of contact
   - Budget
   - Evaluation and acceptance criteria, acceptably modified for vendor's eyes

3. Evaluating vendors' responses to requests for proposals (RFPs) or solicitation

4. Selecting vendor(s) and finalizing contract negotiation with selected vendor(s)

5. Awarding the contract

6. Ensuring that the vendor is willing to make changes when required

All risks identified in the planning phase, as well as any discovered in the contracting phase, should be addressed with plans for their mitigation stated in a binding contract with the selected vendor along with the awarded contract.

Procurement

Procurement applies to COTS, OSS, libraries and packages, and updates and patches. The steps involved in the procurement phase generally follow:

1. Evaluating and selecting:

   - For COTS or OSS, a set of solutions from those that were identified in the planning phase

   - For libraries and packages or updates and patches, the specific version of software that meets your needs

2. Selecting and verifying a trusted source from which to obtain the software. For libraries and packages or updates and patches, this may already be established.

3. Verifying the means of certification of authenticity and integrity of the solution from a trusted source:

   - For OSS, this may be a process of obtaining a source code download from a trusted and approved source and verifying it against a checksum.

   - For COTS software, this is purchasing a shrink-wrapped distribution that comes with a certification of authenticity from a trusted and approved vendor.

4. Obtaining the solution distribution from a trusted source and verifying authenticity and integrity.

All risks identified in the planning phase, as well as any discovered in the procurement phase, should be addressed with plans for their mitigation stated in the acceptance and evaluation criteria and plans.

Implementation and Acceptance

When implementing software, packages, and updates, there are several things an organization can do to improve the security impact. Gathering and evaluating security information can help identify which software best meets the security needs of the organization before acquiring it. Establishing and validating a support contract with a trusted vendor ensures better support and open lines of communication for updates and patches. Developing and executing a test plan based on acceptance and evaluation criteria, including safety and security risks, can produce measurable results for evaluation. Ongoing monitoring of security and performance can reveal problems that might otherwise go undetected.

When dealing with outsourced development, the organization has less direct control of some of these factors. In these situations, the organization can establish a baseline structure to the relationship with the vendor that includes an agreed upon schedule for deliverables, communication channels, and regular progress reports. This facilitates routine deliverables reviews, including security and testing reviews. Ongoing monitoring of security and performance also plays a role here, and in many organizations it is still possible to varying degrees to develop and execute test plans that include safety and security risks.

For each type of software, establish an isolated testing environment for testing purposes. This measure is to contain any negative effects of examining the software from being exposed to other environments.

Follow-On

For the software product under evaluation, follow-on activities are just as important as the initial planning, procuring, implementation, and acceptance. Ongoing maintenance, risk management, and configuration management all need to be performed regularly. Continuous monitoring of security and performance must be maintained. It is also important to routinely update information on security and status. And if any issues arise, it is necessary to request intervention from the vendor.

Relevant Standards

Remember, your organization isn't the first in history to acquire software. Industry standards exist to provide best-practice guidance through this process. Here we examine standards that apply to software acquisition as well as software safety and security standards.

CMMI for Acquisition, Version 1.3

The Capability Maturity Model Integration for Acquisition version 1.3 (CMMI-ACQ V1.3) model provides best practice guidance to an organization for applying CMMI when acquiring products and services. It comes in three parts.

- Part 1, "About CMMI for Acquisition," provides an introduction to concepts, process area components, relationships among process areas, and paths to adoption.

- Part 2, "Generic Goals and Generic Practices, and the Process Areas," contains all of the required and expected components for this model. Additionally, it has related informative components, with examples.

- Part 3, "The Appendices and Glossary," contains informational references useful to understand the process.

Best practices in the model focus on activities for initiating and managing the acquisition of products and services to meet the needs of customers and end users. Although suppliers can provide artifacts useful to the processes addressed in CMMI-ACQ, the focus of the model is on the processes of the acquirer. For more information on CMMI-ACQ V1.3, see `https://resources.sei.cmu.edu/asset_files/TechnicalReport/2010_005_001_15284.pdf`.

Other Standards to Consider with Acquisition

Software acquisition intersects with security of the software lifecycle in different ways depending upon the type of software acquisition and how that acquired software integrates in an organization's processes. For these reasons, as a security practitioner, it is good for you to know of other international standards that may apply to the various situations.

- **ISO/IEC/IEEE 12207:2017, "Systems and software engineering – Software lifecycle processes"**: This standard provides processes that can be employed for defining, controlling, and improving software lifecycle processes within an organization or a project. The processes, activities, and tasks of this document can also be applied during the acquisition of a system that contains software, either alone or in conjunction with ISO/IEC/IEEE 15288:2015. This standard can be found at `https://www.iso.org/standard/63712.html`.

- **ISO/IEC/IEEE 15288:2015, "Systems and software engineering – System lifecycle processes"**: This standard provides a common framework of process descriptions for describing the lifecycle of systems. It also provides processes that support an organization's or project's system lifecycle processes. Organizations and projects can use these processes when acquiring and supplying systems. This standard can be found at `https://www.iso.org/standard/63711.html`.

- **ISO/IEC 25001:2014, "Systems and software engineering – Systems and software Quality Requirements and Evaluation (SQuaRE) – Planning and management"**: This standard helps organizations that have to create and manage SQA requirements and evaluate products by providing requirements and recommendations. This standard can be found at `https://www.iso.org/standard/64787.html`.

Software Safety and Security Standards

To be able to assess the security impact of acquired software, there must be a reference by which to conduct the evaluations. It is essential for you as a security professional to be aware of and seek out industry-accepted security standards to serve as necessary references for your practice, particularly when you are acquiring software.

This section highlights standards that you as a security professional can use either directly, as a reference, or as a starting place for your research. These standards cover software safety and security for electronic and programmable electronic systems, automotive software systems, airborne software systems, space-based software systems, and industrial automation and control systems security.

These were intentionally selected to direct attention to their concentration's significance or rigor, serving as examples of disciplined security standards. Software safety and security standards are useful references when developing software evaluation and acceptance criteria and requirements.

IEC 61508, "Functional Safety"

The International Electrotechnical Commission (IEC) (`http://www.iec.ch/`) is the international standards and conformity body for all fields of electronic-based technology. The IEC defines functional safety for electronic and programmable electronic systems and provides a downloadable brochure at `http://www.iec.ch/functionalsafety/explained/`.

Their IEC 61508 series of standards covers electronic and programmable electronic safety systems. It defines engineering and operational requirements to achieve one of four safety integration levels (SILs). A SIL is based on the risks involved in the system. "IEC 61508-3:2010, Functional safety of electrical/electronic/programmable electronic safety-related systems – Part 3: Software," describes the requirements for software and tooling to configure a software-based safety system.

ISO 26262, "Functional Safety for Automotive Specific Safety Critical Components"

Now that we're solidly in the 21st century, some of the promises of futurists past are coming to fruition. One of these predictions that is imminently becoming manifest is the self-driving car. Notwithstanding this science fiction becoming real, automobiles already are sophisticated and complex mobile computing platforms. One estimate suggests the average high-end automobile uses approximately 100 million lines of code to get from point A to point B. (The full story is available at `https://spectrum.ieee.org/transportation/systems/this-car-runs-on-code.`)

To put this into perspective, Facebook has approximately 70 million lines of code.

Consider for a moment what 100 million lines of code in a high-end automobile means for you now and in the future. Just pondering the potential defect rate and reliability requirements for a software system of this magnitude should rivet you to the ISO 26262 Standard for Functional Safety for Automotive Specific Safety Critical Components. The ISO 26262 standard is described in the National Instrument's whitepaper at `http://www.ni.com/white-paper/13647/en/`. This whitepaper describes the key components of ISO 26262:

- Automotive safety lifecycle (management, development, production, operation, service, decommissioning)

- Automotive risk-based determination of risk classes (Automotive Safety Integrity Levels [ASILs])

- Validation and confirmation requirements to determine an acceptable level of safety being achieved

- Automotive Safety Integrity Levels (ASILs), which are classifications to define safety requirements to align with the ISO 26262 standard

ISA 62443, Series of Standards: Industrial Automation and Control Systems Security

The ISA-99/IEC 62443 global standard for security of Industrial Automation and Control Systems was created by the International Society of Automation (`www.isa.org`). This standard guides an organization to improve the cybersecurity and safety of their process and SCADA environments. It is derived from ISO/IEC 27000 but with an emphasis on Industrial Control Systems environments.

U.S. Federal Acquisition Regulation

In the United States, the Federal Acquisition Regulation (FAR) is the set of rules that regulate how federal government agencies acquire goods and services, including software. This public contracting and procurement regulation is far-reaching and extends to organizations such as the Department of Defense and NASA. It addresses concerns that deal with intellectual property, technical data, service contracts, and further considerations.

Similar to the United States, all governments around the world have their own rules and regulations for public contracting and procurement. It is essential for the security professional to understand the relevant government's rules and their security ramifications when their organization deals with public contracting and procurement.

Software Assurance

Software assurance is the degree of certainty that software is free from vulnerabilities of all kinds and that its functionality meets all expectations required of it.

Software assurance is essential for software development security in that:

- It is the activity to prove that the collective artifacts, processes, and efforts used to produce and sustain software conforms to and complies with all requirements and standards that cover or govern them.

- When assuring the software's conformance and compliance, its activities should prove the safety and security fitness of the software.

- Its activities also cover the safety, conformity, and fitness requirements for acquired or vendor-produced software.

Seven Principles for Software Assurance

The SEI's blog, The Latest Research in Software Engineering and Cybersecurity, shared an October 2016 article called "Seven Principles for Software Assurance" that provides great summary insight into Software Assurance (`https://insights`
`.sei.cmu.edu/sei_blog/2016/10/seven-principles-for-software-assurance.html`).
The SEI blog post began by reminding us of the importance of software assurance.

The following are the SEI's seven principles for software assurance:

1. Risk drives assurance decisions.
2. Risk concerns shall be aligned across all stakeholders and all interconnected technology.
3. Dependencies shall not be trusted until proven trustworthy.
4. Attacks shall be expected.
5. Assurance requires effective communication among technology participants.
6. Assurance shall be well planned and dynamic.
7. A means to measure and audit overall assurance shall be built in.

The SEI principles in detail guide attention and action. The following sections will explore the principles in more detail.

Risk Drives Assurance Decisions

To their detriment, organizations sometimes implement software assurance policies, practices, tools, and constraints based upon the threats they assume they will encounter. Often, threats beyond their modeled predictions exist and pose significant risks to the organization. For software assurance to be effective, it must be reality-based. To achieve this, there must be knowledge sharing of the actual threat landscape. The software assurance practice needs to meet the reality of the risks that exist.

Risk Concerns Shall Be Aligned across All Stakeholders and All Interconnected Technology

You may be familiar with the Target credit card hack of 2013. It stands out in popular memory because the attackers first gained access to Target's network by using credentials from an HVAC vendor.

Organizations must understand that software assurance applies to all stakeholders and interconnected technologies. It also applies to the software supply chain starting with device and software vendors. It is not sufficient just to protect critical assets. Connections with noncritical technology can exist at a variety of levels: network, storage, architecture, and so on. Because of this variety, all the stakeholders must be engaged to assure security effectively.

Dependencies Shall Not Be Trusted Until Proven Trustworthy

Anything that your software depends upon should not be trusted. You should not underestimate the number and scope of dependencies of your software development environment. These dependencies can be software frameworks, libraries, packages, vendor software, certificates, OSS, and so on. Your organization should have a program to verify the safety, integrity, security, and proper functioning of all dependencies. A best practice is to procure dependencies only from trusted sources.

NOTE   One of the ways that the Stuxnet virus was able to penetrate an air-gapped network was via an infected USB memory stick. For more information on Stuxnet, see `https://www.cnet.com/news/stuxnet-delivered-to-iranian-nuclear-plant-on-thumb-drive/`.

Attacks Shall Be Expected

You should assume that any aspect of your information system environment, software, services, and so on, will be attacked. Assurance planning should be done with this fact as a central driver of your plans.

Assurance Requires Effective Communication among Technology Participants

Security of the software development environment involves the expertise and collaboration of many different participants. Security practitioners, software developers, quality assurance, vendors, project development, and project management all have responsibilities to meet this goal. This requires effective communication among all of the technology participants. Effective communication is sharing the right information in the right form with the right people who need to know. This is how the proper participants in the overall effort can do their job.

Assurance Shall Be Well Planned and Dynamic

A software security assurance plan needs to cover each aspect of the software lifecycle. A comprehensive plan considers the assurance requirements dictated by governance, software development, and the operations environment. However comprehensive the planning process and resulting plans may be, the assurance process must still respond to the ongoing changes that result from new situations as they present themselves.

A Means to Measure and Audit Overall Assurance Shall Be Built In

Human nature, for better or worse, aspires to the expectations that are imposed upon it. The software security assurance process is best maintained when it is measured and subject to expectations. For an organization's assurance efforts to be successful, they must be measured and audited on a regular basis.

Software Assurance Guidance and Standards

Having a working definition and knowing its principles is good for a baseline understanding of software assurance. However, for a security practitioner to know how to set up, support, or evaluate a software assurance process, they need to have more information. This section provides guidance and standards material to support these goals. The material points the security practitioner to a security software assurance reference model in SAFECode for an example of successful software assurance process guidance. This is followed by the IEEE Standard for Software Quality Assurance Processes. This standard provides a framework upon which one can understand or build a software assurance capability.

SAFECode

The Software Assurance Forum for Excellence in Code (SAFECode) is a nonprofit organization that promotes the advancement of software assurance methods. SAFECode brings together subject-matter experts from around the globe to share their experiences in the form of best practices in implementing, managing, and supporting product security programs.

Some examples of their work include the following:

- Published practical guidance on significant issues of software security
- Free online software security training courses to be used to support in-house training as well as for an individual's education
- Hosting information-sharing sessions with industry peers in a trusted environment

SAFECode's educational approach is wise guidance for the security professional. For security to keep up with advancing technology and effectively combat increasingly sophisticated threats it needs to improve based upon a set of pragmatic principles.

The SAFECode Principles (`https://safecode.org/safecode-principles/`) are as follows:

- Secure development is an organizational commitment and a holistic process.

- There is no one-size-fits-all approach to software assurance.

- Despite differences, common secure development practices shared across the industry have proven both practical and effective.

- Providing more transparency in the software assurance process and practices helps customers and other key stakeholders manage risk effectively.

- Contributing information about members' own security processes and practices supports SAFECode efforts to advance software assurance and positively impacts the security and reliability of the technology ecosystem.

- Software assurance training should become a required part of any software engineering training program.

By practicing these principles, you and your organization will become more successful in your software assurance efforts. In doing so, the safety and security of software acquisitions will improve significantly as well.

IEEE STD 730-2014

IEEE Standard 730-2014 is the "IEEE Standard for Software Quality Assurance (SQA) Processes." It provides guidance and requirements for software quality assurance. It was the first software engineering standard published in 1979. It fills in the details for the software quality assurance tasks outlined in IEEE 12207, "Standard for Software Life Cycle Processes."

IEEE Standard 730-2014 covers the SQA activity areas of SQA process implementation, product assurance, and process assurance. Product assurance assures that software products conform to established requirements. Process assurance assures the effectiveness and accuracy of a project and that organizational processes and project activities conform to these processes.

For more information on IEEE Standard 730-2014, see `http://ieeexplore.ieee.org/document/6835311/`.

Certification and Accreditation

Certification and accreditation ensure the security of information systems. It is a two-step process that supports the software assurance process.

Certification is a technical evaluation of a software system's security compliance with specific standards to which it should conform. The certification process identifies security weaknesses and ensures that strategies and plans are created to mitigate these weaknesses.

Accreditation in information security has a somewhat different meaning than its meaning for product validation. In information security, accreditation means that management understands the overall security of the evaluated system and formally accepts the risks.

The best guidance for certification and accreditation in an information security environment are formal programs that implement these processes. The U.S. Department of Defense Information Technology Security Certification and Accreditation Process (DITSCAP) is one such program. The SANS Institute provides an overview of DITSCAP at `https://www.sans.org/reading-room/whitepapers/country/ditscap-dods-answer-secure-systems-669`. Also, the National Information Assurance Certification and Accreditation Process (NIACAP) is the U.S. federal government's version of DITSCAP, which offers another program perspective on the process. The National Security Telecommunications and Information Systems Security Committee describes the NIACAP in a whitepaper hosted by New Mexico Tech at `http://infohost.nmt.edu/~sfs/Regs/nstissi_1000.pdf`. Furthermore, NIST SP 800-37, the "Guide for Applying the Risk Management Framework to Federal Information Systems: a Security Life Cycle Approach," provides standard guidance that directs security assessment and authorization at `https://csrc.nist.gov/publications/detail/sp/800-37/rev-1/final`.

In summary, subjecting software artifacts to a formal certification and accreditation (C&A) process has several benefits. It ensures each of the following:

- A set of security requirements is developed and implemented for the software.

- Residual risk is clearly understood, and plans are made to minimize risk.

- All aspects of the development and deployment of security controls and policies are clearly described and documented.

DEFINE AND APPLY SECURE CODING STANDARDS AND GUIDELINES

There are as many styles of coding as there are software developers. Unfortunately, stylistic variety in software development can be an open door to introducing flaws and bugs that lead to weakness and vulnerabilities in programs. Securing the software's API is necessary to protect the software from attacks from untrusted environments. Standardizing coding practices and defining guidelines for secure software development, when applied effectively, serve to improve secure coding practice. Defining and applying secure coding standards and guidelines in an organization's SDLC translates best practices into working software.

Security Weaknesses and Vulnerabilities at the Source-Code Level

While the terms *software security weakness* and *vulnerability* are often used interchangeably, they are not the same. A security weakness at the source code level is not a vulnerability. When an attacker leverages security weakness to compromise a system, the security weakness then becomes a vulnerability. A weakness is a conceptual problem with the software until it is brought into an environment where that problem is exposed and can be exploited.

A software weakness is a bug, flaw, or error in the software. A weakness can be in the architecture, design, or code of a program. Common examples of software weaknesses are buffer overflow, format strings, authentication errors, insufficient data validation, code injection, and the like. Weaknesses can be summed up as what security problems could happen to software. Software weaknesses should be used as guidance to design and construct software in a way that minimizes the chances of the weaknesses being realized.

The Common Weakness Enumeration (CWE) and the OWASP Top Ten are two sources of reference to software weaknesses. They each are valuable references for software weaknesses that you should know about and use as needed in your security practice.

Vulnerabilities are the manifestation of weaknesses in software systems. Unlike situations where software weakness is more of a design concept, a vulnerability is a manifestation of a software weakness that is tied to specific instances of a software product such as a software library, program, or system. The CVE is a searchable database of vulnerabilities and is described in more detail later in this section.

Common Weakness Enumeration (CWE)

The complexity of software, business needs, and desire for usability contributes to the improbability of problem-free code. Categorizing and understanding weaknesses assists security professionals and developers in understanding types of weaknesses. The CWE was created to be a formal reference of software weaknesses. It is intended to be a common language for describing software security weaknesses in architecture, design, or code. It is meant to serve as a standard measuring stick for software security tools that target weaknesses. It is a common baseline standard for weakness identification, mitigation, and prevention efforts.

The CWE listings provide detailed information about software weaknesses. They describe weaknesses and characterize each one, showing how it is possible and may be exploited. In the CWE weakness listings section "modes of introduction," the listing states when the weakness may manifest in SDLC phases. A CWE listing also states the common consequences that are associated with the weakness. These consequences describe the security qualities that are affected, such as confidentiality, integrity, and availability. It describes the impact this weakness will have on the program if exploited and the likelihood of its exploitation. A section in the CWE listing provides code examples of the weakness. Furthermore, it suggests mitigation strategies for the weakness as guidance for the software practitioner to implement.

Developers, designers, and architects can use this information to secure the software. Knowledge, in this case, is power—the power to identify software weaknesses and to mitigate their effects. Using the CWE for this purpose is possible because the CWE is publicly available and free to use. Publicly listing software weaknesses like this may seem risky because it also is a reference to attackers; however, the education it provides software practitioners on how to secure their software against the weaknesses can give security the advantage.

The CWE is organized by three different concept views: research, development, and architecture. Each of these viewpoints organizes software weaknesses into groupings that are useful for different purposes.

The CWE's research concepts view classifies software weaknesses according to their abstract behaviors. The research view overlooks how weaknesses are detected or how they manifest in code. This abstracted view facilitates research on weaknesses. This research format enables discovery of more weaknesses, whether currently captured or ones that are unfilled gaps in the CWE model. The CWE research concept view also helps software security toolmakers improve their products by acting as a content measure. For a more detailed overview of the CWE research concepts, see `https://cwe.mitre.org/data/definitions/1000.html`.

The development concepts view organizes weaknesses around concepts frequently encountered in software development. This view helps software developers understand common code weaknesses. Armed with this knowledge, software developers can avoid making mistakes that cause the weaknesses.

The architectural concepts CWE groups weaknesses by common architectural security practices. This viewpoint helps architects, engineers, and designers to craft architectures and designs with a security focus.

For more information on the CWE, see `https://cwe.mitre.org/about/index.html`.

Common Weakness Risk Analysis Framework (CWRAF)

The OWASP Top Ten Most Critical Web Application Security Risks and the CWE/SANS TOP 25 Most Dangerous Software Errors list are two of the notable software security weakness lists. These types of lists allow us to focus our attention on the vulnerabilities that have the most impact and then to address them with appropriate measures of control for their mitigation. The Common Weakness Risk Analysis Framework (CWRAF) allows organizations to create their own "top-n" list, with "n" being some number that is custom-oriented to its particular concerns.

The CWRAF is a CWE-related project. It offers a customization framework for an organization to construct a view of weaknesses that is most applicable to its type of software through its software lifecycle. This framework has a hierarchical structure for an organization to use to deduce the weaknesses with the most impact on its software concerns. This hierarchical structure consists of domains, technology groups, and vignettes.

Domains in the CWRAF are a broad-strokes categorization of the type of business concern similar to a business sector. Domains in the CWRAF are e-commerce, banking and finance, energy, chemical, manufacturing, shipping and transportation, national defense, homeland security, government other than national defense and homeland security, emergency services, public health, food and water, telecommunications, teleworking, e-voting, social media, and human resources.

For each of the domains, there is a mapping to a technology group. The CWRAF technology groups are web applications, real-time embedded systems, control systems, endpoint computing systems, operating systems, identity management systems, enterprise systems and applications, cloud computing, enterprise security products, and network communications.

Vignettes are ways to communicate an organization's security priorities for software in particular environments. Vignettes exist to support different prioritization of weaknesses.

The CWRAF, through its categorization and structure, allows organizations to measure the risk of security weaknesses in a way that is tied to its business. It enables an organization to prioritize and rank the software weaknesses important to it. It can be used along with the Common Weakness Scoring System (CWSS) to mark the most critical weaknesses of the organization's software.

Common Weakness Scoring System (CWSS)

The CWSS provides a means for prioritizing software weaknesses in a flexible, consistent, and open way. The CWSS can be used to sort through and pick out the highest-priority weaknesses in code when faced with too many results and no clear priorities.

The CWSS uses three different metrics groups: base findings, attack surface, and environmental metrics. The base finding metric group has and represents the weaknesses' inherent risk as well as assessments of the accuracy of its discovery and the effectiveness of controls. The attack surface metric group represents the barriers to attack: what must be overcome to exploit the weakness. The environmental metric group represents specific characteristics of software weaknesses in particular environments or operational contexts.

Weakness scoring calculations are simply a multiplication of the scores of each different metrics group for the weakness. Having the ability to score weaknesses with CWSS in such as fashion makes for consistent ranking and prioritization and thus the ability to effectively direct secure coding activities.

The OWASP Top Ten

The OWASP Top Ten Most Critical Web Application Security Risks list is an essential resource for the security practitioner. It is a fundamental reference of the most common security weaknesses found in web applications. This list helps a security professional understand what security needs to be designed for or applied to web applications to safeguard them against these vulnerabilities being exploited.

The OWASP Top Ten consolidates the 10 most critical web application security risks into one source. It provides salient information on each risk, such as its exploitability, likelihood, and impact. It provides guidance on how to assess whether the software is susceptible to risk. It provides examples of attack scenarios for the risk. It informs the reader how to prevent the web application security risk. It also has references to supplemental guidance, both OWASP and external, to support understanding and how to mitigate the risks effectively.

This Top Ten list undergoes periodic revisions to maintain currency with the state of software security. For instance, the most recent update, the 2017 OWASP Top Ten, takes into account the shift toward microservices, single-page web applications, and the expanding influence of JavaScript. The following is the OWASP Top Ten Most Critical Web Application Security Risks list for 2017:

- **A1:2017-Injection:** An injection flaw is when data that is sent through input channels into software command interpreters has destructive or unintended and malicious effects. These effects are typically to execute an attacker's commands in the interpreter or to obtain unauthorized access to data. The most frequent forms of injection are SQL, NoSQL, OS, and LDAP injection.

- **A2:2017-Broken Authentication:** When authentication or session management functionality is incorrectly implemented in an application, it is considered to be broken. This allows attackers to compromise these mechanisms to hijack users' credentials for their own purposes.

- **A3:2017-Sensitive Data Exposure:** This flaw happens when sensitive data is not properly protected and is at risk of unauthorized exposure. Examples of sensitive data include personally identifiable information, financial data, healthcare data, corporate secrets such as mergers and acquisitions data, or application secrets such as service credentials or API keys. Sensitive data requires extra control in maintaining its confidentiality and integrity.

- **A4:2017-XML External Entities (XXE):** Attackers can exploit an XML processor's XML external entity reference processing. This type of exploit gives an attacker access to resources referred to by the external entities such as internal files and file storage. It can be used to execute remote code or a denial-of-service attack as well.

- **A5:2017-Broken Access Control:** Authenticated users' access control permissions are often incomplete or insufficiently implemented and therefore can be exploited. This opens the potential to access other users' accounts, modify users' data, introduce unauthorized data, and gain access to unauthorized functionality.

- **A6:2017-Security Misconfiguration:** Security misconfiguration is a common concern that manifests in many ways, including using insecure default configurations, incorrect security settings, insecure operating system configuration, uncontrolled cloud storage, or sensitive data leakage in log files. A useful approach to resolving these kinds of issues is to assume that everything should have a secure configuration and to work to make these configurations achieve an acceptable risk level.

- **A7:2017-Cross-Site Scripting (XSS):** Cross-site scripting is when a web application fails to validate or sanitize untrusted data in a web page and this untrusted data, being part of a web page, is then read and executed by the browser, thereby potentially allowing the attacker to execute scripts in the victim's browser to compromise web pages, hijack user sessions, or redirect users to malicious sites. Some sources of this untrusted data can result from including external service-provided data or inclusion of user-supplied data in a web page.

- **A8:2017-Insecure Deserialization:** When software data structures are shared over a network from a source system to a remote system, they often are translated into a form that can be embedded in the communication stream. This process is known as *serialization*. When these data structures are received by the remote system, they are then translated into a form that the recipient software can use. This process is known as *deserialization*. Because the serialization/deserialization processes relate to code, an insecure deserialization can lead to unintended code execution on the remote system. Insecure deserialization can also lead to a number of attacks such as injection, privileged escalation, and replay attacks.

- **A9:2017-Using Components with Known Vulnerabilities:** So much of what makes up software programs are the components included in its deployment. Because these components are a part of the software, their functionality is often executed with the same privileges as the software itself. Using components with known vulnerabilities then is like escorting an attacker inside the fortress. Exploiting these component vulnerabilities can be a means to compromise application security controls or as a vector for attack.

- **A10:2017-Insufficient Logging & Monitoring:** An attack can happen even with the best risk prevention controls in place. This is why logging, monitoring, and integration with incident response is so important. When these controls are insufficient or nonexistent, it allows for an attack to continue undetected and extend to other systems. Most studies show that the time it takes to detect a breach is more than 200 days and that internal processes or monitoring are lacking.

The OWASP Top Ten is one of the industry's gold standard references for web application security. It is often necessary to use multiple sources of information to get a comprehensive map of the threat and vulnerability terrain. In fact, it is useful application security guidance as well. However, as useful as the OWASP Top Ten is, it is not the only source nor the only source of the top threats to consider.

For more information on the OWASP Top Ten for 2017, please see `https://www.owasp` `.org/images/7/72/OWASP_Top_10-2017_%28en%29.pdf.pdf`.

Common Vulnerabilities and Exposures

The CVE is a free authoritative dictionary of vulnerability information that is hosted and curated by the MITRE Organization and sponsored by the US-CERT of the U.S. Department of Homeland Security. The CVE is designed to be used by many cybersecurity products as a source of vulnerability information.

The CVE identifies each vulnerability by a CVE ID. The vulnerabilities are described by the number of exploits, vulnerability types, publish and update dates, and significant security information.

The CVE dictionary is searchable, making it a valuable asset to find vulnerabilities. It is searchable by many parameters, such as language, vendor, software product, version number, vulnerability type, and other criteria. With knowledge of the specific open-source software products that your organization uses, you can search for their vulnerabilities here. See `http://cve.mitre.org` and `https://www.cvedetails.com` to take a closer look at and use the CVE.

Something important to keep in mind is that the CVE information is a dual-edged sword. Although it exists to inform the software security professional what vulnerabilities exists in software, attackers can seek the same information from the CVE and exploit it. It is the responsibility of a software security professional to know and use this information to minimize security risk in software.

Another source of vulnerabilities information is the U.S. Department of Commerce National Institute of Standards and Technology (NIST) National Vulnerability Database (NVD). The NVD builds upon the CVE by incorporating its dictionary and adding analysis and fine-grained search ability.

Security of Application Programming Interfaces

An API defines how to interact with software. Software components interact and work together through the use of an API. An API is a software program's contract that describes how other programs should communicate with it. APIs define the publicly accessible functionality of the program. An API defines how that functionality is invoked, limitations on its use, and expectations when calling it.

An API can act as the front gate for its software. It can protect, log, filter, and approve communication between the software it fronts and external environments.

This section discusses the security of APIs.

Application Programming Interface Types

There are many different types of APIs. There are system-level APIs. There are programming-level APIs for packages or modules with method or function and data structure specifications. These modules can be those of user or system libraries. An API can be the specification of remote calls available to its consumers, like CORBA or RPC. Web-based APIs are based on HTTP/HTTPS. Web-based APIs exchange structured messages, usually in JavaScript Object Notation (JSON) or XML, often in the form Simple Object Access Protocol (SOAP) structures. This section takes a general approach to describe API security and uses a REST-based model as the basis to explain concepts.

Risk Assessment

First, it is necessary to understand an API's risk exposure. Each API should be subject to a risk assessment to determine the risk or residual risk it poses to the organization. An API risk assessment should take into account the data classification, the recovery objectives, and the real and total costs of downtime to the organization, among other things. Make a comprehensive list of the vulnerabilities and threats of the API. Focus on the appropriate risk response by implementing security capabilities to minimize the risks these vulnerabilities and threats pose to the software.

A threat model is useful in determining how an API can be compromised. One should think like an attacker when evaluating an API for its vulnerabilities and desirable targets to attack.

Security of APIs

An API's risks determine what level of protection is appropriate for it. Despite this variety of different APIs, they share many common potential security capabilities. Designing security into an API is a necessity. There are a number of frameworks that offer security features that mitigate the top risks of APIs. Choose a framework that works with the chosen computer language and offers a comprehensive suite of security controls to mitigate the most critical security risks for your application. The following security control areas apply when securing APIs:

- Authentication and access control
- Input validation and sanitization
- Protection of resources
- Protecting communications
- Cryptography
- Security logging, monitoring, and alerting

Authentication and Access Control

Authentication verifies that the consumer calling the API is the entity that they are supposed to be. APIs protect sensitive data. Access to the software resources should be restricted to approved consumers. Authentication performs this activity.

There are many different authentication techniques. These include a username and password-based technique, certificate-based authentication, OAuth, Security Assertion Markup Language (SAML), and others. Some authentication methods have different versions and implementations. Choose the authentication mechanism that best fits the usage patterns of the API. Enforce re-authentication for APIs that grant access to sensitive or privileged functionality.

Basic Authentication

Basic authentication is an authentication scheme that is built into the HTTP protocol. The username and password credentials are sent as base64-encoded strings. Basic authentication is the simplest form of authentication and is the on the weaker side of security. Basic authentication is not recommended when better options are available. If Basic authentication must be used, then it is recommended that effective communication encryption such as Transport Layer Security (TLS) is used as well.

Certificate-Based Authentication

Digital certificates can be used to identify an entity, such as a user, as part of an identity and authentication mechanism. Certificate-based authentication can be used by all endpoints such as users, servers, and the like. Distribution and management of digital certificates should be part of designing a certificate-based implementation.

Dynamic Tokens

Dynamic access tokens are typically tokens issued to users that assert that the bearer has a particular set of privileges for the term restriction of the token.

JWT

When software services are distributed and separated by distance over a network, it presents a challenge on how to communicate a user's authentication and authorization status to various systems. The use of tokens to bear this and other information, collectively known as *claims*, on behalf of the user has been a common and useful strategy in this case. The JavaScript Object Notation (JSON) Web Token (JWT) is a type of dynamic token that uses JSON notation to describe these authentication and authorization claims in a standard format to be used across distributed systems. It is defined by the open standard RFC 7519 (`https://tools.ietf.org/html/rfc7519`).

An example of a claim that a JWT token can represent about a user to an environment could be the assertion of a user's role. An example of this might be when a user is acting as an "administrator" gets presented as part of the user's credentials in a JWT.

JWT is designed to be easy to use. It also can be encrypted based on RFC 7516: JSON Web Encryption (`https://tools.ietf.org/html/rfc7516`) and signed by RFC 7515: JSON Web Signature (`https://tools.ietf.org/html/rfc7515`).

OAuth

OAuth enables delegated authorization. It solves the problem of securely delegating access to a user across multiple resources. There are two OAuth specifications, OAuth 1.0a and OAuth 2.0. These two specifications are incompatible. OAuth 2.0 relies on HTTPS for its security. OAuth 1.0a has security built in to compensate for working with nonsecured protocols. Consider using JWT with OAuth.

Location-Based Access Control Restriction

API access can be restricted by the location of the API caller. This type of access restriction may be used where there are geopolitical or legal constraints on the use of the software, such as sanctions or export controls over data. Restricting access based on geographic location is not foolproof, however, because the caller can spoof the location.

Input Validation and Sanitization

Input validation and sanitization should be among the software security practitioner's primary concerns. Because they accept data from the outside world, input channels expose software systems to potentially destructive or malicious data. Input validation and sanitization are controls against this exposure.

Input validation controls check for the safety and appropriateness of data. Input validation evaluates data for the correct data type, acceptable values, formatting, and particularly for the presence of any data that may be harmful or have unacceptable effects on the system. It also ensures that the input data is safe and secure for the system to accept and prohibits bad input from passing through.

Input sanitization takes this one step further by transforming the input data into a form that neutralizes the potential harm that it could do once accepted into the system. An example of input sanitization is to remove HTML markup or scripting text that may be embedded in input so as to prevent this disallowed content from becoming rendered as a part of subsequent pages that use this input. This is an active control to prevent injection attacks of all kinds.

The API layer is a place to conduct input validation and malicious code injection inspections. An API is the front gate between external entities and the logic. As such, the API is the most important location to perform input validation. However, the software architecture of an API dictates where these controls should be imposed.

It is important to clarify what this means precisely. Often with API calls, there is a client side and a server side. The client side of the API is how the API presents itself to its consumers. This client-side presentation can be any of a number of different representations, such as an HTML web page form or a thick client. Validating and sanitizing input on the client side acts as a convenience for the user by directing them to input correct data. However, it cannot control data that is sent directly to the server side of the API. Thus, it is important for the security practitioner to assume that client-side API input validation and sanitization is insufficient.

It is not exaggerating to state that input validation and sanitization controls should be imposed on every input method to the server side of an API. The server side of the client/server model of an API often can be accessed directly without the client. When the server-side API can be directly accessed, the security practitioner needs to emphasize the importance of imposing input validation and sanitization controls on the inputs accepted by the server-side API.

Protection of Resources

The API protects its program from the external calling environment. Although good software environment security surrounds and protects the software with layers of security, the software itself needs to maintain its self-protective defensive posture. Specifically related to the software itself, a program's API is its first line of defense against hackers.

An API's design should include protecting software and its resources. These protection considerations should include the prevention of invalid input, undesirable data loss, exposure, leakage, destruction, modification, or similar. It serves to hide the internal state and data of its program. While doing so, an API must maintain the availability of program services to its callers.

Protecting Communications

For APIs that have touchpoints with networks (internal to an organization or external on the Internet), sensitive data should be protected while in transit. A network-connected API should require encrypted communication, such as TLS.

Determining which, and to what degree, data protection mechanisms will be employed with the API depends upon its risk assessment. The higher the risk, the more likely it makes sense to use data protection mechanisms.

Cryptography

Cryptographic methods use a number of mechanisms to support the confidentiality, integrity, and availability of API message passing. Cryptographic-related mechanisms essential to API security include encrypted communications, hashing for message integrity, and the use of API keys.

Confidentiality of the message is supported by using encrypted communication protocols such as HTTPS. With HTTPS it is important to consider the role and use of certificates for confidentiality in setting up the encrypted communication channel as well as how they are used to authenticate trusted parties.

Hashing methods such as Message Authentication Codes (MAC) support the integrity of the messages to verify the integrity of authorization tokens passed between systems. This is particularly important with use of authorization tokens such as the JWT, which are used for access control decisions.

API keys are used to support the confidentiality and availability of API services. An API key is a secret key used to authenticate and authorize a client to use an API. Using an API key in this manner allows the API service to base access control on the presence of the key in the API request. Allowing or denying access to clients can be based on the key they use. Also, the use of an API key can reduce the impact of denial-of-service attacks by using the key as a mechanism to manage the volume of requests to the API service. Every request requires an API key, which denies requests that do not have them. Too many requests from the same API key can be remediated by load network controls and use of the HTTP 429 status of "Too Many Requests."

Security Logging, Monitoring, and Alerting

All activities at the various API layers offer valuable information about callers and callees' environment at the times of interaction. These series of events can be correlated to identify patterns of behavior or activities that tell stories about attack pattern attempts or attacks in progress.

Security logging must be part of the API logging. Rank and prioritize the events. These events should then be mapped to appropriate log streams and security event processing endpoints.

Some API event logs related to security are authentication failures, denied authorization, input validation failures, session management events, application errors, and the like. Follow your organization's standard guidelines for the baseline requirements for security event logging.

The best logging is human readable, meaningful, and machine parseable. Events should be logged to the organization's standard log collector mechanisms.

This event stream should be monitored for security events. When attack patterns are discovered in log analysis, it triggers a response such as a status change or an alarm. Rapid notification of security events is a capability that contributes to reducing the time to respond.

Aggregating these event logs and sending them to a SIEM to correlate the API events with other events occurring in the system is an important means to identify, detect, and alert on security events.

Information for the secure coding practitioner: some logging frameworks include functionality that maps log events to additional data or actions.

See "The 10 Commandments of Logging" (`www.masterzen.fr/2013/01/13/the-10-commandments-of-logging/`) for more information.

Security Testing APIs

Testing should be performed to validate the behavior of an API and verify the security and performance characteristics of the API as well. Testing should be comprehensive. It should include a variety of different calling subjects, from the different applicable kinds of endpoints that would call the API, not just web browsers.

A variety of test methods should be employed to see how APIs handle unexpected results.

A comprehensive API testing strategy should consider different degrees of knowledge about the API. Black-box testing, a form of testing that assumes to know nothing about its test targets, is used to test the API as it would usually be called, without knowledge of its internal software environment. White-box testing is done with an intimate knowledge of the API and its software. White-box testing is done because it is best to assume, and assure, that the API can defend against attacks that have the advantage of the full knowledge of the software. White-box testing also provides rapid assessment of potential weaknesses in the software.

Fuzzing, also known as *fuzz testing*, is a testing technique that involves sending large amounts of random data, known as *fuzz*, to an API with the intention of breaking the software. Fuzz testing an API can discover susceptibility to denial of service, program crashes, failing code assertions, and potential memory leaks. Smart fuzzing is used during white-box testing to lower the amount of data and speed up the fuzzing process. Fuzzing generally tries to find and manipulate edge case test data to identify differences in application behavior.

Monkey testing is also a form of testing that intentionally focuses on breaking the software. Monkey testing is different than fuzz testing in that its techniques focus on random actions to break the API. Smart monkey testing is a particularly useful API testing technique because it is monkey testing based on knowledge of the system.

API Design Advantages

Good API design improves security. It defines the contract of how software is to be called and used. An API can also serve as a layer to control access to the software's business logic, its data, and resources. An API promotes good software design by protecting the internal logic, data, and state from the outside environment.

Declare Software Contracts

An application programming interface is the accessible formal contract of a software program that describes how and by what rules other programs should communicate with it. APIs define the publicly accessible functionality of the program. An API defines how that functionality is invoked.

Along with describing the rules and specifications of communication, the API also serves as a protective boundary for the software.

Security Control Layering

Because an API acts as a gate at trust boundaries between the software's internal environment and the software consumers, it is a perfect place to apply security controls.

An API is naturally an access management function. This is a place to ensure only properly authenticated and authorized software users are allowed access to the software resources that the API protects. As a security practitioner, you should also consider whether session management is an appropriate control for the type of API and software functionality.

An API is an excellent place to observe and conduct event activities. Logging and monitoring are essential to a secure API.

Input validation and sanitization should be done at the API. All input into the software should be inspected and made safe for consumption by the internal software environment or disposed through an error handling process. Similarly, all data output through the API should be inspected for safety and security purposes by evaluating the content, format, and encoding. These input and output controls are an important part of a defense-in-depth approach to protecting the software environment from abuse.

Layering security controls at an API is a smart secure software development practice. An API offers a natural point of inspection, management, and control for many safeguards because of its position at a trust boundary. An API also improves software security by promoting good design.

Promote Good Design

An API defines how the software can be called and used by its users and consumers without revealing the implementation details. Because an API defines the contract of how the software is called, the API should rarely change, if at all. Consistency in an API over time is necessary for the stability of systems that are built with dependencies upon the API. An API is a layer of opportunity for the software designer to consider how to design the underlying software.

Because an API both separates and contains its associated software, it can significantly shape the software's design. Designing software through the lens of APIs improves software modularity. Modularity in software design promotes a concentration of business logic and improves reuse. These qualities derive from how an API naturally decouples program logic, separating the code from the API. This in turn encourages a cohesion, which is the grouping of program logic into units.

Modularity

The structure of the API, such as the function or method calls it supports, lends itself to support modularity in the design of the software. Each API function can map to one or more modules that provide its business logic. In this way, an API defines the building blocks of a software system. Designing software in a modular fashion improves the quality and maintainability of the software. Modular software also supports the security of the software, as security mechanisms can be designed and built into the resulting software modular building blocks.

Code Decoupling

Code decoupling, or loose coupling, is a design quality that minimizes implementation dependencies between software libraries and modules. An unchanging API, or slow-changing API, combined with modular-designed software supports the decoupling of the code from the API. The code decoupled from the API has the benefit that the software can be maintained or changed without the API changing. The software can change without its consumers knowing.

Cohesion

In software, cohesion is the design quality that describes the extent to which code logic belongs grouped together. The more similar the software logic is, the more likely it will be a design benefit to associate or package that software together. APIs support cohesion. Using the API as design guidance to implement software in a modular fashion promotes cohesion of the business logic. Similar business logic, supporting the same or similar APIs, is typically packaged together in software modules. Cohesion like this improves software readability, maintainability, and changeability, and thus overall it improves the quality of the software, leading to improved security.

Secure Coding Practices

Secure coding practices are more than just the sum total of keyboard events that a software developer reserves to suffuse security throughout their code. Defensive coding strategies and techniques used to mitigate software risks are only part of secure coding practices. Secure coding practices consist of knowing what to do, understanding the defensive practices, and having an environment that encourages these practices. Secure coding practices require a culture that supports them. Security education, security principles, and security practices are also essential. It is also necessary to implement security practices in appropriate places in the SDLC. All of these issues are part of establishing and following secure coding practices.

Security Culture

It is one thing to know what to do, and it is another thing to do what you know. A secure coding practice is as much an issue of culture as it is of security knowledge and techniques.

Cybersecurity by its nature is a broad discipline. An organization's security culture should reflect its breadth. A good security culture cultivates and imbues its organization and its members with security-related awareness.

It begins with clear and effective security policies and standards. All members and affiliates of an organization should know what security policies and standards apply to their position, both in and out of the office, and these should be known well enough to translate into their day-to-day practice.

Having security policies and standards isn't enough to create a security culture, however. Everyone in the organization must know that they are responsible for supporting the security culture.

Security education and training strengthens this understanding. Security education that engages each constituent in how their role impacts the security culture is an effective way to improve it.

Each of these dimensions is necessary, but what effectively ties all of these together is the organizational philosophy. Having an organizational philosophy that supports a security culture is key to its success. The best organizational philosophy to develop a security culture is to adopt a philosophy of continuous improvement through success and learning. The mentality of the security profession is naturally critical. Unfortunately, negative criticism does not resonate with a human being's motivational imperatives. After people have cleared background checks and have been oriented to your organization, they are more than just a resource, and it is necessary to understand what motivates them. A culture that encourages success or a healthy sense of learning to improve the product, the organization, and the individual will engage people because it demonstrates an emphasis on value. When an organization values continuous improvement, success, and learning and encourages people to grow, it sees a dramatic improvement in the quality of its security culture.

Security Education

When software developers and cybersecurity staff are trained to identify software weaknesses and know how to mitigate the associated risks, there are dramatic improvements in the security of the software being produced. Developers should be trained in how to properly engage in the processes that support security in your secure SDLC, such as secure code reviews. Software developers should also be trained in the proper use of software libraries, frameworks, and tooling to support consistency in how they are used in the organization's development culture.

Security Principles

Secure coding practices depend on principles to guide their application. In *Writing Secure Code*, authors Michael Howard and David LeBlanc recommend a number of security principles. The three key principles are secure by design, secure by default, and secure in deployment.

These three security principles cover the broad strokes of secure coding by bringing emphasis to the areas where a secure coding practitioner should pay attention.

Secure by Design

Security by design guides the software practitioner to identify software weaknesses and prevent them when constructing software. This principle motivates adopting particular practices.

These practices involve activities to identify threats by threat modeling, abuse cases, weakness and vulnerability research, and the like. Furthermore, it makes having a security pattern catalog to address weaknesses, vulnerabilities, and threats a necessary part of a secure coding practice.

Along the lines of software security patterns, a healthy secure coding practice includes the use of coding standards and guidelines. To a software practitioner, code quality and readability make a significant impact on their ability to understand and navigate through it.

Understandable code is more maintainable. Maintainable code is easier to modify and improve security. Here one can read the author's decades of interest in good, clean coding structure. Good, clean software structure is a worthwhile investment in ensuring a solid foundation for the software for its lifetime. Coding standards and guidelines should also include a security focus on the implementation patterns of the languages of choice.

The SEI CERT division publishes and shares coding standards for the following popular software languages: C, C++, Perl, Android, and the Oracle Coding Standard for Java. (See `https://wiki.sei.cmu.edu/confluence/display/seccode/` `SEI+CERT+Coding+Standards` for more information.)

Use software frameworks that emphasize security. Security frameworks that are known and have been proven to reduce the common software vulnerabilities go far toward advancing a secure coding practice because they have security implemented in their design.

Another secure coding practice is to conduct a secure code review of software code that is checked in to source control.

An emphasis on security testing and scanning becomes part of the process as well. Design tests to satisfy the security issues defined in threat model/abuse cases and the like.

Secure by Default

Following the principle of secure by design, secure by default means to configure and deliver the software in a safe and secure state. Secure by default means that only the essential features should be enabled by default. The software's default configurations should match the most secure settings. Secure by default configurations are typically not "user-friendly." To address the "user-unfriendliness" of software secure default configurations, a mechanism to turn on additional features should be added to the software.

Secure in Deployment

Finally, the secure in deployment principle is motivation to think about maintaining a secure operational environment for the software. This principle includes maintaining a mature patching program, a secure deployment process, and sufficient documentation for the user.

Secure Coding Practice in the SDLC

Security activities become more prominently featured in the SDLC processes when secure coding practices are implemented. In the design phase, we see security activities such as threat modeling, attack patterns, weakness and vulnerability research, and the like becoming required parts of the process. The product of these activities supports the collection of security requirements for the software. Any significant threats or vulnerabilities discovered by these activities become the substance of the software's security requirements. Additionally, security design patterns and idioms are necessary components of the design.

During the development phase, things such as secure coding standards, guidelines, and pattern implementation are de rigueur in secure coding practices. An emphasis on security testing and review becomes part of software construction. Tests are written not just to check and verify feature quality but are written against the security requirements as well. Code reviews have an important role in secure coding practices during the development phase but in a particular way. Security code reviews conducted by software development peers at the time of code check-ins to version control are used to share the state of the new code with the team. Software security–educated members of the team review new code for security issues. These issues can then be tracked as software defects to be resolved before release.

Secure coding practices impact the testing phase similarly to how they impact the development phase: with an emphasis on security testing and scanning. In the testing phase, these tests are conducted by someone other than the software developers for the sake of separation of duties. More thorough security scanning and testing may be conducted during the testing phase by specialized staff who are experts in that type of testing. Security testing at this phase includes but is not limited to penetration testing, static analysis, dynamic analysis, and security and compliance user acceptance testing, among others.

OWASP Secure Coding Practices

The OWASP Secure Coding Practices Quick Reference Guide Project is a set of technology-agnostic general secure coding practices. The OWASP Secure Coding Practice recommendations are sets of related security concerns and activities that are grouped into 13 separate categories. Each category represents a secure coding practice focus. It presents to the reader in a checklist format that can be used to instill secure coding practices into the SDLC.

The OWASP Secure Coding Practices cover the following categories:

- Input validation
- Output encoding
- Authentication and password management
- Session management
- Access control
- Cryptographic practices
- Error handling and logging
- Communication security
- System configuration
- Database security

- File management
- Memory management
- General coding practices

This OWASP guidance, similar to OWASP material in general, is oriented to web applications. However, their secure coding practice categories and associated checklists are comprehensive and useful information to serve as a basis for secure coding practice checklists for your organization.

To illustrate the content and utility of the OWASP Secure Coding Practices Checklist, here is a sample of the "Access Control" checklist taken directly from the OWASP Secure Coding Practices Quick Reference Guide:

- Use only trusted system objects, e.g., server-side session objects, for making access authorization decisions.

- Use a single sitewide component to check access authorization. This includes libraries that call external authorization services.

- Access controls should fail securely.

- Deny all access if the application cannot access its security configuration information.

- Enforce authorization controls on every request, including those made by server-side scripts, "includes," and requests from rich client-side technologies like Ajax and Flash.

- Segregate privileged logic from other application code.

- Restrict access to files or other resources, including those outside the application's direct control, to only authorized users.

- Restrict access to protected URLs to only authorized users.

- Restrict access to protected functions to only authorized users.

- Restrict direct object references to only authorized users.

- Restrict access to services to only authorized users.

OWASP's full Secure Coding Practices Quick Reference Guide, including all of its complete checklists, is available at `https://www.owasp.org/index.php/OWASP_Secure_Coding_Practices_-_Quick_Reference_Guide`.

SEI CERT "Top 10 Secure Coding Practices"

A security activity checklist facilitates secure coding practices in a SDLC. However, checklists do not account for an activity that would cover an unknown vulnerability, so using a checklist can give a false sense of confidence. Since there is not yet such a thing as a risk-revealing crystal ball to cover and catch software security concerns that are not known yet, the best practice is to broaden the approach. The SEI CERT Secure Coding Practices take a broader approach.

The SEI CERT Secure Coding Practices can be characterized as secure coding best practices. Whereas the OWASP checklists had particular checklist activities, the SEI CERT Secure Coding Practices are general statements of security truth and principle. The SEI CERT lists 10 Secure Coding Practices and adds two more "bonus" practices.

The 10 SEI CERT Secure Coding Practices are the following:

- Validate input.
- Heed compiler warnings.
- Architect and design for security policies.
- Keep it simple.
- Default to deny.
- Adhere to the principle of least privilege.
- Sanitize data sent to other systems.
- Practice defense in depth.
- Use effective quality assurance techniques.
- Adopt a secure coding standard.

The two SEI CERT Secure Coding Bonus Practices are as follows:

- Define security requirements.
- Model threats.

As you can see by looking at these secure coding practices, they both focus on specific practices, such as validate input, as well as recommend broad practices such as "keep it simple." General security statements like this bring creativity and common sense into the application of the recommended security practices they describe.

The two secure coding practices artifacts presented here complement each other. Where there is overlap, there is also a difference in focus. Combining the OWASP Secure Coding Practices with the SEI CERT Secure Coding Practices is a good practice to create your Secure Coding Practices guidance to use for your SDLC.

Consult the SEI CERT "Top 10 Secure Coding Practices" directly to view all of the checklists (`https://wiki.sei.cmu.edu/confluence/display/seccode/Top+10+Secure+Coding+Practices`).

SUMMARY

It can be said that there is no security without software development security. Software development security is a discipline that has been overlooked for the sake of feature development and software delivery. Writing software is hard. Unfortunately, when software development security is lacking, hacking software is easy, and software applications are increasingly targets of attack.

Software development security is the foundational security for an organization's software and digital data. By protecting software in every aspect of its lifecycle, software development security improves the security posture of an organization. Software security decreases the risk of theft of assets, system compromises, and damage to the brand or assets.

Software development security involves a broad variety of subject matter ranging from how to securely develop software through its lifecycle, to securing the software development environment, to assessing the effectiveness of software security, and finally to knowing and using secure coding guidelines and standards along the way.

Software development security is a necessary component of a comprehensive and effective security strategy.

Index

Numbers

A